To Lucy—my new
shaggy muse

Sherri Jackson

PSYCHOLOGY

A CONCISE INTRODUCTION

Fifth Edition

Richard A. Griggs

University of Florida

worth publishers
Macmillan Learning

New York

Vice President, Social Science: Charles Linsmeier
Publisher, Psychology: Rachel Losh
Executive Editor: Carlise Stembridge
Assistant Editor: Kimberly Morgan Smith
Senior Marketing Manager: Lindsay Johnson
Marketing Assistant: Morgan Ratner
Executive Media Editor: Noel Hohnstine
Media Editor: Anthony Casciano
Director, Content Management Enhancement: Tracey Kuehn
Managing Editor, Sciences and Social Sciences: Lisa Kinne
Senior Project Editor: Jane O'Neill
Senior Photo Editor: Robin Fadool
Permissions Editor: Chelsea Roden
Director of Design, Content Management: Diana Blume
Cover and Interior Designer: Vicki Tomaselli
Art Manager: Matthew McAdams
Illustrations: Eli Ensor, Matthew Holt, Matthew McAdams, Evelyn Pence, and Don Stewart
Senior Production Supervisor: Sarah Segal
Media Producer: Eve Conte
Composition: MPS Limited
Printing and Binding: LSC Communications
Cover Painting: Courtesy of Jackie Saccoccio and 11R, NY

Library of Congress Control Number: 2016951986

ISBN-13: 978-1-4641-9216-6
ISBN-10: 1-4641-9216-2

Second printing

Worth Publishers
One New York Plaza
Suite 4500
New York, NY 10004-1562
www.macmillanlearning.com

About the Author

Richard A. Griggs

Richard A. Griggs is Professor Emeritus of Psychology at the University of Florida. After earning his PhD in cognitive psychology at Indiana University, he went to the University of Florida, where he has spent his entire academic career. He has won numerous teaching awards at the University of Florida and was named APA's Society for the Teaching of Psychology Teacher of the Year for 4-year Colleges and Universities in 1994. He served on the Editorial Board of *Teaching of Psychology* for over a decade, as a *Contemporary Psychology* consulting editor for textbook reviews, and as an associate editor of *Thinking and Reasoning*. His two main research areas are human reasoning and the teaching of psychology. He has published more than 150 journal articles, reviews, and book chapters, including 48 in *Teaching of Psychology*. He was also one of the originators and developers of the Society for the Teaching of Psychology's online resource, *A Compendium of Introductory Psychology Textbooks*, the editor of Volume 3 of the Society's *Handbook for Teaching Introductory Psychology*, and the coeditor of the Society's *Teaching Introductory Psychology: Tips from ToP* and *Teaching Statistics and Research Methods: Tips from ToP*. When he isn't busy with professional activities, he likes to relax at home with his wife, Sherri, also a psychologist, and their dog, Lucy. His main pastimes are reading, puzzles, exercise, and golf.

Brief Contents

About the Author

Johnston Photography

Richard A. Griggs

Richard A. Griggs is Professor Emeritus of Psychology at the University of Florida. After earning his PhD in cognitive psychology at Indiana University, he went to the University of Florida, where he has spent his entire academic career. He has won numerous teaching awards at the University of Florida and was named APA's Society for the Teaching of Psychology Teacher of the Year for 4-year Colleges and Universities in 1994. He served on the Editorial Board of *Teaching of Psychology* for over a decade, as a *Contemporary Psychology* consulting editor for textbook reviews, and as an associate editor of *Thinking and Reasoning.* His two main research areas are human reasoning and the teaching of psychology. He has published more than 150 journal articles, reviews, and book chapters, including 48 in *Teaching of Psychology.* He was also one of the originators and developers of the Society for the Teaching of Psychology's online resource, *A Compendium of Introductory Psychology Textbooks,* the editor of Volume 3 of the Society's *Handbook for Teaching Introductory Psychology,* and the coeditor of the Society's *Teaching Introductory Psychology: Tips from ToP* and *Teaching Statistics and Research Methods: Tips from ToP.* When he isn't busy with professional activities, he likes to relax at home with his wife, Sherri, also a psychologist, and their dog, Lucy. His main pastimes are reading, puzzles, exercise, and golf.

Brief Contents

Contents

Preface

Those of us who teach introductory psychology have the privilege and the challenge of introducing students to our discipline, which is more expansive than ever as psychological research continues to proliferate in the many subareas covered in the course. This task has become increasingly problematic as the authors of introductory textbooks have struggled to keep pace, resulting in books that are more encyclopedic, too long, and thus seemingly impossible to complete in one term. The choices of which topics to assign and to what depth to cover them have become more difficult for teachers. Teachers end up either omitting entire chapters or asking students to read chapters at a pace too hurried for optimal learning. Further, introductory textbooks have become much more expensive, with many priced over $200, leading many students to not even purchase them. As an introductory psychology teacher, I grappled with these critical issues. *Psychology: A Concise Introduction* is the result of my own search for a textbook that includes the essential core content in psychology but is also economical in both size and cost.

Chapter Topics. To make the most informed choices of chapter topics for the first edition of this text, I consulted Benjamin Miller and Barbara Gentile's national survey of 761 introductory psychology teachers at 490 schools (Miller & Gentile, 1998). They asked teachers to rate the importance of and need for coverage of 25 different topics in their courses. Since my first chapter covered psychology as a science, I chose the highest-rated topics in Miller and Gentile's study as the subjects of the other nine chapters. To maintain the book's brevity, I paired sensation with perception and cognitive development with social development in single chapters. The topic order is the standard one—introduction/methods, neuroscience, sensation/perception, learning, memory, thinking/intelligence, developmental psychology, personality, social psychology, and abnormal psychology. Because the topics of emotion, motivation, and states of consciousness were rated just below the chosen topics, I included sections on emotion and consciousness in the neuroscience chapter and on motivation in the learning chapter. My choices of chapter topics were further validated by Scott Bates's analysis of topic coverage for 107 introductory psychology course syllabi (Bates, 2004). His topic coverage findings based on syllabi analysis match my chapter topic choices almost perfectly.

These 10 chapter topic choices also fit nicely with the American Psychological Association's Board of Educational Affairs Working Group's new model for teaching the introductory psychology course (Gurung et al., 2016). They recommend covering at least two topics in each of five specified pillars (groups) of topics (see Figure 1, page 120), and my 10 chapter topics allow introductory course teachers to meet this recommendation, even without teaching all 10 chapters.

This is because some of the chapter topics are members of more than one pillar. A good example is the sensation and perception chapter. These two topics are members of different pillars (pillars 1 and 2). Thus, if you teach this chapter, a topic in each of two pillars is covered. In sum, although there are only 10 chapters in my book, the particular chapter topics that I chose allow teachers flexibility in how they meet this recommendation, if they choose to do so. It is also important to point out that this APA working group cautions against attempting to provide exhaustive coverage of all the various topics in the five pillars given the one-term nature of the vast majority of introductory courses. This caution resonates well with the logic behind the concise nature of my text.

Pedagogical Program. In writing *Psychology: A Concise Introduction*, I have tried to offer solid topical coverage in an engaging, conversational style. The content in each chapter has been reduced to the core content within that topic domain. Illustrations are full-color and pedagogically sound. Students will find this book easy to learn from. It incorporates both pedagogical aids and study guide exercises to structure their learning. My choice of pedagogical aids was primarily based on research findings about student perception of the use and importance of the many aids employed in textbooks. I included the aids that students report valuing and using in their learning. Each chapter begins with an overview in the form of a topical outline, and key terms are identified by boldface type and then defined both in the text and in a marginal glossary. Detailed summaries are provided at the end of each major chapter section. Study guide exercises begin with ConceptCheck questions at the end of each chapter section. These questions lead students to think more deeply about the material in that section. For example, a question may ask students to contrast concepts to understand differences between them or to demonstrate their understanding of a concept by applying it in a novel situation. At the end of each chapter there is a list of Key Terms and a Key Terms Exercise to test student knowledge of these terms. A multiple-choice Practice Test on the chapter's content follows the Key Terms Exercise. Answers to this test along with answers to the Key Terms Exercise and the sectional ConceptChecks are provided at the end of each chapter. These exercises combined with the pedagogical aids should foster sufficient review and self-assessment, eliminating the need for and additional expense of a separate study guide.

Fifth Edition Changes. Reaching the goal of a textbook that could be covered in a single term at a reasonable price without sacrificing essential content was and continues to be a challenge, but based on the overwhelmingly positive market response, the publisher and I seem to have been successful. With only 10 chapters, *Psychology: A Concise Introduction* has fit nicely into introductory courses on both semester and quarter systems. The breadth of the audience for the text has also been gratifying. It has been used successfully at all types of colleges and universities, from 2-year schools to research institutions. Given this success and to maintain the text's basic goal of conciseness, the content was expanded and revised only where necessary. The 10 chapters (those topics taught most frequently by introductory teachers) remain the same, and content additions were made judiciously.

The fourth edition revisions were well received, so my fifth edition revisions are mostly along the same lines. I'll describe some examples of the types of revisions that I made. I updated content where necessary (e.g., evidence of Phineas Gage's probable psychosocial recovery in Chapter 2; Nobel prize–winning cognitive mapping research on the inner GPS in rats and humans in Chapter 4; meta-analytic findings that indicate the Rorschach Inkblot Test is not as invalid as previously thought in Chapter 8; and recent criticisms, studies, and theoretical developments that argue that Milgram's obedience experiments were not really about following orders from an authority in Chapter 9). I added content that provides better closure on a topic (e.g., a discussion of red-green color blindness to facilitate the understanding of the theories of color vision in Chapter 3, a discussion of the recent discovery of Little Albert's identity resulting in a happier ending to his story in Chapter 4, and a discussion of the research using the visual cliff apparatus to help understand infant perceptual abilities in Chapter 7). I also added content that has value to students in their everyday lives (e.g., coverage of the regression toward the mean phenomenon and how it relates to our perception of patterns in the real world in Chapter 1 and an explanation of The Dress color illusion that went viral on the Internet recently and how it relates to brightness constancy in Chapter 3). I also added new concepts if they served to strengthen a discussion of a related concept (e.g., addition of the concept of spurious correlations to facilitate understanding of the third-variable problem present in correlational studies in Chapter 1, the addition of working memory to strengthen understanding of short-term memory in Chapter 5, and the addition of the concepts of experimenter bias and demand characteristics to strengthen understanding of the impact of methodological flaws on drawing conclusions from research findings in Chapter 9). Lastly, I have revised and noticeably lengthened my discussions of Milgram's obedience study and Zimbardo's Stanford prison study in Chapter 9 and Rosenhan's pseudopatient study in Chapter 10. All three studies are now discussed as "contentious classics" (Tavris, 2014), and coverage of the substantial criticism that has been levied against each of these studies is now included, severely limiting and modifying the conclusions that can be soundly drawn from their findings. I also revised the discussion in Chapter 2 on the numerical relationship of glial cells to neurons to reflect the latest research indicating it is 1 to 1 rather than 10 or more to 1, and I updated the discussion in Chapter 4 on mirror neuron systems to reflect the current debate about whether these systems are present in humans, and if so, exactly what they do.

In this new edition, the visual pedagogical program was expanded and strengthened throughout the text. Because this program is an integral part of the learning process, I carefully examined each figure, table, illustration, photo, and cartoon to ensure that it served a clear pedagogical function, and any that needed improvement were either revised or replaced. In addition, the tables were redesigned to facilitate their use, and new illustrations, historical photos, and cartoons were added where necessary to further improve the pedagogical value of the visual program. The text's interior design was also revised to have a cleaner look and thus enhance its use. Because of their success in the first four editions, the specific pedagogical aids employed (those that research has found students report valuing and using in their learning) and the structure of the integrated study guide remain the same. All of the questions in the ConceptCheck sections, Key Terms Exercises, and multiple-choice Practice Tests were reevaluated and revised if necessary. In sum, I think that students will find this new edition even easier to learn from than previous editions.

As with the first four editions, the textbook's smaller size and lower cost allow teachers the option of adding supplemental readings to customize their courses to fit their own goals and interests. To facilitate the task of finding supplemental materials, Worth offers several options. They are described in the next section, and each of them can be packaged with the textbook for a nominal additional cost.

Supplements and Instructor Resources

Digital Resources for Students

LaunchPad for *Psychology: A Concise Introduction*, Fifth Edition, includes an e-Book version of the text for students as well as many other features for students and instructors, including LearningCurve quizzing, student self-assessment, simulations, videos, instructor resources, and an easy-to-use gradebook. **LaunchPad** is described in more detail below in the **Resources for Instructors** section.

A PDF-style e-Book version of *Psychology: A Concise Introduction*, Fifth Edition, offers the complete text in an easy-to-use format. Students can choose to purchase the **PDF-style e-Book** from one of our many publishing partners. The e-Book offers online and downloadable options and provides students with the ability to read, highlight, take notes, search, and share. For a list of our e-Book partners, go to www.macmillanlearning.com/ebooks.

Supplementary Reading for Students

Each of the following Worth supplementary books can be packaged with *Psychology: A Concise Introduction*, **Fifth Edition,** for a nominal additional cost.

New! *Worth Expert Guide to Scientific Literacy: Thinking Like a Psychological Scientist*, Kenneth Keith, Ithaca College, and Bernard Beins, Ithaca College Exposes students to the solid habits of scientific thought and teaches them to apply an empirical attitude and data-driven decision making in their everyday lives (e.g., seeing through pseudoscientific claims). Classic and current research findings are used throughout the book to explain the various scientific literacy concepts.

New! *The Horse That Won't Go Away: Clever Hans, Facilitated Communication, and the Need for Clear Thinking,* **Thomas E. Heinzen, William Patterson University of New Jersey, Scott O. Lilienfeld, Emory University, and Susan A. Nolan, Seton Hall University** An engaging and accessible introduction to the need for psychological science. From the strange case of Clever Hans, the horse that supposedly could count and do math, to the unsupported claim that facilitated communication could allow persons with autism to communicate, the authors take the student on a tour of cases that show just how important it is to rely on the scientific method as we navigate our way through everyday life.

New! *Pursuing Human Strengths: A Positive Psychology Guide,* **Second Edition, Martin Bolt, Calvin College** Martin Bolt's workbook aims to help students build up their strengths. Closely following the research, this book provides a brief overview of nine positive traits, such as hope, self-respect, commitment, and joy. It also offers self-assessment activities that help students gauge how much of the trait they have developed, and research-based suggestions for how they might work further toward fostering these traits.

New! *The Critical Thinking Companion,* **Third Edition, Jane Halonen, University of West Florida, and Cynthia Gray, Alverno College** Tied to the introductory psychology course, this engaging and concise companion book takes an active learning approach to developing students' critical thinking skills. The authors include a wealth of hands-on exercises that span the complete spectrum of chapter topics in the introductory course, from neuroscience to abnormal psychology.

Resources for Instructors

LaunchPad with LearningCurve Quizzing Built to solve key challenges in the course, LaunchPad gives students everything they need to prepare for class and exams, while giving instructors everything they need to quickly set up a course, shape the content to their syllabus, craft presentations and lectures, assign and assess homework, and guide the progress of individual students and the class as a whole.

- An interactive e-Book integrates the text and all student media.

- LearningCurve adaptive quizzing gives individualized question sets and feedback based on each student's correct and incorrect responses. All the questions are tied back to the e-Book to encourage students to read the book in preparation for class time and exams.

- PsychSim 6 has arrived! Tom Ludwig's (Hope College) fabulous new tutorials further strengthen LaunchPad's abundance of helpful student activity resources.

- The Video Assignment Tool makes it easy to assign and assess video-based activities and projects, and provides a convenient way for students to submit video coursework.

- LaunchPad Gradebook gives a clear window on performance for the whole class, for individual students, and for individual assignments.

- A streamlined interface helps students manage their schedule of assignments, while social commenting tools let them connect with classmates and learn from each other. 24/7 help is a click away, accessible from a link in the upper right-hand corner.

- Curated optional pre-built chapter units can be used as is or customized. Or you may choose not to use them and build your course from scratch.

- Book-specific instructor resources include PowerPoint® sets, textbook graphics, lecture and activity suggestions, test banks, and more.

- Offers easy LMS integration into your school's learning management system.

Downloadable Instructor's Resource Manual Mallory Malkin, Mississippi University for Women; Andrew N. Christopher, Albion College; Pam Marek, Kennesaw State University; and Scott Cohn, Western Colorado State University. Thoroughly updated from the last edition, this manual provides a variety of resources to help you plan your course and class sessions. Resources include annotated chapter outlines and lecture guides with tips on how to present the material, effective classroom activities (including both in-class activities and homework assignments) drawn from established sources as well as the authors' own experiences, and suggestions for using Worth courseware, including LaunchPad, Worth's online course space, and all of Worth's video resources for introductory psychology. The Instructor's Resource Manual is downloadable from LaunchPad and the online catalog.

Downloadable Test Bank Richard D. Platt and Cynthia S. Koenig, St. Mary's College of Maryland; Pam Marek, Kennesaw State University; Sherri L. Jackson, Jacksonville University; Richard A. Griggs, University of Florida; and Adrienne Williamson, Kennesaw State University. Tied to the pages of *Psychology: A Concise Introduction,* **Fifth Edition**, the Downloadable Test Bank provides over 1,500 multiple-choice factual/definitional and conceptual questions. Powered by Diploma, it guides you through the process of creating a test, allowing you to add an unlimited number of questions, edit questions, create new questions, format a test, scramble questions, and include pictures and multimedia links. The Diploma Test Bank is downloadable from our online catalog and LaunchPad.

The Video Collection is now the single resource for all videos for introductory psychology from Worth Publishers. Available on flash drive and in LaunchPad, this includes over 130 clips.

Interactive Presentation Slides for Introductory Psychology is an extraordinary series of PowerPoint® lectures. This is a dynamic yet easy-to-use new way to engage students during classroom presentations of core psychology topics. This collection provides opportunities for discussion and interaction, and includes an unprecedented number of embedded video clips and animations.

Lecture and Illustration Slides In addition to the Interactive Presentation Slides, there are two other PowerPoint® slide sets to accompany the text. For each chapter, we offer a set that includes chapter art and illustrations and a final lecture presentation set that merges detailed chapter outlines with text illustrations and artwork from outside sources. Each set can be used directly or customized to fit your needs.

Macmillan Community Created by instructors for instructors, this is an ideal forum for interacting with fellow educators—including Macmillan authors—in your discipline. Join ongoing conversations about everything from course prep and presentations to assignments and assessments to teaching with media, keeping pace with—and influencing—new directions in your field. Includes exclusive access to classroom resources, blogs, webinars, professional development opportunities, and more.

Acknowledgments

First, I would like to thank all of the reviewers who have given generously of their time and expertise in working on the various editions of *Psychology: A Concise Introduction*. I am also indebted to my supplements author team. I truly appreciate their hard work and commitment to excellence.

At Worth Publishers, I am indebted to the many talented editorial and production people who worked on this revision. I would like to thank Carlise Stembridge (Executive Editor), Tracey Kuehn (Director of Content Management Enhancement), Lisa Kinne (Managing Editor), Jane O'Neill (Senior Project Editor), Sarah Segal (Senior Production Supervisor), Diana Blume (Director of Design, Content Management), Vicki Tomaselli (Senior Design Manager), Matthew McAdams (Art Manager), Robin Fadool (Photo Editor), Anthony Casciano (Media Editor), and Kimberly Morgan Smith (Assistant Editor) for all of their respective contributions to the production of this fifth edition. Special thanks go to Jackie Saccoccio for allowing us to use her beautiful paintings for the cover and the chapter opening art. In addition, I appreciate the dedication and meticulous efforts of my copy editor Deborah Heimann, proofreader Maria Vlasak, and indexer Ellen Brennan. My deepest thanks go to my publisher Rachel Losh (now Director of Personalized Learning) for her invaluable support and insightful guidance on this fifth edition.

Finally, my thanks extend to my wife, Sherri. Her love, encouragement, and unflagging support have kept me going through all five editions of this text.

Courtesy of Jackie Saccoccio and 11R, NY

1 The Science of Psychology

What do you think psychologists do? If you are like most people, when you think of a psychologist, you think of a therapist counseling people who have problems. If I asked you to name a psychologist, you would probably name Sigmund Freud. However, Freud and psychologists who work as therapists are not the focus of this book. They will be discussed, but they are only a part of psychology's story. Psychology is a science, not just a mental health profession. The subjects of this scientific study are you, me, all humans. Some psychologists may use other animals in their research, but their main goal is still predominantly to understand humans. **Psychology** is the science of human behavior and mental processes. Psychologists attempt to understand all aspects of both our observable behavior, such as speech and physical movement, and internal mental processes, such as remembering and thinking, which cannot be directly observed. Psychologists may be found in any number of roles, including teaching, researching, consulting, and yes, counseling troubled people. This book, however, will focus on the research done by psychological scientists, the process by which they've accomplished that research, and what we've learned from their work.

Psychological researchers study everything about us from how our brain works and how we see and hear to how we reason and make decisions. The American Psychological Association lists 54 different divisions of psychology, and psychologists specialize in studying each of these different aspects of our behavior and mental processing. To learn more about these various subfields and careers in psychology, visit www.apa.org/careers/resources/guides/careers.aspx. Although there are many diverse areas within psychology, there are only four major research perspectives for studying these topics. We will begin with a general overview of these four perspectives and then provide descriptions of the major research methods that psychologists use regardless of their perspective. Understanding these perspectives and the research methods used by psychologists will allow you to start thinking like a psychologist (like a scientist).

Note that there are other perspectives in psychology that are primarily clinical in nature (related to psychological therapy). We will discuss the psychoanalytic perspective (which emphasizes the interaction of unconscious forces and childhood experiences in personality development) and the humanistic perspective (which emphasizes the personal growth motive) in Chapter 8, Personality Theories and Assessment, and the psychotherapies based on these two perspectives in Chapter 10, Abnormal Psychology.

The Four Major Research Perspectives

There are four major research perspectives—biological, cognitive, behavioral, and sociocultural. It's important to understand that these perspectives are complementary. The research findings from the major perspectives fit together like the pieces of a jigsaw puzzle to give us a more complete picture. No particular perspective is better than the others, and psychologists using the various perspectives work together to provide a more complete explanation of our behavior and mental processing.

The best way to understand how the major research perspectives differ is to consider the major goal of psychologists—to explain human behavior and mental processes. To explain means to know the causes of our behavior and mental processes. To facilitate your

psychology The science of human behavior and mental processes.

1

understanding of these perspectives, I discuss them in two different pairs based on the type of causal factors that they emphasize—internal factors or external factors. The biological perspective and the cognitive perspective focus on causes that stem from within us (internal factors); the behavioral perspective and the sociocultural perspective focus on causes that stem from outside us (external factors). We'll also briefly consider developmental psychology, a research field that provides a nice example of how these perspectives complement one another.

Perspectives Emphasizing Internal Factors

The biological perspective and the cognitive perspective focus on internal factors. In the case of the **biological perspective,** our physiological hardware (especially the brain and nervous system) is viewed as the major determiner of behavior and mental processing. The genetic and evolutionary bases of our physiology are also important. In contrast, for the **cognitive perspective,** the major explanatory focus is on how our mental processes, such as perception, memory, and problem solving, work and impact our behavior. To contrast this perspective with the biological perspective, you can think of these mental processes as the software, or programs, of the brain (the wetware, the biological corollary to computer hardware).

The biological perspective. We are biological creatures; therefore, looking for explanations in terms of our biology makes sense. Biological psychologists look for causes within our physiology, our genetics, and human evolution. They argue that our actions and thoughts are functions of our underlying biology. Let's consider an example of what most people would term a "psychological" disorder, depression. Why do we get depressed? A biological psychologist might focus on a deficiency in the activity of certain chemicals in the nervous system as a cause of this problem. Therefore, to treat depression using this perspective, the problem with the chemical deficiency would have to be rectified. How? Antidepressant drugs such as Prozac or Zoloft might be prescribed. These drugs increase the activity of the neural chemicals involved, and this increased activity might lead to changes in our mood. If all goes well, a few weeks after beginning treatment, we begin to feel better. Thus, our mood is at least partly a function of our brain chemistry. Of course, many nonbiological factors can contribute to depression, including unhealthy patterns of thinking, learned helplessness, and disturbing life circumstances. It's important to remember that employing psychology's complementary perspectives in addressing research and clinical issues provides the most complete answer.

In addition to the impact of brain chemistry, biological psychologists also study the involvement of the various parts of the brain and nervous system on our behavior and mental processes. For example, they have learned that our "eyes" are indeed in the back of our head. Biological psychologists have found that it is the back part of our brain that allows us to see the world. So, a more correct expression would be that "our

biological perspective A research perspective whose major explanatory focus is how the brain, nervous system, and other physiological mechanisms produce behavior and mental processes.

cognitive perspective A research perspective whose major explanatory focus is how mental processes, such as perception, memory, and problem solving, work and impact behavior.

eyes are in the back of our brain." The brain is not only essential for vision, but it is also the control center for almost all of our behavior and mental processing. In Chapter 2, Neuroscience, you will learn how the brain manages this incredibly difficult task as well as about the roles of other parts of our nervous system and the many different chemicals that transmit information within it, and in Chapter 3, Sensation and Perception, you will learn how our two major senses, vision and audition, work.

The cognitive perspective. Cognitive psychologists study all aspects of cognitive processing from perception to the higher-level processes, such as problem solving and reasoning. Let's try a brief exercise to gain insight into one aspect of our cognitive processing. I will name a category, and you say aloud as fast as you can the first instance of that category that comes to mind. Are you ready? The first category is FRUIT. If you are like most people, you said apple or orange. Let's try another one. The category is PIECE OF FURNITURE. Again, if you are like most people, you said chair or sofa. Why, in the case of FRUIT, don't people say pomegranate or papaya? How do we have categories of information organized so that certain examples come to mind first for most of us? In brief, cognitive research has shown that we organize categorical information around what we consider the most typical or representative examples of a category (Rosch, 1973). These examples (such as apple and orange for FRUIT) are called prototypes for the category and are retrieved first when we think of the category.

A broader cognitive processing question concerns how memory retrieval in general works. Haven't you been in the situation of not being able to retrieve information from memory that you know you have stored there? This can be especially frustrating in exam situations. Or think about the opposite—an event or person comes to mind seemingly out of the blue. Why? Even more complex questions arise when we consider how we attempt to solve problems, reason, and make decisions. For example, here's a series problem with a rather simple answer, but most people find it very difficult: What is the next character in the series OTTFFSS_? The answer is not "O." Why is this problem so difficult? The progress that cognitive psychologists have made in answering such questions about cognitive processing will be discussed in Chapter 5, on memory, and Chapter 6, on thinking and intelligence (where you can find the answer to the series problem).

Perspectives Emphasizing External Factors

Both the behavioral perspective and the sociocultural perspective focus on external factors in explaining human behavior and mental processing. The **behavioral perspective** emphasizes conditioning of our behavior by environmental events, and there is more emphasis on explaining observable behavior than on unobservable mental processes. The **sociocultural perspective** also emphasizes the influence of the external environment, but it more specifically focuses on the impact of other people and our culture as the major

behavioral perspective A research perspective whose major explanatory focus is how external environmental events condition observable behavior.

sociocultural perspective A research perspective whose major explanatory focus is how other people and the cultural context impact behavior and mental processes.

determiners of our behavior and mental processing. In addition to conditioning, the sociocultural perspective equally stresses cognitive types of learning, such as learning by observation or modeling, and thus focuses just as much on mental processing as observable behavior.

The behavioral perspective. According to the behavioral perspective, we behave as we do because of our past history of conditioning by our environment. There are two major types of conditioning, classical (or Pavlovian) and operant. You may be familiar with the most famous example of classical conditioning—Ivan Pavlov's dogs (Pavlov, 1927/1960). In his research, Pavlov sounded a tone and then put food in a dog's mouth. The pairing of these two environmental events led the dog to salivate to the tone in anticipation of the arrival of the food. The salivary response to the tone was conditioned by the sequencing of the two environmental events (the sounding of the tone and putting food in the dog's mouth). The dog learned that the sound of the tone meant food was on its way. According to behaviorists, such classical conditioning can explain how we learn fear and other emotional responses, taste aversions, and many other behaviors.

Classical conditioning is important in determining our behavior, but behaviorists believe operant conditioning is even more important. Operant conditioning involves the relationship between our behavior and its environmental consequences (whether they are reinforcing or punishing). Simply put, if we are reinforced for a behavior, its probability will increase; if we are punished, the probability will decrease. For example, if you ask your teacher a question and he praises you for asking such a good question and then answers it very carefully, you will tend to ask more questions. However, if the teacher criticizes you for asking a stupid question and doesn't even bother to answer it, you will probably not ask more questions. Environmental events (such as a teacher's response) thus control behavior through their reinforcing or punishing nature. Both types of conditioning, classical and operant, will be discussed in Chapter 4. The point to remember here is that environmental events condition our behavior and are the causes of it.

The sociocultural perspective. This perspective focuses on the impact of other people (individuals and groups) and our cultural surroundings on our behavior and mental processing. We are social animals; therefore other people are important to us and thus greatly affect what we do and how we think. None of us is immune to these social "forces." Haven't your thinking and behavior been impacted by other people, especially those close to you? Our coverage of sociocultural research will emphasize the impact of these social forces on our behavior and mental processing.

To help you understand the nature of sociocultural research, let's consider a famous set of experiments that attempted to explain the social forces operating during a tragic, real-world event—the Kitty Genovese murder in 1964 (Latané & Darley, 1970). Kitty was returning home from work to her apartment in New York City when she was brutally attacked, raped, and stabbed to death with a hunting knife. With the headline "37 Who Saw Murder Didn't Call Police," Martin Gansberg (1964) reported in the *New York Times* that "For more than an hour 38 respectable, law-abiding citizens in Queens watched a killer stalk and stab a woman in three sep-arate attacks in Kew Gardens. . . . Not one person telephoned the police during the assault; one witness called after the woman was dead" (p. 1). A. M. Rosenthal, the *New York Times* editor for Gansberg's article, later developed the story into a short book, *Thirty-Eight Witnesses* (1964). Although recent research (Manning, Levine, & Collins, 2007) has shown that there is no evidence for the key features of this story, such as the large number of witnesses, the story stimulated Bibb Latané and John Darley to explain why the reported 38 witnesses didn't help until it was too late. In fact, according to Levitt and Dubner (2009), the story inspired more research on bystander apathy than on the Holocaust during the 20 years following the murder.

In their attempt to explain why so many people witnessed the murder but didn't help, Latané and Darley manipulated the number of bystanders witnessing the emergencies that they created in their experiments. Their general finding is called the bystander effect (and sometimes the Genovese Syndrome)—the probability of a victim receiving help in an emergency is higher when there is only one bystander than when there are many. In brief, the presence of other bystanders leads us not to help. How did Latané and Darley apply this effect to the Kitty Genovese murder? They explained that social forces present in that situation kept the bystanders from help-ing. Each felt that someone else would do something and that surely someone else had already called the police. Hence, no one helped. Bystander research, along with studies of other intriguing topics that also involve social forces, such as why we con-form and why we obey even when it may lead to destructive behavior, will be detailed in Chapter 9, on social psychology.

Now you have at least a general understanding of the four major research perspectives, summarized in Table 1.1. Remember, these perspectives are comple-mentary, and, when used together, help us to gain a more complete understanding of our behavior and mental processes. Developmental psychology (the scientific study of human develop-ment across the lifespan) is a research area that nicely illustrates the benefits of using multiple research per-spectives to address experi-mental questions. A good example is the study of how children acquire language. Initially, behavioral learning principles of reinforcement and imitation were believed to be sufficient to account for language acquisition. Although these principles

Table 1.1	The Four Major Research Perspectives in Psychology
Research Perspective	**Major Explanatory Focus**
Biological	How our physiology (especially the brain and nervous system) produces our behavior and mental processes and how genetics and evolution have impacted our physiology
Cognitive	How our mental processes, such as perception, memory, and problem solving, work and how they impact our behavior
Behavioral	How external environmental events condition our observable behavior
Sociocultural	How other people and the cultural context impact our behavior and mental processes

clearly do play a role (Whitehurst & Valdez-Menchaca, 1988), most developmental language researchers now recognize that biology, cognition, and the sociocultural context are also critical to language learning (Pinker, 1994; Tomasello, 2003). Studies of the brain, for example, indicate that specific brain areas are involved in language acquisition. Research has also revealed that cognitive processes are important as well. For example, as children acquire new concepts, they learn the names that go with them and thus expand their vocabulary. In addition, it has been shown that the sociocultural context of language helps children to learn about the social pragmatic functions of language. For instance, they use a variety of pragmatic cues (such as an adult's focus of attention) for word learning. Thus, by using all four research perspectives, developmental researchers have gained a much better understanding of how children acquire language. We will learn in Chapter 7, Developmental Psychology, that our understanding of many developmental questions has been broadened by the use of multiple research perspectives.

Subsequent chapters will detail the main concepts, theories, and research findings in the major fields of psychology. As you learn about these theories and research findings, beware of the **hindsight bias (I-knew-it-all-along phenomenon)**—the tendency, after learning about an outcome, to be overconfident in one's ability to have predicted it. Per the old adage, "Hindsight is 20/20." Hindsight bias has been widely studied, having been featured in more than 800 articles (Roese & Vohs, 2012). It has been observed in various countries and among both children and adults (Blank, Musch, & Pohl, 2007). Research has shown that after people learn about an experimental finding, the finding seems obvious and very predictable (Slovic & Fischhoff, 1977). Almost any conceivable psychological research finding may seem like common sense after you learn about it. Hindsight bias can even make a pair of opposite research conclusions both seem obvious (Teigen, 1986). If you were told that research indicates that "opposites attract," you would likely nod in agreement. Isn't it obvious? Then again, if you had been told that research indicates that "birds of a feather flock together," you would probably have also agreed and thought the finding obvious. Be mindful of hindsight bias as you learn about what psychologists have learned about us. It may lead you to think that this information is more obvious and easier than it actually is. You may falsely think that you already know much of the material and then not study sufficiently, leading to disappointment at exam time. The hindsight bias even works on itself. Don't you feel like you already knew about this bias? Incidentally, social psychology researchers have found that birds of a feather DO flock together and that opposites DO NOT attract (Myers, 2013).

Psychologists' conclusions are based upon scientific research and thus provide the best answers to questions about human behavior and mental processing. Whether these answers sometimes seem obvious or sometimes agree with common sense is not important. What is important is understanding how psychologists conduct this scientific research in order to get the best answers to their questions. In the next section, we discuss their research methods.

hindsight bias (I-knew-it-all-along phenomenon) The tendency, after learning about an outcome, to be overconfident in one's ability to have predicted it.

Section Summary

In this section, we learned that there are four major research perspectives in psychology. Two of them, the biological perspective and the cognitive perspective, focus on internal causes of our behavior and mental processing. The biological perspective focuses on causal explanations in terms of our physiology, especially the brain and nervous system. The cognitive perspective focuses on understanding how our mental processes work and how they impact our behavior. The biological perspective focuses on the physiological hardware, while the cognitive perspective focuses more on the mental processes or software of the brain.

The behavioral perspective and the sociocultural perspective emphasize external causes. The behavioral perspective focuses on how our observable behavior is conditioned by external environmental events. The sociocultural perspective emphasizes the impact that other people (social forces) and our culture have on our behavior and mental processing.

Psychologists use all four perspectives to get a more complete explanation of our behavior and mental processing. None of these perspectives is better than the others; they are complementary. Developmental psychology is a research field that nicely illustrates their complementary nature.

We also briefly discussed the hindsight bias, the I-knew-it-all-along phenomenon. This bias leads us to find outcomes as more obvious and predictable than they truly are. You need to beware of this bias when learning the basic research findings and theories discussed in the remainder of this text. It may lead you to think that this information is more obvious and easier to understand and remember than it actually is. It is important that you realize that psychologists have used scientific research methods to conduct their studies, thereby obtaining the best answers possible to their questions about human behavior and mental processing.

ConceptCheck | 1

Explain how the biological and cognitive research perspectives differ in their explanations of human behavior and mental processing.

Explain how the behavioral and sociocultural research perspectives differ in their explanations of human behavior and mental processing.

Research Methods Used by Psychologists

Regardless of their perspective, psychology researchers use the same research methods. These methods fall into three categories—descriptive, correlational, and experimental. The experimental method is used most often because it allows the researcher to explore cause–effect relationships. Remember, the goal of psychology is to explain (through cause–effect relationships) behavior and mental processes. However, sometimes researchers can't conduct experiments. For example, it is obviously unethical to set up an experiment studying the effects of passive smoking on children. Who would knowingly put a group of children to a lot by employing the cigarette smoke? In such situations, psychologists other methods—descriptive and correlational. Researchers can carefully observe and describe the health effects on one child in a family of smokers, or they can study many families in search of relationships (correlations) between parental smoking and childhood infections. These other research methods also provide data for developing hypotheses (testable predictions about cause–effect relationships) to examine in experimental research. We'll discuss the three types of methods in the following order: descriptive, correlational, and experimental.

Descriptive Methods

There are three types of **descriptive methods:** observational techniques, case studies, and survey research. The main purpose of all three methods is to provide objective and detailed descriptions of behavior and mental processes. However, these descriptive data only allow the researcher to speculate about cause–effect relationships—to develop hypotheses about causal relationships. Such hypotheses must then be tested in experiments. With this important limitation in mind, we'll consider the three descriptive methods one at a time.

Observational techniques. Observational techniques exactly reflect their name. The researcher directly observes the behavior of interest. Such observation can be done in the laboratory. For example, children's behavior can be observed using one-way mirrors in the laboratory. However, behavior in the laboratory setting may not be natural. This is why researchers often use **naturalistic observation,** a descriptive research method in which behavior is observed in its natural setting, without the researcher intervening in the behavior being observed. Researchers use naturalistic observation when they are interested in how humans or other animals behave in their natural environments. The researcher attempts to describe both objectively and thoroughly the behaviors that are present and the relationships among these behaviors. There have been many well-known observational studies of other species of animals in their natural habitats. You are probably familiar with some of them—Dian Fossey's study of mountain gorillas in Africa, on which the movie, *Gorillas in the Mist,* was based, and Jane Goodall's study of chimpanzees in Africa (Fossey, 1983; Goodall, 1986).

This method is not used only for the observation of other species of animals. Observational studies of human behavior are conducted in many natural settings such as the workplace and school and in social settings such as bars.

Observational techniques do have a major potential problem, though. The observer may influence or change the behavior of those being observed. This is why observers must remain as unobtrusive as possible, so that the results won't be contaminated by their presence. To overcome this possible shortcoming, researchers use participant observation. In **participant observation,** the observer becomes part of the group being observed. Sometimes naturalistic observation studies that start out with unobtrusive observation end up as participant observation studies. For example, Dian Fossey's

descriptive methods research methods whose main purpose is to provide objective and detailed descriptions of behavior and mental processes.

naturalistic observation a descriptive research method in which behavior of interest is observed in its natural setting, and the researcher does not intervene in the behavior being observed.

participant observation A descriptive research method in which the observer becomes part of the group being observed.

study of gorillas turned into participant observation when she was finally accepted as a member of the group. However, in most participant observation studies, the observer begins the study as a participant, whether in a laboratory or natural setting. You can think of this type of study as comparable to doing undercover work. A famous example of such a study involved a group of people posing as patients with symptoms of a major mental disorder to see if doctors at psychiatric hospitals could distinguish them from real patients (Rosenhan, 1973). According to Rosenhan, it turned out that the doctors and staff couldn't do so, but the patients could. Once admitted, these "pseudopatients" acted normally and asked to be released. We will find out what happened to them in Chapter 10, on abnormal psychology.

Lady studying chimps, chimp studying lady

Case studies. Detailed observation is also involved in a case study. In a **case study,** the researcher studies an individual in depth over an extended period of time. In brief, the researcher attempts to learn as much as possible about the individual being studied. A life history for the individual is developed, and data for a variety of tests are collected. The most common use of case studies is in clinical settings with patients suffering specific deficits or problems. The main goal of a case study is to gather information that will help in the treatment of the patient. The results of a case study cannot be generalized to the entire population. They are specific to the individual that has been studied. However, case study data do allow researchers to develop hypotheses that can then be tested in experimental research. A famous example of such a case study is that of the late Henry Molaison, a person with amnesia (Scoville & Milner, 1957). He was studied by nearly 100 investigators (Corkin, 2002) and is often referred to as the most studied individual in the history of neuroscience (Squire, 2009). For confidentiality purposes while he was alive (he died in 2008 at the age of 82), only his initials, H. M., were used to identify him in the hundreds of studies that he participated in for over five decades. Thus, we will refer to him as H. M. His case will be discussed in more detail in Chapter 5, Memory, but let's consider some of his story here to illustrate the importance of case studies in the development of hypotheses and the subsequent experimental work to test these hypotheses.

For medical reasons, H. M. had his hippocampus (a part of the brain below the cortex) and the surrounding areas surgically removed at a young age. His case study included testing his memory capabilities in depth after the operation. Except for some amnesia for a period preceding his surgery (especially events in the days immediately before the surgery), he appeared to have normal memory for information that he had learned before the operation, but he didn't

> **case study** A descriptive research method in which the researcher studies an individual in depth over an extended period of time.

survey research A descriptive research method in which the researcher uses questionnaires and interviews to collect information about the behavior, beliefs, and attitudes of particular groups of people.

population The entire group of people that a researcher is studying.

sample The subset of a population that actually participates in a research study.

seem to be able to form any new memories. For example, if he didn't know you before his operation, he would never be able to remember your name regardless of how many times you met with him. He could read a magazine over and over again without ever realizing that he had read it before. He couldn't remember what he had eaten for breakfast. Such memory deficits led to the hypothesis that the hippocampus plays an important role in the formation of new memories; later experimental research confirmed this hypothesis (Cohen & Eichenbaum, 1993). We will learn exactly what role the hippocampus plays in memory in Chapter 5. Remember, researchers cannot make cause–effect statements based on the findings of a case study, but they can formulate hypotheses that can be tested in experiments.

Survey research. The last descriptive method is one that you are most likely already familiar with, survey research. You have probably completed surveys either online, over the phone, via the mail, or in person during an interview. **Survey research** uses questionnaires and interviews to collect information about the behavior, beliefs, and attitudes of particular groups of people. It is assumed in survey research that people are willing and able to answer the survey questions accurately. However, the wording, order, and structure of the survey questions may lead the participants to give biased answers (Schwartz, 1999). For example, survey researchers need to be aware of the social desirability bias, our tendency to respond in socially approved ways that may not reflect what we actually think or do. This means that questions need to be constructed carefully to minimize such biases. Developing a well-structured, unbiased set of survey questions is a difficult, time-consuming task, but one that is essential to doing good survey research.

Another necessity in survey research is surveying a representative sample of the relevant **population,** the entire group of people being studied. For many reasons (such as time and money), it is impossible to survey every person in the population. This is why the researcher only surveys a **sample,** the subset of people in a population participating in a study. For these sample data to be meaningful, the sample has to be representative of the larger relevant population. If you don't have a representative sample, then generalization of the survey findings to the population is not possible.

One ill-fated survey study of women and love (Hite, 1987) tried to generalize from a nonrepresentative sample (Jackson, 2016). Shere Hite's sample was drawn mainly from women's organizations and political groups, plus some women who requested and completed a survey following the researcher's talk-show appearances. Because such a sample is not representative of American women in general, the results were not either. For example, the estimates of the numbers of women having affairs and disenchanted in their relationships with

"Next question: I believe that life is a constant striving for balance, requiring frequent tradeoffs between morality and necessity, within a cyclic pattern of joy and sadness, forging a trail of bittersweet memories until one slips, inevitably, into the jaws of death. Agree or disagree?"

men were greatly overestimated. To obtain a representative sample, survey researchers usually use random sampling.

In **random sampling,** each individual in the population has an equal opportunity of being in the sample. To understand the "equal opportunity" part of the definition, think about selecting names from a hat, where each name has an equal chance of being selected. In actuality, statisticians have developed procedures for obtaining a random sample that parallel selecting names randomly from a hat. Think about how you would obtain a random sample of first-year students at your college. You couldn't just sample randomly from those first-year students in your psychology class. If you did, all first-year students wouldn't have an equal opportunity to be in your sample. You would have to get a complete list of all first-year students from the registrar and then sample randomly from it. The point to remember is that a survey study must have a representative sample in order to generalize the research findings to the population.

Correlational Studies

In a **correlational study,** two variables are measured to determine if they are related (how well either one predicts the other). A **variable** is any factor that can take on more than one value. For example, age, height, grade point average, and intelligence test scores are all variables. In conducting a correlational study, the researcher first gets a representative sample of the relevant population. Next, the researcher takes the two measurements on the sample. For example, the researcher could measure a person's height and their weight.

The correlation coefficient and predictability. To see if the variables are related, the researcher calculates the **correlation coefficient,** a statistic that tells us the type and the strength of the relationship between two variables. Correlation coefficients range in value from –1.0 to +1.0. The sign of the coefficient, + or –, tells us the type of relationship, positive or negative. A **positive correlation** indicates a direct relationship between two variables—low scores on one variable tend to be paired with low scores on the other variable, and high scores on one variable tend to be paired with high scores on the other variable. Think about the relationship between height and weight. These two variables are positively related. Taller people tend to be heavier. SAT scores and first-year college grades are also positively correlated (Linn, 1982). Students who have higher SAT scores tend to get higher grades during their first year of college.

A **negative correlation** is an inverse relationship between two variables—low scores on one variable tend to be paired with high scores on the other variable, and high scores on one variable tend to be paired with low scores on the other variable. A good example of a negative correlation is the relationship for children between time spent watching television and grades in school—the more time spent watching television, the lower the school grades (Ridley-Johnson, Cooper, & Chance, 1983).

random sampling A sampling technique that obtains a representative sample of a population by ensuring that each individual in a population has an equal opportunity to be in the sample.

correlational study A research study in which two variables are measured to determine if they are related (how well either one predicts the other).

variable Any factor that can take on more than one value.

correlation coefficient A statistic that tells us the type and the strength of the relationship between two variables. The sign of the coefficient (+ or –) indicates the type of correlation—positive or negative, respectively. The absolute value of the coefficient (0.0 to 1.0) represents the strength of the correlation, with 1.0 being the maximum strength.

positive correlation A direct relationship between two variables.

negative correlation An inverse relationship between two variables.

As you know if you have ever climbed a mountain, elevation and temperature are negatively correlated—as elevation increases, temperature decreases. In summary, the sign of the coefficient tells us the type of the relationship between the two variables—positive (+) for a direct relationship or negative (–) for an inverse relationship.

The second part of the correlation coefficient is its absolute value, from 0 to 1.0. The strength of the correlation is indicated by its absolute value. Zero and absolute values near zero indicate no relationship. As the absolute value increases to 1.0, the strength of the relationship increases. Please note that the sign of the coefficient does not tell us anything about the strength of the relationship. Coefficients do not function like numbers on the number line, where positive numbers are greater than negative numbers. With correlation coefficients, only the absolute value of the number tells us about the relationship's strength. For example, –.50 indicates a stronger relationship than +.25. As the strength of the correlation increases, researchers can predict the relationship with more accuracy. If the coefficient is + (or –) 1.0, we have perfect predictability. A correlation of +1.0 means that every change in one variable is accompanied by an equivalent change in the other variable in the same direction, and a correlation of –1.0 means that every change in one variable is accompanied by an equivalent change in the other variable in the opposite direction. Virtually all correlation coefficients in psychological research have an absolute value less than 1.0. Thus, we usually do not have perfect predictability so there will be exceptions to these relationships, even the strong ones. These exceptions do not, however, invalidate the general trends indicated by the correlations. They only indicate that the relationships are not perfect. Because the correlations are not perfect, such exceptions have to exist.

It is also important to realize that when two variables are correlated, but imperfectly so, extreme values on one of the variables tend to be matched on average with less extreme values on the other variable. This is called **regression toward the mean** (the **mean** is the statistical name for the numerical average of a set of values). Probability theory tells us that an extreme value, either far above or below average, is likely to be followed by a value that is more consistent with the long-term average. Regression toward the mean holds for both high and low extreme values. Hence, an extreme low value will move up toward the mean, and an extreme high value will move down toward the mean. A good example of regression toward the mean that you can relate to involves students' exam scores on two exams in a class. The students' scores on the two exams are not perfectly correlated. Regression toward the mean tells us that an unusually high or low score on the first exam will likely be followed by a less extreme score on the second exam. Thus, a student who aced the first exam with a score of 100 will likely get a lower score on the second exam, and a student who failed miserably on the first exam will likely get a higher score on the second exam. There are many factors that impact exam scores for you and other students and thus create this imperfect relationship between the two sets of exam

regression toward the mean The tendency for extreme or unusual values on one variable to be matched on average with less extreme values on the other variable when the two variables are not perfectly correlated.

mean The numerical average for a set of values.

scores. I'm sure that you are familiar with these factors, such as not feeling well when you took one of the exams, studying more for one of the exams, the exam questions overlapping more with the material you emphasized in your study on one exam than the other, and so on. It is important to note that regression toward the mean does not mean that all of the extreme scores have to regress toward the mean but rather that on average the extreme scores will do so. Thus, for example, a student who got a score of 100 on the first exam might also get a perfect score on the second exam. However, if you averaged the scores on the second exam of all of the students who got 100 on the first exam, the average would have regressed toward the mean.

Although regression toward the mean seems straightforward, we do not seem to recognize it when it is operating in our everyday lives. A good example is the widespread belief in the "*Sports Illustrated* jinx"—that it is bad luck for an athlete to be pictured on the cover of *Sports Illustrated* magazine because it will lead to a decline in the athlete's performance afterward (Gilovich, 1991). Many athletes do suffer declines in their performance after being pictured on the cover, but the cause of this decline is regression toward the mean and not a jinx. The athletes pictured on the cover have accomplished outstanding performances in their respective sports. This is why they are on the cover. Regression toward the mean would predict that this extremely high level of performance would followed by a more normal level of performance because performance levels of an athlete over time vary and thus are not perfectly correlated. Hence, such regression in performance would be expected. Failure to recognize regression toward the mean is not only the reason for belief in the *Sports Illustrated* jinx but also the reason for other superstitious beliefs that people hold and many other events that we all experience in our everyday lives (Kruger, Savitsky, & Gilovich, 1999; Lawson, 2002). Extreme events tend to be followed by more ordinary ones. When this happens, the important point to remember is that regression toward the mean is likely operating, and no extraordinary explanation is necessary. Not only do people fail to recognize regression toward the mean when it occurs, they also tend to make nonregressive or insufficiently regressive predictions (Gilovich, 1991; Kahneman & Tversky, 1973). Thus, when trying to explain or predict changes in scores, levels of performance, and other events over time, remember regression toward the mean is likely operating so extreme or extraordinary events will tend to be followed by more normal ones.

Scatterplots. A good way to understand the predictability of a coefficient is to examine a **scatterplot**—a visual depiction of correlational data. In a scatterplot, each data point represents the scores on two variables for each participant. Several sample scatterplots are presented in Figure 1.1 (page 14). Correlational studies usually involve a large number of participants; therefore, there are usually a large number of data points in a scatterplot. Because those in Figure 1.1 are just examples to illustrate how to interpret scatterplots, there are only 15 points in each one. This means there were 15 participants in each of the hypothetical correlational studies leading to these scatterplots.

The scatterplots in Figure 1.1(a) and (b) indicate perfect 1.0 correlations—(a) a perfect positive correlation and (b) a

> **scatterplot** A visual depiction of correlational data in which each data point represents the scores on the two variables for each participant.

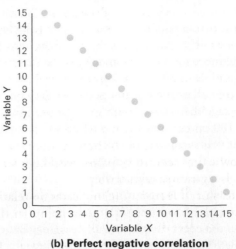

(a) Perfect positive correlation

(b) Perfect negative correlation

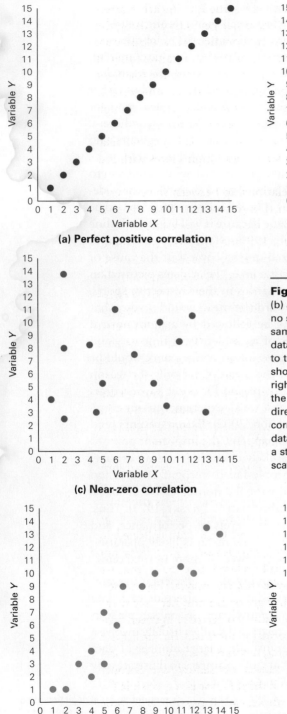

(c) Near-zero correlation

Figure 1.1 | Some Sample Scatterplots | (a) and (b) are examples of perfect correlations because there is no scatter—all of the data points in each plot fall on the same line. The correlation in (a) is positive because the data points show an increasing trend (go from bottom left to top right) and is negative in (b) because the data points show a decreasing trend (go from top left to bottom right). (c) is an example of a near-zero correlation because the data points are scattered all over and do not show a directional trend. (d) is an example of a strong positive correlation because there is not much scatter and the data points have an increasing trend. (e) is an example of a strong negative correlation because there is not much scatter and the data points show a decreasing trend.

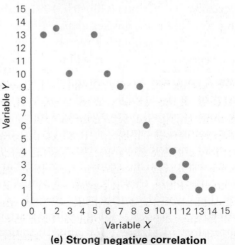

(d) Strong positive correlation

(e) Strong negative correlation

perfect negative correlation. All of the points fall on the same line in each scatterplot, which allows us to predict one variable from the other perfectly by using the equation for the line. This means that you have maximal predictability. Please note that the difference between (a) and (b) is the direction of the data points (line). If the data points show an increasing trend (go from the bottom left to the top right of the scatterplot) as in (a), it is a positive relationship. Low scores on one variable tend to be paired with low scores on the other variable, and high scores with high scores. This is a direct relationship. However, if the data points show a decreasing trend (go from the top left to the bottom right) as in (b), there is a negative relationship. Low scores tend to be paired with high scores, and high scores with low scores. This is an inverse relationship.

The scatterplot in Figure 1.1(c) indicates no relationship between the two variables. There is no direction to the data points in this scatterplot. They are scattered all over in a random fashion. This means that we have a correlation near 0 and minimal predictability. Now consider Figure 1.1(d) and (e). First, you should realize that (d) indicates a positive correlation because of the direction of the data points from the bottom left to the top right and that (e) indicates a negative correlation because of the direction of the scatter from the top left to the bottom right. But what else does the scatter of the data points tell us? Note that the data points in (d) and (e) neither fall on the same line as in (a) and (b), nor are they scattered all about the graph with no directional component as in (c). Thus, scatterplots (d) and (e) indicate correlations with strengths somewhere between 0 and 1.0. As the amount of scatter of the data points increases, the strength of the correlation decreases. So, how strong would the correlations represented in (d) and (e) be? They would be fairly strong because there is not much scatter. Remember, as the amount of scatter increases, the predictability also decreases. When the scatter is maximal as in (c), the strength is near 0, and we have little predictability.

The third-variable problem. Strong correlations give us excellent predictability, but they do not allow us to draw cause–effect conclusions about the relationships between the variables. I cannot stress this point enough. Correlation is necessary but not sufficient for causation to exist. Remember, correlational data do not allow us to conclude anything about cause–effect relationships. Only data collected in well-controlled experiments allow us to draw such conclusions. This does not mean that two correlated variables cannot be causally related, but rather that we cannot determine this from correlational data. Maybe they are; maybe they are not. Correlational data do not allow you to decide if they are or are not. Let's see why.

To understand this point, let's consider the negative correlation between self-esteem and depression. As self-esteem decreases, depression increases. But we cannot conclude that low self-esteem causes depression. First, it could be the reverse causal relationship. Isn't it just as likely that depression causes low self-esteem? Second, and of more consequence, isn't it possible that some third factor is responsible for the relationship between the two variables? For example, isn't it possible that some people have a biological predisposition for both low self-esteem and depression or that both self-esteem and depression are the result of a brain chemistry problem?

Both self-esteem and depression could also stem from some current very stressful events. Such alternative possibilities are examples of the **third-variable problem**—another variable may be responsible for the relationship observed between two variables. In brief, such "third variables" are not controlled in a correlational study, making it impossible to determine the cause for the observed relationship.

To make sure you understand the third-variable problem, here is a very memorable example (Li, 1975, described in Stanovich, 2004). Because of overpopulation problems, a correlational study was conducted in Taiwan to identify variables that best predicted the use of contraceptive devices. Correlational data were collected on many different variables, but the researchers found that use of contraceptive devices was most strongly correlated with the number of electrical appliances in the home! Obviously having electrical appliances such as television sets, microwave ovens, and toasters around does not cause people to use birth control. What third variable might be responsible for this relationship? Think about it. A likely one is level of education. People with a higher education tend both to be better informed about birth control and to have a higher socioeconomic status. The former leads them to use contraceptive devices, and the latter allows them to buy more electrical appliances. Charles Wheelan (2013) describes a similar example of the third-variable problem in his book *Naked Statistics*. Consider the positive correlation between a student's SAT scores and the number of television sets that his family owns. Obviously this does not mean that parents can boost their children's test scores by buying another half-dozen television sets. Nor does it likely mean that watching lots of television is good for academic achievement (we have already learned that it isn't). The most logical explanation would be that highly educated people can afford a lot of television sets and tend to have children who test better than average. Thus, both the number of television sets and the test scores are likely the result of a third variable, parental education.

Now that you are aware of the third-variable problem, think about the following finding of a positive correlation between ice cream sales and forest fires (Silver, 2012). What is the third variable driving this correlation? It is the summer heat. Both occur more often in the summer. Correlations that are the results of third variables are called spurious correlations. A **spurious correlation** is one in which the variables are related through their relationship with one or more other

third-variable problem An explanation of a correlation between two variables in terms of another (third) variable that could possibly be responsible for the observed relationship between the two variables.

spurious correlation A correlation in which the variables are related through their relationship with one or more other variables but not through a causal mechanism.

variables but not through a causal mechanism. *Spurious* comes from the Latin word *spurius,* which means false or illegitimate. Let's think through an example of a spurious correlation. There is a positive correlation between shoe size and reading performance in elementary school children. Certainly having bigger feet doesn't cause a child to read better. What's the third variable operating in this example? If you said age, you are right. Older children on average have larger shoe sizes and read better. Tyler Vigen provides hundreds of examples of spurious correlations at his website, www.TylerVigen.com/spurious-correlations and in his book *Spurious Correlations* (2015). Reviewing some of these examples will help to cement your understanding that correlation does not equal causation.

Given the examples of spurious correlations that we have discussed, such as ice cream sales and forest fires, you may think that such correlations do not have any significance in the real world, but they do. To help you understand why they do, I'll describe a famous example from medical research in which the researchers were led astray by a spurious correlation in their search for the cause of a deadly disease, pellagra. In the early 1900s, pellagra victims (pellagrins) had a mortality rate of 1 in 3, and overall, the disease was killing roughly 100,000 people a year in the southeastern United States (Bronfenbrenner & Mahoney, 1975; Kraut, 2003). Medical researchers were scrambling to find its cause so that a treatment could be found. One correlational study found that the incidence of the disease was negatively correlated with the quality of sanitary conditions (Stanovich, 2010). In geographical areas with higher quality plumbing and sewerage, there was hardly any disease, and in areas with poor plumbing and sewerage, there was an extremely high incidence of the disease. Because this correlation fit the infectious disease model in which the disease is spread by a microorganism, these researchers forgot that there could be a spurious correlation stemming from the third-variable problem and concluded that pellagra was being spread by a microorganism in the feces of victims due to poor sanitary conditions. Enter Joseph Goldberger, assigned by the U.S. Surgeon General to determine the cause of pellagra. He realized that the correlation that had been observed could be a spurious one. If so, he asked, what was the third variable? Goldberger's answer—poverty, which was prevalent in much of the southern United States at that time. People living in areas with high-quality sanitary conditions were economically advantaged, and those living in areas with poor-quality sanitary conditions were economically disadvantaged. But how else could poverty lead to the disease, he wondered? Goldberger's answer was that it led to a dietary deficiency that caused the disease. Economically disadvantaged people were eating a corn-based, high-carbohydrate diet with no animal proteins. It consisted mainly of corn, grits, and cornmeal mush with no meat, eggs, or milk, whereas the diet of the economically advantaged was more balanced and included animal proteins.

But why should a dietary deficiency hypothesis be preferred over an infectious disease hypothesis? Both were congruent with the available correlational data. Most medical researchers ignored Goldberger's proposal and continued to pursue the infectious disease hypothesis. Given the urgency of the situation, with thousands dying from the disease, a frustrated Goldberger felt compelled to squash that hypothesis once and for all by exposing himself and some volunteers to its proposed cause in a series of dramatic demonstrations. He, his wife, and 14 volunteers engaged in a series of what were termed "filth parties" because the participants were "feasting on filth" (Kraut, 2003, p. 147). Urine, fecal matter, and liquid feces were taken from pellagrins and then were mixed with wheat flour and formed into dough balls that were swallowed by Goldberger and the volunteers (Kraut, 2003). For complete refutation of the infectious disease hypothesis, they also mixed scabs taken from the rashes of pellagrins into the dough balls, allowed themselves to be injected with blood taken from pellagrins, and applied secretions from the throats and noses of pellagrins with swabs to their own noses and throats. What happened? No one developed pellagra. The infectious disease hypothesis was put to rest. You are likely wondering why Goldberger and these volunteers had so much faith in the dietary deficiency hypothesis that they would participate in these "filthy" demonstrations. Goldberger had collected enough supporting data from dietary studies that he had conducted at orphanages, a state prison, and a state asylum to convince his wife and the volunteers, but not his opponents, that he was right (Kraut, 2003). Sadly, Goldberger died from kidney cancer in 1929 before the specific dietary cause of pellagra, a niacin deficiency, was identified in the 1930s.

In sum, it is important to realize that correlational studies only allow researchers to develop hypotheses about cause–effect relationships. To test these hypotheses so that cause–effect relationships can be determined, researchers conduct experiments in which they manipulate one variable and measure its effect upon another variable while controlling other potentially relevant (third) variables. For example, one of Goldberger's studies preceding the "filth parties" was an experiment with volunteer inmates in a state prison (Kraut, 2003). Goldberger manipulated the diet of the prisoners by having a group of volunteer prisoners eat the corn-based, no-animal-protein diet that he hypothesized caused the disease and measured the incidence of pellagra development in these prisoners. He found that the majority of the 11 prisoners who ate this diet developed pellagra whereas none of the prison population who ate the normal, more balanced prison diet did. Because the only difference between the prisoners was their diets, Goldberger concluded that a dietary deficiency was the cause of pellagra. What happened to the prisoners who developed pellagra? They had volunteered in exchange for pardons after the study ended. Goldberger offered all of those who had developed pellagra treatment until they were well, and most stayed and were successfully treated. However, some refused and left the prison without treatment. Obviously this was an unusual, ethically questionable experiment that involved a serious disease, but it does illustrate the key elements of experimental research—control, manipulation, and measurement. These elements and the experimental research method are the topics we discuss next.

Experimental Research

The key aspect of experimental research is that the researcher controls the experimental setting. The only factor that varies is what the researcher manipulates. It is this control that allows the researcher to make cause–effect statements about the experimental results. This control is derived primarily from two actions. First, the experimenter controls for the possible influence of third variables by making sure that they are held constant across all of the groups or conditions in the experiment. Second, the experimenter controls for any possible influences due to the individual characteristics of the participants, such as intelligence, motivation, and memory, by using **random assignment**—randomly assigning the participants to groups in an experiment in order to equalize participant characteristics across the various groups in the experiment. If the participant characteristics of the groups are on average equivalent at the beginning of the experiment, then any differences between the groups at the end of the experiment cannot be attributed to such characteristics.

> **random assignment** A control measure in which participants are randomly assigned to groups in order to equalize participant characteristics across the various groups in an experiment.
>
> **independent variable** In an experiment, the variable that is a hypothesized cause and thus is manipulated by the experimenter.
>
> **dependent variable** In an experiment, a variable that is hypothesized to be affected by the independent variable and thus is measured by the experimenter.

Please note the differences between random assignment and random sampling. Random sampling is a technique in which a sample of participants that is representative of a population is obtained. Hence it is used not only in experiments but also in other research methods such as correlational studies and surveys. Random assignment is only used in experiments. It is a control measure in which the researcher randomly assigns the participants in the sample to the various groups or conditions in an experiment. Random sampling allows you to generalize your results to the relevant population; random assignment controls for possible influences of individual characteristics of the participants on the behavior(s) of interest in an experiment. These differences between random sampling and random assignment are summarized in Table 1.2.

Designing an experiment. When a researcher designs an experiment, the researcher begins with a hypothesis (the prediction to be tested) about the cause–effect relationship between two variables. One of the two variables is assumed to be the cause, and the other variable is the one to be affected. The **independent variable** is the hypothesized cause, and the experimenter manipulates it. The **dependent variable**

Table 1.2 Differences Between Random Sampling and Random Assignment	
Random Sampling	**Random Assignment**
A sampling technique in which a sample of participants that is representative of the population is obtained	A control measure in which participants in a sample are randomly assigned to the groups or conditions in an experiment
Used in experiments and some other research methods such as correlational studies and surveys	Used only in experiments
Allows researcher to generalize the findings to the relevant population	Allows researcher to control for possible influences of individual characteristics of the participants on the behavior(s) of interest

is the variable that is hypothesized to be affected by the independent variable and thus is measured by the experimenter. Thus, in an **experiment** the researcher manipulates the independent variable and measures its effect on the dependent variable while controlling other potentially relevant variables. If there is a causal relationship between the independent and dependent variables, then the measurements of the dependent variable are dependent on the values of the independent variable, hence the name dependent variable. Sometimes the researcher hypothesizes more than one cause or more than one effect so he manipulates more than one independent variable or measures more than one dependent variable. To help you understand this terminology and the mechanics of an experiment, I'll describe an example.

Let's consider the simplest experiment first—only two groups. For control purposes, participants are randomly assigned to these two groups. One of the groups will be exposed to the independent variable, and the other will not. The group exposed to the independent variable is called the **experimental group,** and the group not exposed to the independent variable is called the **control group.** Let's say the experimenter's hypothesis is that aerobic exercise reduces anxiety. The independent variable that will be manipulated is aerobic exercise, and the dependent variable that will be measured is level of anxiety. The experimental group will participate in some aerobic exercise program, and the control group will not. To measure any possible effects of the aerobic exercise on anxiety, the experimenter must measure the anxiety levels of the participants in each group at the beginning of the study before the independent variable is manipulated, and then again after the manipulation. If the two groups are truly equivalent, the level of anxiety for each group at the beginning of the study should be essentially the same. If the aerobic exercise does reduce anxiety, then we should see this difference in the second measurement of anxiety at the end of the experiment.

The independent and dependent variables in an experiment must be operationally defined. An **operational definition** is a description of the operations or procedures the researcher uses to manipulate or measure a variable. In our sample experiment, the operational definition of aerobic exercise would include the type and the duration of the activity. For level of anxiety, the operational definition would describe the way the anxiety variable was measured (for example, a participant's score on a specified anxiety scale). Operational definitions not only clarify a particular experimenter's definitions of variables but also allow other experimenters to attempt to replicate the experiment more easily, and replication is the cornerstone of science (Moonesinghe, Khoury, & Janssens, 2007).

Let's go back to our aerobic exercise experiment. We have our experimental group and our control group, but this experiment really requires a second control group. The first control group (the group not participating in the aerobic exercise program) provides a baseline level of anxiety to which the anxiety of the experimental group can then be compared. In other words, it controls for changes over time in the level of anxiety not due to

experiment A research method in which the researcher manipulates one or more independent variables and measures their effect on one or more dependent variables while controlling other potentially relevant variables.

experimental group In an experiment, the group exposed to the independent variable.

control group In an experiment, the group not exposed to the independent variable.

operational definition A description of the operations or procedures that a researcher uses to manipulate or measure a variable.

aerobic exercise, such as regression toward the mean. However, we also need to control for what is called the **placebo effect**—improvement due to the expectation of improving because of receiving treatment. The treatment involved in the placebo effect, however, only involves receiving a **placebo**—an inactive pill or a sham treatment that has no known effects. The placebo effect can arise not only from a conscious belief in the treatment but also from subconscious associations between recovery and the experience of being treated (Niemi, 2009). For example, stimuli that a patient links with getting better, such as a doctor's white lab coat or the smell of an examining room, may induce some improvement in the patient's condition. In addition, giving a placebo a popular medication brand name, prescribing more frequent doses, using placebo injections rather than pills, or indicating that it is expensive can boost the effect of a placebo (Niemi, 2009; Stewart-Williams, 2004; Waber, Shiv, Carmon, & Ariely, 2008). Recent research has even found that the placebo effect may not require concealment or deception (Kaptchuk et al., 2010); in the case of pain, that its size may be impacted by personality traits, such as altruism and resilience (Peciña et al., 2013); and for migraine headache drugs, that it may account for greater than 50% of the drug's effectiveness (Kam-Hansen et al., 2014). Given such findings, it is not surprising that almost half of the physicians recently surveyed reported that they prescribed placebo treatments on a regular basis, and over 60% of the surveyed physicians found this to be an ethically permissible practice (Tilburt, Emanuel, Kaptchuk, Curlin, & Miller, 2008).

You might be puzzled by physicians prescribing placebos, but consider the following. Combining the research finding that the placebo response to pain is very large (Kam-Hansen et al., 2014) with the fact that painkiller addiction has become a major problem in our society, suggests that prescribing placebos might be a viable first course of action for the treatment of pain (Marchant, 2016). Given this large placebo effect, a prescription for an active painkiller might then not be necessary, lessening the possibility of addiction. A recent finding that placebo effects for chronic pain have gotten stronger over time in the United States though not elsewhere in the world (Tuttle et al., 2015) makes the use of placebos in the treatment of pain in this country even more viable. According to Tuttle et al., clinical trials in 2013 for drugs to treat chronic pain produced on average only 9% more pain relief than placebos. In 1996, it was 27%. You may be wondering why the placebo effect for chronic pain has become so strong. One likely explanatory factor is that we have come to have a stronger belief in the effectiveness of painkilling drugs because of the media advertising the effectiveness of these drugs and drugs in general, thereby leading us to have a stronger placebo effect because belief plays a crucial role in the

placebo effect Improvement due to the expectation of improving because of receiving treatment.

placebo An inactive pill or a sham treatment that has no known effects.

placebo effect for pain (Benedetti, 2014). It is difficult, for example, to watch commercial television without being bombarded with such drug advertisements. But don't other countries have such advertising? No, such direct-to-consumer advertising for prescription drugs is only legal here in the United States and in New Zealand. There is also evidence for increased placebo responses in clinical trials for some other drugs, such as antidepressants (Rief et al., 2009). Consequently, prescribing placebos as the first step in treatment of medical problems, such as chronic pain, and mental disorders, such as depression, instead of drugs that are addictive or have serious side effects seems to be a very promising possibility.

The placebo (Latin for "I will please) effect, however, does have an evil twin, the **nocebo** (Latin for "I will harm") **effect**, whereby expectation of a negative outcome due to treatment leads to adverse effects (Benedetti, Lanotte, Lopiano, & Colloca, 2007; Kennedy, 1961). Expectations can also do harm; hence, the nocebo effect is sometimes referred to as a negative placebo effect. For example, when a patient anticipates a drug's possible side effects, he can suffer them even if the drug is a placebo. Because of ethical reasons, the nocebo effect has not been studied nearly as much as the placebo effect, but recently Häuser, Hansen, and Enck (2012) reviewed 31 studies that clearly demonstrated the nocebo effect in clinical practice. They concluded that the nocebo effect creates an ethical dilemma for physicians and therapists—how do they fully inform patients of the potential complications of treatment and at the same time minimize inducing these complications through nocebo effects? Similarly, Petersen et al. (2014) reviewed 10 studies on the nocebo effect on pain and found the effect sizes to be similar to those for placebo effects (moderate to large), thereby indicating the importance of minimizing these effects in actual clinical practice. Thus, research on the nocebo effect has mainly centered on its critical role in clinical practice, whereas much of the research on the placebo effect has been concerned with controlling for improvement due to participant expectations in clinical drug trials and experimental studies, as in our aerobic exercise experiment.

The reduction of anxiety in the experimental group participants in our aerobic exercise experiment may be partially or completely due to a placebo effect. This is why researchers add a control group called the placebo group to control for the possible placebo effect. A **placebo group** is a group of participants who believe they are receiving treatment, but they are not. They get a placebo. For example, the participants in a placebo group in the aerobic exercise experiment would be told that they are getting an antianxiety drug, but they would only get a placebo (in this case, a pill that has no active ingredient). The complete design for the aerobic exercise experiment, including the experimental, placebo, and control groups, is shown in Figure 1.2 For the experimenter to conclude that there is a placebo effect, the reduction of anxiety in the placebo group would have to be significantly greater than the reduction for the control group. This is because the control group provides a baseline of the reduction in symptom severity over time caused by factors other than that caused

nocebo effect A negative placebo effect due to the expectation of adverse consequences from receiving treatment.

placebo group A control group of participants who believe they are receiving treatment, but who are only receiving a placebo.

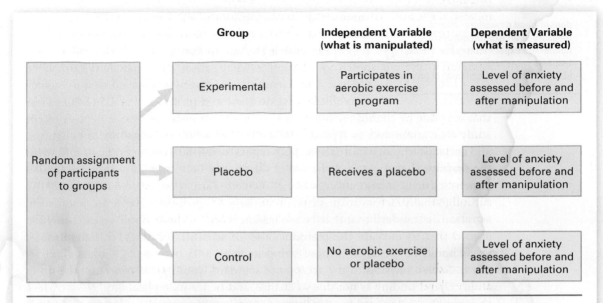

Figure 1.2 | Design of Aerobic Exercise and Anxiety Experiment | Participants are randomly assigned to groups in order to equalize participant characteristics across the groups. The placebo group controls for the placebo effect, and the control group provides a baseline level of anxiety reduction for participants who do not participate in the aerobic exercise program or receive a placebo. The level of anxiety reduction for each group is determined by comparing the measurements of the dependent variable (level of anxiety) before and after manipulating the independent variable (aerobic exercise).

by the placebo (Benedetti, 2014). A good example of such a factor is one that we discussed earlier in the chapter, regression toward the mean. In this example, it would translate to your anxiety regressing naturally toward its normal level over time. If a control group was not included in the study, then the measurement of the placebo effect would be confounded because it would include the improvement due to these other factors and not just the placebo. Similarly, for the experimenter to conclude that the reduction of anxiety in the experimental group is due to aerobic exercise and not a placebo effect or other factors leading to a reduction in anxiety, the reduction would have to be significantly greater than that observed for the placebo and control groups because the reduction in the experimental group is due not only to the effect of the aerobic exercise but also to a placebo effect created by the expectation of getting better by engaging in the aerobic exercise and to natural factors leading the body to reduce anxiety and return to its normal state.

Now you may be wondering what is meant by "significantly greater." This is where statistical analysis enters the scene. We use what are called **inferential statistical analyses**—statistical analyses that allow researchers to draw conclusions about the results of their studies. Such analyses tell the researcher the probability that the results of the study are due to random

inferential statistical analyses
Statistical analyses that allow researchers to draw conclusions about the results of a study by determining the probability that the results are due to random variation (chance). The results are statistically significant if this probability is .05 or less.

double-blind procedure A control measure in an experiment in which neither the experimenters nor the participants know which participants are in the experimental and control groups.

variation (chance). Obviously, the experimenter would want this probability to be low. Remember, the experimenter's hypothesis is that the manipulation of the independent variable (not chance) is what causes the dependent variable to change. The scientific community has agreed that a "significant" finding is one that has a probability of .05 (1/20) or less that it is due to chance. Possibly, this acceptance standard is too lenient. A recent study that attempted to replicate 100 research findings reported in top cognitive and social psychology journals failed to replicate over 60% of the findings, and when the findings were replicated, the size of the observed effects were on average smaller (Open Science Collaboration, 2015; cf. Gilbert, King, Pettigrew, & Wilson, 2016). Although many factors are involved in this large-scale failure to replicate, a statistical significance standard that may be too lenient is one of them. Some researchers have argued that to increase the reproducibility of scientific findings, this significance level should be raised to a more stringent level, .005 or less (e.g., Johnson, 2013, 2014). Such a revision to the acceptance standard would greatly increase the probability that a finding is not due to chance, and hence its replicability. Nevertheless, the acceptance standard for significance at present remains .05 or less.

Statistical significance tells us the probability that a finding did not occur by chance, but it does not insure that the finding has practical significance or value in our everyday world. A statistically significant finding with little practical value sometimes occurs when very large samples are used in a study. With such samples, very small differences among groups may be significant. Belmont and Marolla's (1973) finding of a birth-order effect for intelligence test scores is a good example of such a finding. Belmont and Marolla analyzed intelligence test data for almost 400,000 19-year-old Dutch males. There was a clear birth-order effect: First borns scored significantly higher than second borns, second borns higher than third borns, and so on. However, the score difference between these groups was very small (only a point or two) and thus not of much practical value. So remember, statistically significant findings do not always have practical significance.

The aerobic exercise experiment would also need to include another control measure, the double-blind procedure. In the **double-blind procedure,** neither the experimenters nor the participants know which participants are in the experimental and control groups. This procedure is called "double-blind" because both the experimenters and participants are blind to (do not know) the participant group assignments. It is not unusual for participants to be blind to which group they have been assigned. This is especially critical for

Sidney Harris/ScienceCartoonsPlus.com

"It was more of a 'triple-blind' test. The patients didn't know which ones were getting the real drug, the doctors didn't know, and I'm afraid, <u>nobody</u> knew."

the placebo group participants. If they were told that they were getting a placebo, there would be no expectation for getting better and hence no (or a much reduced) placebo effect. But why should the experimenters not know the group assignments of the participants? This is to control for the effects of experimenter expectation (Rosenthal, 1966, 1994). If the experimenter knew which condition the participants were in, she might unintentionally treat them differently and thereby affect their behavior. In addition, the experimenter might interpret and record the behavior of the participants differently if she needed to make judgments about their behavior (their anxiety level in the example study). The key for the participant assignments to groups is kept by a third party and then given to the experimenter once the study has been conducted.

Now let's think about experiments that are more complex than our sample experiment with its one independent variable (aerobic exercise) and two control groups. In most experiments, the researcher examines multiple values of the independent variable. With respect to the aerobic exercise variable, the experimenter might examine the effects of different amounts or different types of aerobic exercise. Such manipulations would provide more detailed information about the effects of aerobic exercise on anxiety. An experimenter might also manipulate more than one independent variable. For example, an experimenter might manipulate diet as well as aerobic exercise. Different diets (high-protein vs. high-carbohydrate diets) might affect a person's level of anxiety in different ways. The two independent variables (diet and aerobic exercise) might also interact to determine one's level of anxiety. An experimenter could also increase the number of dependent variables. For example, both level of anxiety and level of depression could be measured in our sample experiment, even if only aerobic exercise were manipulated. If aerobic exercise reduces anxiety, then it might also reduce depression. As an experimenter increases the number of values of an independent variable, the number of independent variables, or the number of dependent variables, the possible gain in knowledge about the relationship between the variables also increases. Thus, most experiments are more complex in design than our simple example with an experimental group and two control groups. In addition, many experimental studies, including replications, must be conducted to address any experimental question. Researchers have a statistical technique called **meta-analysis** that combines the results for a large number of studies on one experimental question into one analysis to arrive at an overall conclusion. Because a meta-analysis involves the results of numerous experimental studies, its conclusion is considered much stronger evidence than the results of an individual study in answering an experimental question.

The various research methods that have been discussed are summarized in Table 1.3 (page 26). Their purposes and data-gathering procedures are described. Make sure you understand each of these research methods before going on to the next section, where we'll discuss how to understand research results. If you feel that you don't understand a particular method, go back and reread the information about it until you do.

meta-analysis A statistical technique that combines the results of a large number of studies on one experimental question into one analysis to arrive at an overall conclusion.

Table 1.3	Summary of Research Methods	
Research Method	**Goal of Method**	**How Data Are Collected**
Laboratory observation	Description	Unobtrusively observe behavior in a laboratory setting
Naturalistic observation	Description	Unobtrusively observe behavior in its natural setting
Participant observation	Description	Observer becomes part of the group whose behavior is being observed
Case study	Description	Study an individual in depth over an extended period of time
Survey	Description	Representative sample of a group completes questionnaires or interviews to determine behavior, beliefs, and attitudes of the group
Correlational study	Prediction	Measure two variables to determine whether they are related
Experiment	Explanation	Manipulate one or more independent variables in a controlled setting to determine their impact on one or more measured dependent variables

Section Summary

Research methods fall into three categories—descriptive, correlational, and experimental. There are three descriptive methods—observation, case studies, and surveys. Observational studies can be conducted in the laboratory or in a natural setting (naturalistic observation). Sometimes participant observation is used. In participant observation, the observer becomes a part of the group being observed. The main goal of all observation is to obtain a detailed and accurate description of behavior. A case study is an in-depth study of one individual. Hypotheses generated from case studies in a clinical setting have often led to important experimental findings. Surveys attempt to describe the behavior, attitudes, or beliefs of particular populations (groups of people). It is essential in conducting surveys to ensure that a representative sample of the population is obtained for the study. Random sampling in which each person in the population has an equal opportunity to be in the sample is used for this purpose.

Descriptive methods only allow description, but correlational studies allow the researcher to make predictions about the relationships between variables. In a correlational study, two variables are measured and these measurements are compared to see if they are related. A statistic, the correlation coefficient, tells us both the type of the relationship (positive or negative) and the strength of the relationship. The sign of the coefficient (+ or –) tells us the type, and the absolute value of the coefficient (0 to 1.0) tells us the strength. Zero and values near zero indicate no relationship. As the absolute value approaches 1.0, the strength increases. Correlational data may also be depicted in scatterplots. A positive correlation is indicated by data points that extend from the bottom left of the plot to the top right. Scattered data points going from the top left to the bottom right indicate a negative correlation. The strength is reflected in the amount of scatter—the more the scatter, the lower the strength. When two variables are not perfectly correlated, regression toward the mean will be observed. This means that extreme values on one of the variables tend to be matched on average with less extreme values on the other variable. Thus, when trying to explain or predict changes in scores, levels of performance, and other events over time, remember regression toward the mean is likely operating so extreme or extraordinary events will tend to be followed by more normal ones. A correlation of 1.0 gives us perfect predictability about the two variables involved, but it does not allow us to make cause–effect statements about the variables. This is because "third variables" may be responsible for the observed relationship, making the correlation a spurious one.

To draw cause–effect conclusions, the researcher must conduct well-controlled experiments. In a simple experiment, the researcher manipulates the independent variable (the hypothesized cause) and measures its effect upon the dependent variable (the variable hypothesized to be affected). These variables are operationally defined so that other researchers understand exactly how they were manipulated or measured. In more complex experiments, more than one independent variable is manipulated or more than one dependent variable is measured. The experiment is conducted in a controlled environment in which possible third variables are held constant; the individual characteristics of participants are controlled through random assignment of participants to groups or conditions. Other controls employed in experiments include using a control group that is not exposed to the experimental manipulation, a placebo group that receives a placebo to control for the placebo effect, and the double-blind procedure that controls for the effects of experimenter and participant expectation. The researcher uses inferential statistics to interpret the results of an experiment. These statistics determine the probability that the results are due to chance. For the results to be statistically significant, this probability has to be .05 or less, but this significance standard may be too lenient. In addition, statistically significant results may or may not have practical significance or value in our everyday world. Because researchers have to conduct many studies, including replications, to address an experimental question, meta-analysis, a statistical technique that combines the results of a large number of experiments on one experimental question into one analysis, can be used to arrive at an overall conclusion.

ConceptCheck | 2

Explain why the results of a case study cannot be generalized to a population.

Explain the differences between random sampling and random assignment.

Explain how the scatterplots for correlation coefficients of +.90 and –.90 would differ.

Waldman, Nicholson, Adilov, and Williams (2008) found that autism prevalence rates among school-aged children were positively correlated with annual precipitation levels in various states. Autism rates were higher in counties with higher precipitation levels. Try to identify some possible third variables that might be responsible for this correlation.

Explain why a double-blind procedure is necessary in an experiment in which there is a placebo group.

How to Understand Research Results

Once we have completed an experiment, we need to understand our results and to describe them concisely so that others can understand them. To do this, we need to use statistics. There are two types of statistics—descriptive and inferential. We described inferential statistics when we discussed how to interpret the results of experimental studies. In this section, we will be discussing **descriptive statistics**—statistics used to describe the data of a research study in a concise fashion. The correlation coefficient that we discussed earlier is a descriptive statistic that allows us to describe the results of a correlational study precisely. For experimental findings, we need two types of descriptive statistics to summarize our data—measures of central tendency and measures of variability. In addition, a researcher often constructs a frequency distribution for the data. A **frequency distribution** depicts, in a table or a graph, the number of participants receiving each score for a variable. The bell curve, or normal distribution, is the most famous frequency distribution. We begin with the two types of descriptive statistics necessary to describe a data set: measures of central tendency and measures of variability.

Descriptive Statistics

In an experiment, the data set consists of the measured scores on the dependent variable for the sample of participants. A listing of this set of scores, or any set of numbers, is referred to as a distribution of scores, or a distribution of numbers. To describe such distributions in a concise summary manner, we use two types of descriptive statistics: measures of central tendency and measures of variability.

Measures of central tendency. The measures of central tendency define a "typical" score for a distribution of scores. There are three measures of central tendency (three ways to define the "typical" score)—mean, median, and mode. The first, the mean, is one that you are already familiar with from our earlier discussion of the regression toward the mean phenomenon. Remember, the mean is the numerical average for a distribution of scores. To compute the mean, you merely add up all of the scores and divide by the number of scores. A second measure of central tendency is the **median**—the score positioned in the middle of the distribution of scores when all of the scores are listed from the lowest to the highest. If there is an odd number of scores, the median is the middle score. If there is an even number of scores, the median is the halfway point between the two center scores. The final measure of central tendency, the **mode**, is the most frequently occurring score in a distribution of scores. Sometimes there are two or more scores that occur most frequently. In these cases, the distribution has multiple modes. Now let's consider a small set of scores to see how these measures are computed.

descriptive statistics Statistics that describe the results of a research study in a concise fashion.

frequency distribution A depiction, in a table or figure, of the number of participants (frequency) receiving each score for a variable.

median The score positioned in the middle of a distribution of scores when all of the scores are arranged from lowest to highest.

mode The most frequently occurring score in a distribution of scores.

Let's imagine a class with five students who just took an exam. That gives us a distribution of five test scores: 70, 80, 80, 85, and 85. First, let's compute the mean or average score. The sum of all five scores is 400. Now divide 400 by 5, and you get the mean, 80. What's the median? It's the middle score when the scores are arranged in ascending order. Because there is an odd number of scores (5), it's the third score—80. If there had been an even number of scores, the median would be the halfway point between the center two scores. For example, if there had been only four scores in our sample distribution (70, 80, 85, and 85), the median would be the halfway point between 80 and 85, 82.5. Now, what's the mode or most frequently occurring score? For the distribution of five scores, there are two numbers that occur twice, so there are two modes—80 and 85. This kind of distribution is referred to as a bimodal distribution (a distribution with two modes). Remember that a distribution can have one or more than one mode.

Of the three measures of central tendency, the mean is the one that is most commonly used. This is mainly because it is used to analyze the data in many inferential statistical tests. The mean can be distorted, however, by a small set of unusually high or low scores. In this case, the median, which is not distorted by such scores, should be used. To understand how atypical scores can distort the mean, let's consider changing one score in our sample distribution of five scores. Change 70 to 20. Now, the mean is 70 (350/5). The median remains 80, however; it hasn't changed. This is because the median is only a positional score. The mean is distorted because it has to average in the value of any unusual scores.

Measures of variability. In addition to knowing the typical score for a distribution, you need to determine the variability between the scores. For example, two distributions might have the same mean, but one distribution might have little variability between scores and the other, considerable variability between scores. So how is such variability measured? There are two measures of variability—the range and the standard deviation. The range is the simpler to compute. The **range** is simply the difference between the highest and lowest scores in the distribution. For our sample distribution with five scores, it would be 85 minus 70, or 15. However, like the mean, unusually high or low scores distort the range. For example, if the 70 in the distribution had been a 20, the range would change to be 85 minus 20, or 65. This would not be a good measure of the distribution's variability because four of the five scores are 80 or 85, not very different.

The measure of variability used most often is the standard deviation. In general terms, the **standard deviation** is the average extent that the scores vary from the mean of the distribution. In other words, how spread out are the scores? If the scores do not vary much from the mean, the standard deviation will be small. If they vary a lot from the mean, the standard deviation will be larger. In our example of five test scores with a mean of 80, the scores (70, 80, 80, 85, and 85) didn't vary much from this mean, therefore the standard deviation would not be very large. However, if the scores had been 20, 40, 80, 120, and 140, the mean would still be 80;

range The difference between the highest and lowest scores in a distribution of scores.

standard deviation The average extent that the scores vary from the mean for a distribution of scores.

Table 1.4	Summary of Descriptive Statistics
Descriptive Statistic	**Explanation of Statistic**
Correlation coefficient	A number between −1.0 and +1.0 whose sign indicates the type (+ = positive and − = negative) and whose absolute value (0 to 1.0) indicates the strength of the relationship between two variables
Mean	Numerical average for a distribution of scores
Median	Middle score in a distribution of scores when all scores are arranged in order from lowest to highest
Mode	Most frequently occurring score or scores in a distribution of scores
Range	Difference between highest and lowest scores in a distribution of scores
Standard deviation	Average extent to which the scores vary from the mean for a distribution of scores

but the scores vary more from the mean, therefore the standard deviation would be much larger.

The standard deviation and the various other descriptive statistics that we have discussed are summarized in Table 1.4. Review this table to make sure you understand each statistic. The standard deviation is especially relevant to the normal distribution, or bell curve. We will see in Chapter 6, on thinking and intelligence, that intelligence test scores are actually determined with respect to standard deviation units in the normal distribution. Next we will consider the normal distribution and the two types of skewed frequency distributions.

Frequency Distributions

A frequency distribution organizes the data in a score distribution so that we know the frequency of each score. It tells us how often each score occurred. These frequencies can be presented in a table or visually in a figure. We'll consider visual depictions. For many human traits (such as height, weight, and intelligence), the frequency distribution takes on the shape of a bell curve. For example, the heights of American adult men are distributed in a bell-shaped manner around a mean of 5 feet 10 inches (Wheelan, 2013). In fact, if a large number of people are measured on almost anything, the frequency distribution will visually approximate a bell-shaped curve. Statisticians call this bell-shaped frequency distribution, shown in Figure 1.3, the **normal distribution**.

normal distribution A frequency distribution that is shaped like a bell. About 68% of the scores fall within 1 standard deviation of the mean, about 95% within 2 standard deviations of the mean, and over 99% within 3 standard deviations of the mean.

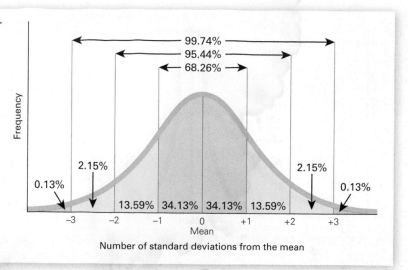

Figure 1.3 | The Normal Distribution | In a normal distribution, the mean, the median, and the mode are all equal because the distribution is perfectly symmetrical about its center. In addition, about 68% of the scores fall within 1 standard deviation of the mean, about 95% within 2 standard deviations of the mean, and over 99% within 3 standard deviations of the mean.

Normal distributions. There are two main aspects of a normal distribution. First, the mean, the median, and the mode are all equal because the normal distribution is symmetric about its center. You do not have to worry about which measure of central tendency to use because all of them are equal. The same number of scores fall below the center point as above it. Second, the percentage of scores falling within a certain number of standard deviations of the mean is set. About 68% of the scores fall within 1 standard deviation of the mean; about 95% within 2 standard deviations of the mean; and over 99% within 3 standard deviations of the mean. So what does this mean for the normal distribution of the heights of American adult men with a mean of 5 feet 10 inches? First, we have to know the standard deviation for this distribution. It is 3 inches. Thus, 68% of the heights of American men fall between 5 feet 7 inches (5 feet 10 inches – 3 inches) and 6 feet 1 inches (5 feet 10 inches + 3 inches), 95% between 5 feet 4 inches (5 feet 10 inches – 6 inches) and 6 feet 4 inches (5 feet 10 inches + 6 inches), and 99% between 5 feet 1 inch (5 feet 10 inches – 9 inches) and 6 feet 7 inches (5 feet 10 inches + 9 inches).

These percentages falling within a certain number of standard deviations are what give the normal distribution its bell shape. The percentages hold regardless of the size of the standard deviation for a normal distribution. Figure 1.4 (page 32) shows two normal distributions with the same mean but different

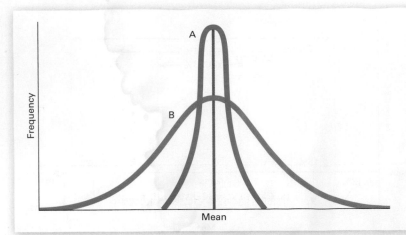

Figure 1.4 | Normal Distributions with Different Standard Deviations | These are normal distributions with the same mean but different standard deviations. Normal distribution A has a smaller standard deviation than normal distribution B. As the standard deviation for a normal distribution gets smaller, its bell shape gets narrower and taller.

standard deviations. Both have bell shapes, but the distribution with the smaller standard deviation (A) is taller. As the size of the standard deviation increases, the bell shape becomes shorter and wider (like B).

The percentages of scores and the number of standard deviations from the mean always have the same relationship in a normal distribution. This allows you to compute percentile ranks for scores. A **percentile rank** is the percentage of scores below a specific score in a distribution of scores. If you know how many standard deviation units a specific score is above or below the mean in a normal distribution, you can compute that score's percentile rank. For example, the percentile rank of a score that is 1 standard deviation above the mean is roughly 84%. Remember, a normal distribution is symmetric about the mean so that 50% of the scores are above the mean and 50% are below the mean. This means that the percentile rank of a score that is 1 standard deviation above the mean is greater than 50% (the percent below the mean) + 34% (the percent of scores from the mean to +1 standard deviation).

Now I'll let you try to compute a percentile rank. What is the percentile rank for a score that is 1 standard deviation below the mean? Remember that it is the percentage of the scores below that score. Look at Figure 1.3. What percentage of the scores is less than a score that is 1 standard deviation below the mean? The answer is about 16%. You can never have a percentile rank of 100% because you cannot outscore yourself, but you can have a percentile rank of 0% if you have the lowest score in the distribution. The scores on intelligence tests and the SAT are based on normal distributions, so percentile ranks can be calculated for these scores. We will return to the normal distribution when we discuss intelligence test scores in Chapter 6.

Skewed distributions. In addition to the normal distribution, two other types of frequency distributions are important. They are called skewed distributions, which are frequency distributions that are asymmetric in shape. The two major types of skewed distributions are illustrated in

percentile rank The percentage of scores below a specific score in a distribution of scores.

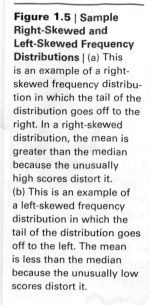

Figure 1.5 | Sample Right-Skewed and Left-Skewed Frequency Distributions | (a) This is an example of a right-skewed frequency distribution in which the tail of the distribution goes off to the right. In a right-skewed distribution, the mean is greater than the median because the unusually high scores distort it. (b) This is an example of a left-skewed frequency distribution in which the tail of the distribution goes off to the left. The mean is less than the median because the unusually low scores distort it.

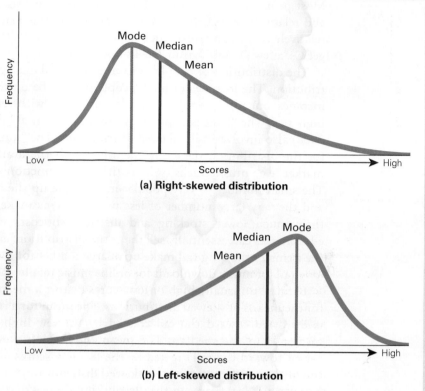

Figure 1.5. A **right-skewed distribution** is a frequency distribution in which there are some unusually high scores [shown in Figure 1.5(a)]. A **left-skewed distribution** is a frequency distribution in which there are some unusually low scores [shown in Figure 1.5(b)]. An easy way to remember the difference is that the tail of the right-skewed distribution goes off to the right, and the tail of the left-skewed distribution goes off to the left. A right-skewed distribution is also called a positively skewed distribution (the tail goes toward the positive end of the number line); a left-skewed distribution is also called a negatively skewed distribution (the tail goes toward the negative end of the number line).

Now that we have defined right-skewed and left-skewed distributions, let's consider some examples of each type of distribution so that we get a better understanding of these distributions. As you read these examples, visually think about what the distributions would look like. Remember, the tail of a right-skewed distribution goes to the right (the high end of the scale), and the tail of a left-skewed distribution goes to the left (the low end of the scale). Also, remember that the tails of these skewed distributions can be very long. Age at retirement is a good example of a left-skewed distribution.

right-skewed distribution An asymmetric frequency distribution in which there are some unusually high scores that distort the mean to be greater than the median.

left-skewed distribution An asymmetric frequency distribution in which there are some unusually low scores that distort the mean to be less than the median.

Most people retire in their mid to late 60s or early 70s, some retire in their 50s, and relatively few in their 40s or earlier. Another example would be scores on a relatively easy exam. Most students would get As or Bs (high scores), some would get Cs, a few Ds, and hardly any Fs (low scores).

The distribution of people's incomes is a good example of a right-skewed distribution. The incomes of most people tend to be on the lower end of possible incomes, but some people make a lot of money, with very high incomes increasingly rare. The "long tail" phenomenon in the digital business world (Anderson, 2008) also involves right-skewed distributions. The "long tail" referred to is that for the distribution depicting the sales of all the available items in a specific market (e.g., music tracks or book titles) as a function of their popularity rank. The small number of very popular items make up the head of the distribution, and the very large number of less popular items make up the long tail. Given their much lower stocking and distribution costs versus physical retailers, e-businesses can essentially sell the entire distribution; and the aggregate of all of the items in the long tail make up a large market for sales. Figure 1.6 shows the long tail for music downloads for online music retailer Rhapsody versus Walmart.

Because unusually high or low scores distort a mean, such distortion occurs for the means of skewed distributions. The mean for a right-skewed distribution is distorted toward the tail created by the few high scores and therefore is greater than the median. The mean for the left-skewed distribution is distorted toward the tail created by the few low scores and therefore is less than the median. When you have a skewed distribution, you should use the median because atypical scores in the distribution do not distort the median. Consider

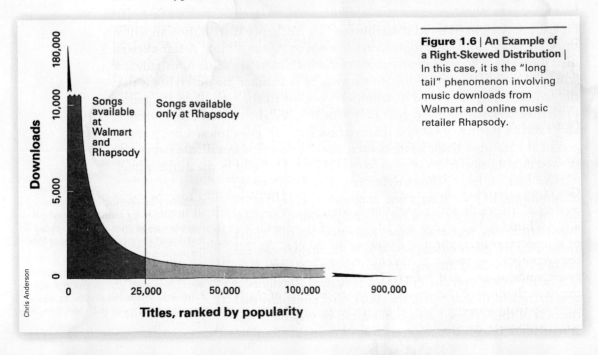

Figure 1.6 | An Example of a Right-Skewed Distribution | In this case, it is the "long tail" phenomenon involving music downloads from Walmart and online music retailer Rhapsody.

this example from Wheelan (2013). The median annual income for 10 guys sitting at a bar is \$35,000 (each earns \$35,000 a year). When multibillionaire Bill Gates walks in and sits at the bar, the median remains \$35,000. If another multibillionaire comes in and sits at the bar, the median still does not change. Why? Atypical scores do not distort the median. This means that you need to know the type of frequency distribution before deciding which measure of central tendency—mean or median—is more appropriate. Beware, sometimes the inappropriate measure of central tendency for skewed distributions (the mean) is used to mislead you (Huff, 1954).

Skewed distributions are also important to understand because various aspects of everyday life, such as medical trends (mortality rates for various diseases), are often skewed. Let's consider a famous example of the importance of understanding skewed distributions (Gould, 1985). Stephen Jay Gould, a noted Harvard scientist, died of cancer in 2002. However, this was 20 years after he was diagnosed with abdominal mesothelioma cancer and told that this type of cancer had "a median mortality rate of 8 months after diagnosis." Most people would think that they would only have about 8 months to live if given this median statistic. However, Gould realized that his expected chances depended upon the type of frequency distribution for the deaths from this disease. Because the statistic is reported as a median rather than a mean, the distribution is skewed. Now, if you were Gould, which type of skewed distribution would you want—right or left? Many people at first think they would want left-skewed, but you wouldn't want this distribution because everyone would be dead within less than a year. Look at its shape in Figure 1.5(b). If it is 8 months from the origin to the median, then it is less than 4 months from the median to the end of the distribution. You would want a severely right skewed distribution with a long tail to the right, going on for years. This is what Gould found the distribution to be when he examined the medical literature on the disease. The distribution had a tail that stretched out to the right for many years beyond the median, and Gould was fortunate to be out in this long tail, living for 20 more years after getting the diagnosis. When he did die, it was from a different type of cancer (Blastland & Dilnot, 2009).

Gould wrote a famous article called "The Median Isn't the Message," in which he argued that his knowledge of statistics saved him from the erroneous conclusion that he would necessarily be dead in 8 months. In confronting his illness, Gould was thinking like a scientist. Such thinking provided him and the many readers of his article with a better understanding of a very difficult medical situation. Thinking like a scientist allows all of us to gain a better understanding of ourselves, others, and the world we all inhabit. Such thinking, along with the accompanying research, has enabled psychological scientists to gain a much better understanding of human behavior and mental processing. We describe the basic findings of this research in the remainder of the book. You will benefit not only from learning about these findings but also from thinking more like a scientist in your daily life.

Section Summary

To understand research findings, psychologists use statistics—a branch of mathematics that provides procedures for the description and analysis of data. In this section, we were concerned with descriptive statistics. Measures of central tendency allow a researcher to describe the "typical" score for a distribution of scores concisely. There are three such measures: mean, median, and mode. The mean is merely the arithmetical average. The median is the middle score when the distribution is arranged in ascending or descending order. The mode is the most frequently occurring score. Of these three measures, the mean is used most often. However, if unusually high or low scores in the distribution distort the mean, then the median should be used. In addition to describing the typical score, we need to determine the variability of the scores. We could use the range—the difference between the highest and lowest scores—but unusually low or high scores distort it. The measure of variability most often used is the standard deviation, the average extent that the scores vary from the mean of the distribution.

The standard deviation is especially relevant to the normal (bell-shaped) frequency distribution. Sixty-eight percent of the scores in a normal distribution fall within 1 standard deviation of the mean, 95% within 2 standard deviations, and over 99% within 3 standard deviations. These percentages hold true regardless of the value of the standard deviation. They also enable us to compute the percentile rank for a specific score in a normal distribution. The percentile rank for a score is the percentage of the scores below it in the distribution of scores. All distributions are not symmetric like the normal distribution. Two important nonsymmetric distributions are the right-skewed and left-skewed distributions. In a right-skewed distribution, there are some unusually high scores, leading to the mean being greater than the median; in a left-skewed distribution, there are some unusually low scores, leading to the mean being less than the median. In both cases, the median should be used because the mean is distorted toward the tail of the distribution.

ConceptCheck | 3

Explain what measures of central tendency and measures of variability tell us about a distribution of scores.

Explain why the normal distribution has a bell shape.

Explain the relationship between the mean and median in a right-skewed distribution and in a left-skewed distribution.

Study Guide

Chapter Key Terms

You should know the definitions of the following key terms from the chapter. They are listed in the order in which they appear in the chapter. For those you do not know, return to the relevant section of the chapter to learn them. When you think that you know all of the terms, complete the matching exercise based on these key terms.

psychology
biological perspective
cognitive perspective
behavioral perspective
sociocultural perspective
hindsight bias (I-knew-it-all-
   along phenomenon)
descriptive methods
naturalistic observation
participant observation
case study
survey research
population
sample
random sampling
correlational study
variable

correlation coefficient
positive correlation
negative correlation
regression toward the mean
mean
scatterplot
third-variable problem
spurious correlation
random assignment
independent variable
dependent variable
experiment
experimental group
control group
operational definition
placebo effect
placebo

nocebo effect
placebo group
inferential statistical analyses
double-blind procedure
meta-analysis
descriptive statistics
frequency distribution
median
mode
range
standard deviation
normal distribution
percentile rank
right-skewed distribution
left-skewed distribution

Key Terms Exercise

Identify the correct term for each of the following definitions. The answers to this exercise follow the answers to the ConceptChecks at the end of the chapter.

1. An explanation of a correlation between two variables in terms of another variable that could possibly be responsible for the observed relationship between the two variables.

_____

2. A control measure in an experiment in which neither the experimenters nor the participants know which participants are in the experimental and control groups.

_____

3. The score positioned in the middle of a distribution of scores when all of the scores are arranged from lowest to highest.

_____

4. An asymmetric frequency distribution in which there are some unusually high scores that distort the mean to be greater than the median.

_____

5. Improvement due to the expectation of improving because of receiving treatment.

_____

6. An inverse relationship between two variables.

_____

7. A control measure in an experiment in which participants are randomly assigned to groups in order to equalize participant characteristics across the various groups in the experiment.

_____

8. The percentage of scores below a specific score in a distribution of scores.

_____

9. A research perspective whose major explanatory focus is how the brain, nervous system, and other physiological mechanisms produce our behavior and mental processes.

_____

10. A description of the operations or procedures that a researcher uses to manipulate or measure a variable.

_____

11. The tendency, after learning about an outcome, to be overconfident in one's ability to have predicted it.

_____

12. A visual depiction of correlational data in which each data point represents the scores on the two variables for each participant.

_____

13. The entire group of people that a researcher is studying.

_____

14. The difference between the highest and lowest scores in a distribution of scores.

_____

15. Statistical analyses that allow researchers to draw conclusions about the results of a study by determining the probability the results are due to random variation (chance).

_____

Practice Test Questions

The following are practice multiple-choice test questions on some of the chapter content. The answers are given after the Key Terms Exercise answers at the end of the chapter. If you guessed on a question or incorrectly answered a question, restudy the relevant section of the chapter.

1. Which of the following major research perspectives focuses on conditioning by external environmental events as the major cause of our behavior?
   a. biological
   b. cognitive
   c. behavioral
   d. sociocultural

2. Which of the following would be the best procedure for obtaining a representative sample of the students at your school?
   a. sampling randomly among students in the student union
   b. sampling randomly among students studying in the library
   c. sampling randomly among the students who belong to Greek organizations
   d. sampling randomly from a list of all the students enrolled at your school

3. Which of the following research methods allow(s) the researcher to draw cause–effect conclusions?
   a. descriptive
   b. correlational
   c. experimental
   d. all of the above

4. Height and weight are _____ correlated; elevation and temperature are _____ correlated.
   a. positively; positively
   b. positively; negatively
   c. negatively; positively
   d. negatively; negatively

5. Which of the following correlation coefficients indicates the STRONGEST relationship?
   a. +.75
   b. –.81
   c. +1.25
   d. 0.00

6. Manipulate is to measure as _____ is to _____.
   a. positive correlation; negative correlation
   b. negative correlation; positive correlation
   c. independent variable; dependent variable
   d. dependent variable; independent variable

7. In an experiment, the _____ group participants receive an inactive treatment but are told that the treatment will help them.
   a. experimental
   b. control
   c. placebo
   d. third-variable

8. The most frequently occurring score in a distribution of scores is the _____, and the average score is the _____.
   a. mode; mean
   b. mean; mode
   c. median; mean
   d. mean; median

9. About _____ % of the scores in a normal distribution are between −1 standard deviation and +1 standard deviation of the mean.
   a. 34
   b. 68
   c. 95
   d. 99

10. In a left-skewed distribution, the mean is _____ than the median; in a right-skewed distribution, the mean is _____ than the median.
    a. greater; greater
    b. greater; less
    c. less; greater
    d. less; less

11. Shere Hite's failure to use _____ resulted in misleading findings for her women and love survey study.
    a. a placebo group
    b. a double-blind procedure
    c. random assignment
    d. random sampling

12. Professor Jones noticed that the distribution of students' scores on his last biology exam had an extremely small standard deviation. This indicates that:
    a. the exam was given to a very small class of students.
    b. the exam was a poor measure of the students' knowledge.
    c. the students' scores tended to be very similar to one another.
    d. the students' mean exam score was less than the median exam score.

13. In a normal distribution, the percentile rank for a score that is 1 standard deviation below the mean is roughly _____%.
    a. 16
    b. 34
    c. 68
    d. 84

14. Dian Fossey's study of gorillas is an example of _____.
    a. naturalistic observation
    b. participant observation
    c. naturalistic observation that turned into participant observation
    d. a case study

15. Which of the following types of scatterplots depicts a weak, negative correlation?
    a. a lot of scatter with data points going from top left to bottom right
    b. very little scatter with data points going from top left to bottom right
    c. a lot of scatter with data points going from bottom left to top right
    d. very little scatter with data points going from bottom left to top right

Chapter ConceptCheck Answers

ConceptCheck | 1

• Both of these research perspectives emphasize internal causes in their explanations of human behavior and mental processing. The biological perspective emphasizes the role of our actual physiological hardware, especially the brain and nervous system, while the cognitive perspective emphasizes the role of our mental processes, the "programs" of the brain. For example, biological explanations will involve actual parts of the brain or chemicals in the brain. Cognitive explanations, however, will involve mental processes such as perception and memory without specifying the parts of the brain or chemicals involved in these processes. Thus, the biological and cognitive perspectives propose explanations at two different levels of internal factors, the actual physiological mechanisms and the mental processes resulting from these mechanisms, respectively.

- Both of these research perspectives emphasize external causes in their explanations of human behavior and mental processing. The behavioral perspective emphasizes conditioning of our behavior by external environmental events while the sociocultural perspective emphasizes the impact of other people and our culture on our behavior and mental processing. Thus, these two perspectives emphasize different types of external causes. In addition, the behavioral perspective emphasizes the conditioning of observable behavior while the sociocultural perspective focuses just as much on mental processing as observable behavior and on other types of learning in addition to conditioning.

ConceptCheck | 2

- The results of a case study cannot be generalized to a population because they are specific to the individual who has been studied. To generalize to a population, you need to include a representative sample of the population in the study. However, the results of a case study do allow the researcher to develop hypotheses about cause–effect relationships that can be tested in experimental research to see if they apply to the population.

- Random sampling is a method for obtaining a representative sample from a population. Random assignment is a control measure for assigning the members of a sample to groups or conditions in an experiment. Random sampling allows the researcher to generalize the results from the sample to the population; random assignment controls for individual characteristics across the groups in an experiment. Random assignment is used only in experiments, but random sampling is used in experiments and some other research methods such as correlational studies and surveys.

- There would be the same amount of scatter of the data points in each of the two scatterplots because they are equal in strength (.90). In addition, because they are strong correlations, there would not be much scatter. However,

the scatter of data points in the scatterplot for +.90 would go from the bottom left of the plot to the top right; the scatter for −.90 would go from the top left of the plot to the bottom right. Thus, the direction of the scatter would be different in the two scatterplots.

- Some possible third variables that could serve as environmental triggers for autism among genetically vulnerable children stem from the children being in the house more and spending less time outdoors because of the high rates of precipitation. According to the authors of the study, such variables would include increased television and video viewing, decreased vitamin D levels because of less exposure to sunlight, and increased exposure to household chemicals. In addition, there may be chemicals in the atmosphere that are transported to the surface by the precipitation. All of these variables could serve as third variables and possibly account for the correlation.

- The double-blind procedure is necessary in experiments with placebo groups for two reasons. First, the participants in the placebo group must think that they are receiving a treatment that will help, or a placebo effect would be negatively impacted. Thus, they cannot be told that they received a placebo. Second, the experimenter must be blinded in order to control for the effects of experimenter expectation (e.g., unintentionally judging the behavior of participants in the experimental and placebo groups differently because of knowing their group assignments).

ConceptCheck | 3

- Measures of central tendency tell us what a "typical" score is for the distribution of scores. The three central tendency measures give us different definitions of "typical." The mean is the average score; the median is the middle score when all of the scores are ordered by value; and the mode is the most frequently occurring score. Measures of variability tell us how much the scores vary from one another, the variability between scores. The range is the difference between the highest and lowest scores, and the standard deviation is the average extent that the scores vary from the mean for the set of scores.

- It has a bell shape because the scores are distributed symmetrically about the mean with the majority of the scores (about 68%) close to the mean (from −1 standard deviation to +1 standard deviation). As the scores diverge from the mean, they become symmetrically less frequent, giving the distribution the shape of a bell.

- In a right-skewed distribution, the mean is greater than the median because the unusually high scores in the distribution distort it. The opposite is true for the left-skewed distribution. The mean is less than the median because the unusually low scores in the distribution distort it.

Answers to Key Terms Exercise

1. third-variable problem
2. double-blind procedure
3. median
4. right-skewed distribution
5. placebo effect
6. negative correlation
7. random assignment
8. percentile rank
9. biological perspective
10. operational definition

11. hindsight bias (I-knew-it-all-along phenomenon)
12. scatterplot
13. population
14. range
15. inferential statistical analyses

Answers to Practice Test Questions

1. c; behavioral
2. d; sampling randomly from a list of all the students enrolled at your school
3. c; experimental
4. b; positively; negatively
5. b; −.81
6. c; independent variable; dependent variable
7. c; placebo
8. a; mode; mean
9. b; 68
10. c; less; greater
11. d; random sampling
12. c; students' scores tended to be very similar to one another
13. a; 16
14. c; naturalistic observation that turned into participant observation
15. a; a lot of scatter with data points going from top left to bottom right

Courtesy of Jackie Saccoccio and 11R, NY

2

Neuroscience

Our brain controls almost everything we do. It is responsible for our perception, consciousness, memory, language, intelligence, and personality—everything that makes us human. This would seem to be a daunting job for an organ that only weighs about three pounds. The brain, however, has typically been estimated to consist of about 100 billion nerve cells, called neurons. A recent study of the cellular composition of the brain, for example, estimated 86 billion (Azevedo et al., 2009). Each neuron may receive infor-

"The body is made up of millions and millions of crumbs"

mation from thousands of other neurons; therefore, the number of possible communication connections between these billions of neurons is in the trillions! One estimate goes as high as one thousand trillion, the number 1 followed by 15 zeroes (Sweeney, 2009). Just as your genome is the entire sequence of nucleotides in your DNA, the totality of the connections between neurons in your nervous system is referred to as your connectome (Seung, 2012). Unlike your genome, which is fixed at conception, your connectome changes throughout your life. With this vast collection of changing neuronal connections, the human brain is the most complex device in the known universe (Buonomano, 2011). Hence, this complexity may never be completely understood, but it's an intriguing puzzle—human brains trying to understand how human brains work.

In this chapter on **neuroscience** (the scientific study of the brain and nervous system), we will first examine neurons, the cellular building blocks of the nervous system. We will look at how neurons transmit and integrate information, and how drugs and poisons interrupt these processes (and change our behavior and mental processes). We will also consider how some diseases and disorders are related to transmission problems.

Once we understand how neurons work, we will consider the hierarchical structure of the nervous system, discussing its various subsystems—the central nervous system and the peripheral nervous system—along with the body's other major communication system, the endocrine glandular system. We will also consider emotions and the role of the autonomic nervous system, a division of the peripheral nervous system, in explaining how our emotional experiences are generated.

Next, the major parts of the brain (vast collections of neurons) and their functions will be detailed. We will focus mainly on the cerebral cortex, the seat of higher mental functioning in humans. Last, we will consider what consciousness is and what brain activity during sleep (a natural break from consciousness) tells us about the five stages of sleep and the nature of dreaming.

neuroscience The scientific study of the brain and nervous system.

The Neuron

Why are psychologists interested in how neurons work? Isn't this biology and not psychology? The answer is that it's both. Humans are biological organisms. To understand our behavior and mental processes, we need to understand their biological underpinnings, starting with the cellular level, the neuron. How we feel, learn, remember, and think all stem from neuronal activity. So, how a neuron works and how neurons communicate are crucial pieces of information in solving the puzzle of human behavior and mental processing.

In explaining how a neuron works, we will talk about how neurons communicate with one another. We have a fairly good understanding of how information is transmitted, but we do not have as good an understanding of exactly how these vast communication networks of neurons oversee what we do and make us what we are. These more complex questions are the remaining key pieces of the puzzle to be solved. In this section, we will cover the part of the story that is best understood—how the building blocks of the nervous system, the neurons, work. We begin with a discussion of the neuron's structure and parts.

The Structure of a Neuron

The brain and the nervous system are composed of two types of cells—neurons and glial cells. **Neurons** are responsible for information transmission throughout the nervous system. They receive, send, and integrate information within the brain and the rest of the nervous system. **Glial cells** (or **glia,** Greek for "glue") constitute the support system for the neurons. For example, glial cells take away the waste products of neurons, keep the neurons' chemical environment stable, and insulate them, allowing neurons to do their work more efficiently. Given the impressive number of neurons that we have, there must be a similar number of glial cells to support the work of these billions of neurons. Recent research has shown this to be true. The ratio of glial cells to neurons has been estimated to be roughly 1:1, so we have about 100 billion glial cells (Azevedo et al., 2009; Hilgetag & Barbas, 2009). It is important to note that though the overall ratio is around 1:1, this ratio varies across different areas in the brain (Herculano-Houzel, 2014). Previous estimates of the overall ratio of glial cells to neurons have ranged as high as 10:1 to 50:1, but after surveying the research literature, Yuhas and Jabr (2012) did not find a single published study supporting such ratios. Hence, at present the claim that there are far more glial cells than neurons seems to be a brain myth (Jarrett, 2015).

Recent research is also questioning the idea that glial cells merely provide a support system for neurons (Barres, 2008; Fields, 2009, 2011; Koob, 2009). It appears that not only do neurons and glial cells communicate but also that glial cells communicate with one another in a separate but parallel network to the neuronal network, influencing the brain's performance. Glial cells also appear to influence the formation of neuronal connections and to aid in determining which neuronal connections get

neurons Cells that transmit information within the nervous system.

glial cells (glia) Cells in the nervous system that comprise the support system for the neurons.

stronger or weaker over time, both essential to learning and to storing memories. In addition, glial cells may play an important role in mental disorders such as schizophrenia and depression and in neurodegenerative diseases such as Parkinson's and Alzheimer's. Whereas neuroscientists are excited by all of these possibilities and the prospect of doing research on these cells that have been largely ignored until recently, neurons are still viewed as the most important cells for communication within the human nervous system and thus will be the focus of our discussion.

dendrites Fibers projecting out of the cell body of a neuron whose function is to receive information from other neurons.

cell body The part of the neuron that contains its nucleus and the other biological machinery to keep the cell alive and that decides whether to generate a neural impulse in order to pass incoming information on to other neurons.

Neurons all have the same basic parts and structure, and they all operate the same way. A generic neuron with all of the important parts identified is depicted in Figure 2.1. The three main components of a neuron are the dendrites, cell body, and axon. Let's first get a general idea of the main functions of these three parts and their relationships to one another.

Dendrites are the fibers that project out of the cell body like the branches of a tree. Their main function is to receive information from other neurons. The dendrites pass this information on to the **cell body,** which contains the nucleus of the cell and the other biological machinery that keeps the cell alive. The cell body also decides whether to pass the information from the dendrites on to other neurons. If the cell body decides to pass along the information, it does so by way

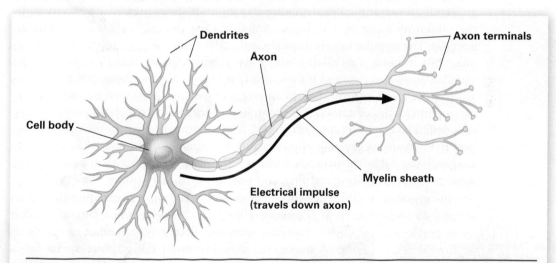

Figure 2.1 | The Structure of a Neuron | The three main parts of a neuron are the dendrites, cell body, and axon. The dendrites receive information from other neurons and pass it along to the cell body. The cell body decides whether the information should be passed on to other neurons. If it decides it should, then it does so by means of an electrical impulse that travels down the axon—the longer, thin fiber coming out of the cell body. The pictured neuron has a myelinated axon. Please note that there are periodic gaps where there is no myelin. The impulse jumps from one gap to the next down the axon. When the impulse reaches the axon terminals, it triggers chemical communication with other neurons.

of the **axon**—the long, singular fiber leaving the cell body. At its end, the axon subdivides into axon terminals, branchlike endings. The main function of the axon is to conduct information from the cell body to the axon terminals in order to trigger the transmission of information with other neurons. Axons vary greatly in length, with the longest ones going from the spinal cord to the toes. Given this general understanding of the parts of the neuron, let's look more closely at exactly how they are involved in transmitting information.

How Neurons Communicate

The first point to note in learning about how neurons communicate with one another (and sometimes with muscles and glands) is that the process is partly electrical and partly chemical. Within a neuron, it's electrical—an actual electrical impulse is generated and travels down the axon. Communication between neurons, however, is chemical. The neurons don't actually touch one another. They are separated by a microscopic gap that chemical molecules travel across to carry their message. We'll first describe the electrical part and then explain this "chemistry" between neurons.

The electrical impulse. The electrical part of the story begins with the messages received by the dendrites from other neurons. These inputs are either excitatory (telling the neuron to generate an electrical impulse) or inhibitory (telling the neuron not to generate an electrical impulse). The cell body decides whether to generate an impulse by continually calculating this input. If the excitatory input outweighs the inhibitory input by a sufficient amount, then the cell body will generate an impulse. The impulse travels from the cell body down the axon to the axon terminals. This impulse is an all-or-nothing event, which means that there is either an impulse or there is not; and if there is an impulse, it always travels down the axon at the same speed regardless of the intensity of the stimulus input. So, how are the varying intensities of stimuli (for example, a gentle pat on the cheek versus a slap) encoded? The answer is straightforward. The intensity of the stimulus determines how many neurons generate impulses and the number of impulses that are generated each second by the neurons. Stronger stimuli (a slap rather than a pat) lead to more neurons generating impulses and generating those impulses more often.

The impulses in different neurons travel down the axon at varying rates up to around 200 miles per hour (Dowling, 1998). This may seem fast, but it is much slower than the speed of electricity or computer processing. A major factor determining the impulse speed for a particular neuron is whether its axon is encased in a **myelin sheath**—an insulating layer of a white fatty substance. The myelin sheath is composed of glial cells that wrap around the neuron's axon. With no myelin sheath, the impulse travels slowly down the axon in a continuous fashion, like a fuse burning down on a stick of dynamite. The rate is faster in axons encased in myelin because the impulse can only be

axon The long, singular fiber projecting out of the cell body of a neuron, whose function is to conduct the neural impulse from the cell body to the axon terminals, triggering chemical communication with other neurons.

myelin sheath An insulating layer covering an axon that allows for faster neural impulses.

regenerated at the periodic gaps in the sheath where there is no myelin. A myelin-ated axon (like the one in Figure 2.1) looks like a string of sausages with gaps between the sausages. The impulse "leaps" from gap to gap instead of traveling continuously down the axon. To understand why this is faster, think about walk-ing across a room in a heel-to-toe fashion (continuously touching the heel of your advancing foot to the toes of your lagging foot) versus taking long strides to get to the other side. Striding is clearly much faster.

Damage to this myelin sheath will result in serious problems. For example, multiple sclerosis causes deterioration of the myelin sheath that encases neuronal axons. This means that impulses can no longer leap down the axon, or eventually even travel down the axon, so information transmission is greatly slowed. People with multiple sclerosis experience incapacitating behavioral changes, such as difficulty in moving. Sadly, there is presently no cure for multiple sclerosis, but recent research using stem cell (an unspecialized cell in the body that can develop into a specialized cell) transplantation has found some preliminary encouraging results (Burt et al., 2015).

Given its white color, myelin is also responsible for the distinction between white matter and gray matter in the brain. Myelinated axons make up the "white" matter; unmyelinated axons, cell bodies, and dendrites make up the "gray" mat-ter. Why the distinction? Myelination creates a whitish appearance because of the white color of the myelin. Unmyelinated parts of a neuron appear grayish. If we were able to look at the two cerebral hemispheres of the brain, they would appear grayish because we are mainly looking at the billions of cell bodies that make up their outside layer. Hence, the expression, "Use your gray matter."

Chemical communication between neurons. What happens when the electrical impulse reaches the axon terminals? The answer is depicted in Figure 2.2 (page 48). In the axon terminals, there are tiny vesicles (sacs) containing a **neurotransmitter,** a naturally occurring chemical in our nervous system that specializes in transmit-ting information. When the impulse reaches the sending neuron's axon terminals, it causes the vesicles to open and the neurotransmitter molecules to come out and go into the **synaptic gap** (or **synapse**), the microscopic gap (less than a millionth of an inch wide) between neurons. Two thousand of these tiny synaptic gaps would fit comfortably inside the thinnest of human hairs (Lynch & Granger, 2008). The neurotransmitter molecules cross the gap and enter receptor sites on the dendrites of other neurons. This is achieved by what is termed binding—neurotransmitter molecules fit into the dendrite receptor sites on the receiving neuron like a key fits into a lock. It's sort of like sex at the molecular level (Pert, 1997). After delivering their message, the molecules go back into the gap. Some are destroyed by enzymes in the gap, but others undergo reuptake—they are taken back into the axon terminals of the sending neuron to be used again. Because synapses are the channels of communication between neu-rons and the means by which the brain accomplishes most of what it does, they are vital to our well-being. Our mind and

neurotransmitter A naturally occurring chemical in the nervous system that specializes in transmitting information between neurons.

synaptic gap (synapse) The micro-scopic gap between neurons across which neurotransmitters travel to carry their messages to other neurons.

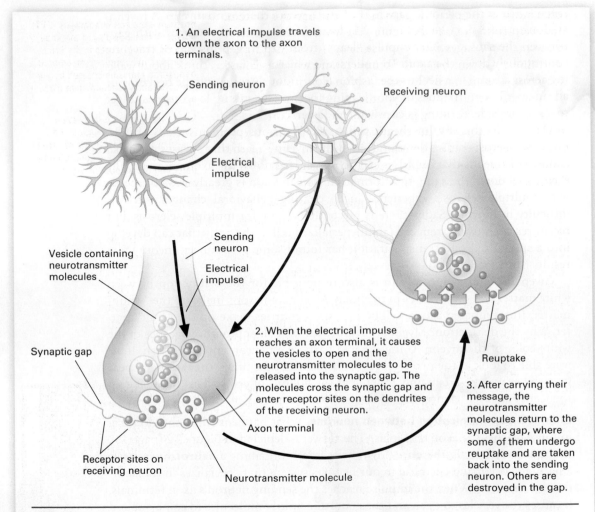

1. An electrical impulse travels down the axon to the axon terminals.

Sending neuron

Receiving neuron

Electrical impulse

Vesicle containing neurotransmitter molecules

Sending neuron

Electrical impulse

Synaptic gap

2. When the electrical impulse reaches an axon terminal, it causes the vesicles to open and the neurotransmitter molecules to be released into the synaptic gap. The molecules cross the synaptic gap and enter receptor sites on the dendrites of the receiving neuron.

Axon terminal

Reuptake

3. After carrying their message, the neurotransmitter molecules return to the synaptic gap, where some of them undergo reuptake and are taken back into the sending neuron. Others are destroyed in the gap.

Receptor sites on receiving neuron

Neurotransmitter molecule

Figure 2.2 | Synaptic Communication Between Neurons | Neurons communicate with each other chemically. As explained in the figure, there are three steps. (1) When the electrical impulse in a neuron reaches the axon terminals, it causes neurotransmitter molecules in the terminal vesicles to be released into the synaptic gap between neurons. (2) These molecules cross the gap and fit into receptor sites on the dendrites of other neurons, thereby carrying their messages. (3) The neurotransmitter molecules then go back into the gap, where they are either taken up by the sending neuron (reuptake) to be used again or are destroyed by enzymes.

behavior are controlled by our synapses. Neuroscientist Joseph LeDoux sums this up very succinctly in his book *Synaptic Self* (2002)—"You are your synapses" (p. ix).

So who discovered the synapse, which is so critical to our existence? Synapses were first documented by Spanish anatomist Santiago Ramón y Cajal in the nineteenth century (Rapport, 2005). Ramón y Cajal, often referred to as the father of neuroscience, shared the Nobel Prize in Physiology or Medicine in 1906 for his contributions to our understanding of the nervous system. However, Ramón y Cajal did not use the word synapse to refer to the microscopic gap between neurons. It was Sir Charles Scott Sherrington, another Nobel Prize winner, who coined this term. According to Rapport (2005), when Sherrington was writing material for a new edition of Michael Foster's *A Textbook of Physiology,* he grew tired of having to continually invent ways to describe the conduction of an impulse across a gap to dendrites. To eliminate this problem, Sherrington coined the term *synapse,* which appeared for the first time in Foster's seventh edition in 1897.

positron emission tomography (PET) scans A visual display of the activity levels in various areas in the brain generated by detecting the amount of positron emission created by the metabolization of radioactive glucose in each area.

functional magnetic resonance imaging (fMRI) A computerized image of the activity levels of various areas in the brain generated by detecting the amount of oxygen brought to each area.

Brain scans. In order to carry out their essential communication work, neurons require oxygen and other nutrients such as blood sugars. This is why about 20% of the body's blood supply is pumped to the brain (Gazzaniga, Ivry, & Mangun, 2002), and the brain consumes about a quarter of the body's oxygen (Ackerman, 2004). Without oxygen, neurons die within minutes. Neurons doing more work require even more oxygen and nutrients. This fact is the key to how various types of brain scans work. There are several types of brain scans, but we will discuss two that are often used by psychology researchers.

In **positron emission tomography (PET) scans,** a harmless dose of radioactive glucose (sugar) is introduced into the bloodstream. The radioactive glucose moves to those areas that are more active, and when the glucose is metabolized by the neurons, it emits positrons (atomic particles emitted by radioactive substances) that are detected and measured by a computer. Active areas show up on the computer-generated image as brighter colors than less active areas. In this manner, PET scans are used to tell us which areas are most active, and thus more involved, while a person performs some task, such as reading or talking.

Another type of scan that has become popular, **functional magnetic resonance imaging (fMRI),** does not require radioactivity being introduced into the bloodstream, but rather focuses on the amount of oxygen brought to the various areas. The areas that are more active are provided with more oxygen through

Tony Zuvela/Cartoonstock.com

increased blood flow to them. The fMRI detects these areas with increased blood flow and highlights them in its computerized image of brain activity. Variations in blood flow are depicted as variations in color in the image. Like PET scans, fMRI scans are used to study the functions of various brain parts and locations. Actually, fMRI is preferred over a PET scan because it is noninvasive and produces a much sharper picture.

Historically, we learned about brain function only by observation of brain-damaged individuals and postmortem comparisons of damaged and normal brains. Modern brain scans have allowed us to learn about structures and functions while the neurons are still healthy and active. Whereas brain scans have definitely helped to gain new insights into the brain and are invaluable to brain research, some researchers think that the explanatory power of brain scans has been vastly overstated (Legrenzi & Umiltà, 2011; Satel & Lilienfeld, 2013). Shermer (2008) and Uttal (2003) provide discussions of the limitations of brain scanning and what it can and cannot show.

Neurotransmitters, Drugs, and Poisons

Fifty to 100 different chemicals in our nervous system function as neurotransmitters (Valenstein, 2005). In this section, we will look at seven of them that we know quite a bit about—acetylcholine, dopamine, serotonin, norepinephrine, GABA (gamma-aminobutyric acid), glutamate, and endorphins. We'll identify some of the behaviors and mental processes in which each of these neurotransmitters plays a major role, provide some examples of how poisons and drugs bring about their effects by impacting the synaptic communication process for particular neurotransmitters, and explain how some disorders and diseases may result from excessive activity or a deficit in activity for particular neurotransmitters. In the discussions of drugs and poisons, we will use the agonist versus antagonist distinction. An **agonist** is a drug or poison that increases the activity of one or more neurotransmitters; an **antagonist** is a drug or poison that decreases the activity of one or more neurotransmitters. We'll see that agonists and antagonists bring about their effects in many different ways.

Acetylcholine. Acetylcholine (ACh) is a neurotransmitter involved in learning, memory, and muscle movement. When it is located in the brain, it impacts learning and memory. Alzheimer's patients tend to have lower levels of ACh. At muscle junctures throughout our body, ACh leads to muscle contractions, allowing us to move the various parts of our body. Its role in muscle movement shows how poisons work in agonistic or antagonistic ways to impact the normal level of neurotransmitter activity. There are several poisons that paralyze us (prevent muscle movement) by preventing ACh from fulfilling its movement function. Let's look at three such poisons and see how they achieve this same effect, but in different ways.

agonist A drug or poison that increases the activity of one or more neurotransmitters.

antagonist A drug or poison that decreases the activity of one or more neurotransmitters.

acetylcholine (ACh) A neurotransmitter involved in learning, memory, and muscle movement.

First, consider botulinum poison (sometimes called botulin), a toxin involved in food poisoning. Botulinum poison is an antagonist that blocks the release of ACh at muscle junctures, leading to paralysis and, if not treated, death. The chest and diaphragm muscles become paralyzed, so the victim cannot breathe. An extremely mild form of this poison is what is used in the Botox treatment for facial wrinkling, where the facial muscles are temporarily paralyzed, thus smoothing them. Curare, the poison that South American Indians put on the tips of their spears and arrows, paralyzes by occupying the receptor sites for ACh, thereby preventing the ACh molecules from getting in and delivering their message. Like botulinum poison, curare is an antagonist for ACh and can kill by paralyzing critical muscles. Another poison, black widow spider venom, is an agonist for ACh, and can also lead to death by paralysis. Black widow spider venom causes the continuous release of ACh, flooding the synapse. This initial effect is agonistic, leading to uncontrollable convulsive movement due to the heightened ACh activity. Death occurs through paralysis after the supply of ACh has been exhausted. But don't worry. Though there's enough poison in a black widow spider bite to kill other insects, humans rarely die from such bites.

Dopamine. **Dopamine** is a neurotransmitter that impacts our arousal and mood states, thought processes, and physical movement, but in a very different way than ACh. Low levels of dopamine in the basal ganglia, brain structures that we will discuss later in the chapter, lead to **Parkinson's disease,** which causes movement problems such as muscle tremors, difficulty initiating movements, and rigidity of movement. Actor Michael J. Fox has Parkinson's disease and so did Muhammad Ali, who died recently. Physicians first attempted to treat Parkinson's disease by injecting dopamine through the bloodstream. This did not work, however, because dopamine could not get through the **blood–brain barrier**—a protective mechanism by which the blood capillaries supplying the brain create a barrier that prevents dangerous substances from accessing the brain. The downside is that some good substances, such as dopamine in the case of Parkinson's disease, also cannot gain access. However, **L-dopa,** a drug for Parkinson's disease, can pass through the blood–brain barrier. It contains the precursors to dopamine, so once in the brain, L-dopa is converted to dopamine. Thus, L-dopa functions as an agonist for dopamine by increasing its production. However, L-dopa is not effective for all Parkinson's patients, and as Parkinson's disease progresses, L-dopa becomes less effective for those it does help.

There are also side effects of L-dopa that resemble some of the symptoms of schizophrenia—a psychotic disorder in which a person loses touch with reality and suffers from perceptual and cognitive processing deficits, such as hallucinations, false beliefs, and deficits in attention. This makes sense, however, because one of the main explanations for schizophrenia involves an excess of dopamine activity, and dopamine impacts our thought processes. In fact, traditional

dopamine A neurotransmitter involved in arousal and mood states, thought processes, and physical movement.

Parkinson's disease A disease in which the person has movement problems such as muscle tremors, difficulty initiating movements, and rigidity of movement. These movement problems stem from a scarcity of dopamine in the basal ganglia.

blood–brain barrier A protective mechanism by which the blood capillaries supplying the brain create a barrier that prevents dangerous substances access to the brain.

L-dopa A drug for Parkinson's disease that contains the precursors to dopamine so that once it is in the brain, it will be converted to dopamine.

antipsychotic drugs for schizophrenia work antagonistically by globally blocking receptor sites for dopamine so that dopamine cannot enter them, thereby reducing its level of activity. Conversely, some of the side effects of these antipsychotic drugs resemble the movement symptoms of Parkinson's disease, because these powerful drugs also lessen the activity of the dopamine in the movement system involving the basal ganglia.

The effects of addictive stimulants (such as amphetamines and cocaine) illustrate dopamine's involvement in our arousal and mood states. For example, amphetamines act as agonists for dopamine activity by continually stimulating the release of dopamine from axon terminals, thereby depleting it. Similarly, cocaine creates an agonistic effect by blocking the reuptake of dopamine, which means dopamine accumulates in the synapse. Cocaine thus prolongs its effect on other neurons by forcing dopamine to deliver its message to these neurons repeatedly, thereby using it up. The downside is that these dopamine-caused "high" arousal states are temporary and are followed by "crashes" created by the shortage of dopamine that follows. The pleasurable mood effects of these addictive stimulants are thought to arise from the release of dopamine in the brain's reward centers. Other addictive drugs such as painkillers, caffeine, and nicotine also increase dopamine activity in these centers.

Serotonin and norepinephrine. In addition to dopamine, cocaine blocks the reuptake of **serotonin** and **norepinephrine**—neurotransmitters involved in levels of arousal and mood, sleep, and eating. These two neurotransmitters play a major role in mood disorders such as depression. The best-known and most prescribed antidepressant drugs, such as Prozac, Paxil, and Zoloft, are **selective serotonin reuptake inhibitors (SSRIs)**—antidepressant drugs that achieve their agonistic effect by selectively blocking just the reuptake of serotonin. SSRIs only partially block reuptake (unlike cocaine) so they do not exhaust the neurotransmitter supply, and there are no subsequent "crashes." Some other antidepressant drugs, such as Cymbalta, Pristiq, and Effexor, work by blocking the reuptake of both serotonin and norepinephrine. These drugs are called **selective serotonin and norepinephrine reuptake inhibitors (SSNRIs)**. SSRIs, SSNRIs, and other types of antidepressant drugs will be discussed more fully in the section on biomedical therapies in Chapter 10.

GABA and glutamate. GABA (gamma-aminobutyric acid) is the main inhibitory neurotransmitter in the nervous system. Thus, its primary role is to keep the brain from becoming too aroused. It works like the brakes on a car by preventing mental processes or behavior from going unchecked. For example, it lowers arousal and anxiety and helps regulate movement. Antianxiety drugs (tranquilizers) are agonists for GABA, increasing GABA activity and thereby lowering anxiety. Lack of GABA activity may also contribute to

serotonin and norepinephrine Neurotransmitters involved in levels of arousal and mood, sleep, and eating.

selective serotonin reuptake inhibitors (SSRIs) Antidepressant drugs that achieve their agonistic effect on serotonin by selectively blocking its reuptake.

selective serotonin and norepinephrine reuptake inhibitors (SSNRIs) Antidepressant drugs that achieve their agonistic effect on serotonin and norepinephrine by selectively blocking their reuptake.

GABA (gamma-aminobutyric acid) The main inhibitory neurotransmitter in the nervous system. It is involved in lowering arousal and anxiety and regulating movement.

epilepsy, a brain disorder leading to uncontrolled movement and convulsions. Tranquilizers, such as Valium and Librium, sometimes also serve as antiepileptic treatments because they have been found to block epileptic convulsions.

Glutamate is the main excitatory neurotransmitter in the nervous system. It is involved in memory storage and pain perception. Excessive glutamate activity, however, can be dangerous, leading to the death of neurons. For example, strokes lead to overstimulation of glutamate synapses and the subsequent loss of neurons that literally excite themselves to death. Deficient glutamate activity can also cause problems. Glutamate levels that drop too low can even cause coma. Research has also found that abnormal levels of glutamate activity may play a central role in the neurochemistry of schizophrenia (Goff & Coyle, 2001; Javitt & Coyle, 2007). Hence, some pharmaceutical companies are examining the potentiality of antipsychotic drugs that impact glutamate activity levels (Papanastasiou, Stone, & Shergill, 2013; Stone, 2011).

glutamate The main excitatory neurotransmitter in the nervous system. It is involved in memory storage, pain perception, strokes, and schizophrenia.

endorphins A group of neurotransmitters that are involved in pain relief and feelings of pleasure.

Endorphins. **Endorphins** are a group of neurotransmitters that are involved in pain relief and feelings of pleasure. They represent the nervous system's natural painkillers. When endorphins are released, we feel less pain and experience a sense of euphoria. Endorphins, therefore, help explain good feelings such as the "runner's high." Higher than normal endorphin levels have been found in runners following a marathon (Mahler, Cunningham, Skrinar, Kraemer, & Colice, 1989). Morphine and heroin are painkilling drugs that achieve their agonistic effects by binding to endorphin receptors, thereby increasing endorphin activity (Pert & Snyder, 1973). (Actually, the word "endorphin" is a contraction of the words "endogeneous," which means originating within, and "morphine.") These painkillers also trigger the brain's reward centers, causing the release of dopamine.

Endorphins may also play a role in biologically explaining placebo effects on pain. Remember, as we discussed in Chapter 1, a placebo drug is an inert substance that has no pharmacological effect. The expectation of improvement created by taking the placebo may stimulate the release of endorphins, resulting in an actual decrease in pain. Similarly, stimulation of endorphins may partially explain how acupuncture, the Chinese medical practice of inserting needles at specified sites of the body, leads to pain relief (Pert, 1997).

Frank and Ernest

Table 2.1	Neurotransmitters and Some of Their Functions
Neurotransmitter	**Involved in:**
Acetylcholine (ACh)	Learning, memory, muscle movement
Dopamine	Arousal and mood states, thought processes, physical movement
Serotonin and Norepinephrine	Levels of arousal and mood, sleep, eating
GABA (main inhibitory neurotransmitter)	Lowering arousal and anxiety, regulating movement
Glutamate (main excitatory neurotransmitter)	Memory storage, pain perception, strokes, schizophrenia
Endorphins	Pain relief and feelings of pleasure

All of the neurotransmitters that we have discussed are summarized in Table 2.1 along with some of the behaviors and mental processes in which they play a major role.

Section Summary

In this section, we discussed how billions of neurons, the building blocks of the nervous system, work and communicate with each other. All three parts of a neuron are involved. The dendrites receive the information from other neurons and pass it on to the cell body, which decides whether to pass the information on to other neurons. If the information is to be passed on, an electrical impulse is generated and travels down the axon. When this impulse reaches the axon terminals, neurotransmitter molecules are released and travel across the synaptic gap, carrying the message to other neurons, and then are destroyed or return to the sending neuron to be used again. It is this chemical communication that allows the neurons to transmit and integrate information within the nervous system, giving us our perceptions, feelings, memories, and thoughts, as well as our ability to move. Glial cells aid in this information transmission process by serving as a support system for the neurons.

Acetylcholine (ACh), dopamine, serotonin, norepinephrine, GABA, glutamate, and endorphins are seven major neurotransmitters that impact many important aspects of our behavior and mental processing. Some disorders and diseases involve excessive activity or a deficit in activity for particular neurotransmitters. In addition, drugs and poisons achieve their effects by changing the activity level of particular neurotransmitters in either agonistic or antagonistic ways. Agonists increase the level of neurotransmitter activity; antagonists decrease it. This neuronal chemistry is the source of all of our behavior and mental processes, but we are only aware of its products (our behavior and mental processing) and not the intercellular chemistry itself. In the next section, we will consider the nervous system at a more global level by examining its major subdivisions—the central nervous system and the peripheral nervous system. We will also discuss the body's other major communication system—the endocrine glandular system.

ConceptCheck | 1

Explain why you can think of a neuron as a miniature decision-making device.

Explain why neural impulses are faster in neurons with myelinated axons than in those with unmyelinated axons.

Explain why drugs that block the reuptake of neurotransmitters are considered agonists.

Explain why treatment of Parkinson's disease with L-dopa leads to some side effects that resemble the thought disorder symptoms of schizophrenia and why the side effects of traditional antipsychotic drugs lead to side effects resembling Parkinson's disease.

The Nervous System and the Endocrine System

In this section, we will present an overview of the nervous system and the other major communication system of the body, the endocrine glandular system. We will also discuss the three types of neurons in the nervous system. An overview diagram of the major subdivisions of the nervous system is given in Figure 2.3 (page 56). The two major parts are the **central nervous system (CNS),** made up of the brain and spinal cord, and the **peripheral nervous system (PNS),** the remainder of the nervous system throughout the body, linking the CNS with the body's sensory receptors, muscles, and glands. One part of the peripheral nervous system, the autonomic nervous system, plays an important role in emotional experiences. We will learn how it does so once we learn more about the general nature of the nervous system and its major divisions and the body's other major communication system, the endocrine glandular system.

There are three types of neurons in the nervous system. **Interneurons,** which integrate information within the CNS by communicating with one another, are only in the CNS. Interneurons also intervene within the spinal cord between sensory and motor neurons that are only in the PNS. **Sensory neurons** carry information to the CNS from sensory receptors (such as the rods and cones in the eyes), muscles, and glands. **Motor neurons** carry movement commands from the CNS out to the rest of the body. Bundles of sensory neurons are called sensory nerves. Most enter the CNS through the spinal cord, while some (from the head) enter the brain directly through holes in the cranium (the skull around the brain). Collections of the motor neurons are called motor nerves. They exit the CNS through the spinal cord or, for the head, from the cranium. To begin to understand the role that these neurons play, we'll next discuss the CNS and the role of the spinal cord.

central nervous system (CNS) The brain and spinal cord.

peripheral nervous system (PNS) The part of the nervous system that links the CNS with the body's sensory receptors, muscles, and glands.

interneurons Neurons that integrate information within the CNS through their communication with each other and between sensory and motor neurons in the spinal cord.

sensory neurons Neurons in the PNS that carry information to the CNS from sensory receptors, muscles, and glands.

motor neurons Neurons in the PNS that carry movement commands from the CNS out to the rest of the body.

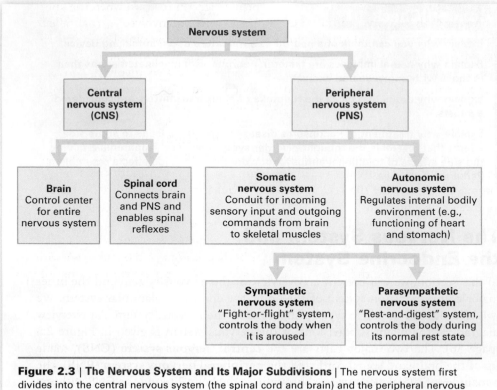

Figure 2.3 | The Nervous System and Its Major Subdivisions | The nervous system first divides into the central nervous system (the spinal cord and brain) and the peripheral nervous system (the remainder of the nervous system throughout the body). The peripheral nervous system has two parts—the somatic (or skeletal) nervous system and the autonomic nervous system. The autonomic nervous system also has two parts—the sympathetic nervous system and parasympathetic nervous system.

The Central Nervous System

Both parts of the CNS, the spinal cord and the brain, are totally encased in bone—the spinal cord within the spinal column and the brain within the cranium—for protective reasons. In addition, for further protection, both are surrounded by cerebrospinal fluid for cushioning. We will detail the spinal cord's role in the CNS here, and then discuss the brain in the last section of this chapter.

The **spinal cord** spans from the stem of the brain down through the neck and the center of the spinal column. It has two main functions. First, it serves as the conduit for both incoming sensory data and outgoing movement commands to the muscles in the body. This is why a spinal cord injury, such as that suffered by actor Christopher Reeve, may result in paralysis and in difficulty breathing. Second, it provides for spinal reflexes. A **spinal reflex** is a simple automatic action not requiring involvement of the brain.

spinal cord The conduit between the brain and the PNS for incoming sensory data and outgoing movement commands to the muscles.

spinal reflex A simple automatic action of the spinal cord not requiring involvement of the brain, such as the knee-jerk reflex.

A good example is the knee-jerk reflex in which a leg jerks forward when the knee is tapped. Only sensory neurons and motor neurons are involved in this reflex. The knee-jerk reflex might appear to have no use, but it is an example of a stretch reflex that is important to maintaining our posture and for lifting objects.

For most spinal reflexes, however, interneurons are also involved. Sensory neurons connect with interneurons in the spinal cord, which then connect with motor neurons. The sensory information is also sent up to the brain by way of interneurons, but the brain is usually not involved. A good example of such a spinal reflex is the withdrawal reflex. When we touch something extremely hot or painful, we jerk away. These reflexes normally occur without interference from the brain so that they can occur rapidly. The brain can stop a spinal reflex by sending commands to override the reflexive response, but for obvious reasons it usually chooses not to interfere.

The brain is the control center for the entire nervous system, but it couldn't perform this job without agents to carry out its commands and to provide information about the activities of the rest of the body and the world outside. We will next discuss the PNS, the system that provides these supportive functions for the brain.

The Peripheral Nervous System

Not only does the PNS gather information for the brain about the external environment and the body's internal environment through the sensory nerves, it also serves as the conduit for the brain's commands to the rest of the body through the motor nerves. To carry out these tasks, the PNS has two parts working in concert with each other—the somatic (or skeletal) nervous system and the autonomic nervous system.

The **somatic (skeletal) nervous system** carries sensory input from receptors to the CNS and relays commands from the CNS to the skeletal muscles to control their movement. Skeletal muscles are those that are attached to bone, such as the muscles of the arms and legs. As we have already discussed, the primary neurotransmitter for these muscles is acetylcholine. The **autonomic nervous system** regulates the functioning of our internal environment (glands and organs such as the stomach, lungs, and heart). The somatic nervous system is thought of as voluntary, but the autonomic system is usually thought of as involuntary, operating on automatic (hence the name, autonomic) to maintain our internal functioning such as heartbeat, respiration, and digestion. This is why we are generally unaware of what the autonomic nervous system is doing.

The autonomic system has two parts—the sympathetic nervous system and the parasympathetic nervous system. These two systems normally work together to maintain a steady internal state. However, the **sympathetic nervous system** is

somatic (skeletal) nervous system
The part of the PNS that carries sensory input from receptors to the CNS and relays commands from the CNS to skeletal muscles to control their movement.

autonomic nervous system The part of the PNS that regulates the functioning of our internal environment (glands and organs like the heart, lungs, and stomach).

sympathetic nervous system The part of the autonomic nervous system that is in control when we are highly aroused, as in an emergency, and need to prepare for defensive action.

Table 2.2	Some Functions of the Sympathetic and Parasympathetic Nervous Systems	
Sympathetic Nervous System	**Parasympathetic Nervous System**	
Dilates pupils	Contracts pupils	
Contracts blood vessels	Dilates blood vessels	
Speeds heart rate	Slows heart rate	
Speeds breathing	Slows breathing	
Inhibits salivation	Activates salivation	
Inhibits digestion	Stimulates digestion	
Activates sweat glands	Inhibits sweat glands	

The sympathetic and parasympathetic divisions of the autonomic nervous system work together to coordinate our internal functioning, including our heart, stomach, and glandular activity. In general, the sympathetic system arouses and expends energy while the parasympathetic system calms and conserves energy.

in control when we are very aroused, as in an emergency, and prepares us for defensive action. The **parasympathetic nervous system** takes over when the aroused state ends to return the body to its normal resting state. Some effects of each part of this dual autonomic system on the glands and muscles that they impact are shown in Table 2.2. In general, the sympathetic nervous system expends energy, and the parasympathetic nervous system conserves energy. The two systems are connected to essentially the same glands and organs, but generally lead to opposite effects. For example, the sympathetic leads to pupil dilation, accelerated heartbeat, and inhibited digestion; the parasympathetic leads to pupil contraction, slowed heartbeat, and stimulated digestion. Given these actions, the sympathetic nervous system is usually referred to as the "fight-or-flight" system; it prepares us for one of these two actions in times of emergency. In contrast, the parasympathetic nervous system has sometimes been called the "rest-and-digest" system (Dowling, 1998).

parasympathetic nervous system The part of the autonomic nervous system that returns the body to its normal resting state after having been highly aroused, as in an emergency.

endocrine glandular system The body's other major communication system. Communication is achieved through hormones that are secreted by the endocrine glands and travel through the bloodstream to their target sites.

The Endocrine Glandular System

The **endocrine glandular system,** the body's other major communication system, is not part of the nervous system, but these two systems are connected in order to maintain normal internal functioning. The endocrine glandular system works with the autonomic nervous system in responding to stress, and it also plays an important role in such basic behaviors as having sex and eating and in normal bodily functions, such as metabolism, reproduction, and growth.

The endocrine glandular system communicates through messengers in the bloodstream. Endocrine glands secrete chemical substances within the body into the bloodstream; exocrine glands (such as sweat and tear glands) secrete substances outside the body. The substances secreted by the endocrine glands are hormones. A **hormone** is a chemical messenger produced by the endocrine glands and carried by the bloodstream to target sites throughout the body. Some hormones (adrenalin and noradrenalin secreted by the adrenal glands) are chemically similar to some neurotransmitters (epinephrine and norepinephrine), but neurotransmitters are released at their targets (other neurons), while hormones have to travel through the bloodstream to reach their targets. For example, the male sex hormone, testosterone, travels from the male sex glands through the bloodstream to target sites in facial skin to stimulate hair growth.

The endocrine glandular system is controlled by its connection with a part of the brain called the hypothalamus (to be discussed in the next section). The hypothalamus controls the most influential gland in the endocrine system, **the pituitary gland,** which releases hormones essential for human growth and also releases hormones that direct other endocrine glands to release their hormones. For example, it is the pituitary gland that directs a male's sex glands to secrete testosterone. The pituitary gland, located near the base of the brain, thus functions like the master of the endocrine system, which is why it is sometimes referred to as the "master gland." The hypothalamus, through its control of the pituitary gland, is thus able to regulate the endocrine glandular system.

Other endocrine glands—such as the thyroid gland, the adrenal glands, the pancreas, and the sex glands—are located throughout the body. The thyroid gland, which affects our growth and maturation among other things, is located in the neck. The adrenal glands, which are involved in our metabolism and help to trigger the "fight-or-flight" response with commands from the autonomic nervous system, are situated above the kidneys. The pancreas, located between the kidneys, is involved in digestion and maintaining our blood-sugar levels. The testes (in males) and ovaries (in females) secrete sex hormones. The major endocrine glands along with their main functions are depicted in Figure 2.4 (page 60).

Emotions and the Autonomic Nervous System

Most of us experience anger, fear, joy, love, hate, and many other emotions. Emotions play an important part in our lives, and the autonomic nervous system, especially the sympathetic division, plays an important role in how we experience and express emotions. Think about the heightened state of arousal and the bodily feelings that accompany various emotions. For example, we may feel our blood pressure rising, our heart pounding, our body trembling, or butterflies

hormone A chemical messenger that is produced by an endocrine gland and carried by the bloodstream to target tissues throughout the body.

pituitary gland The most influential gland in the endocrine glandular system. It releases hormones for human growth and hormones that direct other endocrine glands to release their hormones.

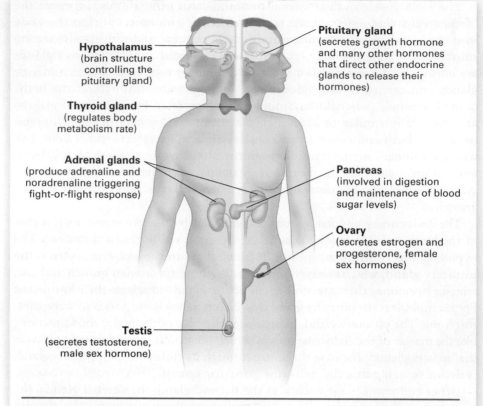

Hypothalamus
(brain structure
controlling the
pituitary gland)

Thyroid gland
(regulates body
metabolism rate)

Adrenal glands
(produce adrenaline and
noradrenaline triggering
fight-or-flight response)

Testis
(secretes testosterone,
male sex hormone)

Pituitary gland
(secretes growth hormone
and many other hormones
that direct other endocrine
glands to release their
hormones)

Pancreas
(involved in digestion
and maintenance of blood
sugar levels)

Ovary
(secretes estrogen and
progesterone, female
sex hormones)

Figure 2.4 | The Endocrine Glandular System | The endocrine glandular system works with the autonomic nervous system in responding to stress. It also plays an important role in such basic behaviors as having sex and eating and in such normal bodily functions as metabolism, reproduction, and growth.

in our stomach. Such bodily arousal and feelings stem from autonomic nervous system activity, which prepares us for our emotional reactions. But exactly what is an emotion, and how do emotions arise?

The three components of emotion. Psychologists usually define an **emotion** as a complex psychological state that involves three components: (1) a physical component—a state of physiological arousal triggered by the autonomic nervous system; (2) a behavioral component—outward expression of the emotion, including facial expressions, movements, and gestures; and (3) a cognitive component—our appraisal of the situation to determine which emotion we are experiencing and how intensely we are experiencing it.

First, let's consider the physical component of emotion. In emotional situations the autonomic nervous system

emotion A complex psychological state that involves a state of physiological arousal, an outward behavioral expression of the emotion, and a cognitive appraisal of the situation to determine the specific emotion and its intensity.

increases our physiological arousal. The sympathetic nervous system goes into its "fight-or-flight" mode—our heart rate and breathing increase, our blood pressure surges, we start sweating, our pupils dilate, we begin trembling, our digestion stops, and so on. This aroused state prepares us to react emotionally to the situation, whether our reaction is to run from an attacker, hug a loved one, or laugh at a roommate's joke. Different emotions seem to lead to subtly different patterns of autonomic nervous system arousal (Levenson, 1992). The language we use to describe different emotional states reflects the different patterns in arousal states for these emotions (Oatley & Duncan, 1994). For example, we say we are "hot under the collar" when angry, but that we have "cold feet" when afraid. These descriptions parallel differences in body temperature for these two basic emotions; we have a higher than normal body temperature when we are angry and a lower one when we are afraid.

The behavioral component of emotion is the product of the somatic nervous system. It provides the nonverbal, expressive behavior for the emotion—our facial expressions, such as smiles and frowns, and our body language, such as clenching our fists. Some emotion researchers have proposed a facial-feedback hypothesis, which assumes that the facial muscles send messages to the brain, allowing the brain to determine which emotion is being experienced (Izard, 1990; Soussignan, 2002). For example, when we see someone we truly care for and haven't seen for some time, we automatically start smiling; signals about this facial expression are sent to the brain to help the brain determine what emotion is being experienced. In fact, there is even evidence that watching another person's facial expressions causes a reciprocal change in our own facial muscles (Dinberg & Thunberg, 1998). If they smile, we smile. Signals are sent not only from the facial muscles but also from the entire motor nervous system to the brain, contributing to the cognitive appraisal component of the emotion.

The cognitive component of emotion appraises the situation to determine what emotion we are experiencing. We perceive the changes in bodily arousal and behavioral responses within the situational context, and then, using the knowledge we have stored in memory about emotions, we determine what emotion we are experiencing. For example, if your hands are sweating, you feel butterflies in your stomach, your mouth is dry, and you are about to give a speech to a large crowd, then your brain will easily deduce that you are anxious.

Next, we will consider how this cognitive component interacts with the physical and behavioral components to produce our emotional experiences as we contrast some of the major theories of emotion.

Theories of emotion. Many theories have been proposed over the last century to explain emotion. We'll consider three of them—the James-Lange theory, the Cannon-Bard theory, and the Schachter-Singer two-factor theory. To see how these theories differ, we'll contrast them with what is referred to as the "common-sense" explanation of emotion, which proposes that the subjective experience of the emotion triggers the physiological arousal and behavioral response. For example, you are out hiking and you see a bear (an emotion-provoking stimulus).

William James

Carl Lange

Walter Cannon

Philip Bard

The commonsense view would say that you cognitively recognize a dangerous situation and react emotionally by realizing you are afraid. This emotional feeling of fear triggers the arousal of the autonomic nervous system—for example, your heart races and you start sweating—and a behavioral response—you back away slowly. (Don't run from a bear. It triggers their chase instincts.) The commonsense view proposes the following order of events—you realize you are afraid, and then the physiological arousal and behavioral response follow. Your heart races and you start sweating and back away because you are afraid.

American psychologist William James and Danish psychologist Carl Lange developed one of the earliest theories of emotion (Lange & James, 1922). They disagreed with the order of events proposed by the commonsense theory and argued that the emotional feeling does not precede, but rather follows, the physiological arousal and behavioral response. According to the **James-Lange theory,** physiological arousal and backing away are responses to the stimulus of seeing the bear. You then interpret these autonomic and behavioral responses as the emotion fear. You determine that you are afraid because you are sweating, your heart is racing, and you are backing away. The emotional feeling occurs after, and as a result of, the arousal and behavioral responses. The particular emotion experienced depends upon the specific arousal and response patterns.

Walter Cannon, the physiologist most responsible for discovering the functions of the autonomic nervous system, had different ideas about the role of arousal in emotion. He and another physiologist, Philip Bard, developed what is called the **Cannon-Bard theory** (Bard, 1934; Cannon, 1927). This theory argues that arousal patterns for different emotions are too physiologically alike to be used to determine which emotion is being experienced. Instead, they proposed that an emotion-provoking stimulus (the bear) sends messages simultaneously to the peripheral nervous system and the brain. The autonomic nervous system produces the physiological arousal responses such as our heart racing; the motor nervous system produces the behavioral response (backing away); and the brain produces the emotional feeling (fear). These three responses occur simultaneously, but independently. So, according to the Cannon-Bard theory, the arousal and behavioral responses do not cause the emotional feeling, and the emotional feeling does not cause the responses. They all happen at the same time.

Subsequent research on these two theories has not strongly supported either one but has indicated that the cognitive component may play a larger role than previously thought. These early theories did not emphasize this component. The last theory of emotion that we will discuss, Stanley Schachter and Jerome Singer's two-factor theory, illustrates the emerging importance of the cognitive component (Schachter & Singer, 1962). Schachter and Singer agreed with the James-

Lange theory that arousal was a central element in our experience of emotion, but also with the Cannon-Bard theory that physiological arousal is too similar to distinguish different emotions. According to the **Schachter-Singer two-factor theory,** there are two important ingredients in determining the emotion—physiological arousal and cognitive appraisal. The physiological arousal tells us how intense the emotion is, while the cognitive appraisal of the entire situation (the arousal responses such as our heart racing, the behavioral response of backing away, and the situational aspect of being alone with the bear) allows us to identify (label) the emotion, leading to the emotional feeling (fear). In the two-factor theory, cognitive appraisal precedes the emotion. This is different from the Cannon-Bard assumption that arousal and the emotion occur simultaneously. The two-factor theory is contrasted with the three earlier theories in Figure 2.5.

James-Lange theory A theory of emotion proposing that an emotion is determined from a cognitive appraisal of the physiological arousal and behavioral responses, which occur first.

Cannon-Bard theory A theory of emotion proposing that an emotion is determined from simultaneously occurring physiological arousal, behavioral responses, and cognitive appraisal.

Schachter-Singer two-factor theory A theory of emotion proposing that an emotion is determined by cognitive appraisal of the physiological arousal and the entire environmental situation.

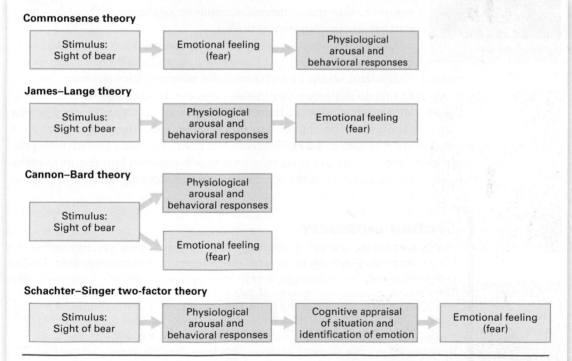

Figure 2.5 | Theories of Emotion | The commonsense theory argued that our feeling of fear causes our physiological arousal and behavioral responses. The James-Lange theory proposed just the opposite—our physiological arousal and behavioral responses cause us to feel afraid. According to the Cannon-Bard theory, the physiological and behavioral responses and the feeling of fear occur simultaneously. The Schachter-Singer two-factor theory asserted that cognitive appraisal of the physiological arousal and behavioral responses and the entire situation leads to the identification (labeling) of the emotion (fear), which leads to our feeling of fear.

Stanley Schachter

Jerome E. Singer

Schachter and Singer's experimental work to test their theory only provided partial support, but their theory has spurred much discussion and research on the role of cognitive appraisal in emotion. As mentioned earlier, the autonomic arousal patterns for some emotions are not the same, but some argue that these pattern differences may be too small to allow the differentiation of most emotions (Lang, 1994). However, these emotions also lead to different patterns of brain activity (Damasio et al., 2000). Could these patterns be used to differentiate emotions?

To help resolve this question, Joseph LeDoux (1996, 2000) proposes that there are different brain systems for different emotions. Some emotional responses might be the product of a brain system that operates as a reflex system without cognitive appraisal. Fear is probably such an emotion. LeDoux actually has some evidence that the fear response can be generated almost instantaneously—before higher-level cognitive appraisal of the situation could occur. Such fast responding would have survival value from an evolutionary point of view by allowing us to make quick, defensive responses to threats without having to wait on slower, cognitive appraisal.

Other emotions, however, may entail using a brain system that relies on cognitive appraisal and the use of past emotional experiences in this appraisal. This system would be responsible for more complex emotions, such as love or guilt, that do not require an instant response. In sum, this theory not only accommodates much of what we know about emotion but also provides a general framework for research on the roles of various brain structures in generating our emotions. We now turn to a discussion of these brain structures and what we presently know about them and their roles not only in emotion but also in thought, language, memory, and the many other information-processing abilities we possess.

Section Summary

In this section, we discussed the two major communication systems within the body—the nervous system, which uses neurotransmitters to communicate, and the endocrine glandular system, which uses slower-acting hormones to communicate. The nervous system is composed of two main divisions—the central nervous system (CNS), which consists of the brain and spinal cord, and the peripheral nervous system (PNS), which links the CNS with the body's sensory receptors, muscles, and glands. Sensory neurons carry information from the PNS to the CNS, and motor neurons carry movement commands from the CNS to parts of the PNS. The spinal cord not only serves as the conduit for this information but also is responsible for spinal reflexes, automatic actions not requiring involvement of the brain. Interneurons integrate all information processing within the CNS.

The PNS has two parts that work in concert with each other—the somatic nervous system carries sensory information to the CNS and relays commands from the CNS to skeletal muscles to control their movement, and the autonomic nervous system regulates our internal environment. To do this, the autonomic system has two parts working together—the sympathetic nervous system, which expends energy, and the parasympathetic nervous system, which conserves energy. The sympathetic is in control during emergencies to help us prepare for defensive action; once the emergency is over, the parasympathetic helps us return to our normal resting state.

The endocrine glandular system is not part of the nervous system, but the two systems work together to maintain normal internal functioning. The endocrine glandular system plays an important role in many basic behaviors, such as eating and having sex, and normal bodily functions, such as metabolism, growth, and reproduction. The brain controls the endocrine glandular system through the hypothalamus, which controls the master gland within the system, the pituitary gland.

We also discussed how the autonomic nervous system plays a critical role in the physical component of our emotional experiences by triggering a state of physiological arousal, which prepares us for our emotional reactions. An emotion is the result of the interplay between this physical component, a behavioral component (the outward expression of the emotion), and a cognitive component (an appraisal of the entire situation to determine which emotion we are experiencing). The major explanations of emotion have varied in the proposed relationships among these three components, as well as their importance. More recent theories of emotion, such as Schachter and Singer's two-factor theory, have emphasized the importance of the cognitive appraisal component, and the idea that cognition must precede emotion. However, this is not always the case. LeDoux's proposal that different brain systems may be responsible for different emotional responses (those that require cognitive appraisal versus those that do not) can account for both emotional reactions in which cognition precedes emotion, and those in which emotion precedes cognition.

ConceptCheck | 2

Explain the differences between sensory neurons, motor neurons, and interneurons with respect to location and function.

Explain why the sympathetic nervous system has been referred to as the "fight-or-flight" system and the parasympathetic nervous system as the "rest-and-digest" system.

Explain how hormones differ from neurotransmitters. Explain why the pituitary gland is referred to as the "master gland."

Explain how the James-Lange theory and the Cannon-Bard theory of emotion differ.

The Brain

The brain has evolved from the brain stem structures that link the brain to the spinal cord all the way up to the cerebral cortex. As we go up the brain stem, processing gets more complex. In fact, it is the very top, the cerebral cortex, that differentiates our brains from those of all other animals. The cerebral cortex enables such complex processes as decision making, language, and perception. Even so, all of the structures below the cerebral cortex are essential for normal behavior and mental

medulla A brain stem structure involved in many essential body functions, such as heartbeat, breathing, blood pressure, digestion, and swallowing.

processing. This will become clearer as we discuss each structure's role in this complex, interactive system we call the brain.

Going Up the Brain Stem

Between the spinal cord and the cortex, there are two sets of brain structures—the central core and the limbic system. The brain stem and structures near the brain stem (cerebellum, thalamus, and basal ganglia) can be thought of as the central core of the brain. Surrounding the top border of the brain stem are the limbic system structures—the hypothalamus, hippocampus, and amygdala. Our discussion will start with the central core structures going up the brain stem to the limbic system structures.

The central core. Figure 2.6 shows the central core brain structures. The brain stem spans from the spinal cord up to the thalamus. The first brain stem structure is the **medulla,** which links the spinal cord to the brain. The medulla is involved

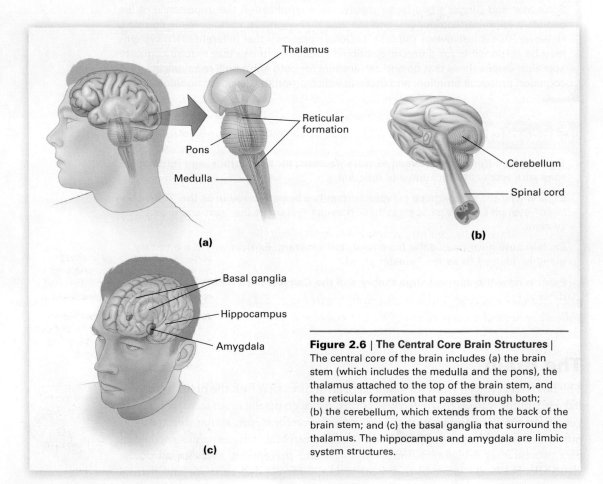

(a)

(b)

(c)

Figure 2.6 | The Central Core Brain Structures | The central core of the brain includes (a) the brain stem (which includes the medulla and the pons), the thalamus attached to the top of the brain stem, and the reticular formation that passes through both; (b) the cerebellum, which extends from the back of the brain stem; and (c) the basal ganglia that surround the thalamus. The hippocampus and amygdala are limbic system structures.

in regulating essential body functions such as heartbeat, breathing, blood pressure, digestion, and swallowing. This is why damage to the medulla can result in death. A drug overdose that suppresses proper functioning of the medulla can also lead to death. Just above the medulla, where the brain stem bulges, sits the **pons.** Along with the medulla, the pons serves as a passageway for neural signals to and from higher areas in the brain. The pons (Latin for "bridge") functions as a bridge between the cerebellum and the rest of the brain and is involved in sleep and dreaming.

The **reticular formation,** a network of neurons running up the center of the brain stem and into the thalamus, is involved in controlling our different levels of arousal and awareness. This function was demonstrated by Moruzzi and Magoun (1949) in research with cats. When they stimulated a sleeping cat's reticular formation, the cat awoke and entered a very alert state. When they severed the connections of the reticular formation with higher brain structures, however, the cat went into a coma from which it could never be awakened. The reticular formation also plays a role in attention by deciding which incoming sensory information enters our conscious awareness.

The **cerebellum** is involved in the coordination of our movements, our sense of balance, and motor learning. Cerebellum means "little brain" in Latin, and it looks like two minihemispheres attached to the rear of the brain stem. The cerebellum has roughly the same surface area (if unfolded) as a single cerebral hemisphere does (Bower & Parsons, 2007), but it is composed of smaller neurons so it takes up far less space. Only making up about 10% of the brain's weight (Rilling & Insel, 1998), it has more neurons, an estimated 70 billion (Azevedo et al., 2009), than the rest of the brain combined. This is because the great majority of cerebellar neurons are granule neurons, which are very small and can be densely packed into a smaller space. The cerebellum coordinates all of our movements, such as walking, running, and dancing. Damage to the cerebellum will lead to very unsteady, unbalanced movement. Alcohol depresses the functioning of the cerebellum, leading to the uncoordinated movements typical of someone who is drunk. This is why some of the tests for being drunk involve coordinated movement. In addition, the cerebellum is the location of motor learning, such as how to ride a bicycle or to type. There is also some emerging evidence indicating that the cerebellum not only coordinates movement but may also play a role in integrating and coordinating sensory input and in mental functions such as planning (Bower & Parsons, 2007). Lastly, recovery from cerebellar damage, and even from removal of the cerebellum at a young age, is relatively good. Why this is so remains unanswered.

The **thalamus,** located at the top of the brain stem, serves as a relay station for incoming sensory information. As such, it sends each type of sensory information (visual, auditory, taste, or touch) to the appropriate location in the cerebral cortex.

pons A brain stem structure that serves as a bridge between the cerebellum and the rest of the brain and is involved in sleep and dreaming.

reticular formation A network of neurons running up the center of the brain stem that is responsible for our different levels of arousal and consciousness.

cerebellum A part of the brain involved in the coordination of our movements, sense of balance, and motor learning.

thalamus A part of the brain that serves as a relay station for incoming sensory information.

basal ganglia A part of the brain that is involved in the initiation and execution of movements.

limbic system A group of brain structures (hypothalamus, hippocampus, and amygdala) that play an important role in our survival, memory, and emotions.

hypothalamus A part of the brain that is involved in regulating basic drives such as eating, drinking, and having sex. It also directs the endocrine glandular system through its control of the pituitary gland and the autonomic nervous system to maintain the body's internal environment.

The only type of sensory information that does not pass through the thalamus is olfactory (smell) information. Smell information goes directly from the receptors in our nose to the cortex. The **basal ganglia** are on the outer sides of the thalamus and are concerned mainly with the initiation and execution of physical movements. Like the cerebellum, the basal ganglia are affected by alcohol, and so make the movements required by tests for drunken driving difficult to execute. The basal ganglia are actually a group of various interacting brain regions. As we discussed earlier in this chapter, abnormally low dopamine activity in one region of the basal ganglia results in Parkinson's disease. Another disease that involves difficulty in controlling movements is Huntington's chorea, which stems from problems in another region of the ganglia in which there are GABA and acetylcholine deficits.

All of the various central core structures are summarized in Table 2.3 along with some of their major functions.

The limbic system. Surrounding the top border (or *limbus* in Latin) of the brain stem is the **limbic system,** which is made up of the hypothalamus, the amygdala, and the hippocampus. These limbic structures play an important role in our survival, memory, and emotions. Figure 2.7 shows the three parts of the limbic system. The **hypothalamus** is a very tiny structure, weighing about half an ounce, which is named after its location—below the thalamus (*hypo* means "below" in Greek). The hypothalamus controls the pituitary gland (and so directs activity in the endocrine glandular system) and the autonomic nervous system to maintain

Table 2.3	Central Core Structures and Some of Their Functions
Central Core Structure	**Functions**
Medulla	Involved in essential body functions, such as heartbeat, breathing, blood pressure, and swallowing
Pons	Serves as bridge between cerebellum and rest of brain and involved in sleep and dreaming
Reticular Formation	Responsible for our different levels of arousal and consciousness
Cerebellum	Involved in coordination of our movements, sense of balance, and motor learning
Thalamus	Serves as relay station for incoming sensory stimuli (except for olfactory sensory information)
Basal Ganglia	Involved in initiation and execution of movements

the body's internal environment, such as regulating body temperature. It also plays a major role in regulating basic drives such as eating, drinking, and having sex. Thus, this tiny structure plays a huge role in both our behavior and our survival.

The **hippocampus** is involved in the formation of memories. Hippocampus may seem like a rather strange name, but like many parts of the brain, it was given a name that matched its visual appearance. The hippocampus looks somewhat like a sea-horse, and *hippocampus* means "seahorse" in Greek. Recall the case study of H. M. that we discussed in Chapter 1. H. M. had his left and right hippocampal structures removed for medical reasons and as a result suffered severe memory deficits (Corkin, 1984). Subsequent research on H. M. and other people with amnesia has shown the hippocampus to be critical for the formation of certain types of new memories (Cohen & Eichenbaum, 1993), which we will discuss in Chapter 5.

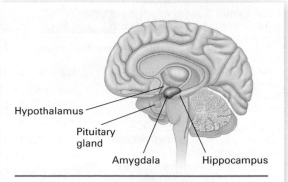

Figure 2.7 | The Limbic System | Positioned around the top of the brain stem is the limbic system—the hypothalamus, hippocampus, and amygdala.

The hippocampus has also been found to have the capacity to generate new neurons, a process called neurogenesis (Gage, 2003; Kempermann & Gage, 1999). The research group most responsible for demonstrating neurogenesis in humans was led by Fred Gage. Given that brain-imaging techniques cannot detect neuronal growth and that ethics prohibit neurosurgery to detect such growth in humans, Gage and his colleagues developed a very clever way to demonstrate that such growth exists. BrdU is a traceable substance that has been used in cancer treatment to track how rapidly the disease is spreading. BrdU is integrated into the DNA of cells preparing to divide. Hence it becomes part of the DNA of the new cells and all future descendants of the original dividing cells. Thus, BrdU functions as a marker for new cells. Because BrdU cannot be administered to healthy people, Gage and his colleagues examined postmortem hippocampal tissue of cancer patients who had been injected with BrdU before their deaths, and new noncancerous cells with BrdU were found (Eriksson et al., 1998; van Praag et al, 2002). Although the purposes of neurogenesis in the hippocampus of humans are not yet clear, some research suggests that it may play a key role in depression (Jacobs, van Praag, & Gage, 2000a, 2000b). We will consider this hypothesis in Chapter 10, Abnormal Psychology.

Located just in front of the hippocampal structures are the **amygdala** left and right structures. Amygdala means "almond" in Greek, and these structures look like almonds. The amygdala plays a major role in regulating our emotional experiences, especially fear, anger, and aggression. It is also responsible for generating quick emotional responses

hippocampus A part of the brain involved in the formation of memories.

amygdala A part of the brain that is involved in emotions by influencing aggression, anger, and fear and by providing the emotional element of our memories and the interpretation of emotional expressions in others.

Table 2.4	Limbic System Structures and Some of Their Functions
Limbic System Structure	**Functions**
Hypothalamus	Involved in regulating basic drives such as eating, drinking, and having sex; directing the endocrine glandular system; and maintaining the body's internal environment
Hippocampus	Involved in the formation of memories and via neurogenesis may play a role in depression
Amygdala	Involved in emotions by influencing aggression, anger, and fear and by providing emotional element of our memories and the interpretation of emotional expressions in others

directly, without cortical involvement (LeDoux, 2000). The first evidence for the amygdala's role in emotional behavior was done on wild, rather violent rhesus monkeys (Klüver & Bucy, 1939). The monkeys' amygdalas were surgically removed. The surgery transformed the monkeys into calm, tame animals, clearly changing their emotional behavior. Other research has indicated that the amygdala also provides the emotional element in our memories and guides our interpretation of the emotional expressions of others (LeDoux, 1996).

All three structures in the limbic system are summarized in Table 2.4 along with some of their major functions.

Processing in the Cerebral Cortex

All of the brain structures that we have discussed so far are important to our behavior and survival. The most important brain structure, however, is the **cerebral cortex,** the control and information-processing center for the nervous system. This is where perception, language, memory, decision making, and all other higher-level cognitive processing occur. The cerebral cortex physically envelops all of the other brain structures, except for the lowest parts of the brain stem and cerebellum. It is by far the largest part of the brain, accounting for about 80% of its total volume (Kolb & Whishaw, 2001). The cerebral cortex consists of layers of interconnected cells that make up the "bark" or covering of the brain's two hemispheres, which are called cerebral hemispheres. The two hemispheres are separated on top by a deep gap but joined together farther down in the middle by the **corpus callosum,** a bridge of neurons that allows the two hemispheres to communicate.

The cerebral cortex is very crumpled in appearance with all sorts of bulges and gaps. This allows more cortical

cerebral cortex The layers of interconnected cells covering the brain's two hemispheres. This is the control and information-processing center for the nervous system; it is where perception, memory, language, decision making, and all other higher-level cognitive processing occur.

corpus callosum The bridge of neurons that connects the two cerebral hemispheres.

surface area to fit inside our rather small skull. If we were to unfold the cerebral cortex to check the amount of surface area, we would find the area to be about the size of four sheets of notebook paper or one newspaper page. Think about this. You couldn't fit four sheets of paper into your pants pocket unless you crumpled them up. This is the same principle that applies to fitting the large surface area of the cerebral cortex into the small space within the skull. It is this large amount of surface area in the cerebral cortex that not only allows our complex cognitive processing but also differentiates our brains from those of all other animals. To see where different types of processing occur in the cerebral cortex, we need to learn the geography of the two hemispheres. This geography is rather simple in that the outer surface of each hemisphere is divided into four defined parts, called lobes, which we will discuss first.

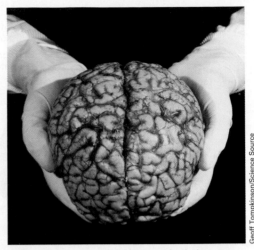

The cerebral cortex of the human brain is very crumpled. This allows more cortical surface area to fit inside our rather small skull. The actual surface area, if unfolded, is about the size of four sheets of notebook paper.

The four lobes. Figure 2.8 (page 72) shows the four lobes in the left hemisphere. They are the same in the right hemisphere and are named after the specific bone area in the skull covering each of them. Two distinctive fissures (gaps) serve as boundary markers for three of the lobes. The central fissure (also called the fissure of Rolando) runs down the center of each hemisphere, and the lateral fissure (also called the Sylvian fissure) runs back along the side of each hemisphere. The four lobes are named for the four bones of the skull that overlie them. The **frontal lobe** is the area in front of the central fissure and above the lateral fissure, and the **parietal lobe** is the area located behind the central fissure and above the lateral fissure. The **temporal lobe** is located beneath the lateral fissure. The remaining lobe is the **occipital lobe,** which is located in the lower back of each hemisphere. Brynie (2009) explains how to find your occipital lobes. Run your hand up the back of your neck until you come to a bump and then place your palm on the bump. Your palm is squarely over the occipital lobes. The frontal lobes are the largest of the lobes. Their location is easy to remember because they are in the front of the hemispheres and directly behind the forehead. Now that we know these four areas, we can see what we have learned about what type of processing occurs in each of them. We begin with the well-defined areas for producing voluntary movement of different parts of the body, such as raising a hand or making a fist, and for processing various types of sensory input, such as touch, visual, and auditory information.

frontal lobe The area in each cerebral hemisphere in front of the central fissure and above the lateral fissure. The motor cortex is in this lobe.

parietal lobe The area in each cerebral hemisphere in back of the central fissure and above the lateral fissure. The somatosensory cortex is in this lobe.

temporal lobe The area in each cerebral hemisphere located beneath the lateral fissure. The primary auditory cortex is in this lobe.

occipital lobe The area located in the lower back of each cerebral hemisphere. The primary visual cortex is in this lobe.

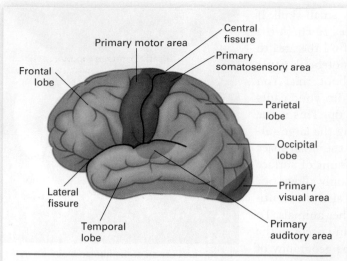

Figure 2.8 | The Four Lobes and the Sensory-Motor Processing
Areas | This figure shows the four lobes in the left hemisphere.
They are exactly the same areas in the right hemisphere. The
central fissure separates the frontal lobe from the parietal lobe,
and the temporal lobe is located beneath the lateral fissure running
along the side of the hemisphere. The occipital lobe is toward the
lower back of the hemisphere. The motor cortex is the strip in the
frontal lobe directly in front of the central fissure; the somatosensory cortex is the strip in the parietal lobe directly behind the central
fissure. Primary auditory processing occurs in the temporal lobe,
and primary visual processing in the occipital lobe.

The motor cortex. The **motor cortex,** the frontal lobe strip of cortex directly in front of the central fissure in each hemisphere, allows us to move different parts of our body. The two motor cortex strips are related to the body by contralateral control—each hemisphere controls the voluntary movement of the opposite side of the body. This means that the motor strip in the left hemisphere controls movement in the right side of the body, and the motor strip in the right hemisphere controls movement in the left side of the body. It is also interesting that the amount of space allocated to a specific body part in the motor cortex is not related to the actual size of the body part, but rather to the complexity and precision of movement of which that part is capable. Smaller parts that can make complex movements, such as our fingers, get a large amount of space, and larger parts, such as our torso, that cannot make complex movements do not get much space. Figure 2.9 illustrates this with what is called a homunculus ("little man" in Greek)—a body depiction with the size of each body part proportional to its amount of area in the motor cortex and not its actual size. Note that the body parts are arranged in a toe-to-head fashion spanning from the top of the motor strip to the bottom. It is as if the homunculus is hanging by its toes over the side of the hemisphere.

motor cortex The strip of cortex in each cerebral hemisphere in the frontal lobe directly in front of the central fissure, which allows us to move different parts of our body.

somatosensory cortex The strip of cortex in each cerebral hemisphere in the parietal lobe directly in back of the central fissure, which allows us to sense pressure, temperature, and pain in different parts of our body as well as the position of our body parts.

The somatosensory cortex. The **somatosensory cortex,** the parietal lobe strip of cortex directly behind the central fissure in each hemisphere, is where our body sensations of pressure, temperature, limb position, and pain are processed. *Somato* is Greek for body. Somatosensory, then, refers to the body senses. In addition to information about touch, the somatosensory cortex receives input about temperature and pain and information from the muscles and joints that allow us to monitor the positions of the various parts of the body. As in the motor cortex, there are contralateral relationships between the somatosensory strips and

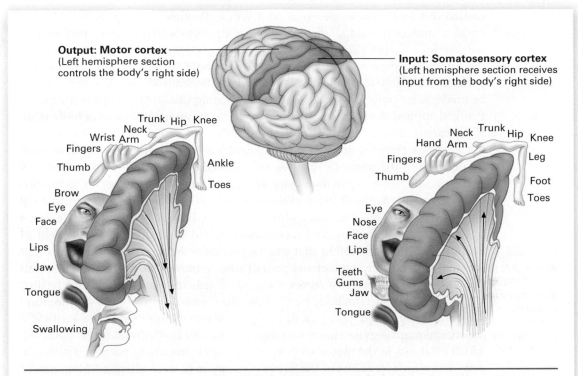

Output: Motor cortex
(Left hemisphere section controls the body's right side)

Input: Somatosensory cortex
(Left hemisphere section receives input from the body's right side)

Figure 2.9 | Homunculi for the Motor Cortex and the Somatosensory Cortex | These homunculi are for the left hemisphere. This means that the motor strip controls the right side of the body, and the somatosensory strip receives signals from the right side of the body. The amount of space for each body part in the motor strip is based on the complexity and precision of movement for that part, and the amount of space for each body part in the somatosensory strip is related to the part's sensitivity. For both strips, the body is arranged from foot to head starting from the top of the hemisphere. (Adapted from Penfield/Rasmussen, *The Cerebral Cortex of Man* ©1950, Gale, A part of Cengage Learning, Inc. Reproduced by permission www.cengage.com/permissions)

sides of the body. The somatosensory strip in the left hemisphere interprets the body sensory information for the right side of the body, and the strip in the right hemisphere interprets this information for the left side of the body. In addition, the amount of space within these strips is not allocated by the size of the body part. In the somatosensory cortex, it is allocated in accordance with the sensitivity of the body part—the more sensitive, the more space. For example, the lips and other parts of the face are more sensitive, so they have larger processing areas than body parts, such as our torso, that are not as sensitive. The homunculus for the somatosensory strip is given in Figure 2.9. Like the motor strip, the body is arranged from toe to head, starting at the top of the strip.

You may be wondering how the homunculi for the motor and somatosensory strips were determined. They were the result of pre-surgical brain evaluations carried out by Canadian neurosurgeon Wilder Penfield who applied mild electrical stimulation via a single electrode to a patient's brain before performing surgery for epilepsy (Buonomano, 2011; Seung, 2012). Because the brain itself does not have pain receptors, these surgeries could be performed in conscious patients with only local anesthesia applied to the scalp where incisions were to be made. After pulling back the scalp and opening the skull to expose the brain, Penfield applied electrical probes to different locations in the brains of more than 500 patients. By carrying out multiple stimulations and meticulously recording the patient's response to each one, Penfield was able to identify the abnormal tissue causing the patient's seizures and delineate those areas surrounding the tissue that he had to avoid damaging during the surgery. In using this technique to carry out pre-surgical brain evaluations of his patients, Penfield amassed a large body of stimulation data, which led to the first detailed large-scale functional map of the human cerebral cortex (Penfield & Boldrey, 1937; Penfield & Rasmussen, 1968). He found that when a particular area in the motor cortex was stimulated, a specific part of the patient's body moved, and when a particular area in the somatosensory cortex was stimulated, the patient reported feeling a sensation in a specific body part. These data were used to create the homunculi for the two strips. Using fMRI images, researchers have replicated Penfield's functional mappings for these two strips (Seung, 2012). The researchers observed which locations in the motor strip were activated by touching parts of a subject's body and which locations in the somatosensory strip were activated when a subject moved parts of the body.

The visual cortex and the auditory cortex. There are two other important areas for processing sensory information in Figure 2.8 that we haven't discussed yet. These are the primary processing areas for our two major senses, seeing and hearing. The visual cortex is located in the occipital lobes at the back of the hemispheres, and the auditory cortex is in the temporal lobes. Figure 2.8 shows where they are located in the left hemisphere. They have the same locations in the right hemisphere. The size of the primary visual cortex varies between individuals over a threefold range in surface area and volume (Dougherty et al., 2003). The reasons for this variability are not known. Interestingly, Schwartzkopf, Song, and Rees (2011) found a strong negative correlation between the magnitude of two context illusions and the surface area of the primary visual cortex. Thus, the smaller your primary visual cortex, the more dramatic some visual illusions appear. The primary visual cortex and the primary auditory cortex are only the locations of the initial processing of visual and auditory information. These primary areas pass the results of their analyses on to areas in the other lobes to complete the brain's interpretation of the incoming visual or auditory information. These secondary cortical processing areas are part of what is termed the **association cortex**—all the areas of the cerebral cortex, except for those devoted to primary sensory or motor processing.

association cortex All of the cerebral cortex except those areas devoted to primary sensory processing or motor processing. This is where all the higher-level cognitive processing that requires the association (integration) of information, such as perception and language, occurs.

Table 2.5	The Four Cerebral Lobes and Type of Sensory/Motor Processing in Each Lobe
Cerebral Lobe	**Type of Sensory/Motor Processing**
Frontal	Includes motor cortex, which allows us to move the different parts of our body
Parietal	Includes somatosensory cortex where our body sensations of touch, temperature, limb position, and pain are processed
Temporal	Includes primary auditory cortex where auditory sensory information is initially processed
Occipital	Includes primary visual cortex where visual sensory information is initially processed

The four cerebral lobes and the type of sensory/motor processing that occurs in each lobe are summarized in Table 2.5.

Given the different locations of the visual cortex and the auditory cortex, you may think that seeing and hearing function entirely separately from each other. The reality, however, is that there is plenty of crosstalk between them. A good example of this interaction is the McGurk effect, which demonstrates that the brain integrates visual and auditory information when processing spoken language (McGurk & MacDonald, 1976). The McGurk effect arises out of conflicting auditory and visual information. A person's lip movements influence what we hear. For example, if you listen to an audio track of a syllable ("ba") spoken repeatedly while you watch a video clip of a person making the lip movements as if repeatedly saying another syllable ("ga"), you actually hear a third syllable "da," the brain's best guess after merging the information from the two senses. You will have a much better understanding of the McGurk effect if you experience it, and you can find several Web sites that allow you to do so just by doing an online search for the McGurk effect. The McGurk effect is a good example of how visual information can exert a strong influence on what we hear, but it is just one example of how our senses interact. There are many others, such as the smell of food influencing its taste. In interpreting the world, the brain blends the input from all of our senses.

It is important not to confuse sensory interaction in general and the McGurk effect, which all of us with normal sensory capabilities can experience, with synesthesia, a rare neurological condition in which otherwise normal people have cross-sensory experiences in which stimulation in one modality leads to automatic, involuntary experiences in another modality. For example, in synesthesia, sounds may evoke tastes, and colors may evoke smells. In addition, perception of a form (e.g., a number) may induce an unusual perception in the same modality (e.g., a color). Although grapheme-color synesthesia (seeing letters, words, and numbers in colors) and sound-color synesthesia (seeing sounds as colors) are the most common types of synesthesia (Brang & Ramachandran, 2011), there are many other types. The exact number is not known. Some people with synesthesia appear to use this union of the senses to inspire their art (Ramachandran & Blakeslee, 1998). For example, Russian artist Wassily Kandinsky said that when he saw colors, he also heard music, leading him to develop his style of abstract painting (Blakeslee & Blakeslee, 2008). It was as if he was capturing music on canvas. Synesthesia affects only 2% to 4% of the population and is believed to stem from some type of cross-wiring in the brain in which normally separate areas of the brain elicit activity in one another (Brang & Ramachandran, 2011). Although familial linkage analyses have shown a strong genetic component, the precise genes involved in synesthesia have not been identified, and why this sensory anomaly has remained in our gene pool remains a mystery. As Eagleman (2011, p. 80) points out in discussing the tiny genetic changes that cause synesthesia, "microscopic changes in brain wiring can lead to different realities," demonstrating once again that reality is more subjective than most people realize.

The association cortex. Most of the cortex (about 70%) is association cortex. This is where all the higher-level processing such as decision making, reasoning, perception, speech, and language occurs. These areas were named the association cortex because higher-level processing requires the association (integration) of various types of information. Scientists have studied the association cortex for over a century, but they are only beginning to understand the functions of some of the association areas (helped greatly by scanning technologies, such as PET scans and fMRI). For example, Sergent, Ohta, and MacDonald (1992) and Kanwisher, McDermott, and Chun (1997) used PET scans and fMRI, respectively, and found a small region on the underside of the temporal lobe near the intersection of the temporal and occipital lobes that responded most strongly to faces. Kanwisher and her colleagues named it the fusiform face area (FFA). Subsequent fMRI studies have confirmed the engagement of the FFA during a range of facial perception tasks (Tong, Nakayama, Moscovitch, Weinrib, and Kanwisher, 2000). The asymmetry of the FFA (it is much larger in the right hemisphere) leads to a right-hemisphere specialization for face recognition (Kanwisher, 2006; Kanwisher & Yovel, 2009). Hence, it is the right hemisphere that is mainly at work when we process faces.

Damage to the FFA has also been found to play a role in prosopagnosia (sometimes called face blindness), a condition that impacts a person's ability to recognize faces including relatives, friends, and acquaintances or even oneself in a mirror (Greuter, 2007; Hadjikhani & de Gelder, 2002). Although a person with prosopagnosia cannot consciously recognize faces, some part of their brain does unconsciously distinguish familiar faces from unfamiliar ones because they show a higher skin conductance response to familiar faces (Tranel & Damasio, 1985). Sadly, prosopagnosia cannot be cured, but people with prosopagnosia learn other ways of recognizing people, such as memorizing people's different speech patterns, their gaits, how they wear their hair, and so on. Surprisingly, prosopagnosia also occurs among people without brain damage and is highly heritable (Wilmer et al., 2010).

During the nineteenth century and most of the twentieth century, however, brain scans obviously weren't available, so scientists had to learn about the association areas by other methods. One major method was to study the behavior of people who had suffered brain damage in accidents and strokes, or had brain surgery for medical reasons. Their behavioral and mental processing deficits were then related to the particular cortical areas where damage or surgery had occurred. A railroad worker's tragic accident in 1848 gave us some hints as to what type of processing occurs in our frontal lobes (Macmillan, 2000). Phineas Gage was taking a break from tamping some blasting powder into a rock with a metal tamping iron. He was distracted and the tamping iron slipped, generating some sparks that caused the powder to explode. The explosion caused the metal tamping iron, which was 3 feet 7 inches long, 1¼ inches in diameter, and 13½ pounds in weight, to fly through his left cheek and head, exiting through his left frontal lobe (Ratiu, Talos, Haker, Lieberman, & Everett, 2004; Van Horn et al., 2012). Before Ratiu et al.'s study, most researchers believed that both frontal lobes were damaged, but Ratiu et al. showed that the cerebral injury was limited to the left frontal lobe. Their computerized tomography scan of Gage's skull clearly shows this, and Van Horn et al. later verified the damage was localized to the left frontal lobe.

Gage survived, but his personality appeared to be greatly changed. According to his doctor and friends, Gage was "no longer Gage" (Macmillan, 2000). He became very irresponsible, impulsive, and disorderly; had great difficulty making decisions and reasoning; and cursed regularly. This led neuroscientists to hypothesize that the frontal lobes played a major role in such behaviors. Subsequent collaborative evidence from similar cases and from studies using other techniques such as brain scans confirmed that this is the case (Klein & Kihlstrom, 1998). The frontal lobes play a major role in our planning, decision making, judgment, impulse control, and personality, especially its emotional aspects. Actually, the cortical area destroyed in Gage's left frontal lobe (the prefrontal cortex just behind the forehead and in front of the primary motor cortex) was essentially the left portion of the cortex that was disconnected from the rest of the brain in the infamous

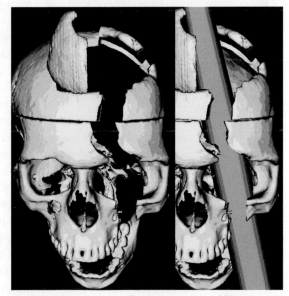

The left panel shows a 3-D reconstruction of Phineas Gage's injuries, and the right panel shows the 3-D reconstruction of the injuries with the tamping iron in place. These reconstructions are based on a computerized tomography scan of Phineas Gage's exhumed skull. As you can clearly see in the reconstructions, the cerebral injury was limited to the left frontal lobe, contrary to previous claims that both the left and right frontal lobes were damaged. (Peter Ratiu, Ion-Florin Talos, Steven Haker, Daniel Lieberman, and Peter Everett, "The Tale of Phineas Gage, Digitally Remastered," *Journal of Neurotrauma 21*, no. 5, 2004 © Mary Ann Liebert, Inc., pp. 637–643.)

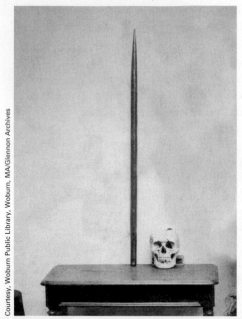

Courtesy, Woburn Public Library, Woburn, MA/Glennon Archives

Phineas Gage's doctor had this picture of the tamping iron and Phineas's skull taken in 1868 to document the case. Seeing the iron and the skull side by side makes it difficult to believe that Gage survived, but he did. He died 12 years later in 1860 at age 36, probably from hypothermia stemming from an epileptic seizure (Fleischman, 2002).

lobotomies performed on hundreds of patients in mental hospitals in the middle part of the twentieth century. The frontal lobes may also be partially responsible for the bad decisions and risky behavior of teenagers, because frontal lobe development is not complete until the late teens and possibly even the early 20s (Sabbagh, 2006).

What happened to Phineas Gage? While it has proved very difficult to fill in the exact details of Gage's subsequent life, Fleischman (2002) provides a general account. Following his recovery, Phineas tried to return to his job as railroad foreman, but because of the "new" Gage's vulgar, unreliable behavior, the railroad let him go. It appears that for a brief period of time he traveled around New England exhibiting himself along with the tamping iron, possibly ending up in P. T. Barnum's American Museum sideshow in New York City. After this, because he got along very well with horses, he worked for a while in a livery stable in New Hampshire near his hometown. In 1852 he traveled, taking the tamping iron with him, to South America to care for horses and be a stagecoach driver in Chile. Because of health issues he returned in 1859 to California where his family had moved; and after recovering, he found work as a farmhand. In 1860 he began suffering epileptic seizures (likely due to slow changes in his brain tissue damaged in the railroad accident), and at that time, physicians could not control such seizures. These seizures killed him, 11½ years after the accident. The immediate cause of death was probably hypothermia created by the seizures (during which the body cannot control its internal temperature).

Macmillan and Lena (2010) provide a detailed argument that Gage seems to have made a surprisingly good psychosocial adaptation to his injury and that his mental changes were not as permanent as was once thought and that over time, he became a higher functioning, more socially adapted person. According to Macmillan and Lena, major factors in this rehabilitation were Gage's highly structured employment and life over a period of nearly 8 years as a stagecoach driver in Chile and the social skills, responsibilities, and challenges entailed in this work. For example, driving a six-horse stagecoach team in which each horse was controlled separately by differing movements of the reins over steep and rough terrain clearly required complex sensory-motor/cognitive skills, and dealing with the non–English-speaking passengers in a foreign country clearly required social skills. With respect to Gage's recovery, Kotowicz (2007) pointed out that a Harvard surgeon, Henry Bigelow, is the only person known to have observed Gage for an appreciable time (well over a year) after his accident and to have published his observations (Bigelow, 1850), and he reported Gage as fully recovered. Bigelow arranged to have Gage under his care and at his expense for purposes of observation for 8 to 9 weeks. Bigelow described Gage as having "quite recovered in his faculties of body and mind" and does not mention anything strange or unusual about his behavior (Macmillan, 2000). In addition, Macmillan and Lena found a statement from Dr. Henry Trevitt, a doctor who lived in Chile at the time Gage was there and knew Gage well. The doctor reported that Gage "was in the enjoyment of good health with no impairment whatever of his mental faculties (p. 648)," which strongly supports the argument that Gage made a good recovery. Given the long-term post-accident reports of Drs. Bigelow and Trevitt about Gage, Kotowicz argues that some of Gage's short-term post-accident behavior is understandable in the context of his adjustment to his facial disfigurement, which obviously takes time. In addition, recently discovered photos of Gage, such as the one included here, are supportive of Macmillan and Lena's recovery hypothesis in that they show Gage as a well-dressed man who appears confident and even handsome despite his facial disfigurement (Kean, 2014). Macmillan and Lena concluded that although they did not think that Gage recovered completely and became

Collection of Jack and Beverly Wilgus

This photo of Phineas Gage is a compensating reversal of a daguerreotype discovered in 2009 by Jack and Beverly Wilgus. The daguerreotype showed Gage laterally (left-right) reversed so a reversal had to be applied to the daguerreotype in order to see Gage correctly as he appeared in real life. Wilgus and Wilgus (2009) provide an explanation of the photographic process involved in creating a daguerreotype. As Kean (2014) points out, this photo contradicts the conception of Gage as a "dirty, disheveled misfit" but rather shows that the post-accident Gage was a "proud, well-dressed, and disarmingly handsome" man.

Gage again, "he seems to have come much closer to being so than is commonly believed" (p. 655). Such a recovery fits well with our current state of knowledge about neuroplasticity and the brain's ability to heal itself. If you want to find out more about Phineas Gage, go to www.uakron.edu/gage/, a Web site devoted to him that was created by Malcolm Macmillan, the world's leading authority on Gage.

Early brain researchers also analyzed the brains of deceased people, relating a person's brain analysis to their behavior while living. Using this technique, two nineteenth-century researchers, Paul Broca and Karl Wernicke, studied people with aphasias—speech and language dysfunctions—and made some major discoveries about where speech and language abilities occur in the brain. By examining the brains of deceased persons who had lost their ability to speak fluently while alive, Paul Broca, a French brain researcher, identified an area in the left frontal lobe that is named after him, **Broca's area,** which is

Broca's area An area in the cerebral cortex responsible for fluent speech production. It is in the left frontal lobe of the majority of people, regardless of handedness.

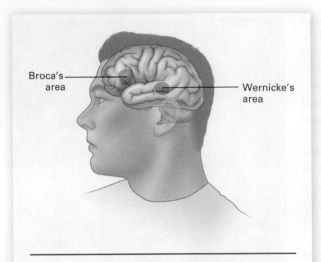

Broca's area

Wernicke's area

Figure 2.10 | Broca's Area and Wernicke's Area | Broca's area and Wernicke's area are responsible for speech production and the comprehension of speech and text, respectively. They are located only in the left hemisphere for the majority of both left- and right-handed people.

responsible for fluent speech production (see Figure 2.10). Damage to Broca's area leads to Broca's aphasia—the inability to generate fluent speech while maintaining the ability to understand speech and read silently.

Broca's area is only in the left hemisphere in the majority of people, both right-handed and left-handed (unlike the sensory and motor processing areas that are in each hemisphere). This means that speech production seems to be a specialization of the left hemisphere (the comparable area in the right hemisphere is usually not used for speech production). So, what is this area in the right hemisphere used for? One possible answer that has been offered is singing and music. People with Broca's area damage often retain these abilities (Besson, Faita, Peretz, Bonnel, & Requin, 1998). This means that singing and speaking seem to originate from different areas of the brain. What about Broca's area in deaf people who use sign language? Will damage to Broca's area impact their ability to use sign language? The answer is yes. Broca's area seems important for both the production of speech and its complement in the deaf, sign language (Corina, 1998).

People with damage to Broca's area do not have a problem understanding the speech of other people or reading silently, which means these skills must involve other areas. One of these areas is in the left temporal lobe and is named after its discoverer, Karl Wernicke, a German researcher. **Wernicke's area** is responsible for the comprehension of speech and reading. Figure 2.10 shows exactly where this area is located. Damage to this area leads to Wernicke's aphasia—incoherent speech and the inability to understand the speech of others and to read. Wernicke's area functions as the understanding center for incoming speech and text. To sum up, Broca and Wernicke together discovered a double dissociation of speech production and comprehension. Damage to Broca's area stops speech production but leaves speech comprehension intact, and damage to Wernicke's area stops speech comprehension but spares speech production, though the speech is nonsensical.

Wernicke's area An area in the cerebral cortex responsible for comprehension of speech and text. It is in the left temporal lobe of the majority of people, regardless of handedness.

Like Broca's area, Wernicke's area is only in the left temporal lobe of the majority of people (regardless of handedness). Many people have the misconception that these speech and language centers normally reside in the hemisphere opposite to a person's handedness. This is only the case for a very small number of right-handers and some left-handers, however. Speech and language centers are located in the left hemisphere for about 95% of right-handers and 70% of left-handers (Springer & Deutsch, 1998).

Broca and Wernicke examined the brains of deceased people who had speech and language dysfunctions in order to identify the speech and language centers in the brain. So perhaps this cortical localization technique could be used with highly intelligent people to identify the keys to their genius, the neural basis of intellect? What about the brain of acclaimed genius Albert Einstein? Was it studied after his death in 1955? The answer is a much qualified yes, because

This is a photo of Dr. Thomas Harvey with a jar containing pieces of Albert Einstein's brain.

his brain was not studied in the careful, systematic manner that you would think it would be. The journey that Einstein's brain took was indeed a bizarre odyssey (Abraham, 2001). With the exception of his brain and eyes, his body was cremated on the day of his death; but to this day no one seems to know where the ashes are (Lepore, 2001). The examining pathologist at Princeton Hospital where Einstein died, Dr. Thomas Harvey, removed the brain and took dozens of photographs of the whole and partially dissected brain before having it partitioned into 240 blocks of tissue, preparing a roadmap of the locations in the brain that yielded the dissected blocks, and sectioning and staining histological slides from the blocks.

Despite Harvey's meticulous preservation of Einstein's brain and the distribution of some brain sections to a few researchers, nothing had yet been published 23 years later when Harvey was interviewed in 1978 (Lepore, 2001). During this time period, Harvey kept most of the brain hidden away for his own personal research. He stored these remaining dissected and labeled brain pieces in glass jars of formaldehyde in a cider box in his office. Einstein's brain usually accompanied him when he traveled. In fact, Dr. Harvey made a trip across America to visit Einstein's granddaughter with some of the photographs and slides and some pieces of the brain floating in formaldehyde in a Tupperware bowl in a duffel bag in the trunk of a car (Paterniti, 2000).

Starting in the 1980s Harvey did dole out some more of the slides and photographs to researchers. This led to six peer-reviewed publications and a few speculative differences between Einstein's brain and those of people with normal intelligence (Falk, Lepore, & Noe, 2012). For example, Diamond, Scheibel, Murphy, and Harvey (1985) found a higher glia to neuron ratio in the left parietal lobe, and Witelson, Kigar, and Harvey (1999) found that the gross anatomy of Einstein's brain seemed within normal limits with the exception of his parietal lobes. These findings led to the hypothesis that Einstein's unusual parietal lobes might have provided the neural basis for his visuospatial and mathematical skills, consistent with the finding of an enlarged parietal lobe in the preserved brain of Carl Gauss, one of the greatest mathematicians ever (Seung, 2012). In 2007 Harvey died, but fortunately Dr. Harvey's Estate donated 14 of Harvey's photographs of Einstein's whole brain (last seen in 1955) along with some of the histological slides and the roadmap that identifies the brain locations that yielded the slides to the National Museum of Health and Medicine (Falk, Lepore, & Noe, 2012).

Granted access to these materials, Falk et al. (2012) were able to describe the external gross neuroanatomy of Einstein's entire cerebral cortex in comparison to 85 normal human brains. Many of the photographs show structures that were not visible in the photographs previously analyzed. Falk et al. found that Einstein's brain was of unexceptional size but had very unusual morphology. The complexity and pattern of convolutions and folds in the prefrontal lobe, parietal lobe, visual cortex, and primary motor and somatosensory cortices gave these parts a much larger surface area than in normal brains. Falk et al. also speculated on the meaning of their findings. For example, the expanded prefrontal cortex may have contributed to the neurological substrates for some of Einstein's remarkable abilities, and the unusual parietal lobes are consistent with the earlier hypothesis that they may have provided the neurological underpinnings for his visuospatial and mathematical abilities. But the long, strange journey for Einstein's brain hasn't ended. In 2012, digital preservations of some of the slides of Einstein's brain became available to the general public as an iPad application. You have to wonder whether Einstein would have wanted images of his brain sold to nonscientists for $9.99.

Specializations of the Left and Right Hemispheres

Next, we will consider the question of whether there are any hemispheric specializations other than speech, language, and face perception. To try to answer this question, researchers have examined patients who have had their corpus callosum, the cortical bridge between the two hemispheres, severed as a medical treatment for severe cases of epilepsy. William Van Wagenen performed the first split-brain surgery in 1940 (Gazzaniga, 2008). Not many people have had this surgery, and because of improved medications and other modes of treatment for epilepsy, it is done even more rarely now. The rationale behind this surgery was that the epileptic seizures would be lessened in severity if they were confined to only one hemisphere. Indeed, the surgery did provide this benefit. However, it also created a group of people (usually referred to as "split-brain" patients) in which the two hemispheres of the brain could not communicate, composing an ideal group for studying the question of hemispheric specialization. According to Gazzaniga (2008), there have only been 10 split-brain patients who have been well tested. First, we will discuss the general experimental procedure that has been used to study the hemispheric specialization question with these patients.

Studying the two hemispheres. To understand the experimental procedure for studying the two hemispheres, we first need to understand how the visual fields, the eyes, and the cerebral hemispheres are related. These relationships are shown in Figure 2.11. Our field of vision has two halves—the left visual field (what is to the left of center in our field of vision) and the right visual field (what is to the right of center in our field of vision). Light waves from the left visual field go to the right half of each eye, and those from the right visual field go the left half of each eye. Each visual field is processed by half of each eye. The right half of each eye connects with the right hemisphere, and the left half of each eye with the left hemisphere. This means that the eyes and the hemispheres, with respect to processing incoming visual information, are not contralaterally related. Rather, the visual information in half of each eye goes to each hemisphere. The visual information in the right halves goes to the right hemisphere, and the visual information in the left halves goes to the left hemisphere. Thus, information in the left visual field goes only to the right hemisphere, and information in the right visual field goes only to the left hemisphere. The following diagram should help you remember this processing sequence:

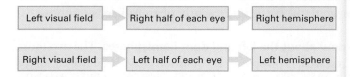

This relationship between the visual fields and the hemispheres is important because it allows information that is presented briefly in one visual field to go to only one hemisphere. With split-brain patients, the information cannot be transferred to the other hemisphere because the corpus callosum connecting their two hemispheres has been severed. By examining how split-brain patients can identify the presented information (orally, visually, or by touch), researchers can study the hemispheric specialization question.

Recall that the speech and language centers (Broca's and Wernicke's areas) are only in the left hemisphere of the vast majority of people. This would mean that a split-brain patient should only be able to identify information orally when it is presented briefly in the right visual field (it is this field that feeds information to the left hemisphere). In fact, this is what has been found with split-brain patients. For example, if a picture of a

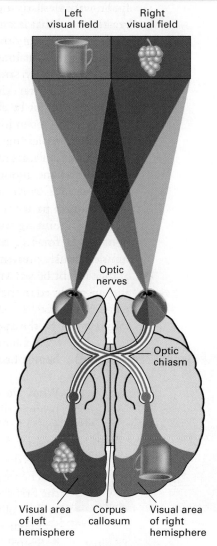

Figure 2.11 | The Pathways for Processing Information in the Left and Right Visual Fields | The information from the left visual field goes to the right half of each eye and then to the right hemisphere. The information in the right visual field goes to the left half of each eye and then to the left hemisphere. Half of the fibers from each eye cross over at the optic chiasm to go to the opposite hemisphere—the right half in the left eye go to the right hemisphere and the left half in the right eye go to the left hemisphere.

spoon were flashed briefly in the left visual field, a split-brain patient would not be able to say that it was a spoon. But if we blindfolded the split-brain patient and asked her to identify the flashed object from a group of objects by touch with the left hand, the split-brain patient can do this (Gazzaniga, 1992). Remember that the somatosensory strip in the right hemisphere is connected to the left hand. However, even after identifying the spoon as the object presented, a split-brain patient would not be able to identify it orally if asked what was in her left hand. What would happen if the blindfolded split-brain patient were asked to move the object from her left hand to her right hand? She would now say that she was holding a spoon. The information that it was a spoon would be gathered through touch by her right hand and sent to the somatosensory strip in her left hemisphere, allowing her to transfer this information to the speech centers in the left hemisphere.

Split-brain patients are also sometimes asked to identify the presented information by pointing with the appropriate hand (left hand for right hemisphere, right hand for left hemisphere). A clever use of this methodology involves simultaneously presenting different objects to each hemisphere. For example, an orange might be shown in the right visual field so it goes to the left hemisphere, and an apple in the left visual field so it goes to the right hemisphere. If then asked to use the left hand to identify what was presented, the split-brain patient would point to the apple; but if she had been asked to use the right hand, she would have pointed to the orange. In each case, the nonresponding hemisphere would be baffled by the other hemisphere's response.

Roger Sperry

Michael Gazzaniga

What we know about the left and right hemispheres. The two most prominent researchers on split-brain questions have been Roger Sperry and Michael Gazzaniga. Sperry led most of the early split-brain research and in 1981 won the Nobel Prize in Physiology or Medicine for his discoveries concerning the functional specializations of the cerebral hemispheres. Sperry's student, Michael Gazzaniga, who conducted the first studies with human split-brain participants in the early 1960s at the California Institute of Technology under the guidance of Sperry and neurosurgeon Joseph Bogen (Gazzaniga, 2015; Gazzaniga, Bogen, & Sperry, 1962), has continued this line of inquiry for the past five decades (Gazzaniga, 2005, 2008). Now let's see what these studies with split-brain participants have told us about hemispheric specialization.

We know that the speech and language centers are specialties of the left hemisphere. This is why the left hemisphere is sometimes referred to as the verbal hemisphere. This does not mean, however, that the right hemisphere has no verbal ability. It can't produce speech, but it can understand simple verbal material. In addition, the left hemisphere is better at mathematical skills and logic, while the right is better at spatial perception, solving spatial problems (e.g., block design), and drawing. The right hemisphere is also better at face recognition. Due to the asymmetry in the fusiform face area, recognition of faces is faster when faces are presented in the left- than the right-visual field of both split-brain patients (Stone, Nisenson, Eliassen, & Gazzaniga, 1996) and normal people (Yovel, Tambini, & Brandman, 2008). In general, the left hemisphere is more analytic, analyzing wholes into their elements or pieces; the right hemisphere processes information in a more holistic fashion, combining pieces into wholes (Reuter-Lorenz & Miller, 1998). The right gets the big picture (the "forest"); the left focuses on the smaller details (the "trees"). This information-processing style difference between the two hemispheres is sometimes referred to as global versus local processing.

Support for this general processing style difference between the hemispheres has been corroborated by research with brain-damaged patients using hierarchical stimuli developed by David Navon (1977). These hierarchical stimuli consist of a large letter (the global, holistic level) that is composed of smaller versions of another letter (the local or analytic level). See the example in Figure 2.12a in which the large letter **H** is composed of smaller **A**s. Delis, Robertson, and Efron (1986) used such stimuli to study perceptual encoding in brain-damaged patients. The patients were asked to study the hierarchical stimulus and then redraw it from memory after a brief period of distraction. The patients with right hemisphere damage who were dependent on their left hemisphere often drew **A**s unsystematically scattered about the page (see Figure 2.12b). They remembered the constituent elements of the original stimulus but not the overall pattern. In contrast, the patients with left hemisphere damage who were dependent on their right hemisphere often drew a large capital **H** but with no **A**s (see Figure 2.12c). They remembered the global pattern but not the constituent elements. Thus, the right hemisphere specializes in synthesizing global, holistic patterns, whereas the left hemisphere specializes in analyzing the details of a stimulus. Fink et al. (1996) have also observed this hemispheric processing style difference in PET scan data when normal participants were attending to either the global or local level of Navon hierarchical figures.

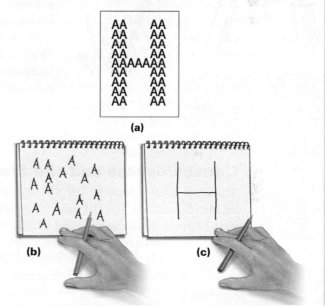

Figure 2.12 | Sample Hierarchical Stimulus and Recall Results for Such Stimuli by Brain-Damaged Patients | (a) The sample hierarchical stimulus is a capital **H** made up of little **A**s. (b) Patients with right hemisphere damage (dependent on the left hemisphere) could remember the details of the hierarchical stimulus (the **A**s) but not the overall pattern (**H**). (c) Patients with left hemisphere damage (dependent upon the right hemisphere) could remember the overall pattern (**H**) but not its details (the **A**s).

Andrew Swift

WHAT HAPPENS WHEN THE RIGHT SIDE OF THE BRAIN CRASHES...

Steamy Raimon/Cartoonstock.com

This processing difference along with all of the other specialization differences that have been observed in split-brain patients have led to the expressions "left-brained" and "right-brained" to refer to people who seem to excel at the skills normally attributed to left and right hemispheres, respectively. We must remember, however, that these differences in hemispheric performance are for people whose two hemispheres can no longer communicate. When normal people are performing a task, the two hemispheres are constantly interacting and sharing information. There is no forced separation of labor as in the split-brain patient. Each hemisphere contributes in a complementary, not exclusive, way. It may be the case that one hemisphere tends to play a larger role depending on what mental activity we are currently engaged in, but both hemispheres are involved (Corballis, 2007; Hellige, 1993; Jarrett, 2015; Nielsen, Zielinski, Ferguson, Lainhart, & Anderson, 2013). This is why it is not accurate to say someone is "left-brained" or "right-brained." It is best not to make the distinction. Nearly all of us are "whole-brained."

Consciousness and the Sleeping Brain

There are many questions left for neuroscientists to answer about the brain and its many functions, but the most intriguing questions concern human consciousness—What is consciousness and what underlies it? Probably the best way to think about **consciousness** is as a person's subjective awareness of his inner thinking and feeling as well as his immediate surroundings. Thus, consciousness is both internal (one's thoughts and feelings) and external (what's going on in one's environment).

Most brain (and bodily) functioning goes on without our conscious awareness. For example, you are presently recognizing the letters and words in this paragraph, but you are not consciously aware of the actual processing required to accomplish this recognition. You are only consciously aware of the results of the recognition process (the meaningful collection of words). Even if you wanted to, you couldn't become consciously aware of this processing by the brain. Think about the billions of neurons communicating with one another within your brain and nervous system at this very moment. You cannot become aware of activity at this neuronal level of processing. Our consciousness is privy to only some of the results of this processing.

consciousness An individual's subjective awareness of their inner thinking and feeling and their external environment.

We can describe waking consciousness as our tuning in to both our internal and external worlds, but questions about exactly what underlies it (how it is generated) or why it evolved remain open for debate. Dehaene (2014) and Kaku (2014) provide some interesting theorizing about answers to these questions. Similarly, we are still pondering the question of why we experience sleep—a natural, altered state of consciousness. We do, however, have some better answers to questions about what the brain is doing during sleep. Electrical recordings of brain activity during sleep allow us to measure different stages of sleep and to tell us when we are dreaming. So first we'll examine the stages of sleep and how they are related to dreaming. Then, we will briefly discuss theories that have been proposed to explain why we sleep and why we dream.

The five stages of sleep. The various stages of sleep have been determined by monitoring the electrical activity in the brain using an electroencephalograph (EEG). Small electrodes are attached to the scalp and connected to recording equipment that produces a real-time graph of electrical activity in the cortex of the brain. In Figure 2.13, a sample EEG for the awake, relaxed state is shown along with sample EEGs for the five stages of sleep. As we slip into sleep and pass through the first four stages, our brain waves change, in general becoming progressively slower, larger, and more irregular, especially in Stages 3 and 4. Stage 1 sleep, which lasts about 5 minutes, is followed by about 20 minutes of Stage 2 sleep, which is characterized by periodic bursts of rapid activity called sleep spindles. Some researchers believe these spindles represent the activity of a mechanism that lessens the brain's sensitivity to sensory input and thus keeps the person asleep. The fact that older people's sleep contains fewer spindles and is interrupted by more awakenings during the night is consistent with this explanation.

Next are the two stages composed of slow-wave sleep—the brief, transitional sleep of Stage 3 and then the deep sleep of Stage 4. These two stages, especially Stage 4, are characterized by delta waves—large, slow brain waves. You are now completely asleep and this initial period of slow-wave sleep lasts for about 30 minutes. In deep sleep, the parasympathetic nervous system

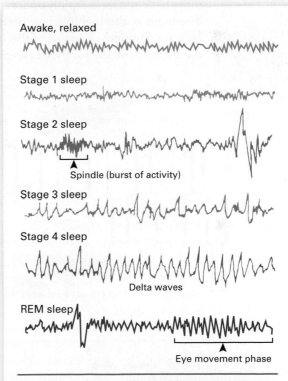

Figure 2.13 | Sleep Stages and the Brain Waves Associated with Each Stage | The various stages of sleep are indicated by changes in the brain waves in the EEG recordings. As you pass from awake to deep sleep (Stages 3 and 4), the brain waves get larger and slow down. After deep sleep, you ascend back through Stages 3 and 2 into REM sleep, for which the waves are more rapid and resemble those of Stage 1.

REM (rapid eye movement) sleep The stage of sleep that is characterized by rapid eye movements and brain wave patterns that resemble those for an awake state and in which most dreaming occurs. REM sleep is sometimes referred to as paradoxical sleep because the bodily muscles are immobilized but much of the brain is highly active.

dominates. So, muscles relax, heart rate slows, blood pressure declines, and digestion is stimulated. Mysteriously, the brain is still monitoring environmental information, though it is outside our conscious awareness. If a sensory stimulus is important, such as a baby's cry, or very strong, such as a slamming door or a breaking glass, it will break through the perceptual barrier created by sleep and awaken us.

Near the end of your first period of deep sleep (about an hour after falling asleep), you return through Stages 3 and 2 and enter **REM (rapid eye movement) sleep,** the most fascinating stage of sleep. REM sleep is characterized by very rapid waves somewhat like those of Stage 1 sleep. However, you are still sound asleep. REM sleep is sometimes referred to as paradoxical sleep because the muscles are relaxed but other body systems and the brain are active, following a waking pattern. Heart rate rises, breathing is more rapid, eyes move back and forth rapidly under closed eyelids, and one's genitals become aroused. The brain is also highly active; both oxygen consumption and cerebral blood flow increase. Strangely, given all of this internal activity, the muscles are relaxed, leaving the body essentially paralyzed except for occasional muscle twitching.

REM sleep indicates the beginning of dreaming; it is the stage during which most dreaming occurs. How do we know this? If people are awakened during Stages 1 through 4, they only occasionally report dreaming; but if awakened during REM sleep, people usually recall dreams that they were having. This is as true for people who say they dream as for those who say they rarely do so, which means that we all dream whether we realize it or not. This first bout of REM sleep typically lasts about 10 minutes and completes the first sleep cycle of the night. The cycle of stages, in which we move out of and back into REM sleep, repeats itself about every 90 minutes throughout the night. Deep sleep (Stages 3 and 4) gets briefer and eventually disappears, as Stage 2 and REM sleep periods get longer with each sleep cycle. Over the course of the night, you have four or five REM sleep periods, amounting to about 20% to 25% of your sleep time (Figure 2.14).

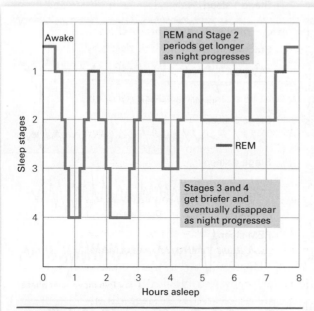

Figure 2.14 | The Pattern of Sleep-Stage Cycles During a Night's Sleep | After passing through the first four stages of sleep, we return through Stages 3 and 2 to enter REM sleep. This completes the first sleep-stage cycle. As this cycle is repeated throughout a typical night's sleep, the deep sleep stages (3 and 4) get briefer and disappear, and the Stage 2 and REM sleep periods get longer.

We spend on average about 2 hours a night dreaming, which works out to about 6 years of dreaming across our lifetime, given current life expectancies. We don't remember many of our dreams, though. The dreams we do remember are usually from our last phase of REM sleep, right before we wake up. Many dreams are highly emotional and unpleasant. For example, people often dream of being attacked or pursued. This may be due to the fact that the frontal lobes (responsible for rational thought) are shut down during REM sleep, but the amygdala and the hippocampus, the limbic system structures responsible for emotion and memory, are active, creating the irrational imagery and emotional experiences of our dream world. Given the strong visual nature of dreams, what are the dreams of blind people like? Research indicates that people born blind or who go blind very early in life do not have visual dreams. Their dreams are just as emotional, but involve other sensations, especially sounds.

Why do we sleep and dream? We do not know why we sleep, but we know that we need sleep. You cannot cheat sleep; it will always overcome you. Inadequate sleep has a high cost. Sleep-deprived people have impaired concentration and a general bodily feeling of weakness and discomfort, and they may even hallucinate. Sleep deprivation also suppresses your immune system, lessening your ability to fight off infection and disease. Sleep-deprived people are also more vulnerable to accidents. For example, traffic accidents increase following the shortened sleep accompanying the 1-hour time change in the spring (Coren, 1993). All of this may help explain why people who typically sleep 7 or 8 hours outlive those who are chronically sleep deprived (Dement, 1999). College students are notorious for being sleep deprived, with as many as four out of five not getting adequate sleep. Beware of sleep deprivation and its negative effects. Sleep deprivation makes it more difficult to concentrate, study, and take exams. So, creating a large sleep debt will, in simple terms, "make you stupid" (Dement, 1999, p. 231).

We clearly need sleep. How much, however, varies greatly with individuals. On the average, though, we spend about a third of our lives sleeping. Why? Four possible answers have been proposed, and the actual answer probably involves all four. First, sleep seems to serve a restorative function by allowing the brain and body time to rest and recuperate from the daily wear and tear of our existence. For example, recent research has shown that during sleep the brain cleans itself of toxic metabolic byproducts (Xie et al., 2013). This finding that sleep ensures metabolic homeostasis also has implications for many neurological disorders, many of which, such as Alzheimer's disorder, are associated with sleep disturbances. These disturbances would prevent the brain from cleaning itself, and toxic byproducts would build up and cause brain damage. Second, gene activity during sleep ramps up the production of myelin, which as you have learned, protects our brain's circuitry and facilitates neuronal transmission (Bellisi et al., 2013). Thus, sleep fortifies the brain over the long term by leading to the production of myelin, the brain's insulating material. Third, sleep helps us process what we learn. It allows the brain the opportunity to consolidate our day's experiences into our memory banks for later retrieval and use. Indeed, there is research evidence that memory is often strengthened and enhanced following a period of sleep (Stickgold & Ellenbogen, 2009). REM sleep is especially important in relation to memory. Disruption of REM sleep (by being constantly awakened during this stage) following learning impairs our memory for this learning (DuJardin, Guerrien, & LeConte, 1990). Disruption of other sleep stages does not similarly impair memory. Fourth, sleep may have evolved as an adaptive process. It served a protective function for our ancestors, increasing their survival by keeping them safe from predators during the night and from the dangers of wandering around cliffs in the dark. Those who stayed in their caves and slept had a better chance of surviving and passing on their genes.

So, sleep has clear advantages. But why do we dream? One answer is the critical role of REM sleep in learning—providing the opportunity for memory consolidation of new information (Stickgold, Hobson, Fosse, & Fosse, 2001). Other answers to the question of why we dream have also been proposed. About a hundred years ago, Sigmund Freud proposed that dreams were disguised outlets for the inner conflicts of our unconscious (Freud 1900/1953a). But given its lack of scientific support, the Freudian view has been rejected by most contemporary sleep researchers. There are many contemporary theories of why we dream, and all have their critics. One explanation that has received much attention is the activation-synthesis theory (Hobson, 2003; Hobson & McCarley, 1977; Hobson, Pace-Scott, & Stickgold, 2000). This physiological theory proposes that neurons in the pons fire spontaneously during REM sleep, sending random signals to various areas in the cortex and the emotional areas in the limbic system. The signals are random, but the brain tries to make sense of them and produce a meaningful interpretation. Thus, a dream is the brain's synthesis of these signals. However, because the signals evoke random memories and visual images, the brain has a difficult time weaving a coherent story, often resulting in the bizarre and confusing nature of our dreams. This relates to a major criticism of the theory: dream content is more coherent, consistent over time, and concerned with waking problems and anxieties than the activation-synthesis theory would predict (Domhoff, 2003). Criticisms aside, this theory has led to a wide body of research on the neurological stuff that dreams are made of and thus greatly increased our knowledge of the physiological basis of dreaming.

In contrast to the activation-synthesis theory of dreaming, the neurocognitive theory of dreaming emphasizes the parallels between waking cognition and dreaming (Domhoff, 2011). Neurocognitive theory argues that explaining dreams as our subjective interpretations of random neural firing is too simple and that dreams are meaningful products of our cognitive abilities, with continuity between waking and dreaming cognition. Most dreams are about people and activities that are well-known to the dreamer and reflect our waking concerns, personality, emotions, and interests (Domhoff, 1996; Nir & Tononi, 2010). According to neurocognitive theory, the dreams of children younger than 9 or 10 years old are simpler and less emotional and bizarre than adult

dreams. Why? Children's dream development parallels the gradual development of advanced cognitive abilities, such as visual imagination. Once their
cognitive abilities are more advanced, their dreams become more complex. In
brief, dreams are a product of our normal cognitive processes, but they use self-
generated sensory data during sleep rather than external sensory input as they
do when we are awake.

Although sleep researchers do not agree about why we dream, they do agree
that REM sleep is essential. This is clearly demonstrated by the REM sleep
rebound effect—a significant increase in the amount of REM sleep following
deprivation of REM sleep. The fact that REM sleep and the rebound effect are
observed in other mammals implies a definite biological need for this type of
sleep. Exactly what that need is, however, remains an open question.

Section Summary

In this section, we discussed many of the major structures in the brain. Between the
spinal cord and the cerebral hemispheres, there are two sets of brain structures—the
central core and limbic system. The central core is made up of the medulla, pons,
and reticular formation (parts of the brain stem) and the cerebellum, thalamus, and
basal ganglia (structures near the brain stem). The medulla regulates essential body
functions, such as breathing and blood pressure, and the pons serves as a bridge
between the cerebellum and the rest of the brain. The reticular formation is involved
in controlling different levels of arousal and awareness. The cerebellum is involved
in the coordination of movement and motor learning, the thalamus serves as a relay
station for incoming sensory information, and the basal ganglia are involved in the
initiation and execution of physical movements. Surrounding the top of the brain,
the limbic system structures (hypothalamus, hippocampus, and amygdala) play
important roles in our survival, memory, and emotions.

As we move up the brain stem to the cerebral hemispheres, the functioning gets
more complex. It is the top cortical layer that gives us all of our complex abilities
(such as language, perception, and decision making) and makes us "human." Each
cerebral hemisphere is divided into four lobes—frontal, parietal, temporal, and occipital. The motor cortex in the frontal lobes allows us to move different parts of our
body. The somatosensory cortex in the parietal lobes is where our body sensations of
touch, temperature, limb position, and pain are processed. Both the motor cortex and
the somatosensory cortex are related to the two sides of our body in a contralateral
fashion—the left hemisphere controls the movement of, and processes body sensations from, the right side of the body, and the right hemisphere does so for the left
side of the body. The primary visual cortex is in the occipital lobes, and the primary
auditory cortex is in the temporal lobes. The remaining area in the two hemispheres,
about 70% of the cortex, is called the association cortex. All of the higher-level cognitive processing, including perception and decision making, occurs in the association
cortex. Such processing requires the association of various types of information.

Research has shown that the frontal lobes play a major role in our planning, reasoning, impulse control, and personality—especially its emotional aspects. We have
also learned that the speech and language areas are only in the left hemisphere in

the majority of people, regardless of handedness. Broca's area in the left frontal lobe is responsible for speech production, and Wernicke's area in the left temporal lobe is responsible for the comprehension of speech and text. In addition, research on split-brain patients (whose hemispheres cannot communicate because they have had their corpus callosum surgically severed) has shown that there are processing differences between the two hemispheres. For example, the left specializes in speech, language, mathematical skills, and logic; the right specializes in spatial perception, face recognition, and drawing. In addition, the right hemisphere specializes in processing stimuli at the holistic, global level, whereas the left hemisphere analyzes stimuli into their elements or pieces. We must remember, however, that in normal people, the two hemispheres are constantly interacting. One hemisphere may play a more major role in some tasks, but both hemispheres are involved.

Neuroscientists have much more to learn not only about the brain but also about consciousness, a person's awareness of his inner thinking and feeling and his external environment. We have learned much about sleep, a natural altered state of consciousness, through the use of EEG recordings of the brain's electrical activity while sleeping. Such recordings indicate the occurrence of five different stages of sleep, with the REM (rapid eye movement) sleep stage as the one during which most dreaming occurs. We can't yet explain definitively why we sleep or why we dream, but both are clearly essential. Sleep-deprived people suffer many consequences ranging from impaired concentration to weakened immune systems. A rebound effect for REM sleep (a significant increase in REM sleep) follows REM sleep deprivation.

ConceptCheck | 3

Explain where in the cerebral cortex (which hemisphere, lobe, area in the lobe, and part of that area) is active when you feel a slap on the left cheek of your face.

Explain which areas in the cerebral cortex are involved and how they are involved when you shadow (repeat aloud) someone's speech.

Explain what types of behavioral deficits would be observed in a person who suffered damage to her cerebellum.

Explain how you could demonstrate that a split-brain patient knows what was briefly flashed in his left visual field, even though he cannot say what was flashed.

This 400-year-old painting, *Vertumnus*, was done by Giuseppe Arcimboldo, a sixteenth-century Italian painter who is best known for creating imaginative portraits from such objects as fruits, vegetables, flowers, books, and other objects. *Vertumnus* is a portrait of Rudolf II of Prague made from fruits, flowers, and vegetables. Let's use this portrait to test your understanding of both the processing differences between the two hemispheres and the relationship between the visual fields and the hemispheres. Suppose *Vertumnus* is flashed briefly in the left visual field of a split-brain patient and he is instructed to point with the appropriate hand to what he saw given the choice of the two words "face" and "fruits." Which hand would he use and which word would he point to? Why? Now suppose the painting had been flashed briefly in his right visual field. Which hand would he use and which word would he point to? Why?

The Art Archive at Art Resource, NY

Explain why REM sleep is sometimes referred to as paradoxical sleep.

Study Guide

Chapter Key Terms

You should know the definitions of the following key terms from the chapter. They are listed in the order in which they appear in the chapter. For those you do not know, return to the relevant section of the chapter to learn them. When you think that you know all of the terms, complete the matching exercise based on these key terms.

neuroscience

neurons

glial cells (glia)

dendrites

cell body

axon

myelin sheath

neurotransmitter

synaptic gap (synapse)

positron emission tomography (PET) scan

functional magnetic resonance imaging (fMRI)

agonist

antagonist

acetylcholine (ACh)

dopamine

Parkinson's disease

blood–brain barrier

L-dopa

serotonin

norepinephrine

selective serotonin reuptake inhibitors (SSRIs)

selective serotonin and norepinephrine reuptake inhibitors (SSNRIs)

GABA (gamma-aminobutyric acid)

glutamate

endorphins

central nervous system (CNS)

peripheral nervous system (PNS)

interneurons

sensory neurons

motor neurons

spinal cord

spinal reflex

somatic (skeletal) nervous system

autonomic nervous system

sympathetic nervous system

parasympathetic nervous system

endocrine glandular system

hormone

pituitary gland

emotion

James-Lange theory

Cannon-Bard theory

Schachter-Singer two-factor theory

medulla

pons

reticular formation

cerebellum

thalamus

basal ganglia

limbic system

hypothalamus

hippocampus

amygdala

cerebral cortex

corpus callosum

frontal lobe

parietal lobe

temporal lobe

occipital lobe

motor cortex

somatosensory cortex

association cortex

Broca's area

Wernicke's area

consciousness

REM (rapid eye movement) sleep

Key Terms Exercise

Identify the correct term for each of the following definitions. The answers to this exercise follow the answers to the ConceptChecks at the end of the chapter.

1. A chemical messenger that is produced by an endocrine gland and carried by the bloodstream to target sites throughout the body.

2. The part of the brain involved in the coordination of our movements, sense of balance, and motor learning.

3. An insulating layer of a white fatty substance on an axon that allows for faster neural impulses.

4. A visual display that shows the activity of various areas in the brain by detecting the level of positron emission arising from radioactive glucose being metabolized in each area.

5. A naturally occurring chemical within the nervous system that specializes in transmitting information between neurons.

6. The areas in the cerebral cortex not devoted to primary sensory processing or motor processing.

7. A drug or poison that decreases the activity of one or more neurotransmitters.

8. The part of the peripheral nervous system that carries sensory input from receptors to the CNS and relays commands from the CNS to skeletal muscles to control their movement.

9. The bridge of neurons that connects the two cerebral hemispheres.

10. The major inhibitory neurotransmitter in the nervous system.

11. Cells in the nervous system that comprise the support system for the neurons.

12. Drugs that achieve their agonistic effect on serotonin by selectively blocking its reuptake.

13. A group of neurotransmitters that are involved in pain relief and feelings of pleasure.

14. A brain stem structure involved in many essential body functions, such as heartbeat, breathing, blood pressure, digestion, and swallowing.

15. The area in each cerebral hemisphere in back of the central fissure and above the lateral fissure. The somatosensory cortex is in this lobe.

Practice Test Questions

The following are practice multiple-choice test questions on some of the chapter content. The answers are given after the Key Terms Exercise answers at the end of the chapter. If you guessed or incorrectly answered a question, restudy the relevant section of the chapter.

1. The main function of the _____ is to receive information from other neurons.
   a. dendrites
   b. cell body
   c. axon
   d. axon terminals

2. Which of the following is an agonist?
   a. curare
   b. GABA
   c. botulinum poison
   d. amphetamine

3. An SSRI works by blocking the reuptake of _____.
   a. dopamine
   b. serotonin
   c. norepinephrine
   d. GABA

4. Which type of neuron carries information from the CNS to the PNS?
   a. sensory neuron
   b. motor neuron
   c. interneuron
   d. glial

5. Which of the following is an action of the parasympathetic nervous system?
   a. pupil dilation
   b. stimulation of digestion
   c. accelerated heartbeat
   d. raised blood sugar levels

6. The actions of the pituitary gland are controlled by the _____.
   a. hippocampus
   b. amygdala
   c. hypothalamus
   d. medulla

7. The limbic system consists of the _____.
   a. thalamus, hypothalamus, and amygdala
   b. hypothalamus, medulla, and reticular formation
   c. amygdala, hypothalamus, and hippocampus
   d. basal ganglia, amygdala, and cerebellum

8. In the majority of people, Broca's area is located in the _____ hemisphere, and Wernicke's area is located in the _____ hemisphere.
   a. right; right
   b. right; left
   c. left; right
   d. left; left

9. Information in a person's left visual field goes to the _____ half of each eye and then to the _____ hemisphere.
   a. left; left
   b. left; right
   c. right; right
   d. right; left

10. Which of the following stages of sleep is referred to as paradoxical sleep?
    a. Stage 2
    b. Stage 3
    c. Stage 4
    d. REM sleep

11. The _____ theory of emotion proposes that the physiological arousal and behavioral responses and the emotional feeling all occur simultaneously but independently.
    a. Schachter-Singer two-factor
    b. Cannon-Bard
    c. James-Lange
    d. "commonsense"

12. At dinner, when John picks up his fork, his _____ nervous system controls the movement of his fingers. His _____ nervous system regulates his stomach and controls the digestion of food.
    a. autonomic; autonomic
    b. autonomic; somatic
    c. somatic; autonomic
    d. somatic; somatic

13. Damage to the right hemisphere will most likely disrupt a person's ability to _____.
    a. balance a checkbook
    b. recognize faces
    c. do logic problems
    d. give speeches

14. Botulinum poisoning (food poisoning) causes paralysis by blocking the release of _____, and curare paralyzes by occupying the receptor sites for _____.
    a. acetylcholine; acetylcholine
    b. acetylcholine; GABA
    c. GABA; acetylcholine
    d. GABA; GABA

15. The amount of space devoted to each part of the body in the motor cortex is _____.
    a. proportional to the actual size of that part of the body
    b. proportional to the complexity and precision of movement of which that part of the body is capable
    c. the same for all body parts
    d. greater for your torso than for your hands

Chapter ConceptCheck Answers

ConceptCheck | 1

- We can think of the neuron as a miniature decision-making device because the cell body of the neuron has to decide whether to generate an electrical impulse based on the incoming information from other neurons. If the excitatory input outweighs the inhibitory input by a sufficient amount, the cell body will decide to generate an impulse.

- Neural impulses are faster in neurons with myelinated axons than unmyelinated axons because the electrical impulse leaps from gap to gap in the myelin sheath rather than traveling continuously down the axon.

- Drugs that block the reuptake of neurotransmitters are considered agonists because they keep the neurotransmitters active in the synaptic gap (they keep carrying their messages over and over again to the receiving neuron), which increases the activity of the neurotransmitters.

- L-dopa leads to side effects that resemble the thought disorder symptoms of schizophrenia because L-dopa increases the activity of dopamine in the brain and the schizophrenic symptoms are the result of too much dopamine activity. Similarly, traditional antipsychotic drugs lead to side effects resembling Parkinson's disease symptoms because these drugs globally reduce the activity of dopamine in the brain. Thus, dopamine activity in the movement system involving the basal ganglia is reduced, leading to movement problems similar to those of Parkinson's disease.

ConceptCheck | 2

- With respect to location, sensory neurons and motor neurons are only in the PNS, and interneurons are only in the CNS. With respect to function, sensory neurons carry information to the CNS from the sensory receptors and internal organs, muscles, and glands of the body. Motor neurons carry movement commands from the CNS out to the rest of the body. Interneurons integrate the information within the CNS.

- The sympathetic nervous system is referred to as the "fight-or-flight" system because it prepares us for these actions in an emergency situation. The parasympathetic nervous system is referred to as the "rest-and-digest" system because its actions (the opposite of those in the sympathetic nervous system) allow us to rest and let functions such as digestion go back to normal.

- Both hormones and neurotransmitters are chemical messengers, but the hormones are much slower because they carry their message through the bloodstream to their distant targets. Neurotransmitters are released within the nervous system directly to their targets.

- The pituitary gland is referred to as the "master gland" because it releases hormones that direct the other endocrine glands to release their hormones. It functions like the master of the endocrine system.

- According to the James-Lange theory of emotion, we use the autonomic arousal and behavioral responses to determine the emotion. The emotional feeling occurs after and as a result of these responses. The specific emotion experienced depends upon the particular pattern of the arousal and behavioral responses. But, according to the Cannon-Bard theory, arousal patterns are too similar to be used to differentiate specific emotions. Cannon and Bard propose that arousal, behavioral response, and emotional feeling occur simultaneously and independently. Thus, contrary to the James-Lange theory, the arousal and behavioral responses and the emotional feeling happen at the same time.

ConceptCheck | 3

- To feel a slap on the left cheek of your face, the area devoted to the cheek in the lower half of the somatosensory cortical strip in the parietal lobe in the right hemisphere would be activated. Refer to Figure 2.9 to see the exact location of the cheek in the somatosensory homunculus and thus the activation. Remember that the activation would be at this location in the right hemisphere because your left cheek was slapped.

- When you shadow someone's speech, the auditory sensory input from the person's speech goes first to the primary auditory cortex in the temporal lobes, next to Wernicke's area to be understood, and then to Broca's area to produce the appropriate motor programs, which are then sent to the motor cortex, which then executes the programs to activate your speech muscles to produce the speech.

- A person who suffered damage to her cerebellum would have problems in motor coordination and balance. Her movements would be jerky and uncoordinated, and she would have great difficulty maintaining her balance.

- You would ask him to identify the object by the sense of touch with his left hand. He could identify it by matching the tactile input (the information gathered from touching the object) with his knowledge of what had been presented, both in the right hemisphere.

- If *Vertumnus* were flashed briefly in a split-brain person's left visual field, it would be processed in his right hemisphere. Hence he would use his left hand to respond because the right hemisphere's motor cortex controls that hand. Because the right hemisphere specializes in face recognition and engages in visual, holistic processing, he would point to "face" because the overall global impression of the painting is a face. However, if the painting had been flashed briefly in his right visual field, he would use his right hand because the painting would be processed in the left hemisphere, which controls that hand. Because the left hemisphere engages in analytic processing of the elements of a stimulus, the painting would be analyzed into its component elements (fruits, flowers, and vegetables) so he would point to "fruits," one of the main elements of the face. Gazzaniga has actually conducted some experimental trials using some of Arcimboldo's paintings with a split-brain participant and found these predicted results.

- REM sleep is sometimes referred to as paradoxical sleep because your bodily muscles are relaxed and immobilized, but many parts of your brain are active with both oxygen consumption and cerebral blood flow increasing. The brain appears to be awake, but you are behaviorally asleep.

Answers to Key Terms Exercise
1. hormone
2. cerebellum
3. myelin sheath
4. positron emission tomography (PET) scan
5. neurotransmitter
6. association cortex
7. antagonist
8. somatic (skeletal) nervous system
9. corpus callosum
10. GABA (gamma-aminobutyric acid)
11. glial cells (glia)
12. selective serotonin reuptake inhibitors (SSRIs)
13. endorphins
14. medulla
15. parietal lobe

Answers to Practice Test Questions
1. a; dendrites
2. d; amphetamine
3. b; serotonin
4. b; motor neuron
5. b; stimulation of digestion
6. c; hypothalamus
7. c; amygdala, hypothalamus, and hippocampus
8. d; left; left
9. c; right; right
10. d; REM sleep
11. b; Cannon-Bard
12. c; somatic; autonomic
13. b; recognize faces
14. a; acetylcholine; acetylcholine
15. b; proportional to the complexity and precision of motor movement of which that part of the body is capable

Courtesy of Jackie Sacoccio and 11R, NY

3

Sensation and Perception

How the Physical World Relates to the Psychological World

The Detection Question

The Difference Question

The Scaling Question

How We See and How We Hear

How the Eye Works

How We See Color

How the Ear Works

How We Distinguish Pitch

How We Make Sense of What We See

Bottom-up Processing and Top-down Processing

Perceptual Organization and Perceptual Constancy

Depth Perception

Imagine what you would be like if you couldn't see, hear, taste, smell, or feel. You could be described as alive only in the narrowest sense of the word. You would have no perceptions, memories, thoughts, or feelings. We understand the world through our senses, our "windows" to the world. Our reality is dependent upon the two basic processes of sensation and perception. To understand this reality, we must first understand how we gather (sense) and interpret (perceive) the information that forms the foundation for our behavior and mental processing. Sensation and perception provide us with the information that allows us

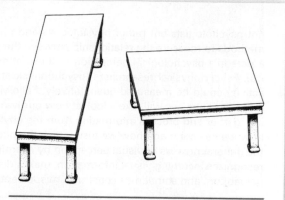

Figure 3.1 | Turning the Tables, an Example of a Misperception | The two tabletops appear to have different dimensions and shapes. Surprisingly, however, they are identical. To convince yourself, measure one and then compare it to the other. Even knowing this, you cannot make your brain see them as identical. (From *Mind Sights: Original Visual Illusions, Ambiguities, and Other Anomalies*, by R. N. Shepard, 1990, New York: W.H. Freeman/Henry Holt.)

both to understand the world around us and to live in that world. Without them, there would be no world; there would be no "you."

Perception does not exactly replicate the world outside. As Martinez-Conde and Macknik (2010, p. 4) point out, "It is a fact of neuroscience that everything we experience is actually a figment of our imagination. Although our sensations feel accurate and truthful, they do not necessarily reproduce the physical reality of the outside world." Our "view" of the world is a subjective one that the brain constructs by using assumptions and principles, both built-in and developed from our past perceptual experiences (Hoffman, 1998). We perceive what the brain tells us we perceive. This means that sometimes our view of the world is inaccurate. Consider the tops of the two tables depicted in Figure 3.1. Do they appear to be the same shape and size? They don't appear to be identical, but they are! If you trace one of the tabletops and then place the tracing on the other one, it will fit perfectly. As pointed out by Lilienfeld, Lynn, Ruscio, and Beyerstein (2010), "Seeing is believing, but seeing isn't always believing correctly" (p. 7). We will revisit this illusion and its explanation later in the chapter; but, in general, this illusion is the result of the brain's misinterpretation of perspective information about the two tables (Shepard, 1990). The important point for us is that the brain is misperceiving reality and that even with the knowledge that these two tabletops are identical, you will not be able to suppress the misperception your brain produces. What we perceive is generated by parts of the brain to which we do not have access. Your brain, not you, controls your perception of the world. The brain doesn't work like a photocopy machine during perception. The brain interprets during perception; our perception is its interpretation. Beauty is not in the eye of the beholder, but rather in the brain of the beholder.

To understand how sensation and perception work, we must first look at how the physical world outside and the psychological world within relate to each other. This pursuit will take us back to the experimental roots of psychology and the work of nineteenth-century German researchers in psychophysics. These researchers were not psychologists but rather physiologists and physicists. They used experimental methods to measure the relationship between the physical properties of stimuli and a person's psychological perception of those stimuli (hence the term psychophysics). Psychophysical researchers (psychophysicists) demonstrated that our mental activity could be measured quantitatively. Following a discussion of some of their major findings, we will take a look at how our two primary senses, vision and hearing, gather and process information from the environment, specifically focusing on how we see color and how we distinguish the pitch of a sound. Last, we will detail the general process of visual perception by examining how the brain organizes and recognizes incoming visual information, makes distance judgments to enable depth perception, and sometimes constructs misperceptions (illusions) as in Figure 3.1.

How the Physical World Relates to the Psychological World

Just as the name implies, psychophysical research focuses on the relationship between the physical world and the psychological world. Early psychophysical researchers attempted to answer basic questions concerning how we process the intensities of physical energy forms such as light waves and sound waves. We will discuss three questions that they addressed in their research—the detection question, the difference question, and the scaling question.

The detection and difference questions examine limits on our sensory processing. The detection question is concerned with the limits on our ability to detect very faint signals. How intense does a light have to be for us to see it? How intense does a sound have to be for us to hear it? Similarly, the difference question is concerned with limits on our detection abilities, but in this case with our ability to detect very small differences between stimuli. What is the smallest difference in brightness between two lights that we can see? What is the smallest difference in loudness between two sounds that we can hear? The scaling question is not concerned with sensory processing limits, but rather with how we perceive the magnitudes (intensities) of clearly detectable stimuli. What is the relationship between the actual physical intensities of stimuli and our psychological perceptions of these intensities? For example, if we double the physical intensity of a light, do we see it as twice as bright? If we double the intensity of a sound, do we hear it as twice as loud? The answer to both of these questions is, surprisingly, "no." If our perception does not reflect the actual changes in intensities, then how are the perceived changes related to the actual changes? The scaling question asks how our perceptual scaling of stimulus intensities is related to the actual physical scaling of stimulus intensities.

The Detection Question

What's the dimmest light we can see or the softest sound we can hear? To answer such questions about the limits of our detection abilities, early

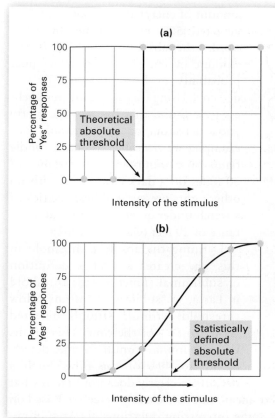

Figure 3.2 | Theoretical and Observed Absolute Thresholds | (a) This is a depiction of the result that psychophysical researchers thought they would observe in their detection studies. Theoretically, the absolute threshold is the minimum amount of physical energy in a stimulus (the minimum intensity of a stimulus) necessary to detect it. If a stimulus does not have this much energy, it should never be detected. If it has this much energy or more, it should always be detected. (b) This is a depiction of the result that psychophysical researchers actually obtained. There was no amount of physical energy in a stimulus that led to the kind of responding depicted in (a). Instead, the responding looked more like a flattened S shape. Thus, the absolute threshold was defined statistically as the minimum amount of energy in a stimulus detected 50% of the time.

psychophysicists varied the amount of energy in a sensory stimulus (for example, the intensity of a light or sound) and asked a person to answer "yes" or "no" as to whether the stimulus (the light or the sound) was detected. They attempted to measure the minimum amount of energy necessary for detection, what they called the absolute threshold. They reasoned that a person would always detect a stimulus that contained at least this threshold amount of energy. In other words, the person would say "no" to all stimuli with less than this amount of energy and "yes" to all stimuli with this amount or more. Figure 3.2(a) depicts a plot of the result that psychophysical researchers thought they would observe.

Absolute threshold. The experimental results, however, did not fit this prediction. There was no abrupt transition point from responding "no" to responding "yes." Instead, the percentage of the time that a person said "yes" increased gradually as the amount of energy in the stimulus increased. This pattern of responding is depicted in Figure 3.2(b). Given this result, psychophysicists had to use a statistical definition to define the **absolute threshold,** the minimum

absolute threshold The minimum amount of energy in a sensory stimulus detected 50% of the time.

Betsy Streeter/Cartoonstock.com

amount of energy in a sensory stimulus detected 50% of the time. In other words, the absolute threshold is the amount of energy that has an equal probability of being detected or not detected. Using this definition, researchers have found that humans are pretty good detectors of weak stimuli. For example, we are able to see a candle flame on a mountain at a distance of 30 miles on a dark clear night with no other lights present and hear the tick of a watch under quiet conditions at a distance of 20 feet (Galanter, 1962).

Defining the absolute threshold in this way creates a strange definition of subliminal (*limen* means threshold in Latin, so "subliminal" means below threshold) stimuli—stimuli detected less than 50% of the time. This means that subliminal stimuli are ones detected up to 49% of the time. Such a definition clearly does not match what people commonly take subliminal to mean: not consciously detected. Based on this everyday definition, however, some interesting questions about subliminal processing arise. Is there any empirical evidence for subliminal perception (perception without conscious awareness)? Is there any empirical evidence for subliminal persuasion (advertisers influencing consumer behavior with subliminal stimuli)? The answer to this last question is a clear "no" (Moore, 1988, 1992; Pratkanis, 1992; Pratkanis & Greenwald, 1988; Trappey, 1996). There is no need to worry that television, music, and other media are subliminally manipulating us. But what about those claims that subliminal tapes can improve your memory, help you to lose weight, and so on? Research has also shown that the tapes don't have the effects claimed (Greenwald, Spangenberg, Pratkanis, & Eskenazi, 1991).

Research in well-controlled laboratory settings (Bar & Biederman, 1998; Marcel, 1983), however, has demonstrated, with respect to subliminal perception, that sensory input can definitely be registered without our conscious awareness. Such perception is short-lived, though, and doesn't seem to have any consequential, long-term impact on our behavior (Greenwald, Draine, & Abrams, 1996; Greenwald, Klinger, & Schuh, 1995). Subliminal perception should not be confused with extrasensory perception (ESP), perception without using our known senses, such as mental telepathy (perceiving another person's thoughts). Just as there is no reliable evidence for subliminal persuasion, neither is there any such evidence for ESP (Druckman & Swets, 1988; Milton & Wiseman, 1999; Galak, LeBoeuf, Nelson, & Simmons, 2012). After decades of research, no one has ever demonstrated a single, reproducible ESP finding. In 1964, James Randi, a magician and master debunker of paranormal claims, offered $1,000 to any person who could demonstrate any psychic, supernatural, or paranormal ability under controlled conditions. The prize has since grown to be $1 million. Although hundreds have applied, Randi still has his money. (For more information, go to the "The Million Dollar Challenge" icon at Randi's Web site, www.randi.org.)

Signal detection theory. Contemporary psychophysical researchers believe that the detection of faint signals involves decision making, as well as sensory processing, so they use signal detection theory to examine a person's detection of very faint sensory stimuli (Green & Swets, 1966; Swets, 1964). According to **signal detection theory,** our ability to detect a faint sensory signal (stimulus) is a decision-making process that depends upon a person's physiological sensitivity to the signal and upon a person's decision-making criterion, which is based on nonsensory factors such as personality traits, expectations, alertness, and motivation. A person must make a decision about the sensory evidence that is available. Is there sufficient evidence to say a signal was present? This is like the decision a juror has to make in a trial. The juror has to decide, based upon the evidence presented, whether the defendant is guilty or not guilty. Based on their personalities and beliefs, jury members may use very different decision-making criteria (need varying amounts of evidence before deciding guilt). Similarly, people may have equal physiological sensitivity to sensory signals, but come to different decisions about whether they detected them or not because they use different criteria for their decisions.

The task used by signal detection researchers is different from that used to measure the absolute threshold. Instead of presenting a faint signal of varying intensity on each trial, either a signal of constant faint intensity is presented on a trial or no signal is presented, and the observer decides that a signal was presented and responds "yes" or that no signal

signal detection theory A theory that assumes that the detection of faint sensory stimuli depends not only upon a person's physiological sensitivity to a stimulus but also upon his decision criterion for detection, which is based on nonsensory factors.

Table 3.1	Four Possible Outcomes in a Signal Detection Study	
	Signal	
	Present	**Absent**
Observer's Response "No" "Yes"	Hit	False Alarm
	Miss	Correct Rejection

was presented and responds "no." Thus, there are four possible events that could occur on a trial: detecting a signal when one was presented (a hit), saying a signal was presented when it was not (a false alarm), failing to detect a signal when one was presented (a miss), or correctly saying a signal was not presented when it was not (a correct rejection). Two of these events (hit and correct rejection) are correct responses by the observer, and two (false alarm and miss) are errors. All four events are depicted in Table 3.1.

Using the data for these four outcomes over a large number of trials, a signal detection theoretical analysis provides two quantitative measures, one for a person's physiological sensitivity to faint sensory signals and one for his decision criterion (how much evidence is needed for a "yes" response). The importance of the former measure is obvious, but why is the latter measure of value? Consider a sample detection task in the real world—looking at an X-ray to determine whether a faint spot indicating cancer is present. Remember, there are two possible errors in a detection decision—saying a signal is present when it is not (a false alarm) and saying a signal is not present when it is (a miss). The costs of either of these errors could be great. In the X-ray example, a false alarm might lead to additional (and unnecessary) clinical tests and possibly unnecessary surgery; a miss might lead to no treatment and death.

The measurement of a person's decision criterion tells us about these two error rates. For example, a person with a very lax decision criterion (a tendency to say "yes" with little evidence, a "yea" sayer) will make many false alarms but have few misses because he is saying "yes" most of the time. The opposite is true for a person with a very strict decision criterion (a tendency to only say "yes" when there is much evidence, a "nay" sayer). A strict criterion leads to many misses but few false alarms because the observer is saying "no" most of the time. So, depending upon the cost of each type of error, a person can change his decision criterion to lessen the cost. The bottom line is that our perception of even a faint signal is a subjective process impacted by nonsensory factors. With this understanding of limitations on our ability to detect faint sensory signals, let's see what psychophysical researchers have found out about our ability to detect very small differences between signals—the difference question.

The Difference Question

What's the smallest difference in brightness between two lights or in loudness between two sounds that we can detect? To answer such questions about how much difference there needs to be between stimuli to perceive them as different, psychophysicists vary the amount of difference in physical energy between two clearly detectable stimuli (for example, two lights or two sounds) and ask a person to answer "yes" or "no" as to whether the stimuli (lights or sounds) are different. With this procedure, these early psychophysical researchers thought that they could measure a person's threshold for perceiving a difference in intensity between two stimuli. However, as with absolute threshold measurement, the results did not reveal a set threshold amount, so the **difference threshold** had to be defined statistically as the minimum difference between two stimuli detected 50% of the time. Another name for the difference threshold is the just noticeable difference, or jnd.

Weber's law. When measuring a person's difference threshold, psychophysicists presented two stimuli on each trial and varied the amount of difference between them across trials. It is important to understand how they manipulated the amount of difference across trials. To do this, they kept the intensity of one stimulus the same on every trial and changed the intensity of the other stimulus across trials. They called the stimulus whose intensity remained the same the standard stimulus, and the stimulus whose intensity changed across trials the comparison stimulus. For example, the standard stimulus for judging differences in lifted weights might be 20 pounds, and the comparison stimuli would be various weights less than or greater than 20 pounds. On one trial the comparison weight might be 19.5 pounds, 21 pounds on the next trial, and so forth.

Ernst Weber, a nineteenth-century German psychophysicist, discovered that difference thresholds and the standard stimulus intensities used to measure them have a very lawful relationship. Simply put, **Weber's law** says that for each type of sensory judgment that we can make, the measured difference threshold is a constant fraction of the standard stimulus value used to measure it. Psychophysicists have determined the constants for the various types of sensory judgment. For example, for judging brightness of lights the constant is .08, but it is .05 for loudness of tones (Teghtsoonian, 1971). A smaller constant means that smaller differences can be detected for that type of sensory judgment. To understand Weber's law, let's consider perceiving differences in lifted weights. The constant for lifted weights is .02, or 1/50. If the standard stimulus used to determine the difference threshold were 100 pounds, the threshold would be 2 pounds. If the standard were 200 pounds, the threshold would be 4 pounds. What would the difference threshold be for a standard stimulus of 1,000 pounds? It would be 20 pounds (1/50 of 1,000). Researchers have found that Weber's law holds for most types of sensory judgments but not for very low-intensity or very high-intensity stimuli (Gescheider, 1976).

In everyday life, Weber's law means that our ability to perceive a difference is relative to the constant background intensity. For example, in a dimly lit room, a little bit of light will be noticed; but in a brightly lit room, it will take a much

difference threshold The minimum difference between two sensory stimuli detected 50% of the time. The difference threshold is also sometimes referred to as the just noticeable difference, or jnd.

Weber's law For each type of sensory judgment that we can make, the measured difference threshold is a constant fraction of the standard stimulus value used to measure it. This constant fraction is different for each type of sensory judgment.

greater increase in light to be noticed. In both cases, however, the proportion of the background intensity necessary to see an increase in brightness will be the same. The bottom line is that we notice proportional differences and not absolute differences. But when we perceive differences between stimuli that are well above threshold level, are the perceived differences in magnitude the same as the actual differences in the physical intensities of the stimuli? This is the scaling question.

The Scaling Question

The detection question and the difference question were concerned with thresholds and with the perception of very weak stimulus intensities or very small differences between stimulus intensities. The events occurring in normal perception, however, are well above threshold levels; therefore, it is important to understand how we perceive the changing intensities of these everyday events that are well above our thresholds. To do so, we need to understand the scaling question—How do perceptual scales of measurement relate to physical scales of measurement? For almost all types of sensory judgment, the scales of measurement are not equivalent. They are lawfully related, however.

Stevens's power law. S. S. Stevens, a twentieth-century American researcher, conducted experiments in which he had people estimate the magnitudes of many types of sensory stimuli. Through these experiments, he discovered how the perceived magnitude of a stimulus is related to its actual physical magnitude (Stevens, 1962, 1975). By relating the perceived magnitude judgments to the actual physical intensities, Stevens found that the perceived magnitude of a stimulus (for example, the perceived brightness of a light or loudness of a sound) is equal to its actual physical intensity raised to some constant power for each type of sensory judgment. This relationship is called **Stevens's power law.**

Now let's try to figure out what this means by considering some different types of sensory judgment. First, if the constant power for a type of sensory judgment were 1, the perceived magnitude would actually equal the physical magnitude. However, this is seldom the case, though it does happen when we judge line lengths. If a line is doubled in length, we perceive its length as doubled. For almost all types of sensory judgments, however, the constant power that the physical intensity has to be raised to is either less than or greater than 1, which means that the perceived magnitude is less or greater, respectively, than the actual physical magnitude. Brightness and loudness magnitude judgments are good examples of when the perceived magnitude is less than the actual magnitude.

To perceive a light as twice as bright, its actual intensity has to be increased eight- to ninefold. A good example of the perceived magnitude being greater than actual physical magnitude is the judgment of electric shock intensities. If shock intensity is doubled, we perceive the increase as much more than double, about 10 times as great. The bottom line is that for almost all types of sensory judgments, our

Stevens's power law The perceived magnitude of a stimulus is equal to its actual physical intensity raised to some constant power. The constant power is different for each type of sensory judgment.

perception of stimulus magnitude does not match the actual physical world. Our perception is a transformation that is created within us.

> **sensory adaptation** Our sensitivity to unchanging and repetitious stimuli disappears over time.

Another phenomenon that helps us to understand how we process the intensity of stimuli is **sensory adaptation**—our sensitivity to unchanging and repetitious stimuli disappears over time. For example, when we first put our watch on our wrist, we are aware of it, but that sensitivity disappears quickly. Why? Our senses are set to detect changes in the environment, and therefore they adapt to continuous or repeated presentation of a stimulus with decreasing responsiveness. Sensory adaptation makes sense from an evolutionary viewpoint. It is more important for our survival to detect environmental changes than things that don't change. Changes are more likely to signal danger. There are some limits on sensory adaptation, though. We don't adapt to extremely intense, especially painful stimuli, such as a severe toothache or incredibly loud noises. We also don't usually adapt to unchanging visual stimuli; our eyes are constantly moving so their visual images continue to change.

To help you to integrate the information in this section, the three psychophysical questions along with the answers we have described are summarized in Table 3.2. If anything in this table is not clear to you, restudy the relevant text material before going on to the next section.

Table 3.2	Three Psychophysical Questions and Answers
Psychophysical Questions	**Answers**
Detection Question: What is the minimum amount of energy in a stimulus that humans can detect?	Absolute threshold: The minimum amount of energy in a stimulus that can be detected 50% of the time
	Signal detection theory: Detection of faint stimuli depends not only upon physiological sensitivity to a stimulus but also upon a person's decision criterion for detection, which is based on nonsensory factors
Difference Question: What is the minimum difference in stimulus energy between two stimuli that humans can detect?	Difference threshold: The minimum difference in stimulus energy between two stimuli that can be detected 50% of the time
	Weber's law: The measured difference threshold is a constant fraction of the standard stimulus used to measure it and this constant is different for each type of sensory judgment
Scaling Question: How are human perceptual scales of measurement related to physical scales of measurement?	Stevens's power law: The perceived magnitude of a stimulus is equal to its actual physical intensity raised to some constant power for each type of sensory judgment

Section Summary

In this section, we discussed some of the basic findings from psychophysical research. We considered three psychophysical questions—the detection, difference, and scaling questions. To answer the detection question, psychophysical researchers measured the absolute threshold, the minimum stimulus intensity that can be detected 50% of the time. Using this definition, researchers have found humans to be pretty good detectors of faint signals. However, because they view the detection task as a decision-making process involving a response criterion, contemporary sensory researchers prefer to use signal detection theory to describe our detection abilities. Using this type of analysis, both an observer's decision criterion and her sensitivity to faint sensory stimuli can be identified. Thus, if the costs of a particular observer's errors (false alarms or misses) are high, the observer's criterion can be changed to reduce these rates. Regardless of the type of analysis, researchers have failed to find any reliable evidence for subliminal persuasion or extrasensory perception.

To answer the difference question, psychophysicists measured the difference threshold, the minimum difference in stimulus intensity between two stimuli that can be detected 50% of the time. It turns out that difference thresholds and the standard stimulus intensities used to measure them have a relationship called Weber's law—the measured difference threshold is a constant proportion of the standard stimulus value used in its measurement. This constant is different for each type of sensory judgment, and a smaller constant indicates that smaller differences can be detected for that type of sensory judgment.

Surprisingly, research on the scaling question has indicated that the relationship between perceived stimulus magnitudes and the actual physical magnitudes is almost always not an equivalent one. According to Stevens's power law, to equal the perceived intensity, the actual physical intensity has to be raised to some constant power, and this constant is different for each type of sensory judgment. When this constant power is 1, the perceived intensity equals the actual intensity. This, however, seldom occurs, but it is the case for line-length judgments. Almost all of the time the constant is less or greater than 1, which means that the perceived intensity is less or greater, respectively, than the actual physical intensity. Brightness and loudness are examples of perceived magnitude judgments being less than the actual physical magnitudes, and electric shock is an example of magnitude judgments being greater. Sensory adaptation, our decreasing sensory responsiveness to constant, nonextreme stimuli, also helps us to understand how we process the intensity of stimuli.

ConceptCheck | 1

Why were absolute and difference thresholds given statistical definitions?

According to signal detection theory, what would happen to a person's false alarm and miss rates if the person switched from a very lax to a very strict decision criterion?

What does a really large constant fraction in Weber's law tell us about our ability to judge differences?

What does Stevens's power law tell us about our perception of the physical intensities of stimuli?

How We See and How We Hear

Our two most dominant senses are vision and hearing. This section will first discuss how our eyes and ears gather and process information from the environment. Visual and auditory stimuli are physical energies in the form of waves—light waves and sound waves. We need to understand the characteristics of these waveforms to understand how visual and auditory stimuli are processed, so we need to discuss them first. A typical waveform and its primary characteristics (wavelength, frequency, and amplitude) are illustrated in Figure 3.3.

wavelength The distance in one cycle of a wave, from one crest to the next.

amplitude The amount of energy in a wave, its intensity, which is the height of the wave at its crest.

frequency The number of times a wave cycles in one second.

Wavelength refers to the distance in one cycle of a wave, from one crest to the next. Different wavelengths of light lead to varying perceptions of color. Humans can perceive wavelengths roughly from 400 to 700 nanometers (nm), or billionths of a meter. As the wavelengths decrease from 700 nm, the resulting hues go from red through the colors of the spectrum down to violet. One way to remember the order of these colors is by remembering the name ROY G. BIV, which stands for Red, Orange, Yellow, Green, Blue, Indigo, and Violet. **Amplitude** refers to the amount of energy in a wave, its intensity, which is the height of the wave at its crest. For light waves, the amplitude determines the brightness of the light. Different amplitudes lead to different levels of brightness; the greater the amplitude, the brighter the light.

For auditory stimuli, the frequency of the waveform rather than its length is used. **Frequency** refers to the number of times the waveform cycles in one second. Longer wavelengths have lower frequencies, and shorter wavelengths have higher frequencies. The frequency of a sound wave determines its pitch, the quality of sound that we describe as high or low. For example, female voices usually have a higher pitch than male voices. Humans can perceive sound wave frequencies from

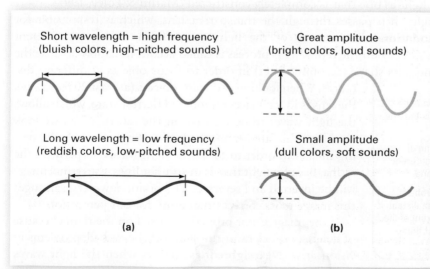

Short wavelength = high frequency
(bluish colors, high-pitched sounds)

Long wavelength = low frequency
(reddish colors, low-pitched sounds)

(a)

Great amplitude
(bright colors, loud sounds)

Small amplitude
(dull colors, soft sounds)

(b)

Figure 3.3 | A Typical Waveform and Its Characteristics | Wavelength is the distance of one complete cycle of the wave, from one crest to the next. A wave's frequency refers to the number of times it can cycle in one second—the longer the wave, the lower the frequency. The amplitude of the wave refers to the amount of energy in the wave, which is the height of the wave at its crest.

about 20 to 20,000 hertz (Hz), the number of cycles of the sound wave in one second. This unit of measurement's name, hertz, comes from a nineteenth-century German physicist named Heinrich Hertz, who studied sound. The amplitude of a sound wave corresponds to our perception of its loudness. As the amplitude of a wave increases, its perceived loudness increases.

The brain cannot process physical energies such as light waves and sound waves. There are receptor cells in our eyes and ears that specialize in **transduction**—converting physical energy into neural signals that the brain can understand. This conversion is the first step in processing incoming sensory information. Following transduction, the incoming visual and auditory signals undergo further processing on their way to the brain, and within the brain before we see and hear the brain's interpretations of these signals. Next, we will take a closer look at transduction and the initial information processing in the eyes and ears, focusing on how we see color and how we distinguish the pitches of sounds.

How the Eye Works

The light-sensitive receptor cells are located in the retina at the very back of the eye; therefore, light waves have to travel through almost the entire eye before transduction occurs. Figure 3.4 shows the path of the light and each of the parts of the eye that we will discuss. The cornea is the clear, tough covering on the front of the eye that starts bending the light waves that will eventually have to be focused on the retina. The light waves pass through the cornea and the pupil, a tiny hole through which the light waves enter the eye. The iris is a colored muscle that both gives eyes their color and controls the size of the pupil, which determines how much light enters. To lessen the amount of entering light, the iris will constrict (lessen) the size of the pupil, and to increase the amount of entering light, it will dilate (increase) the pupil's size. A completely dilated pupil lets in about 16 times as much light as one that is completely constricted (Matlin & Foley, 1997).

The light then passes through the transparent lens, which is responsible for **accommodation**—the focusing of the light waves from objects of different distances directly on the retina. This process is called accommodation because the lens changes its shape (accommodates) in order to focus objects at different distances. When looking at distant objects (at least 20 feet away), the lens is in its unaccommodated flattest state, which allows the light waves to be focused on the retina. When we look at objects that are nearer, the lens accommodates by becoming thicker in order to focus the light waves properly on the retina. Because light travels in straight lines, the retinal image will be inverted and reversed. The brain, however, rearranges this image to its correct orientation for our perception.

If the image is not properly focused on the retina because of defects in the lens or the shape of the eyeball, problems in vision arise. **Nearsightedness** occurs when the light waves

transduction The conversion of physical energy into neural signals that the brain can understand.

accommodation The focusing of light waves from objects of different distances directly on the retina.

nearsightedness A visual problem in which the light waves from distant objects come into focus in front of the retina, blurring the images of these objects.

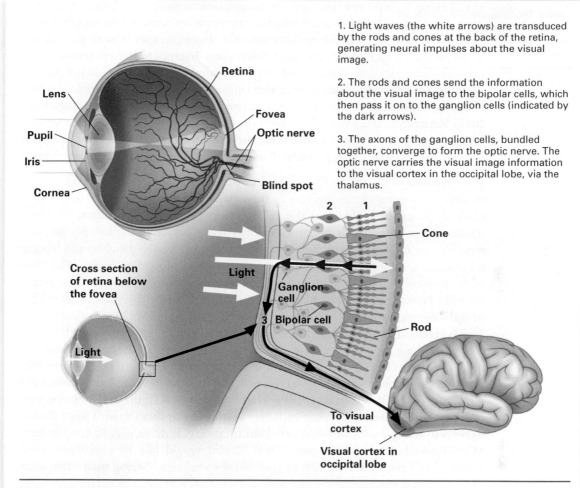

1. Light waves (the white arrows) are transduced by the rods and cones at the back of the retina, generating neural impulses about the visual image.

2. The rods and cones send the information about the visual image to the bipolar cells, which then pass it on to the ganglion cells (indicated by the dark arrows).

3. The axons of the ganglion cells, bundled together, converge to form the optic nerve. The optic nerve carries the visual image information to the visual cortex in the occipital lobe, via the thalamus.

Figure 3.4 | The Path of Light Through the Eye and the Structure of the Retina | The light travels through the cornea, enters through the pupil whose size is controlled by the iris, and is focused on the retina by the lens. Here, as explained in the figure, the light waves are (1) transduced into neural signals describing the visual image; and (2) these signals are sent to the bipolar cells, which forward them to the ganglion cells whose axons bundle together to form the optic nerve, which (3) carries the signals back to the occipital lobes in the brain, via the thalamus, to be interpreted.

from distant objects come into focus in front of the retina, which blurs the images of these objects. **Farsightedness** is created by the opposite focusing problem— light waves from nearby objects come into focus behind the retina, resulting in blurred images. So, in nearsightedness, we have difficulty viewing distant objects, but can see near objects well; in farsightedness, we have difficulty viewing near objects, but can see far objects well. Farsightedness is similar

farsightedness A visual problem in which the light waves from nearby objects come into focus behind the retina, blurring the images of these objects.

retina The light-sensitive layer of the eye that is composed of three layers of cells—ganglion, bipolar, and receptor (rods and cones).

to what happens to our vision as we age; the lens loses its ability to accommodate for nearby objects. Older people find it difficult to focus on near objects, so they have to get reading glasses and hold objects at a distance to help in seeing them.

It is also important to realize that our brains do not process everything in the physical world but rather only a tiny bit of it. For example, the part of the light spectrum that is visible to us is less than a ten-trillionth of it (Eagleman, 2011). We have no awareness of the rest of the spectrum carrying X-rays, radio signals, gamma rays, and so on. No matter how hard you try, your senses are not equipped to tune into the rest of the spectrum. There is far more out there than meets the eye.

The structure of the retina. Except for the visual image being reversed and inverted, no visual processing occurs until the light waves reach the retina, which is only a mere half-millimeter thick (Brynie, 2009). As shown in Figure 3.4, the **retina,** the light-sensitive layer of the eye, is composed of three layers of cells—ganglion, bipolar, and receptor (the rods and cones). The light waves pass through the ganglion and bipolar cells before reaching the rods and cones, where visual processing begins. The light waves are absorbed by photopigments (light-sensitive chemicals) within these receptor cells, creating patterns of neural impulses that describe the visual image. This neural information is conveyed to the bipolar cells, which in turn send it along to the ganglion cells. The optic nerve, the axons of the ganglion cells bundled together, exits the eye carrying the information along the visual pathways to the brain. Where the optic nerve exits each eye, we have a blind spot—a retinal area with no receptor cells, preventing us from seeing anything there (Ramachandran, 1992). To experience the blind spots in each of your eyes, follow the instructions in Figure 3.5. Why don't we normally notice the blind spot in each eye? The brain fills them in with what should be there by using the surrounding visual information (Churchland & Ramachandran, 1996; Ramachandran & Gregory, 1991). If you would like to experience some examples of how your brain fills in your blind spots, visit "Seeing more than your

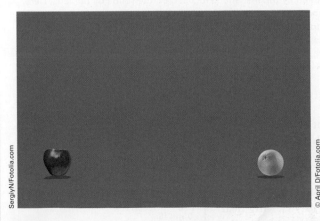

SergiyN/Fotolia.com

© April D/Fotolia.com

Figure 3.5 | Find Your Blind Spots | To find the blind spot in your left eye, hold the book at arm's length in front of you, close your right eye and stare at the orange on the right with your left eye, and keep staring at the orange while you move the book slowly toward you. The apple should disappear when it falls on the blind spot in your left eye, somewhere between 6 to 12 inches from your eye. To find the blind spot in your right eye, this time close the left eye and stare at the apple on the left with your right eye as you move the book slowly toward you. This time the orange should disappear when it falls upon the blind spot in your right eye.

eye does" at serendip.brynmawr
.edu/bb/blindspot1.html. It provides examples of how your brain
uses colors and patterns in the
area surrounding the blind spot
to make the best guess about
what should be in the blind
spot itself.

David Hubel (left) and Torsten Wiesel (right)

The optic nerve carries the
visual information to the thalamus, which is responsible for
directing it to the primary visual
cortex in our occipital lobes
to be processed. But how does
the visual cortex interpret this
message from the retina? David
Hubel and Torsten Wiesel's innovative research in which they recorded patterns
of electrical impulses in individual neurons in the visual cortex of cats provided
the answer. They were awarded the Nobel Prize in Physiology or Medicine in 1981
for their discoveries concerning information processing in the visual system. The
story of their collaboration along with reprints of all of their key publications can
be found in Hubel and Wiesel's *Brain and Visual Perception: The Story of a 25-Year
Collaboration* (2004). Because this cortical visual processing is very involved, we'll
just describe the general nature of this very counterintuitive processing.

Essentially, the brain recognizes a visual object (a process called pattern recognition) by breaking it down into its elementary features, such as angles and
diagonal lines. Cortical cells called feature detectors then recognize these elementary features. Finally, the elementary features are put back together again, so that
the whole object can be recognized. For example, to recognize a triangle, $\triangle$, it
is broken down into its features (possibly, /, __, and \), which are recognized and
then regrouped into the proper relationship. Strange isn't it? To recognize an
object, the object is broken down into its parts and then these parts are put back
together again in order to identify object. Even stranger is that there are separate
processing systems for form, color, distance, and motion information, which the
brain somehow coordinates and unifies into our seamless perception of the world
(Ratey, 2001).

But what if your primary visual cortex were severely damaged? You would
be blind in the conventional sense, but you might possibly have what is
called **blindsight** (seeing without knowing)—a condition in which a blind
person has some spared visual capacities in the absence of
any visual awareness (Weiskrantz, 2009). The oxymoron
blindsight was coined by Lawrence Weiskrantz of Oxford
University, who has studied this condition for more than
40 years (Weiskrantz, Warrington, Sanders, & Marshall, 1974).

blindsight A condition in which a
blind person has some spared visual
capacities in the absence of any
visual awareness.

rods Receptor cells in the retina that are principally responsible for dim light and achromatic vision.

cones Receptor cells in the retina that are principally responsible for bright light and color vision.

fovea A tiny pit in the center of the retina filled with cones.

People with blindsight respond to a visual stimulus without consciously experiencing it. For example, they claim that they do not see an object, but when asked to reach out and touch it, they can do so far more often than what chance would predict. If you put a large object in their path, they will walk around it but insist that they do not see anything. The experimental evidence concerning blindsight has sometimes been controversial (Cowey, 2010), and the explanation for blindsight remains unsettled. Some researchers believe that the blindsight responses stem from the flow of visual information through neural pathways that bypass the damaged visual cortex (a kind of information detour) to brain areas that do not convey the conscious perception but enable the blindsight responses (Ptito & Leh, 2007; Schmid et al., 2010). An alternative explanation is that a small amount of healthy tissue remains within the damaged visual cortex, not enough to provide conscious perception but sufficient for blindsight responses (Gazzaniga, Fendrich, & Wesainger, 1994). It is also possible that both hypotheses are correct. Because there is much variability between those with blindsight, each hypothesis might explain different cases. One conclusion that can be made, however, is that normal visual perception requires a healthy visual cortex.

Rods and cones. There are two types of visual receptor cells, rods and cones, in the retina. They are called rods and cones because of their actual physical shapes. Their functions are also very different. Rods are principally responsible for dim light and achromatic (colorless) vision, and cones for bright light and color vision. **Rods** outnumber cones about 20 to 1 (Kalat, 2007). There are about 120 million rods and only 6 million or so cones in each eye. **Cones** are more centrally located in the retina than rods. They are located in the **fovea,** a tiny pit in the center of the retina, and in the periphery of the retina on each side of the fovea. Rods are only located in the periphery, and the proportion of rods to cones increases with increasing distance from the fovea. The major differences between rods and cones are summarized in Table 3.3.

Table 3.3	Differences Between Rods and Cones
Rods	**Cones**
120 million in each eye	6 million in each eye
Located mainly in periphery of retina	Located mainly in fovea and central retina
Primarily responsible for dim light vision	Primarily responsible for bright light vision
Responsible for achromatic (colorless) vision	Responsible for chromatic (color) vision
Lead to low visual acuity	Lead to high visual acuity

The difference in location of rods (peripheral) and cones (central) helps us to determine where we should focus an object for the best visual acuity (resolution of detail). In normal or brighter light when the cones are mainly responsible for our vision, the object should be focused on the fovea, which is packed with cones. Cones provide a clearer picture of an object. Why? Cones, especially foveal cones, tend to have more direct routes than the rods to the bipolar and ganglion cells for the retinal information that they process. For example, typically one foveal cone communicates with one bipolar cell, but several rods communicate with one bipolar cell. This means that the information that the rods send forward has been averaged across several retinal positions, leading to a less clear picture of the retinal image. Foveal cones do not have to do such averaging; therefore, the retinal

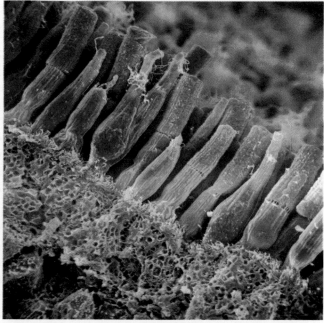

This is a highly magnified and colorized electromicrograph that clearly shows the difference between the rods and cones. The rods are the longer, thinner green receptors, and the cones are the shorter, more tapered blue receptors.

Science Source

image they send forward is more detailed and clearer. The cones in the periphery just outside of the fovea do some averaging but far less than the rods. A good example of the foveal cones' role in the resolution of detail concerns the changes in French artist Edgar Degas's paintings as his retinal disease worsened in his later years. As his central vision grew blurry, his paintings became less detailed and coarser and lost refinement (Marmor, 2006). He could not see the detail so he could not paint it.

But where should we focus an object in dim light conditions? The answer is in the periphery of the retina rather than the fovea. Why? This is where the rods are more densely located, and they are mainly responsible for our vision when not much light is available. We shouldn't look directly at the object when there isn't much light, but rather focus a little to the side of it so that it will be projected onto the periphery of the retina. The image won't be as clear as when we can use our cones, but it is the best we can do in dim light. The major role of the rods in dim light vision is also apparent in **dark adaptation,** the process by which the rods and cones through internal chemical changes become more and more sensitive to light in dim light conditions. The cones adapt quickly (in 5 to 10 minutes), but need more light to function, so they do not really help us to see in dim light. It takes longer for the rods to adapt (20 minutes or so), but they slowly help us to see in dim light. Normally, however, we have enough light for our cones to be working. That is why we see the world in vivid color.

dark adaptation The process by which the rods and cones through internal chemical changes become more and more sensitive to light in dim light conditions.

But how do the cones do this, and what else is involved in producing our perception of color? These are the questions we discuss next.

How We See Color

How many different colors can humans discriminate? Hundreds? Thousands? These estimates are not even close. It has been estimated that the human eye can discriminate about 7.5 million different colors (Fineman, 1996). How can we differentiate so many colors? Actually our color vision can be explained by combining two rather simple theories of color vision, the trichromatic theory and the opponent-process theory. We will consider each one separately and then how the two work together to explain color vision.

Trichromatic theory of color vision. Trichromatic theory, as the word trichromatic implies, proposes that there are three colors involved. It assumes that there are three types of cones, activated best by short, medium, or long wavelengths of light, roughly corresponding to blue, green, and red. Indeed, physiological research indicates that there are three types of cones, each containing a slightly different photopigment that is maximally sensitive to blue, green, or red wavelengths of light (Wald, 1964). The trichromatic theory assumes that all of the many colors that we can perceive are mixtures of various proportions of these three cone activities. If all three types of cones are equally active, we see white (the sum of the three wavelengths of light). Trichromatic theory played a role in the creation of the television screen, which consists of microscopic red, green, and blue dots. The colors we see on the screen are the product of how these three types of dots are activated by the television broadcast and how the light-emitting dots activate our three types of cones.

It is important to realize that the proposed mixtures of the primary colors are **additive mixtures**—different wavelengths of light are directly mixed together. In additive mixtures, all of the wavelengths of light reach the retina and are added together. The resulting colors are very different from those for **subtractive mixtures,** such as mixing paints. In subtractive mixtures, some wavelengths are absorbed (subtracted) and so do not get reflected from the mixture to the retina. For example, if we mix red, green, and blue paints together in equal amounts, the result is black (no light reflected). A mixture of equal proportions of red, green, and blue wavelengths of light, however, appears white. These subtractive and additive mixtures are shown in Figure 3.6.

The trichromatic theory provides a good explanation of the most prevalent type of color blindness—red-green color blindness in which red and green cannot be discriminated. Approximately 10% of males and less than 1% of females are red-green colorblind (Livingstone, 2002). According to trichromatic theory, a person with red-green color blindness has normal blue-sensitive cones but has deficient red- or green-

trichromatic theory A theory of color vision that assumes that there are three types of cones, each only activated by wavelength ranges of light corresponding roughly to blue, green, and red. It further assumes that all of the various colors that we can see are mixtures of various levels of activation of the three types of cones. If all three are equally activated, we see white.

additive mixtures Direct mixtures of different wavelengths of light in which all of the wavelengths reach the retina and are added together.

subtractive mixtures Mixtures of wavelengths of light in which some wavelengths are absorbed (subtracted) and so do not get reflected from the mixtures to the retina.

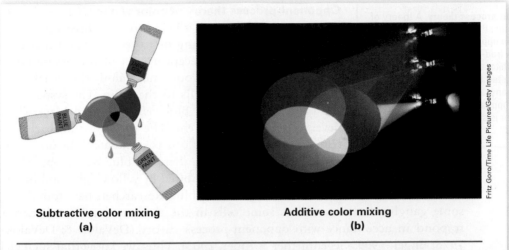

Subtractive color mixing
(a)

Additive color mixing
(b)

Fritz Goro/Time Life Pictures/Getty Images

Figure 3.6 | Subtractive and Additive Mixtures | (a) In a subtractive mixture, some wavelengths are absorbed (subtracted) and so do not get reflected from the mixture. For example, mixing equal amounts of red, green, and blue paints is a subtractive mixture. The intersection of all three colors appears black. (b) Mixing equal amounts of red, green, and blue wavelengths of light, however, is an additive mixture in which all the wavelengths are directly mixed together, producing different results than mixing paints of these three colors. For example, the intersection of all three wavelengths appears white. The binary additive mixtures are also counterintuitive. For example, the additive mixture of equal proportions of red and green wavelengths of light appears yellow.

sensitive cones, which would explain their inability to discriminate red and green. Why, however, is this type of color blindness more prevalent in males than in females? As Livingstone explains, the genes responsible for producing the photopigments in the red- and green-sensitive cones are located on the X chromosome. Females have two X chromosomes, but males have only one. Thus, for females carrying a defect in the gene that produces the photopigment for the red- or green-sensitive cones in one of these chromosomes, the other chromosome will likely be normal, and consequently, they will have normal color vision. Males who carry such a defective gene, however, do not have another X chromosome (no backup) so their color vision will be abnormal.

There are, however, color phenomena that trichromatic theory has difficulty explaining. We know that red-green and blue-yellow are pairs of **complementary colors,** wavelengths that when added together produce white. This means we cannot produce an additive mixture that is perceived to be reddish-green or a bluish-yellow. Trichromatic theory can't explain why such colors can't be produced if every color is an additive mixture of the three primary colors. In addition, this theory has difficulty explaining how we see complementary-color afterimages. For example, if we stare at a solid red square for a while and then look at a white sheet of paper, we will see a solid green square. Why? To explain such phenomena, researchers developed a second theory of color vision, the opponent-process theory (Hurvich & Jameson, 1957), which we will discuss next.

complementary colors Wavelengths of light that when added together produce white.

opponent-process theory A theory of color vision that assumes that there are three opponent-process cell systems (red-green, blue-yellow, and black-white) that process color information after it has been processed by the cones. The colors in each system oppose one another in that if one color is stimulated, the other is inhibited.

Opponent-process theory of color vision. The **opponent-process theory** assumes that there are three opponent-process cell systems helping us to see color and that they are located at the post-receptor level of processing (after cone processing), which would mean along the visual pathways from the bipolar cells to the brain. The systems are the pairs, red-green and blue-yellow, plus a black-white (levels-of-brightness) system. The colors within each system oppose each other—if one is stimulated, the other one is inhibited. For example, there are blue-yellow opponent-process cells stimulated by blue light and inhibited by yellow light, and others that are stimulated by yellow and inhibited by blue. Researchers have found that some ganglion cells as well as some cells in the thalamus and visual cortex respond in accordance with opponent-process theory (DeValois & DeValois, 1975; Engel, 1999; Gegenfurtner & Kiper, 2003). Thus, we know that such cell systems exist.

Opponent-process theory can easily explain why we can't see a reddish-green or a bluish-yellow. The complementary colors involved in each case cannot both be simultaneously stimulated. They cancel each other out. The theory can also explain complementary color afterimages. When you stare at one of the two colors in an opponent-process system for a while, the part of that system responsible for processing this color gets fatigued and has to stop and recover. This is why we see the complementary color in the system when we look at a white surface—the other color is recovering and cannot oppose it. A good example is the American red, white, and blue flag. If we stare at a picture of this flag for a while and then switch our attention to a white sheet of paper, we see a complementary green, black, and yellow flag! If you stare at the green, black, and yellow flag in Figure 3.7 for about 40 seconds and then look at the white space next to it, what do you see?

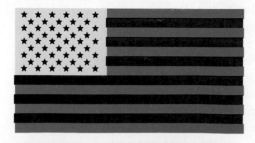

Figure 3.7 | Demonstration of Complementary Afterimage | Stare at the flag above for a while and then look at the white space to its right. You should see the American flag.

Table 3.4	Three Theories of Color Vision
Theory	**Explanation of Color Vision**
Trichromatic theory	There are three types of cones, each only activated by wavelength ranges of light corresponding roughly to blue, green, and red; all colors are mixtures of various levels of activation of these three types of cones
Opponent-process theory	There are three opponent-process cell systems (red-green, blue-yellow, and black-white) that process color information after it has been processed by the cones; the colors in each system oppose one another (if one is stimulated, the other is inhibited)
Composite theory	Color information is processed by the cones according to trichromatic theory, but color information is processed at the post-receptor cell level according to opponent-process theory

There is research that supports both trichromatic theory and opponent-process theory, so the best explanation for how we see color involves both theories, but at different locations in the visual pathways (Boynton, 1988). Color information is processed by the cones according to trichromatic theory, but color information is processed at the post-receptor cell level (by bipolar, ganglion, thalamic, and cortical cells) according to the opponent-process theory. This simple composite theory is a good example of competing theories becoming complementary theories. All three theories of color vision are summarized in Table 3.4.

This brief discussion of how we see color shows how visual input from the environment is processed, analyzed, and reconfigured, starting with its initial processing in the retina and as it continues along the visual pathways to the brain to be interpreted. Next, we will consider how such processing of auditory information enables us to hear.

How the Ear Works

The auditory sensory system is a mechanical (vibratory) system with the receptor cells located in the inner portion of each ear. As you can see in Figure 3.8 (page 122), the ear is divided into three sections—the outer ear, middle ear, and inner ear. The parts of each section are also shown in Figure 3.8. The pinna, the external part of the ear, collects sounds and funnels them through the auditory canal to the tympanic membrane (the eardrum), which marks the boundary between the outer ear and middle ear. The sound waves produce vibrations in the eardrum, and these vibrations create a chain reaction that moves the malleus, incus, and stapes (more commonly referred to as the hammer, anvil, and stirrup given their shapes), the three tiny bones in the middle ear (the three smallest bones in the human body). The movement of the stapes creates vibrations of the oval window, a membrane covering an opening into the inner ear.

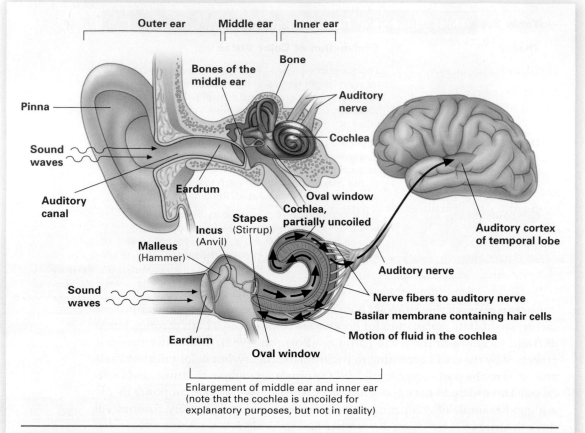

Figure 3.8 | The Path of Sound Through the Ear | Sound is conducted through the ear by way of air pressure changes. After entering through the pinna, the sound waves create vibrations in the eardrum that lead to movement of the three tiny bones in the middle ear. This movement leads to vibration of the oval window that leads to movement of the fluid in the inner ear, displacement along the basilar membrane, and movement of the hair cells within the membrane. The movement of these hair cells creates the neural signals that are taken to the primary auditory cortex in the temporal lobes by the auditory nerve via the thalamus.

The **cochlea** is a snail-shaped structure in the inner ear that contains the receptor cells for hearing. Tiny **hair cells** that line the basilar membrane (a membrane that extends the length of the cochlea) are the receptors for hearing. There are not nearly as many hair cells in the ears as there are rods and cones in the eyes, only about 16,000 hair cells in each ear (Matlin & Foley, 1997). The vibrations of the oval window displace fluid within the cochlea, which causes movement of the basilar membrane and thus movement of the hair cells in the membrane. The auditory message is coded according to how these tiny hair cells move. This motion of the hair cells

cochlea A snail-shaped structure in the inner ear that contains the receptor cells for hearing.

hair cells The receptor cells for hearing. They line the basilar membrane inside the cochlea.

gets translated into neural impulses that get passed on to the auditory nerve cells that carry the information to the thalamus, which directs the information to the primary auditory cortex in the temporal lobes.

Hearing loss caused by damage to these hair cells or the auditory nerve fibers is called **nerve deafness.** The most common causes of such damage are aging and continued exposure to extremely loud noises. Nerve deafness is much more difficult to treat than **conduction deafness,** hearing loss caused by damage to the mechanical system carrying the auditory information to the cochlea. For example, puncturing an eardrum can lead to conduction deafness. Hearing aids can often help to alleviate this type of deafness.

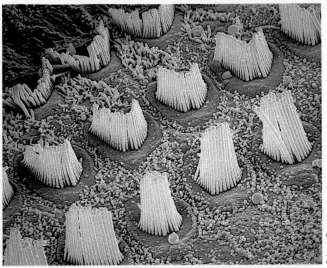

This image of hair cells lining the cochlea has been greatly magnified and colorized. The hair cells vibrate in response to sound, and this motion gets translated into neural impulses that get carried to the primary auditory cortex.

It is important to realize that just as we learned that we only process a small part of the light spectrum, parts of the auditory spectrum are outside the range of human hearing. We cannot process ultrasound stimuli, those above 20,000 Hz, and infrasound stimuli, those below 20 Hz. Other animals, however, have different windows on the auditory world. For example, elephants, whales, and giraffes can hear infrasound stimuli; and dolphins and bats, ultrasound stimuli. Whales and elephants use infrasound to communicate over long distances, possibly up to hundreds of miles in the case of whales. Dolphins communicate using ultrasound frequencies, and bats use them to navigate and hunt in darkness. Dogs and cats can hear frequencies above 40,000 and 50,000 Hz, respectively; and the upper range for dolphins may extend to 150,000 Hz (Goldstein, 2007). Thus, the outside world is really noisy; we just lack the ability to process it.

Now, given our basic understanding of how the ear works and how auditory information gets coded and processed, we'll consider an important aspect of this complex coding, how we distinguish different pitches.

How We Distinguish Pitch

Remember that pitch is the quality of sound that we describe as high or low and is determined by the frequency of a sound wave. We can perceive sound wave frequencies from about 20 to 20,000 Hz. Each of the frequencies in this rather large range corresponds to a different pitch that we can perceive.

nerve deafness Hearing loss created by damage to the hair cells or the auditory nerve fibers in the inner ear.

conduction deafness Hearing loss created by damage to one of the structures in the ear responsible for mechanically conducting the auditory information to the inner ear.

The best explanation of how we perceive this range of pitches parallels the story of how we see different colors. We will find that to get the best explanation, two theories will need to be combined—place theory and frequency theory. First, we will consider each of the two theories, and then how they go together.

Place theory. Place theory assumes that there is a specific place along the basilar membrane, starting from the oval window, which will respond maximally to a particular frequency. Thus, the brain will know the frequency by knowing the location of peak activity along the basilar membrane. In some ingenious experiments on the cochleas from human cadavers, Georg von Békésy discovered that each frequency generates a traveling wave that moves along the basilar membrane and peaks at a particular location (Békésy, 1960). Starting at the oval window and 20,000 Hz, the pitch goes down as the peak activity moves down the basilar membrane. These peak locations tell the brain the frequencies of the incoming auditory stimuli.

Frequency theory. Frequency theory assumes that the frequency of the sound wave is mimicked by the firing rate of the hair cells across the entire basilar membrane. For example, if the frequency were 100 Hz, the firing rate for the membrane would be 100 impulses per second. The brain would know the frequency by the basilar membrane's firing rate in reaction to the auditory stimulus.

Now let's see why and how we put theories together to get a better explanation of pitch perception. First, research has found that specific locations along the basilar membrane correlate well with the frequencies of sound waves, except for lower pitches (< 500 Hz). For these lower pitches, the firing rate of the basilar membrane mimics the frequency. This means that place theory can explain how we hear the entire range of pitches except for low pitches, but frequency theory can explain how we hear these low pitches. Is frequency theory only able to explain how we perceive pitches below 500 Hz? No, the upper limit on firing rate is 5,000 times per second. There is a maximum firing rate for nerve cells, about 1,000 times per second. However, with the addition of the **volley principle,** in which the cells take turns firing to increase the maximum firing rate for the group of cells, frequency theory could explain our perception of frequencies up to about 5,000 Hz (Zwislocki, 1981). Because 5,000 times per second is the upper limit for the firing rate using the volley principle, frequency theory would not be able to explain how we perceive higher frequencies of 5,000 to 20,000 Hz.

Combining the two theories gives us a composite theory that fits the research findings on pitch perception. Frequency theory explains the perception of lower frequencies (< 500 Hz), and place theory explains how we perceive higher frequencies (> 5,000 Hz). This means that the brain uses the firing rate to differentiate the low frequencies and the location of maximal hair cell activity along the basilar membrane to distinguish the high frequencies. For the range

place theory A theory of pitch perception that assumes that there is a specific location along the basilar membrane that will maximally respond to a particular frequency, thereby indicating the pitch to the brain. As this location goes down the basilar membrane from the oval window, the pitch goes down from 20,000 Hz to 20 Hz.

frequency theory A theory of pitch perception that assumes that the frequency of the sound wave is mimicked by the firing rate of the entire basilar membrane.

volley principle Cells taking turns firing will increase the maximum firing rate for a group of cells.

Table 3.5	Theories of Pitch Perception
Theory	**Explanation of Pitch Perception**
Place theory	There is a specific location along the basilar membrane that will maximally respond to a particular frequency, thereby indicating the pitch to the brain
Frequency theory	The frequency of the sound wave is mimicked by the firing rate of the entire basilar membrane, thereby indicating the pitch to the brain
Composite theory	Lower frequencies ($<$ 500 Hz) are processed according to frequency theory, higher frequencies ($>$ 5,000 Hz) are processed according to place theory, and for frequencies between from 500 to 5,000 Hz, both theories are working

of frequencies in between (roughly 500 to 5,000 Hz), both sources of information work, giving us double coverage and better pitch perception. This is fortunate because this range of frequencies contains the sounds most important to us—for example, human speech. All three theories of pitch perception are summarized in Table 3.5.

Section Summary

In this section, we discussed our two most dominant senses—vision and hearing. Stimuli for both senses occur in the form of waves, light waves and sound waves, respectively. For light waves, different wavelengths lead to the perception of different colors, and the amplitude of the wave determines the level of perceived brightness. With respect to sound waves, wave frequency determines the pitch that we perceive, and wave amplitude determines our perception of loudness. The brain cannot process such physical energy forms, hence receptor cells (rods and cones in the retina and hair cells in the basilar membrane within the cochlea) transduce (convert) the physical energy into neural signals that the brain can understand.

Light waves pass through many parts of the eye before being transduced by the rods and cones at the back of the retina. Once transduced, the neural signals are carried by the optic nerve to the thalamus, which sends them to the primary visual cortex where they are interpreted. In this interpretation process, the object is broken down into its elemental features, which are recognized by feature detectors, and then the features are combined so that the whole object can be recognized. The cones and rods divide the initial visual processing. Cones are responsible for bright light and color vision; rods are responsible for dim light and achromatic vision.

There are two competing explanations for how we see color—trichromatic theory and opponent-process theory. Trichromatic theory proposes three types of cones, each responding to ranges of wavelengths corresponding to red, green, and blue. All other colors are derived from varying proportions of these three primaries. Research indicates that we do have these three types of cones. Opponent-process theory assumes that there are three types of cell systems (red-green, blue-yellow, and black-white) at the post-receptor level that help us to see color. Being complementary pairs, the colors within each system oppose (cancel) each other. Opponent-process theory can explain complementary color phenomena that the trichromatic theory cannot. The combination of these two theories provides the best explanation of color vision. The trichromatic theory explains how the cones operate, and the opponent-process theory explains how cells in the visual pathways operate after the cones have done their initial processing.

The auditory system is a mechanical vibratory system with the hair cell receptors located within the basilar membrane in the cochlea. Incoming vibrations result in fluid displacement in the cochlea that causes movement of these hair cells. The nature of these hair cell movements creates the auditory message that gets carried by the auditory nerve, by way of the thalamus, to the primary auditory cortex for interpretation. Damage to these hair cells or the auditory nerve results in nerve deafness, which is very difficult to treat. Damage to one of the structures conducting the auditory information to the inner ear causes conduction deafness, which is easier to treat.

To explain how we perceive pitch, two theories are necessary. We can perceive a fairly large range of frequencies, 20 to 20,000 Hz. Place theory, which assumes that there are specific locations along the basilar membrane correlated with each frequency, explains how we hear high pitches (frequencies above 5,000 Hz). Frequency theory, which assumes that the firing rate of the hair cells mimics the incoming frequency information, explains how we hear low pitches (frequencies less than 500 Hz). Frequency theory (with the addition of the volley principle) and place theory both operate to give us better pitch perception for moderate pitches (frequencies from 500 to 5,000 Hz).

ConceptCheck | 2

Explain the difference between nearsightedness and farsightedness with respect to focusing problems.

Explain what opponent-process theory would predict that you would see if you stared for a minute at a flag with alternating yellow and white stripes and a rectangular patch of green in the center and then looked at a white sheet of paper.

Explain why longer sound waves lead to lower frequencies and shorter ones lead to higher frequencies.

Explain why neither the place theory nor the frequency theory by itself can explain human perception of pitch from 20 to 20,000 Hz.

How We Make Sense of What We See

So far we have learned that sensory structures such as the eyes and ears are designed to receive and begin processing various aspects of stimuli from our external environment. These structures transduce the raw data from the environment into neural impulses that the brain can understand. This initial information gathering and recoding by the sensory structures is usually referred to as

sensation, and the resulting interpretation by the brain, **perception.** These two processes, however, are not quite as distinct as their definitions make them sound. They work together in more of an interactive way. A consideration of bottom-up and top-down processing for visual perception should help you to understand this interaction. Following this discussion, we'll consider perceptual organization and constancy, two processes essential for bringing order to incoming visual information. Last, we'll discuss distance perception, how the brain manages to give us the third dimension of depth in our perception of the world.

Bottom-up Processing and Top-down Processing

Perception is the product of bottom-up and top-down processing. **Bottom-up processing** refers to the processing of incoming sensory input as it travels up from the sensory structures to the brain. It is called bottom-up because it is coming from the senses up to the brain. Bottom-up processing starts with the transduction of the incoming sensory signals. You can think of bottom-up processing as bringing the sensory input from the environment to the brain to be interpreted. However, the perceptual systems in the brain do not just randomly search through billions of possibilities to recognize the sensory input that is sent up. The search is greatly narrowed by **top-down processing**—the brain's use of knowledge, beliefs, and expectations to interpret the sensory information. It is referred to as top-down because it is coming from the top (the brain) back down to the lower sensory structures. To understand the difference between these two types of processing, think about listening to someone speak in a language that is foreign to you. You have bottom-up processing in that you hear the sounds. You cannot interpret this sensory input, however, because you do not have top-down processing (comprehension of the foreign language is not part of your knowledge base). Because top-down processing is so critical to perception, there are more top-down neural connections than bottom-up connections, about a 10:1 ratio (Hickok, 2014).

To further your understanding of these two types of processing, look at Figure 3.9 (page 128). Do you see a meaningful pattern? If not, then your top-down processing is letting you down. There is a cow staring directly at you. The head is on the left side of the image. To see it, your top-down processing has to organize various features in the figure successfully to fit your knowledge of what such a cow looks like. Once your brain does this, you won't have trouble seeing it the next time you look at this figure. You'll have the necessary top-down processing. In fact, using similar stimuli, Tovee, Rolls, and Ramachandran (1996) found that neurons in the temporal lobes permanently altered their connections once the meaningful pattern (such as the cow in our example) has been seen. In addition, using a jumble of black and white splotches from which you eventually see a dog, Ramachandran, Armel, and Foster (as reported in Ramachandran & Blakeslee, 1998, p. 297)

sensation The initial information gathering and recoding by the sensory structures.

perception The interpretation by the brain of sensory information.

bottom-up processing The processing of incoming sensory information as it travels up from the sensory structures to the brain.

top-down processing The brain's use of knowledge, beliefs, and expectations to interpret sensory information.

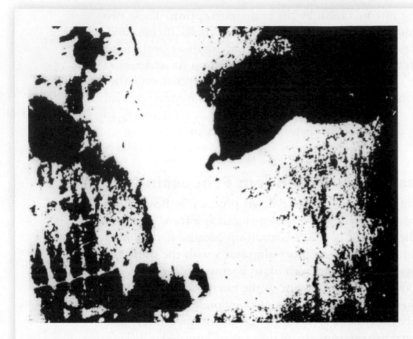

Figure 3.9 | Perceptual Organization and Top-down Processing | Do you see a meaningful object in this figure? There is one. It is a cow staring directly at you. Can you find it? To do so, your perceptual top-down processing mechanisms will have to organize some of the features of the figure to match your knowledge of what a cow looks like. If you are having trouble locating the cow, its head occupies most of the left half of the figure, and its body, the right half. Once you see it, you won't have any difficulty seeing it the next time. Your top-down processing mechanisms will know how to organize the features so you perceive it. (From *American Journal of Psychology.* Copyright 1951 by the Board of Trustees of the University of Illinois. Used with permission of the University of Illinois Press.)

found that if two completely different views of this dog are presented in rapid succession, naive subjects can see only incoherent motion of the black and white splotches; but if they have already seen the dog, it is seen to jump or turn in the appropriate manner, demonstrating the role of top-down object knowledge in motion perception. If you are still having trouble locating the cow, the dark splotches at the bottom of the figure, just to the left of center, represent her nose and mouth. Up higher are other dark areas that are her eyes and ears.

The subjective nature of perception is due to this top-down processing. Our past experiences, beliefs, and expectations bias our interpretations of sensory input. As the French novelist Anais Nin observed, "We do not see things as they are, we see things as we are" (Tammet, 2009). Perceptual set and the use of contextual information in perception are two good examples of this biasing effect of top-down processing. **Perceptual set** occurs when we interpret an ambiguous stimulus in terms of how our past experiences have "set" us to perceive it. Our top-down processing biases our interpretation so that we're not even aware of the ambiguity.

Let's consider how we perceive close plays in sporting events. Don't we usually see them in favor of "our" team? We are set by past experiences to see them in this biased way. This means that past experiences guide our perception with top-down processing. In other words, we see it "our way."

perceptual set The interpretation of ambiguous sensory information in terms of how our past experiences have set us to perceive it.

A, B, C, D, E, F
10, 11, 12, 13, 14

Figure 3.10 | A Context Effect on Perception |
The interpretations of the ambiguous characters
composing the second item in the first series and
the fourth item in the second series are determined
by the context created by the items on each side of
them. In the first series, these items are letters so
the interpretation of the ambiguous characters is a
letter, B. In the second series, the items are numbers so the interpretation is a number, 13. (*Sensation
and Perception* (6th ed.), by S. Coren, L. M. Ward, & J. T. Enns, 2004, New York:
Wiley. ISBN: 0471272558.)

Contextual effects are even stronger examples of top-down processing guiding perception. A **contextual effect** on perception occurs when we use the present context
of sensory input to determine its meaning. Figure 3.10 shows a simple example of
such contextual effects. Most people see the top line of characters as the alphabetic
sequence A, B, C, D, E, F, and the second line as the numeric sequence 10, 11, 12, 13,
14. But if we now look at the characters creating the B and the 13, they are the same
in each case. The context created by each line (alphabetic versus numeric) determined
our interpretation. If surrounded by letters, the characters were interpreted as the letter B; if surrounded by numbers, the characters were interpreted as the number 13.

Context is a crucial contributor to perception. Without contextual information, the brain may not be able to decide upon an interpretation. What about
the following characters: IV? They could be alphabetical (the letters I and V) or
numeric (the Roman numeral for 4). Inserted into a sentence with other words,
such as "Jim was in the hospital and hooked up to an IV," we would perceive
them as letters. However, if they were inserted into the sentence, "Edward IV was
the King of England in the fifteenth century," we would perceive their numerical
meaning. The addition of contextual information provides top-down processing
that allows the brain to resolve such ambiguities in normal perception.

Perceptual Organization and Perceptual Constancy

Perceptual organization and constancy are essential processes for bringing order
to the incoming sensory input. Let's consider perceptual organization first. To be
interpreted, the bits of incoming sensory data must be organized into meaningful
wholes—shapes and forms. Some German psychologists working in the early part of
the twentieth century developed many principles that explain how the brain automatically organizes visual input into meaningful holistic objects. Because the German
word gestalt translates as "organized whole," these psychologists became known
as Gestalt psychologists. To the Gestalt psychologists, these
organized wholes are more than just the sum of their parts. A
good example of this is stroboscopic movement, the perceptual
creation of motion from a rapidly presented series of slightly

contextual effect The use of the present context of sensory information to
determine its meaning.

figure-and-ground principle The Gestalt perceptual organizational principle that the brain organizes sensory information into a figure or figures (the center of attention) and ground (the less distinct background).

varying images. For example, we see smooth motion when watching a movie, but in actuality there are only still picture frames being shown rapidly in succession. The motion we perceive emerges from the parts, the still frames, but is not present in them. You have already experienced another example of the whole being greater than the sum of its parts in the last question in ConceptCheck 3, Chapter 2. The whole (a portrait of Rudolf II of Prague) is greater than the sum of its parts (fruits, flowers, and vegetables). To explain how we organize our visual input into holistic objects, Gestalt psychologists proposed many different organizational principles. We will consider two major ones—the figure-and-ground principle and the principle of closure.

Gestalt psychologists developed a basic rule for perceptual organization, the **figure-and-ground principle**—the brain organizes the sensory input into a figure or figures (the center of attention) and ground (the less distinct background). To get a better understanding of this principle, let us examine the image in Figure 3.11. This reversible figure-ground pattern was introduced by Danish Gestalt psychologist Edgar Rubin in 1915 (Rubin, 1921/2001). What is the figure and what is the ground? These keep changing. We see a vase as a white object on a colored background, but then we see two faces in silhouette facing each other on a white background. What you see is determined by which side of the wavy lines extending down either side of the image your brain focuses on to form the figure (Restak & Kim, 2010). If you concentrate laterally (outwardly), then you'll see the faces. If you concentrate medially (inwardly), then you'll see the vase. This is what is called border ownership (Rubin, 2001). When you perceive the faces, you see the blue region as owning the border (the wavy lines); but when you perceive the vase, you see the white region as owning the border. With each switch in perspective, the brain keeps switching its figure and ground organization for these sensory data. This is called a reversible pattern because the figure and ground reverse in the two possible interpretations. What is figure in one interpretation becomes the background in the other. Without any context, top-down processing cannot determine which interpretation is the correct one.

Figure 3.11 | An Example of Figure-Ground Ambiguity | Do you see a white vase or two blue facial silhouettes looking at each other? You can see both, but only one at a time. When you switch your perception from one to the other, your brain is switching how the input is organized with respect to figure and ground. When you see a vase, the vase is the object, but when you see the two faces, the vase becomes the background.

This is an example of a bistable perception—an unchanging visual stimulus that leads to repeated alternation between two different perceptions (Yantis, 2014).

John O'Brien/The New Yorker Collection/www.cartoonbank.com

The ambiguous vase–silhouettes illustration helps us to understand the figure-and-ground principle, but ambiguity can also be due to the possibility of more than one object on the same background. The features of the object may allow more than one interpretation. A classic example of such an ambiguity is given in Figure 3.12. Do you see an old woman or a young woman? The young woman is looking back over her right shoulder, and the old woman's chin is down on her chest. The young woman's ear is the left eye of the old woman. Actually, depending upon how you organize the features, you can see both, but not simultaneously. If you are able to see both, your top-down processing will keep switching your perception because there is no contextual information to determine which interpretation is correct.

W. E. Hill, 1915.

Figure 3.12 | An Example of an Organizational Perceptual Ambiguity | Do you see the head and shoulders of an old woman or a young woman? If you're having trouble seeing the old woman, she has a large nose, which is located below and to the left of the center of the figure. The old woman's large nose is the chin and jaw of the younger woman. Now can you see both of them? Because there is no contextual information to determine a correct interpretation, your perception will keep switching from one interpretation to the other.

Figure 3.13 | Two More Organizational Perceptual Ambiguities | On the left is a young/old woman ambiguity taken from a German postcard from 1888. The ambiguity on this postcard is like the one in Figure 3.12. Can you see both the young woman and the old woman? Their head positions are just like those in Figure 3.12. The old woman's big nose is the chin and jaw of the younger woman. On the right is a similar perceptual ambiguity that allows the perception of both a young man and an old man. If you're having difficulty seeing both men, the old man's big nose is the chin and jaw of the younger man just like in the ambiguous women's version. The two men, however, are facing to the right and not to the left like the two women. ((a) Science Source; (b) Drawn by Mr. George P. Marsden, Chief, Medical Arts Section, DRS, NIH)

This young/old woman organizational ambiguity is often credited to British cartoonist W. E. Hill who published it in a humor magazine in 1915, but it appears that Hill adapted it from an original concept that was popular throughout the world on postcards and trading cards in the nineteenth century. The earliest known depiction of the young/old woman ambiguity is on an anonymous German postcard from 1888 shown on the left in Figure 3.13 (Weisstein, 2009). Can you perceive both the young woman and the old woman? Having identified them in Hill's illustration should have facilitated their perception on this card. As in Hill's illustration, the old woman's large nose is the chin and lower jaw of the younger woman. Botwinick (1961) created the male version of this figure (shown on the right in Figure 3.13) and entitled it "Husband and Father-in-Law" because the title of Hill's female ambiguous figure was "Wife and Mother-in-Law." If you're having trouble perceiving the two men, the older man's big nose (like the older woman's big nose) is the chin and lower jaw of the younger man; but the two men are facing in the opposite direction of the two women in Hill's illustration.

Another important Gestalt perceptual organizational principle is **closure,** which refers to the tendency to complete (close) incomplete figures to form meaningful objects. You've already seen some examples of closure in Figures 3.9 and 3.10. Closure was used to perceive the cow in Figure 3.9 (page 128) and to perceive the ambiguous characters in Figure 3.10 (page 129) as the letter B in the alphabetic context. The French artist Paul Cézanne used the principle of closure in his paintings by leaving bare patches of canvas in them for the viewer to fill in the blanks (Lehrer, 2007; Sweeney, 2011). Significantly, he worked at about the same time as the Gestalt psychologists developed their principles of perceptual organization. In order to close a figure, we use top-down knowledge. Sometimes, however, the brain goes too far in using closure and creates figures where none exist. Such figures are called **subjective contours**—lines or shapes that are perceived to be present but do not really exist (Kanizsa, 1976). The white

closure The Gestalt perceptual organizational principle that the brain completes (closes) incomplete figures to form meaningful objects.

subjective contour A line or shape that is perceived to be present but does not really exist. The brain creates it during perception.

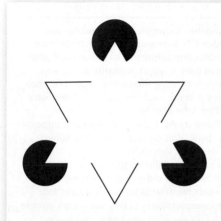

Figure 3.14 | An Example of a Subjective Contour | Does there appear to be a very bright triangle overlying three black circles and another triangle? This brighter-appearing triangle isn't really there. It is a subjective contour created by your brain in its perception of the three black circles with a chunk missing (the three Pac Man–like characters). To demonstrate that this overlying brighter triangle is truly not there, cover up everything in the display but the horizontal blank center. When you do this, you will not see any difference in level of brightness across the horizontal center of the display. If the whiter triangle were really there, you would see differences in brightness.

triangle that seems to be overlying three black circles and another triangle in Figure 3.14 is a subjective contour. Only three 45° angles and three black circles with a chunk missing are present. In perceiving these stimuli, the brain creates an additional object, the second triangle, by filling in the missing parts of the sides of this triangle; but this triangle doesn't really exist. The caption for Figure 3.14 explains how to demonstrate that the overlying triangle is really not there. Because 4-month-old infants also see such subjective contours (Ghim, 1990), it appears that our brains are hardwired to make sense of missing information by using top-down processing to fill in what should be there (Hood, 2009). The visual cortex also responds to the illusory contours as if they are real. Von der Heydt, Peterhans, and Baumgartner (1984) found that illusory contours evoked responses in cells in the visual cortex that responded as if the contours were real lines and edges.

Not only does the brain create subjective contours, but it also creates ones that are ambiguous. An example of an ambiguous subjective contour is the Necker cube in Figure 3.15 on page 134 (from Bradley, Dumais, & Petry, 1976). In perceiving a Necker cube, you have filled in the nonexistent lines that connect its corners. The cube seems to float in front of the page, with green circles behind it. All that is really there are green circles with white lines in them. Your brain constructs the cube's subjective edges and its three-dimensional shape. You can show that this is a subjective contour by placing your finger over a green circle. The lines emanating from that circle will vanish. You can also reverse the orientation of this phantom cube just as you can for a true Necker cube (another example of a bistable perception). Focus on the "x." It will move from the front edge of the cube to the back edge when the cube reverses orientation. This phantom cube not only illustrates an ambiguous subjective contour, but it also allows you to remove the subjective edges of the cube from your perception. Imagine that the green circles are holes and that you are looking at the cube through these holes. The cube is actually suspended behind the page. This perception

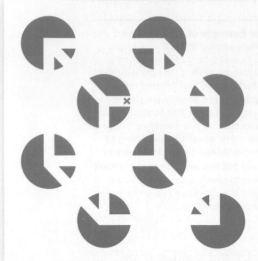

Figure 3.15 | Another Example of an Ambiguous Subjective Contour | This phantom Necker cube is an example of an ambiguous subjective contour. Instead of seeing green circles with white lines inside them, you see a cube, seemingly floating above the page. The lines between the circles that connect the corners of the cube are nonexistent. The cube also reverses orientation. Focus on the "x," and it will move from the front edge of the cube to the back. You can also make the subjective segments of the cube vanish by viewing the circles as holes in the page and imagining that you are looking through the holes to see the cube suspended below. The cube below also reverses orientation so there are four different possible interpretations of this seemingly simple stimulus. (Reprinted by permission from Macmillan Publishers Ltd: "Reply to Cavonius," by D. R. Bradley, S. T. Dumais, & H. M. Petry, 1976, *Nature, 261*, p. 78.)

may take a little longer to achieve, but be patient. Once you are able to perceive this interpretation, the illusory contour lines vanish, but the cube continues to reverse. Thus, there are four perceptions possible for this seemingly simple visual display, demonstrating that perception is a process of active construction. This display also demonstrates that the brain constructs our three-dimensional view of the world from the visual cues available in a visual stimulus, in this case a two-dimensional one (Hoffman, 1998). We will discuss how we perceive depth in the next section.

In addition to being able to organize and group sensory input to form meaningful objects, the brain must be able to maintain some type of constancy in its perception of the outside world, and it does. **Perceptual constancy** refers to the perceptual stability of the size, shape, brightness, and color for familiar objects seen at varying distances, different angles, and under different lighting conditions. These various types of constancy are referred to as size, shape, brightness, and color constancy, respectively. The retinal images for familiar objects change under different visual conditions such as different viewing angles or distances. For example, the size of a car doesn't shrink in our perception as it drives away. The size of its retinal image shrinks, but its size in our perception doesn't change. The brain adjusts our perceptions in accordance with what we have learned about the outside world. We know that the car's size doesn't change and realize that it is just farther away from us. Perceptual constancy must override this changing sensory input to maintain an object's normal size, shape, brightness, and color in our perception of the object. Perceptual constancy is a very adaptive aspect of visual perception. It brings order and consistency to our view of the world.

perceptual constancy The perceptual stability of the size, shape, brightness, and color for familiar objects seen at varying distances, different angles, and under different lighting conditions.

Using our understanding of how the brain achieves these constancies, however, we can create situations that fool the brain, creating an illusion. Consider brightness constancy (also called lightness constancy). The brightness of an object depends upon the amount of light the object reflects relative to its surroundings. Look at Figure 3.16a. Which checker square is brighter, Square A or Square B? Doesn't Square B appear brighter to you? It is not. The two squares are the same shade of gray. Edward H. Adelson at MIT created this illusion. What causes our illusory perception that the two squares are not the same brightness? Whereas there are other factors involved (e.g., how the brain uses shadow information because B is in the shadow and A is not), the primary one is that the two squares have different surrounding contexts. Square A appears darker because it is surrounded by lighter squares, and Square B appears lighter because it is surrounded by darker squares. The brain uses the surroundings of the two squares to determine their brightness and is led astray in this case. Look at Figure 3.16b. Now the surroundings of the two squares are the same so your brain judges their brightness to be the same and you perceive them as the same. Perceived brightness of an object depends upon its surrounding context. Remember that even knowing that the two tables in the Turning the Tables illusion given in Figure 3.1 (see page 101) were the same size, you could not make your brain perceive them as equal. The same holds here. Even knowing that the two squares in Figure 3.16a are the same, you cannot make your brain perceive them to be the same. If you are

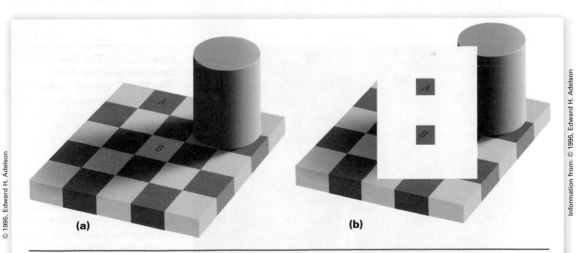

© 1995, Edward H. Adelson

Information from: © 1995, Edward H. Adelson

(a)

(b)

Figure 3.16 | Adelson's Checker Shadow Illusion | (a) Which checker square is brighter—Square A or Square B? It certainly appears that Square B is brighter. However, the two squares are the same shade of gray. Whereas there are other factors involved in this brightness illusion, an important one is that the two squares have different surrounding contexts. Square A appears darker because it is surrounded by lighter squares, and Square B appears lighter because it is surrounded by darker squares. The message: Perceived brightness is relative. (b) The two squares are now surrounded by the same context, allowing you to see that they are indeed the same shade of gray.

still not convinced that Squares A and B in Figure 3.16a are the same, then photocopy the page, cut the two squares out, and compare them. This will convince you.

Perceiving constancies also seems to have subjective components that can lead different people to see the same stimulus differently, but each person would still see it in a constant fashion. A good example is "The Dress" color debate (also known as "Dressgate") that went viral on the Internet in February 2015. A photo of the dress to be worn by a mother-in-law-to-be was posted online in an attempt to solve the disagreement between the future bride and groom about the color of the dress in the photo. The bride saw the dress as white and gold, and the groom as blue and black (the actual colors of the dress). Indeed, the public also seemed to be firmly entrenched into white-and-gold and blue-and-black camps with the vast majority of people not being able to switch their color interpretations. These two perceptions of the dress are given in Figure 3.17. Why the difference in color perception? Whereas there are many explanations that have been proposed for this difference and perceptual researchers are still in disagreement about the explanation, one of the most plausible proposals argues that it stems from individual differences in color constancy (Macknik & Martinez-Conde, 2015). To achieve color constancy, the brain has to determine what the illumination source is for an object. Thus, it is possible that the differing color perceptions of the dress stem from people differing in their interpretation of what the illumination source for the dress is. According to Macknik and Martinez-Conde, light in the natural world comes from either direct golden sunlight or from the blue sky so the cortical color

Figure 3.17 | The Two Color Interpretations of "The Dress" | These are the two color interpretations of the photo of "The Dress" that went viral on the Internet in early 2015. People became firmly entrenched in their perception of the dress as white and gold or blue and black. The dress was actually blue and black. As explained in the text, the two interpretations may stem from subjective assumptions made by the brain about the illumination source for the dress.

processing areas in the brain assume that most illumination has these colors. Thus, people looking at The Dress could assume that it is lit either by blue sky or golden sunlight. If the brain assumes it is blue sky, then it will subtract the blue from its perception of the dress, and the dress would appear white and gold. If it assumes illumination by sunlight, then it would subtract gold, and the dress would appear blue and black. It has also been proposed that the brains of people who stay up later (night owls) have more experience with artificial lighting which has more reddish light in it, so to achieve color constancy the brains of these people would subtract the red from their perception of the dress, which also results in seeing the dress as blue and black (Lafer-Sousa, Hermann, & Conway, 2015). In sum, to achieve color constancy different people make different assumptions about the light source that lead to different color perceptions of the dress. As Macknik and Martinez-Conde concluded, "The dress demonstrates that we can see the world in strikingly different ways depending on what our individual brain brings to the table" (p. 20).

Perceptual organization and perceptual constancy are essential processes in perception. Without them, our perceptions would be meaningless fragments in a constant state of flux. Constancy and organization bring meaning and order to them. However, neither of these aspects explains another crucial part of visual perceptual processing—how we perceive the third dimension: depth.

Depth Perception

Depth perception involves the judgment of the distance of objects from us. The brain uses many different sources of relevant information or cues to make judgments of distance. These cues may require both eyes (binocular cues) or only one eye (monocular cues).

The major binocular cue is retinal disparity. To understand retinal disparity, first consider that our two eyes are not in the same place on our face. Each eye (retina) takes in a slightly different view of the world. The difference (disparity) between these two views of each retina provides information about the distance of an object from us. It allows the brain to triangulate the distance from us. The **retinal disparity** cue refers to the fact that as the disparity (difference) between the two retinal images increases, the distance from us decreases.

To understand this, hold up your right hand in front of you and form a fist but extend your index finger upward. If you hold it stationary and focus on it, and now close one eye, and then rapidly open it and close the other one a few times, your finger will appear to move. If you now move the finger closer to you and repeat the rapid closing and opening of the eyes one at a time, again, the finger appears to move, but now much more because the retinal views of the finger are more disparate. When right in front of your eyes, you see maximal movement because the disparity between the two retinal images is at its maximum.

There are several monocular cues, but we will discuss only a couple of them so that you have some understanding

depth perception Our ability to perceive the distance of objects from us.

retinal disparity A binocular depth cue referring to the fact that as the disparity (difference) between the two retinal images of an object increases, the distance of the object from us decreases.

I have no depth perception. Is there a cop standing on the corner, or do you have a tiny person in your hair?

Dan Piraro, reprinted with permission of King Features Syndicate

of how such cues work. **Linear perspective** (sometimes called perspective convergence) refers to the fact that as parallel lines recede away from us, they appear to converge—the greater the distance, the more they converge. For example, think about looking down a set of railroad tracks or a highway. The tracks and the two sides of the road appear to converge as they recede away from us. Because convergence is involved, this cue is sometimes referred to as perspective convergence. Another monocular cue that is easy to understand is **interposition**—if one object partially blocks our view of another, we perceive it as closer. Near objects partially overlap farther ones.

Monocular cues, binocular cues, and various distance-judging principles the brain uses are normally valid distance indicators. However, sometimes these cues and principle lead the brain to create misperceptions. We refer to such misperceptions as illusions—misperceptions of reality. Two illusions are illustrated in Figure 3.18. The first (a) is called the Ponzo illusion because it was first demonstrated by the Italian psychologist Mario Ponzo in 1913. The two horizontal bars are identical in size, but the top one appears larger. The other illusion (b) is the Terror Subterra illusion (Shepard, 1990). The pursuing monster (the higher one) looks larger than the pursued monster, but the two monsters are identical in size. In addition to this size illusion, the identical faces of the two monsters are sometimes misperceived as expressing different emotions, such as rage in the pursuer and fear in the pursued monster. How are distance cues involved in these misperceptions of size in these two illusions?

To understand how distance cues are involved in these illusions, we must first consider how the brain relates the retinal image size of an object to the object's distance from us. As an object gets farther away from us, its size on the retina decreases. This is simple geometry, and the brain uses this geometric principle in creating our perception of the object. Now consider the situation in which two objects have equal retinal image sizes, but distance cues indicate to the brain that one of the objects is farther away. What would the brain conclude from this information? Using the principle relating retinal image size to distance, it would conclude that the object farther away must be larger. This is the only way that its retinal image size could be equal to that of the object closer to us. Thus, the brain enlarges the size of the more

linear perspective A monocular depth cue referring to the fact that as parallel lines recede away from us, they appear to converge—the greater the distance, the more they seem to converge. Sometimes referred to as perspective convergence.

interposition A monocular depth cue referring to the fact that if one object partially blocks our view of another, we perceive it as closer to us.

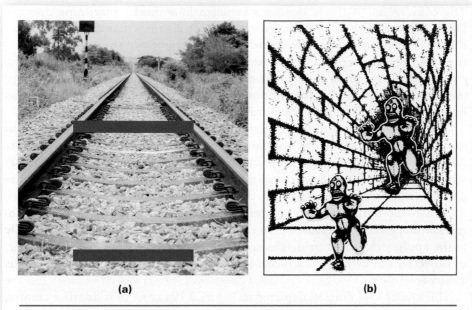

(a)   **(b)**

Figure 3.18 | The Ponzo and Terror Subterra Illusions | (a) The two red bars in the
Ponzo illusion are identical in size. However, the top bar appears to be larger. (b) The
two monsters in the Terror Subterra illusion are identical in size, but the pursuing monster (the top one) appears to be larger. To convince yourself that the two bars and the
two monsters are identical, trace one of the bars (monsters) on a thin sheet of paper
and then slide the tracing over the other bar (monster). Both illusions seem to be
caused by the brain's misinterpretation of the relative distance from us of the two bars
in (a) and the two monsters in (b). ((a) Sorapop Udomsri/Shutterstock; (b) *Mind Sights: Original Visual Illusions,
Ambiguities, and Other Anomalies,* by R. N. Shepard, 1990, New York: W.H. Freeman/Henry Holt.)

distant object in our perception of the objects. However, if the cues provided incorrect distance information and the objects were really equidistant from us, then we
would see a misperception, an illusion. The brain incorrectly enlarged the object that
it had mistakenly judged to be farther away. This is comparable to something we
have experienced in working math problems: plug an incorrect value into an equation and get the problem wrong. This is essentially what the brain is doing when
it uses incorrect information about distance, leading to a mistake in perception.
It is important to realize that our brain's computing of the retinal image size and
distance from us of objects is done at the unconscious level of processing. We are
privy only at a conscious perceptual level to the product of our brain's calculations.

Now let's apply this explanation to our sample illusions. Think about
the Ponzo illusion shown in Figure 3.18a. If this illusion is due to the
brain's using incorrect distance information about the two horizontal bars,
which cue that we described is responsible? That's right—linear perspective.

The convergence of the railroad tracks normally indicates increasing distance. Given this cue information, the brain incorrectly assumes that the top bar is farther away. Because the two horizontal bars are the same size and truly equidistant from us, they are the same size on our retinas. Because their retinal images are of equal size but the brain thinks that the bars are at varying distances from us, it incorrectly distorts the top bar (the one assumed to be farther away) to be larger in our perception, or, should I say, misperception.

The Terror Subterra illusion shown in Figure 3.18b can be explained in the same way. Monocular depth cues, mainly linear perspective, lead the brain to judge the pursuing monster to be farther away. Given that the retinal image sizes of the two monsters are equal because the two monsters are identical and equidistant from us and that the pursuing monster is incorrectly judged to be farther away, the brain enlarges the pursuing monster in our conscious perception, resulting in the illusion. As in the Ponzo illusion, the brain applies the valid principle relating retinal image size to the distance of objects from us, but uses incorrect distance information and thus creates a misperception.

The Müller-Lyer illusion depicted in Figure 3.19 (a and b) is another example of an illusion created by the brain misapplying the geometry relating retinal image size to distance from us (Gregory, 1968). As in the other two illusions, the brain mistakenly thinks that the line on the right with arrow feather endings is farther away than the line on the left with arrowhead endings. Why? In this case, the brain is using a relationship between distance and different types of corners that it has learned from its past perceptual experience. The line with arrow feather endings has the appearance of a corner that is receding away from us (like the corners where two walls meet in a room), while the line with arrowhead endings has the appearance of a corner that is jutting out toward us (like the corners where two sides of a building meet). These two types of corners are illustrated in Figure 3.19 (c and d). Thus, based on its past experience with such corners, the brain believes that the line with arrow feather endings is farther away.

However, in reality, the line with the arrow feather endings is not farther away. The two vertical lines are identical in length and equidistant from us; therefore, their two retinal images are identical. Given the identical retinal images and the incorrect judgment about relative distance, the brain incorrectly enlarges the line with arrow feather endings so that we perceive it as being longer. In support of this explanation, cross-cultural researchers have found that people who live in physical environments without such distance-indicating corners are far less susceptible to seeing the illusion (Segall, Campbell, & Herskovits, 1963, 1966; Stewart, 1973).

The Turning the Tables illusion in Figure 3.1 also arises because our brain gives us a three-dimensional interpretation of a two-dimensional drawing (Shepard, 1990). Perspective cues indicate that the long side of the table on the left goes back in depth whereas the long side of the table on the right is more nearly at right angles to our line of sight. Thus, if the table

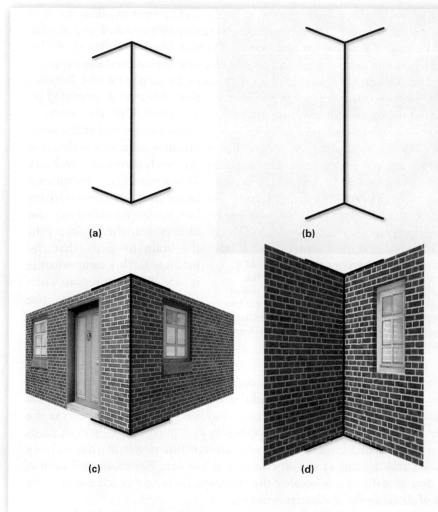

(a)

(b)

(c)

(d)

Figure 3.19 | The Müller-Lyer Illusion | (a and b) The two vertical line segments are equal in length. However, the one with the arrow feather endings on the right appears longer than the one with the arrowhead endings on the left. (c and d) Like the illusions in Figure 3.18, this illusion is created by the brain misapplying the geometry relating the retinal image size of objects and their distance from us. Based on its experiences with receding and projecting corners as illustrated here, our brain mistakenly thinks that the line with arrow feather endings is a receding corner and thus farther from us than the line with arrowhead endings, which our brain thinks is a projecting corner. Because the retinal images of the two lines are identical, the brain incorrectly lengthens the arrow feather line in our conscious perception. (Data from *The Intelligent Eye*, by R. L. Gregory, 1970, Orion Publishing Group Ltd., p. 80.)

on the left goes back in depth, the brain will think that its retinal image must be foreshortened (appear shorter than it really is) because this is what happens in true three-dimensional viewing. The fact that the retinal images of the two tabletops, however, are identical in length thus implies that the real length of the table on the left must be greater than the real length of the table on the right (and vice versa for the short sides of the two tables given their depth interpretations by the brain). Because these inferences about orientation, depth, and length are made automatically by the brain, we remain powerless to eliminate the illusion even though we know that the tabletops are identical. The drawing of the tables automatically triggers the brain to make a three-dimensional interpretation, and we cannot choose to see the drawing as what it is, patterns of lines on a flat piece of paper.

Paul Souders/The Image Bank/Getty Images

The Moon Illusion | The moon on the horizon appears much larger than it does when it is overhead, higher up in the sky, but this is an illusion. The moon is the same size and remains the same distance from us regardless of where it is in the sky. Objects near the horizon lead the brain to think that the horizon moon is farther away than when it is overhead, so the brain mistakenly enlarges its size in our perception because the retinal images of the horizon and overhead moons are the same size.

The moon illusion can also be explained in a similar way (Restle, 1970). The illusion is that the moon appears to be larger on the horizon than when it is overhead at its zenith. But the moon is the same size and at the same distance from us whether it is on the horizon or overhead. This means that the moon's larger size on the horizon has to be an illusion. The objects near the horizon lead the brain to think that the moon is farther away when it is near the horizon than when it is overhead. Because the retinal images of the moon at these two locations are the same and the brain mistakenly thinks that the horizon moon is farther away, it distorts the moon's size to appear much larger in our perception than when it is overhead, and this increase in apparent size makes it appear nearer (Gregory, 2009). It really isn't, and it is easy to see that this is the case. To make the moon on the horizon shrink, we can roll up a sheet of cardboard into a viewer and look at the moon through this viewer so that we only see the moon and not any of the objects on the horizon. The moon will appear to shrink dramatically in size because the brain will no longer be led astray in its judgment of distance for the horizon moon.

Linear perspective (parallel lines converging as they recede away from us) plays a major role in many illusions, but what would the brain do if it were led to believe that parallel lines weren't converging as they receded away from us? Look at Figure 3.20, the leaning tower illusion (Kingdom, Yoonessi, & Gheorghiu, 2007). The same exact photo of the Leaning Tower of Pisa is shown in both panels. Yet the tower on the right appears to be leaning more. Why? Our visual system treats the two images as if they are part of a single scene, rather than as two separate images of the same tower. Normally, if two adjacent towers rise at the same angle, they appear to converge as the tops of the towers recede from view; but because these are identical photos, the projections of the towers on the retina are parallel and do not converge in the distance (increasing height in this case). Thus, the brain decides that they are diverging. It employs its rule that lines receding away from us must diverge if their projections are parallel. Even knowing that these are identical photographs, you will not be able to

Fred Kingdom

Figure 3.20 | The Leaning Tower Illusion | These are duplicate pictures of the Leaning Tower of Pisa, but the one on the right seems to be leaning more. It isn't, but you cannot override your brain's interpretation to see these pictures as the same. To convince yourself that they are identical, photocopy the figure and then cut out one of the panels and compare it to the other panel.

override your brain's misinterpretation and see them as such. They will remain the "Twin Towers of Pisa," with one tower leaning more than the other.

In creating the visual illusions that we have discussed, the brain is using valid principles, but faulty information about such factors as relative distance or perspective. The overall result (our perception) is incorrect. In summary, the distance cues and principles the brain uses to give us an accurate view of the external world work almost all of the time, but these same cues and principles sometimes cause misperceptions.

Section Summary

In this section, we looked at visual perception in more detail. Bottom-up and top-down processing are both necessary for smooth and efficient perception. While top-down processing is adaptive, as illustrated by perceptual constancy, it is also responsible for the subjective nature of perception. Perceptual bias and contextual perceptual effects are good examples of how our past experiences, beliefs, and expectations guide our interpretation of the world.

Perceptual organization and perceptual constancy are essential processes for giving order to incoming sensory input. Gestalt psychologists proposed many principles that guide the organization of sensory input into meaningful holistic objects, such as the figure-and-ground and closure principles. In addition to organizing the sensory input into meaningful objects, the brain must maintain constancy in its perception of the world. To achieve perceptual constancy, the brain uses top-down processing to change sensory input to maintain an object's normal size, shape, brightness, and color in our perception of the object.

Depth perception (the judgment of the distance of objects from us) is a crucial part of visual perception. To judge depth, the brain uses information from binocular cues, such as retinal disparity, and monocular cues, such as linear perspective and interposition. The brain's perception of object size is related to its distance from us. As an object gets farther away from us, its size on our retina decreases. However, sometimes the brain applies this geometric principle relating retinal image size to distance and creates a misperception (an illusion). The Ponzo, Terror Subterra, Müller-Lyer, Turning the Tables, and moon illusions are good examples of such misapplication. In each case, the brain incorrectly judges that the two objects involved in the illusion, which have equal retinal image sizes, are at varying distances, and so it mistakenly makes the object judged to be farther away larger in our perception.

ConceptCheck | 3

Explain why perceptual processing requires both bottom-up and top-down processing.

Explain how the top-down processing involved in context effects on perception is similar to that involved in using the Gestalt organizational principle of closure.

Explain why seeing one of your professors in a local grocery store makes it more difficult to recognize her.

Explain why the brain's application of the geometric relationship between retinal image size of an object and its distance from us leads the brain to create the Ponzo, Müller-Lyer, and moon illusions.

Study Guide

Chapter Key Terms

You should know the definitions of the following key terms from the chapter. They are listed in the order in which they appear in the chapter. For those you do not know, return to the relevant section of the chapter to learn them. When you think that you know all of the terms, complete the matching exercise based on these terms.

absolute threshold	rods	volley principle
signal detection theory	cones	sensation
difference threshold	fovea	perception
Weber's law	dark adaptation	bottom-up processing
Stevens's power law	trichromatic theory	top-down processing
sensory adaptation	additive mixtures	perceptual set
wavelength	subtractive mixtures	contextual effect
amplitude	complementary colors	figure-and-ground principle
frequency	opponent-process theory	closure
transduction	cochlea	subjective contour
accommodation	hair cells	perceptual constancy
nearsightedness	nerve deafness	depth perception
farsightedness	conduction deafness	retinal disparity
retina	place theory	linear perspective
blindsight	frequency theory	interposition

Key Terms Exercise

Identify the correct term for each of the following definitions. The answers to this exercise follow the answers to the ConceptChecks at the end of the chapter.

1. The focusing of light waves from objects of different distances directly on the retina.

2. A visual problem in which the light waves from nearby objects are focused behind the retina, blurring the images of these objects.

3. A theory of color vision that assumes that there are three types of cones, each activated only by wavelength ranges of light corresponding roughly to blue, green, and red.

4. The brain's use of knowledge, beliefs, and expectations to interpret sensory information.

5. The Gestalt perceptual organizational principle that the brain completes incomplete figures to form meaningful objects.

6. Our sensitivity to unchanging and repetitious stimuli disappears over time.

7. Hearing loss created by damage to one of the structures in the ear responsible for carrying the auditory information to the inner ear.

   _____

8. The number of times a waveform cycles in 1 second.

   _____

9. The perceived magnitude of a stimulus is equal to its actual physical intensity raised to a constant power, and this constant power is different for each type of sensory judgment.

   _____

10. The minimum difference between two sensory stimuli detected 50% of the time.

    _____

11. Wavelengths of light that when added together produce white.

    _____

12. A theory of pitch perception which assumes that the frequency of the sound wave is mimicked by the firing rate of the entire basilar membrane.

    _____

13. A line or shape that is perceived to be present but does not really exist. The brain creates it during perception.

    _____

14. The perceptual stability of the size, shape, brightness, and color for familiar objects seen at varying distances, different angles, and under different lighting conditions.

    _____

15. The process by which the rods and cones, through internal chemical changes, become more and more sensitive to light in dim light conditions.

    _____

Practice Test Questions

The following are practice multiple-choice test questions on some of the chapter content. The answers are given after the Key Terms Exercise answers at the end of the chapter. If you guessed on a question or incorrectly answered a question, restudy the relevant section of the chapter.

1. The amount of energy in a sensory stimulus detected 50% of the time is called the _____.
   a. difference threshold
   b. absolute threshold
   c. false alarm rate
   d. miss rate

2. If a person is using a very strict criterion for a signal detection task, the false alarm rate will be _____, and the miss rate will be _____.
   a. high; high
   b. high; low
   c. low; high
   d. low; low

3. According to Weber's law, if the difference threshold constant = 1/50, then the difference threshold for a standard stimulus of 100 units would be _____.
   a. 1
   b. 2
   c. 5
   d. 10

4. Red wavelengths of light are _____, and violet wavelengths of light are _____.
   a. long; long
   b. long; short
   c. short; long
   d. short; short

5. The rods in the retina are responsible for _____ vision, and the cones are responsible for _____ vision.
   a. color; dim light
   b. bright light; dim light
   c. color; bright light
   d. dim light; color

6. According to the opponent-process theory of color vision, if you stared at a blue circle for a while and then looked at a white surface, you would see a circular _____ afterimage.
   a. blue
   b. green
   c. yellow
   d. black

7. Transduction of sound waves into neural impulses is performed by the _____.
   a. eardrum
   b. oval window
   c. malleus, incus, and stapes
   d. hair cells in the basilar membrane

8. The best explanation for how we perceive low pitches (< 500 Hz) is the _____ theory, and the best explanation for how we perceive high pitches (> 5,000 Hz) is the _____ theory.
   a. place; place
   b. place; frequency
   c. frequency; place
   d. frequency; frequency

9. Perceptual set is a good example of _____.
   a. the figure-ground principle
   b. perceptual constancy
   c. bottom-up processing
   d. top-down processing

10. Which of the following is a binocular depth cue?
   a. linear perspective
   b. interposition
   c. retinal disparity
   d. all of the above

11. What is the purpose of transduction?
   a. increasing the intensity of a stimulus so it is easier for the brain to detect
   b. translating physical energy into neural signals that the brain can understand
   c. determining whether or not a stimulus is detectable
   d. integrating visual signals with auditory signals

12. Damage to the hair cells in the cochlea causes _____ deafness, and _____ occurs when light waves from distant objects come into focus in front of the retina.
   a. nerve; nearsightedness
   b. conduction; nearsightedness
   c. nerve; farsightedness
   d. conduction; farsightedness

13. Even though the image of your dog on your retina changes as your dog runs to fetch a stick, you do not perceive your dog as getting smaller. Which process of perception explains this phenomenon?
   a. perceptual set
   b. perceptual constancy
   c. dark adaptation
   d. accommodation

14. Perceiving either a vase or two facial silhouettes looking at each other was used to illustrate the Gestalt principle of _____; perceiving two ambiguous characters numerically as 13 or alphabetically as the letter B was used to illustrate _____.
   a. closure; subjective contours
   b. figure and ground; contextual effects
   c. closure; contextual effects
   d. figure and ground; subjective contours

15. Although Henry's watchband was bothering him when he first put it on, a short while later he did not even notice he was wearing it. This illustrates _____.
   a. accommodation
   b. sensory adaptation
   c. subliminal perception
   d. perceptual constancy

Chapter ConceptCheck Answers
ConceptCheck | 1

- The two types of threshold were given statistical definitions because the experimental data did not permit an absolute definition. There was no none-to-all point of change in the results that were observed when psychophysical researchers attempted to measure the absolute and difference thresholds.

- In switching from a very lax to a very strict decision criterion, a person's false alarm rate would go down and the miss rate would go up. These changes would be due to the person's changing from saying "yes" most of the time to saying "no" most of the time.

- A really large constant fraction in Weber's law would indicate that difference judgments for that type of sensory judgment are not very good; a larger proportion of the standard stimulus is necessary for a difference to be perceived.

- Stevens's power law tells us that our perceptions of the magnitudes of the physical intensities of stimuli are seldom equivalent to the actual physical intensities. Our perceived magnitude of a stimulus is usually equal to the actual physical intensity raised to some power. Hence, our perception of a physical intensity is a transformation of it created within us. Sometimes the perceived magnitude is greater than the actual physical intensity, and sometimes it is less.

ConceptCheck | 2

- In nearsightedness, we have difficulty viewing distant objects because their images come into focus in front of the retina; in farsightedness, we have difficulty viewing near objects because their images come into focus behind the retina. The focusing problems could be due to defects in the lens or the shape of the eyeball.

- After staring at the flag with alternating yellow and white stripes and a block of green in the middle, the yellow, white, and green parts of the three opponent-process systems would be fatigued and thus unable to oppose the blue, black, and red parts of these systems when you stared at the white sheet of paper. Thus, instead of seeing white, you would see an afterimage of a flag with alternating blue and black stripes and a block of red in the middle. Once the opposing parts of the three systems recovered, the flag afterimage would disappear, and you would see the white surface.

- Longer wavelengths lead to lower frequencies because such wavelengths can only cycle a small number of times per second. Similarly, shorter wavelengths lead to higher frequencies because they can cycle more times per second.

- Neither theory by itself can explain how we hear the entire range of pitches, 20 to 20,000 Hz, because each theory is unable to explain pitch perception for a particular part of this range. Place theory cannot explain how we perceive low pitches ($<$ 500 Hz) because there are no places of maximal firing along the basilar membrane for these frequencies. The firing rate of the entire membrane mimics these frequencies. Similarly, frequency theory cannot explain how we perceive high pitches, those greater than 5,000 Hz, because there is a physiological limit on the firing rate for cells. Even if the volley principle is employed, this limit is about 5,000 times per second. This means that the hair cells could not generate firing rates to match the high frequencies.

ConceptCheck | 3

- Perceptual processing requires both types of processing because without bottom-up processing you would have nothing to perceive and without top-down processing you would have no knowledge to use to interpret the bottom-up input.

- The similarity is that, in both cases, the brain uses top-down processing to complete the perception. In context effects, the brain uses the present context to complete the perception by determining what would be meaningful in that particular context. In closure, the brain uses the incomplete part of an object to determine what the remaining part should be in order for it to be a meaningful object.

- It is more difficult to recognize your professor because she is in a very different context. Your brain is thrown for a "perceptual loop" because she doesn't fit in this context (outside the classroom). This is why it takes your brain longer to find the relevant top-down knowledge.

- The retinal image sizes of the two objects in each case are equal because the two objects are actually equal in size and are equidistant from us. Available distance cues, however, lead the brain to believe mistakenly that one of the two objects in each case is farther away. Therefore, the brain enlarges the size of the object that it thinks is more distant because this would have to be the case in order for the geometric relationship between retinal image size and distance from us to hold. For example, in the Ponzo illusion, the linear perspective distance cue leads the brain to think that the top horizontal bar is farther away. Because the two horizontal bars have identical retinal image sizes, the brain then uses the geometric relationship and mistakenly creates an illusion by making the top bar larger in our perception.

Answers to Key Terms Exercise

1. accommodation
2. farsightedness
3. trichromatic theory
4. top-down processing
5. closure
6. sensory adaptation
7. conduction deafness
8. frequency
9. Stevens's power law
10. difference threshold
11. complementary colors
12. frequency theory
13. subjective contour
14. perceptual constancy
15. dark adaptation

Answers to Practice Test Questions

1. b; absolute threshold
2. c; low; high
3. b; 2
4. b; long; short
5. d; dim light; color
6. c; yellow
7. d; hair cells in the basilar membrane
8. c; frequency; place
9. d; top-down processing
10. c; retinal disparity
11. b; translating physical energy into neural signals that the brain can understand
12. a; nerve; nearsightedness
13. b; perceptual constancy
14. b; figure and ground; contextual effects
15. b; sensory adaptation

4 | Learning

Our ability to learn seems boundless. We continue to learn new things every day, and we continually use the products of our past learning. Our learning affects how we perceive, remember, think, and behave. In this chapter, we will focus on what psychologists have learned about how we learn.

In general, two types of psychologists—behavioral psychologists and cognitive psychologists—have studied learning, and they have gone about their research in very different ways. Behavioral psychologists have focused on the learning of associations through classical conditioning and operant conditioning. Classical conditioning involves learning associations between events in our environment, such as that the smell of the turkey roasting in the oven signals that a delicious meal will follow. Operant conditioning focuses on learning associations between our behavior and its environmental consequences, such as that additional studying usually leads to better grades. Cognitive psychologists studying learning are interested in the more complex type of learning involved in human memory—how we encode information into our memory system, store it over time, and later retrieve it for use. A cognitive psychologist would be interested in how you learn the information in this textbook and what type of study technique would lead to the best memory for this information.

In this chapter, we will first focus on what behavioral psychologists have discovered about learning associations through classical conditioning and operant conditioning. Then we will consider some of the biological constraints upon such learning and also begin a discussion of the cognitive approach to learning (covered in detail in the next chapter, on how we remember).

Learning Through Classical Conditioning

Does the name "Pavlov" ring a bell? If you understand this really bad joke, then you are already somewhat familiar with **classical conditioning**—learning that one stimulus signals the arrival of another stimulus. A stimulus (plural: stimuli) is any sight, sound, smell, taste, or body sensation that a human or animal can perceive. You know from Chapter 1 that Pavlov's dogs salivated to the sound of a tone (the first stimulus) because they learned to expect food in their mouth (the second stimulus) after hearing the tone. This may not sound like the research of a Nobel Prize-winning scientist, but it was important work that had a great impact on our understanding of how we learn. Classical conditioning is sometimes referred to as Pavlovian conditioning because Pavlov was the first researcher to study this type of learning systematically. So, let's take a closer look at Pavlov's research to gain an understanding of classical conditioning and its importance in learning.

The Elements and Procedures of Classical Conditioning

Ivan Pavlov was a Russian physiologist who won a Nobel Prize in 1904 for his earlier work on the physiology of digestion. Pavlov studied the digestive processes of dogs. During these

classical conditioning Acquiring a new response (the conditioned response) to a previously neutral stimulus (the conditioned stimulus) that reliably signals the arrival of an unconditioned stimulus.

This is a photograph of Pavlov's experimental laboratory. Look at the dog's left cheek. Pavlov devised a surgical insert that diverted the dog's saliva to exit its cheek so the saliva could be measured accurately.

experiments, the dogs were strapped into harnesses and had tubes inserted in their cheeks to measure salivation, the initial step in the digestive process. Pavlov had cleverly found a way to divert the saliva so that it was excreted through the dogs' cheeks. As part of this research, the dogs were given food (meat powder), and then the amount of saliva excreted was measured. During this research, Pavlov made an accidental discovery. He noticed that the dogs started to salivate before the meat powder was even put in their mouths. For example, the dogs salivated when they heard the footsteps of his assistants bringing the meat powder. Pavlov wanted to know why, and this became the focus of his research for the remainder of his career. So what exactly did he do?

Unconditioned stimulus (UCS) and unconditioned response (UCR). First, let's consider why the dogs salivated when the meat powder was put in their mouths. This is a reflexive response—when food is put in your mouth, you salivate. Dogs do it, I do it, you do it. This is called a **reflex**—a stimulus-response pair (food in the mouth and salivation) in which the stimulus automatically elicits the response. The reflexive stimulus (food in the mouth) that elicits the automatic response (salivation) is referred to as the **unconditioned stimulus (UCS)**, and the response automatically elicited by the UCS is referred to as the **unconditioned response (UCR)**. The key word is "unconditioned." This means that no learning was necessary for this stimulus (the food, in our example) to elicit the response (salivation, in our example). It's a naturally occurring reflex. Now let's examine how such reflexes are used to achieve conditioning.

Conditioned stimulus (CS) and conditioned response (CR). Pavlov began with a neutral stimulus, a stimulus that does not naturally elicit the to-be-conditioned response. Pavlov used various neutral stimuli, such as a tone generated by a tuning fork, a light, and a touch on the leg, in his conditioning research on dogs (Pavlov, 1927/1960). Before conditioning, his dogs did not automatically salivate to these stimuli. They had to learn (be conditioned) to do this. To achieve such conditioning, the neutral stimulus (for example, a tone) is presented just before the UCS (the food). What does "just before" mean? This can mean a few seconds, but the optimal time interval between the onsets of the two stimuli is usually very brief, only a half-second to a full second (Mazur, 1998). In addition, the two stimuli usually need to be paired together for several trials. Nevertheless, there are

reflex A stimulus-response pair in which the stimulus (the unconditioned stimulus) automatically elicits the response (the unconditioned response).

unconditioned stimulus (UCS) The stimulus in a reflex that automatically elicits an unconditioned response.

unconditioned response (UCR) The response in a reflex that is automatically elicited by the unconditioned stimulus.

some exceptions in which classical conditioning can be obtained without a close temporal pairing of the CS and UCS and in only a small number of trials, sometimes only one. The primary exception is taste aversion, which we will discuss in the last section of this chapter when we discuss biological constraints on learning.

Once the conditioning occurs (signaled in Pavlov's research by the dog salivating to the sound of the tone before the meat powder is put into its mouth), the neutral stimulus is referred to as the **conditioned stimulus (CS)**. This previously neutral stimulus (the tone) comes to elicit a new response (salivating) after repeated pairings with the unconditioned stimulus (meat powder in the dog's mouth). The learned response (salivating) to the conditioned stimulus (the tone) is called the **conditioned response (CR)**. The conditioned response (salivating) is a preparatory response for the impending UCS (meat powder in the dog's mouth).

To firm up your understanding of the elements of classical conditioning, let's consider another example, conditioning of the eyeblink response, which is often used in classical conditioning research with humans. A neutral stimulus, such as a tone, is presented just before a mild puff of air to a person's eye (the UCS). Initially, an eyeblink (the UCR) occurs reflexively in response to the air puff (the UCS), but with repeated pairings of the tone followed shortly thereafter by the air puff, the previously neutral stimulus (the tone) becomes the conditioned stimulus (the CS) and now elicits a new response, an eyeblink (the CR), in advance of the air puff. In this case, the eyeblink serves as an adaptive, defensive response to the air puff. Instead of an air puff to a person's eye as the UCS, Clark Hull, a major behavioral psychologist in the first half of the twentieth century, used a slap to the face as the UCS and his graduate students at Yale University as his subjects (Gluck, Mercado, & Myers, 2011). Thus, Hull trained his students to blink in anticipation of a slap to the face. For obvious ethical reasons, researchers have not followed in Hull's footsteps and do not use the face slap as the UCS in human classical conditioning.

Delayed and trace conditioning. The timing of the relationship of the CS and UCS is a critical factor in classical conditioning. The conditioned stimulus (the tone) is presented just before the UCS (the meat powder in Pavlov's experiments) because the conditioning involves learning that this stimulus is a reliable predictor for the arrival of the UCS (Rescorla, 1988). Thus, presenting the UCS before the CS (called backward conditioning) or presenting the UCS and

conditioned stimulus (CS) The stimulus that comes to elicit a new response (the conditioned response) in classical conditioning.

conditioned response (CR) The response that is elicited by the conditioned stimulus in classical conditioning.

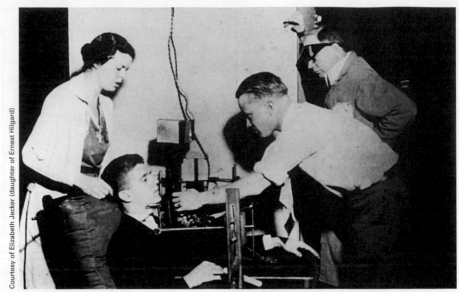

Courtesy of Elizabeth Jecker (daughter of Ernest Hilgard)

Clark Hull (standing with visor) supervising a classical conditioning experiment at Yale University in the 1920s. The seated graduate student is being conditioned to blink at the sound of a tone in anticipation of a slap to the face. Given that there is a brief interval between the tone and the slap to the face, this is an example of trace conditioning. Actually this particular graduate student, Ernest Hilgard, went on to become one of the most famous psychologists of the twentieth century.

CS at the same time (called simultaneous conditioning) typically leads to no conditioning or poor conditioning because the CS in these two cases would not be a good predictor of the UCS (Powell, Symbaluk, & MacDonald, 2002). The CS has to clearly predict the UCS by being presented first or conditioning usually will not occur. There are two ways to present the CS first: delayed and trace conditioning.

In **delayed conditioning**, the CS remains on until after the UCS is presented, so that the two stimuli occur at the same time. The tone would be turned on and not turned off until after the meat powder was placed in the dog's mouth. This procedure is called "delayed" because turning off (taking away) the CS is delayed until after the UCS starts. In **trace conditioning**, there is a period of time between turning off the CS and the onset of the UCS (called the trace interval), when neither stimulus is present. In Pavlov's case, this would mean turning the tone on and then off, waiting a brief period of time, and then putting the meat powder in the dog's mouth. For the association between stimuli to be learned, the animal or human (dog in Pavlov's case) must maintain a "memory trace" of the CS (the tone) to pair with the later-occurring UCS (the meat powder). This is why it is called trace conditioning.

Delayed conditioning is the most effective procedure for classical conditioning, but trace conditioning can be almost

delayed conditioning A classical conditioning procedure in which the conditioned stimulus precedes the unconditioned stimulus and remains present until after the unconditioned stimulus is presented so that the two stimuli occur together.

trace conditioning A classical conditioning procedure in which the conditioned stimulus precedes the unconditioned stimulus but is removed before the unconditioned stimulus is presented so that the two stimuli do not occur together.

Before Conditioning

| Unconditioned Stimulus (UCS) | elicits | Unconditioned Response (UCR) |

| Neutral Stimulus (NS) | Does not elicit to-be-conditioned response

During Conditioning Trials

Present | Neutral Stimulus (NS) | just before

| Unconditioned Stimulus (UCS) | (which automatically elicits UCR)

After Conditioning

| Conditioned Stimulus (CS; former NS) | elicits | Conditioned Response (CR) |

Figure 4.1 | The Elements of Classical Conditioning | In classical conditioning, you start with a reflex—an unconditioned stimulus (UCS) that automatically elicits an unconditioned response (UCR). To condition a new response to a neutral stimulus, the neutral stimulus is presented just before the unconditioned stimulus. After several pairings, the neutral stimulus elicits a new response called the conditioned response (CR). The neutral stimulus is now referred to as the conditioned stimulus (CS).

as effective if the trace interval between stimuli is very short (Powell, Symbaluk, & MacDonald, 2002). It also appears that for trace conditioning, processing by both the cerebellum and hippocampus is essential for successful conditioning whereas for delayed conditioning, only processing by the cerebellum is necessary (Clark & Squire, 1998). In trace conditioning, processing by the hippocampus is necessary to establish a memory trace of the CS so that it can be associated with the UCS following the trace interval (Bangasser, Waxler, Santollo, & Shors, 2006). In addition, it appears that delayed conditioning can be accomplished without conscious awareness of the temporal relationship between the CS and UCS, but trace conditioning cannot (Clark & Squire, 1998).

The entire classical conditioning process is diagrammed in Figure 4.1. Study the diagram to make sure you understand the four elements that are involved in classical conditioning—the UCS, UCR, CS (the former neutral stimulus), and CR. To ensure that you understand, next we'll consider another famous example of classical conditioning, the Little Albert study.

The Little Albert study. John Broadus Watson, an American psychologist in the early part of the twentieth century, was the founder of behavioral psychology (Watson, 1913, 1919). He was very impressed with classical conditioning and its potential use to make psychology an objective science of behavior. To examine the possible role of such conditioning in human emotional responses such as fear, Watson and his research assistant, Rosalie Rayner, conducted a fear-conditioning study on an infant they referred to as Albert B. (Watson & Rayner, 1920). When the study began, Albert was about 9 months old, and when the study ended, he was almost 13 months old. Because Albert was just an infant, over time the study has become known as the Little Albert study.

Let's think about the Little Albert study in terms of the four elements of classical conditioning—UCS, UCR, CS, and CR. As a neutral stimulus, the researchers used a white rat. Albert was not afraid of the rat. In fact, when he saw the rat before the conditioning, he moved toward it and touched it. What was the reflex that Watson and Rayner used? While Albert was looking at the white rat, Watson quietly sneaked behind him with an iron bar and a hammer and clanged them together. Albert's reflexive response, the UCR, was the fear-avoidance response (crying and trying to crawl away) to this unexpected loud noise, the UCS. Watson and Rayner paired the sight of the white rat (the neutral stimulus that became the CS) with the unexpected loud noise (the UCS) until the sight of the white rat alone (the unexpected loud noise did not follow) elicited the fear-avoidance response. It took only seven pairings (done over two sessions, one week apart) for Albert to learn to fear the rat. This study was unethical, of course, and psychologists would not be allowed to conduct such a study today. Making it more unethical, Watson and Rayner did not even attempt to decondition the fear-avoidance response in Albert although they knew a month in advance when Albert and his mother were leaving the hospital where she worked, she and Albert resided, and the experiment was conducted. Ironically, however, at that time Watson was criticized more by animal rights activists for his research with rats than he was for the Little Albert study (Buckley, 1989). Although the Little Albert study has many limitations (e.g., it had only one subject), it has become one of psychology's most famous (infamous) studies and contributed greatly to promoting the behavioral psychology movement in the first half of the twentieth century.

You may be wondering what became of Albert and whether there were lasting effects of his fear-conditioning experiences? Until recently, no one knew Albert's identity or

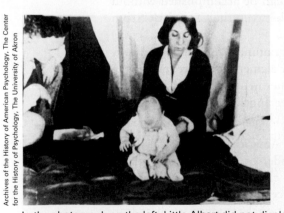

In the photograph on the left, Little Albert did not display any fear of the white rat before the classical conditioning trials but rather attempted to play with it. However, following the conditioning trials in which the sight of the white rat was paired with an unexpected loud noise, he acquired a fear response to the rat. In the second photograph, he is generalizing this conditioned fear response to a rabbit.

Archives of the History of American Psychology, The Center for the History of Psychology, The University of Akron

Courtesy of Professor Benjamin Harris, University of New Hampshire his fate, but now we do. After much historical detective work that took years, two possible identifications were proposed, but one fit the available evidence about Albert much better than the other (Griggs, 2015). We now know with reasonable certainty that Albert was Albert Barger (remember, he was named Albert B. in the study), the infant son of a wet nurse working and residing at the hospital where the Watson and Rayner study was conducted (Bartlett, 2014; Powell, Digdon, Harris, & Smithson, 2014). It turns out that Albert Barger lived a long life, dying in 2007 at the age of 87. Powell and his colleagues were surprised when they first learned from Barger's niece that her uncle had an aversion (but not a particularly strong one) to dogs and animals in general. The aversion, however, appears to have been more of a general dislike of animals and not due to his fear-conditioning experiences. In addition, according to Powell et al., Albert's conditioning experiences did not appear to have had any adverse effects on his personality. Albert died without knowing that it was highly likely that he was the famous Little Albert in the psychological literature. His niece thought that he would have been thrilled about this, but sadly, we will never know what his reaction would have been when learning that he was Little Albert, one of the most famous subjects in psychological research.

This is the only published photo of Little Albert (Albert Barger) as an adult. He died in 2007 at the age of 87, and he never learned that he was the famous Little Albert in the Watson and Rayner fear-conditioning study in 1920.

Photo courtesy of Doroty Parthree

Although Watson and Rayner did not decondition Little Albert, one of Watson's former students, Mary Cover Jones, demonstrated that such a fear could be deconditioned (Jones, 1924). She deconditioned a preexisting fear of rabbits in a 3-year-old boy named Peter. In Chapter 10, we will discuss a behavioral therapy for treating fear disorders (called phobias) that is based upon Jones's work. In addition, Elsie Bregman in 1934 showed that there could be limits to conditioning such fear responses. In her study, she was unable to condition infants to fear inanimate objects such as wooden blocks and cloth curtains. These results suggest possible biological predispositions to learn certain fears more easily than others. We will return to this idea in the last section of this chapter in our discussion of biological constraints on learning.

It is important to realize that classical conditioning is not only involved in conditioning negative emotional responses such as fear, but can also be used to develop positive emotional responses to stimuli. For example, classical conditioning is used in advertising in order to condition positive attitudes and feelings toward products (Allen & Shimp, 1990; Grossman & Till, 1998; Olson & Fazio, 2001). Think about advertisements that pair celebrities with products. Pairing popular professional basketball players like Michael Jordan and LeBron James with Nike products in advertisements is a good example. Both of these athletes were paid millions of dollars for their Nike endorsements. Why? The advertisers attempt to use our positive feelings about these celebrities to condition positive responses to their products. The celebrity serves as the UCS, and the product as the CS. Advertising campaigns using this evaluative classical conditioning technique have proved very effective (Hofmann, De Houwer, Perugini, Baeyens, & Crombez, 2010). John Watson pioneered this type of advertising when he worked as a psychology consultant for the J. Walter Thompson advertising agency in New York following his dismissal from academics (Buckley, 1989). Watson was forced to leave the academic life after he had an extramarital affair with his research assistant on the Little Albert study, Rosalie Rayner.

General Learning Processes in Classical Conditioning

We have seen how classical conditioning works: A new, learned response (the CR) is elicited by the CS in preparation for the arrival of the UCS. This response learning is also referred to as **acquisition**, acquiring a new response—the CR to the CS. But what happens after acquisition? Will this new response (for example, fear-avoidance in the Little Albert study) be generalized to other stimuli (say, white rabbits) that are similar to the CS (a white rat)? If so, can we learn to discriminate and respond this way only to specific stimuli (white rats)? Will this response (fear-avoidance) continue to occur when the CS (a white rat) is no longer paired with the UCS (the unexpected loud noise)? To answer such questions, we now turn to a discussion of the other general learning processes that follow acquisition in classical conditioning.

Extinction and spontaneous recovery. What do you think would happen to the CR if the UCS no longer followed the CS? Would the CR now be "unlearned"? Remember that in classical conditioning the CS reliably signals that the UCS is coming. If the CS no longer serves this function, then the CR is no longer necessary so it is no longer made. No preparation is needed because the UCS is no longer presented. For example, in Pavlov's work the dog would eventually stop salivating to the tone when the tone no longer signaled that the meat powder was coming. In the Little Albert study, Albert's fear of a white rat would have diminished and eventually stopped over time if it no longer signaled that the loud, unexpected noise was coming, but remember, Watson and Rayner never did this. He left without being deconditioned. This unlearning or deconditioning process is called **extinction**, the diminishing of the CR when the UCS no longer follows the CS.

A visual comparison of the acquisition and extinction processes is given in Figure 4.2 (a and b). The strength of the CR increases during acquisition, but it decreases during extinction. Note, however, that during the extinction process, the CR mysteriously increases somewhat in strength

acquisition (in classical conditioning) Acquiring a new response (the conditioned response) to the conditioned stimulus.

extinction (in classical conditioning) The diminishing of the conditioned response when the unconditioned stimulus no longer follows the conditioned stimulus.

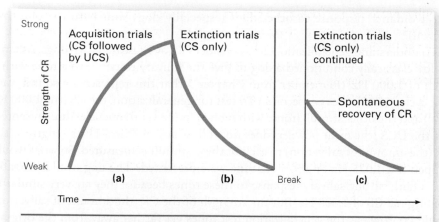

Figure 4.2 | Acquisition, Extinction, and Spontaneous Recovery | Panel (a) depicts the acquisition of the CR. Note that during acquisition, the UCS follows the CS on each trial. Acquisition of the CR is reflected in the increase in its strength across conditioning trials. Extinction is depicted in panel (b). On extinction trials, the UCS never follows the CS. This process is reflected in the decrease of the strength of the CR across extinction trials. Note, however, that when a break is taken during extinction training, there is a temporary partial recovery in strength of the CR following the break, depicted in panel (c). This partial recovery is called spontaneous recovery. The amount of recovery lessens as extinction training continues.

following a rest interval. This is called **spontaneous recovery**, a partial recovery in strength of the CR following a break during extinction trials (see Figure 4.2c). As extinction continues, however, the recovery observed following the rest intervals continues to decrease until it is minimized. For example, the dog would salivate very little or not at all to the tone. The spontaneous recovery that occurs during the extinction process indicates, as Pavlov had concluded, that the CR may not be totally lost during extinction, but only greatly weakened or inhibited. Research since Pavlov's time has demonstrated that this is indeed the case (Bouton, 1994; Rescorla, 1996).

Stimulus generalization and discrimination. In addition to acquisition, extinction, and spontaneous recovery, there are two other general learning processes involving the CR—stimulus generalization and discrimination. Let's consider generalization first. After acquisition of a CR (salivating) to a CS (a tone), we observe generalization. In **stimulus generalization**, stimuli similar to the CS elicit the CR. The more similar the stimulus is to the CS, the stronger the response will be. Generalization is an adaptive process. Classical conditioning would not be a very useful type of learning if it only allowed us to learn relationships between specific stimuli. If a dog bites you, isn't it more adaptive to generalize the

spontaneous recovery (in classical conditioning) A partial recovery in strength of the conditioned response following a break during extinction training.

stimulus generalization (in classical conditioning) The elicitation of the conditioned response to stimuli that are similar to the conditioned stimulus. The more similar the stimulus is to the conditioned stimulus, the stronger the response.

fear-avoidance response to other dogs (especially dogs similar to the one that bit you)?

To understand generalization, let's consider Pavlov's research with dogs. Assume Pavlov classically conditioned a dog to give the salivary response to a tone with a pitch of 1,000 Hz. (Remember from Chapter 3 that this represents a sound wave that cycles 1,000 times per second.) To test for generalization, the CS (the 1,000 Hz tone) and the other stimuli (tones with higher and lower frequencies) are presented, but the UCS (the meat powder) does not follow any of them. The strength of the CR (the amount of salivation) to each of these stimuli is measured. So what would happen if a 1,025 Hz or a 975 Hz tone were presented? The dog would probably give a fairly strong salivary response to these tones because they are very similar to the original CS of 1,000 Hz. But the strength of the CR (the amount of salivation) would go down as the generalization test tones get farther away from the original CS of 1,000 Hz. This generalization function is illustrated in Figure 4.3. Ignore the discrimination function in the figure for now. We will discuss it shortly.

Notice how symmetric the generalization test results are around the original CS value (1,000 Hz) in Figure 4.3. This is because the generalization test tones could be varied symmetrically in frequency above and below the original CS tone.

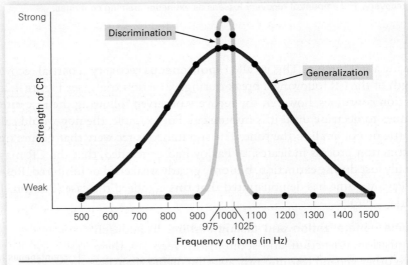

Figure 4.3 | Stimulus Generalization and Discrimination | These are idealized stimulus generalization and discrimination results following classical conditioning of the salivary response (CR) in dogs to a tone of 1,000 Hz (CS). The strength of the CR to generalization test stimuli (all tones except the 1,000 Hz tone) decreases as the similarity of the test stimulus to the original CS decreases. These generalization responses, however, can be extinguished through discrimination training in which the UCS (food) only follows the 1,000 Hz tone. The CR to each of the other tones will be extinguished except for the tones so similar to the 1,000 Hz tone (975 Hz and 1,025 Hz) that the dog does not perceive them as different.

But think about the Little Albert study by Watson and Rayner. Their original CS was a white rat so the generalization stimuli could not be varied symmetrically around it. What do you think they used to test for generalization? The main objects that they used were other animals—a rabbit, as you can see in the photos of the experiment, and a dog (neither was white)—and Rayner's furry sealskin coat (also nonwhite), but they also used some less similar inanimate objects—for example, a white-bearded Santa Claus mask, a package of white cotton, and some wooden toy blocks. Even though the generalization stimuli did not vary symmetrically around the white rat and the reporting of the generalization data was somewhat imprecise given that it was descriptive (e.g., "pronounced withdrawal of the body and whimpering") and not quantitative, the characteristic pattern of generalization results was by and large observed—as the generalization test stimuli became less similar to the CS (the white rat), the strength of the CR (the fear-avoidance response) decreased. Albert's responses to the animals and the sealskin coat (furry stimuli) were all strongly negative. He showed a much weaker negative response to the bearded Santa Claus mask and only a mild negative response to the white cotton, indicating that Albert generalized his fear more to furry stimuli than to white stimuli (at least the ones used in the study). As would be predicted because of their dissimilarity to the white rat, Albert showed no fear of the toy blocks and actually played with them.

Sometimes we overgeneralize and need to narrow our responding to a specific stimulus or smaller set of stimuli. In the case of the dog bite, we might overgeneralize and fear any dog. This wouldn't be rational, so we would need to learn to discriminate dogs that might bite us from those that would not. Such discrimination learning can be thought of as the opposite of generalization. Generalization leads to the CR being given to a broader set of stimuli; discrimination leads to the CR being given to a narrower set of stimuli. In classical conditioning, **stimulus discrimination** is the elicitation of the CR only by the CS or only by a small set of highly similar stimuli that includes the CS. In the dog bite example, this would be learning only to fear potentially dangerous dogs.

Discrimination training is used to teach stimulus discrimination. We will discuss the simplest case—learning to give the CR only to the original CS. This is the same procedure used to determine the sensory abilities of animals. In this type of discrimination training, the UCS follows only the original CS, the one stimulus to which you want the animal or human to respond (give the CR). None of the other stimuli used in the training are followed by the UCS. During discrimination training, you present many different stimuli numerous times, but the UCS only follows the original CS. What do you think happens? What normally happens to the CR when the UCS is removed in classical conditioning? It is extinguished. This is what discrimination training does; it diminishes the responding to the other stimuli.

Idealized results of stimulus discrimination training for a CS tone of 1,000 Hz in our Pavlovian classical conditioning example are shown in Figure 4.3. As you can see,

stimulus discrimination (in classical conditioning) The elicitation of the conditioned response only by the conditioned stimulus or only by a small set of highly similar stimuli that includes the conditioned stimulus.

Table 4.1	General Learning Processes in Classical Conditioning
Learning Process	**Explanation of Process**
Acquisition	Acquiring a new response (the conditioned response) to the conditioned stimulus
Extinction	Diminishing of the conditioned response when the unconditioned stimulus no longer follows the conditioned stimulus
Spontaneous recovery	Partial recovery in strength of the conditioned response following a break during extinction training
Stimulus discrimination	Elicitation of the conditioned response by stimuli that are similar to the conditioned stimulus (the more similar, the stronger the response)
Stimulus generalization	Elicitation of the conditioned response only by the conditioned stimulus or only by a small set of highly similar stimuli that includes the conditioned stimulus

responding is centered at 1,000 Hz, as it is for the stimulus generalization results. However, unlike the generalization results, the responding following discrimination training is to a much narrower range of stimulus frequencies. The animal has learned only to salivate to the 1,000 Hz tone and tones very similar to it (975 Hz and 1,025 Hz). Why does the animal salivate at all to any stimulus other than the 1,000 Hz tone? It wouldn't if it had perfect pitch perception and could discriminate all frequencies, but it can't. Thus, the animal salivates to this narrow range of frequencies because it has difficulty differentiating them. This is why discrimination training can be used to learn what nonverbal animals (and human infants) can discriminate. If they respond to stimuli the same way, then it is assumed that they cannot differentiate between the stimuli.

All five of the general learning processes for classical conditioning are summarized in Table 4.1. If any of these processes are not clear to you, restudy the discussions of those processes in the text and their visual depictions in Figures 4.2 and 4.3 to solidify your understanding. You want to ensure that you understand these learning processes for classical conditioning, because they will be redefined for operant conditioning in the next section.

Section Summary

In this section, we discovered that one way we learn about the world is by noting associations between various stimuli in our environment. This is called classical conditioning. Classical conditioning occurs when a conditioned stimulus (CS) reliably predicts the arrival of an unconditioned stimulus (UCS), which reflexively elicits an unconditioned response (UCR). In Pavlov's research, for example, a tone (CS) predicted the arrival of meat powder (UCS) that automatically elicited a salivary response (UCR). The optimal way to pair the two stimuli together in classical conditioning is called delayed conditioning. The CS is presented shortly before the UCS, but the CS continues so that the two stimuli occur together (the tone is turned on and left on until the meat powder is put in the dog's mouth). The learning is the acquisition of a new response, the conditioned response (CR) to the CS (the dog starts salivating to the sound of the tone).

Once this new response is acquired, it will be generalized to stimuli similar to the CS (tones similar in frequency to the particular tone used as the CS in conditioning). Although this generalization of the CR is an adaptive process, we can learn to discriminate the CS (the particular tone used in conditioning) from other stimuli (tones) except those highly similar to the CS. In discrimination learning, we learn that the CS is the only stimulus that is followed by the UCS. When the UCS no longer follows a stimulus, the CR (salivation) is extinguished (no longer given). However, the CR temporarily increases in strength following breaks during the extinction process. This is known as spontaneous recovery and indicates that the CR may still be available in a weakened or inhibited form.

ConceptCheck | 1

At about the same time that Pavlov accidentally discovered classical conditioning and began studying it, an American graduate student at the University of Pennsylvania, Edwin Twitmyer, was conducting his doctoral research (see Twitmyer, 1974). Twitmyer was examining the strength of the knee-jerk reflex and how this reflex might be affected by other physiological factors, such as clenching one's fists. During some of his trials, a bell would ring to signal to the participant to clench his fists, then a hammer would strike the participant's knee, the knee would jerk, and the amount of knee jerk would be measured. After many of these trials, Twitmyer noticed that a participant's knee might jerk before the hammer hit it. It jerked in response to the bell! Like Pavlov, he had accidentally discovered a case of classical conditioning. Identify the UCS, UCR, CS, and CR in this strange case of classical conditioning.

Explain why Watson and Rayner's Little Albert study is an example of the delayed conditioning procedure, not the trace conditioning procedure.

Explain why generalization and discrimination can be thought of as opposites.

Explain which other general learning process is used in discrimination training.

Learning Through Operant Conditioning

In the previous section, we described classical conditioning—learning about associations between stimuli in our environment. In this section, we will consider another important type of conditioning, **operant conditioning**—learning to associate behaviors with their consequences. Behaviors that are reinforced (lead to satisfying consequences) will be strengthened, and behaviors that are punished (lead to unsatisfying consequences) will be weakened. The behavior that is reinforced or punished is

operant conditioning Learning to associate behaviors with their consequences. Behaviors that are reinforced (lead to satisfying consequences) will be strengthened, and behaviors that are punished (lead to unsatisfying consequences) will be weakened.

law of effect A principle developed by Edward Thorndike that says that any behavior that results in satisfying consequences tends to be repeated and that any behavior that results in unsatisfying consequences tends not to be repeated.

referred to as the operant response because it "operates" on the environment by bringing about certain consequences. We are constantly "operating" on our environment and learning from the consequences of our behavior. For example, in meeting someone whom you like and want to date, your behavior (what you say and how you act) will either lead to satisfying consequences (a date) or unsatisfying consequences (no date). Satisfying consequences will lead you to act that way again in the future; unsatisfying consequences will lead you to change your behavior.

Research on how we learn associations between behaviors and their consequences started around the beginning of the twentieth century. American psychologist Edward Thorndike studied the ability of cats and other animals to learn to escape from puzzle boxes (Thorndike, 1898, 1911). In these puzzle boxes, there was usually only one way to get out (for example, pressing a lever would open the door). Thorndike would put a hungry animal in the box, place food outside the box (but in sight of the animal), and then record the animal's behavior. If the animal pressed the lever, as a result of its behavior it would manage to escape the box and get the food (satisfying effects). The animal would tend to repeat such successful behaviors in the future when put back into the box. However, other behaviors (for example, pushing the door) that did not lead to escaping and getting the food would not be repeated.

Based on the results of these puzzle box experiments, Thorndike developed what he termed the **law of effect**—any behavior that results in satisfying consequences tends to be repeated, and any behavior that results in unsatisfying consequences tends not to be repeated. In the 1930s, B. F. (Burrhus Frederic) Skinner, the most influential of all behaviorists, redefined the law in more objective terms and started the scientific examination of how we learn through

Edward Thorndike used puzzle boxes like the one shown here in his classic learning studies with cats. The boxes varied in how difficult they were for the cats to escape from. The puzzle box was one of the easier boxes—pulling on a looped string raised the bolt to open the door. More difficult boxes required the cat to make more than one response. The results of these puzzle box experiments led Thorndike to develop the law of effect.

operant conditioning (Skinner, 1938). Let's move on to Skinner's redefinition and a description of how operant conditioning works.

Learning Through Reinforcement and Punishment

To understand how operant conditioning works, we first need to learn Skinner's redefinitions of Thorndike's subjective terms, "satisfying" and "unsatisfying" consequences. A **reinforcer** is defined as a stimulus that increases the probability of a prior response, and a **punisher** as a stimulus that decreases the probability of a prior response. Therefore, **reinforcement** is defined as the process by which the probability of a response is increased by the presentation of a reinforcer following the response, and **punishment** as the process by which the probability of a response is decreased by the presentation of a punisher following the response. "Reinforcement" and "punishment" are terms that refer to the process by which certain stimuli (consequences) change the probability of a behavior; "reinforcer" and "punisher" are terms that refer to the specific stimuli (consequences) that are used to strengthen or weaken the behavior.

Let's consider an example. If you operantly conditioned your pet dog to sit by giving her a food treat each time she sat, the food treat would be the reinforcer, and the process of increasing the dog's sitting behavior by using this reinforcer would be called reinforcement. Similarly, if you conditioned your dog to stop jumping on you by spraying her in the face with water each time she did so, the spraying would be the punisher, and the process of decreasing your dog's jumping behavior by using this punisher would be called punishment.

Just as classical conditioning is best when the CS is presented just before the UCS, immediate consequences normally produce the best operant conditioning (Gluck, Mercado, & Myers, 2011). Timing affects learning. If there is a significant delay between a behavior and its consequences, conditioning is very difficult. This is true for both reinforcing and punishing consequences. The learner tends to associate reinforcement or punishment with recent behavior; and if there is a delay, the learner will have engaged in many other behaviors during the delay. Thus, a more recent behavior is more likely to be associated with the consequences, hindering the conditioning process. For instance, think about the examples we described of operantly conditioning your pet dog to sit or to stop jumping on you. What if you waited 5 or 10 minutes after she sat before giving her the food treat, or after she jumped on you before spraying her. Do you think your dog would learn to sit or stop jumping on you very easily? No, the reinforcer or punisher should be presented right after the dog's behavior for successful conditioning.

Normally then, immediate consequences produce the best learning. However, there are exceptions. For example, think about studying now for a psychology exam in two weeks. The consequences (your grade on the exam) do not immediately follow your present study behavior. They come two weeks later. Or think about any job that you have had. You likely didn't get paid immediately. Typically, you are

reinforcer A stimulus that increases the probability of a prior response.

punisher A stimulus that decreases the probability of a prior response.

reinforcement The process by which the probability of a response is increased by the presentation of a reinforcer.

punishment The process by which the probability of a response is decreased by the presentation of a punisher.

appetitive stimulus A stimulus that is pleasant.

aversive stimulus A stimulus that is unpleasant.

positive reinforcement Reinforcement in which an appetitive stimulus is presented.

positive punishment Punishment in which an aversive stimulus is presented.

paid weekly or biweekly. What is necessary to overcome the need for immediate consequences in operant conditioning is for the learner to have the cognitive capacity to link the relevant behavior to the consequences regardless of the delay interval between them. If the learner can make such causal links, then conditioning can occur over time lags between behaviors and their consequences.

Positive and negative reinforcement and punishment. Both reinforcement and punishment can be either positive or negative, creating four new terms. Let's see what is meant by each of these four new terms—positive reinforcement, negative reinforcement, positive punishment, and negative punishment. To understand these terms, we first have to understand that positive and negative do not have their normal meanings in this context. The word "positive" means that a stimulus is presented; the word "negative" means that a stimulus is removed. In both positive reinforcement and positive punishment, a stimulus is presented; in both negative reinforcement and negative punishment, a stimulus is removed. Next, we need to understand that there are two types of stimuli that could be presented or removed: appetitive and aversive stimuli. An **appetitive stimulus** is a stimulus that the animal or human finds pleasant (has an appetite for). An **aversive stimulus** is a stimulus that the animal or human finds unpleasant, the opposite of appetitive. Food, money, and good grades are examples of appetitive stimuli for most of us, and strong electric shock, bad grades, and sickness are examples of aversive stimuli for most people.

Now that we know what positive and negative mean, and the difference between appetitive and aversive stimuli, we can understand the meanings of positive and negative reinforcement and punishment. General explanations for each type of reinforcement and punishment are given in Figure 4.4. In **positive reinforcement**, an appetitive stimulus is presented, but in **positive punishment**, an

	Positive	Negative
Reinforcement	Appetitive stimulus presented	Aversive stimulus removed
Punishment	Aversive stimulus presented	Appetitive stimulus removed

Figure 4.4 | Positive and Negative Reinforcement and Punishment | "Positive" means that something is presented, and "negative" means that something is taken away. Reinforcement means that the behavior is strengthened, and punishment means that the behavior is weakened. In positive reinforcement, an appetitive (pleasant) stimulus is presented, and in positive punishment, an aversive (unpleasant) stimulus is presented. In negative reinforcement, an aversive stimulus is removed, and in negative punishment, an appetitive stimulus is removed.

aversive stimulus is presented. An example of positive reinforcement would be praising a child for doing the chores. An example of positive punishment would be spanking a child for not obeying the rules.

What type of operant conditioning is going on here? Be careful. Think about it from the perspectives of both the child and the parents. For the child, it's positive reinforcement. The child is crying to get something pleasant (sleeping with the parents). For the parents, it's negative reinforcement. They let the child sleep with them in order to remove something they find unpleasant, the crying.

Similarly, in negative reinforcement and negative punishment, a stimulus is taken away. In **negative reinforcement**, an aversive stimulus is removed; in **negative punishment**, an appetitive stimulus is removed. An example of negative reinforcement would be taking Advil to get rid of a headache. The removal of the headache (an aversive stimulus) leads to continued Advil-taking behavior. An example of negative punishment would be taking away a teenager's driving privileges after she breaks curfew. The removal of the driving privileges (an appetitive stimulus) leads to better adherence to the curfew in the future.

In all of these examples, however, we only know if a stimulus has served as a reinforcer or a punisher and led to reinforcement or punishment if the target behavior keeps occurring (reinforcement) or stops occurring (punishment). For example, the spanking would be punishment if the disobedient behavior stopped, and the praise reinforcement if the chores continued to be done. However, if the disobedient behavior continued, the spanking would have to be considered reinforcement; and if the chores did not continue to be done, the praise would have to be considered punishment. This is an important point. What serves as reinforcement or punishment is relative to each individual, in a particular context, and at a particular point in time. While it is certainly possible to say that certain stimuli usually serve as reinforcers or punishers, they do not inevitably do so. Think about money. For most people, $100 would serve as a reinforcer, but it might not for Bill Gates (of Microsoft), whose net worth is in the billions. Remember, whether the behavior is strengthened or weakened is the only thing that tells you whether the consequences were reinforcing or punishing, respectively.

Given the relative nature of reinforcement, it would be nice to have a way to determine whether a certain event would function as a reinforcer. The **Premack principle** provides us with a way to make this determination (Premack, 1959, 1965). According to David Premack, you should view reinforcers as behaviors rather than stimuli (e.g., eating food rather than food). This enables the conceptualization of reinforcement as a sequence of two behaviors—the behavior that is being reinforced followed by the behavior that is the reinforcer. But what is the principle? The principle is that

negative reinforcement Reinforcement in which an aversive stimulus is removed.

negative punishment Punishment in which an appetitive stimulus is removed.

Premack principle The principle that the opportunity to perform a highly frequent behavior can reinforce a less frequent behavior.

the opportunity to perform a highly frequent behavior can reinforce performing a less frequent behavior. For example, children typically spend more time watching television than doing homework. Thus, watching television could be used as a reinforcer for doing homework. In sum, the Premack principle allows us to identify potential reinforcers by focusing on the relative probabilities of behaviors. To determine these probabilities, you observe how often the person or animal engages in various behaviors. The Premack principle has proved to be a very useful tool in applied work with clinical populations, situations in which normal reinforcers seem to have little effect, by enabling the identification of which behaviors will serve as reinforcers.

Primary and secondary reinforcers. Behavioral psychologists make a distinction between primary and secondary reinforcers. A **primary reinforcer** is innately reinforcing, reinforcing since birth. Food and water are good examples of primary reinforcers. Note that "innately reinforcing" does not mean "always reinforcing." For example, food would probably not serve as a reinforcer for someone who has just finished eating a five-course meal. Innately reinforcing only means that the reinforcing property of the stimulus does not have to be learned. In contrast, a **secondary reinforcer** is not innately reinforcing, but gains its reinforcing property through learning. Most reinforcers fall into this category. Examples of secondary reinforcers are money, good grades, and applause. Money would not be reinforcing to an infant, would it? Its reinforcing nature has to be learned through experience.

Behaviorists have employed secondary reinforcers in token economies in a variety of institutional settings, from schools to institutions for the mentally challenged (Allyon & Azrin, 1968). Physical objects, such as plastic or wooden tokens, are used as secondary reinforcers. Desired behaviors are reinforced with these tokens, which then can be exchanged for other reinforcers, such as treats or privileges. Thus, the tokens function like money in the institutional setting, creating a token economy. A token economy is an example of **behavior modification**—the application of conditioning principles, especially operant principles, to eliminate undesirable behavior and to teach more desirable behavior. Like token economies, other behavior modification techniques have been used successfully for many other tasks, from toilet training to teaching children who have autism (Kazdin, 2001).

primary reinforcer A stimulus that is innately reinforcing.

secondary reinforcer A stimulus that gains its reinforcing property through learning.

behavior modification The application of classical and operant conditioning principles to eliminate undesirable behavior and to teach more desirable behavior.

Reinforcement without awareness. According to behavioral psychologists, reinforcement should strengthen operant responding even when people are unaware of the contingency between their responding and the reinforcement. Evidence that this is the case comes from a clever experiment by Hefferline, Keenan, and Harford (1959). Participants were told that the purpose of the study was to examine the effects of stress on body tension and that muscular tension would be evaluated during randomly alternating periods of harsh noise and soothing music. Electrodes were attached to different areas of the participants' bodies to measure muscular tension. The duration of the harsh noise, however, was not really random. Whenever a participant contracted a very small muscle in their left thumb, the noise was terminated. This muscular response was imperceptible and could only be detected by the electrode mounted at the muscle. Thus, the participants did not even realize when they contracted this muscle.

There was a dramatic increase in the contraction of this muscle over the course of the experimental session. The participants, however, did not realize this, and none had any idea that they were actually in control of the termination of the harsh noise. This study clearly showed that operant conditioning can occur without a person's awareness. It demonstrated this using negative reinforcement (an increase in the probability of a response that leads to the removal of an aversive stimulus). The response rate of contracting the small muscle in the left thumb increased and the aversive harsh noise was removed when the response was made. Such conditioning plays a big role in the development of motor skills, such as learning to ride a bicycle or to play a musical instrument. Muscle movements below our conscious level of awareness but key to skill development are positively reinforced by our improvement in the skill.

Pessiglione et al. (2008) provide a more recent demonstration of operant conditioning without awareness for a decision-making task. In brief, participants learned to choose contextual cues predicting monetary reinforcement (winning money) relative to those predicting punishment (loss of money) without conscious perception of these cues. Thus, they learned cue-outcome associations without consciously perceiving the cues. The procedure involved visual masking. When a visual stimulus is masked, it is exposed briefly (for maybe 50 milliseconds) and followed immediately by another visual stimulus that completely overrides it, thereby masking (preventing conscious perception of) the first stimulus.

In this experiment, after being exposed to a masked contextual cue (an abstract novel symbol masked by a scrambled mixture of other cues) flashed briefly on a computer screen, a participant had to decide if he wanted to take the risky response or the safe response. The participant was told that the outcome of the risky response on each trial depended upon the cue hidden in the masked image. A cue could either lead to winning £1 (British currency), losing £1, or not winning or losing any money. If the participant took the safe response, it was a neutral outcome (no win or loss). Participants were also told that if they never took the risky response or always took it, their winnings would be nil and that because they could not consciously perceive the cues, they should follow their intuition in making their response decisions. All of the necessary precautions and assessments to ensure that participants did not perceive the masked cues were taken. Overall, participants won money in the task, indicating that the risky response was more frequently chosen following reinforcement predictive cues relative to punishment predictive cues.

In addition to this recent demonstration of operant conditioning without awareness, there have been several demonstrations of classical conditioning without awareness (Clark & Squire, 1998; Knight, Nguyen, & Bandettini, 2003;

Craig Swanson/www.perspicuity.com

Morris, Öhman, & Dolan, 1998; Olsson & Phelps, 2004). Using delayed conditioning, Clark and Squire, for example, successfully conditioned the eyeblink response in both normal and amnesic participants who were not aware of the tone–air puff relationship. Participants watched a movie during the conditioning trials, and postconditioning testing indicated that they had no knowledge of the CS-UCS association.

General Learning Processes in Operant Conditioning

Now that we have a better understanding of how we learn through reinforcement and punishment, let's consider the five general learning processes in operant conditioning that we discussed in the context of classical conditioning—acquisition, extinction, spontaneous recovery, generalization, and discrimination. Because some of the examples of these processes are concerned with operant conditioning of animals, it's important to know how such animal research is conducted. It's also important to learn how to read cumulative records because they are used to measure and depict operant responding in the general learning processes.

For control purposes, behavioral psychologists conduct much of their laboratory research on nonhuman animals. In conducting their experiments with animals, operant conditioning researchers use operant chambers, which resemble large plastic boxes. These chambers are far from simple boxes, though. Each chamber has a response device (such as a lever for rats to press or a key for pigeons to peck), a variety of stimulus sources (such as lamps behind the keys to allow varying colors to be presented on them), and food dispensers. Here, "key" refers to a piece of transparent plastic behind a hole in the chamber wall. The key or other response device is connected to a switch that records each time the animal responds. Computers record the animal's behavior, control the delivery of food, and maintain other aspects of the chamber. Thus, the operant chamber is a very controlled environment for studying the impact of the animal's behavior on its environment. Operant chambers are sometimes referred to as "Skinner boxes" because B. F. Skinner originally designed this type of chamber.

What if the animal in the chamber does not make the response that the researcher wants to condition (for example, what if the pigeon doesn't peck the key)? This does happen, but behavioral researchers can easily deal with this situation. They use what they call **shaping**; they train the animal to make the

Nina Leen/Time-Life Pictures/Getty Images

B. F. Skinner and one of his operant conditioning chambers, a "Skinner box." When the rat presses the lever, an electrical relay system is activated and reinforcement (such as a food pellet) is delivered. In addition to a lever, operant chambers may contain other response mechanisms, such as a key for a pigeon to peck.

response they want by reinforcing successive approximations of the desired response. For example, consider the key-peck response for a pigeon. The researcher would watch the behavior of the pigeon and would begin the shaping by reinforcing the pigeon for going in the general area of the key. This would get the pigeon near the key. The researcher would then reinforce the pigeon any time its head was in the area of the key. The pigeon would keep its head near the key and would probably occasionally touch the key. Then the researcher would reinforce the pigeon for touching the key. As you can see, by reinforcing such successive approximations of the desired behavior, the animal can be shaped to make the desired response. This training by successive approximations is just as successful with humans and is also used to shape human operant responding.

shaping Training a human or animal to make an operant response by reinforcing successive approximations of the desired response.

cumulative record A record of the total number of operant responses over time that visually depicts the rate of responding.

acquisition (in operant conditioning) The strengthening of a reinforced operant response.

Responding in an operant conditioning experiment is depicted in a **cumulative record**. A cumulative record is a record of the total number of responses over time. As such, it provides a visual depiction of the rate of responding. Figure 4.5 shows how to read a cumulative record. The slope of the record indicates the response rate. Remember that the record visually shows how the responses cumulate over time. If the animal is making a large number of responses per unit of time (a fast response rate), the slope of the record will be steep. The cumulative total is increasing quickly. When there is no responding (the cumulative total remains the same), the record is flat (no slope). As the slope of the record increases, the response rate gets faster. Now let's see what cumulative records look like for some of the general learning processes.

Acquisition, extinction, and spontaneous recovery. The first general process, **acquisition**, refers to the strengthening of the reinforced operant response. What would this look like on the cumulative record? Figure 4.6(a, page 172) shows that

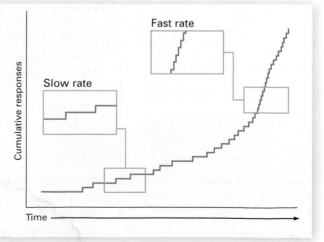

Figure 4.5 | How to Understand a Cumulative Record | By measuring how responses cumulate over time, a cumulative record shows the rate of responding. When no responses occur, the record is flat (has no slope). As the number of responses increases per unit of time, the cumulative total rises more quickly. The response rate is reflected in the slope of the record. The faster the response rate, the steeper the slope of the record.

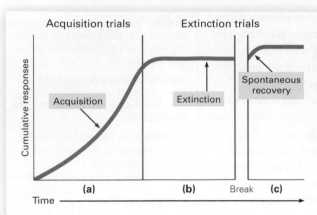

Figure 4.6 | Cumulative Record Illustrations of Acquisition, Extinction, and Spontaneous Recovery | (a) This is an acquisition cumulative record; the responding rate increases as learning occurs so the cumulative record has a fairly steep slope reflecting this increase. (b) This is an extinction cumulative record; the responding rate has essentially fallen to zero. A flat cumulative record indicates extinction. (c) This is an example of spontaneous recovery—a burst of responding following a break in extinction training. As the extinction training continues, the record will return to flat (no responding).

the response rate increases over time. This looks very similar to the shape of the acquisition figure for classical conditioning (see Figure 4.2), but remember the cumulative record is reporting cumulative responding as a function of time, not the strength of the response. Thus, **extinction**, the diminishing of the operant response when it is no longer reinforced, will look different than it did for classical conditioning. Look at Figure 4.6(b). The decreasing slope of the record indicates that the response is being extinguished; there are fewer and fewer responses over time. The response rate is diminishing. When the record goes to flat, extinction has occurred. However, as in classical conditioning, there will be **spontaneous recovery**, the temporary recovery of the operant response following a break during extinction training. This would be indicated in the record by a brief period of increased responding following a break in extinction training. However, the record would go back to flat (no responding) as extinction training continued. This is shown in Figure 4.6(c).

Let's think about acquisition, extinction, and spontaneous recovery with an example that is familiar to all of us—vending machines. We learn that by putting money into a certain vending machine, we can get a candy bar. We acquire the response of inserting money into this particular machine. One day, we put in money, but no candy comes out. This is the case the next few times we visit the machine. Soon, we stop putting our money in the machine. Our responding is being extinguished. However, after a few more days (a break), we go back and try again. This is comparable to spontaneous recovery. We hope the machine has been repaired, and we'll get that candy bar. If so, our response rate will return to its previous level; if not, our response rate will continue along the extinction trail.

extinction (in operant conditioning) The diminishing of the operant response when it is no longer reinforced.

spontaneous recovery (in operant conditioning) The temporary recovery of the operant response following a break during extinction training.

discriminative stimulus (in operant conditioning) The stimulus that has to be present for the operant response to be reinforced.

Discrimination and generalization. Now let's consider discrimination and generalization. To understand discrimination in operant conditioning, we need first to consider the **discriminative stimulus**—the stimulus that has to be present for the operant response to be reinforced or punished. The discriminative stimulus "sets the occasion" for the response to be reinforced or punished (rather than elicits the response as in classical conditioning). Here's an example. Imagine a rat in an experimental operant chamber. When a light goes on and the rat presses the lever, food is delivered. When the light is not on, pressing the lever does not lead to food delivery. In brief, the rat learns the conditions under which pressing the lever will be reinforced with food. This is **stimulus discrimination**— learning to give the operant response (pressing the lever) only in the presence of the discriminative stimulus (the light). A high response rate in the presence of the discriminative stimulus (the light) and a near-zero rate in its absence would indicate that the discrimination was learned.

Now we can consider **stimulus generalization**, giving the operant response in the presence of stimuli similar to the discriminative stimulus. Let's return to the example of the rat learning to press the lever in the presence of a light. Let's make the light a shade of green and say that the rat learned to press the lever only in the presence of that particular shade of green light. What if the light were another shade of green, or a different color, such as yellow? Presenting similar stimuli (different-colored lights) following acquisition constitutes a test for generalization. The extent of responding to a generalization stimulus reflects the amount of generalization to that stimulus. As with classical conditioning (see Figure 4.3), there is a gradient of generalization in operant conditioning—as the generalization test stimulus becomes less similar to the discriminative stimulus, the response rate for the operant response goes down. A stimulus discrimination function similar to the one observed for classical conditioning would also be observed after additional discrimination training that involved teaching discrimination of the discriminative stimulus (the light) from other stimuli of the same class (lights of different colors).

Stimulus discrimination and generalization in operant conditioning are not confined to using simple visual and auditory stimuli such as colored lights and varying tones, even for animals other than humans. For example, Watanabe, Sakamoto, and Wakita (1995) showed that pigeons could successfully learn to discriminate paintings by Monet, an impressionist, and Picasso, a cubist; and that following this training, they could discriminate paintings by Monet and Picasso that had never been presented. Furthermore, the pigeons showed generalization from Monet's paintings to paintings by other impressionists (Cézanne and Renoir) or from Picasso's paintings to paintings by other cubists (Braque and Matisse). In addition, Porter and Neuringer (1984) have reported successful learning of musical discrimination between selections by Bach versus Stravinsky by pigeons followed by generalization to music by similar composers. Otsuka, Yanagi, and Watanabe (2009) similarly showed that even rats could learn this musical discrimination between selections by Bach versus those by Stravinsky. Thus, like

stimulus discrimination (in operant conditioning) Learning to give the operant response only in the presence of the discriminative stimulus.

stimulus generalization (in operant conditioning) Giving the operant response in the presence of stimuli similar to the discriminative stimulus. The more similar the stimulus is to the discriminative stimulus, the higher the operant response rate.

Table 4.2	General Learning Processes in Operant Conditioning
Learning Process	**Explanation of Process**
Acquisition	Strengthening of a reinforced operant response
Extinction	Diminishing of the operant response when it is no longer reinforced
Spontaneous recovery	Temporary recovery in the operant response rate following a break during extinction training
Stimulus generalization	Giving the operant response in the presence of stimuli similar to the discriminative stimulus (the more similar, the higher the response rate)
Stimulus discrimination	Learning to give the operant response only in the presence of the discriminative stimulus

humans, other animals can clearly learn to discriminate complex visual and auditory stimuli and then generalize their learning to similar stimuli.

All five of the general learning processes for operant conditioning are summarized in Table 4.2. If any of these processes are not clear to you, restudy the discussions of those processes in the text to solidify your understanding. Also make sure that you understand how these learning processes in operant conditioning differ from those in classical conditioning (summarized in Table 4.1).

Now that we understand the general processes involved in operant conditioning, we need to consider the question of how operant responding is maintained following acquisition. Will the responding be maintained if it is reinforced only part of the time? If so, what's the best way to do this? Such questions require an understanding of what are called reinforcement schedules.

Partial-Reinforcement Schedules in Operant Conditioning

The reinforcement of every response is called a **continuous schedule of reinforcement**. But we aren't reinforced for every response in everyday life. In real life, we experience **partial schedules of reinforcement**, in which a response is only reinforced part of the time. Partial-reinforcement schedules lead to the **partial-reinforcement effect**. Responses that are reinforced according to a partial schedule rather than a continuous schedule are more resistant to extinction. Incidentally, Skinner accidentally discovered the partial-reinforcement effect when he was short of food reinforcement for his experimental work and was forced to use partial reinforcement instead of continuous reinforcement (Skinner, 1956). To understand this effect, we first need to consider the four major aspects of

continuous schedule of reinforcement Reinforcing the desired operant response each time it is made.

partial schedule of reinforcement Reinforcing the desired operant response only part of the time.

partial-reinforcement effect The finding that operant responses that are reinforced on partial schedules are more resistant to extinction than those reinforced on a continuous schedule.

partial-reinforcement schedules—ratio, interval, fixed, and variable.

Partial-reinforcement schedules can be based on either the number of responses made or on the amount of time that has elapsed. A ratio schedule is based on the number of responses made, and an interval schedule is based on the amount of time that has elapsed. In addition, the number of responses or the amount of elapsed time can be fixed or variable. In a fixed schedule, the number of responses required for a ratio schedule or the amount of time needed for an interval schedule is fixed. Similarly, for a variable schedule, the number of responses required for a ratio schedule and amount of time for an interval schedule varies on each trial. In summary, there are four types of partial schedules—fixed ratio, variable ratio, fixed interval, and variable interval. Let's look first at ratio schedules.

Ratio schedules. In a **fixed-ratio schedule**, a reinforcer is delivered after a fixed number of responses are made. The number of responses must be greater than one. (A fixed-ratio schedule that only required one response to get a reinforcer would be a continuous schedule of reinforcement). In a laboratory experiment, for example, a rat might have to press the lever 10 times (the fixed ratio) before the delivery of a reinforcer (usually food). To get another reinforcer, 10 more presses would be necessary, and so on. A good example from everyday life is piecework in a factory in which a worker has to make a certain number of items (say two wallets) before receiving any pay. The worker makes two wallets and then receives a certain amount of money. Then he or she must make two more to be paid that amount of money again. Just as the rat has to make responses (press the lever), the worker has to make responses (in this case, make actual products) to get reinforced.

In a **variable-ratio schedule**, the number of responses it takes to obtain a reinforcer varies on each trial but averages to be a certain number across trials. The human, rat, or other animal never knows exactly how many responses will be necessary to get the next reinforcer. A rat might have to press a lever 10 times to get a reinforcer, then 21 times, then

Researchers at MIT study the effects of casino gambling on laboratory rats.

John McPherson/Universal Press UClick

fixed-ratio schedule A partial schedule of reinforcement in which a reinforcer is delivered each time a fixed number of responses is made. The fixed number can be any number greater than one.

variable-ratio schedule A partial schedule of reinforcement in which the number of responses it takes to obtain a reinforcer varies on each trial but averages to a set number across trials.

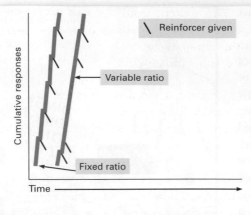

Figure 4.7 | Cumulative Records for Fixed-Ratio and Variable-Ratio Schedules of Partial Reinforcement | Both ratio schedules lead to high rates of responding as indicated by the steep slopes of the two cumulative records. Each tick mark indicates when a reinforcer was delivered. As you can see, the tick marks appear regularly in the record for the fixed-ratio schedule, but irregularly in the record for the variable-ratio schedule. A fixed-ratio schedule leads to short pauses after reinforcement, but these pauses don't occur as often for a variable-ratio schedule.

6 times, and so on. The exact number of responses necessary to get a reinforcer varies. A good example in everyday life is the way a slot machine is programmed. The person playing the slot machine knows that it will eventually pay off but does not know how many responses (insertions of money into the slot machine) are necessary to get that payoff.

Ratio schedules lead to high rates of responding because the number of responses determines reinforcement; the more they respond, the more they are reinforced. Cumulative records for the two ratio schedules are given in Figure 4.7. The slopes for the two ratio schedules are steep, which indicates a high rate of responding. Look closely after each reinforcement presentation (indicated by a tick mark), and you will see very brief pauses after reinforcement, especially for the fixed-ratio record. These pauses indicate that the animal took a short break from responding following the reinforcement. These pauses occur more often for the fixed-ratio schedule because the number of responses that must be made to get another reinforcer is known. Thus, the animal or human can rest before starting to respond again. These pauses get longer as the fixed number of responses gets larger.

Interval schedules. Now let's consider interval schedules. Do you think the cumulative records for the two interval schedules will have steep slopes like the two ratio schedules? Will there be any flat sections in the record indicating no responding? Let's see. In a **fixed-interval schedule**, a reinforcer is delivered following the first response after a set interval of time has elapsed. Please note that the reinforcement does not automatically appear after the fixed interval of time has elapsed; the reinforcement merely becomes obtainable after the fixed interval. A response must be made in order to get the reinforcement. Let's consider an example. We could fix the time interval at one minute for our example of a rat pressing a lever in an operant chamber. This means that a food pellet would be delivered following the first lever press after one minute had elapsed. After another minute elapsed following the response and another lever press was made,

fixed-interval schedule A partial schedule of reinforcement in which a reinforcer is delivered after the first response is given once a set interval of time has elapsed.

another reinforcer would be delivered. This pattern would continue—one minute elapses, a response is made, a reinforcer is given. Before predicting what the cumulative record for this type of schedule should look like, let's think about a fixed-interval schedule example with students.

In most of your classes, you are given periodic scheduled exams (for example, an exam every four weeks). To understand how such periodic exams represent a fixed-interval schedule, think of studying as the targeted response, and an acceptable grade on the exam as the reinforcer. Think about how much you would study during each of the four-week intervals before each test. Think about the average study behavior across students in the class for each day during that four-week interval. There probably wouldn't be much studying during the first week or two, and the amount of study would increase dramatically (cramming) right before each exam. Think about what the cumulative record for this sort of responding would look like. There would be long periods with little responding (essentially flat sections) right after each exam, and then there would be a dramatic burst of responding (a steep slope) right before each exam. Now look at the record for the fixed-interval schedule in Figure 4.8. It looks just like this. This is also what the record would look like for a rat pressing a lever on this type of schedule for a food reinforcer.

Now imagine that you are the teacher of a class in which students had this pattern of study behavior. How could you change the students' study behavior to be more regular? The answer is to use a **variable-interval schedule** in which a reinforcer is delivered following a response after a different time interval on each trial (in our example, each exam), but the time intervals across trials average to be a set time. This would translate in our example to unscheduled surprise exams. Think about how students' study behavior would have to change to do well on the exams with this new schedule. Students would have to study more regularly because a test could be given at any time. Their studying would be steadier over each interval. They wouldn't have long periods of little or no studying. Now look

> **variable-interval schedule** A partial schedule of reinforcement in which the time that must elapse on each trial before a response will lead to the delivery of a reinforcer varies from trial to trial but averages to a set time across trials.

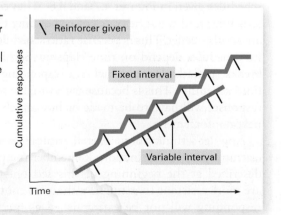

Figure 4.8 | Cumulative Records for Fixed-Interval and Variable-Interval Schedules of Partial Reinforcement | As in Figure 4.7 the tick marks indicate when reinforcers were delivered for each of the two schedules. The flat sections following reinforcements for the fixed-interval schedule indicate periods when little or no responding occurred. Such pauses do not occur for a variable-interval schedule. A variable-interval schedule leads to steady responding.

Table 4.3	Four Partial-Reinforcement Schedules and Their Effects on Response Rate
Schedule	**Effect on Response Rate**
Fixed-ratio (reinforcer is delivered after a fixed number of responses are made)	High rate of responding with pauses after receiving reinforcement
Variable-ratio (reinforcer is delivered after a variable number of responses are made)	High rate of responding with fewer pauses after receiving reinforcement than for a fixed-ratio schedule
Fixed-interval (reinforcer is delivered after the first response is given once a fixed interval of time has elapsed)	Little or no responding followed by a high rate of responding as the end of the interval nears
Variable-interval (reinforcer is delivered after the first response is given once a variable interval of time has elapsed)	Steady rate of responding during the interval

at the cumulative record for the variable-interval schedule in Figure 4.8. The flat sections appearing in the fixed-interval schedule are gone. The slope of the record indicates a steady rate of responding (studying). Why? The answer is simple—the length of the interval varies across trials (between exams in the example). It might be very brief or very long. The students don't know. This is why the responding (studying) becomes steady.

The four types of partial-reinforcement schedules and their respective effects on response rate are summarized in Table 4.3. As you review the information in this table for each type of schedule, also review the cumulative record for the schedule in either Figure 4.7 or 4.8 to see visually the impact of that type of schedule upon responding.

Let's compare the cumulative records for the four types of partial-reinforcement schedules given in Figures 4.7 and 4.8. What conclusions can we draw? First, ratio schedules lead to higher rates of responding than interval schedules. Their slopes are much steeper. This is because ratio schedules depend on responding, and interval schedules depend on time elapsing. Second, variable schedules lead to fewer breaks (periods during which no responding occurs) after reinforcements than fixed schedules. This is because with variable schedules it is not known how many responses will have to be made or how much time will have to elapse before the next reinforcement.

Now let's think about partial-reinforcement schedules in terms of a general learning process—extinction. Remember the partial-reinforcement effect that we described at the beginning of this section—partial schedules of reinforcement are more resistant to extinction than are continuous schedules. This means that responding will not be extinguished as quickly after using one of the partial schedules as it would be with a continuous schedule. Obviously, it is easier to extinguish the response if the reinforcement had been given continuously for every response in the past. If a response is made and doesn't get reinforced, the responder knows immediately something is wrong because they have always been reinforced after each response. With partial schedules, if a response is made and doesn't get reinforced, the responder doesn't know that anything is wrong because they have not been reinforced for every response. Thus, it will take longer before extinction occurs for the partial schedules because it will take longer to realize that something is wrong.

Do you think there are any differences in this resistance to extinction between the various partial schedules of reinforcement? Think about the fixed schedules versus the variable schedules. Wouldn't it be much more difficult to realize that something is wrong on a variable schedule? On a fixed schedule, it would be easy to notice that the reinforcement didn't appear following the fixed number of responses or fixed time interval. On a variable schedule, however, the disappearance of reinforcement would be very difficult to detect because it's not known how many responses will have to be made or how much time has to elapse. Think about the example of a variable-ratio schedule with the rat pressing a lever. Because there is no fixed number of responses that have to be made, the rat wouldn't realize that its responding was being extinguished. It could be that the number of lever presses necessary to get the next reinforcement is very large. Because of such uncertainty, the variable schedules are much more resistant to extinction than the fixed schedules.

Motivation, Behavior, and Reinforcement

We have just learned about how reinforcement works and that partial-reinforcement schedules are powerful. But what initiates our behavior and guides it toward obtaining reinforcement? The answer is **motivation,** the set of internal and external factors that energize our behavior and direct it toward goals. Its origin is the Latin word *movere,* meaning to set in motion. Motivation moves us toward reinforcement by initiating and guiding our goal-directed behavior. There are several explanations of how motivation works. We will first consider a few general theories of motivated behavior and then a distinction between two types of motivation and reinforcement, extrinsic versus intrinsic.

Theories of motivation. One explanation of motivation, **drive-reduction theory,** proposes that first, a bodily need (such as hunger) creates a state of bodily tension called a drive; then, motivated behavior (seeking food) works to reduce this drive by obtaining reinforcement (food) to eliminate this need and return the body to a balanced internal state. Drives are disruptions of this balanced bodily state. We are "pushed" into action by these unpleasant drive states. They motivate our behavior to reduce the drive. Drive-reduction theory does a

motivation The set of internal and external factors that energize our behavior and direct it toward goals.

drive-reduction theory A theory of motivation that proposes that our behavior is motivated to reduce drives (bodily tension states) created by unsatisfied bodily needs to return the body to a balanced internal state.

good job of explaining some of our motivated behaviors, especially those concerned with biological needs, such as hunger and thirst; but it cannot explain all motivated behavior. Our behaviors are clearly motivated by factors other than drive reduction. Even eating and drinking aren't always cases of drive-reduction motivation. What if you accidentally run into someone that you really want to date and she/he asks you to lunch, but you had eaten a full lunch 15 minutes earlier? You would probably eat another lunch, wouldn't you? We eat for reasons other than hunger. Similarly, I'm sure that you often drink beverages without being truly thirsty. And is it really a "thirst" for knowledge that motivates your study behavior? A complementary theory, the incentive theory of motivation, has been proposed to account for such behavior.

In contrast to being "pushed" into action by internal drive states, the **incentive theory** of motivation proposes that we are "pulled" into action by incentives, external environmental stimuli that do not involve drive reduction. The source of the motivation, according to incentive theory, is outside the person. Money is an incentive for almost all of us. Good grades and esteem are incentives that likely motivate much of your behavior to study and work hard. Incentive theory is much like operant conditioning. Your behavior is directed toward obtaining reinforcement.

Another explanation of motivation, **arousal theory**, extends the importance of a balanced internal environment in drive-reduction theory to include our level of physiological arousal and its regulation. According to arousal theory, our behavior is motivated to maintain an optimal level of arousal, which varies within individuals (Zuckerman, 1979). When below the optimal level, our behavior is motivated to raise our arousal to that level. We seek stimulation. We might, for example, go see an action movie. If overaroused, then our behavior is motivated to lower the arousal level. We seek relaxation, so we might take a nap or a quiet walk. So in arousal theory, motivation does not always reduce arousal as in drive-reduction theory, but rather regulates the amount of arousal (not too much, not too little).

incentive theory A theory of motivation that proposes that our behavior is motivated by incentives, external stimuli that we have learned to associate with reinforcement.

arousal theory A theory of motivation that proposes that our behavior is motivated to maintain an optimal level of physiological arousal

Yerkes-Dodson law A law describing the relationship between the amount of arousal and the performance quality on a task—increasing arousal up to some optimal level increases performance quality on a task, but increasing arousal past this point is detrimental to performance.

In addition, arousal theory argues that our level of arousal affects our performance level, with a certain level being optimal. Usually referred to as the **Yerkes-Dodson law** because Robert Yerkes and James Dodson (1908) originally proposed it, this relationship between level of arousal and performance quality is rather simple. Shown in Figure 4.9, it is an inverted U-shaped relationship. Increased arousal will aid performance to a point (the optimal amount of arousal), after which further arousal impairs performance. Think about exams. You need to be aroused to do well on them; but if you are too aroused, your performance will be negatively affected.

To solidify your understanding of these three theories of motivation, they are summarized in Table 4.4.

Figure 4.9 | The Yerkes-Dodson Law | The Yerkes-Dodson law is very straightforward. As arousal increases, the quality of performance increases—up to the point of optimal arousal. Further increases in arousal are detrimental to performance.

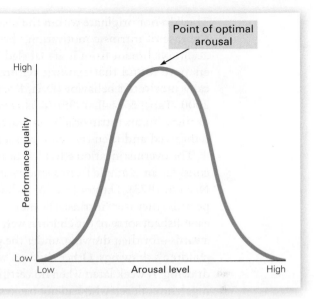

Extrinsic motivation versus intrinsic motivation. Motivation researchers make a distinction between **extrinsic motivation,** the desire to perform behavior to obtain an external reinforcer or to avoid an external aversive stimulus, and **intrinsic motiva-tion,** the desire to perform a behavior for its own sake. In cases of extrinsic motivation, reinforcement is not obtained from the behavior, but is a result of the behavior. In intrinsic

Table 4.4	Theories of Motivation
Theory	**Explanation**
Drive-reduction theory	Our behavior is motivated to reduce drives (bodily tension states) created by unsatisfied bodily needs to return the body to a balanced internal state
Incentive theory	Our behavior is motivated by incentives (external stimuli that we have learned to associate with reinforcement)
Arousal theory	Our behavior is motivated to maintain an optimal level of physiological arousal

motivation, the reinforcement is provided by the activity itself. Think about what you are doing right now. What is your motivation for studying this material? Like most students, you want to do well in your psychology class. You are studying for an external reinforcer (a good grade in the class), so your behavior is extrinsically motivated. If you enjoy reading about psychology and studying it for its own sake and not to earn a grade (and I hope that you do), then your studying would be intrinsically motivated. It is not an either-or situation. Both types of motivation are probably involved in your study behavior, but the contribution of each type varies greatly for each student.

The reinforcers in cases of extrinsic motivation—such as food, money, and awards—are called extrinsic reinforcers.

extrinsic motivation The desire to perform a behavior for external reinforcement.

intrinsic motivation The desire to perform a behavior for its own sake.

They do not originate within the task itself, but come from an external source. In the case of intrinsic motivation, the enjoyment of the behavior and the sense of accomplishment from it are labeled intrinsic reinforcers. Paradoxically, researchers have found that extrinsic reinforcement will sometimes undermine intrinsically motivated behavior (Deci, Koestner, & Ryan, 1999; Lepper & Henderlong, 2000; Tang & Hall, 1995). This is referred to as the **overjustification effect**, a decrease in an intrinsically motivated behavior after the behavior is extrinsically reinforced and then the reinforcement is discontinued.

The overjustification effect has been demonstrated for people of all ages, but let's consider an example from a study with nursery-school children (Lepper, Greene, & Nisbett, 1973). The children liked drawing with felt-tip pens and did so during play periods (they were intrinsically motivated to engage in such drawing). Once this was established, some of the children were given extrinsic reinforcement—"Good Player" awards—for their drawing, under the guise that someone was coming to look at the children's drawings. Other children were not given this extrinsic reinforcement for drawing. A week later, when no certificates were being offered for the felt-tip drawings, the children who had not been extrinsically reinforced continued to draw with the felt-tip pens, but those who had been reinforced spent much less time drawing, illustrating the overjustification effect. What leads to this effect?

In our example, extrinsic reinforcement (the awards for the children) provides unnecessary justification for engaging in the intrinsically motivated behavior (drawing with the felt-tip pens). A person's intrinsic enjoyment of an activity provides sufficient justification for their behavior. With the addition of the extrinsic reinforcement, the person may perceive the task as overjustified and then attempt to understand their true motivation (extrinsic versus intrinsic) for engaging in the activity. It is this cognitive analysis of motivation that leads to the decrease in engaging in the activity. In this cognitive analysis, the person overemphasizes the importance of the extrinsic motivation to their behavior. For example, the person may perceive the extrinsic reinforcement as an attempt at controlling their behavior, which may lead them to stop engaging in the activity to maintain their sense of choice. A person might also think that the reinforcement makes the activity more like work (something one does for extrinsic reinforcement) than play (something one does for its own sake), lessening their enjoyment of the activity and leading them to cease engaging in it.

The overjustification effect indicates that a person's cognitive processing influences their behavior and that such processing may lessen the effectiveness of extrinsic reinforcers. Don't worry, though, about the overjustification effect influencing your study habits (assuming that you enjoy studying). Research has shown that performance-contingent extrinsic reinforcers (such as your grades, which are contingent upon your performance) are not likely to undermine studying (Eisenberger & Cameron, 1996; Tang & Hall, 1995). This means that the extrinsic reinforcement is not likely to impact intrinsic motivation if the extrinsic reinforcement is dependent upon doing something well versus just doing it.

overjustification effect A decrease in an intrinsically motivated behavior after the behavior is extrinsically reinforced and then the reinforcement is discontinued.

The overjustification effect imposes a limitation on operant conditioning and its effectiveness in applied settings. It tells us that we need to be careful in our use of extrinsic motivation so that we do not undermine intrinsic motivation. It also tells us that we must consider the possible cognitive consequences of using extrinsic reinforcement. In the next section, we continue this limitation theme by first considering some biological constraints on learning and then some cognitive research that shows that reinforcement is not always necessary for learning.

Section Summary

In this section, we learned about operant conditioning, in which the rate of a particular response depends on its consequences, or how it operates on the environment. Immediate consequences normally produce the best operant conditioning, but there are exceptions to this rule. If a particular response leads to reinforcement (satisfying consequences), the response rate increases; if a particular response leads to punishment (unsatisfying consequences), the rate decreases. In positive reinforcement, an appetitive (pleasant) stimulus is presented, and in negative reinforcement, an aversive (unpleasant) stimulus is removed. In positive punishment, an aversive (unpleasant) stimulus is presented; in negative punishment, an appetitive (pleasant) stimulus is removed.

In operant conditioning, cumulative records (visual depictions of the rate of responding) are used to report behavior. Reinforcement is indicated by an increased response rate on the cumulative record, and extinction (when reinforcement is no longer presented) is indicated by a diminished response rate leading to no responding (flat) on the cumulative record. As in classical conditioning, spontaneous recovery of the response (a temporary increase in response rate on the cumulative record) is observed following breaks in extinction training. Discrimination and generalization involve the discriminative stimulus, the stimulus in whose presence the response will be reinforced. Thus, discrimination involves learning when the response will be reinforced. Generalization involves responding in the presence of stimuli similar to the discriminative stimulus—the more similar the stimulus, the greater the responding.

We learned about four different schedules of partial reinforcement—fixed ratio, variable ratio, fixed interval, and variable interval. All of these partial-reinforcement schedules, especially the variable ones, lead to greater resistance to extinction than does a continuous reinforcement schedule. This is the partial-reinforcement effect. In addition, we learned that ratio schedules lead to faster rates of responding than interval schedules and that variable schedules lead to fewer pauses in responding.

We also learned about motivation, which moves us toward reinforcement by initiating and guiding our goal-directed behavior. We considered three theories of motivation. First, drive-reduction theory proposes that drives—unpleasant internal states of tension—guide our behavior toward reinforcement so that the tension is reduced. Second, incentive theory asserts that our behavior is motivated by incentives—environmental stimuli that are associated with reinforcement. Third, arousal theory emphasizes the importance of physiological arousal and its regulation to motivation. Our behavior is motivated to maintain an optimal level of arousal. In addition, our level of arousal affects how well we perform tasks and solve problems. According to the Yerkes-Dodson law, increased arousal up to some optimal amount aids performance, but additional arousal is detrimental.

We also learned about the overjustification effect, in which extrinsic (external) reinforcement sometimes undermines intrinsic motivation, the desire to perform a behavior for its own sake. In the overjustification effect, there is a substantial decrease in an intrinsically motivated behavior after this behavior is extrinsically reinforced and then the reinforcement is discontinued. This effect seems to be the result of the cognitive analysis that a person conducts to determine the true motivation for their behavior. The importance of the extrinsic reinforcement is overemphasized in this cognitive analysis, leading the person to stop engaging in the behavior. Thus, the overjustification effect imposes a cognitive limitation on operant conditioning and its effectiveness.

ConceptCheck | 2

Explain what "positive" means in positive reinforcement and positive punishment and what "negative" means in negative reinforcement and negative punishment.

Explain why it is said that the operant response comes under the control of the discriminative stimulus.

Explain why a cumulative record goes to flat when a response is being extinguished.

Explain why the partial-reinforcement effect is greater for variable schedules than fixed schedules of reinforcement.

Explain why the overjustification effect is a cognitive limitation on operant conditioning.

Biological and Cognitive Aspects of Learning

In our discussion of the classical conditioning of emotional responses, we mentioned biological predispositions to learning certain fears. Humans seem prepared to learn fears of animals or heights much easier than fears of toy blocks or curtains. Animals (snakes or spiders) are more dangerous to us than toy blocks, so such predispositions make evolutionary sense (Seligman, 1971). Are there any other predispositions that affect classical conditioning and are there any biological constraints on operant conditioning? In addition to addressing these questions about the biological aspects of learning, we will also discuss cognitive research on latent learning and learning through modeling that questions whether reinforcement is necessary for learning. Let's start with the biological research.

Biological Preparedness in Learning

Do you have any taste aversions? Have you stopped eating a certain food or drinking a certain liquid because you once got miserably sick after doing so? If you have a really strong aversion, you may feel ill even when you think about that food or drink. If the illness involved a specific food from a particular restaurant, you may have even generalized the aversion to the restaurant. Just as we are biologically prepared to learn certain fears more than others (Öhman & Mineka, 2001), we are also prepared to learn taste aversions. Our preparedness to learn to fear objects and situations dangerous to us (animals and heights) and to avoid foods and drinks that make us sick has adaptive significance. Such learning enhances our chances of survival. It makes biological sense then that we should be predisposed to such learning. To see how psychologists have studied such predispositions, let's take a closer look at some of the early research on taste aversion.

Taste aversion. John Garcia and his colleagues conducted some of the most important early research on taste aversion in the 1960s. Their research challenged the prevailing behaviorist argument that an animal's capacity for conditioning is not limited by its biology (Garcia, 2003). Garcia benefited from an accidental discovery while studying the effects of radiation on rats (Garcia, Kimeldorf, Hunt, & Davies, 1956). The rats would be moved from their home cages to experimental chambers for the radiation experiments. The radiation made the rats nauseated, and they would get very sick later back in their home cages. The rats, however, would still go back into the experimental chambers where they had been radiated, but they would no longer drink the water in these chambers. Why? The water bottles in the chambers were made of a different substance than those in the home cages—plastic versus glass. So, the water the rats drank in the experimental chambers had a different taste than that in their home cages, and the rats had quickly learned an aversion to it. They paired the different taste with their later sickness. Rats do not have the cognitive capacity to realize that they were radiated and that it was the radiation that made them sick. Note that the rats did not get sick immediately following the drinking or the radiation. The nausea came hours later. This means that learning a taste aversion is a dramatic counterexample to the rule that the UCS (sickness) in classical conditioning must immediately follow the CS (the different-tasting water) for learning to occur (Etscorn & Stephens, 1973). In fact, if the CS-UCS interval is less than a few minutes, a taste aversion will not be learned (Schafe, Sollars, & Bernstein, 1995). This makes sense because spoiled or poisoned food typically does not make an animal sick until a longer time period has elapsed.

So how did Garcia and his colleagues use these taste aversion results for rats to demonstrate biological preparedness in learning? Garcia and Koelling (1966) showed that the rats would not learn such aversions for just any pairing of cue and consequences. Those that seemed to make more biological sense (different-tasting water paired with later sickness) were easily learned, but other pairings that didn't make biological sense did not even seem learnable. For example, they examined two cues that were both paired with sickness through radiation: (1) sweet-tasting water, or (2) normal-tasting water

John Garcia

accompanied by clicking noises and flashing lights when the rats drank. The rats who drank the sweet-tasting water easily learned the aversion to the water, but the rats who drank normal-tasting water with the accompanying clicking noises and flashing lights did not. The rats just couldn't learn to pair these environmental auditory and visual cues with their later sickness; this pairing didn't make any biological sense to the rats. It's important for rats to learn to avoid food and water that will make them sick, but in a natural environment, noises and lights don't typically cause sickness for rats.

This doesn't mean that other animals might not be predisposed to learn auditory or visual aversions. For example, many birds, such as quail, seem to learn visual aversions rather easily. A clever study demonstrated this difference among animals in types of learning predispositions. In this study, both quail and rats drank dark blue, sour-tasting water prior to being made ill (Wilcoxon, Dragoin, & Kral, 1971). Later, the animals were given a choice between dark blue water that tasted normal and sour-tasting water that visually appeared normal. The birds only avoided the dark blue water, and the rats only avoided the sour-tasting water. In general, an animal is biologically predisposed to learn more easily those associations that are relevant to its environment and important to its survival (Staddon & Ettinger, 1989). Rats are scavengers, so they eat whatever is available. They encounter many novel foods, so it makes biological sense that they should be prepared to learn taste aversions easily to enhance their survival. Birds hunt by sight, so visual aversions are more relevant to their survival. There are also biological preparedness effects on operant conditioning. We'll take a look at one of the most important—instinctual drift.

Instinctual drift. Keller and Marian Breland, two of Skinner's former students, discovered an important biological preparedness effect on operant conditioning

As shown in these photos, pigs are biologically predisposed to root out their food, and raccoons are biologically predisposed to wash their food. Thus, when the Brelands operantly conditioned pigs and raccoons to pick up oversized coins and put them in a bank using food reinforcement, the animals sometimes "misbehaved" (reverted back to these instinctual responses that were part of their food gathering behaviors). The pigs pushed the coins with their snouts, and the raccoons rubbed the coins together in their forepaws. Reverting back to an innate, instinctual response from a learned operant response is called instinctual drift.

(Breland & Breland, 1961). The Brelands, who became animal trainers, employed operant conditioning to train thousands of animals to do all sorts of tricks. In doing this training, they discovered what has become known as **instinctual drift**—the tendency of an animal to drift back from a learned operant response to an object to an innate, instinctual response. For example, the Brelands used food reinforcement to train some animals to pick up oversized coins and put them in a bank. The Brelands did this with both pigs and raccoons. However, they observed that once the coins became associated with the food reinforcement, both types of animal drifted back to instinctual responses that were part of their respective food-gathering behaviors. The pigs began to push the coins with their snouts, and the raccoons started to rub the coins together in their forepaws. These more natural responses interfered with the Brelands' operant training.

> **instinctual drift** The tendency for an animal to drift back from a learned operant response to an innate, instinctual response to an object.
>
> **latent learning** Learning that occurs but is not demonstrated until there is incentive to do so.

The important point of these findings is that biologically instinctual responses sometimes limit or hinder our ability to condition other, less natural responses. The Brelands' work demonstrates a biological preparedness effect upon operant conditioning. Biological predispositions show that animals will learn certain associations (those consistent with their natural behavior) more easily than others (those less consistent with their natural behavior). Also note that this "misbehavior" of the pigs and the raccoons (their instinctual responses) continued without reinforcement from the trainers. In fact, it prevented the animals from getting reinforcement. This aspect of the Brelands' work relates to the more general question of whether we can learn without reinforcement, which we will discuss in the next section.

Latent Learning and Observational Learning

Cognitively oriented learning researchers are interested in the mental processes involved in learning. These researchers have examined the question of whether we can learn without reinforcement in their studies of latent learning and observational learning. We'll consider some of the classic research on these two types of learning.

Latent learning. Think about studying for an exam in one of your courses. What you have learned is not openly demonstrated until you are tested on it by the exam. You learn, but you do not demonstrate the learning until reinforcement for demonstrating it (a good grade on the exam) is available. This is an example of what psychologists call **latent learning,** learning that occurs but is not demonstrated until there is incentive to do so. This is what Edward Tolman was examining in his pioneering latent-learning research with rats.

In this research, food-deprived rats had to negotiate a maze, and the number of wrong turns (errors) that a rat made was

Edward Tolman

"Bathroom? Sure, it's just down the hall to the left, jog right, left, another left, straight past two more lefts, then right, and it's at the end of the third corridor on your right."

counted (Tolman & Honzik, 1930a, b, and c). In one study, there were three different groups of rats and about three weeks (one trial per day) of maze running. Food (reinforcement) was always available in the goal box at the maze's end for one group but never available for another group. For the third group, there was no food available until the eleventh day. What happened? First, the number of wrong turns decreased over trials, but it decreased much more rapidly for the group who always got food reinforcement through the first 10 trials. Second, the performance for the group that only started getting food reinforcement on the eleventh day improved immediately on the next day (and thereafter), equaling that of the group that had always gotten food reinforcement (Figure 4.10). It appears that the third group of rats had been learning the maze all along, but did not demonstrate their learning until the food reinforcement was made available. The rats' learning had been latent. They had learned a cognitive map (a mental representation) of the maze,

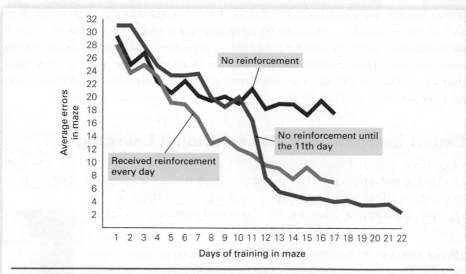

Figure 4.10 | Latent Learning | There were three different groups of rats, and each rat received one trial per day in a maze. Latent learning is evident for the rats who did not receive reinforcement until Day 11. Once reinforcement (a food reward in the goal box at the end of the maze) was given, these rats demonstrated their prior learning of the maze on the first 11 days by immediately (on Day 12) doing as well as the rats that had been regularly reinforced. They had learned a cognitive map of the maze, and when reinforcement became available, they used it. This learning remained latent (present but not evident) until their maze-running behavior was reinforced. (Data from "Introduction and Removal of Reward, and Maze Performance in Rats," by E. C. Tolman & C. K. Honzik, 1930, *University of California Publication in Psychology*, 4, pp. 257–275.)

and when they needed to use it (when reinforcement became available), they did. This explanation was tested further by blocking the optimal route to the goal box to see if the rats would use their cognitive map to take the next best route. The rats did.

> **observational learning (modeling)**
> Learning by observing others and imitating their behavior.

How would such a map be created in the rat's brain and how would it allow the rat to navigate its way through a complex environment, such as a maze? A few decades elapsed after Tolman's research before these questions were answered. The answer involves the discovery of two types of neurons in the brain, place cells and grid cells. Physiological psychologist John O'Keefe identified the place cells located in the hippocampus that function to build an inner map of the environment (O'Keefe, 1976; O'Keefe & Dostrovsky, 1971), and May-Britt and Edvard Moser identified the grid cells located in the entorhinal cortex, a cortical region next to the hippocampus, that generate a coordinate system and allow precise positioning and pathfinding, a sort of inner GPS (Fyhn, Molden, Witter, Moser, & Moser, 2004; Hafting, Fyhn, Molden, Moser, & Moser, 2005; Moser and Moser, 2016; Sargolini et al., 2006). For their key contributions to our understanding of this system, John O'Keefe and May-Britt and Edvard Moser shared the 2014 Nobel Prize in Physiology or Medicine. Brain imaging research along with studies of patients undergoing neurosurgery have provided evidence that place and grid cells also exist in the human brain and work as in the rat brain to provide us with an inner GPS (Ekstrom et al., 2003; Jacobs et al., 2013). Other research has shown that this is true also for bats and monkeys (Finkelstein et al., 2014), suggesting that this navigational system arose early in mammalian evolution and that similar neural positional algorithms are used across various mammalian species.

Observational learning. Much learning by humans is more cognitive in nature and does not involve conditioning through direct experience. Observational learning, sometimes called modeling, is a good example. By watching a model, we learn through vicarious reinforcement and punishment without being conditioned directly. We learn to anticipate a behavior's consequences in situations like those that we have observed. **Observational learning (modeling)**—learning by observing others and imitating their behavior— plays a major role in human learning (Bandura, 1973). For example, observational learning helps us learn how to play sports, write the letters of the alphabet, and drive a car. We observe others and then do our best to imitate their behavior. We also often learn our attitudes and appropriate ways to act out our feelings by observing good and bad models. Today's sports and movie stars are powerful models for such learning. In sum, imitation is pervasive in humans, even infants (Jones, 2007).

Albert Bandura

Courtesy of Albert Bandura

Albert Bandura's famous experiments on learning through modeling involved a Bobo doll, a large inflated clown doll, and

Courtesy of Albert Bandura

These photographs of the children in the Bobo doll experiments imitating the violent behavior of the adult model show the powerful influence of observational learning.

kindergarten-age children as participants (Bandura, 1965; Bandura, Ross, & Ross, 1961, 1963a, 1963b). In one experiment, some of the children in the study were exposed to an adult who beat, kicked, and yelled at the Bobo doll. After observing this behavior, each child was taken to a room filled with many appealing toys, but the experimenter upset the child by saying that these toys were being saved for other children. The child was then taken to a room that contained a few other toys, including the Bobo doll. Can you guess what happened? The child started beating on the Bobo doll just as the adult model had done. The children even repeated the same words that they heard the model use earlier while beating the doll. Children who had not observed the abusive adult were much less likely to engage in such behavior.

But what would happen if a child were exposed to a model that acted gently toward the Bobo doll? In another experiment, Bandura had children observe either an aggressive model, a gentle model, or no model. When allowed to play in a toy room that included a Bobo doll, what happened? The children exposed to the aggressive model acted more aggressively toward the doll than the children with no model, and the children with the gentle model acted more gently toward the doll than the children with no model. In general, the children's behavior with the doll was guided by their model's behavior. But the models in these experiments were not reinforced or punished for their behavior. Would this make a difference?

Bandura examined this question in another experiment. The young children watched a film of an adult acting aggressively toward the Bobo doll, but there were three different versions of the film. In one version, the adult's behavior was reinforced; in another, the behavior was punished; and in the third, there were no consequences. Each child's interactions with the Bobo doll varied depending upon which film the child had seen. The children who had watched the adult get reinforced for aggressive behavior acted more aggressively toward the Bobo doll than those who had seen the model act with no consequences. In addition, the children who had watched the adult get punished were less likely to act aggressively toward the doll than the children who had not been exposed to any consequences for acting aggressively toward the doll. The children's behavior was affected by the consequences witnessed in the film. Then Bandura cleverly asked the children if they could imitate the behavior in the film for reinforcement (snacks). Essentially, all of the children could do so. This is an important point. It means that the children all learned the behavior through observation regardless of whether the behavior was reinforced, punished, or neither.

According to Lansford (2012), researchers subsequently questioned the generalizability of Bandura's findings both with respect to the context (the studies were conducted in a laboratory setting) and the temporal proximity between the children's observation of the adult model's aggression and their own aggression (there was a close temporal proximity in the studies). Would children imitate aggression in other settings and after lengthier delays? It turns out that they do. More recent studies have found that Bandura's finding of children imitating aggression does hold in a variety of nonlaboratory settings and after lengthy delays between observing the aggression and then acting aggressively (Bushman & Huesmann, 2010; Guerra, Huesmann, & Spindler, 2003; Slater, Henry, Swaim, & Anderson, 2003).

Much of the research on observational learning since Bandura's pioneering studies has focused on the question of whether exposure to violence in media leads people to behave more aggressively. There is clearly an abundance of violence on television and in other media. It has been estimated that the average child has viewed 8,000 murders and 100,000 other acts of violence on television alone by the time he finishes elementary school (Huston et al., 1992), and more recent research indicates that the amount of violence on television and in other media has increased since Huston et al.'s study. For example, the Parents Television Council (2007) found that violence in prime-time television increased 75% between 1998 and 2006, and the National Television Violence Study evaluated almost 10,000 hours of broadcast programming from 1995 through 1997 and found that 61% of the programming portrayed interpersonal violence, much of it in an entertaining or glamorized manner, and that the highest proportion of violence was in children's shows (American Academy of Pediatrics, 2009). But do we learn to be more aggressive from observing all of this violence on television and in other media?

Literally hundreds of studies have addressed this question, and as you would expect, the findings are both complicated and controversial. Leading scientists reviewing this literature, however, came to the following general conclusion: "Research on violent television and films, video games, and music reveals unequivocal evidence that media violence increases the likelihood of aggressive and violent behavior in both immediate and long-term contexts" (Anderson et al., 2003). Similarly, the authors of a recent meta-analysis of over 130 studies of video game play with 130,296 participants across Eastern and Western cultures concluded that exposure to violent video games is a causal risk factor for increased aggressive behavior, aggressive cognition, and aggressive affect and for decreased empathy and prosocial behavior (Anderson et al., 2010). Huesmann (2010, p. 179) argues that this meta-analysis "proves beyond a reasonable doubt that exposure to video game violence increases the risk that the observer will behave more aggressively and violently in the future" (cf. Ferguson & Kilburn, 2010). Finally, based on a review of research findings on the exposure to violence in television, movies, video games, cell phones, and on the Internet since the 1960s, Huesmann (2007) concluded that such exposure significantly increases the risk of violent behavior on the viewer's or game player's part, and that the size of this effect is large enough to be considered a public health threat (cf. Ferguson & Kilburn, 2009). Per the effect sizes for many common threats to public health given in Bushman & Huesmann (2001), there is only one greater than exposure to media violence and aggression and that is smoking and lung cancer.

The empirical evidence linking exposure to media violence to increased risk of aggressive behavior seems clear-cut (e.g., Murray, 2008; cf. Grimes, Anderson, & Bergen, 2008). However, as with other learned behaviors, many factors at the individual, family, and broader community levels contribute to the development of aggression. We must also remember that media exposure is not a necessary and sufficient cause of violence—not all viewers will be led to violence, with some more susceptible than others; but this is also true for other public health threats, such as exposure to cigarette smoke and the increased risk of lung cancer. It is also very difficult to determine whether cumulative exposure leads to increased aggression over the long term (cf. Hasan, Bègue, Scharkow, & Bushman, 2013). Regardless, it seems clear that exposure to media violence is a risk factor for aggression. In this vein, the American Academy of Pediatrics (2009, p. 1222) concluded that "exposure to violence in media, including television, movies, music, and video games, represents a significant risk to the health of children and adolescents. Extensive research evidence indicates that media violence can contribute to aggressive behavior, desensitization to violence, nightmares, and fear of being harmed."

Recent research has also identified neurons that provide a possible neural basis for observational learning. These **mirror neurons** are neurons that fire both when performing an action and when observing another person perform that same action. When you observe someone engaging in an action, similar mirror neurons are firing in both your brain and in the other person's brain. Thus, these neurons in your brain are "mirroring" the behavior of the person you are observing. Mirror neurons were first discovered in macaque monkeys via electrode recording by Giacomo Rizzolatti and his colleagues at the University of Parma in the mid-1990s (Iacoboni, 2009b), but it is not normally possible to study single neurons in humans because that would entail attaching neurons directly to the brain; therefore, most of the evidence for such neurons in humans is indirect. For example, using fMRI and other scanning techniques, neuroscientists have observed that the same cortical areas in humans are involved when performing an action and observing that action (Rizzolatti & Craighero, 2004). These areas are referred to as mirror neuron systems because groups of neurons firing together rather than single neurons firing separately were observed in these studies. A recent study, however, claimed to provide direct evidence for mirror neurons in humans by recording the activity of individual neurons (Mukamel, Ekstrom, Kaplan, Iacoboni, &

mirror neurons Neurons that fire both when performing an action and when observing another person perform that same action.

Fried, 2010). Mukamel et al. recorded from the brains of 21 patients who were being treated for intractable epilepsy. The patients had been implanted with electrodes to identify seizure locations for surgical treatment. With the patients' consent, the researchers used the same electrodes for their study. They found neurons that behaved as mirror neurons, showing their greatest activity both when the patients performed a task and when they observed a task. However, in another human study at about the same time (Lingnau, Gesierich, & Caramazza, 2009), no evidence was found that neurons in the proposed mirror neuron areas functioned as mirror neurons should function. Specifically, the cells did not show adaptation to viewing and executing the same movements over and over again. In sum, whereas some researchers now claim that we now know for sure that humans have mirror neurons (Keysers & Gazzola, 2010), other researchers doubt that these supposed mirror neuron systems function as supporters claim they do (Hickok, 2014).

Because both human and nonhuman primates learn much through observation and imitation, mirror neuron systems, if they function as their proponents claim they do, would provide a way through which observation could be translated into action (Cattaneo & Rizzolatti, 2009; Iacoboni, 2005, 2009b). Indeed, some studies claim that mirror neurons have proved useful in the rehabilitation of motor deficits in people who have had strokes (Ertelt et al., 2007). For example, patients who watch videos of people demonstrating various arm and hand movements (action observation) improved faster than those who did not watch the videos (Binkofski & Buccino, 2007). In addition to providing a neural basis for observational learning, some researchers have speculated that mirror neuron systems may also play a major role in both empathy (the ability to feel and understand the feelings of others) and understanding the intentions of others (Iacoboni, 2009a). In addition, mirror neurons have been proposed to be the basic neural mechanism from which language evolved (Rizzolatti & Arbib, 1998; Rizzolatti & Craighero, 2004). Some other researchers even think that there may be a link between mirror neuron deficiency and social disorders, namely autism, in which individuals have difficulty in social interactions (Dapretto et al., 2006). All of these claims for mirror neurons, especially the more speculative ones, such as the links to autism and language, are very controversial (Hickok, 2014; Jarrett, 2015). For example, a review of the results from 25 relevant studies concluded that there was little evidence for a global dysfunction of the mirror neuron system in autism (Hamilton, 2013). It is clear that most people with autism have no problem understanding other people's actions and have normal imitation abilities and thus do not have dysfunctional mirror neuron systems (Gallese, Gernsbacher, Heyes, Hickok, & Iacoboni, 2011, p. 290). In sum, researchers not only disagree about the presence of mirror neuron systems in humans but also, if they do exist, about what exactly they do (Jarrett, 2015).

Lastly, observational learning, like latent learning, emphasizes the role of cognitive processes in learning. As demonstrated by our examples, just as Tolman's rats seemed to have a cognitive map of the maze, Bandura's children seemed to have a cognitive model of the actions of the adult models and their consequences.

Cognitive psychologists have studied the development of such mental representations and their storage in memory and subsequent retrieval from memory in their attempts to understand how the human memory system works. We will take a detailed look at the human memory system in Chapter 5.

Section Summary

In this section, we learned about some of the effects of biological preparedness on learning and about latent learning and observational learning in which direct reinforcement is not necessary. Research on taste aversion indicated that rats could easily learn aversion to different-tasting water when it was paired with later sickness, but could not learn to pair auditory and visual cues with such sickness. This finding indicates that animals may be biologically predisposed to learn those associations that are important to their survival more easily than arbitrary associations. Similarly, the Brelands found in their animal training work that animals drift back to their instinctual responses from conditioned arbitrary ones, a phenomenon called instinctual drift. Findings such as these highlight the impact of biological predispositions upon learning.

Research has shown that reinforcement is not necessary for learning to occur. Tolman's research with rats running mazes showed that without reinforcement, rats could learn a cognitive map of the maze that they could then use very efficiently when reinforcement became available at the end of the maze. This was an instance of latent learning, learning that is not demonstrated until there is an incentive to do so. Albert Bandura's pioneering research on observational learning showed that much of human learning also doesn't involve direct experience. The children in his study all learned a model's behavior through observation, regardless of whether the behavior was reinforced, punished, or neither. Research in observational learning since Bandura's studies has extended his findings by linking exposure to media violence to an increased likelihood of aggression in viewers. Other recent research by neuroscientists has led to the discovery of mirror neuron systems that may provide a possible neural basis for observational learning. However, their existence and functions in humans are controversial and have not been established by current research findings.

ConceptCheck | 3

Explain why the ease of learning taste aversions is biologically adaptive for humans.

Given Garcia and Koelling's (1966) findings (discussed in this section) for rats' pairing the cues of sweet-tasting water and normal-tasting water accompanied by clicking noises and flashing lights when the rats drank with a sickness consequence, what do you think they observed when they paired these two cues with an immediate electric shock consequence instead of a sickness consequence? Justify your answer in terms of biological preparedness in learning.

Explain why it would be easier to operantly condition a behavior that is "natural" for an animal than one that isn't natural.

Explain the relationship between latent learning and reinforcement.

Explain how reinforcing and punishing models influenced observers in Bandura's research.

Study Guide

Chapter Key Terms

You should know the definitions of the following key terms from the chapter. They are listed in the order in which they appear in the chapter. For those you do not know, return to the relevant section of the chapter to learn them. When you think that you know all of the terms, complete the matching exercise based on these key terms.

classical conditioning
reflex
unconditioned stimulus (UCS)
unconditioned response (UCR)
conditioned stimulus (CS)
conditioned response (CR)
delayed conditioning
trace conditioning
acquisition (in classical conditioning)
extinction (in classical conditioning)
spontaneous recovery (in classical conditioning)
stimulus generalization (in classical conditioning)
stimulus discrimination (in classical conditioning)
operant conditioning
law of effect
reinforcer
punisher
reinforcement
punishment

appetitive stimulus
aversive stimulus
positive reinforcement
positive punishment
negative reinforcement
negative punishment
Premack principle
primary reinforcer
secondary reinforcer
behavior modification
shaping
cumulative record
acquisition (in operant conditioning)
extinction (in operant conditioning)
spontaneous recovery (in operant conditioning)
discriminative stimulus (in operant conditioning)
stimulus discrimination (in operant conditioning)
stimulus generalization (in operant conditioning)

continuous schedule of reinforcement
partial schedule of reinforcement
partial-reinforcement effect
fixed-ratio schedule
variable-ratio schedule
fixed-interval schedule
variable-interval schedule
motivation
drive-reduction theory
incentive theory
arousal theory
Yerkes-Dodson law
extrinsic motivation
intrinsic motivation
overjustification effect
instinctual drift
latent learning
observational learning (modeling)
mirror neurons

Key Terms Exercise

Identify the correct term for each of the following definitions. The answers to this exercise follow the answers to the ConceptChecks at the end of the chapter.

1. A classical conditioning procedure in which the conditioned stimulus precedes the uncon-

ditioned stimulus but the two stimuli do not occur together.

_____

2. A stimulus that gains its reinforcing property through learning.

_____

3. In operant conditioning, giving the operant response in the presence of stimuli similar to the discriminative stimulus.

_____

4. The stimulus that comes to elicit a new response in classical conditioning.

_____

5. The finding that operant responses reinforced on partial schedules are more resistant to extinction than those reinforced on a continuous schedule.

_____

6. A stimulus that is unpleasant.

_____

7. Training an animal or human to make an operant response by reinforcing successive approximations to the desired response.

_____

8. A partial schedule of reinforcement in which the number of responses it takes to obtain a reinforcer varies on each trial but averages to a set number across trials.

_____

9. A partial schedule of reinforcement in which the time that must elapse on each trial before a response will lead to the delivery of a reinforcer varies from trial to trial but averages to a set time across trials.

_____

10. The application of classical and operant conditioning principles to eliminate undesirable behavior and to teach more desirable behavior.

_____

11. The desire to perform a behavior for external reinforcement.

_____

12. Punishment in which an aversive stimulus is presented.

_____

13. A principle developed by Edward Thorndike that says that any behavior that results in satisfying consequences tends to be repeated and that any behavior that results in unsatisfying consequences tends not to be repeated.

_____

14. A partial recovery in strength of the conditioned response following a break during extinction training.

_____

15. The diminishing of the operant response when it is no longer reinforced.

_____

Practice Test Questions

The following are practice multiple-choice test questions on some of the chapter content. The answers are given after the Key Terms Exercise answers at the end of the chapter. If you guessed on a question or incorrectly answered a question, restudy the relevant section of the chapter.

1. In Pavlov's classical conditioning research, a tone was used as the _____, and food inserted in the mouth served as the _____.
   a. UCS; CS
   b. CS; UCS
   c. UCR; CR
   d. CR; UCR

2. In classical conditioning, the diminishing of the CR following removal of the UCS is called _____.
   a. acquisition
   b. discrimination
   c. extinction
   d. generalization

3. In stimulus generalization in classical conditioning, the strength of the CR _____, as the similarity of the generalization stimulus to the _____ increases.
   a. increases; CS
   b. decreases; CS
   c. increases; UCS
   d. decreases; UCS

4. In reinforcement, the probability of a behavior _____; in punishment the probability of a behavior _____.
   a. increases; increases
   b. increases; decreases
   c. decreases; increases
   d. decreases; decreases

5. Negative reinforcement occurs when an _____ stimulus is _____.
   a. appetitive; presented
   b. appetitive; removed
   c. aversive; presented
   d. aversive; removed

6. Which of the following is the best example of a primary reinforcer?
   a. a cheeseburger
   b. a grade of "A" on an exam
   c. praise from your teacher
   d. winning the lottery

7. The stimulus in whose presence a response will be reinforced is called the stimulus _____ in operant conditioning.
   a. generalization
   b. discriminative
   c. acquisition
   d. extinction

8. Piecework in a factory is an example of a _____ schedule of reinforcement; a slot machine is an example of a _____ schedule of reinforcement.
   a. variable-ratio; fixed-interval
   b. fixed-interval; variable-ratio
   c. fixed-ratio; variable-ratio
   d. variable-ratio; fixed-ratio

9. The Brelands' difficulties in training animals were the result of _____.
   a. the partial-reinforcement effect
   b. instinctual drift
   c. a token economy
   d. latent learning

10. Tolman's research with rats in mazes indicated the occurrence of _____.
    a. observational learning
    b. latent learning
    c. the partial-reinforcement effect
    d. instinctual drift

11. Which of the following is an example of a secondary reinforcer?
    a. money
    b. a money order
    c. a check
    d. all of the above

12. The _____ effect is a decrease in an intrinsically motivated behavior after the behavior is extrinsically reinforced and the reinforcement discontinued.
    a. overjustification
    b. partial reinforcement
    c. shaping
    d. instinctual drift

13. A steep cumulative record in operant conditioning indicates _____, and a flat cumulative record indicates _____.
    a. a slow rate of responding; no responding
    b. a slow rate of responding; a fast rate of responding
    c. a fast rate of responding; no responding
    d. a fast rate of responding; a slow rate of responding

14. The results of Bandura's Bobo doll studies illustrate _____, and Tolman and Honzik's studies of latent learning indicate the importance of _____ in maze learning by rats.
    a. observational learning; the overjustification effect
    b. observational learning; cognitive maps
    c. the partial-reinforcement effect; the overjustification effect
    d. the partial-reinforcement effect; cognitive maps

15. Continuing to take Advil because it alleviates headaches is an example of _____, and no longer parking in "No Parking" zones because you lost money in fines for doing so is an example of _____.
    a. positive punishment; positive reinforcement
    b. positive reinforcement; positive punishment
    c. negative punishment; negative reinforcement
    d. negative reinforcement; negative punishment

Chapter ConceptCheck Answers

ConceptCheck | 1

- The UCS was the hammer striking the participant's knee, and the UCR was the participant's knee jerk in response to the hammer strike. The CS was the bell ringing, and the CR was the participant's knee jerk in response to this bell.

- The Little Albert study is an example of using the delayed classical conditioning procedure because the CS (the white rat) was presented before the UCS (the loud, unexpected noise) and remained there until the UCS was presented. If the white rat had been taken away before the unexpected loud noise, then the study would have been an example of using the trace conditioning procedure.

- Generalization and discrimination can be thought of as opposites because generalization is the broadening of the conditioned response to other stimuli, whereas discrimination is the narrowing of the response to only the stimulus followed by the UCS and those stimuli so similar to this stimulus that they cannot be discriminated from it.

- Extinction is used during discrimination training. The responses to all stimuli except the original CS are diminished because the UCS does not follow any of them. However, if a stimulus cannot be discriminated from the CS, the response to it is not extinguished.

ConceptCheck | 2

- "Positive" refers to the presentation of a stimulus. In positive reinforcement, an appetitive stimulus is presented; in positive punishment, an aversive stimulus is presented. "Negative" refers to the removal of a stimulus. In negative reinforcement, an aversive stimulus is removed; in negative punishment, an appetitive stimulus is removed.

- The operant response comes under the control of the discriminative stimulus because it is only given in the presence of the discriminative stimulus. The animal or human learns that the reinforcement is only available in the presence of the discriminative stimulus.

- A cumulative record goes flat when a response is extinguished because no more responses are made; the cumulative total of responses remains the same over time. Thus, the record is flat because this total is not increasing at all. Remember that the cumulative record can never decrease because the total number of responses can only increase.

- The partial-reinforcement effect is greater for variable schedules than fixed schedules because there is no way for the person or animal to know how many responses are necessary (on a ratio schedule) or how much time has to elapse (on an interval schedule) to obtain a reinforcer. Thus, it is very difficult to realize that reinforcement has been withdrawn and so the responding is more resistant to extinction. On fixed schedules, however, you know how many responses have to be made or how much time has to elapse because these are set numbers or amounts of time. Thus, it is easier to detect that the reinforcement has been withdrawn, so fixed schedules are less resistant to extinction.

- The overjustification effect is a cognitive limitation on operant conditioning because it is the result of a person's cognitive analysis of their true motivation (extrinsic versus intrinsic) for engaging in an activity. In this analysis, the person overemphasizes the importance of the extrinsic reinforcement. For example, the person might now view the extrinsic reinforcement as an attempt at controlling their behavior and stop the behavior to maintain their sense of choice.

ConceptCheck | 3

- Learning taste aversions quickly and easily is adaptive because it increases our chances of survival. If we eat or drink something that makes us terribly sick, it is adaptive to no longer ingest that food or drink because we might die. We have a greater probability of surviving if we learn such aversions easily.

- The rats easily learned (stopped drinking the water) when the normal-tasting water accompanied by clicking noises and flashing lights was paired with immediate electric shock, but they did not when the sweet-tasting water cue was paired with this consequence. In terms of biological preparedness, the former pairing makes biological sense to the rats whereas the latter pairing does not. In a natural environment, audiovisual changes typically signal possible external dangers, but sweet-tasting water typically does not. External cues (noises and flashing lights) paired with an external dangerous consequence (shock) makes more biological sense than an internal cue (taste) paired with an external consequence (shock). For learning to occur, external cues should be paired with external consequences, and internal cues with internal consequences.

- It would be easier to operantly condition a "natural" response because it would lower the probability that instinctual drift will interfere with the conditioning. Because an animal would already be making its natural response to the object, there would be no other response to drift back to. In addition, the natural response to the object would be easier to shape because it would be given sooner and more frequently than an unnatural response.

- Latent learning occurs without direct reinforcement, but such learning is not demonstrated until reinforcement is made available for the learned behavior.

- In Bandura's work, reinforcing the model increased the probability that the observed behavior would be displayed, and punishing the model decreased the probability that the observed behavior would be displayed. But Bandura demonstrated in both cases that the behavior was learned. The reinforcement or punishment only affected whether it was displayed.

Answers to Key Terms Exercise

1. trace conditioning
2. secondary reinforcer
3. stimulus generalization
4. conditioned stimulus
5. partial-reinforcement effect
6. aversive stimulus
7. shaping
8. variable-ratio schedule
9. variable-interval schedule
10. behavior modification
11. extrinsic motivation
12. positive punishment
13. law of effect
14. spontaneous recovery (in classical conditioning)
15. extinction (in operant conditioning)

Answers to Practice Test Questions

1. b; CS; UCS
2. c; extinction
3. a; increases; CS
4. b; increases; decreases
5. d; aversive; removed
6. a; a cheeseburger
7. b; discriminative
8. c; fixed-ratio; variable-ratio
9. b; instinctual drift
10. b; latent learning
11. d; all of the above
12. a; overjustification
13. c; a fast rate of responding; no responding
14. b; observational learning; cognitive maps
15. d; negative reinforcement; negative punishment

5 | Memory

Imagine what life would be like without memory. Everything would be constantly new. There would be no past experiences. We would have no top-down processing. Even the present would be a state of massive confusion because we couldn't use what we know, our memory, to interpret the world. Everything would be new and unfamiliar. So, instead of being critical of memory when we forget things, we should be thankful that we have it. Our memories may fail us sometimes, but they are essential for life as we currently experience it. Without memory, we would be lost in the present.

The study of memory is not only an extension of the study of sensation and perception discussed in Chapter 3 (top-down processing using stored memories enables current perceptions, and new memories are formed from these perceptions), but it is also an extension of the discussion of the learning processes in Chapter 4 (the learning involved in human memory is more complex than the associational learning involved in conditioning). In this chapter, we will focus on the memory processes essential to learning as we normally think about it—learning from books and other media. The material in this chapter will have a practical use—by finding out how memory works, you will be able to improve yours.

To help understand how your memory works, we begin with a discussion of the most influential model of our memory system—the three-stage model. Then, the focus will turn to how we get information into our memory system—a process called encoding. In this section, we will examine ways to improve memory through better encoding. Next, we will consider encoding's companion process—retrieval, the process of getting information out of memory. In this section on retrieval, we will learn that memory is a constructive process and can be manipulated. We will also consider the question of whether information stored in memory is ever lost. Is the information truly no longer available or is it just not accessible at a particular point in time? Here we will also discuss false memories and the controversial topic of repressed memories of childhood abuse. But before considering these more complex issues in memory, let's get a basic overview of how our memory system works by considering the classic three-stage model.

Three-Stage Model of Memory

The three-stage model of our memory system has guided much of the research on memory since the late 1960s (Atkinson & Shiffrin, 1968). Diagrams depicting this memory model typically use a series of boxes to indicate the stages of information processing, and arrows connecting the boxes to show the flow of information within the system. Figure 5.1 (page 202) is an informational flow chart for the three-stage memory model. In general, information enters from the physical environment through our senses into sensory memory and flows from sensory memory to short-term memory to long-term memory and then back to short-term memory when we need to use it. In this section, we will discuss each of these three stages of information processing and how the stages interact to provide us with memory. The initial stage of processing, sensory memory, is roughly comparable to what we called sensation in Chapter 3. Information in this stage is bottom-up sensory input that hasn't been recognized yet. So let's begin by

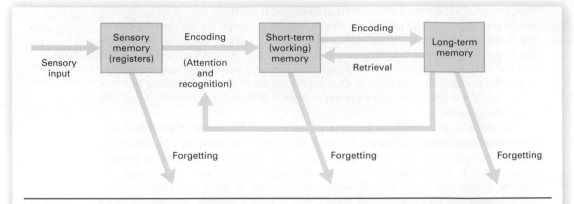

Figure 5.1 | Three-Stage Model of Memory | Information from the physical environment enters the sensory registers through each of our senses (vision, hearing, taste, smell, and touch). This set of registers is referred to collectively as sensory memory. These registers are temporary storage places for sensory information until it can be attended to, recognized, and moved further along in the memory system. Sensory information that is not attended to is quickly forgotten. The information in each register that we attend to goes on to be recognized and enters the second stage of memory, short-term memory, which is comparable to our present awareness. Top-down processing (using information stored in long-term memory) guides this encoding of sensory input from sensory memory into short-term memory. If attended to and studied, information in short-term memory will be encoded into long-term memory where it is stored for later use. If not attended to, the information will be forgotten. To use the information stored in long-term memory, we bring it back into short-term memory (a process called retrieval). If we cannot retrieve such information, it is said to be forgotten. Later in the chapter we will consider explanations for such forgetting.

discussing how memory researchers have demonstrated that a sensory-memory stage exists and how information is processed in this stage.

Sensory Memory

Sensory memory (SM) consists of a set of registers, where we temporarily store incoming sensory information from the physical environment until we can attend to it, interpret it, and move it to the next stage of memory processing (short-term memory). We have a register for each of our senses—vision, hearing, taste, smell, and touch. The sensory information stored temporarily in these registers has not yet been recognized. Once it is recognized and we are consciously aware of it, it has moved into the next memory stage, short-term memory. Vision is our dominant sense, so we'll focus on the visual sensory register, commonly referred to as iconic memory, to help you understand how these registers work.

A good way to think about **iconic memory** is that it is photographic memory but for less than 1 second. An exact copy of the visual information exists in iconic memory, but only for a very brief period of time. We cannot attend to

sensory memory (SM) The set of sensory registers, one for each of our senses, that serve as holding places for incoming sensory information until it can be attended to, interpreted, and encoded into short-term memory.

iconic memory The visual sensory register that holds an exact copy of the incoming visual input but only for a brief period of time, less than 1 second.

everything we see; therefore, the visual information in the register that we attend to gets recognized and goes on to short-term memory, and the unattended information in the register fades away and is quickly forgotten. We said that iconic memory lasts less than a second. This means that its duration (how long information can remain in a memory stage if not attended to) is less than a second. How do we know this? We will examine how research psychologists have answered this duration question and a similar capacity question (how much information can be held in a memory stage at one time) for each of the three memory stages. We'll start with a discussion of how the capacity and duration answers for iconic memory were found. Two different experimental procedures, one direct and one inferential, were used. We'll consider the direct one, the temporal integration procedure, first, because it is easier to understand.

> **temporal integration procedure**
> An experimental procedure in which two meaningless visual patterns that produce a meaningful pattern if integrated are presented sequentially with the time delay between their presentations varied.

The temporal integration procedure. In the **temporal integration procedure,** two random meaningless dot patterns are presented sequentially at the same visual location with a brief time delay between them. When these two meaningless patterns are integrated, a meaningful pattern is produced. So, if the meaningful pattern is seen, this means that the two patterns must have been integrated in our memory system (since the two patterns were not presented simultaneously).

To see how this works, let's consider an example. Look at the first two dot patterns (a and b) in Figure 5.2. Neither has any meaning by itself. Each is just a random dot pattern. However, if you integrate the two patterns (as shown in c), you see a meaningful pattern—the letters V O H. If the first two patterns were shown simultaneously in the same visual location on a screen so that they were integrated, you would see V O H; but if they were presented sequentially, the only way you could see the three letters is if the two meaningless dot patterns are integrated somewhere within your memory system. This is exactly what happens. The two patterns are integrated in iconic memory. However, this is only the case if the interval between the two patterns is very brief, less than a second (Eriksen & Collins, 1967). Participants in experiments such as this do not see the meaningful pattern when the

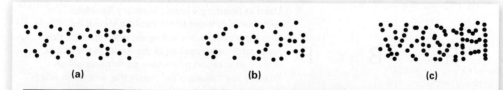

(a) (b) (c)

Figure 5.2 | An Example of the Temporal Integration Procedure | In this experimental procedure, two meaningless patterns (such as a and b) are shown sequentially at the same visual location. If the time interval between the two patterns is less than a second, a meaningful pattern (in this example, the letters V O H) is seen. The meaningful pattern can only be perceived when the two other patterns are integrated, so this integration must be taking place within our memory system, in what we call the visual sensory register or iconic memory.

Sperling's full-report procedure An experimental procedure in which, following the brief presentation of a matrix of unrelated consonants, the participant has to attempt to recall all of the letters in the matrix.

Sperling's partial-report procedure An experimental procedure in which, following the brief presentation of a matrix of unrelated consonants, the participant is given an auditory cue about which row of the matrix to recall.

two dot patterns are separated by more than a second. The first pattern has already faded from the visual register, and the two patterns cannot be integrated in iconic memory.

This pattern of results using the temporal integration procedure is also observed for larger, more complex dot patterns (Hogben & Di Lollo, 1974). People see the meaningful integrated pattern if the interval between these larger patterns is less than a second. Hence the capacity of the visual sensory register must be fairly large or these more complex patterns couldn't be integrated in iconic memory. Thus, the capacity of iconic memory is large, but its duration is very brief, less than a second.

Sperling's full- and partial-report procedures. We find the same results when we use a very different experimental procedure devised by George Sperling (1960). On each trial in Sperling's research, participants were presented with a different matrix of unrelated consonants for 50 milliseconds, a very brief interval but long enough to process visual information. Different size matrices were used, but in our explanation we will consider 3 × 3, nine-letter matrices (as illustrated in Figure 5.3). The task was to report the letters in the matrix briefly flashed on each trial, but Sperling used two different report procedures. In **Sperling's full-report procedure,** the participant had to try to report the entire matrix of letters. Over trials, participants recalled 4.5 letters on average, usually those letters in the top row and the left section of the second row. However, participants also reported (subjectively) that they sensed the entire matrix, but that it had faded from memory by the time they reported the 4 or 5 letters. This sounds like iconic memory, doesn't it? Let's see how Sperling indirectly demonstrated through inference that the remaining unreported letters were indeed in iconic memory by using his partial-report procedure.

In **Sperling's partial-report procedure,** the participant only had to report a small part of the presented letter matrix, a row indicated by an auditory cue on

Figure 5.3 | A 3 × 3 Letter Matrix Like Those Used in Sperling's Iconic Memory Research | On each trial, a different letter matrix is shown for 50 milliseconds. In the full-report procedure, participants attempt to recall all of the letters in the matrix. In the partial-report procedure, participants get an auditory cue following the matrix that tells them which row to report—high-pitched tone, recall top row; medium-pitched tone, recall middle row; and low-pitched tone, recall bottom row. The row that is cued is varied randomly across trials, so the participant has no way of knowing which row will be cued on any particular trial. In addition, the time between the letter matrix presentation and the auditory cue is varied.

each trial. A high-pitched tone indicated that the top row was to be recalled, a medium-pitched tone the middle row, and a low-pitched tone the bottom row. These tones were easy to discriminate, so the participant had no difficulty in determining which row was indicated for recall. The letter matrix was different on every trial; therefore, the participant could not learn the matrix. In addition, the cued row was varied randomly across trials; therefore, the participant had no way of knowing which row would be cued on any particular trial. Regardless, when the auditory cue was given immediately after the brief presentation of the letter matrix, participants recalled the indicated row 100% of the time. From this result, we can infer that all of the rows must have been present in iconic memory; that is, an exact copy of the letter matrix must have been in iconic memory. Sheingold (1973) replicated Sperling's findings with children ages 5, 8, and 11 years old and with adults. He argued that the initial capacity of iconic memory was invariant across age. More recently, Blaser and Kaldy (2010), using a modified partial report technique, found that by 6 months of age, infants' iconic memory capacity nearly matches that of adults. Given this finding of its early development, it appears that iconic memory is an essential component of our flexible, multifaceted visual system. We will learn about infants' visual memory in Chapter 7, Developmental Psychology.

Based on the experimental results for the temporal integration procedure, what do you think would happen when Sperling inserted a time delay between the letter matrix and the auditory cue? Remember, the duration of iconic memory was estimated to be less than a second. Sperling found that as this time delay increased (up to 1 second), participants' recall of the cued row worsened. This meant that the matrix was fading quickly from memory. We can conclude, then, based on two very different experimental procedures, that there is a visual sensory register and that it seems to hold an exact copy of the visual stimulus (indicating a large capacity), but only for a very brief time, less than a second (a very brief duration). In addition, this duration does not seem to decrease much across the lifespan. Walsh and Thompson (1978) found a decrease of only 41 milliseconds on average for older adults (mean age of 67) versus young adults (mean age of 24).

To get a feel for how iconic memory works in nonlaboratory situations, let's think about seeing a bolt of lightning. It's not really a singular, continuous bolt. It is actually three or more bolts that overlap in our iconic memory and lead to the perception of the single flash of lightning. If you turn off the lights and have a friend quickly move a flashlight in a circular motion, you see a circle of light. Why? Again, iconic memory is at work; it isn't a

Three or four bolts of lightning overlap in our iconic memory, leading to the perception of one continuous bolt.

continuous stream of light, but that's what you see. This has larger implications. It is iconic memory that allows us to see the world as continuous and not as a series of unconnected snapshots.

All of our senses have sensory registers that have large capacities with very brief durations. For example, the auditory sensory register, called echoic memory, that processes sounds has a duration of 4–5 seconds, slightly longer than the duration of iconic memory (Darwin, Turvey, & Crowder, 1972; Glucksberg & Cowen, 1970). These sensory registers are what enable continuous perception of the physical environment. Collectively, these registers make up sensory memory, the first step of information processing in the three-stage memory model. However, when we think about memory, we aren't usually thinking about sensory memory. We're thinking about memory with a much longer duration. So let's take a look at the next major stage of processing in the memory system—short-term memory, which has a little longer duration.

Short-Term Memory

Short-term memory (STM) is the memory stage in which the recognized information from sensory memory enters consciousness. We rehearse the information in short-term memory so we can transfer it into more permanent storage (long-term memory) and remember it at some later time. We also bring information from long-term memory back into short-term memory to use it to facilitate rehearsal, solve problems, reason, and make decisions; thus short-term memory is often thought of as working memory (Baddeley, 2012; Engle, 2002). It is the workbench of the memory system. It is where you are doing your present conscious cognitive processing. What you're thinking about right now as you read this sentence is in your short-term memory. As you work to understand and remember what you are reading, you are using your short-term working memory. The capacity of this type of memory is rather small. Humans just can't process that many pieces of information simultaneously in consciousness. In addition, new information in this stage is in a rather fragile state and will be quickly lost from memory (in less than 30 seconds) if we do not concentrate on it. This is why it is called short-term memory. Now that we have a general understanding of the nature of this stage of memory, let's see how researchers have learned about its capacity and duration.

short-term memory (STM) The memory stage with a small capacity (7 ± 2 chunks) and brief duration (< 30 seconds) that we are consciously aware of and in which we do our problem solving, reasoning, and decision making.

memory span task A memory task in which the participant is given a series of items one at a time and then has to recall the items in the order in which they were presented.

The capacity of short-term memory. To assess the capacity of short-term memory, researchers have used the **memory span task.** In this task, the participant is presented a series of items one at a time and has to remember the items in the order that they were presented. The list items could be any of several types of stimuli such as unrelated letters or words. On each trial, the specific list items change. For example, if words are used, then it is a different list of words on each trial. What have researchers found? George Miller provided the answer in his classic 1956 paper, "The Magical Number Seven, Plus or Minus Two: Some Limits on Our Ability to Process Information." Your **memory span** is defined as the average number of items you can remember across a series of memory span trials. Humans remember 7 ± 2 (5 to 9) chunks of information on memory span tasks. To see what Miller meant by the term "chunk," let's consider the memory span task.

In the memory span task, different types of items can be used. If the items were unrelated letters, most participants would remember 5 to 9 unrelated letters. But if the items were three-letter acronyms (meaningful abbreviations like ABC or USA) or words (like dog or boy), participants would remember 5 to 9 three-letter acronyms or words (15 to 27 letters). In this latter case, participants remember more letters than in the first case, but they remember the same number of meaningful units. This is what is meant by the term "chunk." A **chunk** is a meaningful unit in memory. The capacity limit in short-term memory is in terms of chunks, 7 ± 2 chunks. So if the chunks are larger for a particular type of material (words vs. letters), we remember more information but not more chunks. Experts in a particular area, such as chess masters, have larger chunks for information in their area of expertise (Chase & Simon, 1973). In the case of a chess master, for example, several chess pieces on the board form a chunk whereas for chess novices, each piece is a separate chunk.

The duration of short-term memory. Now let's consider the duration of short-term memory, less than 30 seconds. Why is the duration of short-term memory said to be less than 30 seconds if this type of memory is equivalent to our conscious workspace? If we choose to do so, we could keep information in our consciousness for as long as we want, clearly longer than 30 seconds. The duration estimate refers to how long information can stay in short-term memory if we cannot attend to it. To measure this duration, researchers developed the distractor task (Brown, 1958; Peterson & Peterson, 1959). In the **distractor task,** a small amount of information (three unrelated consonants such as CWZ) is presented, the participant is immediately distracted from concentrating on the information for a brief interval of time, and then the information must be recalled. How is the participant distracted? A number is immediately presented, and the participant has to count rapidly aloud backward by 3s (or by some other interval). Counting backward rapidly occupies the short-term work space and prevents the participant from attending to the three letters. The experimenter varies the length of the distraction period. When the distraction period is over, the participant must try to recall the letters. What happens? Some typical data are presented in Figure 5.4.

As you can see in Figure 5.4 (page 208) the estimated duration for information in short-term memory is rather brief, less than 30 seconds. To relate this to everyday life, think about looking up a new phone number. You find the number in the phone book. It goes into your iconic memory, and you attend to it and recognize it.

memory span The average number of items an individual can remember across a series of memory span trials.

chunk A meaningful unit in a person's memory.

distractor task A memory task in which a small amount of information is briefly presented and then the participant is distracted from rehearsing the information for a variable period of time, after which the participant has to recall the information.

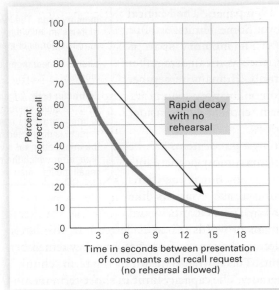

Figure 5.4 | Results for the Short-Term Memory Distractor Task | This figure shows how forgetting in short-term memory occurs over time. As the length of the distractor interval increases, forgetting increases very rapidly. In less than 30 seconds, recall is essentially zero. (Data from: Peterson, L. R., & M. J. Peterson, M. J. (1959). Short-term retention of individual verbal items. *Journal of Experimental Psychology, 58,* 193–198.)

It enters your conscious short-term memory. You start to concentrate on it so you can dial the number. Now what would happen to that number if you heard someone screaming outside and you ran to see what had happened? Chances are that you would forget the phone number (just like participants forget the three consonants in studies using the distractor task), and then have to look it up again. Information in short-term memory is in a temporary storage state, and we need to concentrate on it to prevent it from being lost. Usually we use maintenance rehearsal to accomplish this. **Maintenance rehearsal** is repeating the information in short-term memory over and over again in order to maintain it. For example, in the case of the phone number, we rehearse it over and over again to ourselves until we dial it.

Maintenance rehearsal is just one type of work (processing and manipulating information) performed in short-term memory. As we pointed out earlier, because of all of the various types of work done in short-term memory, it is now often referred to as working memory. For our purposes here, you can think of **working memory** as a more detailed description of short-term memory that includes the mechanisms that allow short-term memory to accomplish its tasks. To explain how working memory does this, researchers have proposed differing models of the mechanisms in working memory (Miyake & Shah, 1999). The most influential explanatory model is that of Alan Baddeley (2007, 2012; Baddeley & Hitch, 1974). In brief, Baddeley proposes that there are four components of working memory: (1) a phonological loop, (2) a visuospatial sketchpad, (3) an episodic buffer, and (4) a central executive. The phonological

maintenance rehearsal A type of rehearsal in short-term memory in which the information is repeated over and over again in order to maintain it.

working memory A more detailed version of short-term memory that includes the mechanisms that allow short-term memory to accomplish its tasks.

loop allows you to work with verbal information for a short period of time. It is what allows us to repeat the phone number in the maintenance rehearsal example over and over in order to maintain it. Similarly, the visuospatial sketchpad works with visual and spatial information, such as the figures and illustrations on a page in this book, as well as their spatial positions on the page. The episodic buffer integrates information from the phonological loop, the visuospatial sketchpad, and long-term memory, such as the integration of the visual information of your teacher writing on the blackboard, the verbal input from his lecture, and the meaning of all of this input from long-term memory. It is called the episodic buffer because it represents a temporary storage place (a buffer) for the integrated representation of what is happening at any moment in time (an episode). Lastly, the central executive component is responsible for coordinating the activities of and distributing resources to the other three components so that the work (the processing and manipulation of information) can be optimally accomplished. It is also the mechanism for controlling our attention and communicating with long-term memory. In brief, it is the CEO of working memory.

Now that we have a better understanding of how short-term memory works, we need to think about what our goal is when we are trying to learn. It is not merely to maintain information in short-term memory. Our goal is to put that information into long-term storage so that we can retrieve and use it in the future, and our short-term memory plays a large role in this task. In the last two major sections of this chapter, we will look at the process of encoding information from short-term memory into long-term memory and of retrieving that information from long-term memory back into short-term memory at some later time. But first we need to get an overview of long-term memory, the last memory stage in the three-stage model.

Long-Term Memory

When we use the word "memory," we normally mean what psychologists call long-term memory. **Long-term memory (LTM)** allows storage of information for a long period of time (perhaps permanently), and its capacity is essentially unlimited. Remember the trillions of possible synaptic connections in the brain that we discussed in Chapter 2? They represent the capacity of long-term memory. The brain's memory storage capacity has been estimated to be around 2.5 petabytes (a million gigabytes), which would be enough to hold 3 million hours of television shows if your brain worked like a video recorder (Reber, 2010). You would have to leave the television running continuously for more than 300 years to use up all that storage. We will consider the duration or permanence of information in long-term memory in more detail later in this chapter when we consider theories of forgetting.

The durations and capacities for all three stages of memory are summarized in Table 5.1 (page 210). Review these so that you have a better understanding of how these three stages differ. Next, let's consider different types of long-term memories.

long-term memory (LTM) The memory stage in which information is stored for a long period of time (perhaps permanently) and whose capacity is essentially unlimited.

Table 5.1	Durations and Capacities of the Three Memory Stages	
Memory Stage	Duration	Capacity
Sensory memory	< 1 sec for iconic memory; 4–5 secs for echoic memory	Large
Short-term memory	Up to 30 secs without rehearsal	7 ± 2 chunks
Long-term memory	A long time (perhaps permanently)	Essentially unlimited

Types of long-term memories. Memory researchers make many distinctions between various types of long-term memories (Squire, 2004). The first distinction is between memories that we have to recall consciously and make declarative statements about and those that don't require conscious recall or declarative statements (see Figure 5.5). What if someone asked you, "Who was the first president of the United States?" You would retrieve the answer from your long-term memory and consciously declare, "George Washington." This is an example of what is called **explicit (declarative) memory**—long-term memory for factual knowledge and personal experiences. Explicit memory requires a conscious explicit effort to remember.

explicit (declarative) memory
Long-term memory for factual knowledge and personal experiences. This type of memory requires a conscious effort to remember and entails making declarations about the information remembered.

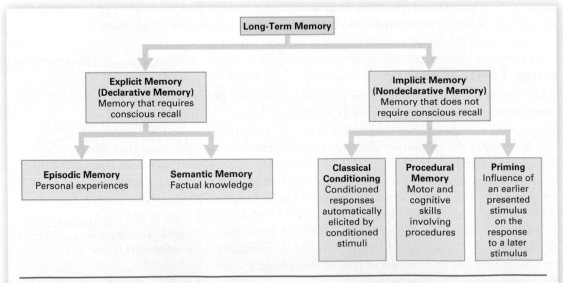

Figure 5.5 | Types of Long-Term Memory | Memory researchers make a distinction between two major types of long-term memory—explicit memory, which requires conscious recall, and implicit memory, which does not. Each of these two major types of long-term memory is further subdivided into more specific types of long-term memory, as defined in the figure.

Tulving (1972) made a further distinction in explicit memory between **semantic memory,** memory for factual knowledge, and **episodic memory,** memory of your personal life experiences (the episodes in your life). Remembering that George Washington was the first president of the United States (semantic memory) is very different than remembering your first kiss (episodic memory). Semantic and episodic memories blend together in autobiographical memory (Williams, Conway, & Cohen, 2008). Autobiographical memories obviously include episodic memories of your past personal experiences, but they can also be about factual, semantic aspects of your personal history, such as remembering your birth date or what high school you attended.

Explicit memory is contrasted with **implicit (nondeclarative) memory.** Implicit memory is long-term memory that influences our behavior but does not require conscious awareness or declarative statements. Implicit memory happens automatically, without deliberate conscious effort. For example, you remember how to drive a car and you do so without consciously recalling and describing what you are doing as you drive. Some implicit memories (like driving a car, typing, or hitting a tennis ball) are referred to as **procedural memories** because they have a physical procedural aspect (the execution of an ordered set of movements) to them. In contrast with declarative explicit memories, procedural implicit memories are like knowing "how" versus knowing "what." Not all implicit memories, however, are procedural memories (see Figure 5.5). We learned about another type of implicit memory, classical conditioning, in Chapter 4. Classically conditioned responses elicited automatically by conditioned stimuli are also implicit memories.

Another type of nonprocedural implicit memory is priming. In **priming,** an earlier stimulus influences the response to a later stimulus. Priming is classed as implicit memory because it occurs independent of a person's conscious memory for the priming stimulus. There are several experimental priming procedures, but let's consider one called repetition priming so that you can gain a better understanding of how priming works. In repetition priming, a person first studies a list of words and then at some later time is asked to complete a list of word fragments with the first word that comes to mind for each fragment. For example, the fragment s _ c _ _ _ might be presented. The likelihood that the person answers s o c i a l (the primed word because the word social was on the earlier word list) is much higher than for unprimed words, such as s o c c e r or s o c k e t, that fit the fragment but were not on the list. Such priming occurs even when people had not recognized the list word on an earlier recognition test (Tulving, Schacter, & Stark, 1982). Thus, priming occurs when explicit memory for the word does not, which means that priming is an involuntary, nonconscious

semantic memory Explicit memory for factual knowledge.

episodic memory Explicit memory for personal experiences.

implicit (nondeclarative) memory Long-term memory for procedural tasks, classical conditioning, and primary effects. This type of memory does not require conscious awareness or the need to make declarations about the information remembered.

procedural memory Implicit memory for cognitive and motor tasks that have a physical procedural aspect to them.

priming The implicit influence of an earlier presented stimulus on the response to a later stimulus. This influence is independent of conscious memory for the earlier stimulus.

amnesic A person with severe memory deficits following brain surgery or injury.

implicit process. Graf, Squire, and Mandler (1984) provided further evidence that priming is an implicit, nonconscious type of memory. They found that amnesics who had no explicit memory for new information could perform as well as normal adults on a repetition priming word fragment task even though the amnesics had no conscious memory of having seen the words before.

Next we'll see how other memory research with amnesics has allowed us to further differentiate explicit and implicit memory and even discover what parts of the brain seem to be involved in each type of memory.

Amnesia, the loss of long-term memories. There is some evidence from the studies of **amnesics,** people with severe memory deficits following brain surgery or injury, that explicit and implicit memories are processed in different parts of the brain. We will focus our discussion of amnesics on the most studied amnesic in psychological research, H. M., whom we discussed briefly in Chapter 1. When H. M. was 7 years old, he was hit by a bicyclist and suffered a brain injury that later led to severe epileptic seizures in his teens (Hilts, 1995). In 1953 at the age of 27, H. M. had his hippocampus and surrounding temporal lobe areas removed with the hope of reducing his epileptic seizures (Corkin, Amaral, Gonzalez, Johnson, & Hyman, 1997). The seizures were reduced, but the operation drastically affected his long-term memory. Before the operation, he had normal short-term memory and long-term memory. After the operation, he had normal short-term memory, above-average intelligence, and no perceptual or language deficits, but he didn't seem able to store any new information in long-term memory (Scoville & Milner, 1957). For example, H. M. could read the same magazine over and over again and think it was a new magazine each time. He could no longer follow the plot of a television show because the commercials would interfere with his memory of the story line. If he did not know someone before his operation and that person introduced herself to him and then left the room for a few minutes, he would not know the person when she returned. Even Brenda Milner and Suzanne Corkin, the two neuroscientists who studied H. M. for decades, had to introduce themselves anew each time they met with him.

© Suzanne Corkin, used by permission of the Wylie Agency LLC

Henry Molaison, shown above, is often referred to as the best known and most studied individual in the history of neuroscience. He died in 2008 at the age of 82. For confidentiality purposes while he was alive, only his initials, H. M., were used to identify him in the hundreds of studies that he participated in for over five decades. Following his death, his brain was sliced into razor-thin histological sections for preservation and digital imaging, allowing researchers to create a 3D model of his brain (Annese et al., 2014) and hence to determine more accurately the neuroanatomical extent of his 1953 bilateral surgical ablation to treat severe epilepsy.

H. M. had **anterograde amnesia**—the inability to form new explicit long-term memories following surgery or trauma to the brain. Anterograde amnesia is contrasted with **retrograde amnesia**—the disruption of memory for the past, especially episodic information for events before, especially just before, brain surgery or trauma. Such amnesia is typical in cases of brain concussions. H. M. had some retrograde amnesia, especially for the several days preceding the surgery, but this was mild compared with his severe, pervasive anterograde amnesia.

Remember, as we just learned, amnesics have shown implicit repetition priming effects. So what about H. M.? Although he didn't form any new explicit long-term memories (but see O'Kane, Kensinger, & Corkin, 2004, and Skotko et al., 2004), did he too form new implicit memories? The answer is a resounding "yes" (Corkin, 2013). Let's briefly consider some of the experiments demonstrating this. H. M. demonstrated implicit procedural memory on a mirror-tracing task. In this task, you have to trace a pattern that can be seen only in its mirror image, which also shows your tracing hand moving in the direction opposite to its actual movement. This is a difficult motor task, but there is a practice effect in that the number of errors decreases across practice sessions. H. M.'s performance on this task showed a normal practice effect even when months elapsed between the sessions (Gabrieli, Corkin, Mickel, & Growdon, 1993). However, he did not remember ever having done this task and had to have the instructions repeated for each session. Corkin (1968) also found that H. M. improved with practice on another manual skill learning task, one in

anterograde amnesia The inability to form new explicit long-term memories for events following surgery or trauma to the brain. Explicit memories formed before the surgery or trauma are left intact.

retrograde amnesia The disruption of memory for the past, especially episodic information for events before, especially just before, surgery or trauma to the brain.

The Mirror-Tracing Task | The task is to trace the outline of a star (or some other shape) with a metal stylus when the star and your hand can be seen only in the mirror. Thus, the tracing movements have to be made in the direction opposite from the way in which they appear in the mirror. When the stylus moves off of the star outline (each red section in the illustrated tracing), it makes electrical contact with the underlying aluminum plate and a tracing error is recorded. There is nonconducting tape on the star outline, so as long as the stylus stays on the outline, no electrical contact is made. Just like we would, H. M. improved from session to session (the number of errors he made decreased) as he gained more experience in this task. However, unlike us, he could not remember ever having performed the task before and had to have the task explained to him each session. As explained in the text, this means that he formed new implicit procedural memories for how to do the task, but he did not form new explicit episodic memories of having performed the task.

which he had to keep a stylus on a small dot that was spinning around on a turntable. H. M. got better at this task with practice, but he had no conscious memory of his earlier experiences that led to his improved performance.

H. M. also demonstrated implicit repetition priming effects on a word fragment completion task without conscious awareness of the earlier presented priming words (Corkin, 2002) and implicit memory for a classically conditioned eyeblink response (Woodruff-Pak, 1993). In the latter case, after he was classically conditioned to give an eyeblink response to a tone, he could not consciously remember the conditioning episodes; however, he stored an implicit memory of the conditioned association between the tone and eyeblink response. Thus, he blinked when he was exposed to the tone but had no idea why he did so. LeDoux (1996) tells the story of a similar finding with a female amnesic with memory deficits like those of H. M. She was unable to recognize her doctor (Edouard Claparède), so each day Dr. Claparède shook her hand and introduced himself. One day, however, the doctor concealed a tack in his hand so that when shaking hands, the tack pricked her. The next time the doctor tried to introduce himself and shake hands, she refused to do so but didn't know why. She had been conditioned without any explicit awareness of it.

How is it possible that H. M. and other amnesics like him can form new implicit but not explicit memories? Research indicates that other parts of the brain, such as the cerebellum and basal ganglia and not the hippocampus, are important for implicit memory formation and storage (Green & Woodruff-Pak, 2000; Knowlton et al., 1996; Krebs, Hogan, Hening, Adamovich, & Poizner, 2001; Krupa, Thompson, & Thompson, 1993; Squire, 2004). Implicit memory formation is functional in these amnesics because the cerebellum, basal ganglia, and the other parts of the brain necessary for such memories are intact, but explicit memory formation isn't functional because the hippocampus has been removed. Findings congruent with the major processing differences between the left and right hemispheres that we discussed in Chapter 2 are observed for people with only left or right hemisphere damage. Schacter (1996) reported that people with left hippocampal damage have difficulty recalling verbal information, but they do not have difficulty remembering visual information, and the opposite is true for those with right hippocampal damage.

A hippocampal explanation has also been proposed for **infantile/child amnesia,** our inability as adults to remember events that occurred in our lives before about 3 years of age. According to this explanation, we cannot remember our experiences during this period because the hippocampus, which is crucial to the formation of episodic explicit long-term memories, is not yet fully developed. Remember, as we discussed in Chapter 2, neurogenesis, the generation of new neurons, occurs in the hippocampus. During infancy, neurogenesis levels are high because the hippocampus is developing. Akers et al. (2014) found evidence that such high levels of neurogenesis disrupt hippocampus-dependent memories, causing them to degrade. It is also important to realize that although the hippocampus is critical to the formation of explicit memories, it is not the final repository for these memories, but is more like a holding zone for them.

infantile/child amnesia Our inability as adults to remember events that occurred in our lives before about 3 years of age.

As explicit memories age, the hippocampus's participation wanes (Smith & Squire, 2009). These memories are distributed throughout many areas in the cortex, a process called memory consolidation (the storage of long-term memories). How this happens and how these memories are represented remain questions to be answered (Miller, 2005).

Evidence for short-term versus long-term memory distinction. The memory findings for amnesics like H. M. also indicate that short-term memory and long-term memory are different stages of memory. H. M.'s short-term memory did not suffer any substantial deficits after the operation. For example, his memory span was within the normal range. He could repeat a telephone number with no difficulty. Researchers examining the free recall task have found additional evidence that long-term memory and short-term memory are different stages. In the **free recall task,** participants are given a list of words one at a time and then asked to recall them in any order they wish. Kirkpatrick (1894) introduced the free recall task, noting that some word positions are recalled much better than others. If recall performance for the words is plotted in terms of the order the words were presented (their position in the list— first, second, . . . , last), the figure has a very distinctive shape (Figure 5.6). The ends of the list are recalled much more often than the middle of the list. The superior recall of the early portion of the list is called the **primacy effect.** The superior recall of the latter portion of the list is called the **recency effect.**

How do the primacy effect and recency effect relate to the distinction between short-term and long-term memory? The recency effect is caused by recall from short-term memory. Items at the end of the list, the most recent items, have a high probability of still being in short-term memory, so they can be recalled

free recall task A memory task in which a list of items is presented one at a time and then the participant is free to recall them in any order.

primacy effect The superior recall of the early portion of a list relative to the middle of the list in a one-trial free recall task.

recency effect The superior recall of the latter portion of a list relative to the middle of the list in a one-trial free recall task.

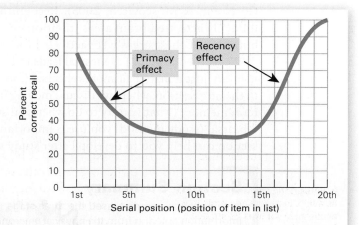

Figure 5.6 | Serial Position Effects for a One-Trial Free Recall Task | The superior recall of the first few items presented relative to those in the middle of the list is called the primacy effect. This effect is due to the fact that the primary items in the list are studied more and so have a higher probability of being in long-term memory for later recall. The recency effect refers to the superior recall of the last few items presented versus those in the middle of the list. This effect is due to the easy immediate recall of the items presently in short-term memory (those recently presented).

immediately and very well. The primacy effect, however, is the result of superior recall from long-term memory of the first few words in the list versus those in the middle (Rundus & Atkinson, 1970). Let's think about the task. The words are presented one at a time. The first word comes into your empty short-term memory to be rehearsed. It gets 100% of your attention. Then the second word appears and is rehearsed with the first word (each gets 50% of your attention). This goes on until short-term memory capacity is reached and each new word causes a word already in short-term memory to be bumped out. This results in the first few items on the list being rehearsed more than the later words in the middle and thus having a higher probability of being stored in long-term memory and recalled better. The items in the middle of the list come into a filled short-term memory, get little rehearsal, and thus have a low probability of being stored in long-term memory and recalled later. This is similar to what sometimes happens to students on exams. They study one topic more than another, and this translates to better test performance on the more-studied topic.

How do we know that this is so? Researchers have demonstrated that the primacy effect and the recency effect can be manipulated independently, indicating that different memory stages are involved. For example, if recall is delayed by having the participants count rapidly backward by 3s for 30 seconds, the recency effect is eliminated, but the primacy effect remains (Glanzer & Cunitz, 1966). Thus, the distractor period only disturbed recall from short-term memory. Similarly, we can eliminate the primacy effect but still observe a recency effect if we force participants to rehearse each of the list items equally by having them only rehearse each word aloud after it is presented. With equal rehearsal, the primary and middle items are recalled equally well, so there is no primacy effect, and because amount of rehearsal is not critical to recall from short-term memory, a recency effect (although smaller) remains. In addition, fMRI neuroimaging data indicate that both short-term memory and long-term memory are involved in these serial position effects (Talmi, Grady, Goshen-Gottstein, & Moscovitch, 2005). Recognition of early items in the word list uniquely activated brain areas traditionally associated with long-term memory, but none of these areas were activated for retrieval of late items in the list.

We learned that more rehearsal leads to better long-term memory, but is better memory just a matter of more rehearsal (more study)? This question is addressed in the next section, where we discuss moving information from short-term to long-term memory (what you try to do when you study). You will learn that the type of rehearsal (study method) you use is important. Thus, the information in the next section can help you to develop better study strategies and better memory.

Section Summary

In this section, we discussed the three-stage model that describes the processing of information entering from the physical environment through our senses into our memory system. In general, sensory information enters the sensory registers that comprise the first stage of processing—sensory memory. These temporary storage registers have large capacities and hold essentially exact copies of the information until we can attend to it and process it further. The duration of these registers is very brief, however. In the case of the visual sensory register, the duration is less than a second. We can only attend to part of the information in each register to process it farther into the memory system. The rest of the information fades quickly from the register and is forgotten.

The information that we attend to gets recognized and moves into our short-term memory, the second stage in the three-stage memory model. Short-term memory is like our conscious workspace. It has a small capacity (7 ± 2 chunks of information) and a brief duration (less than 30 seconds). Short-term memory is sometimes referred to as working memory, because it is here that we do the work necessary to encode new information into long-term memory and to accomplish all of our other conscious activities, such as problem solving and decision making. Working memory can be thought of as the collection of mechanisms in short-term memory that allows it to accomplish these tasks. According to Baddeley's model of working memory, the mechanisms are a phonological loop, a visuospatial sketchpad, an episodic buffer, and a central executive. The central executive coordinates the activities of the other three components and the storing and retrieval of information from long-term memory.

The third stage of processing, long-term memory, is what we normally mean when we use the word "memory." It is our long-term (perhaps permanent) repository for information. In addition, the capacity of long-term memory is essentially limitless. There are different types of long-term memories. The major distinction is between explicit memories (those that require conscious recall and declaration) and implicit memories (those that do not require conscious recall and declaration). There are two types of explicit memories—semantic memories (our factual knowledge base) and episodic memories (our personal life experiences). There are three types of implicit memories—procedural memories that involve some type of physical or cognitive procedure, classical conditioning memories, and memories leading to priming effects.

Research findings with amnesics who have suffered hippocampal damage indicate that the hippocampus is important for explicit memory formation but not implicit memory formation. These findings also support the distinctiveness of short-term and long-term memories because these amnesics have relatively normal short-term memory. Further evidence for these two stages is provided by the primacy effect and the recency effect for free recall. The independent manipulation of these effects indicates that they are the products of recall from different memory stages.

ConceptCheck | 1

Explain why you can think of the information in sensory memory as bottom-up input and the information in long-term memory as top-down input.

Explain why the very brief duration of iconic memory is necessary for normal visual perception.

Explain what is meant by the term "chunk" with respect to the capacity of short-term memory, 7 ± 2 chunks.

Explain how the studies of H. M. indicate that he could not form any new explicit long-term memories but could form new implicit long-term memories.

Encoding Information into Memory

There are three essential processes in our memory system—encoding, storage, and retrieval. **Encoding** is the process of transferring information from one memory stage to the next (from sensory into short-term memory and from short-term into long-term memory). **Storage** refers to the process of maintaining information in a particular stage. Storage is temporary except for in long-term memory. **Retrieval** is the process of bringing information stored in long-term memory to the conscious level in short-term memory. Let's go back to the flow chart of the three-stage model of memory in Figure 5.1. Encoding and retrieval determine the flow of information within the three-stage system. Information is first encoded from sensory memory to short-term memory, where it can be stored temporarily. Information is then encoded from short-term to long-term memory, where it is stored more permanently but can be retrieved and brought back into short-term memory when we need to use it.

In this section, we will cover encoding and its role in moving information from short-term into long-term memory. Our focus will be on the best ways to achieve this transfer. We begin with a consideration of general encoding strategies.

How We Encode Information

The first distinction to consider is automatic versus effortful processing (Hasher & Zacks, 1979). **Automatic processing** is processing that occurs subconsciously and does not require attention. In contrast, **effortful processing** is processing that occurs consciously and requires attention. For a particular type of processing to become automatic, much practice is needed. A good example is reading. At first, learning to read is very effortful, but after years of practice it becomes easier and more automatic. Wouldn't it be nice if encoding to learn (studying) were an automatic process? It is unlikely that studying can become as automatic as reading, but we can get better at it by using better encoding strategies and practicing these strategies. In this section, we'll discuss some better ways to encode.

This distinction between automatic and effortful processing can also be applied to the three-stage memory model and the explicit versus implicit long-term memory difference that we discussed in the last section. The three-stage memory model is an explanation of how we process explicit memories, which require conscious effortful processing. Subconscious automatic processing, however, is responsible for storing implicit memories. If this automatic processing were to be represented in the three-stage memory model depicted in Figure 5.1, it would be an arrow going straight from the sensory input to long-term memory, bypassing the first two memory stages and hence our conscious awareness. The encoding strategies that we will discuss next, however, involve effortful processing leading to explicit memories, so

encoding The process of moving information from one memory stage to the next (from sensory memory into short-term memory or from short-term memory to long-term memory).

storage The process of maintaining information in a memory stage.

retrieval The process of bringing information stored in long-term memory into short-term memory.

automatic processing Memory processing that occurs subconsciously and does not require attention.

effortful processing Memory processing that occurs consciously and requires attention.

they require conscious awareness. If you practice them, your encoding (and your memory) will improve.

Levels-of-processing theory. Remember that encoding is the process of transferring information from one memory stage into another. Here we are interested in encoding from short-term to long-term memory. Encoding information into long-term memory is related to retrieving information from long-term memory. Some types of encoding lead to better retrieval. The **levels-of-processing theory** describes what types of encoding lead to better retrieval (Craik & Lockhart, 1972). This theory assumes that incoming information can be processed at different levels, from the simplistic physical level to the semantic level, and that semantic processing, especially elaborative semantic processing, leads to better memory. According to this theory, there are three general levels of processing—physical, acoustic, and semantic. To understand the differences among these three levels, consider processing the word "brain." We can process it as a string of lowercase letters. This would be the physical level. Next we could process "brain" by how it sounds, the acoustic level, which is a little deeper than the physical level. Third, we can process what "brain" means and then elaborate upon that meaning by relating it to what we know about parts of the brain and brain chemistry.

Let's consider an experiment to see how these three levels may lead to different levels of memory performance. Researchers presented participants with a long list of words one at a time, but manipulated the level of processing of the words by manipulating the task to be performed on each word (Craik & Tulving, 1975; Experiment 2). For each word, one of three types of questions had to be answered. One type of question required processing the word at a physical level (for example, "Is this word in capital letters?"). A second type of question required acoustic processing (for example, "Does the word rhyme with bear?"). The third type of question required semantic processing (for example, "Will the word fit in the sentence, The man placed the _____ on the table?"). Participants did not know that they would be tested for their memory of the words. They only thought that they had to answer a question about each word. However, the experimenter later surprised the participants with a memory test for the words. Levels-of-processing theory predicts that memory for the words that had to be processed semantically should be best, those processed acoustically next best, and those only processed physically worst. This is exactly what was found (see Figure 5.7). Long-term recognition memory was the best for the words encoded semantically, next best for those encoded acoustically, and worst for those only encoded physically.

> **levels-of-processing theory** A theory of information processing in memory that assumes that semantic processing, especially elaborative semantic processing, leads to better long-term memory.

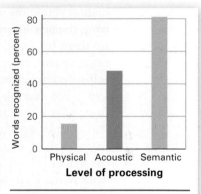

Figure 5.7 | Differences in Recognition Memory for Words Processed at Different Levels | Participants were presented a long list of words one at a time and had to answer a question about each word as it was presented. The nature of the questions led to different levels of processing—physical (how it was printed), acoustic (how it sounded), or semantic (what it meant). The level of processing dramatically affected the participants' later ability to recognize the word as one that had been on this list. (Data from: Craik, F. I. M., & Tulving, E. (1975). Depth of processing and the retention of words in episodic memory. *Journal of Experimental Psychology: General, 104,* 268–294.)

Elaborative rehearsal. Maintenance rehearsal, the repetitive cycling of information in short-term memory, was discussed earlier in the chapter. This type of rehearsal serves to maintain information in short-term memory. Levels-of-processing theory, however, views this type of rehearsal as shallow, acoustic rehearsal. It is not very effective in producing good long-term memory for information. Semantic processing is much better. Once at the semantic level of processing, though, we should engage in **elaborative rehearsal**—rehearsing by relating the new material to information already in long-term memory. The memory organization created by the integration of the new information with existing information leads to more successful retrieval of the information than shallower processing. This organization provides more retrieval cues (links with other information in long-term memory) for the new information, thereby facilitating its retrieval. For example, to elaborately encode the concept of elaborative rehearsal, you could relate it to other concepts that you learned recently by thinking about such things as how elaborative rehearsal is different from maintenance rehearsal, how it relates to levels-of-processing theory, and how it is an example of effortful processing. Such elaboration enables much better long-term memory.

In elaborative rehearsal, you should try to relate the new information to information you know well. Because you know yourself so well, you should elaborate by tying the new information to yourself. To learn new concepts, you should personalize them by thinking of examples of these concepts in your own experiences. It is easier to remember information that you have related to yourself. This is called the **self-reference effect,** and it is a well-established research finding (Symons & Johnson, 1997). For example, researchers have found that people can remember more words from a list if they related the words to themselves (Rogers, Kuiper, & Kirker, 1977). Participants were asked whether list words such as "generous" applied to them. Later recall of such words was very good, even better than for words processed at the semantic level (as in the Craik and Tulving study). Think about how this might work. What if the word were "honest"? You would start thinking about incidents in your life in which you were honest and in which you were not. The word would then

be linked to all of these incidents, facilitating its later recall. So when you are studying a new concept, try to find examples of it in your own life. For some concepts this is easy to do; for others it isn't. However, it's worth the effort because such connections will help you to remember the concept through the self-reference effect.

Environmental effects on encoding. The fact that elaborative rehearsal improves memory stems from a larger principle—the encoding specificity principle (Tulving, 1983). In simple terms, the **encoding specificity principle** proposes that the cues present during encoding serve as the best cues for retrieval. This is why the various concepts and examples that you relate to a new concept during

elaborative rehearsal A type of rehearsal in short-term memory in which incoming information is related to information from long-term memory to encode it into long-term memory.

self-reference effect The superior long-term memory for information related to oneself at time of encoding into long-term memory.

encoding specificity principle The principle that the environmental cues (both internal and external) present at the time information is encoded into long-term memory serve as the best retrieval cues for the information.

Callahan

John Callahan/Levin Represents

"I wonder if you'd mind giving me directions. I've never been sober in this part of town before."

elaborative rehearsal help you remember the concept. They were present during encoding so they serve as good retrieval cues. Such cues are internal environmental cues; they refer to internal cognitive processing, what you were thinking about during rehearsal. Encoding specificity also applies to the external environmental cues present during encoding. Many research studies have shown that long-term memory is better when the physical study and test environments are as similar as possible. For example, in one rather dramatic demonstration of this, participants learned and were tested either underwater or on land (Godden & Baddeley, 1975). The two groups that had the same study and test environments (both were underwater or both were on land) remembered significantly better than the two groups that had their study and test environments reversed (one underwater and the other on land, or vice versa). However, you need not rush to classrooms to study. Classroom environmental effects on college exam performance are not very strong (Saufley, Otaka, & Bavaresco, 1985). Why? External environmental effects on learning diminish when the learning has taken place in several environments (Smith, Glenberg, & Bjork, 1978). In the case of exams, students have successfully learned the relevant information in a variety of environments ranging from the classroom to nonclassroom environments such as the library and dormitory rooms, thereby overriding the classroom environmental effect.

We have limited our discussion so far to a rather narrow definition of internal environment—a person's mental activities at the time of encoding. Broader internal environmental factors, such as a person's physiological state or mood, also impact encoding and retrieval. These effects lead to a phenomenon known as **state-dependent memory,** memory that depends upon the relationship of one's physiological state at time of encoding and retrieval. The best memory occurs when people are in the same state at retrieval as they were at encoding, and memory is hindered by state differences. For example, people under the influence of alcohol at time of encoding would recall best if under the influence at the time of retrieval. Please note, however, that memory under the influence of alcohol, regardless of the state at the time of retrieval, is very poor. It is best to encode and retrieve in a nonalcoholically influenced state.

state-dependent memory Long-term memory retrieval is best when a person's physiological state at the time of encoding and retrieval of the information is the same.

mood-dependent memory Long-term memory retrieval is best when a person's mood state at the time of encoding and retrieval of the information is the same.

mood-congruence effect Tendency to retrieve experiences and information that are congruent with a person's current mood.

mnemonic A memory aid.

method of loci A mnemonic in which sequential pieces of information to be remembered are encoded by associating them with sequential locations in a very familiar room or place and then the pieces of information are retrieved by mentally going around the room (place) and retrieving the piece at each location.

There are similar effects on memory that depend on the relationship between a person's emotional states, such as being happy or sad, at time of encoding and retrieval. Because one's mood is involved, these effects are referred to as **mood-dependent memory,** the retrieval of a particular memory is better when a person's mood at retrieval is the same as it was during encoding. Like state-dependency effects, mood-dependency effects furnish support for the encoding specificity principle—context is important for successful memory retrieval. There is also a related phenomenon called the **mood-congruence effect**—the tendency to recall memories that are congruent with a person's current mood. A particular mood cues memories that are consistent with that mood (Eich, 1995). We tend to remember more positive events when we are feeling good and more negative events when we are feeling down. These events have been associated with the accompanying emotions. Thus, the emotions serve as retrieval cues for the events. This congruence effect may hinder recovery in depressed people because they will tend to remember negative events and not positive ones. In fact, this is the case. Depressed patients report more memories related to illness, injury, and death than nondepressed people (Schacter, 2000). Think positively, and the mood-congruence effect will help maintain that positive attitude.

In summary, elaborative rehearsal is the most effective strategy for encoding. Research has found that actors working to learn their lines use elaborative rehearsal including encoding specificity, mood-congruence effects, and the self-reference effect (Noice & Noice, 1997). They do not use shallow processing and just memorize their lines. (Neither should students try this in their courses!) Elaborative rehearsal is the key to more effective learning. It is important to practice this type of rehearsal. You should integrate information that you are trying to learn with as much other information in your knowledge base as you can, especially relating it to yourself. You will get better at this elaboration strategy as you practice it, and learning will become easier.

How to Improve Encoding

In this section, we will discuss a few more specific ways to improve memory. We'll start with some techniques to improve memory for lists and more organized sets of concepts. These techniques use a **mnemonic,** a memory aid. Mnemonics are useful for remembering lists of items, especially ordered lists, speeches, and long passages of text. We'll start with a mnemonic that was used by ancient Greek orators to remember speeches.

The Greek orators used a mnemonic called the **method of loci** (Yates, 1966). "Loci" is the plural of "locus," which means place or location. In the method of loci, the sequential pieces of information to be remembered are first associated with sequential locations in a very familiar room or place. Then, when retrieving the information, one would merely mentally go around the room (or place) and retrieve the item stored at each sequential location. The Greek orators would mentally store the major points of a speech at sequential locations in the room where they were speaking. Then, during the speech an orator would go from location to location within the room to retrieve the key points of his speech. If you were trying to remember an ordered list of items for an exam, you could pair the items system-

MEMORY SCHOOL

MNEMONICS

"You simply associate each number with a word, such as 'table' and 3,476,029."

atically with locations within the classroom and then during the exam mentally go from location to location within the classroom to retrieve them. The method of loci is a type of elaborative rehearsal using mental imagery. You elaborate upon items that you want to remember by visually associating them with a series of locations that you already know well or that will be available at the time of recall.

All mnemonics work by using some type of elaboration. In another mnemonic, the **peg-word system,** you visually associate the items in a list with a jingle that you first memorize. The jingle is "One is a bun, two is a shoe, three is a tree, four is a door, five is a hive, six is sticks, seven is heaven, eight is a gate, nine is swine, and ten is a hen." You then associate each successive item in the list with the object for each successive number. For example, the first item on the list would be associated visually in a mental image with bun. If the word to be remembered were "dog", then you might construct an image of a big bun with a dog in it. Then, as you go through the peg words, you retrieve the associated image, so you can retrieve the list.

One might think that these mnemonic techniques require much more effort than just memorizing the information that we want to remember. But researchers have found that people using mnemonics demonstrate much better memory than those who have just attempted to memorize a list. Why? As we discussed earlier, elaborative rehearsal is better for encoding into long-term memory. Professional memory experts do not have exceptional intelligence or structural brain differences but rather have their own unique mnemonic techniques and are superior at using them (Maguire, Valentine, Wilding, & Kapur, 2003). Their techniques, like the ones that we have described, are all essentially based on elaborative encoding,

peg-word system A mnemonic in which the items in a list to be remembered are associated with the sequential items in a memorized jingle and then the list is retrieved by going through the jingle and retrieving the associated items.

spacing (distributed study) effect Superior long-term memory for spaced study versus massed study (cramming).

the key to superior memory. For a fascinating journey into the world of these memory experts, you should read Joshua Foer's engaging book, *Moonwalking with Einstein: The Art and Science of Remembering Everything* (2011). Under the tutelage of some of these experts, Foer went from being a journalist with an average memory to winning the U.S. Memory Championship in 2006, testifying to the effectiveness of mnemonic techniques.

Mnemonics that involve little elaboration have not been found to be very effective. A good example is the first-letter technique (Gruneberg & Herrmann, 1997). In the first-letter technique, you compose a word, acronym, or sentence from the first letters of the words you want to remember. This is the mnemonic that we suggested in Chapter 3 to use to remember the colors of the spectrum (the name ROY G. BIV—**R**ed, **O**range, **Y**ellow, **G**reen, **B**lue, **I**ndigo, **V**iolet). This mnemonic helps, but it is not as effective as the other, more elaborative mnemonics, especially for more complex information.

So what else—in addition to elaborative rehearsal and the use of mnemonics—improves encoding and retrieval? There are three concepts that will help: (1) distributed study is better than cramming, (2) practice makes perfect, and (3) testing enhances memory. The superior memory for spaced study versus cramming is called the **spacing (distributed study) effect.** Your memory will improve if you distribute your studying for an exam over the entire preparation interval and not just the few days before the exam (Payne & Wenger, 1996). Hundreds of experiments have shown the benefits of distributed study (Cepeda, Pashler, Vul, Wixted, & Rohrer, 2006). In fact, for best results, distribute your studying *and* cram. The more you study, the more you learn. Overlearning, continuing to study material past the point of initial learning, improves memory (Rohrer & Taylor, 2006). Remember what we said about practice and automatic processing. Continued practice will make retrieval more automatic. Such practice may not make you "perfect," but you'll definitely do better. Lastly, don't just study. Incorporate repeated self-testing during your distributed study periods. Such testing will enhance your memory by allowing you to practice retrieval, which is what exams require (Roediger & Karpicke, 2006). Don't wait for an exam to test your retrieval; test it regularly during study. It will not only help you to practice retrieval but also help you to guide your study by pointing out what you have learned and what you have not learned.

Section Summary

In this section, we discussed the most effective encoding strategy, elaborative rehearsal, which is relating new information to well-known information in long-term memory. Elaboration is most effective when we relate the new information to ourselves, the self-reference effect. Elaborative rehearsal leads to better memory because we create good retrieval cues when we integrate the new information with older, well-known information. This relates to the encoding specificity principle, which states that the best retrieval cues are those present during encoding.

We learned that state-dependent memory, mood-dependent memory, and mood-congruent memory are special cases of this principle. In these cases, the physiological state and the emotional mood provide strong retrieval cues.

We also discussed how mnemonic devices, memory aid techniques, are especially effective for remembering ordered information in a list, speech, or text. The method of loci, which originated in ancient Greece, and the peg-word system are both very effective because of their use of elaboration and visual imagery. In addition, to improve memory we should engage in spaced study—distributing our elaborative study over time rather than cramming. Overlearning and self-testing are also beneficial.

ConceptCheck | 2

Explain why elaborative encoding is more effective than just memorizing.

Explain how state-dependent memory and mood-dependent memory stem from the encoding specificity principle.

Explain what the method-of-loci mnemonic and the peg-word system mnemonic have in common.

Retrieving Information from Memory

In the last section, we focused on how to encode information into long-term memory. In this section, we will examine how we retrieve encoded information. First, we will consider the various ways that retrieval is measured. This will be followed by a discussion of forgetting, the failure to retrieve. Here we will discuss the major theories of why our memories fail us. Then, we will examine the reconstructive nature of the retrieval process by considering the role of schemas, source misattribution, and the misinformation effect. Finally, we will discuss the problem of "false" memories.

How to Measure Retrieval

The three main methods for measuring our ability to retrieve information from long-term memory are recall, recognition, and relearning. **Recall** is a measure of retrieval that requires the reproduction of the information with essentially no retrieval cues. Common recall measures would be short-answer and essay test questions. **Recognition** is a measure of retrieval that only requires the identification of the information in the presence of retrieval cues. In a recognition test you do not have to reproduce the information, you only have to identify it. Multiple-choice and matching test questions are examples of recognition test questions. Usually such questions are easier because retrieval cues (the answers

recall A measure of long-term memory retrieval that requires the reproduction of the information with essentially no retrieval cues.

recognition A measure of long-term memory retrieval that only requires the identification of the information in the presence of retrieval cues.

relearning The savings method of measuring long-term memory retrieval in which the measure is the amount of time saved when learning information for the second time.

themselves) are present to help you remember the information. The third method, **relearning,** is sometimes called the savings method because it is a measure of the amount of time saved when learning information for the second time. The most relevant example of relearning for students is studying for a comprehensive final examination in a course. You must relearn the material. It will take you less time to relearn it, but how much less depends upon how well you learned it the first time.

Hermann Ebbinghaus conducted the first experimental studies on human memory more than 100 years ago in Germany using the relearning method (Ebbinghaus, 1885/1964). His stimulus materials were lists of nonsense syllables, groupings of three letters (consonant-vowel-consonant such as BAV) that are not words or acronyms. He used meaningless nonsense syllables because he wanted to study pure memory for the list items. His familiarity with and knowledge of words and acronyms would have affected his ability to learn and remember the lists. His experimental procedure was very straightforward. He would study a list of nonsense syllables until he could correctly recite the complete list without any hesitations. He then put the list aside and waited some period of time (from 20 minutes up to 31 days) and then relearned the list to the same criterion (one complete recitation without any hesitations).

To get a measure of relearning, Ebbinghaus computed what he called a savings score—the reduction in the number of trials it took him to reach criterion. For example, if it took him 10 trials to learn a list initially and only 5 to relearn it, he saved 50% (5 vs. 10 trials). He used many different lists of nonsense syllables and many different retention intervals (the different amounts of time between initial learning and relearning). The results were like those shown in Figure 5.8. The forgetting curve in this figure shows that the greatest amount of forgetting occurs rather quickly and then tapers off. In Ebbinghaus's case, after about 2 days, little more forgetting occurred. This type of forgetting curve for long-term memory has been obtained over and over again in memory research (Bahrick, 1984). What causes this forgetting? Let's consider some possible explanations.

© Corbis

Hermann Ebbinghaus

Why We Forget

There is no question that we forget. Our memories clearly fail us. This is especially problematic for exams. Haven't we all taken an exam and forgotten some information and then retrieved it after the exam was over? To understand forgetting,

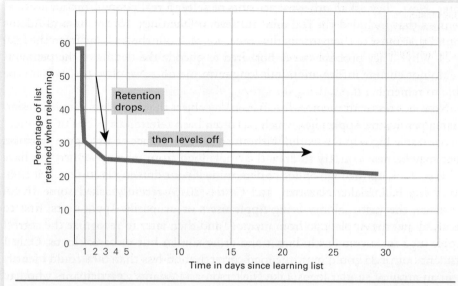

Figure 5.8 | Forgetting Curve for Long-Term Memory | The course of long-term forgetting usually takes on the shape of this figure—a rapid steep decrease that then levels off. In Ebbinghaus's memory research with nonsense syllables, the amount of time he saved relearning the material decreased dramatically for the first 2 days following initial learning and then leveled off after that. (Data from: Ebbinghaus, H. (1964). *Memory: A contribution to experimental psychology* (H. A. Ruger & C. E. Bussenius, Trans.). New York: Dover. (Original work published 1885.)

we must confront two questions. First, why do we forget? Second, do we really ever truly forget or do we just fail to retrieve information at a particular point in time? To answer these questions, we'll take a look at four theories of forgetting—encoding failure theory, storage decay theory, interference theory, and cue-dependent theory.

Encoding failure theory states that sometimes forgetting is not really forgetting but rather encoding failure (sometimes called pseudoforgetting). The information in question never entered long-term memory. We can't forget information that never entered long-term memory (that we never encoded into long-term memory). This would be like trying to locate a particular book in a library when the library never purchased it. There are many studies that have found encoding failure, even for the details of everyday objects, such as coins and numerical keypads (Rinck, 1999; Rubin & Kontis, 1983). Let's consider a classic study by Nickerson and Adams (1979). They found that our memory, both recall and recognition, for the common penny is not very good. The participants in the study found it incredibly difficult to draw the front and back of a penny. There are eight critical features on a penny, and Nickerson and Adams found the median number recalled and located correctly to be just

encoding failure theory A theory of forgetting that proposes that forgetting is due to the failure to encode the information into long-term memory.

three. Next, they asked other participants to select a real penny from an array of pennies that included the real one and several fake ones. Nickerson and Adams found that most of the participants could not pick out the real one from the fake ones. Why? They probably never bothered to encode the details of the penny. If we do not encode information into long-term memory, we obviously will not be able to remember it.

Now let's test your memory for an everyday object that has a less detailed design than a penny, the Apple logo, which has often been referred to as one of the most recognizable logos in the world. Without sneaking a glance at any Apple products that may be near you, try to draw the Apple logo from memory. Once you have done so, look up the logo online to determine if your drawing is correct. If it isn't, don't feel bad. Blake, Nazarian, and Castel (2015) recently asked some UCLA students, the vast majority being Apple users or primarily Apple users, first to recall (draw) the Apple logo from memory and then later to recognize the correct Apple logo in an array including it and other similar but incorrect logos. Only 1 student out of 85 could draw the logo correctly, and less than 50% could identify it in an array of similar logos. Like Nickerson and Adams's participants who had not encoded the details of the penny, the UCLA students had not encoded the details of the Apple logo. Given that we do not seem to remember details unless we consciously make an effort to encode them, make sure that you do encode them in studying for your exams. If the details are not encoded, then they cannot be remembered.

The other three theories of forgetting deal with information that was encoded into long-term memory but that we cannot retrieve. The **storage decay theory** suggests that forgetting occurs because of a problem in the storage of the information. The storage decay theory assumes that the biological representation of the memory gradually decays over time and that periodic use of the information will help to maintain it in storage. This latter assumption reflects the "use it or lose it" principle. This theory proposes that we forget because the information is no longer available in long-term memory. We forget because we cannot possibly remember it. The memory trace has decayed away. This would be like trying to get a particular book from a library, but finding that its pages had rotted away.

storage decay theory A theory of forgetting that proposes that forgetting is due to the decay of the biological representation of the information and that periodic usage of the information will help to maintain it in storage.

interference theory A theory of forgetting that proposes that forgetting is due to other information in memory interfering and thereby making the to-be-remembered information inaccessible.

The other two theories of forgetting propose that there are retrieval problems and not problems with storage. Both assume that the forgotten information is still available in long-term memory but cannot be retrieved. Each of the theories proposes a different reason for why the information cannot be retrieved. **Interference theory** proposes that other information interferes and makes the forgotten information inaccessible. In our library book example, this would be comparable to boxes of books blocking access to the location where the book is located. This theory proposes two types of such interference:

(1) **proactive interference**—the disruptive effect of prior learning on the retrieval of new information, and (2) **retroactive interference**—the disruptive effect of new learning on the retrieval of old information. To help you understand the difference between these two types of interference, remember that proactive is forward acting and retroactive is backward acting interference. Let's consider a couple of examples. Think about changing phone numbers after having a particular number for many years. When asked for your phone number, remembering the old one interferes with retrieving the new one. This would be proactive interference. The disruptive effect is from prior learning (your old phone number). For an example of retroactive interference, think about being at a party with many people you do not know. You meet someone who you want

Speed Bump   Dave Coverly

Dave Coverly/Speed Bump

to talk to later, but after meeting her, you are introduced to several other people. Now you cannot remember her name. The names of the people that you met after her are interfering with your retrieval of her name. This is retroactive interference because it is a case of the disruptive effect of new learning on the retrieval of old information. An additional example of each type of interference is given in Figure 5.9 (page 230).

Cue-dependent theory also assumes that forgetting stems from not gaining access to the desired information (Tulving, 1974). According to cue-dependent theory, we forget because the cues necessary for retrieval are not available. The information is available, but we cannot access it because we cannot find it. This is like trying to find a particular book in a library without its call number and a map of the library stacks. We wouldn't have the cues necessary to locate it, so it is likely we would not be able to do so. Successful retrieval is dependent upon the availability of the retrieval cues. An example of forgetting involving inaccessibility due to insufficient cues that all of us have experienced is the **tip-of-the-tongue (TOT) phenomenon** in which we can almost recall something, but the memory eludes us (Brown & McNeill, 1966). The phenomenon's name comes from the colloquial

proactive interference The disruptive effect of prior learning on the retrieval of new information.

retroactive interference The disruptive effect of new learning on the retrieval of old information.

cue-dependent theory A theory of forgetting that proposes that forgetting is due to the unavailability of the retrieval cues necessary to locate the information in long-term memory.

tip-of-the-tongue (TOT) phenomenon The failure to recall specific information from memory combined with partial recall and the feeling that recall is imminent.

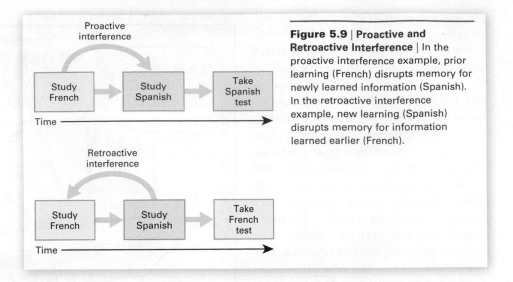

Figure 5.9 | Proactive and Retroactive Interference | In the proactive interference example, prior learning (French) disrupts memory for newly learned information (Spanish). In the retroactive interference example, new learning (Spanish) disrupts memory for information learned earlier (French).

saying, "It's on the tip of my tongue." You feel like you know the inaccessible information and are on the brink of retrieving it. Diary research indicates that college students experience roughly one or two TOT states per week, compared with two to four per week for elderly adults; middle-aged adults fall somewhere in between (Schacter, 2000). TOT experiences occur most often for names of people. You may remember what letter begins a person's name, but you still cannot retrieve the name. You are confident that you know it, but you just don't seem able to pull it out of your memory. Partial information about the name often helps to resolve the TOT state by providing cues that lead to successful recall.

So, there are many reasons why we forget. The four major theories are summarized in Table 5.2, but how can you apply this knowledge to enhance your learning? First, sometimes we forget because we do not encode the information into long-term memory. You should be especially wary of this reason when you are preparing for your class exams. You need to study thoroughly to avoid encoding failure on exams. Second, we may forget if information that is encoded and stored in long-term memory isn't periodically recalled and refreshed. The information can fade away over time. Think about what you have learned in the various courses that you have taken so far in college. After a course is over, you may sometimes feel like you retained little of that information for very long. If you want to retain more of it for a longer period of time, you need to regularly recall and use it. Third, the information that we are trying to retrieve may still be there, but we forget because other information may interfere with our retrieval of it or we may not have the necessary retrieval cues available to find it. Both elaboration during encoding and overlearning will help to reduce these retrieval problems.

The next section concerns the information that we do retrieve. Is it accurate or is it distorted? The answer is that it is often distorted. How does this

Table 5.2	Four Theories of Forgetting
Theory	**Explanation of Forgetting**
Encoding failure theory	Forgetting is due to the failure to encode the information into long-term memory
Storage decay theory	Forgetting is due to the decay of the biological representation of the information in long-term memory
Interference theory	Forgetting is due to the interference of other information in long-term memory, making the forgotten information inaccessible
Cue-dependent theory	Forgetting is due to the unavailability of the retrieval cues necessary to locate the information in long-term memory

occur? It occurs because retrieval is reconstructive and not exact. Let's take a look at the retrieval process to see how its reconstructive nature may distort our memories.

The Reconstructive Nature of Retrieval

The act of remembering is an act of reconstruction. Memory does not work like a tape recorder or a video recorder. Retrieval is not like playback. Our memories are far from exact replicas of past events. If you read a newspaper this morning, do you remember the stories that you read in the paper word for word? We usually encode the gist or main theme of the story along with some of the story's highlights. Then, when we retrieve the information from our memory, we reconstruct a memory of the story using the theme and the highlights.

Our retrieval reconstruction is guided by what are called **schemas**—frameworks for our knowledge about people, objects, events, and actions. These schemas allow us to organize our world. For example, what happens when you enter a dentist's office or what happens when you go to a restaurant to eat? You have schemas in your memory for these events. The schemas tell us what normally happens. For example, consider the schema for eating out in a restaurant (Schank & Abelson, 1977). First, a host or hostess seats you and gives you a menu. Then the waitperson gets your drink order, brings your drinks, and then takes your meal order. Your food arrives, you eat it, the waitperson brings the bill. You pay it, leave a tip, and go. These schemas allow us to encode and retrieve information about the world in a more organized, efficient manner.

schemas Frameworks for our knowledge about people, objects, events, and actions that allow us to organize and interpret information about our world.

The first experimental work on schemas and their effects on memory was conducted by Sir Frederick Bartlett in the first half of the twentieth century (Bartlett, 1932). Bartlett had his participants study some stories that were rather

source misattribution Attributing a memory to the wrong source, resulting in a false memory.

unusual. He then tested their memory for these stories at varying time intervals. When the participants recalled the stories, they made them more consistent with their own schemas about the world. For example, one story did not say anyone was wounded in the battle described, but participants recalled that many men were wounded, fitting their schemas for battles. Unusual details were normalized. For example, participants recalled incorrectly that the men in another story were fishing rather than hunting seals. In addition, the stories were greatly shortened in length when recalled. Strangely, the participants did not even realize that they were changing many of the details of the stories. In fact, the parts that they changed were those that they were most confident about remembering.

Bartlett's participants had reconstructed the stories using their schemas and did not even realize it. The main point to remember is that they distorted the stories in line with their schemas. Why? Schemas allow us to encode and retrieve information more efficiently. It would be impossible to encode and retrieve the exact details of every event in our lives. That's why we need organizing schemas to guide us in this task, even though they do not provide an exact copy of what happened. This seems a small cost given the benefits provided by organizing memory in terms of schemas.

Memory can be further distorted in reconstruction by source misattribution and the misinformation effect. **Source misattribution** occurs when we do not remember the true source of a memory and attribute the memory to the wrong source. Maybe you dream something and then later misremember that it actually happened. You misattribute the source to actual occurrence rather than occurrence in a dream. Source information for memories is not very good. You need to beware of this when writing papers. You may unintentionally use another person's ideas and think they are yours. You have forgotten their source. Even if source misattribution is unintentional, it is still plagiarism. Source misattribution also helps to explain déjà vu, that eerie sense that you have been in the exact same situation before, but in actuality you have not (Cleary, 2008). You have a feeling of familiarity because you have previously experienced elements in the situation in other contexts, but you cannot make the correct source attributions for them. Thus, déjà vu may result from feelings of familiarity that occur in a new situation without proper identification of their sources.

Source misattribution can also lead to other problems. A famous case of source misattribution involved noted developmental psychologist Jean Piaget (Loftus & Ketcham, 1991). For much of his life, Piaget believed that when he was a child, his nursemaid had thwarted an attempt to kidnap him. He remembered the attempt, even remembered the details of the event. When the nursemaid finally admitted to making up the story, Piaget couldn't believe it. He had reconstructed the event from the many times the nursemaid recounted the incident and had misattributed the source to actual occurrence. This is like thinking that something we dreamed really

Salvatore Cullari

"Well, I'm here to develop some false memories so I can forget about my own rotten past!"

occurred. The source of the memory is misattributed. Source misattribution results in what is called a **false memory,** an inaccurate memory that feels as real as an accurate memory. False memories can also be the result of imagination and observation inflation and the misinformation effect.

Imagination inflation is increased confidence in a false memory of an event caused by repeatedly imagining the event. For example, imagining performing an action often induces a false memory of having actually performed it (Garry, Manning, Loftus, & Sherman, 1996; Goff & Roediger, 1998). Repeated imagining inflates the confidence the person has that he actually performed the action, the imagination inflation effect. What might cause this disconcerting memory failure? Several factors likely contribute to the formation of these false memories. First, actually perceiving something and imagining it activate the same brain areas, leading to similar neural events that when tested might cause confusion as to whether the event was imagined or real (Gonsalves et al., 2004). Second, repeatedly imagining an event makes it seem increasingly familiar. This sense of familiarity can then be misinterpreted as evidence that the event actually occurred (Sharman, Garry, & Beuke, 2004). Lastly, the more vividly we are able to imagine events, the more likely it is that the imagined events feel like real events (Loftus, 2001; Thomas, Bulevich, & Loftus, 2003).

There is now evidence for a similar false memory effect in which a false memory of self-performance of an action is induced by merely observing another person's actions (Lindner, Echterhoff, Davidson, & Brand, 2010). It has been named the observation inflation effect because of its similarity to the imagination inflation effect. What could account for this effect? The controversial mirror neuron

false memory An inaccurate memory that feels as real as an accurate memory.

Jodi Hilton, POOL/AP Photo

Dr. Elizabeth Loftus has conducted research on eyewitness testimony and the inaccuracies in memory retrieval for over 30 years. Given her expertise in this area, she has testified as an expert witness in over 200 court cases, including many high-profile cases such as the trial of serial killer Ted Bundy (Neimark, 1996).

systems that we discussed in Chapter 4 may be involved. Some mirror neuron research suggests that observation of another person's action may trigger a covert simulation of the action and thus activate motor representations similar to those produced during actual self-performance of the action (Iacoboni, 2009b). Other evidence suggests that the neural correlates for such mirrored motor representations are similar to those for self-performed actions (Senfor, Van Petten, & Kutas, 2002). Thus, when a person is tested about actually performing the observed action, the mirrored action representations could erroneously be reactivated, leading to the observation inflation effect (Lindner et al., 2010).

The **misinformation effect** occurs when a memory is distorted by subsequent exposure to misleading information (Loftus, 2005). Elizabeth Loftus and her colleagues have provided numerous demonstrations of the misinformation effect, involving thousands of subjects, over the past four decades (Frenda, Nichols, & Loftus, 2011). These studies usually involve witnessing an event and then being tested for memory of the event but being given misleading information at the time of the test. Let's consider an example. Loftus and John Palmer (1974) showed participants a film of a traffic accident and then later tested their memory for the accident. The test included misleading information for some of the participants. For example, some participants were asked, "How fast were the cars going when they smashed into each other?" and others were asked, "How fast were the cars going when they hit each other?" Participants who were asked the question with the word "smashed" estimated the speed to be much higher than those who were asked the question with the word "hit." In addition, when brought back a week later, those participants who had been questioned with the word "smashed" more often thought that they had seen broken glass in the accident when in fact there was none. The key theme of this line of research is that our memories for events are distorted by exposure to misinformation. The resulting false memories seem like real memories.

False memories have important implications for use of eyewitness testimony in criminal cases and for the

misinformation effect The distortion of a memory by exposure to misleading information.

controversy over memories of childhood sexual abuse that have supposedly been repressed but then are "recovered" in adulthood. The Loftus and Palmer research example shows us that eyewitness testimony is subject to error and manipulation by misleading information. Between 1989 and 2007, for example, 201 prisoners in the United States were freed because of DNA evidence; and 77% of these prisoners had been mistakenly identified by eyewitnesses (Hallinan, 2009). Many of these overturned cases rested on the testimony of two or more mistaken eyewitnesses. Eyewitnesses not only often misidentify innocent people as criminals but they also often do so with the utmost confidence, and jurors tend to heavily weigh an eyewitness's confidence when judging their believability.

Clearly, certain types of interrogation, including the way questions are worded, could lead to false memories. With respect to the repressed memory controversy, many memory researchers are skeptical and think that these "recovered" memories may describe events that never occurred (like the kidnapping attempt on Piaget as a child). Instead, they may be false memories that have been constructed and may even have been inadvertently implanted by therapists during treatment sessions. In fact, researchers have demonstrated that such implanting is possible (Loftus, Coan, & Pickrell, 1996; Loftus & Ketcham, 1994). We must remember, however, that demonstrating the possibility of an event does not demonstrate that it actually happened. So, are all memories of childhood sexual abuse false? Absolutely not. Sexual abuse of all kinds is unfortunately all too real. The important point for us is that the research on false memory has provided empirical evidence to support an alternative explanation to the claims for recovered memories, and this will help to sort out the true cases from the false.

Section Summary

In this section, we considered the three ways to measure retrieval—recall, recognition, and relearning. In recall, the information has to be reproduced, but in recognition it only has to be identified. In relearning, the time one saves in relearning information is the measure of memory. For all three retrieval measures, forgetting from long-term memory levels off after a rapid initial burst of forgetting.

There are four major theories that address the question of why we forget. Encoding failure theory assumes that the information is never encoded into long-term memory, so it is not there to be retrieved. The storage decay theory assumes that the information is encoded but that it decays during storage so that it is no longer available to be retrieved. The other two theories assume that the information is still available in long-term memory but cannot be accessed. Interference theory assumes that the retrieval failure is due to other information blocking our retrieval. This interfering information could be older information interfering with the retrieval of new information (proactive interference) or new information interfering with the retrieval of older information (retroactive interference). The other theory, cue-dependent theory, assumes that the cues necessary to retrieve the information are not available, meaning that the information cannot be located in long-term memory.

Memory is a reconstructive process guided by our schemas—organized frameworks of our knowledge about the world. The use of schemas along with source misattribution problems, imagination and observation inflation, and the misinformation effect can lead to false memories, inaccurate memories that feel as real as accurate memories. Such false memories create questions about the accuracy of eyewitness testimony and the validity of supposed repressed memories of childhood abuse.

ConceptCheck | 3

Explain the difference between recall and recognition as methods to measure retrieval.

Explain how the four major theories of forgetting differ with respect to the availability versus accessibility of the forgotten information.

Explain how schemas help to create false memories.

Explain how source misattribution and the misinformation effect lead to false memories.

Study Guide

Chapter Key Terms

You should know the definitions of the following key terms from the chapter. They are listed in the order in which they appear in the chapter. For those you do not know, return to the relevant section of the chapter to learn them. When you think that you know all of the terms, complete the matching exercise based on these key terms.

sensory memory (SM)
iconic memory
temporal integration procedure
Sperling's full-report procedure
Sperling's partial-report procedure
short-term memory (STM)
memory span task
memory span
chunk
distractor task
maintenance rehearsal
working memory
long-term memory (LTM)
explicit (declarative) memory
semantic memory
episodic memory
implicit (nondeclarative) memory
procedural memory

priming
amnesic
anterograde amnesia
retrograde amnesia
infantile/child amnesia
free recall task
primacy effect
recency effect
encoding
storage
retrieval
automatic processing
effortful processing
levels-of-processing theory
elaborative rehearsal
self-reference effect
encoding specificity principle
state-dependent memory
mood-dependent memory
mood-congruence effect

mnemonic
method of loci
peg-word system
spacing (distributed study) effect
recall
recognition
relearning
encoding failure theory
storage decay theory
interference theory
proactive interference
retroactive interference
cue-dependent theory
tip-of-the-tongue (TOT) phenomenon
schemas
source misattribution
false memory
misinformation effect

Key Terms Exercise

Identify the correct term for each of the following definitions. The answers to this exercise follow the answers to the ConceptChecks at the end of the chapter.

1. The principle that states that the cues (both internal and external) present at the time information is encoded into long-term memory serve as the best retrieval cues for the information.

   _____

2. A measure of long-term memory retrieval that requires the reproduction of the information with essentially no retrieval cues.

   _____

3. The disruptive effect of new learning on the retrieval of old information.

   _____

4. The visual sensory register that holds an exact copy of the incoming visual input but only for a very brief period of time—less than a second.

   _____

5. A meaningful unit in memory.

_____

6. Long-term memory for factual knowledge and personal experiences that requires a conscious effort to remember and that entails making declarations about the information remembered.

_____

7. The inability to form new explicit long-term memories for events following surgery or trauma to the brain.

_____

8. A type of rehearsal in short-term memory in which incoming information is related to information from long-term memory to encode it into long-term memory.

_____

9. Superior long-term memory for spaced study versus massed study (cramming).

_____

10. Frameworks of knowledge about people, objects, events, and actions that allow us to organize and interpret information about our world.

_____

11. Explicit memory for personal experiences.

_____

12. A theory of forgetting that proposes that forgetting is due to the unavailability of the retrieval cues necessary to locate the information in long-term memory.

_____

13. An experimental procedure in which, following the brief presentation of a matrix of unrelated consonants, the participant is given an auditory cue about which row of the matrix to recall.

_____

14. Our inability as adults to remember events that occurred in our lives before about 3 years of age.

_____

15. A memory task in which the participant is given a series of items one at a time and then has to recall the items in the order in which they were presented.

_____

Practice Test Questions

The following are practice multiple-choice test questions on some of the chapter content. The answers are given after the Key Terms Exercise answers at the end of the chapter. If you guessed on a question or incorrectly answered a question, restudy the relevant section of the chapter.

1. Which of the following types of memory holds sensory input until we can attend to and recognize it?
   a. short-term memory
   b. sensory memory
   c. semantic memory
   d. episodic memory

2. Our short-term memory capacity is _____ ± 2 chunks.
   a. 3
   b. 5
   c. 7
   d. 9

3. Which of the following types of memory has the shortest duration?
   a. sensory memory
   b. short-term memory
   c. semantic memory
   d. episodic memory

4. Procedural memories are _____ memories and thus are probably processed in the _____ .
   a. explicit; hippocampus
   b. explicit; cerebellum
   c. implicit; hippocampus
   d. implicit; cerebellum

5. Which of the following leads to the best long-term memory?
   a. maintenance rehearsal
   b. elaborative rehearsal
   c. physical processing
   d. acoustic processing

6. The primacy and recency effects in free recall demonstrate that we have the greatest difficulty recalling the words _____ of a list.
   a. at the beginning
   b. at the end
   c. in the middle
   d. at the beginning and end

7. Which of the following is not a mnemonic aid?
   a. method of loci
   b. peg-word system
   c. temporal integration procedure
   d. first-letter technique

8. An essay test measures _____, and a multiple-choice test measures _____.
   a. recall; recall
   b. recall; recognition
   c. recognition; recall
   d. recognition; recognition

9. Which of the following theories of forgetting argues that the forgotten information was in long-term memory but is no longer available?
   a. encoding failure theory
   b. storage decay theory
   c. interference theory
   d. cue-dependent theory

10. Piaget's false memory of a kidnapping attempt when he was a child was the result of _____.
   a. infantile amnesia
   b. source misattribution
   c. encoding failure
   d. storage decay

11. After learning the phone number for Five Star Pizza, Bob cannot remember the phone number he learned last week for the Donut Connection. After living in Los Angeles for three years, Jim is unable to remember his way around his hometown in which he had lived the previous 10 years prior to moving to Los Angeles. Bob is experiencing the effects of _____ interference, and Jim is experiencing the effects of _____ interference.
   a. proactive; proactive
   b. proactive; retroactive
   c. retroactive; proactive
   d. retroactive; retroactive

12. Per the levels-of-processing theory, which of the following questions about the word "depressed" would best prepare you to correctly remember tomorrow that you had seen the word in this practice test question today?
   a. How well does the word describe you?
   b. Does the word consist of 10 letters?
   c. Is the word typed in capital letters?
   d. Does the word rhyme with obsessed?

13. The forgetting curve for long-term memory in Ebbinghaus's relearning studies with nonsense syllables indicates that _____.
   a. the greatest amount of forgetting occurs rather quickly and then it levels off
   b. little forgetting occurs very quickly and the greatest amount occurs later, after a lengthy period of memory storage
   c. forgetting occurs at a uniform rate after learning
   d. little forgetting ever occurs

14. In the Loftus and Palmer experiment, participants were shown a film of a traffic accident and then later tested for their memory of it. The finding that memory differed based upon the specific words used in the test questions illustrated _____.
   a. state-dependent memory
   b. source misattribution
   c. the self-reference effect
   d. the misinformation effect

15. The results for the experiment in which word lists were studied either on land or underwater and then recalled either on land or underwater provide evidence for _____.
   a. source misattribution
   b. encoding specificity
   c. proactive interference
   d. retroactive interference

Chapter ConceptCheck Answers
ConceptCheck | 1
- As pointed out in Chapter 3, bottom-up processing is the processing of incoming sensory information from the physical environment. This is what occupies sensory memory so it is bottom-up input. Also, as pointed out in Chapter 3, top-down processing uses the

information in our long-term knowledge base to interpret the bottom-up input. Thus, long-term memory can be thought of as providing top-down input because it is the repository of our knowledge base and past experiences.

- The duration of iconic memory must be very brief because if it were not, our visual sensory register would get overloaded quickly, leading to successive visual images overlapping in the register. Thus, we wouldn't perceive the world normally because it would be a constant mix of conflicting overlapping images.

- A "chunk" is a meaningful unit in our memory; for example, a single letter, an acronym, and a word each comprise one chunk. We have a memory span of 7 ± 2 unrelated letters, acronyms, or words.

- H. M. demonstrated a practice effect on the mirror-tracing task and the manual skill learning task in which he had to keep a stylus on a small dot that was spinning around on a turntable, but he did not consciously remember ever having done either task. This shows that he formed new implicit long-term memories for how to do these tasks because his performance on the tasks improved as he gained experience on them but that he did not form new explicit long-term memories for actually having done the tasks because he could not remember ever doing these tasks. H. M. also demonstrated repetition priming effects on a word fragment completion task without conscious awareness of the earlier presented priming words. Thus, he demonstrated implicit long-term memory for the words on the word fragment completion task but he had no explicit long-term memory for having seen them before. In another study, he was classically conditioned to give an eyeblink response to a tone. After the conditioning, whenever he was exposed to the tone, he gave the eyeblink response, but he did not consciously remember ever having been conditioned. This finding shows that he formed new implicit long-term memories of the association between the tone and eyeblink but did not form any new explicit long-term memories for the conditioning episodes.

ConceptCheck | 2

- Elaborative encoding is more effective than memorizing because the process of elaboration ties the new information to older, well-known information. This older information provides many good retrieval cues for the new information. Thus, elaborative encoding provides both more retrieval cues and better ones than memorizing.

- State-dependent memory and mood-dependent memory are both instances of the encoding specificity principle operating because in each case, maximal similarity in study-test physiological states or moods leads to the best long-term memory.

- Both mnemonics relate the new information to a well-known sequence. In each mnemonic you step through the sequence and retrieve the list item tied to that step. In the case of the method of loci, sequential locations within a well-known room or place are used, whereas in the peg-word system, the steps are part of a well-learned jingle (one is a bun, two is a shoe, . . .). Thus, both mnemonics use elaborative rehearsal.

ConceptCheck | 3

- In recall, the information has to be reproduced. In recognition, the information only has to be identified.

- Encoding failure theory and storage decay theory assume the forgotten information is not available in long-term memory. Both the interference and cue-dependent theories of forgetting assume it is still available but not accessible.

- Schemas help to create false memories because in using them, we tend to replace the actual details of what happened with what typically happens in the event that the schema depicts. As Bartlett found in his schema research, this is especially true for unusual details. This means that schemas tend to normalize our memories and lead us to remember what usually happens and not exactly what did happen.

- Source misattribution leads to false memories because we don't really know the source of a memory. The event may never have occurred, but we think that it did because we misattributed the source of the memory. The misinformation effect leads to false memories through the effect of misleading information being given at the time of retrieval. We incorporate this misleading information for an event into our memory and thus create a false memory for it.

Answers to Key Terms Exercise

1. encoding specificity principle
2. recall
3. retroactive interference
4. iconic memory
5. chunk
6. explicit memory
7. anterograde amnesia
8. elaborative rehearsal
9. spacing (distributed study) effect
10. schemas
11. episodic memory
12. cue-dependent theory
13. Sperling's partial-report procedure
14. infantile/child amnesia
15. memory span task

Answers to Practice Test Questions

1. b; sensory memory
2. c; 7
3. a; sensory memory
4. d; implicit; cerebellum
5. b; elaborative rehearsal
6. c; in the middle
7. c; temporal integration procedure
8. b; recall; recognition
9. b; storage decay theory
10. b; source misattribution
11. d; retroactive; retroactive
12. a; How well does the word describe you?
13. a; the greatest amount of forgetting occurs rather quickly and then it levels off
14. d; the misinformation effect
15. b; encoding specificity

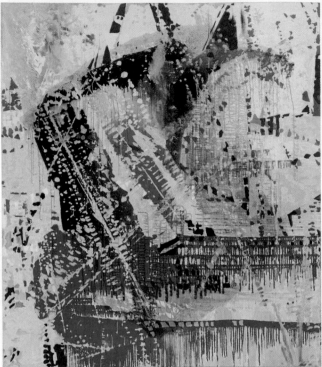

Courtesy of Jackie Saccoccio and 11R, NY

6 | Thinking and Intelligence

In this chapter, we will consider how we use the information in our memories to think. **Thinking** is the processing of information to solve problems and make judgments and decisions. Because these processes are important aspects of intelligent thinking, we will also consider intelligence testing and some of the controversies surrounding the concept of intelligence. We will start our discussion with the most basic, higher-level cognitive process—problem solving. You will be asked to solve several problems. You will learn more from these exercises if you try to solve each problem before reading about its solution.

Problem Solving

A problem is a situation in which there is a goal, but it is not clear how to reach the goal. There are well-defined and ill-defined problems (Gilhooly, 1996). A **well-defined problem** is a problem with clear specifications of the start state (where you are), goal state (where you want to be), and the processes for reaching the goal state (how to get there). An **ill-defined problem** is a problem lacking clear specification of the start state, goal state, or the processes for reaching the goal state. Board games such as Monopoly and Scrabble represent well-defined problems. Their start states and goal states, along with the processes of moving from one to the other (the rules of the game), are all clearly specified. Getting your roommate to help clean the apartment would be an ill-defined problem. The start state and goal state are fairly well-defined, but the processes for moving between them are not. Most problems we confront are ill-defined, and to solve them we need to define the missing parts. We'll see that some blocks to solving problems may arise in this definition process before we even attempt to solve a problem.

Before learning about some of these obstacles to problem solving, I would like you to attempt to solve the following problems. You may recognize one of the series problems from Chapter 1. Don't worry if you find these problems difficult; most people do. I will explain why.

thinking The processing of information to solve problems and make judgments and decisions.

well-defined problem A problem with clear specifications of the start state, goal state, and the processes for reaching the goal state.

ill-defined problem A problem lacking clear specification of either the start state, goal state, or the processes for reaching the goal state.

(a) **Instructions: For each of these two series problems, your goal is to predict the next alphabetic character in each of the series. The answer to the first series is not "O."**

O T T F F S S ?
E O E R E X N ?

(b) Instructions: **Connect the nine circles using four straight lines without lifting your pen or pencil from the paper or retracing any of your lines. You should attempt this problem on a separate sheet of paper so that you can keep a record of your attempts. Once you have a four-straight-line solution, the next goal is to connect the nine circles with three straight lines using the same constraints as in the four-straight-line version.**

Blocks to Problem Solving

Problem solving can be divided into two general steps: (1) interpreting the problem and (2) trying to solve the problem. For many problems, the path to a solution is blocked in the first step by incorrectly interpreting the problem. This is like answering a test question too quickly, only to find out later that you misinterpreted the question. If you are working with such a misinterpretation, you will probably fail to solve the problem. The two nine-circle problems are good examples of problems that often lead to misinterpretations. Let's see how.

Interpreting the problem. Look at your failed attempts at solving the nine-circle problem involving four straight lines. Did you try to keep your lines within the mental square created by the circles? Most people do, and you cannot solve the problem this way (Wickelgren, 1974). Not only do most people create this misinterpretation, but they also continue to use it even though they make no progress toward solving the problem. This inability to "think outside the box" and create a new interpretation of a problem is called **fixation**. Reread the instructions. You were not required to keep your lines within this mental square. Any or all of the four lines can extend outside this space. The lines only have to be straight and connect all nine circles. Knowing this, try again to solve the problem. Draw a straight line that goes down through the first column of circles and continues on outside of the mental square. When you bring your next line back up, also continue it outside of the mental square. This should start you on your way to a solution, though it may still be elusive (Weisberg & Alba, 1981).

What about the second nine-circle problem—connecting all nine circles with three straight lines? If you didn't solve it, think about the assumptions that you made when you interpreted the problem. This problem is even more difficult, because you may have made two mistakes in your interpretation and fixated on them, making the problem impossible to solve. First, as in the four-straight-line problem, you might have assumed that you need to keep your lines within the mental

fixation The inability to create a new interpretation of a problem.

square created by the circles. Second, you might have assumed that the lines need to go through the centers of the circles. Neither assumption is valid. Now try to solve this problem knowing that both of these assumptions are misinterpretations. Try drawing three straight lines that do not go through the centers of the circles and that travel outside the mental square. It might help to imagine using a very long ruler to draw your lines. If you're still stumped on either one of these problems, look at the sample solutions at the end of the chapter.

"Thinking outside of the box is difficult for some people. Keep trying."

Another obstacle to problem solving is **functional fixedness**—the inability to see that an object can have a function other than its typical one. This type of fixation also occurs during the problem definition stage. Functional fixedness limits our ability to solve problems that require using an object in a novel way (Duncker, 1945). This often happens to us in our everyday life. Maybe we need a screwdriver, but one isn't available. We have other things such as coins that could function as a screwdriver, but we may not think about using them in this novel way. Or, what if you just did some grocery shopping, and as you are about to walk out of the store it starts raining hard. You have no umbrella. How can you avoid getting soaked? You bought some large trash bags, but you may not think about using one as a raincoat to protect you from the rain. To combat functional fixedness, we should systematically think about the possible, novel uses of all the various objects in the problem environment. This is bound to increase our ability to solve the continual problems that come up in our daily lives.

Solving the problem. Problem misinterpretation and functional fixedness are good examples of the negative impact that our past experiences can have on our ability to solve current problems. Our past experience with problem solving can also lead to a phenomenon known as **mental set**—the tendency to use previously successful solution strategies without considering others that are more appropriate for the current problem. Mental set is especially common for strategies that have been used recently. Consider the two letter-series problems on page 243. If you had difficulty solving them, mental set may be what hindered you (Griggs, 2003). You probably attempted to solve these two problems with strategies that you have used successfully in the past with series problems. You may have viewed the letters in the series as single entities and looked for relationships between them. This strategy does not include viewing each of the letters as part of some larger entity. You cannot solve the series unless you do so. For the first series problem, you should think of the letters as the first letters in the words of a well-known ordering. It's as easy as 1-2-3.

functional fixedness The inability to see that an object can have a function other than its typical one in solving a problem.

mental set The tendency to use previously successful problem-solving strategies without considering others that are more appropriate for the current problem.

insight A new way to interpret a problem that immediately yields the solution.

The solution: These are the first letters in the sequence of number words—**O**ne, **T**wo, **T**hree, **F**our, **F**ive, **S**ix, **S**even—so the answer is E for **E**ight. This should help you to solve the second series problem, but don't fall prey to mental set and try to find another well-known ordering in which these are the first letters of the words in the sequence. You need to look for another solution strategy. Because of mental set, you probably don't see the strategy, but it's directly related to the solution to the first series. The letters in the second series are the last letters in the number words—on**E**, tw**O**, thre**E**, up to seve**N**. The answer is T for eigh**T**. What's the lesson to be learned? Don't cling to solution strategies that have worked in the past, but which are not presently working. Try new approaches.

Sometimes when searching for new approaches to a problem, we may experience what has been called **insight**—a new way to interpret a problem that immediately gives the solution. This rapid understanding is the key to the solution. Insight is sometimes referred to as an "Aha!" or "Eureka!" experience. Try the following problem from Knoblich and Oellinger (2006). You may experience insight in solving it. The solution is given at the end of the chapter.

Instructions: The equation shown is not correct. To create a correct equation, you can move only one matchstick (but not remove it). Only Roman numerals and the three operators, +, −, and = are allowed.

For insight problem solving tasks such as matchstick problems, the frontal cortex (home to executive processes such as planning, judging, evaluating, and deciding) may actually hinder insight rather than facilitate it (Restak & Kim, 2010). Reverberi, Toraldo, D'Agostini, and Skrap (2005) found that patients with damage to their lateral frontal cortex actually outperformed healthy participants on insight problems. While only 43% of healthy participants could solve some very difficult matchstick problems, 82% of patients with frontal lobe damage did so. Thus, our intact frontal lobes may lock us into less than optimal solution strategies (a mental set effect) for insight problems. In the Reverberi et al. study, the patients with frontal lobe damage were freed from this constraint and were more successful in solving the problems, indicating that other brain regions may be more critical to solving insight problems.

Recent research indicates that the right anterior temporal lobe (directly above the right ear) may be such a region. Chi and Snyder (2011) found that noninvasive transcranial direct current stimulation of the anterior temporal lobes (inhibiting the left anterior temporal lobe and activating the right anterior temporal lobe) facilitated the solution of insight problems. The stimulation led to a threefold increase in solving difficult matchstick problems. Hence, maybe the advice to "think outside the box" should be amended to be "think outside the frontal lobes." Chi and Snyder (2012) also found that this same transcranial stimulation of the anterior temporal lobes will facilitate the solution of the nine-circle problem. None of the participants solved the problem before stimulation; 14 of 33 broke fixation and solved it as a result of receiving the stimulation. Chi and Snyder calculated that the probability that this fraction of the participants could solve it by chance is less than one in a billion.

You might wonder if there is any validity to prescriptive advice such as to "think outside the box." Metaphors such as this (and others such as to consider a problem "on one hand and then on the other") suggest a connection between concrete bodily experiences and creative problem solving in which physically enacting the metaphor would enhance creative problem solving. Leung et al. (2012) have provided the first evidence that such embodiment might activate cognitive processes that facilitate creativity. For example, subjects trying to solve an innovative verbal thinking task performed much better if they sat and thought outside rather than inside a 125-cubic-foot box made of plastic pipe and cardboard. Similar results were observed for another creativity task for subjects solving the task while walking freely outside a fixed rectangular path indicated by duct tape on the floor (marking out a box of about 48 square feet in area) versus walking along the path. Obviously much more research is needed on this experimental question, but these initial findings indicate that thinking "outside the box" may not be a cliché; you might just need to use an actual box.

We have discussed many potential blocks to problem solving, and it takes a very conscious, concerted effort to overcome them. What can you do? Ask yourself questions such as the following: Is my interpretation of the problem unnecessarily constraining? Can I use any of the objects in the problem in novel ways to solve the problem? Do I need a new type of solution strategy? If we do not make this effort, we are engaged in what is called mindless behavior—rigid, habitual behavior in which we fail to attend carefully to the details of the present situation (Langer, 1989, 1997). To be good problem solvers, we will need to be open to new interpretations of problems and to new ways of using objects to solve problems. We will also need to develop a broader, more effective set of solution strategies, which is our next topic.

Solution Strategies

Just as problem solving can be divided into two steps, solution strategies can be divided into two types—algorithms and heuristics. An **algorithm** is a step-by-step procedure that guarantees a correct answer to a problem. For example, when we solve a math problem with long division, we are using an algorithm. If we execute the steps correctly, we will get the correct answer. For many problems, however, we may not know the algorithm or an algorithm for the problem may not exist. To solve the

algorithm A step-by-step problem-solving procedure that guarantees a correct answer to a problem.

heuristic A problem-solving strategy that seems reasonable given one's past experience with solving problems, especially similar problems, but does not guarantee a correct answer to a problem.

problem in such cases, we have to use a **heuristic**, a solution strategy that seems reasonable given our past experiences with solving problems, especially similar problems. Think of a heuristic as an educated guess.

Sometimes you may even know the algorithm for a problem, but you don't use it because its execution would be too time-consuming. Instead you may try some heuristics, and they might pay off with a quicker answer, or they may lead to no answer or an incorrect one. This is the crucial difference between an algorithm and a heuristic. An algorithm guarantees a correct answer (if it's the correct algorithm for the problem and you execute it correctly), but a heuristic makes no guarantees. Let's consider some problems (anagram word puzzles) for which you likely know the algorithm, but because it would usually be too difficult to execute, you use heuristics instead. In an anagram puzzle, the letters of a word are presented in a scrambled order, and the problem is to rearrange them to determine the word. Now, what's the algorithm for such puzzles? Generate each possible sequence of the letters and check to see if each sequence is a word. This sounds simple, but it isn't. For example, there are over 5,000 possible sequences of the letters for a seven-letter anagram! So unless there are only a few letters in the anagram, we use heuristics based upon our knowledge of the English language. For example, we know that the letter U usually follows the letter Q and that certain letters such as B and C don't follow one another in words. We attempt to create words with the letters following such principles. To understand this strategy, let's work a couple of anagram puzzles. As you try to solve them, think about the strategy you are using.

Instructions: Rearrange the letters in each anagram puzzle to form a meaningful word in the English language.

1. L O S O G C Y H Y P   **2. T E R A L B A Y**

The first puzzle is rather easy. The answer is especially relevant to this text. It's PSYCHOLOGY. Your use of heuristics was probably successful and led to a quick answer. The second puzzle is more difficult. Your use of heuristics may have failed and didn't yield a solution. Even so, you probably didn't switch to using the algorithm. You probably kept trying to find a solution by using heuristics. As you can see, heuristics might pay off with quick answers, but they may lead to no answer as in the second anagram puzzle. Now think about the algorithmic strategy. There are over 40,000 sequences for the eight letters in the second anagram puzzle; therefore, generating each of them to check if it's a word would take far more time and effort than we are willing to spend. However, if you did so, you would find that the answer is BETRAYAL.

Now let's consider three particular heuristics that are used fairly often in problem solving—the anchoring and adjustment, working backward, and means–end analysis heuristics. We'll start with the anchoring and adjustment heuristic.

Anchoring and adjustment. To help you to understand this heuristic, let's try an estimation problem taken from Plous (1993). The task involved in this problem would be impossible to execute. It is only a hypothetical problem that examines how we make estimates.

> **Estimate how thick a sheet of paper that is 0.1 millimeter thick would be if it were folded in on itself 100 times.**

Most people estimate the thickness to be only a few yards or so, which is not even close to the correct answer: 0.1 millimeter $\times$ 2^{100}, which equals 800 trillion times the distance between the earth and the sun (Plous, 1993)! Why do we underestimate this thickness by so much? We are most likely using the **anchoring and adjustment heuristic** in which an initial estimate is used as an anchor and then this anchor is adjusted up or down. The difficulty in using the anchoring and adjustment heuristic is that we tend to attach too much importance to the starting anchor amount and do not adjust it sufficiently (Tversky & Kahneman, 1974). The folding problem is a good illustration of this bias. If you double the thickness of the sheet of paper a few times, you still have a rather small thickness. Using this small thickness as an anchor for making your estimate, you do not adjust the estimate sufficiently and usually guess only a few yards. In this case, the anchoring and adjustment heuristic leads us to ignore the fact that the powers of 2 grow exponentially as we double them and become very large very quickly.

This estimation problem was only a hypothetical exercise, but it shows how we fail to adjust the anchor enough when using the anchoring and adjustment heuristic. Anchoring is a very robust psychological phenomenon and has even been shown to hold when the anchors represent the same physical quantity, 7.3 kilometers and 7,300 meters (Wong & Kwong, 2000). Estimates for the 7.3 km group were much lower than those for the 7,300 m group. Anchoring has been shown to influence judgments in a variety of domains, such as making judgments in personal injury cases (Chapman & Bornstein, 1996), negotiating (Ritov, 1996), and playing the stock market (Paulos, 2003). In the real world, anchoring may have costs attached to it. A good example that you may have experienced is the inclusion of minimum payment information on credit card statements. These minimum payment amounts can act as psychological anchors (Stewart, 2009; Thaler & Sunstein, 2008). In a hypothetical bill-paying experiment manipulating the inclusion of minimum payment information, Stewart (2009) found that the inclusion of this information led to significant reductions in partial payment amounts, which in the real world would lead to increased interest charges. We should also beware of using this heuristic when meeting people. Our first impression of a person is similar to forming an anchor. We must be sure to process subsequent information about the person carefully and adjust our impression (anchor) sufficiently. Remember, the anchoring and adjustment heuristic leads us to fail to adjust the anchor enough. So do not become too attached to an anchor when making judgments and decisions.

anchoring and adjustment heuristic A heuristic for estimation problems in which one uses his or her initial estimate as an anchor estimate and then adjusts the anchor up or down (often insufficiently).

working backward heuristic A problem-solving heuristic in which one attempts to solve a problem by working from the goal state back to the start state.

Working backward. Working backward is a heuristic that you may have learned to use in your math classes. The **working backward heuristic** is attempting to solve a problem by

means–end analysis heuristic A problem-solving heuristic in which the distance to the goal state is decreased systematically by breaking the problem down into subgoals and achieving these subgoals.

working from the goal state backward to the start state (Wickelgren, 1974). In math problems, this translates to working backward from the answer to the given information in the problem. To see how this heuristic would work, consider the following problem (Sternberg & Davidson, 1982):

> Water lilies growing in a pond double in area every 24 hours. On the first day of spring, only one lily pad is on the surface of the pond. Sixty days later, the pond is entirely covered. On what day is the pond half covered?

Did you solve it? It is impossible to solve this problem working in a forward direction. However, if you work backward by starting with the fact that the pond is entirely covered on the sixtieth day, you can solve it rather easily. Just ask yourself how much of the pond would be covered on the fifty-ninth day if the pond were entirely covered on the sixtieth day. The answer is half. The working backward heuristic is ideal for problems that have many possible paths from the start state, but only one path (or a few) going backward from the goal state.

Means–end analysis. A good heuristic for working forward on a problem is means–end analysis. In the **means–end analysis heuristic**, the problem is broken down into subgoals and we work toward decreasing the distance to the goal state by achieving these subgoals. Consider the following Tower of Hanoi problem. It is a well-defined problem. The start state, the goal state, and the rules for moving from the start state to the goal state are all clearly specified.

> **Instructions: The problem is to create the same configuration of disks on Peg C as is on Peg A in the starting state. Rules, however, govern your moves. You can only move one disk at a time, and you cannot place a larger disk on top of a smaller disk. Try to solve this problem efficiently by minimizing the number of moves that have to be made. The most efficient solution involves seven moves.**

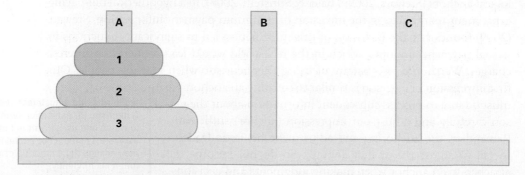

Let's try to use means–end analysis to solve the problem. What would be the first subgoal? You have to get Disk 3 on Peg C. You cannot, however, achieve this immediately, so you have to set up another subgoal. What is it? You have to get

Disk 1 on top of Disk 2 on Peg B. You cannot achieve this immediately either, so what is the next subgoal? Yes, you have to get Disk 2 on Peg B. To achieve this, you need to get Disk 1 off Disk 2 and not on Peg B. How do you achieve this subgoal? By now you should have the idea. Go ahead and finish solving the problem. It takes a minimum of seven moves. (The list of moves is given at the end of this chapter.) Using means–end analysis to solve this problem leads to a recursive subgoaling process. For example, solving the 3-disk version requires solving two 2-disk problems; solving the 4-disk version requires solving two 3-disk problems, each of which requires solving two 2-disk problems, and so on. In brief, this strategy entails building many smaller sub-towers on the way to building the required full tower (Cohen & Eichenbaum, 1993). Using means–end analysis (setting up subgoals and so on) to solve the Tower of Hanoi problem obviously involves planning, and remember from Chapter 2, the frontal lobes play a major role in planning. Thus, patients with frontal lobe damage might have difficulty solving this problem, and this is exactly what Goel and Grafman (1995) and Morris, Miotto, Feigenbaum, Bullock, & Polkey (1997) found.

The specific solution steps to a Tower of Hanoi problem can be varied both by varying the number of disks and the start and goal states (which peg the disks are on and which peg they need to be moved to, respectively) for each number of disks. Such changes allow researchers to see if problem performance is enhanced with practice on various versions of the problem. As you would expect, they found that people do get more efficient in solving these problems with practice. Some early research reported by Squire and Cohen (1984) interestingly found that a practice effect is also shown by anterograde amnesics, such as H. M. (who was described in Chapter 5), even though they had no recollection on each trial of ever having seen the problem before. Remember, as we discussed in Chapter 5, such amnesics form implicit procedural memories from practice in solving a problem because their cerebellum and basal ganglia are intact but no explicit episodic memories of working on the problem are formed because the hippocampus is critical for forming such memories and they had their hippocampus removed. However, these early findings were not replicated (Gabrieli, Keane, & Corkin, 1987), and it was concluded that the findings were due to experimenter–participant coaching interactions. Xu and Corkin (2001) clearly showed that anterograde amnesics are not able to learn the means–end analysis recursive strategy described earlier to solve the problem and hence do not show a practice effect (Xu & Corkin, 2001). Xu and Corkin concluded that learning this strategy requires both implicit procedural memory and explicit episodic memory in that it involves both motor and cognitive learning. Therefore, because anterograde amnesics cannot form new explicit episodic memories, they cannot learn this strategy and do not show a practice effect on the Tower of Hanoi problem.

Given the solution to the 3-disk Tower of Hanoi problem described above, let's consider a 64-disk Tower of Hanoi problem. Everything is the same except the number of disks—64 instead of 3. What is your estimate of the minimum number of moves necessary to solve the 64-disk version? Don't read further until you derive an estimate. If you used the anchoring and adjustment heuristic to derive an estimate, you probably greatly underestimated the answer. You probably derived a rather small anchor based on the 3-disk version that required only seven moves and then failed to adjust it upward sufficiently. The minimum number of moves for the Tower of Hanoi problems is $2^n - 1$, where n is the number of disks (Raphael, 1976). Thus, for 3 disks, the answer is $2^3 - 1$ (which is 7). Now do you see the problem with your estimate? The answer for 64 disks is $2^{64} - 1$, or trillions of moves! Did the anchoring and adjustment heuristic lead you astray again?

The events in our everyday lives are not as well-defined as the allowable moves in a Tower of Hanoi problem. They are uncertain. They have varying probabilities of occurring, and therefore we have to learn how to think in a probabilistic world. Such thinking involves estimating event probabilities (uncertainties). The heuristics we have discussed so far are not usable for this type of judgment. The heuristics that we do use to make these probability judgments and, more generally, how we think under uncertainty are the main topics of the next section.

Section Summary

In this section, we discussed how problems are either well-defined or ill-defined. Well-defined problems provide clear definitions of the start and goal states, and the processes for reaching the goal state from the start state. Ill-defined problems do not. Everyday problems tend to be ill-defined; therefore, interpreting the problem is necessary. Such interpretation may block problem solving. Blocks can be caused by problem misinterpretation, functional fixedness, or mental set. These blocks are all examples of the negative impact of our past experience on problem solving. We must make a mindful effort to overcome these blocks or our problem solving will suffer.

When attempting to solve a problem, we use either an algorithm that guarantees us a correct answer or heuristics that may lead to a quick solution or possibly to no solution. We prefer to use heuristics because they are less time-consuming. In addition, we may not know the appropriate algorithm for a problem or one may not even exist. Sometimes heuristics can lead to errors. A good example is the anchoring and adjustment heuristic for making estimates. The error in this case stems from our failure to adjust our initial anchor sufficiently.

The working backward heuristic is especially useful for problems that have many paths going forward from the start state but only one (or a few) going backward from the goal state. Means–end analysis is a useful heuristic for almost any type of problem. In this heuristic, you move forward by achieving subgoals that continue to reduce the distance between the start state and goal state.

ConceptCheck | 1

Explain how functional fixedness and mental set are examples of the negative impact of past experience.

Explain why we tend to use heuristics and not algorithms even though algorithms guarantee correct solutions.

Explain how the anchoring and adjustment heuristic may lead you to make a serious error in estimation.

Thinking Under Uncertainty

We live in an uncertain world. However, we suffer from an illusion of certainty—an emotional need for certainty when none exists. This need for certainty seems to be a fundamental aspect of human thinking. We also suffer from what Gigerenzer (2002) calls statistical innumeracy—the inability to reason from uncertainties and risk. Thus, our reasoning under uncertainty often goes awry. Such reasoning requires an understanding of probabilities and the ability to make judgments about probabilities. So we will begin with a discussion of probability and then describe how we seem to go about estimating the probabilities of events in the uncertain world we live in.

Everything that happens has a probability. For example, there is a probability for whether it will rain today and another probability for whether you will get an "A" in this class. The probability of an event is the likelihood that it will happen. Probabilities range from 0 (never happens) to 1 (always happens), but they are usually uncertain, somewhere between 0 and 1. An event with a probability of 0.5 is maximally uncertain because it is equally likely to occur and to not occur. Because we live in an uncertain world, we have to learn to estimate the probabilities (uncertainties) of various events. But how do we do this? Let's try to estimate some probabilities.

Consider this: Does the letter *r* occur more often as the first letter or third letter in English words? To answer this question, you need to make a judgment about the probability of one event (*r* occurring as the first letter) in relation to the probability of a second event (*r* occurring as the third letter). Think about how you would estimate these probabilities. One way to proceed would be to compare the ease of thinking of words beginning with *r* versus having *r* in the third position. Isn't it easier to think of words beginning with *r*? Does this mean that such words occur more often and that this event is more probable? If you think so, you are using a heuristic (words that are more available in our memory are more probable) to answer the probability question. When we discuss the main heuristics that humans use to judge probabilities, we'll return to this problem and see if this heuristic led us to the correct answer.

In addition to judging the uncertainty of events in our environment, we attempt to reduce our uncertainty about the world by trying to find out how various events are related to each other. For example, is the amount of arthritis pain related to the weather? To answer such questions, we develop and test hypotheses about how the events in our world are related. Such hypothesis testing allows us to learn about the world. Many of our beliefs are the conclusions that we have arrived at from testing such hypotheses. However, we usually don't test our hypotheses in well-controlled formal experiments the way that psychologists do. Instead we conduct subjective, informal tests of our hypotheses. Obviously, such a nonscientific approach may be biased and result in incorrect conclusions and erroneous beliefs. A good example is belief in the paranormal. If you are like most college students, you probably believe in at least one paranormal phenomenon, such as mental telepathy, clairvoyance, or psychokinesis (Messer & Griggs, 1989).

But, as you learned in Chapter 3, there is not one replicable scientific finding for any of these phenomena. We'll discuss how such erroneous beliefs might arise from our subjective hypothesis testing method.

We also often engage in hypothesis testing in various medical situations. One very common instance is testing the hypothesis that we have a specific disease given a positive result on a medical screening test for the disease. This actually amounts to trying to compute a conditional probability, which for most people (doctors and patients) is not that easy. Research that we will discuss shows that both doctors and patients tend to greatly overestimate such probabilities. To help you more accurately assess your chances of having the disease in this situation, we'll teach you a relatively simple way to compute such probabilities. But first let's see how we judge probabilities in general and how these judgments might be biased.

Judging Probability

Cognitive psychologists Amos Tversky and Daniel Kahneman identified two heuristics that we often use to make judgments about probabilities—the representativeness heuristic and the availability heuristic (Tversky & Kahneman, 1974). It is important to point out that these two heuristics usually lead to reasonably good judgments, but they sometimes lead to errors. Why? The major reason is that a heuristic can lead us to ignore information that is extremely relevant to

Courtesy of Barbara Tversky

Amos Tversky

Andreas Rentz/Getty Images for Burda Media

Daniel Kahneman

Daniel Kahneman was awarded the Nobel Prize in Economic Sciences in 2002 for the groundbreaking research on heuristics that we partially describe here. His collaborator Amos Tversky would surely have shared the Nobel Prize with him, but he died in 1996, and Nobel committees are prohibited from awarding prizes posthumously. As we will learn, Kahneman and Tversky's research demonstrated that people often make decisions using heuristics rather than complete rational analysis. Kahneman's prize was in Economic Sciences because this research had important applications to economic theory and because there is no Nobel Prize awarded in psychological sciences.

the particular probability judgment. To understand, let's consider the following problem (Tversky & Kahneman, 1983).

> You will read a brief description of Linda, and then you will be asked to make a judgment about her. Here's the description:
>
> Linda is 31 years old, single, outspoken, and very bright. She majored in philosophy. As a student, she was deeply concerned with issues of discrimination and social justice, and also participated in antinuclear demonstrations.
>
> Which of the following alternatives is more likely?
>
> Linda is a bank teller.
>
> Linda is a bank teller and active in the feminist movement.

The representativeness heuristic. To decide which alternative is more probable, most people would use what is called the **representativeness heuristic**—a rule of thumb for judging the probability of membership in a category by

representativeness heuristic A heuristic for judging the probability of membership in a category by how well an object resembles (is representative of) that category (the more representative, the more probable).

how well an object resembles (is representative of) that category. Simply put, the rule is: the more representative, the more probable. Using this heuristic, most people, including undergraduates, graduate students, and professors, judge that the second alternative (Linda is a bank teller and active in the feminist movement) is more likely than the first alternative (Tversky & Kahneman, 1983). Why? Linda resembles someone active in the feminist movement more than she resembles a bank teller. However, it is impossible for the second alternative to be more likely than the first. Actually the description of Linda is totally irrelevant to the probability judgment!

Let's look at the set diagram in Figure 6.1. This diagram illustrates what is known as the conjunction rule for two different uncertain events (in this case, being a bank teller and being active in the feminist movement). The conjunction rule is that the likelihood of the overlap of two uncertain events (the green section of the diagram) cannot be greater than the likelihood of either of the two events because the overlap is only part of each event. This means that all of the tellers who are active in the feminist movement make up only part of the set of all bank tellers. Because the set of bank tellers is larger and includes those tellers who are active in the feminist movement, it is more likely that someone is a bank teller than that someone is a bank teller and active in the feminist movement. Judging that it is more likely that Linda is a bank teller and

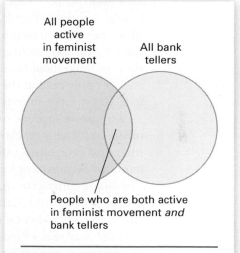

Figure 6.1 | The Overlapping Set Diagram for the Linda Problem | The overlap (the green area) of the two sets (all bank tellers and all people active in the feminist movement) indicates the probability of being both a bank teller and active in the feminist movement. Because this area is a subset (part) of each of the two sets, its probability has to be less than that for either of the two sets. This is the conjunction rule.

conjunction fallacy Incorrectly judging the overlap of two uncertain events to be more probable than either of the two events.

gambler's fallacy Incorrectly believing that a chance process is self-correcting in that an event that has not occurred for a while is more likely to occur.

active in the feminist movement illustrates the **conjunction fallacy**—incorrectly judging the overlap of two uncertain events to be more likely than either of the two events. By using the representativeness heuristic, we overlook a very simple principle of probability, the conjunction rule. This illustrates the shortcoming of using such heuristics—overlooking essential information for making the probability judgment.

Using the representativeness heuristic also leads to the **gambler's fallacy**—the erroneous belief that a chance process is self-correcting in that an event that has not occurred for a while is more likely to occur. Suppose a person has flipped eight heads in a row and we want to bet $100 on the next coin toss, heads or tails. Some people will want to bet on tails because they think it more likely, but in actuality the two events are still equally likely. One of the most famous examples of the gambler's fallacy occurred in a Monte Carlo casino in 1913 when a roulette wheel landed on black 26 times in a row (Lehrer, 2009). During that run, most people bet against black since they felt that red must be "due." They assumed that the roulette wheel would somehow correct the imbalance and cause the wheel to land on red. The casino ended up making millions of francs. "The wheel has no mind, no soul, no sense of fairness . . . Yet, we often treat it otherwise" (Vyse, 1997, p. 98).

Why do people commit the gambler's fallacy? Again, they are using the representativeness heuristic (Tversky & Kahneman, 1971). People believe that short sequences (the series of eight coin tosses or the 26 spins of the roulette wheel) should reflect the long-run probabilities. Simply put, people believe random sequences, whether short or long, should look random. This is not the case. Probability and the law of averages only hold in the long run, not the short run. In addition, the long run is indeed very long—infinity. The representativeness heuristic leads us to forget this.

Why are we so prone to using the representativeness heuristic and making judgments based only on categorical resemblance? The answer is tied to the fact that the mind categorizes information automatically. Categorization is just another name for pattern recognition, an automatic process that we discussed in Chapter 3. The brain constantly recognizes (puts into categories) the objects, events, and people in our world. Categorization is one of the brain's basic operational principles, so it shouldn't be surprising that we may judge categorical probabilities in the same way that we recognize patterns. This is how the brain normally operates. In addition to probability judgments, the representativeness heuristic can lead us astray in judging the people we meet because our first impression is often based on categorical resemblance. We tend to categorize the person based on the little information we get when we meet him or her. Remember that this initial judgment is only an anchor, and we need to process subsequent information carefully in order to avoid misjudgment of the person.

The availability heuristic. Let's go back to the judgment that you made earlier. Does the letter *r* appear more often as the first letter or third letter in English words? Actually, the letter *r* appears twice as often as the third letter in words than as the first letter. However, if you used the availability heuristic that was described, you would judge the reverse to be the case (that *r* occurs more often as the first letter). The **availability heuristic** is the rule of thumb that the more available an event is in our memory, the more probable it is (Tversky & Kahneman, 1973). We can think of more words beginning with the letter *r* than with *r* in the third position because we organize words in our memories

> **availability heuristic** A heuristic for judging the probability of an event by how available examples of the event are in memory (the more available, the more probable).

by how they begin. This does not mean that they are more frequent, but only that it is easier to think of them. They are easier to generate from memory. The opposite is the case—words with *r* in the third position are more frequent. This is actually true for seven letters: *k, l, n, r, v, x,* and *z* (Tversky & Kahneman, 1973).

Remember that a heuristic does not guarantee a correct answer. The availability heuristic may often lead to a correct answer; but as in the letter *r* problem, events are sometimes more easily available in our memories for reasons other than how often they actually occur. An event may be prominent in our memories because it recently happened or because it is particularly striking or vivid. In such cases, the availability heuristic will lead to an error in judgment. Think about judging the risk of various causes of death. Some causes of death (airplane crashes, fires, and shark attacks) are highly publicized and thus more available in our memories, especially if they have occurred recently. Using the availability heuristic, we judge them to be more likely than lesser publicized, less dramatic causes of death such as diabetes and emphysema, which are actually more likely but not very available in our memories (Lichtenstein, Slovic, Fischhoff, Layman, & Combs, 1978). In fact, the probability of dying from falling airplane parts is 30 times greater than

Because airplane crashes are so visually dramatic and highly publicized by the media, they tend to be very available in our memories. This availability leads us to greatly overestimate our likelihood of dying in a plane crash.

that of being killed by a shark (Plous, 1993). The lesson to be learned here is that greater availability in memory does not always equal greater probability.

Availability in memory also plays a key role in what is termed a dread risk. A dread risk is a low-probability, high-damage event in which many people are killed at one point in time. Not only is there direct damage in the event, but there is secondary, indirect damage mediated through how we psychologically react to the event. A good example is our reaction to the September 11, 2001, terrorist attacks (Gigerenzer, 2004, 2006). Fearing dying in a terrorist airplane crash because the September 11 events were so prominent in our memories, we reduced our air travel and increased our automobile travel, leading to a significantly greater number of fatal traffic accidents than usual. It is estimated that about 1,600 more people needlessly died in these traffic accidents (Gigerenzer, 2006). These lives could have been saved had we not reacted to the dread risk as we did. We just do not seem to realize that it is far safer to fly than to drive. National Safety Council data reveal that you are 37 times more likely to die in a vehicle accident than on a commercial flight (Myers, 2001).

Since heuristics may mislead us, you may wonder why we rely upon them so often. First, heuristics are adaptive and often serve us well and lead to a correct judgment. Second, they stem from what cognitive psychologists call System 1 (automatic) processing (Evans, 2008, 2010; Stanovich & West, 2000). System 1 processing is part of a dual processing system and is contrasted with System 2 (reflective) processing. Kahneman (2011) refers to System 1 as fast, intuitive, and largely unconscious thinking and System 2 as slow, analytical, and consciously effortful thinking. Although System 2 is responsible for more rational processing and can override System 1, it is also lazy. System 2 is willing to accept the easy but possibly unreliable System 1 answer. Clearly there are shortcomings with the System 1 heuristics that we use to judge probabilities (uncertainties). Thus, you should work to engage System 2 processing. Slow down your thinking; be more analytical. For example, make sure you have not overlooked relevant probability information when using the representativeness heuristic, and try to think beyond prominence in memory when using the availability heuristic. In brief, don't "rush to judgment." Are there also shortcomings with the way we try to reduce our uncertainty and learn about the world through hypothesis testing? We now turn to this question.

Hypothesis Testing

In Chapter 1, we discussed the experimental research method that psychologists use to test their hypotheses about human behavior and

Could increased smart phone usage lead to even more System 1 fast, intuitive thinking?

Dan Thompson/Universal Press UClick

mental processing. Like psychologists, we too have beliefs about the relationships between the variables in our environment (hypotheses), and we too collect data to test these beliefs. However, we don't use the experimental method discussed in Chapter 1. So what do we do? How do people test their hypotheses and thus reduce their uncertainty about the world? British researcher Peter Wason devised two problems to examine this question—the 2-4-6 task and the four-card selection task.

Confirmation bias. In the 2-4-6 task, you are presented the number sequence "2-4-6" and asked to name the rule that the experimenter used to generate that sequence (Wason, 1960). Before presenting your hypothesized rule (your answer), you are allowed to generate as many sequences of three numbers as you want and get feedback on whether each conforms to the experimenter's rule. When you think that you know the rule, you tell the experimenter. Before we describe how people perform on this task, think about how you would proceed. What would be your first hypothesis for the rule and what sequences of three numbers would you generate to test your hypothesized rule?

Most of the participants do not name the correct rule. They devise a hypothesis (e.g., "numbers increasing by 2") and proceed to test the hypothesis by generating series that conform to it (e.g., 8-10-12). In other words, they test their hypotheses by trying to confirm them. Did you do this? People do not test their hypotheses by trying to disconfirm them (e.g., generating the sequence 10-11-12 for the hypothesis "numbers increasing by 2"). The tendency to seek evidence that confirms one's beliefs is called **confirmation bias**. This bias is pervasive in our everyday hypothesis testing, so it is not surprising that it occurs on the 2-4-6 task. The 2-4-6 task serves to highlight the inadequacy of the confirmation bias as a way to test a hypothesis. To truly test a hypothesis, we must try to disconfirm it. We should attempt to disconfirm each hypothesis that we generate. The experimenter's rule for the 2-4-6 task was a very simple, general rule, so most sequences that people generated conformed to it. What was it? The rule was simply any three increasing numbers; how far apart the numbers were did not matter.

Now let's look at the four-card selection task (Wason, 1966, 1968). Try the problem before reading further.

> **The four cards below have information on both sides. On one side of a card is a letter, and on the other side is a number.**

| A | | K | | 4 | | 7 |

> **Consider this rule: If a card has a vowel on one side, then it has an even number on the other side.**
>
> **Select the card or cards that you definitely must turn over to determine whether the rule is true or false for these four cards.**

confirmation bias The tendency to seek evidence that confirms one's beliefs.

Well, if you're like most people, you haven't answered correctly. The correct response rate for this problem is usually less than 10% (Griggs & Cox, 1982). The most frequent error is to select the cards showing A and 4. The card showing A is part of the correct solution, but the card showing 4 is not. You should select the cards showing A and 7. Why? First, you should decide what type of card would falsify the rule. The rule states that if a card has a vowel on one side, it has to have an even number on the other side. Therefore, a card with a vowel on one side and an odd number on the other side would falsify the rule. Now do you see why the answer is A and 7? An odd number on the other side of the A card would falsify the rule, and so would a vowel on the other side of the 7 card. No matter what is on the other side of the K and 4 cards, the rule is true.

So why do people select the cards showing A and 4? As in the 2-4-6 task, people focus on confirmation and select cards to verify the rule (show that it is true). They choose the cards showing A and 4 because they incorrectly think that the rule must hold in both directions (it doesn't) and they must verify that it does so. They choose the card showing a vowel (A) to verify that it has an even number on the other side and the card showing an even number (4) to verify that it has a vowel on the other side. Instead of deducing what will falsify (disconfirm) the rule, people merely try to confirm it (demonstrating confirmation bias). There is, however, some recent evidence that people motivated to reject a rule because it is personally threatening or disagreeable to them will focus on disconfirmation and thus perform better on the four-card selection task (Dawson, Gilovich, & Regan, 2002).

Research on the 2-4-6 task and the four-card selection task show that people typically try to confirm hypotheses. Confirmation bias, however, is not limited to the 2-4-6 and four-card selection tasks, but extends to many aspects of our daily lives such as jury decisions, physicians' diagnoses, and the justification of governmental policies (Nickerson, 1998). In addition, it leads to other cognitive difficulties. For example, confirmation bias may lead us to perceive illusory correlations between events in our environment (Chapman, 1967; Chapman & Chapman, 1967). An **illusory correlation** is the erroneous belief that two variables are statistically related when they actually are not. If we believe a relationship exists between two things, then we will tend to notice and remember instances that confirm this relationship. Let's consider an example.

Many people erroneously believe that a relationship exists between weather changes and arthritis. Why? They focus on instances when the weather changes and their arthritic pain increases. To determine if this relationship actually exists, we need to consider the frequency of all four possible events, the two that confirm the hypothesis and the two that disconfirm it. In our example, the two confirming instances would be (1) when the weather changes and arthritic pain changes, and (2) when the weather does not change and arthritic

illusory correlation The erroneous belief that two variables are statistically related when they actually are not.

pain does not change. The two disconfirming instances are (1) when the weather changes but arthritic pain does not, and (2) when the weather does not change but arthritic pain does. When the frequencies of all four events are considered, it turns out that there isn't a relationship between these two variables. The confirming events are not more frequent than the disconfirming events (Redelmeier & Tversky, 1996).

> **belief perseverance** The tendency to cling to one's beliefs in the face of contradictory evidence.
>
> **person-who reasoning** Questioning a well-established research finding because one knows a person who violates the finding.

Confirmation bias is likely responsible for many of our erroneous beliefs. Science provides better answers than informal, biased hypothesis testing. When our beliefs are contradicted by science, as in the case of belief in paranormal events, we should think about our hypothesis testing procedure versus that of the scientist. We may have only gathered evidence to support our belief. We have to be willing to accept that our beliefs may be wrong. This is not easy for us to do. We suffer from **belief perseverance**—the tendency to cling to our beliefs in the face of contradictory evidence (Anderson, Lepper, & Ross, 1980). Our beliefs constitute a large part of our identity; therefore, admitting that we are wrong is very difficult. Such denial is illustrated by **person-who reasoning**—questioning a well-established finding because we know a person who violates the finding (Nisbett & Ross, 1980; Stanovich, 2010). A good example is questioning the validity of the finding that smoking leads to health problems, because we know someone who has smoked most of his or her life and has no health problems. Such reasoning also likely indicates a failure to understand that these research findings are probabilities. Such research findings are not certain; they do not hold in absolutely every case. Exceptions to these sorts of research findings are to be expected. Person-who reasoning is not valid, and we shouldn't engage in it.

Testing medical hypotheses. As was pointed out earlier, confirmation bias seems to impact physicians' testing of hypotheses during the diagnostic process (Nickerson, 1998). Physicians (and patients) also seem to have difficulty in interpreting positive test results for medical screening tests, such as for various types of cancer and HIV/AIDS (Gigerenzer, 2002). They often overestimate the probability that a patient has a disease based on a positive test result. This is partially due to the illusion of certainty that we discussed earlier. Such test results are not absolutely certain. When considering what a positive result for a screening test means, you are testing the hypothesis that a patient actually has the disease being screened for by determining the probability that the patient has the disease given a positive test result. This is what is called a conditional probability—the probability of an event (that the patient has the disease) given that another event has occurred (the patient tested positive for the disease). Because you will be considering the results of medical screening tests throughout your lifetime and will inevitably get some positive results, you should understand how to compute this conditional probability in order to know your chances of actually having the disease. Because this computation is not a very

Oliver Hartung/The New York Times/Redux

Gerd Gigerenzer

intuitive process, I will show you a straightforward way to do it, so that you can make more informed medical decisions.

Much of the research that is focused on how successful doctors and patients are at correctly interpreting a positive result for a medical screening test and on how they can improve their performance has been conducted by Gerd Gigerenzer and his colleagues (Gigerenzer, 2002; Gigerenzer & Edwards, 2003; Gigerenzer, Gaissmaier, Kurz-Milcke, Schwartz, & Woloshin, 2007; Gigerenzer & Hoffrage, 1995). Both doctors and patients have been found to overestimate these conditional probabilities. An older study by Eddy (1982) with 100 American doctors as the participants illustrates this overestimation finding; but before considering it, some explanation is necessary. In medicine, probabilities are often expressed in percentages rather than as numbers between 0 and 1.0. Three terms relevant to screening tests, the base rate for a disease and the sensitivity and false positive rates for the test, also need to be explained before we continue. The base rate (prevalence) of a disease is simply the probability with which it occurs in the population. The sensitivity rate for a screening test is the probability that a patient tests positive if she has the disease, and the false positive rate is the probability that a patient tests positive if she does not have the disease. Now consider Eddy's problem. You should try to estimate the probability asked for in the problem before reading on.

> **Estimate the probability that a woman has breast cancer given a positive mammogram result and a base rate for this type of cancer of 1%, a sensitivity rate for the test of 80%, and a false positive rate for the test of 9.6%.**

What was your estimate? If you acted like the doctors, you overestimated the probability. Almost all of the doctors estimated this probability to be around 75%. The correct answer, however, is much less, only around 8%. Hoffrage and Gigerenzer (1998) replicated Eddy's finding with even more shocking results. Physicians' estimates ranged from 1% to 90%, with a 90% chance of breast cancer being the most frequent estimate. Given the doctors' overestimation errors, think of how many women who tested positive in this case would have been unnecessarily alarmed had this been real life and not an experiment. Think about the possible consequences, which are far from trivial—emotional distress, further testing, biopsy, more expense, and maybe even unnecessary surgery. To correctly compute the conditional probability that someone has the disease given a positive test result, Gigerenzer recommends that you convert all of the percentages (probabilities) into natural frequencies, simple counts of events. According to

Gigerenzer, natural frequencies represent the way humans encoded information before probabilities were invented and are easier for our brains to understand. In brief, they make more sense to us. To convert to natural frequencies, we begin by supposing there is a sample of women who have had the screening test. It's best to suppose a large, even number such as 1,000, because such numbers allow an easier conversion to natural frequencies. Assuming a sample of 1,000 women, we can then convert Eddy's percentages into natural frequencies and compute the conditional probability.

> **Given a base rate of 1%, we would expect 10 (1% of 1,000) women to have breast cancer.**
>
> **Of these 10, we expect 8 (80% of 10) to test positive because the test has a sensitivity rate of 80%. The results for these 8 women are called true positives because these women have breast cancer and their test results were positive. The test results for the other 2 women are called false negatives because these women have breast cancer but their test results were negative.**
>
> **Among the 990 (1,000 − 10) women without breast cancer, 95 (9.6% of 990) will test positive given the 9.6% false positive rate. The results for these 95 women are called false positives because these women do not have cancer but their test results were positive. The results for the remaining 895 women are called true negatives because these women do not have cancer and their test results were negative.**
>
> **Thus, 103 (8 + 95) women in the sample of 1,000 will test positive, but only 8 are true positives. Thus, the conditional probability that a woman testing positive actually has cancer is the percentage of positive test results that are true positives, 8/103 = 0.077 (7.7%).**

Hoffrage and Gigerenzer (1998) found that once they presented the numbers as natural frequencies to doctors, the majority suddenly understood how the conditional probability should be calculated. Do you? If not, the solution steps are visually illustrated in the natural frequency tree diagram in Figure 6.2 (page 264). Read through the steps in the tree diagram. This should help.

It should be clear to you now that a positive result for a medical screening test does not necessarily mean that you have the disease. It is not certain. You might or you might not. It is natural to assume the worst (the illusion of certainty) when faced with a positive test result, but it may be more probable that you do not have the disease. It might be a false positive. Combine a low incidence rate (for example, 1% or 2%) with just a modest false positive rate (for example, 10%) for a screening test, and there will be many false positives (Mlodinow, 2008). A good example is mammography for younger women. In this case, a positive mammogram is actually more likely not to indicate cancer. Such findings have recently led the American Cancer Society in 2015 to recommend that women of average risk for breast cancer do not start yearly mammogram screening until the age of 45 (Keating & Pace, 2015), and the U.S. Preventive Services Task Force (the federal panel empowered to evaluate

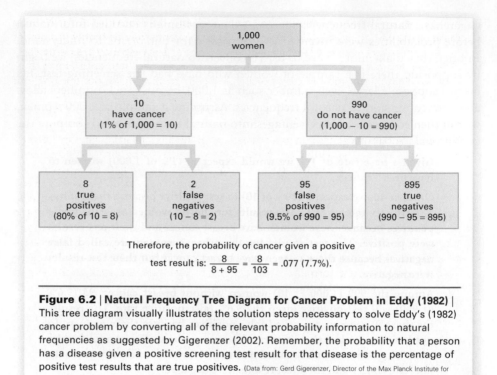

Therefore, the probability of cancer given a positive test result is: $\dfrac{8}{8+95} = \dfrac{8}{103} = .077$ (7.7%).

Figure 6.2 | Natural Frequency Tree Diagram for Cancer Problem in Eddy (1982) | This tree diagram visually illustrates the solution steps necessary to solve Eddy's (1982) cancer problem by converting all of the relevant probability information to natural frequencies as suggested by Gigerenzer (2002). Remember, the probability that a person has a disease given a positive screening test result for that disease is the percentage of positive test results that are true positives. (Data from: Gerd Gigerenzer, Director of the Max Planck Institute for Human Development, Berlin.)

cancer screening tests) in 2016 to recommend not until the age of 50 (Siu, 2016). Of course, screening tests with high false positive rates are also problematic, leading to both overdiagnosis and overtreatment. A good example is the PSA test for prostate cancer in men (Gilligan, 2009). Given that the potential benefits do not outweigh the harms for this test, the U.S. Preventive Services Task Force recommended in 2012 against PSA screening for men, regardless of age (Moyer, 2012). For more detailed coverage of interpreting screening test results and understanding other medical statistics, see Gigerenzer (2002), Gigerenzer, Gaissmeier, Kurz-Milcke, Schwartz, and Wolosin (2007), and Woloshin, Schwartz, and Welch (2008).

Section Summary

In this section, we learned that when we make probability judgments, we often use the representativeness and availability heuristics. When using the representativeness heuristic, we judge the likelihood of category membership by how well an object resembles a category (the more representative, the more probable). This heuristic can lead us to ignore extremely relevant probability information such as the conjunction rule. The availability heuristic leads us to judge the likelihood of an event by its availability in memory (the more available, the more probable). We may make errors with the availability heuristic, because events may be highly prominent in our memories because of their recent occurrence or because they are particularly vivid and not because they occur more often. Using these heuristics arises from System 1 (automatic, intuitive) processing. We need to slow down our thinking and engage System 2 (effortful, analytical) processing to improve our judgment.

We also considered that when we test hypotheses about our beliefs, we tend to suffer from confirmation bias (the tendency to seek evidence that confirms our beliefs). This bias may lead us to have erroneous beliefs based on illusory correlations, believing two variables are related when they actually are not. To prevent this, we should attempt to disconfirm our hypotheses and beliefs rather than confirm them. Even in the face of contradictory evidence, we tend to persevere in our beliefs and ignore the evidence, or we engage in denial through invalid person-who statistical reasoning (thinking that a well-established finding should not be accepted because there are some exceptions to it). Lastly, we discussed medical hypothesis testing, specifically how to compute the conditional probability that a person actually has a disease that is being screened for, given a positive test result. Research indicates that both doctors and patients tend to overestimate such probabilities. The conversion of the relevant probability information, however, to natural frequencies greatly facilitates the computation of these conditional probabilities. The most important point to remember is that a positive medical screening result does not mean you definitely have the disease being screened for. You might or you might not. Computing the conditional probability will tell you the probability that you do have the disease.

ConceptCheck | 2

Explain how using the representativeness heuristic can lead to the conjunction fallacy.

Explain how using the availability heuristic can lead to the misjudgment of the probabilities of various causes of death.

Explain how confirmation bias can lead to the perception of an illusory correlation.

Given a base rate of 2% for a disease and a false positive rate of 10% and a sensitivity rate of 90% for the screening test for the disease, use natural frequencies to compute the conditional probability that a person actually has the disease given a positive test result.

Intelligent Thinking

The types of thinking that we have discussed so far—problem solving, judgment, and hypothesis testing—are important aspects of intelligent thinking, or what we call intelligence. We have a pretty good idea of what intelligence is, and we can recognize examples of intelligent thinking. However, finding a definition of intelligence that most psychologists can agree upon is not that easy. The definition of intelligence is controversial, and intelligence tests and their use are even more controversial. Their fairness and usefulness are constantly questioned. In this section, we will examine two of the major questions concerning intelligence and intelligence tests. First, is intelligence one general ability or is it a set of specific mental abilities? Second, is intelligence due to genetics or experience? To put these two discussions into proper perspective, we will first consider the historical development of intelligence tests and then the characteristics of a good intelligence test.

Intelligence Tests

The first attempts to develop intelligence tests took place in late nineteenth-century England and in early twentieth-century France. From the start, intelligence testing was enmeshed in the nature-versus-nurture controversy—is intelligence innate (set by genetics) or is it nurtured by one's environmental experiences? You will see that the major intelligence theorists tended to favor one side or the other. As each theorist's work is described, his bias will be pointed out.

The history of intelligence tests. In late nineteenth-century England, Sir Francis Galton was trying to develop an intelligence test for the purpose of eugenics, selective reproduction to enhance the capacities of the human race (Fancher, 1985). Galton clearly fell on the nature side of the nature–nurture debate. He believed in the genetic determination of intelligence and thought he could measure intelligence by measuring various aspects of the human brain and nervous system. Galton assumed that more intelligent people would have more acute senses, greater strength, and faster reactions to stimuli, so he devised a series of tests measuring these physical traits and tested thousands of people. As you might guess, Galton's tests were not good predictors of intelligent thinking. Probably more significant to intelligence testing was Galton's invention of the basic mathematics behind correlational statistics (what he termed "co-relations") that are used for numerous aspects of testing from assessing genetic contributions to determining a test's validity (Gardner, Kornhaber, & Wake, 1996). Before Galton, correlational statistics did not exist. Actually, his disciple, Karl Pearson, formalized Galton's ideas to allow computation of the correlation coefficient (Fancher, 1985), which we discussed in Chapter 1.

In France at the beginning of the twentieth century, Alfred Binet and his assistant Theophile Simon were working on the problem of academic retardation. France had recently introduced mass public education, and the French government asked Binet to develop a test to diagnose children whose intellectual development was subnormal and who would not be able to keep up with their peers in school. This test, published in 1905, was the first accepted test of intelligence (Fancher, 1985). The test calculated a child's performance as an intellectual level, or mental age, that then could be used in diagnosing academic retardation. Mental age is the age

Sir Francis Galton

© Corbis

typically associated with a child's level of test performance. If a child's mental age were less than his or her chronological (actual) age, the child would need remedial work. The fact that Binet helped in the development of "mental orthopedics"—mental exercises designed to raise the intelligence of children classified as subnormal—clearly illustrated his bent toward the nurture side of the nature–nurture debate. The Binet-Simon test was revised in 1908 and again in 1911, the year Binet died unexpectedly at the age of 54 from a terminal disease whose exact nature is no longer known (Fancher, 1985). Within 10 years of Binet's death, translations and revisions of the Binet-Simon scale were in use all over the world (Miller, 1962). Ironically, the test was not used extensively in France until the 1940s—and only then when a French social worker who had been working in the United States brought the American version of the test back to France (Kaufman, 2009; Miller, 1962).

Alfred Binet

The next major figure in intelligence test development, Lewis Terman, had Galton's nature bias, but he used Binet and Simon's test. Working at Stanford University, Terman revised the intelligence test for use with American schoolchildren. This revision, first published in 1916, became known as the Stanford-Binet (Terman, 1916). To report Stanford-Binet scores, Terman used the classic intelligence quotient formula suggested by William Stern, a German psychologist (Stern, 1914). The **intelligence quotient (IQ)** formula was the following: IQ = (mental age/chronological age) × 100. Multiplying by 100 centered the scale at 100. When a child's mental age (as assessed by the test) was greater than the child's chronological age (actual age), the child's IQ was greater than 100; when chronological age was greater than mental age, the child's IQ was less than 100. The IQ formula, however, is no longer used to compute a person's intelligence test score on the Stanford-Binet. It is a confounded measure because a year's growth doesn't have a constant meaning from year to year for mental ability. Mental growth levels off, but age keeps increasing. How intelligence test scores are computed is explained in our discussion of the next major figure of intelligence testing, David Wechsler.

intelligence quotient (IQ) (mental age/chronological age) × 100.

David Wechsler was working as chief psychologist at Bellevue Hospital in New York City in the 1930s and was in charge of testing thousands of adult patients from very diverse backgrounds (Fancher, 1985). Like Binet, Wechsler thought that intelligence was nurtured by one's environment. Given that most of his patients were undereducated, he wanted to get a much broader assessment of their abilities. The Stanford-Binet wasn't well-suited for his purposes, because it only

Lewis Terman

David Wechsler

provided a single measure of abilities related to academic performance (IQ). The IQ formula was especially irrelevant for adults because, as we mentioned earlier, at some point mental age levels off but chronological age keeps increasing. Based on the Stanford-Binet, a person's IQ would automatically go down with age regardless of one's mental abilities.

Given all of these problems, Wechsler developed his own test, the Wechsler Bellevue Scale, in 1939 (Gardner, Kornhaber, & Wake, 1996). This test became known as the Wechsler Adult Intelligence Scale (WAIS) in 1955 and is appropriate for ages 16 and older. Wechsler also developed the Wechsler Intelligence Scale for Children (WISC) in 1949 for children aged 6 to 16. Both tests (the WAIS and WISC) provide finer analyses of a person's abilities by providing test scores for a battery of not only verbal tests (such as vocabulary and word reasoning) but also nonverbal, performance tests (such as block design, matrix reasoning, and visual puzzles). An item similar to those on the WAIS nonverbal Visual Puzzles subtest and some similar to those on the WAIS Cancellation subtest are given in Figure 6.3a and 6.3b, respectively.

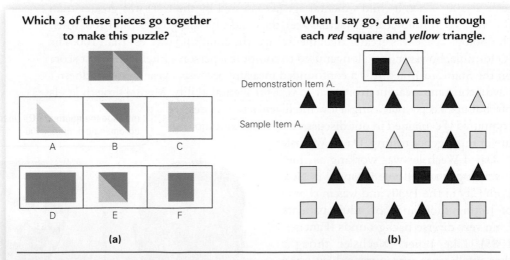

Figure 6.3 | Sample Performance (Nonverbal) Test Items on the WAIS | (a) This is a nonverbal test item similar to those on the WAIS Visual Puzzles subtest that assesses perceptual reasoning ability. (b) These are nonverbal test items similar to those on the WAIS Cancellation subtest that assess perceptual processing speed. (a) Wechsler Adult Intelligence Scale, Fourth Edition (WAIS-IV). Copyright © 2008 NCS Pearson, Inc. Reproduced with permission. All rights reserved. (b) "Wechsler Adult Intelligence Scale®, Fourth Edition" and "WAIS" are trademarks, in the United States and other countries, of Pearson Education, Inc. or its affiliate(s).)

The WAIS is in its fourth edition, and the WISC and Stanford-Binet are now in their fifth editions. Like Wechsler's two tests, the latest edition of the Stanford-Binet provides a broader assessment of intelligence, including nonverbal subtests.

Deviation IQ scores. Wechsler also devised a better way to report intelligence test scores, called deviation IQ scores. Like IQs, deviation IQs involve standardization. **Standardization** is the process that allows test scores to be interpreted by providing test norms. To standardize a test, the test must be given to a representative sample of the relevant population. The scores of this sample then serve as the test norms for interpretation. For example, Terman standardized the original Stanford-Binet on American children of various ages. Any child's raw test score could be compared to the standardization norms to calculate the child's mental age and IQ. Because of the problems in the IQ formula for adults, however, Wechsler decided to use his standardization data differently. He collected standardization data for various adult age groups. The data for each age group form a normal distribution (see Figure 6.4).

To calculate a person's deviation IQ, Wechsler compared the person's raw test score to the normal distribution of raw scores for that person's standardization age group. He calculated how far the raw score was from the mean raw score in terms of standard deviation units from the mean. To make the deviation scores resemble IQ formula scores, he set the mean to 100 and the standard deviation to 15. He then defined a person's **deviation IQ score** as 100 plus or minus (15 × the number of standard deviation units a person's raw test score is from the mean for the relevant age group norms). For example, if a person's raw test

standardization The process that allows test scores to be interpreted by providing test norms.

deviation IQ score 100 plus or minus (15 × the number of standard deviations the person is from the raw score mean for their standardization group).

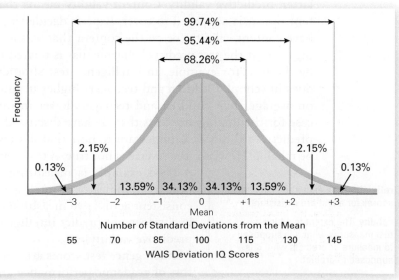

Figure 6.4 | Deviation IQ Scores on the WAIS | Deviation IQ scores for the WAIS are indicated for the mean, and 1 to 3 standard deviations above or below the mean. To make deviation IQ scores resemble IQ scores, the mean was set at 100 points and the standard deviation at 15 points.

score fell 1 standard deviation above the mean for his or her age group, he or she would have a deviation IQ score of 100 plus (15 × 1), or 115. The deviation IQ scale for the WAIS is illustrated in Figure 6.4. The same scale is used for the WISC but with standardization data for various child age groups; a similar deviation IQ scale with the standard deviation set at 15 is now used for scoring the Stanford-Binet intelligence test.

Reliability and validity. In addition to being standardized, a good test must also be reliable and valid. **Reliability** is the extent to which the scores for a test are consistent. This may be assessed in various ways. In the test–retest method, the test is given twice to the same sample, and the correlation coefficient for the two sets of scores is computed. If the test is reliable, this coefficient should be strongly positive. Remember from Chapter 1 that a strong correlation coefficient approaches 1.0, hence acceptable reliability coefficients should be around +0.90 or higher. The reliability coefficients for the major intelligence tests, the WAIS, WISC, and Stanford-Binet, are at this level (Kaufman, 2000).

If multiple forms of the test are available, then alternate-form reliability can be assessed. Alternate-form reliability is determined by giving different forms of the test to the same sample at different times and computing the correlation coefficient for performance on the two forms. A third type of reliability assessment involves consistency within the test. If the test is internally consistent, then performance on the two halves of the test (odd versus even items) should be strongly positively correlated. This type of reliability is called split-half reliability because performance on half of the test items (the odd-numbered items) is compared to performance on the other half (the even-numbered items).

In addition to reliability, a test should have validity. **Validity** is the extent to which a test measures what it is supposed to measure or predicts what it is supposed to predict. The former type of validity is called content validity, and the latter, predictive validity. Content validity means that the test covers the content that it is supposed to cover. Experts decide this. All course exams should have content validity (be on the content that was assigned). Predictive validity means that the test predicts behavior that is related to what is being measured by the test; for example, an intelligence test should predict how well a child does in school. Children and teenagers higher in intelligence should do better on average than children and teenagers lower in intelligence, and this is the case for the intelligence tests that we have discussed. These tests all have good predictive validity. It is important to note that if a test is valid, then it will also be reliable. However, the reverse is not true. A test may be reliable, but not valid.

A good example is measuring the circumference of the head as an indicator of intelligence. This number would be consistent across two measurements and therefore reliable, but it does not predict intelligent behavior (does not have predictive validity).

Intelligence test scores are among the most valid predictors of academic performance and job performance across

reliability The extent to which the scores for a test are consistent.

validity The extent to which a test measures what it is supposed to measure or predicts what it is supposed to predict.

just about every major occupation studied (Neisser et al., 1996; Sackett, Schmitt, Ellingson, & Kabin, 2001; Schmidt & Hunter, 1998). Not only do intelligence tests have good predictive validity, but they also are not biased against women or minorities. The tests' predictive validity applies equally to all. It is roughly the same regardless of gender, race, ethnicity, and so on. Group differences in test scores are accompanied by comparable differences in performance. As Lilienfeld, Lynn, Ruscio, and Beyerstein (2010) point out, the belief that these tests are biased in this way is a widespread myth and the research on this belief indicates that intelligence tests and other standardized abilities tests, such as the SAT, are not biased against either women or minorities. A task force of the American

"I'd have done better on the intelligence test, but it was biased toward intelligent people."

Marty Bucella/Cartoonstock.com

Psychological Association (Neisser et al., 1996) and two National Academy of Science panels (Hartigan & Wigdor, 1989; Wigdor & Garner, 1982) reached this same conclusion. In sum, the question of intelligence test bias with respect to predictive validity has been settled about as conclusively as any scientific controversy can be (Gottfredson, 1997, 2009; Sackett, Bornerman, & Connelly, 2008).

Psychologists agree on what an intelligence test should predict, but they do not agree on how intelligence should be defined. Is intelligence one general ability or many specific abilities? Does intelligence involve more than just mental abilities? Are there multiple types of intelligence? Different psychologists answer these questions in different ways based on their definitions of intelligence. The other major controversy concerning intelligence is the nature–nurture debate on the basis of intelligence. Galton's work marked the beginning of this debate, and the debate is still with us today, over a century later. It is to these two controversies that we now turn.

Controversies About Intelligence

The argument over whether intelligence is a single general ability or a collection of specific abilities has been around for over a hundred years. Many theorists have argued that intelligence comprises multiple abilities, but the exact number of abilities or types of intelligence proposed has varied from 2 to over 100. In our discussion, we'll consider a few of the more prominent theories, first considering those that propose that intelligence is one or more mental abilities and then theories that define intelligence more broadly, including more than just mental abilities as assessed by intelligence tests.

Theories of intelligence. Mental ability theories of intelligence began with Charles Spearman (1927), who argued that intelligence test performance is a function of two types of factors: (1) a *g* factor (general intelligence), and (2) some *s* factors (specific intellectual abilities such as reasoning). Spearman thought that the *g* factor was more important because it was relevant across the various mental abilities that make up an intelligence test, and that the *s* factors were more pertinent to specific subtests of an intelligence test.

Spearman's theory was based on his observation that people who did well on one subtest usually did well on most of the subtests, and people who did poorly usually did so on most of the subtests. Individuals did not do equally well on all of the various subtests, however, indicating the secondary effects of the *s* factors or specific abilities on the various subtests. Contemporary research has shown the *g* factor to be a good predictor of performance both in school and at work (Gottfredson, 2002a, 2002b).

In contrast, one of Spearman's contemporaries, L. L. Thurstone, argued that specific mental abilities (like Spearman's *s* factors) were more important (Thurstone, 1938). Based on his research, he argued that there were seven primary mental abilities—verbal comprehension, number facility, spatial relations, perceptual speed, word fluency, associative memory, and reasoning. Thurstone identified these primary abilities by using **factor analysis,** a statistical technique that identifies clusters of test items that measure the same ability (factor). Spearman also used factor analysis, so why the difference in theories? Basically, they emphasized different aspects of the analysis. Thurstone emphasized the specific factor clusters, whereas Spearman emphasized the correlations across the various clusters.

Later, Raymond Cattell (a student of Spearman) and John Horn proposed a slightly different type of mental ability theory that has mainly influenced researchers focused on aging (Cattell, 1987; Horn & Cattell, 1966, 1967). They proposed that the *g* factor should be viewed as two types of intelligence: (1) fluid intelligence and (2) crystallized intelligence. Fluid intelligence refers to abilities independent of acquired knowledge, such as abstract reasoning, logical problem solving, and the speed of information processing. They defined crystallized intelligence as accumulated knowledge and verbal and numerical skills. This theory has interested researchers focused on aging because crystallized intelligence increases with experience and formal education and grows as we age; fluid intelligence is not influenced by these factors and actually declines with age. However, a recent large-scale study revealed that this differentiation may be too simplistic and that various cognitive abilities that make up intelligence peak at different ages (Hartshorne & Germaine, 2015).We will return to this theory in Chapter 7 when we consider how intelligence changes across the life span.

All of the theories we have discussed thus far focus on definitions of intelligence as mental abilities that can be assessed by standard intelligence tests such as the Stanford-Binet and WAIS. Three major contemporary theories by Howard Gardner (1983, 1993, 1999), Robert Sternberg (1985, 1988, 1999),

factor analysis A statistical technique that identifies clusters of test items that measure the same ability (factor).

and Keith Stanovich (2009a, b) extend this definition to include other types of abilities. We'll consider Gardner's first. According to Gardner's theory of multiple intelligences, there are eight independent intelligences—linguistic, logical-mathematical, spatial, musical, bodily-kinesthetic, intrapersonal, interpersonal, and naturalistic. Brief descriptions of each of these intelligences are given in Table 6.1. The linguistic and logical-mathematical intelligences seem to fit with other definitions of intelligence in terms of mental abilities, but the other six are controversial; many psychologists see these as talents or skills instead of types of intelligence. In addition, many of these intelligences are difficult to quantify (such as intrapersonal intelligence) and present measurement problems.

According to Sternberg's triarchic theory of intelligence, there are three types of intelligence—analytical, practical, and creative. Analytical intelligence is essentially what is measured by standard intelligence tests, the skills necessary for good academic performance. However, the other two types of intelligence are not really measured by standard intelligence tests. Practical intelligence could be equated with good common sense or "street smarts." Creative intelligence is concerned with the ability to solve novel problems and deal with unusual situations. Sternberg's intelligences are all types of mental ability, but the inclusion of practical and creative intelligences broadens our conception of intelligence by including mental abilities that seem to have more applicability in the nonacademic world.

Cognitive researcher Keith Stanovich (2009a, 2009b) argues that intelligence is a meaningful, useful construct and, unlike Gardner and Sternberg, is not interested in expanding the definition of intelligence. Rather he argues that intelligence is only one component of good thinking and thus by itself is not sufficient to explain such thinking. The other critical component is our ability to think and act rationally, which is not assessed by standard intelligence tests. Further, these two components are independent so you can be intelligent and not act rationally and vice versa. This is why smart people sometimes do foolish things. Stanovich

Table 6.1	Brief Descriptions of Gardner's Eight Intelligences
Linguistic	Language ability as in reading, writing, and speaking
Logical-mathematical	Mathematical problem solving and scientific analysis
Spatial	Reasoning about visual spatial relationships
Musical	Musical skills such as the ability to compose and understand music
Bodily-kinesthetic	Skill in body movement and handling objects
Intrapersonal	Understanding oneself
Interpersonal	Understanding other people
Naturalist	Ability to discern patterns in nature

coined the term "dysrationalia" to describe this failure to think and behave rationally despite having adequate intelligence.

One cause of dysrationalia is that we tend to be cognitive misers, using System 1 too much. This is the reason we have developed a whole set of heuristics and biases (many such as anchoring, representativeness, and confirmation bias were discussed earlier in this chapter) to limit the amount of reflective, analytical thinking that we need to engage in. As we have learned, these shortcut strategies provide rough and ready answers that are right sometimes but often wrong. Another source of dysrationalia is what Stanovich calls the mindware gap, which occurs when we haven't learned the appropriate mindware (specific knowledge, such as an understanding of probability, and cognitive rules and strategies, such as scientific thinking, that are necessary to think rationally). According to Stanovich, many intelligent people never acquire the appropriate mindware. Finally, given such causes, Stanovich thinks that rational thinking and behavior can be taught and that they ought to be taught at every stage of the educational system. Richard Nisbett, in his 2015 book *Mindware: Tools for Smart Thinking*, provides a guide to the most essential mindware tools and how to frame common problems so that these tools can be applied to them.

The six theories of intelligence that we have discussed are briefly summarized in Table 6.2. Next we will consider the controversial nature–nurture debate on the basis of intelligence.

Table 6.2	Theories of Intelligence
Theorist	**Theory Summary**
Spearman	Intelligence is mainly a function of a general intelligence (*g*) factor
Thurstone	Intelligence is a function of seven primary mental abilities—verbal comprehension, number facility, spatial relations, perceptual speed, word fluency, associative memory, and reasoning
Cattell and Horn	There are two types of intelligence—crystallized intelligence, which refers to accumulated knowledge and verbal and numerical skills, and fluid intelligence, which refers to abilities independent of acquired knowledge, such as abstract reasoning, logical problem solving, and speed of information processing
Gardner	Intelligence is defined as eight independent intelligences—linguistic, logical-mathematical, spatial, musical, bodily-kinesthetic, intrapersonal, interpersonal, and naturalist
Sternberg	Intelligence is defined as three types of abilities—analytical, creative, and practical
Stanovich	Intelligence is not sufficient for good thinking; rationality, which is independent of intelligence, is also necessary

Nature versus nurture. Not only do psychologists disagree on the definition of intelligence, they also argue about its origins—the nature-nurture debate that we discussed earlier. This debate was popularized by Galton, a strong proponent of the nature side of the argument, over a century ago. Most contemporary psychologists, however, believe that both heredity (nature) and environmental experiences (nurture) are important. The disagreement now is over the relative contribution of each part (nature and nurture) to intelligence. We'll take a brief look at how some psychologists have tried to settle this disagreement.

First, we'll consider the results of genetic similarity studies. Genetic similarity between people varies from 100% similarity between identical twins to 50% between fraternal twins and between siblings (brothers and sisters) to 0% between two unrelated people. If intelligence were due to heredity, the average correlations between intelligence scores should decrease as genetic similarity decreases. Researchers have found this to be the case (Bouchard & McGue, 1981). The average correlation coefficient drops from +0.86 for identical twins to essentially 0 for unrelated people. The data, however, also show effects of environment. For example, if identical twins are raised apart (adopted into different families), the average correlation between their intelligence test scores drops to +0.72, indicating the importance of sharing similar environments.

Let's consider two more of these findings to see how the effects of both heredity and environment are indicated. The average correlation between fraternal twins raised together (+0.60) is less than that for identical twins reared apart (+0.72), indicating the influence of heredity; but the average correlation is greater than that for ordinary siblings reared together (+0.47), indicating environmental influences. Remember that the amount of genetic similarity for fraternal twins and ordinary siblings is the same, 50%. This means that the greater correlation for fraternal twins (+0.60 versus +0.47) must be due to environmental factors. The fraternal twins are the same age; hence their environmental experiences are more similar than those for ordinary siblings of different ages. As these two findings indicate, heredity and environment work together to influence intelligence test scores.

Researchers have also looked at adopted children and the correlations between their scores with both their adoptive and biological parents. The modest correlation between the intelligence test scores of adopted children with their adoptive parents disappears as the children age (McGue, Bouchard, Iacono, & Lykken, 1993). The reverse is true, however, for the correlation between the scores for adopted children and their biological parents. It increases (Plomin, DeFries, McClearn, & Rutter, 1997). This stronger relationship between a person's intelligence and that of his or her biological parents means that nature plays a larger role in determining a person's intelligence than environmental experiences.

The results of genetic similarity studies of intelligence can also be used to estimate its **heritability,** an index of the degree that variation of a trait within a given population is due to heredity. These estimates vary, usually in the range from around 50% up to 70% (Bouchard, Lykken, McGue, Segal, & Tellegen, 1990).

heritability An index of the degree that variation of a trait within a given population is due to heredity.

Mike Twohy/The New Yorker Collection/The Cartoon Bank

"Big deal, an A in math. That would be a D in any other country."

Thus, for a given population, 50% to 70% of the variation in their intelligence test scores is estimated to be due to heredity. However, because heritability is not 100%, this means that heredity and environment work together to determine intelligence (though heredity may make a larger contribution). Given this fact, recent research focuses on how heredity and environment interact to determine a person's intelligence score. The assumption is that heredity determines a **reaction range,** genetically determined limits for an individual's intelligence. Heredity places upper and lower limits on a person's intelligence, but the quality of the person's environment determines where the individual falls within this range. The principle is simple—the higher the environmental quality, the higher the person's intelligence within the reaction range.

Two points about heritability should be made clear. First, it is a group statistic and is not relevant to individual cases. For example, if the heritability estimate for intelligence for a population were 50%, this does not mean that 50% of the intelligence of an individual in the group is determined by genetics and the other 50% by environmental experiences. It means that 50% of the variation in intelligence among people in the population is due to genetics and 50% of the variation is due to environmental experiences. Second, it is important to understand that heritability has nothing to do with the differences that have been observed between populations, such as the difference in scores for Asian schoolchildren versus American schoolchildren. Heritability only applies to the variation within a given population or group, not to variation between groups. Observed group differences must be analyzed individually and in a different way.

Let's examine the gap between Asian and American schoolchildren to see one way such analyses are done (Stevenson, Chen, & Lee, 1993; Stevenson & Stigler, 1992). In this case, researchers examined the group difference for children of different ages and concluded that the gap is likely due to the priority placed on education in Asian countries. Why? There doesn't seem to be a gap before the children enter school. The gap begins and increases as the children proceed through school. The Asian cultures place higher value on education, and so the children spend more time studying and work harder, achieving more in school and higher test scores. There seem to be clear environmental factors operating to explain this particular group difference.

As if there are not enough unanswered questions and debates about intelligence, a recent curious finding has led to

reaction range The genetically determined limits for an individual's intelligence.

yet another. It is called the "Flynn effect" because intelligence researcher James Flynn popularized it. The "Flynn effect" label was coined by Herrnstein and Murray in their book *The Bell Curve* (1994). Actually Flynn (2007) says that if he had thought to name it, he would have called it the "Tuddenham effect" because Tuddenham (1948) was the first to present

Flynn effect The finding that the average intelligence test score in the United States and other industrialized nations has improved steadily over the last century.

convincing evidence of the effect using the intelligence test scores of U.S. soldiers in World Wars I and II. The **Flynn effect** refers to the fact that in the United States and other Western developed nations, average intelligence scores have improved steadily over the past century (Flynn, 1987, 1999, 2007, 2012). For example, the average score in 1918 would be equivalent to a score of 76 when compared to recent standardization norms. This translates to a gain on average of about 3 points per decade on both the Stanford-Binet and Wechsler intelligence scales. A recent meta-analysis (Trahan, Stuebing, Hiscock, & Fletcher, 2014) of 285 studies (N = 14,031) with test score data for a wider range of intelligence tests than Flynn used in his analyses supported Flynn's estimate of about 3 points per decade. Another recent, even larger meta-analysis of the intelligence test score data for almost 4 million participants from 31 countries across more than one century (1909–2013) also found an average of about 3 points per decade in intelligence test scores (Pietschnig & Voracek, 2015).

Proposed explanations for the Flynn effect involve a broad range of environmental factors, from improved nutrition, hygiene, and availability of medical services to better education and smaller average family size, but the explanation of the effect still remains a source of debate, with multiple factors likely contributing to it (Neisser, 1998; Mingroni, 2014; Williams, 2013). Joining this debate, Flynn has recently proposed that the effect is not due to people getting smarter overall but rather to the fact that they are getting smarter at skills that have become more important in our society over the past century, especially abstract, scientific thinking (Flynn, 2007, 2012). Our society has changed from agriculture-based to industry-based to information-based. Thus, the need to develop abstract, scientific thinking has grown as the nature of our society has changed. Flynn's hypothesis is supported by the finding that large intelligence increases have not been observed for all types of cognitive functioning. For example, the largest intelligence gains have come on intelligence subtests that involve abstract, scientific thinking, and the gains on subtests that are related to traditional academic subjects, such as vocabulary, general knowledge, and arithmetic, have been smaller. In agreement with Flynn's proposal, Pietschnig and Voracek (2015) found that the gains for fluid intelligence (abilities such as abstract reasoning that are independent of acquired knowledge) over the past century have been greater than for crystallized intelligence (acquired knowledge and verbal and numerical skills).

James Flynn

Pietschnig and Voracek (2015) also found that although intelligence test score gains have increased over the past few decades, the size of the gain each decade has been decreasing. Consistent with this finding, other researchers have found data that indicate that the Flynn effect may have already ended in some developed countries (for example, Denmark and Norway) but is still alive in the United States and some other developed nations such as Germany and those countries that make up the United Kingdom (Flynn, 2012; Kaufman, 2009). These findings, however, are for developed countries. Has the Flynn effect also been found for intelligence test scores in developing countries and if it has, how does it compare to that for developed countries? The findings of a recent study by Wongupparaj, Kumari, and Morris (2015) address these questions. Their meta-analysis covered 64 years (1950–2014) and used intelligence test data for the Raven's Progressive Matrices test (a measure of nonverbal intelligence that requires mental manipulation of objects, logical inference, and other types of abstract reasoning) for both developed countries and developing countries (mainly from Africa, Asia, and South America). They found evidence of the Flynn effect in both types of countries. Although the average general intelligence score was always higher for developed countries, the size of the gains over time were greater for developing countries, closing the gap between these two types of countries to only about 3 points by 2014. To explain these gains for developing countries, Wongupparaj, Kumari, and Morris discuss possible causal factors, but they are essentially the same factors that have been proposed for the Flynn effect in developed countries. Thus, an explanation of the Flynn effect for developing countries seems just as elusive as it is for developed countries.

Section Summary

In this section, we discussed how the first attempts at developing a valid intelligence test began with Galton in late nineteenth-century England and with Binet and Simon in early twentieth-century France. Galton failed, but Binet and Simon, hired by the French government to develop a test to find children who would have difficulty in school, succeeded in 1905. Lewis Terman, working at Stanford University, revised the Binet-Simon test to use with American schoolchildren in 1916, and this test became known as the Stanford-Binet. Results for the Stanford-Binet were reported in terms of Stern's IQ formula, IQ = (mental age/chronological age) × 100. Subsequently, David Wechsler developed both the WAIS for adults and the WISC for children. Unlike the Stanford-Binet, these tests included both verbal and nonverbal subtests. In addition, Wechsler used deviation IQ scores instead of IQs to report performance on his tests. Deviation IQ scores are based on how many standard deviations a person's raw test score is above or below the raw score mean for his or her age group norms. Wechsler set the mean to 100 and the standard deviation to 15 to create deviation IQ scores that resemble IQ formula scores.

We also learned that these intelligence tests have both reliability (consistency in measurement) and predictive validity (predicting what we suppose they should predict) and are among the most valid predictors of both academic performance and job performance. In addition, research has not supported the claim that they are biased toward women or minorities.

We also considered some of the major theories of intelligence. Most of these theories define intelligence in terms of mental abilities, but differ with respect to how many abilities are proposed. Using the results of factor analysis, Spearman thought that a general intelligence factor (the g factor) was most important, but other theorists, like Thurstone, emphasized multiple, more specific abilities in their definitions. Two recent theories have attempted to broaden the conception of intelligence and another theory points to the limitations of intelligence as a sufficient explanation of good thinking. Howard Gardner has proposed a theory of eight independent types of intelligence, but critics view some of these as talents or skills and not really types of intelligence. Robert Sternberg has also attempted to broaden the conception of intelligence in his triarchic theory of intelligence, which includes analytical, creative, and practical intelligences, with the latter two having more applicability in the nonacademic world. Keith Stanovich does not want to expand the definition of intelligence but rather argues that rationality in addition to intelligence is necessary for good thinking.

Last, we considered the origins of intelligence. We found that genetic similarity studies indicate that both nature (heredity) and nurture (environmental experiences) are important in determining one's intelligence. However, both heritability estimates and the results of adoption studies indicate that nature likely plays a larger role than nurture in determining intelligence. The concept of reaction range attempts to explain how heredity and environmental experiences work together to determine an individual's intelligence—heredity places limits on intellectual development, but the quality of the person's environment determines where the person's intelligence level falls within these limits. Finally, we discussed the Flynn effect—the finding that intelligence, at least as assessed by intelligence tests, has dramatically increased in the United States and other Western developed nations over the past century, about 3 points per decade. Many environmental factors have been proposed to explain this effect, but its explanation, which likely involves multiple factors, remains a source of debate. Recently, Flynn proposed that the effect is not due to people getting smarter overall but rather to the fact that they are getting smarter at skills that have become more important in our society over the past century, especially abstract, scientific thinking. Flynn's proposal is supported by a recent finding that fluid intelligence has increased more than crystallized intelligence over the past century. Other recent studies have found that the size of the effect for developed countries has decreased over the past few decades and that the effect may have ended in some developed countries. The opposite, however, is true for developing countries whose average intelligence test scores have made large gains in the past few decades. The gap between the average intelligence score for developing countries is now only about 3 points lower than the average for developed countries. The explanation for these findings is also a source of debate.

ConceptCheck | 3

Explain why standardization of a test is necessary.

Explain what a deviation IQ score is and how it differs from an IQ score.

Explain how the results of studies examining the impact of genetic similarity on intelligence support both nature and nurture explanations.

Explain how the more contemporary theories of intelligence proposed by Gardner, Sternberg, and Stanovich differ from the more traditional theories of intelligence (e.g., those proposed by Spearman and Thurstone).

Study Guide

Chapter Key Terms

You should know the definitions of the following key terms from the chapter. They are listed in the order in which they appear in the chapter. For those you do not know, return to the relevant section of the chapter to learn them. When you think that you know all of the terms, complete the matching exercise based on these key terms.

thinking

well-defined problem

ill-defined problem

fixation

functional fixedness

mental set

insight

algorithm

heuristic

anchoring and adjustment heuristic

working backward heuristic

means–end analysis heuristic

representativeness heuristic

conjunction fallacy

gambler's fallacy

availability heuristic

confirmation bias

illusory correlation

belief perseverance

person-who reasoning

intelligence quotient (IQ)

standardization

deviation IQ score

reliability

validity

factor analysis

heritability

reaction range

Flynn effect

Key Terms Exercise

Identify the correct term for each of the following definitions. The answers to this exercise follow the answers to the ConceptChecks at the end of the chapter.

1. Incorrectly judging the overlap of two uncertain events to be more probable than either of the two events.

   _____

2. The extent to which a test measures what it is supposed to measure or predicts what it is supposed to predict.

   _____

3. A new way to interpret a problem that immediately yields the solution.

   _____

4. Questioning a well-established research finding because you know a person who violates the finding.

   _____

5. The genetically determined limits for an individual's intelligence.

   _____

6. A problem-solving heuristic in which the distance to the goal state is decreased systematically by breaking the problem down into subgoals and achieving these subgoals.

   _____

7. The tendency to use previously successful problem-solving strategies without considering others that are more appropriate for the current problem.

   _____

8. An index of the degree that variation of a trait within a given population is due to heredity.

    _____

9. The process that allows test scores to be interpreted by providing test norms.

    _____

10. Incorrectly believing that a chance process is self-correcting in that an event that has not occurred for a while is more likely to occur.

    _____

11. A problem lacking clear specification of either the start state, goal state, or the processes for reaching the goal state.

    _____

12. A heuristic for estimation problems in which one uses his or her initial estimate as an anchor estimate and then adjusts the anchor up or down (often insufficiently).

    _____

13. A problem-solving heuristic in which one attempts to solve a problem by working from the goal state back to the start state.

    _____

14. The tendency to cling to one's beliefs in the face of contradictory evidence.

    _____

15. A statistical technique that identifies clusters of test items that measure the same ability (factor).

    _____

Practice Test Questions

The following are practice multiple-choice test questions on some of the chapter content. The answers are given after the Key Terms Exercise answers at the end of the chapter. If you guessed on a question or incorrectly answered a question, restudy the relevant section of the chapter.

1. The tendency to think of only the most typical uses of objects in a problem setting is called _____.
   a. fixation
   b. mental set
   c. functional fixedness
   d. confirmation bias

2. If you compute the area of a room by using the formula length × width = area, you are using a(n)/the _____.
   a. algorithm
   b. heuristic
   c. conjunction rule
   d. anchoring and adjustment heuristic

3. The representativeness heuristic leads us to _____.
   a. judge the probability of an event in terms of its prominence in memory
   b. judge the probability of category membership by resemblance to the category
   c. seek only evidence that confirms our beliefs
   d. maintain our beliefs even though we have been given evidence that contradicts them

4. Overestimating the probability of dying in an airplane crash is likely the result of using the _____.
   a. representativeness heuristic
   b. availability heuristic
   c. anchoring heuristic
   d. conjunction rule

5. In the 2-4-6 task, participants demonstrate _____ in testing their hypotheses.
   a. mental set
   b. confirmation bias
   c. person-who reasoning
   d. belief perseverance

6. Mistakenly believing that two events are related is called _____.
   a. functional fixedness
   b. illusory correlation
   c. the Flynn effect
   d. the conjunction fallacy

7. Which of the following statements about test reliability and validity is false?
   a. A test can be reliable and valid.
   b. A test can be reliable but not valid.
   c. A test can be valid but not reliable.
   d. A test can be neither reliable nor valid.

8. The intelligence test scores for _____ are most strongly correlated.
   a. identical twins reared apart
   b. fraternal twins reared together
   c. siblings reared together
   d. unrelated people reared apart

9. Which of the following intelligence theorists emphasized the *g* factor?
   a. Sternberg
   b. Gardner
   c. Spearman
   d. Thurstone

10. The Flynn effect refers to the observation that average intelligence test scores in the United States and other Western industrialized nations have _____ over the past century.
    a. increased
    b. decreased
    c. stayed the same
    d. first increased but then decreased

11. Which of the following intelligence theorists proposed three types of intelligence—analytical, practical, and creative?
    a. Sternberg
    b. Gardner
    c. Thurstone
    d. Spearman

12. The folding problem in which you were asked to estimate the thickness of a 0.1 millimeter sheet of paper folded in on itself 100 times illustrates how the _____ can lead to dramatic underestimates of the correct answer to an estimation problem.
    a. representativeness heuristic
    b. availability heuristic
    c. anchoring and adjustment heuristic
    d. conjunction rule

13. A person who questions the validity of the research findings that indicate smoking leads to health problems as a result of his knowing someone who has smoked most of their life and has no health problems is using _____.
    a. the representativeness heuristic
    b. the availability heuristic

    c. person-who reasoning
    d. inferential-statistical reasoning

14. A heritability estimate of 100% for intelligence in a given population means that the variation in intelligence for this population is determined _____.
    a. solely by genetics
    b. solely by environmental experiences
    c. 50% by genetics and 50% by environmental experiences
    d. 75% by genetics and 25% by environmental experiences

15. In the Linda problem, if you judge that it is more likely that Linda is a bank teller and active in the feminist movement than that Linda is a bank teller, you are likely using the _____ heuristic and committing the _____ fallacy.
    a. availability; gambling
    b. availability; conjunction
    c. representativeness; gambling
    d. representativeness; conjunction

Chapter ConceptCheck Answers

ConceptCheck | 1

- In functional fixedness, we fixate on the normal function of an object given our past experiences with that object. Our past experience with the object may block us from seeing how to use it in a novel way. Similarly, mental set leads us to approach a problem in the same way we have approached similar problems in the past, especially the recent past. We tend to block developing a new approach because our mental set keeps us locked into the old approach based on our past experiences.

- We use heuristics rather than algorithms because algorithms tend to be time-consuming and more difficult to use. Solving anagram puzzles is a good example of a case where we know the algorithm, but we do not use it unless there are only a few letters, because it is too time-consuming and difficult to use.

- The anchoring and adjustment heuristic leads to a serious error in estimation when we fail to adjust our initial anchor sufficiently either up or down in magnitude. The paper-folding problem is a good example of such a failure.

ConceptCheck | 2

- The representativeness heuristic can lead to the conjunction fallacy by causing us to ignore the conjunction rule when making a probability judgment involving the conjunction of two uncertain events. Use of the heuristic for the Linda problem illustrates how this occurs. We focus on how much Linda resembles a feminist and ignore the conjunction rule that says that the probability that Linda is a bank teller has to be more probable than the conjunction of her being a bank teller and active in the feminist movement.

- The availability heuristic can lead us to overestimate the risk of causes of death that are highly publicized (such as airplane crashes, fires, and shark attacks) and underestimate those that are less publicized and not as dramatic (such as diabetes and emphysema). Because the highly publicized causes are more available in our memories, we misjudge them to be more probable than the less publicized causes.

- Confirmation bias can lead to the perception of an illusory correlation by leading us to confirm our belief about the correlation by focusing only on events that confirm the belief and not on those that disconfirm the belief. To test to see if a relationship exists, we must consider the probabilities of both types of events.

- Assume that 1,000 people are screened for the disease. Given a base rate of 2% for the disease, only 20 (2% of 1,000) would actually have the disease. This means that 980 people (1,000 – 20) would not have the disease. Given a test sensitivity rate of 90%, 18 of the 20 (90% of 20) people who have the disease would test positive. Given a false positive rate of 10%, 98 (10% of 980) people who do not have the disease would test positive. Thus, there would be 116 positives (18 true positives and 98 false positives). Hence the conditional probability that someone testing positive actually has the disease is 18/116, which is 0.155 (15.5%).

ConceptCheck | 3

- Standardization of a test is necessary for the interpretation of test performance. In the standardization process, a representative sample of the relevant population takes the test and their scores are used as the norms for the test. Test takers' scores are compared to those of the standardization group in order to determine an index of performance. For example, on intelligence tests a person's performance is compared to the scores for a representative sample of the person's age group.

- A deviation IQ score is based on the normal distribution of scores for a person's standardization age group. First, a person's raw score is determined in terms of standard deviation units above or below the mean for that normal distribution. Then the person's score in terms of standard deviation units is converted to a score that resembles an IQ score. For example, on the WAIS the mean (or 0 point) is set equal to 100 and the standard deviation to 15. Thus, a person who scores 1 standard deviation above the mean in comparison to his age group norms receives a score of 100 + 15, or 115. IQ scores were based on the following formula, IQ = (mental age/chronological age) × 100. A deviation IQ tells us how well a person did relative to the standardization data for the person's age group. An IQ told us how well a child did relative to the child's own actual age.

- The results of genetic similarity studies support the nature (heredity) explanation of intelligence because as genetic similarity decreases, the average correlation between intelligence test scores also decreases. The average correlation is strongest for identical twins (about 0.90). However, these results also indicate that environment (nurture) plays a role. For example, the average correlation for intelligence test scores for identical twins decreases when the twins are adopted and raised apart in different environments. The twins are 100% genetically similar in both cases; therefore, environmental factors must be responsible for the difference in average correlations.

- The theories proposed by Gardner and Sternberg are different from the traditional theories of intelligence that we discussed in that both theorists broaden the definition of intelligence by proposing types of intelligence that are not measured by standard intelligence tests like the WAIS and Stanford-Binet. In Gardner's case, six of his proposed eight intelligences fall into this category. In Sternberg's case, two of his three proposed types of intelligence do so. However, all three of Sternberg's intelligences are types of mental ability, but this is not true for Gardner's proposed intelligences.

With respect to Stanovich's theory, he doesn't want to expand the definition of intelligence like Gardner and Sternberg do, but rather argues that intelligence is only one component of good thinking. The other critical component is our ability to think and act rationally, which is not assessed by standard intelligence tests.

Answers to Key Terms Exercise

1. conjunction fallacy
2. validity
3. insight
4. person-who reasoning
5. reaction range
6. means–end analysis heuristic
7. mental set
8. heritability
9. standardization
10. gambler's fallacy
11. ill-defined problem
12. anchoring and adjustment heuristic
13. working backward heuristic
14. belief perseverance
15. factor analysis

Answers to Practice Test Questions

1. c; functional fixedness
2. a; algorithm
3. b; judge the probability of category membership by resemblance to the category
4. b; availability heuristic
5. b; confirmation bias
6. b; illusory correlation
7. c; A test can be valid but not reliable.
8. a; identical twins reared apart
9. c; Spearman
10. a; increased
11. a; Sternberg
12. c; anchoring and adjustment heuristic
13. c; person-who reasoning
14. a; solely by genetics
15. d; representativeness; conjunction

Answers to Problems

Solutions to nine-circle problems, p. 244

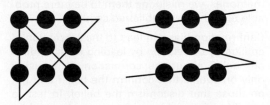

The sample four-straight-line solution is not unique. You may draw your first line from any of the other corner circles and continue from there to achieve a similar solution. The sample three-straight-line solution is taken from Adams (1986).

Solution to insight problem, p. 246

As Knobllch and Oellinger (2006) explain, most people try to create a correct equation by moving a matchstick that changes the numbers because we are taught in school that solving math problems is all about manipulating quantities. This knowledge, however, blinds us to the needed insight. To experience insight on this problem, you need to change your perspective about where the solution might lie—realize that you can also change operators. The solution lies in moving one matchstick to change the operators as shown below.

Most efficient solution to Tower of Hanoi problem, p. 250

Move 1: Move Disk 1 to Peg C
Move 2: Move Disk 2 to Peg B
Move 3: Move Disk 1 to Peg B
Move 4: Move Disk 3 to Peg C
Move 5: Move Disk 1 to Peg A
Move 6: Move Disk 2 to Peg C
Move 7: Move Disk 1 to Peg C

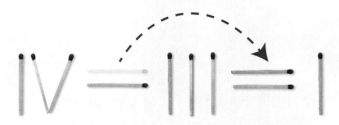

Courtesy of Jackie Saccoccio and 11R, NY

7

Developmental Psychology

So far we have discussed perception, learning, memory, thinking, and intelligence, but we have not considered how these processes develop over the life span. This is what developmental psychologists study—how and why we change as we grow older. They examine our behavior and mental processing from conception until death. **Developmental psychology** is the scientific study of biological, cognitive, social, and personality development throughout the life span. This chapter will focus on three major types of development— biological, cognitive, and social (the next chapter will deal with personality).

Historically, a major issue for all types of development has been the nature-versus-nurture question (which we also confronted in our discussion of intelligence). As with intelligence, most psychologists now believe that nature and nurture interact to influence our development. Lingering controversial issues include exactly how nature and nurture interact and which is more important to the various aspects of our development (Harris, 1998). We will return to the nature–nurture issue at different points in the chapter.

Developmental psychologists usually divide the life span into several stages, beginning with the prenatal stage and ending with late adulthood. Table 7.1 provides a commonly used set of stages, each of which is characterized by different biological, cognitive, and social changes. Most of the major theories in developmental psychology that we will discuss are stage theories. Stage theories organize developmental change by providing the approximate age ranges at which we can expect certain types of behavior and cognitive functioning. Keep in mind, however, that the age at which individuals enter and leave stages can vary, that stage transition is probably more gradual than abrupt, and that stage definitions may vary across cultures.

This chapter is divided into discussions of different types of development, but it is important to remember that the various types of development occur simultaneously and so have an impact on each other. We begin with a discussion of the first two stages of the life span—prenatal development and infancy—to learn how development begins and progresses

developmental psychology The scientific study of biological, cognitive, social, and personality development across the life span.

Table 7.1	Dividing the Life Span Into Developmental Stages
Stage	**Approximate Age Range**
Prenatal	Conception to birth
Infancy	Birth to 2 years
Childhood	2 to 12 years
Adolescence	12 to 18 years
Young adulthood	18 to 40 years
Middle adulthood	40 to 65 years
Late adulthood	65 years and over

very early in our lives. Here we will be mainly concerned with physical development, specifically sensory and motor development. Next we will focus on our cognitive development from birth through adulthood by discussing early language development, Jean Piaget's influential stage theory of cognitive development, Lev Vygotsky's sociocultural approach to such development, and the question of whether intelligence declines across the life span.

In the last section of this chapter, we will consider social development. We will begin with a discussion of Lawrence Kohlberg's influential theory of the development of moral reasoning, then examine early social development with a discussion of the research on attachment formation, parenting styles, and theory of mind development, and conclude with a description of Erik Erikson's stage theory of social-personality development across the life span. This chapter will give you a better idea about where you are in your development, how you got there, and where you can expect to go.

Prenatal Development and Infancy

What happens in the prenatal environment? What sensory abilities do we have at birth? Is our brain fully developed at birth? These are the kinds of questions that we will address in this section. We know, for instance, that the brain is not fully developed at birth. Remember, we learned in Chapter 5, on memory, that we do not have any explicit memories about this period of our life because the hippocampus isn't fully developed until later. Thus, this next section should interest all of us, because we have no memory of our own life in the prenatal stage and infancy. Let's get started with the beginning of all development—the union of sperm and egg.

Prenatal Development

Human conception begins when a sperm (male reproductive cell) penetrates the membrane of an ovum, or egg (female reproductive cell). Each of these reproductive cells contains genetic instructions. When the two combine, a complete set of genetic instructions is formed, half from the father and half from the mother. The fertilized egg that is formed from the union of the sperm and egg cells is called a **zygote**. All other cells in the human body develop from this single cell, and each duplicate cell carries a copy of the genetic instructions of the original zygote. The zygote develops into a growing cluster as the cells duplicate.

The **gene** is the basic unit of genetic instruction. Genes are short segments of **chromosomes,** molecules of DNA (deoxyribonucleic acid) that hold the genetic instructions for every cell in our body. Except for reproductive cells (sperm and eggs), every cell of a normal human has 23 pairs

zygote The fertilized egg that is formed from the union of the sperm and egg cells in human reproduction.

gene The basic unit of genetic instruction.

chromosomes Molecules of DNA that hold the genetic instructions for every cell in the body.

of chromosomes, one of each pair coming from the mother and one from the father. Reproductive cells receive only one member of each pair, giving them only 23 chromosomes. This means that when a sperm combines with an ovum, the zygote will have the complete 46. It is the 23rd pair of chromosomes that determines a person's sex. In a female, there are two X-shaped chromosomes (XX); in a male, there is one X-shaped chromosome and one smaller Y-shaped chromosome (XY). It is the Y chromosome that leads to the development of a male; hence the sex of the zygote is determined by which sperm, X or Y, fertilizes the ovum.

In some cases, the growing cluster of duplicated cells breaks apart early in development, resulting in two clusters with identical genes. These clusters become **identical (monozygotic) twins.** They are identical because they originate from the same zygote. **Fraternal (dizygotic) twins** originate from the fertilization of two eggs at approximately the same time. Thus, fraternal twins are nonidentical and could be of different sexes and just as different as any two children with the same parents. You may be wondering why two children with the same parents can be very different in appearance. The answer is the same reason that children with different parents vary greatly in appearance—chance determines which one of the 23 pairs of chromosomes goes to a reproductive cell. This means that there are 2^{23} (eight million or so) chromosome possibilities for each reproductive cell in each parent. In addition, when the two reproductive cells unite to form the zygote, they interact to further increase the uniqueness of the zygote. This is why children from the same family can look so different.

Prenatal development (conception until birth) is divided into three stages— the germinal stage, the embryonic stage, and the fetal stage. The germinal stage begins with the formation of the zygote and ends after about two weeks, when the outer portion of the zygote's developing cluster of cells has attached itself to the uterine wall. This implantation leads to the formation of the placenta and umbilical cord, which allow oxygen and nutrients from the mother to enter and wastes to exit. The inner portion of the zygote becomes the developing organism, the embryo. During the embryonic stage (from two weeks to about two months), the major structures and organs of the body begin to develop, and the embryo starts to resemble a human being. During the fetal stage (from about two months following conception to birth), the developing organism is called a fetus, and through very rapid growth, the body structures and organs complete their development.

Both genetic and environmental factors impact prenatal development. The nature–nurture issue is relevant, even in prenatal development. This development is mainly a function of the zygote's genetic code (nature), but it is also affected by the mother's environment (nurture). **Teratogens** are environmental agents (such as drugs or viruses), diseases (such as German measles), and physical conditions (such as

identical (monozygotic) twins Twins that originate from the same zygote.

fraternal (dizygotic) twins Twins that originate from the fertilization of two eggs at approximately the same time (two zygotes).

teratogens Environmental agents such as drugs and viruses, diseases, and physical conditions that impair prenatal development and lead to birth defects and sometimes death.

fetal alcohol syndrome (FAS) A syndrome affecting infants whose mothers consumed large amounts of alcohol during pregnancy, resulting in a range of severe effects including intellectual disability and facial abnormalities.

sucking reflex An innate human reflex that leads infants to suck anything that touches their lips.

malnutrition) that impair prenatal development and lead to birth defects or even death. Expectant mothers who drink alcohol, smoke, or take drugs put their developing fetuses at great risk. **Fetal alcohol syndrome (FAS)** occurs when mothers consume alcohol during pregnancy, resulting in a range of severe effects including intellectual disability and facial abnormalities in the child. As alcohol consumption increases, the risk of FAS increases. And since there is no known safe limit of alcohol consumption, the best strategy is to avoid alcohol and other teratogens entirely during pregnancy. The effects of teratogens also vary depending on when during pregnancy the fetus is exposed. Early in pregnancy a teratogen may affect the formation of the eyes, whereas later it may be the brain that is affected. There are other maternal factors that affect prenatal development. Age is one such factor. The probability of health risks to the fetus increases for mothers who are very young, 15 or younger, or older, over 35 (Andersen, Wohlfahrt, Christens, Olsen, & Melbe, 2000; Phipps, Blume, & DeMonner, 2002).

Other risks to newborns include prematurity and low birth weight. Those that are born prematurely, before the 37th week, have a number of problems, which increase with the degree of prematurity. Major health problems of premature infants include immaturity of the lungs and the digestive and immune systems. Premature infants also have low birth weight, although some full-term infants can as well. Low birth weight increases the chances of neurological handicaps and death (Holsti, Grunau, & Whitfield, 2002). Many of the teratogens discussed above increase the likelihood of prematurity, although in about 50% of the cases there is no identifiable cause. So remember, a healthy woman providing a healthy prenatal environment enhances the probability of a healthy child.

How We Develop During Infancy

Motor development and sensory-perceptual development are the two major areas of development during infancy. We will start with an overview of our abilities at birth. Then we will discuss how these processes develop during infancy.

Motor development. The newborn comes equipped with several motor reflexes, which are unlearned responses. Some of these reflexes, such as the breathing reflex that provides us with oxygen, have obvious survival value and are permanent, but others aren't as necessary and disappear within the first year of life. Two examples of reflexes that disappear are the Babinski reflex, in which infants fan their toes upward when their feet are touched, and the grasping reflex, in which infants grasp any object that touches their palms. Two other motor reflexes, the sucking reflex and the rooting reflex, are concerned with getting nourishment and so are obviously related to survival. The **sucking reflex**

© Picture Partners/AGE Fotostock

leads infants to suck anything that touches their lips, and the **rooting reflex** leads infants to turn their mouths toward anything that touches their cheeks and search for something to suck on.

> **rooting reflex** An innate human reflex that leads infants to turn their mouth toward anything that touches their cheeks and search for something to suck on.
>
> **habituation** A decrease in the physiological responding to a stimulus once it becomes familiar.

In this first year or so of life, infants learn to sit, stand, and walk. This is an orderly sequence; each new motor behavior builds upon previous ones. Infants learn to prop up and support their body, then to sit without support, then to crawl, then to stand while holding onto an object, then to stand without support, and finally to walk without support at somewhere around 12 months of age. It was once thought that motor development was primarily a maturational process that unfolded according to a genetic program. However, as with most achievements, the process is more complex. Learning how to walk, for instance, involves the interaction of multiple factors, such as increases in strength, body proportions, and balance (Thelen, 1995). During this first year, infants are also developing their perceptual abilities and learning to coordinate their body movements with perceptual input. In fact, the process infants go through when they learn how to move around by themselves leads to changes in depth perception (our ability to perceive the distance of objects from us). Infants who have experienced crawling develop a fear of heights and falling, whereas infants of the same age who are not yet crawling do not show this fear (Campos, Anderson, Barbu-Roth, Hubbard, Hertenstein, & Witherington, 2000).

Sensory-perceptual development. Psychologists have developed a number of interesting experimental techniques to study sensory-perceptual abilities in nonverbal infants. The preferential-looking technique, a procedure used to study vision, is surprisingly simple (Fantz, 1961, 1963). Two visual stimuli are displayed side by side, and the researcher records how long the infants look at each stimulus. If the infants look at one side longer, it is inferred that they can tell the difference between the two stimuli and have a preference. Another technique involves **habituation,** a decrease in the physiological responding to a stimulus once it becomes familiar. Infants will stare at a novel, unfamiliar stimulus, but this interest habituates and the infants look at it less and less. They get bored with it. If infants look longer at a new stimulus than an old one, then it is inferred that they must be able to perceive the difference between the two stimuli. Researchers may use measures other than viewing time. For example, infants intensify their sucking of a pacifier in their mouth when confronted with a novel, unfamiliar stimulus. When they habituate to the stimulus, the sucking returns to normal. Similarly, a developmental researcher may use changes in biological mechanisms, such as heart rate, to indicate infants' perceptual behavior.

Through these ingenious techniques we have learned that our five senses are functional at birth (though not fully developed). Vision, our dominant sense, is the least developed at birth. Newborns cannot see very clearly. Their visual acuity (resolution of visual detail) is estimated to be about 20/400 to 20/800 (Kellman & Banks, 1998). This means that the visual detail that a person with

Mark Richards/Photo Edit

The visual cliff. This photo shows an infant on the centerboard of the visual cliff apparatus and his mother trying to coax him to crawl toward her over the apparent steep drop-off. Research has shown that almost all infants, ages 6 to 14 months, will not do so.

normal 20/20 vision can see at 400 to 800 feet is what the infant sees at 20 feet. This lack of resolution is due to inadequate connections between the infant's eyes and the brain, but these connections develop quickly. Hence, acuity develops quickly and reaches 20/20 within the first year of life. Color vision develops even sooner, by two to three months, when it becomes comparable to that of adults (Kellman & Arterberry, 1998). We also know that depth perception develops rather quickly (Gibson & Walk, 1960). Demonstrations of this have used an apparatus called the visual cliff, a table with a glass top that gives the illusion of a very steep (cliff-like) drop-off at one end and a very shallow drop-off at the other end. There is a centerboard between the two ends. In experiments using the visual cliff apparatus, an infant is positioned on the centerboard, and the infant's mother is at one of the two ends, coaxing the infant to crawl to her. The infant demonstrates depth perception by refusing to crawl toward what he perceives as a steep drop-off but crawling over the apparent shallow drop-off. Gibson and Walk tested infants, ages 6 to 14 months. All of the infants crawled toward the mother over the apparent shallow drop-off, but almost none would crawl onto the apparent steep drop-off. These findings suggest that depth perception develops early in infancy and may be partially innate. However, more recent research indicates that learning (in the form of locomotor experience) definitely plays a role in in the development of infants' depth perception (Adolph, Kretch, & LoBue, 2014). When placed on the deep side of the visual cliff, crawling infants show accelerated heart rate (a fear response), but prelocomotor (not yet crawling) infants do not (Campos, Bertenthal, & Kermoian, 1992). In addition, infants need a few weeks of locomotor experience before they avoid the deep side of the visual cliff (Bertenthal, Campos, & Barrett, 1984). As infants become more mobile, their locomotor experience leads them to fear heights.

We also know that infants have a visual preference for faces, especially their mother's face, and other complex stimuli (Field, Cohen, Garcia, & Greenberg, 1984; Valenza, Simion, Cassia, & Umiltà, 1996). Infants' preference for such visual complexity may be due to the fact that such stimulation is necessary for proper development of the visual pathways and cortex during infancy (Greenough, Black, & Wallace, 1987). In addition to their visual preference for faces, recent research indicates that the ability to process configural information in upright faces (i.e., the structural relationships between the individual features on the face) may already be present at birth (Leo & Simion, 2009). The manner in which Leo and Simion demonstrated this is interesting because it involves what is called Thatcherization, an illusion created by Peter Thompson (1980) involving images of former Prime Minister Margaret Thatcher. Thatcherization is created by rotating the eyes and mouth 180° within the image of a face, causing the face to appear grotesque. See Figure 7.1. The top row looks like two upside-down Thatchers, but the bottom row looks like a Thatcher on the left and a horrible mutant on the right (her face has been Thatcherized). Although the Thatcher on the right in the top row looks ok, it isn't. It's the image on the bottom right flipped vertically. Turn the page upside down and the mutant Thatcher will reappear.

Adults readily detect changes in face patterns brought about by Thatcherization when the faces are viewed upright but not when they are viewed upside down (Thompson, 1980). This inability to quickly discriminate a Thatcherized face from an unaltered face when viewed upside down is thought to be caused by the disruption of configural processing, so that the structural changes from Thatcherization are no longer apparent (Bartlett & Searcy, 1993). Leo and Simion wanted to know if newborns would respond like adults to such faces. Using the

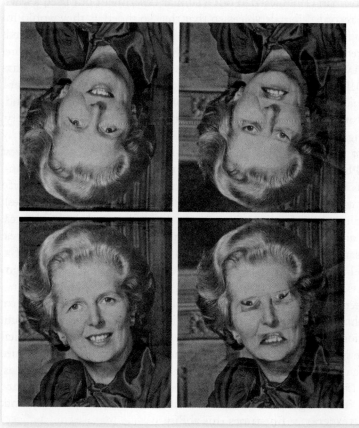

Figure 7.1 | The Margaret Thatcher Illusion | The top and bottom row of images of former Prime Minister Margaret Thatcher are identical to each other but flipped vertically. The top row looks like two upside-down Thatchers, but the bottom row looks like a Thatcher on the left and grotesque mutant Thatcher on the right. You do not notice that the Thatcher at the upper right is the mutant Thatcher because the eyes and mouth are right side up although the overall face is upside down. (Courtesy of Peter Thompson. From P. Thompson, "Margaret Thatcher: A new illusion," *Perception*, 9(1980), 383–384.)

habituation paradigm, they tested newborns' ability to discriminate a normal face and a Thatcherized face when presented upright and also upside down. Newborns could do so when the faces were upright (as in the bottom row of Figure 7.1) but not when the faces were upside down (as in the top row), the same inversion effect observed in adults. Hence, Leo and Simion concluded that newborns were sensitive to configural information in faces.

Hearing in the newborn is even more fully developed than vision. In fact, newborns can distinguish their mother's voice from those of others (DeCasper & Fifer, 1980). Research indicates this ability and several auditory preferences develop in the womb before birth (Dirix, Nijhuis, Jongsma, & Hornstra, 2009). Let's briefly consider one of the most famous studies indicating the effects of prenatal learning on auditory preferences after birth (DeCasper & Spence, 1986). During the final 16 weeks of pregnancy, mothers read Dr. Seuss's *The Cat in the Hat* aloud twice a day. Following birth, the researchers had the babies suck on an artificial nipple that, depending upon the infant's sucking pattern, would activate a tape of their mother reading the Dr. Seuss story or another story that the mother had never read aloud. Most of the infants sucked to hear *The Cat in the Hat*. The infants preferred the familiar story that their mothers had read to them while they were still in the womb. Then, Spence and Freeman (1996) carried out a similar experiment but used a low-pass filter to muffle recorded female voices so that they sounded as they would in the womb. Again, indicating the effects of prenatal learning, the infants preferred their mothers' filtered voices over those of other women. Infants also prefer the sound of the human voice and speech sounds versus other types of sounds (Shultz & Vouloumanos, 2010). By 6 months of age, although auditory perceptual performance remains immature, the infant's processing of the intensity, frequency, and temporal nature of auditory stimuli is nearly adultlike (Werner, 2007). Auditory perceptual processing continues to improve into childhood and adolescence.

One of the most remarkable hearing abilities that infants possess involves speech perception. **Phonemes** are the smallest distinctive speech sounds in a language. They allow us to distinguish between different words. For example, the difference between the words *pat* and *bat* is the difference in the *pa* and *ba* phonemes. In order to learn a language, infants must be able to detect these subtle differences between phonemes, and they are able to do so soon after birth. Different languages do not use all the same phonemes, and adults who are not native speakers of a particular language have difficulty detecting the speech sounds of that language. Japanese adults, for example, have trouble with the English *r* and *l* sounds. Infants, in contrast, can detect all phonemes whether or not they have been exposed to them. By 12 months of age, however, they no longer can easily detect speech sounds not in their native language (Kuhl, 2004). Interestingly though, a brief amount of exposure given through live social interaction is sufficient to maintain the ability to detect nonnative phonemes (Kuhl, Tsao, & Liu, 2003). It seems as though infants come into the world prepared to learn whatever language they happen to find themselves exposed to, and experience fine-tunes this ability.

phonemes The smallest distinctive speech sounds in a language.

The senses of smell, taste, and touch are also fairly well developed at birth. For example, infants can differentiate the smell of their mother from the smells of other people. Researchers discovered this by placing a nursing pad worn by the mother on one side of an infant and a pad worn by another woman on the other side, then measured how long the baby was turned toward each side. The infants spent more time turned toward their mother's pad (MacFarlane, 1975).

Some recent studies have indicated that infants' understanding of the physical world and their cognitive abilities may be much better than was previously thought. Researchers have demonstrated that very young infants may have an innate conceptual understanding of object movement—for instance, that objects cannot simply go through solid surfaces (Baillargeon, 1993, 2002). Other researchers have suggested that infants can perform simple mathematical operations such as addition and subtraction (Wynn, 1992). Needless to say, such claims are not without controversy—trying to understand the mind of a nonverbal infant is not an easy task (see Cohen & Marks, 2002).

Development of an infant's cognitive and perceptual abilities depends upon brain development. The brain contains about 100 billion neurons at birth, but the infant's brain is rather immature, and connections between neurons (neural networks) need to be formed. During the first few months of life, there is a large growth spurt for these connections between neurons, especially those in the cortex that control perception and cognition. Thousands of new connections are established for these neurons. The connections between the retina and the brain are a good example. Without visual experiences, these visual pathways do not develop, and vision will be permanently lost (Kalat, 2007). This is why a baby born with cataracts that prevent vision needs to have them removed as early as possible, so that normal vision will develop. During infancy, the networks of neurons that are used become stronger, and those that are not used disappear (Thompson, 2000).

Section Summary

Our prenatal development starts with conception, the fertilization of an egg by a sperm to form a zygote, and proceeds through the germinal stage (first two weeks), the embryonic stage (two weeks to two months), and the fetal stage (two months to birth). Prenatal development is guided by the zygote's genetic code (nature), but teratogens (environmental agents such as drugs or viruses, diseases, and malnutrition) can impact the prenatal environment (nurture) and result in birth defects and even death. Other factors that affect prenatal development include fetal alcohol syndrome and the age of the mother. Prematurity and low birth weight are also risks to newborns. The newborn comes equipped with several motor reflexes, some critical for survival, such as the rooting and sucking reflexes that lead to nourishment, and some not so critical, such as the grasping reflex, which disappear within the first year of life. Within this first year, the infant learns to sit, stand, and walk in a very orderly sequence; each new motor behavior builds upon previous ones. They also learn to coordinate their body movements with perceptual input.

Although not fully developed, our five senses are functional at birth, with vision being the least developed. To study early sensory-perceptual capabilities in the nonverbal infant, researchers developed special techniques that allow them to determine what an infant can discriminate. Such research has shown, for example, that infants have the remarkable ability to discriminate phonemes, the smallest distinctive speech units in a language. Sensory-perceptual development depends upon brain development in the form of a large growth spurt of neural networks, such as between the retina and the brain. If these visual pathways do not develop in infancy, vision will be permanently lost. The neural networks that are used grow stronger, and those that are not used are eliminated.

ConceptCheck | 1

Explain how the effects of teratogens are due to nurture and not nature.

Explain how habituation is used to study infant sensory-perceptual skills.

How We Think Throughout Our Lives

In this section, we will examine how our cognitive abilities, such as thinking and language, develop. Because we are verbal animals and our language ability differentiates us from all other animals, we will look first at how this ability begins its development, which will lead us back to the nature–nurture issue. Next we will outline one of the most important theoretical contributions to psychology, Swiss psychologist Jean Piaget's theory of cognitive development. According to Piaget, starting at birth all of us go through the same four stages of cognitive development, each of which is qualitatively different. Next we will discuss Russian psychologist Lev Vygotsky's sociocultural approach to cognitive development. Vygotsky's approach has recently become very popular because it emphasizes the importance of social and cultural contexts in development. Last, we will consider the question of whether intelligence declines throughout the adult portion of the life span.

How We Learn Language

Our ability to use language makes us unique. No other animal seems to be able to acquire and develop language ability as humans do. Although speechless at birth, our capacity for language begins to develop soon after. Children in different cultures learn to speak very different languages, but they all seem to go through the same sequence of stages. We will describe these stages of language acquisition and then consider the nature–nurture issue in explaining how language acquisition occurs.

baby talk (parentese) The different format of speech that adults use when talking with babies that involves the use of shorter sentences with a higher, more melodious pitch.

Let's begin with the newborn infant and see how language develops. Infants are speechless, but one way they communicate is through crying. Infants cry differently, for example, to indicate hunger versus pain. Crying, movement, and facial expressions allow infants to communicate fairly well. Infants also prefer **baby talk (parentese),** the different format of speech that adults use when talking with babies that involves the use of shorter sentences with a higher, more melodious pitch than normal speech. Actually, these exaggerated speech melodies parents use when speaking to their babies help the infants grasp the speaker's intentions. Fernald (1993) exposed 5-month-old infants from English-speaking families to approval and prohibition phrases spoken in German, Italian, and both nonsense and regular English parentese. Even though all of this speech was gibberish to the babies, they responded with the appropriate emotion, crying when they heard prohibitions and smiling when they heard approvals. Thus, the melodious nature and not the content of parentese conveys the message to an infant.

By two months or so, infants are making more meaningful noises such as cooing (repeating vowel sounds such as "oo" and "ah") and laughing. Infants use cooing as their response in vocal interactions with their parents. At about six or seven months, **babbling,** the rhythmic repetition of various syllables, including both consonants and vowels, begins. The syllables that are babbled are not limited to the sounds that the infant hears or those from their parents' language. However, this early babbling begins to include more and more sounds from the infant's native language over the next six months. The infant can now also understand some words such as "mommy" and "daddy." For example, the question "Where is mommy?" will lead the infant to look at her mother.

At about 1 year of age, infants begin to speak a few words. Their first words usually refer to their caregivers and objects in their daily environment. Sometimes, infants use a **holophrase,** a word that expresses a complete idea. A good example is a child going to the door and saying "bye-bye." Vocabulary grows slowly until about 18 months, and then there is a vocabulary spurt, maybe of 100 words or more per month. This is also the period during which overextension and under-extension occur. **Overextension** is the application of a newly learned word to objects that are not included in the meaning of the word. **Underextension** is the failure to apply the new word more generally to objects that are included within the meaning of the new word. A couple of examples will make these concepts clearer. A good example of overextension is children's tendency to call any male "dada," overextending the word and deflating the father's ego. Underextension frequently occurs when children do not extend the categories of "dog" and "cat" to dogs and cats beyond the family's pet dog or cat. The words are applied too narrowly. As vocabulary expands, the incidences of overextension and underextension decrease. This expansion of vocabulary reflects the influence of cognitive development; as children acquire new concepts, they learn the names that go with them.

One of the challenges children face in acquiring a vocabulary is determining the meaning of words, because the context in which children hear language is often ambiguous.

babbling The rhythmic repetition of various syllables including both consonants and vowels.

holophrase A word used by an infant to express a complete idea.

overextension The application of a newly learned word to objects that are not included in the meaning of the word.

underextension The failure to apply a new word more generally to objects that are included within the meaning of the word.

Savage Chickens

by Doug Savage

Savage Chickens/Doug Savage

For instance, if a mother points out a bird flying overhead and exclaims "look at the bird," the child has to consider many possibilities as the potential meaning of the word *bird*. For example, *bird* could refer to any object above them or any object in the sky. Research has shown, however, that children use many different types of cues to identify the speaker's intended meaning of *bird*. Some researchers have argued that children are particularly good at using social cues, such as the speaker's eye gaze, pointing, and emotional reactions to determine what the adult means when using a novel word (Baldwin & Moses, 2001; Brooks & Meltzoff, 2008; Golinkoff & Hirsh-Pasek, 2006). For instance, Tomasello, Strosberg, and Akhtar (1996) showed that children could use a speaker's emotional reaction to determine which novel object a speaker is labeling. In their task, an experimenter told 18-month-old infants that she was going to find a "toma" (a novel object). She then picked up a novel object but then rejected it and acted disappointed. She then picked up a second novel object and acted excited. She didn't name either of the two objects. The child was then shown both novel objects and asked to give the experimenter the "toma." If the child was able to use the emotional reaction of the experimenter to determine which object was the toma, she should select the object that the experimenter was excited about; and most 18-month-old children were able to do so even though it was not the first object seen.

The next step in language development is the combining of words into sentences. This begins during the vocabulary spurt between 18 and 24 months. Children engage in what is called **telegraphic speech,** using two-word sentences with mainly nouns and verbs. It is called telegraphic speech because the speech is like that in a telegram, concise and direct. Some examples are "Dada gone" and "Throw ball." These two-word statements begin to be expanded, and between the ages of 2 and 5, children acquire the grammar of their native language. Children learn these rules implicitly and in a very predictable order across all cultures. How they do so returns us to the nature–nurture issue.

Children acquire language early and easily, without direct instruction, and this acquisition process seems to be the same across cultures that have very different languages. This is why there is much support for the argument that language development is a genetically programmed ability (Chomsky, 1965; Pinker, 1994). Children, however, cannot develop normal speech without exposure to

telegraphic speech Using two-word sentences with mainly nouns and verbs.

human speech, and it is clear that caregivers can facilitate and enhance language development, indicating that experience definitely plays a role in language acquisition. As is usually the case with the nature–nurture issue, there is some evidence for both sides; nature and nurture provide interactive influences (Elman, Bates, Johnson, Karmiloff-Smith, Paisi, & Plunkett, 1996).

One of the best illustrations of children's special skill in learning a language is the existence of a critical period for acquiring it. A critical period is a time period when learning certain skills is most easily accomplished and is thought to reflect the influence of biology (brain maturation) on development. If children do not acquire a language by a certain age, usually thought to be around the time of puberty or perhaps earlier, then they will not learn it as well as younger children. For example, children who are isolated from human contact prior to puberty have difficulty learning a language, even after years of later exposure. The best known example of this is a girl known as "Genie" (Fromkin, Krasjen, Curtiss, Rigler, & Rigler, 1974). Genie was kept tied to a potty chair for most of the first 13 years of her life. During this time, Genie heard very little language and had minimal social interactions. After she was rescued, both researchers and therapists worked hard to rehabilitate her. Although she did make some linguistic progress and was able to learn several hundred words, her grammatical development never reached typical developmental levels, even after several years of trying. A similar critical period exists for children acquiring American Sign Language (ASL). Most deaf children of hearing parents are not as adept at ASL as deaf children of deaf parents because they are typically taught ASL later, since their parents are not signers themselves (Newport, 1991; Senghas & Coppola, 2001). A critical period also exists for second language learning. As you may know from your own struggles to learn a second language, children have a much easier time than adults (Birdsong & Molis, 2001; Johnson & Newport, 1989).

Language development occurs during the first few years of life when the brain and cognitive abilities, such as thinking and reasoning, are also developing. When children start talking, it is easy to start thinking of them as miniature adults, but this would be a big mistake. Their cognitive abilities are not at all like those of an adult. To see how these cognitive abilities develop, we'll consider Piaget's stage theory of cognitive development, which tells us how a speechless newborn develops into a cognitively complex adult.

Piaget's Theory of Cognitive Development

Jean Piaget was a twentieth-century Swiss psychologist whose research on children's thinking led to a landmark theory of cognitive development. He was named one of the twentieth century's 20 most influential thinkers by *Time* magazine in 1999. Piaget started his career in France working with Theophile Simon (of Binet-Simon intelligence scale fame) standardizing intelligence tests (Hunt, 1993). However, he soon returned to Switzerland and began his research on how children think. Piaget did not conduct formal experiments. In his loosely structured

Bill Anderson/Science Source

Jean Piaget interacting with a child attempting to solve a problem in one of Piaget's loosely structured studies.

interviews he instead posed problems for children to solve (he used his own three children in his early research), observed their actions carefully, and questioned them about their solutions. He was particularly interested in children's errors, which he thought provided insight into the child's thinking, especially into how it differed from adult thinking. He found that children of roughly the same age often gave the same wrong answers. From such data, he developed a theory of cognitive development that revolutionized our understanding of children's thinking and its development (Piaget, 1926/1929, 1936/1952, 1983).

Piaget's cognitive theory incorporated two of his interests, biology and philosophy. He assumed that cognitive development stems from a child's adaptation to the environment, and that children attempt to promote their survival by trying to learn about their environment. This means that a child is an active seeker of knowledge and gains an understanding of the world by operating in it. The child organizes this knowledge into what Piaget called schemes (now called schemas), which are frameworks for our knowledge about people, objects, events, and actions. Remember, we discussed these in Chapter 5. Schemas are the basic units of our knowledge that allow us to organize and interpret information about our world. In our long-term memories, we have schemas for concepts (such as books or dogs), events (such as going to a restaurant or to the dentist's office), and actions (such as riding a bicycle).

According to Piaget, cognitive adaptation involves two processes, assimilation and accommodation, both of which impact the development of schemas and thus learning. **Assimilation** is the interpretation of new experiences in terms of our existing schemas; **accommodation** is the modification of current schemas to allow for new experiences. Our earlier example of overextension—when infants call all men "dada"—would represent a child's attempt to assimilate. Children learn, however, that they need to accommodate and change their schemas. A child has only one father, but there are many men in the world. It is through accommodation that the number and complexity of a child's schemas increase and learning occurs. In accommodation, either new schemas are created for information that doesn't fit into one's present schemas or existing schemas are modified to include the new information (such as for father and men).

Piaget also proposed that major changes in children's thinking occur in stages. Each stage permits only certain kinds of thinking and involves qualitatively different

assimilation Piaget's term for the interpretation of new experiences in terms of present schemas.

accommodation Piaget's term for the modification of present schemas to fit with new experiences.

Table 7.2	Piaget's Stage of Cognitive Development
Stage (age range)	**Stage Description**
Sensorimotor (birth to 2 years)	Children use senses and motor abilities to learn about the world and develop object permanence.
Preoperational (2 to 6 years)	Children use symbolic thinking to understand the world but remain egocentric and lack the mental operations that allow logical thinking.
Concrete operational (6 to 12 years)	Children gain cognitive operations for logical thinking about concrete events, understand conservation, and perform mathematical operations, but they cannot reason abstractly.
Formal operational (12 years through adulthood)	Further development of cognitive operations enables adolescents to engage in abstract thinking and hypothetical-deductive reasoning.

cognitive functioning. Piaget further assumed that all children go through the same stages in the same order. He proposed four stages, outlined in Table 7.2. As you learn about each stage, realize that you will be changing your own schemas to accommodate all this new information about Piaget's theory. Then, after you have finished reading about the stages, look back at Table 7.2. You should easily be able to assimilate the stage descriptions into your modified schemas for Piaget's theory.

The sensorimotor stage. In the **sensorimotor stage,** from birth to about age 2, infants learn about the world through their sensory and motor interactions with it. Beginning with the simple reflexes that we discussed earlier, infants come to know the world by looking, listening, sucking, grasping, and manipulating. Infants less than 8 to 12 months old lack **object permanence,** the knowledge that an object exists independent of perceptual contact with it. For example, young infants do not understand that a toy continues to exist even if they can no longer see it. Object permanence develops over the first 2 years of life. Very young infants will not search for a toy that vanishes; but at about 4 to 8 months, they will sometimes search for it, especially if it is only partially hidden. At 8 to 12 months, they will search for a toy even if it is completely hidden, indicating that they realize that the toy still exists even if they cannot see it. Children continue to develop their understanding of object permanence and have a fairly complete understanding by 2 years of age. Similarly, symbolic representation of objects and events starts to develop during the latter part of the sensorimotor stage. Infants begin to use words as symbols to represent known objects at around 18 months. By 18 to 24 months, infants use telegraphic

sensorimotor stage The first stage in Piaget's theory of cognitive development, from birth to about age 2, during which infants learn about the world through their sensory and motor interactions with it and develop object permanence.

object permanence The knowledge that an object exists independent of perceptual contact with it.

THE FAMILY CIRCUS   By Bil Keane

"Look what I can do, Grandma!"

The child in this cartoon is demon-strating egocentric behavior, so he would be in Piaget's preoperational stage of cognitive development. Given his egocentrism, he thinks that everybody sees what he sees regardless of where they are.

speech, which represents continuing development of symbolic representation.

The preoperational stage. In the **preoperational stage,** from age 2 to age 6, children's thinking becomes more symbolic and language-based, but remains egocentric and lacks the mental operations that allow logical thinking. Preoperational children can pretend, imagine, and engage in make-believe play. They have the ability to use one thing to represent another. Preoperational children might pretend that a broom is a horse to ride, or that their finger is a tooth-brush. They no longer need to be interacting with an object to think about it. For example, they now can point to a pic-ture of a dog and say "doggie" or crawl around and pretend to be a dog by barking like a dog. Word learning also contin-ues at a rapid pace, and children have learned thousands of words by the end of the preoperational stage. Children also learn to produce narratives, descriptions of past events that have the structure of a story. However, preoperational children's thinking still has major limitations. Let's first consider what it means that their thinking is egocentric.

Egocentrism is the inability to distinguish one's own perceptions, thoughts, and feelings from those of others. This means that a preoperational child cannot perceive the world from another person's perspective. For example, preoperational children don't realize what they are doing when they block the view of the television. They assume that another's view is the same as their view. Egocentric behavior does not stem from selfishness or a lack of consider-ation. Preoperational children just have not developed the cognitive ability to see another person's view. It is important for parents to realize this cognitive limitation in their preoperational children. If not, they may misinterpret their children's behavior in a negative way, leading to unjust punishment of the child.

Next, to understand what Piaget meant by the lack of mental operations that allow a child to think logically, let's consider conservation. Some grasp of conservation marks the end of the preoperational stage and the beginning of the concrete operational stage. **Conservation** is the knowl-edge that the quantitative properties of an object (such as mass and number) remain the same despite changes in appearance. Simply put, the quantitative properties of an object do not change with a change in appearance. There are many Piagetian conservation tests, but a well-known one is the liquid/beakers problem (see Figure 7.2). In this test, the child is first shown two identical short, fat beakers

preoperational stage The second stage in Piaget's theory of cognitive development, from age 2 to 6, during which the child's thinking becomes more symbolic and language-based, but remains egocentric and lacks the mental operations that allow logical thinking.

egocentrism The inability to distinguish one's own perceptions, thoughts, and feelings from those of others.

conservation The knowledge that the quantitative properties of objects (such as mass and number) remain the same despite changes in appearance.

Tests of Various Types of Conservation

Type of Conservation	Initial Presentation	Transformation	Question	Preoperational Child's Answer
Continuous Quantity	Two identical beakers with equal amounts of liquid.	Pour one beaker into a taller, narrower beaker.	Which beaker contains more liquid?	The taller one.
Number	Two identical rows of checkers.	Increase the space between the checkers in one row.	Which row has more checkers?	The longer one.
Mass	Two equivalent lumps of clay.	Squeeze one lump into a long, thin shape.	Which shape has more clay?	The long one.
Length	Two sticks of identical length.	Move one stick.	Which stick is longer?	The one that is farther to the right.

Figure 7.2 | Tests of Conservation | These are examples of tests for conservation of continuous quantity, number, mass, and length. The typical preoperational child's responses are given in the last column.

with equal amounts of liquid in each. With the child watching, the liquid in one of the beakers is poured into a taller, thinner beaker. Then the child is asked if the two beakers have the same amount of liquid or if one has more liquid than the other. If the child understands conservation, then he can explain why the two differently shaped beakers have an equal amount of liquid in them. No liquid was taken away or added. However, a preoperational child will say that the two beakers have different amounts and most often that the taller, thinner beaker has more liquid. Like egocentric thinking, the failure to understand conservation illustrates one of Piaget's main points—a child is not like a miniature adult with less information. A child's way of thinking is very different, and how it is different depends upon the child's stage of cognitive development.

"Cut it up into a LOT of slices, Mom. I'm really hungry!"

A major reason why a preoperational child does not understand conservation is that the child lacks an understanding of **reversibility**—the knowledge that reversing a transformation brings about the conditions that existed before the transformation. As adults, you and I realize that you could easily pour the liquid in the taller beaker back into the shorter beaker to return to the starting state. A preoperational child does not understand this reversibility operation. A preoperational child's thinking also reflects **centration**—the tendency to focus on only one aspect of a problem at a time. In the liquid/beakers problem, for example, the child may only focus on the heights of the beakers and conclude that one has more because it is taller. Obviously, both the height and width of the beakers need to be considered in order to make a correct judgment. Other Piagetian conservation tests in addition to the liquid/beakers problem are illustrated in Figure 7.2. Find a preoperational child around 3 to 4 years of age and try these tests. The child's responses will not only amaze you but will also give you a much better understanding of the cognitive limitations of the preoperational stage of development.

The concrete operational and formal operational stages. During the **concrete operational stage,** from about age 6 to 12, children gain a fuller understanding of conservation and other mental operations that allow them to think logically, but only about concrete events. Different forms of conservation are developed at different times. For example, conservation of continuous quantity, number, and mass are acquired rather early, but conservation of length is more difficult and is acquired later in the concrete operational stage (Vasta, Miller, & Ellis, 2004). In addition to conservation operations, concrete operational children develop other mental operations that allow them to reason logically, such as transitivity (if A > B, and B > C, then A > C) and seriation (the ability to order stimuli along a quantitative dimension, such as a set of pencils by their length).

reversibility The knowledge that reversing a transformation brings about the conditions that existed before the transformation.

centration The tendency to focus on only one aspect of a problem at a time.

concrete operational stage The third stage in Piaget's theory of cognitive development, from age 6 to 12, during which children gain a fuller understanding of conservation and other mental operations that allow them to think logically, but only about concrete events.

formal operational stage The last stage in Piaget's theory of cognitive development, starting at age 12 or so, during which a child gains the capacity for hypothetical-deductive thought.

However, all of these operations are limited to reasoning logically about concrete events. For example, transitivity is limited to having the actual objects present, such as three sticks of different lengths. Children wouldn't be able to solve the transitivity problem without the sticks physically present. Similarly, concrete objects (such as beakers of liquid) would need to be present to solve the conservation of continuous quantity problem. This means that the reasoning of concrete operational children is tied to immediate reality (what is in front of them and tangible) and not with the hypothetical world of possibility. They cannot deal with what-if and if-then problems and abstract thinking. They also do not engage in systematic deduction to solve a problem, but rather use a haphazard trial-and-error strategy.

In the **formal operational stage,** starting at age 12 or so, children gain the capacity for such hypothetical-deductive thought. According to Piaget, this capacity allows adolescents to engage not only in hypothetical thought but also in systematic deduction and tests of hypotheses, what could easily be referred to as scientific thinking. To understand the difference in thinking between concrete and formal operational children, Piaget used several scientific thinking tasks (Inhelder & Piaget, 1958).

In one of these tasks, children or adolescents are shown several flasks of what appear to be the same clear liquid and are told that one combination of two of these liquids would produce a blue liquid. The task is to determine the combination that would produce the blue liquid. The concrete operational children just start mixing different clear liquids together haphazardly. The formal operational children, however, proceed very differently. They develop a systematic plan for deducing what the correct combination must be by determining all of the possible combinations (hypotheses for the correct combination) and then systematically evaluating each one. To accomplish this plan, they systematically mix the liquid in one beaker with each of the other liquids. If none of these combinations produced the blue liquid, they deduce that the liquid in that beaker is not relevant to the sought-after combination and then proceed to test each of the other clear liquids in the same manner until they find the correct combination.

Formal operational adolescents can also evaluate the logic of verbal statements without referring to concrete situations; the concrete operational child can only do so with concrete evidence. For example, in one formal operational study, the experimenter asked whether a statement about some colored poker chips was true, false, or uncertain (Osherson & Markman, 1975). When the experimenter hid a chip in his hand and asked about the statement, "Either the chip is red or it is not red," the formal operational children realized that the statement was true regardless of the color of the hidden chip, but the concrete operational children were uncertain of the statement's truth status. The formal operational children understood the disjunctive logic of the statement, and the concrete operational children did not. Concrete operational children also have difficulty with propositional logic that contradicts reality (Moshman & Franks, 1986). For example, concrete operational children would judge the following reasoning to be faulty, "If cats are bigger than horses and horses are bigger than mice, then cats are bigger than mice," because the first relationship does not hold in real life. Concrete operational children are tied to the realistic truth of the content (what is) in their logical reasoning, but formal operational children are not.

Evaluation of Piaget's theory. Recent research has shown that cognitive development seems to proceed in the general sequence of stages that Piaget proposed (Lourenco & Machado, 1996). This means that Piaget's theory seems to have captured the general nature of cognitive development accurately. However, there are many issues with the specifics of Piaget's stage theory. For example, recent research has demonstrated that rudiments of many of Piaget's key concepts (such as object permanence) may begin to appear at earlier ages than Piaget proposed. Infants and young children may be more cognitively competent than Piaget theorized. Piaget's tests for the understanding of concepts may have been too complex and thus missed partial knowledge of the concept. For example, Piaget's test for object permanence required infants to reach for a hidden object. A complete understanding required the infants to search for the object after several invisible (hidden) movements. Later research that involved tracking infants' eye movements has found that infants (as young as 3 months) continue to stare at the place where the object disappeared from sight, indicating some degree of object permanence (Baillargeon, 1987).

More recent research on the formal operational stage also makes it clear that not all people reach this stage of thinking, especially in cultures that do not emphasize such thinking, and that those that do reach the stage may not always use such thinking (Dasen, 1994; McKinnon & Renner, 1971). For example, people in non-Western cultures do not usually do well on the specific scientific reasoning tasks used by Piaget, but they do very well and demonstrate formal operational thought on comparable tasks involving content that they are familiar with and that is significant within their culture (Vasta, Miller, & Ellis, 2004). Even Piaget, late in his life, realized that there were limitations on achieving formal operations (Piaget, 1972).

Other cognitive developmental researchers question whether Piaget's characterization of distinct stages of development is correct. In particular, the **information-processing approach to cognitive development** questions the existence of stages and argues that development is continuous and not composed of distinct stages. So how do information-processing developmental psychologists explain the growth in children's cognitive abilities? They attribute this growth to developmental changes in children's information-processing abilities—how they take in, store, and use information. The information-processing approach uses a computer metaphor to describe children's thinking. Just as a computer's ability to solve problems is affected by memory and requires specific processing steps, children's problem-solving ability involves similar information processing. Information-processing researchers study factors that affect such processing. For example, developmental improvements in speed of processing (Kail, 1991), storage capacity (Pascual-Leone, 1989), and knowledge base (Schneider, 1993) have all been found to influence improvements in children's memory and thinking. As children grow older, they become increasingly more adept at information processing.

We should mention two other major criticisms of Piaget's stage theory. One is that Piaget did not sufficiently consider the impact of culture and social environment on cognitive development (Miller, 2011; Segall, Dasen, Berry, & Poortinga, 1990). The second is that Piaget's stage theory of cognitive development ends with adolescence and the development of formal operations, instead of continuing through to adulthood. Although Piaget did not address these issues, other developmental psychologists have done so. We will discuss the first issue

information-processing approach to cognitive development An approach to studying cognitive development that assumes cognitive development is continuous and improves as children become more adept at processing information (taking in, storing, and using information).

in the next section when we examine the work of Russian psychologist Lev Vygotsky, whose theory did emphasize the sociocultural aspects of cognitive development. The second issue will be addressed in the section after that when we examine the question of what happens to intelligence from adolescence to old age. Does it decline as we age, especially in late adulthood? This discussion will allow us to examine two major research methods used by developmental psychologists, cross-sectional studies and longitudinal studies.

zone of proximal development According to Vygotsky, the difference between what a child can actually do and what the child could do with the help of others.

scaffolding According to Vygotsky, a style of teaching in which the teacher adjusts the level of help in relation to the child's level of performance while orienting the child's learning toward the upper level of his or her zone of proximal development.

Vygotsky's Sociocultural Approach to Development

Lev Vygotsky was a Russian developmental psychologist who was a contemporary of Piaget. Both were born in 1896, but Vygotsky died of tuberculosis at a very young age, 37, and did not have the opportunity to finish developing his theory. As with Piaget's work, there was little interest in the Western world in Vygotsky's work until the 1960s. Vygotsky's approach has become especially popular recently, however, because of its sociocultural emphasis on development.

Vygotsky (1930, 1933, 1935/1978, 1934/1986) stressed that cognitive abilities develop through interactions with others and represent the shared knowledge of one's culture. The social aspects of Vygotsky's approach are straightforward. We are social animals, and therefore much of our learning occurs within social interactions. In brief, we learn from other people—our parents, siblings, friends, teachers, and others. Vygotsky proposed that culture impacts both the content and the processes of the child's cognitive development, because a child's cognitive development occurs within this cultural context. Now that we have a general idea of Vygotsky's theory, let's take a look at two of his major theoretical concepts—the zone of proximal development and scaffolding.

In Vygotsky's theory, the **zone of proximal development** is the difference between what a child can actually do and what the child could do with the help of others. In Vygotsky's terms, this is the difference between the levels of actual development and potential development. It means that there are thinking skills that the child can display with the help of others but cannot perform independently. It also leads to a style of teaching called **scaffolding.** In scaffolding, the teacher adjusts the level of help in relation to the child's level of performance, while directing the child's learning progress toward the upper level of the child's zone of proximal development. The teacher gauges the amount of assistance necessary based on the learner's needs. The learning is structured in steps so that the child learns to achieve each step independently, but is guided and supported by the teacher throughout the learning process.

Sovfoto/UIG via Getty Images

Lev Vygotsky

To illustrate these two concepts and Vygotsky's theory, let's consider the example of a child trying to solve a jigsaw puzzle (Berger, 2006). A child may appear not to be able to solve the puzzle. However, Vygotsky would say that this particular problem-solving task could be within the child's zone of proximal development, but that she could not achieve it on her own. She needs a teacher to scaffold the task for her. How might this scaffolding proceed? The teacher would break the task down into manageable units; for example, the teacher might ask the child just to look for pieces for a particular section of the puzzle with specific suggestions about the size, shape, and colors of the relevant pieces. If this doesn't work, the teacher might actually place a few pieces in their proper places or move a few relevant pieces to their correct orientations, so their relevance is more obvious to the child. Throughout this scaffolding process, the teacher must be totally supportive of the child's progress and sensitive to how much help the child needs to progress toward solving the puzzle and how best to direct her to succeed in the next step of the solution process. After solving the puzzle, the teacher might have the child do it again, but this time with less guidance. Soon the child will be able to complete the puzzle independently. The teacher builds a scaffold to enable the child's learning. Once the learning is achieved, the scaffold is no longer necessary.

As recommended with Piaget's tests for the various types of conservation, find a young child and try to teach her how to solve a jigsaw puzzle using Vygotsky's scaffolding method. It will not only give you a better understanding of this approach but will also lead you to understand the social aspects of learning that Vygotsky stressed in his theory.

How Intelligence Changes in Adulthood

Piaget's description of intellectual development stops in adolescence with the onset of formal operations (hypothetical thought and systematic deduction), but it is important to examine what happens to intelligence across the various stages of adulthood from youth to old age. Do our cognitive abilities severely decrease across adulthood, especially in old age? The attempt to answer this question illustrates the differences between two major research methods in developmental psychology, cross-sectional studies versus longitudinal studies. In a **cross-sectional study,** people of different ages are studied and compared with one another at a single point in time. In a **longitudinal study,** the same people are studied over a long period of time. This involves collecting data periodically on the same people as they age. Longitudinal studies assess changes in people over time, whereas cross-sectional studies assess differences among age groups at a particular point in time. We will examine the use of both of these developmental research methods to answer the question about intelligence across the life span, learning the advantages and disadvantages of each.

cross-sectional study A study in which the performances of groups of participants of different ages are compared with one another.

longitudinal study A study in which performance of the same group of participants is examined at different ages.

The cross-sectional method. The early studies on this question about intelligence across the life span used the cross-sectional method. These studies used representative samples of people of various ages and consistently found that intelligence declined with age. Later studies, however, used the longitudinal method. When the same people were

> **cohort effects** People of a given age (cohorts) are affected by factors unique to their generation, leading to differences in performance between generations.

retested over a period of years, researchers found that intelligence did not decline with age, but remained rather stable and possibly increased until very late in life when it showed a decline. Now think about why there were two different answers to the intelligence question. First, consider the nature of a cross-sectional study and the possible problems with this method. A cross-sectional study compares people not only of different ages but also of different generations. This difference in generations can lead to what are called **cohort effects**—people of a given age (cohorts) are affected by factors unique to their generation, leading to differences in performance among generations. For example, there were significant differences in education and educational opportunities for the various generations across the twentieth century. Earlier generations generally received less education, which could certainly account for the intellectual decline observed in the cross-sectional studies. So, why would a researcher use the cross-sectional method, given such possible cohort effects? The cross-sectional method is far less time-consuming and less expensive than the longitudinal method. In addition, there is no need for continual retesting, as there is in longitudinal research.

The longitudinal method. Now consider the longitudinal research method. Although there is no possibility of cohort effects when using the longitudinal method, it is time-consuming and expensive, and repeated testing has to be conducted. In addition, another problem arises. Participants may discontinue their participation, move far away, or die. This means that the sample changes across time, which could have an impact on the research findings if those who disappear from the sample are unlike, in some relevant characteristic, those who stay. How might a changing sample lead to the misleading finding that intelligence remains fairly stable? Here's one explanation—those who survived to be tested at the older ages may have been the most intelligent and healthiest participants, those whose intelligence would be the most likely not to decline. This would also mean that the participants whose intelligence was likely to decline may have no longer been in the study. Given the shortcomings of both methods (see Table 7.3 on page 310), it has proven rather difficult to get a clear answer to this question of intelligence across the life span.

The type of intelligence that is being tested is also important and further complicates the search for an answer. Remember from the last chapter, in our discussion of types of intelligence, that we differentiated fluid intelligence and crystallized intelligence. Crystallized intelligence refers to accumulated knowledge, verbal skills, and numerical skills that increase with age; fluid intelligence involves abilities, such as abstract thinking and logical problem solving, that decrease with

Table 7.3	Advantages and Disadvantages for Cross-sectional and Longitudinal Research Methods		
Research Method	**Description**	**Advantages**	**Disadvantages**
Cross-sectional study	People of different ages are studied at a single time	Not very time-consuming or expensive	No need for continued retesting Possible confounding due to cohort effects (differences in performance between age groups caused by generational differences)
Longitudinal study	Same people are studied repeatedly over a long period of time	No possibility of cohort effects	Very time-consuming and expensive Repeated testing has to be conducted Possible confounding due to changes in sample over time

age (Horn, 1982). This difference may help to explain why scientists make their major contributions early, but historians and philosophers make theirs later in their careers.

The Seattle Longitudinal Study was a major attempt to answer the question of whether or not intelligence declines with age (Schaie, 1994, 1995). It was a large-scale longitudinal study of various intellectual abilities (such as inductive reasoning, word fluency, and perceptual speed) across the entire span of adulthood. It started in 1956 with more than 5,000 participants being tested every 7 years through 1998. The study was actually a combination of the longitudinal and cross-sectional methods, since groups of new participants were added periodically. This allowed the researchers to examine the possible shortcomings of both methods.

In general, the researchers found that most intellectual abilities decline somewhat by age 60, but the decline is not great until a person reaches age 80 or more (except for abilities largely dependent upon speed of processing, which clearly declines as we age). There are large individual differences, however. Those who suffer the least decline seem to be those who have stayed healthy, are in the higher socioeconomic categories, and are still involved in intellectually stimulating environments. In brief, it seems that if we work to stay healthy and cognitively stimulated, we won't suffer major deficits in our cognitive abilities until rather late in adulthood.

Section Summary

We are speechless at birth, but our capacity for language develops soon thereafter. Children of different cultures learn different languages, but they seem to go through the same sequence of stages for language acquisition. At about 12 months, infants begin to speak a few words, and then to use holophrases, words that express complete ideas. Their vocabulary grows slowly. Overextension and underextension of a word's meaning occur. A vocabulary spurt starts at about 18 months, and children engage in telegraphic speech, using two-word sentences of mainly nouns and verbs. These brief statements start to expand, and between the ages of 2 to 5, children acquire the grammar of their native language. Children acquire language early and easily, without direct instruction, and this process seems universal. There is much support for the argument that language development is a genetically programmed ability. It is also clear that certain environmental experiences (exposure to human speech) are necessary, and that caregivers can facilitate and enhance language development.

It appears that children's thinking, in general, goes through a universal sequence of development. Jean Piaget's theory proposes distinct stages of cognitive development and emphasizes that the child is trying to adapt to his environment and is an active seeker of knowledge. This knowledge about the world is organized into schemas, and these schemas are developed through the processes of assimilation and accommodation.

During the sensorimotor stage (from birth to 2 years), infants learn and know about their world only through their sensory and motor interactions with it, but during this stage, object permanence develops along with language and the symbolic representation of objects and events. In the preoperational stage (from 2 to 6 years), the child's thought becomes more symbolic and language-based but remains egocentric and lacks the mental operations that allow logical thinking. For example, the child lacks the reversibility operation and so does not understand conservation. In the concrete operational stage (from about 6 to 12 years), the child gains a fuller understanding of conservation and other mental operations that allow logical thinking, but only about concrete events. In the last stage, the formal operational stage (from age 12 through adulthood), the individual gains the capacity for hypothetical and deductive thought.

Recent research indicates that many of Piaget's key concepts (such as object permanence) may begin to appear at earlier ages than Piaget proposed, but that cognitive development seems to proceed in the general sequence that he proposed. It is clear, however, that not everyone reaches formal operational thinking, especially in cultures that do not emphasize such thinking, and that those who do may not always use such thinking. In addition, the information-processing approach to cognitive development questions the existence of stages and argues that cognitive development is continuous and not composed of stages. The information-processing approach argues that cognitive development stems from improvements in children's information-processing abilities—how they take in, store, and use information.

Piaget was not concerned with the sociocultural aspects of cognitive development, but Russian psychologist Lev Vygotsky was. Vygotsky proposed that cognitive abilities develop through interaction with others and represent shared knowledge of one's culture. According to Vygotsky, a child's zone of proximal development is the difference between what a child can actually do and what the child could do with the help of others. This is why Vygotsky recommended a style of teaching called scaffolding.

The teacher structures the child's learning in steps, so that the child learns each step independently but is guided and supported by the teacher toward the upper level of the child's zone of proximal development.

Piaget and Vygotsky didn't really examine what happens to cognitive abilities across the life span, but other developmental researchers have. They have used the cross-sectional (studying people of different ages at a single time) and longitudinal (studying the same people repeatedly over a long period of time) methods, as well as the combination of the two, to do so. In general, developmental researchers have found that the ability to perform tasks that involve crystallized intelligence tends to increase with age, but that the ability to perform tasks that involve fluid intelligence shows a pattern of decline with age. Cognitive abilities that do not involve speed of processing, however, do not show dramatic decline until the age of 80 and beyond; but there are large individual differences. Those people who have stayed healthy, are in the higher socioeconomic levels, and are still involved in intellectually stimulating environments tend to see the smallest declines in intelligence as they age.

ConceptCheck | 2

Explain how overextension and underextension in language development relate to Piaget's concepts of assimilation and accommodation in schema development.

Explain why a child who thought that a pizza cut into eight slices was more than the same pizza cut into six slices would be in the preoperational stage of cognitive development.

Explain how Vygotsky's zone of proximal development and scaffolding are related to learning and teaching.

Explain the difference between the cross-sectional and longitudinal research methods.

Moral Development and Social Development

We develop cognitively and socially simultaneously, so these two types of development are difficult to separate. As Vygotsky stressed, cognitive development is best understood in its social context. In this section, we will discuss moral and social development, but we need to remember that it occurs simultaneously with cognitive development and is affected by it. Moral reasoning that involves both social and cognitive elements is a good illustration of this interactive development. For example, until a child moves away from egocentric thinking, it would be difficult for her to consider different perspectives when reasoning about the morality of a particular action. We begin our discussion of social development with a description of the major theory of moral development, Kohlberg's stage theory of moral reasoning. Then, we examine early social development with a discussion of attachment formation and parenting styles followed by a discussion of one of the most important social developments in early childhood, theory of mind. We conclude with a description of Erik Erikson's stage theory of social-personality development across the life span, from birth through late adulthood.

Kohlberg's Theory of Moral Reasoning

Lawrence Kohlberg

The most influential theory of moral reasoning is Lawrence Kohlberg's stage theory (Kohlberg, 1976, 1984). Building on an earlier theory of moral reasoning proposed by Piaget (1932), Kohlberg began the development of his theory by following in Piaget's footsteps, using stories that involved moral dilemmas to assess a child's or an adult's level of moral reasoning. To familiarize you with these moral dilemmas, consider Kohlberg's best-known story—a dilemma involving Heinz, whose wife was dying of cancer. In brief, there was only one cure for this cancer. A local druggist had developed the cure, but he was selling it for much more than it cost to make and than Heinz could pay. Heinz tried to borrow the money to buy it, but could only get about half of what the drug cost. He asked the druggist to sell it to him cheaper or to let him pay the rest later, but the druggist refused. Out of desperation, Heinz broke into the druggist's store and stole the drug for his wife. Given this story, the person is asked if Heinz should have stolen the drug and why or why not.

Using the responses to and explanations of this and other moral dilemmas, Kohlberg found three levels of moral reasoning—preconventional, conventional, and postconventional. These levels are outlined in Table 7.4. Each level has

Table 7.4	Kohlberg's Stage Theory of Moral Reasoning	
Level I Preconventional Morality		
Stage 1	Punishment orientation	Compliance with rules to avoid punishment
Stage 2	Reward orientation	Compliance with rules to obtain rewards and satisfy own needs
Level II Conventional Morality		
Stage 3	Good-girl/good-boy orientation	Engages in behavior to get approval of others
Stage 4	Law and order orientation	Behavior is guided by duty to uphold laws and rules for their own sake
Level III Postconventional Morality		
Stage 5	Social contract orientation	Obeys rules because they are necessary for social order but understands rules are relative
Stage 6	Universal ethical principles orientation	Concerned about self-condemnation for violating universal ethical principles based on human rights

Lee Lockwood/Time Life Pictures/Getty Images

preconventional level of moral reasoning The first level of reasoning in Kohlberg's theory of moral development in which moral reasoning is based on avoiding punishment and looking out for your own welfare and needs.

conventional level of moral reasoning The second level of reasoning in Kohlberg's theory of moral development in which moral reasoning is based on social rules and laws.

postconventional level of moral reasoning The last level of reasoning in Kohlberg's theory of moral development in which moral reasoning is based on self-chosen universal ethical principles (with human rights taking precedence over laws) and the avoidance of self-condemnation for violating such principles.

two stages. At the **preconventional level of moral reasoning,** the emphasis is on avoiding punishment and looking out for your own welfare and needs. Moral reasoning is self-oriented. At the **conventional level,** moral reasoning is based on social rules and laws. Social approval and being a dutiful citizen are important. At the highest level, the **postconventional level,** moral reasoning is based on self-chosen universal ethical principles, with human rights taking precedence over laws, and on the avoidance of self-condemnation for violating such principles.

It is important to point out that in determining a person's level, it did not matter to Kohlberg whether the person answered yes or no to the dilemma. For example, in the Heinz dilemma, it did not matter whether the person said he should steal the drug or that he should not do so. The reasoning provided in the person's explanation is what mattered. Kohlberg provided examples of such explanations for each level of reasoning. To understand how Kohlberg used these responses to the moral dilemmas, let's consider sample Stage 4 rationales for stealing the drug and for not stealing the drug. The pro-stealing explanation would emphasize that it is Heinz's duty to protect his wife's life, given the vow he took in marriage. But it's wrong to steal, so Heinz would have to take the drug with the idea of paying the druggist for it and accepting the penalty for breaking the law. The anti-stealing rationale would emphasize that you have to follow the rules regardless of how you feel and regardless of the special circumstances. Even if his wife is dying, it is still Heinz's duty as a citizen to follow the law. If everyone started breaking laws, there would be no civilization. As you can see, both explanations emphasize the law-and-order orientation of this stage—if you break the law, you must pay the penalty.

Kohlberg proposed that we all start at the preconventional level as children and as we develop, especially cognitively, we move up the ladder of moral reasoning. The sequence is unvarying, but, as with Piaget's formal operational stage, we all may not make it up to the last stage. That the sequence does not vary and that a person's level of moral reasoning is age-related (and so related to cognitive development) has been supported by research.

Research also indicates that most people in many different cultures reach the conventional level by adulthood, but attainment of the postconventional level is not so clear (Snarey, 1985). There are other problems. First, it is important to realize that Kohlberg was studying moral reasoning and not moral behavior. As we will see in Chapter 9, on social psychology, thought and action are not always consistent. Ethical talk may not equate to ethical behavior. Second, some researchers have criticized Kohlberg's theory for not adequately representing the morality of women. They argue that feminine moral reasoning is more concerned with a morality of care that focuses on interpersonal relationships and the needs of others than a morality of justice, as in Kohlberg's theory. Similarly, critics have questioned the theory's universality by arguing that the higher stages are biased toward Western values. In summary, Kohlberg's theory has both support and criticism, but more impor-

> **attachment** The lifelong emotional bond between infants and their mothers or other caregivers, formed during the first 6 months of life.

tantly, it has stimulated research that continues to develop our understanding of moral development.

Attachment and Parenting Styles

As we have said before, humans are social creatures. Infants' first social relationship—between them and their primary caregivers—is important and has been carefully studied by developmental psychologists (Bowlby, 1969). This lifelong emotional bond that exists between the infants and their mothers or other caregivers is formed during the first 6 months of life and is called **attachment.** Traditionally, the primary caregiver has been the infant's mother, but times have changed; today the primary caregiver could be the mother, father, grandparent, nanny, or day care provider. Because attachment is related to children's later development, it is also important to examine whether children who are put in day care at a young age are at a disadvantage in comparison to those who remain at home. Following a discussion of some of the early research on attachment, we will address this question. First, we consider the question of why the attachment forms. Is it because the caregiver provides food, and the attachment forms as a consequence of reinforcement?

Attachment and Harlow's monkeys. Harry Harlow used newborn monkeys in his attachment research to address this question (Harlow, 1959; Harlow & Harlow, 1962; Harlow & Zimmerman, 1959). These attachment studies were a consequence of an accidental discovery during his learning research using the infant monkeys. The infant monkeys often caught diseases from their mothers, so Harlow had separated the infant monkeys from their mothers. He gave cheese-cloth blankets to the isolated infant monkeys. The infant monkeys became strongly attached to these blankets and were greatly disturbed if their "security" blankets were taken away.

After this observation, Harlow began to separate the infant monkeys from their mothers at birth and put them in cages containing two inanimate surrogate (substitute) mothers—one made of wire and one made of terry cloth. Figure 7.3 (page 316) shows examples of these surrogate mothers and the motherless monkeys. Half of the monkeys received their nourishment from a milk dispenser in the wire mother and half from a dispenser in the terry cloth mother. However, all of the monkeys preferred the cloth monkey regardless of which monkey provided their nourishment. The monkeys being fed by the wire mother would only go to the wire mother to eat and then return to the cloth mother. As shown in Figure 7.3, if possible, the infant monkeys would often cling to the cloth monkey

Harry Harlow

Photo Researchers, Inc.

Photo Researchers, Inc.

Figure 7.3 | Harlow's Motherless Monkeys and Surrogate Mothers | In Harry Harlow's research on the role of feeding in the attachment process, he found that contact comfort, rather than feeding, was the most important factor in an infant monkey's attachment. The infant monkeys spent most of their time on the terry cloth surrogate mother regardless of whether she provided their nourishment or not. The infant monkey would often even cling to the cloth monkey while feeding from the wire mother.

while feeding from the wire mother. In brief, the infant monkeys would spend most of each day on the cloth mother. The monkeys clearly had become attached to the cloth mother. Harlow concluded that "contact comfort" (bodily contact and comfort), not reinforcement from nourishment, was the crucial element for attachment formation.

In addition, the infant monkeys would cower in fear when confronted with a strange situation (an unfamiliar room with various toys) without the surrogate mother. When the surrogate mother was brought into the strange situation, the infant monkeys would initially cling to the terry cloth mother to reduce their fear, but then begin to explore the new environment and eventually play with the toys. Harlow concluded that the presence of the surrogate mother made the monkeys feel secure and therefore sufficiently confident to explore the strange situation. This situation is very similar to the Strange Situation procedure developed by Mary Ainsworth to study the attachment relationship in human infants (Ainsworth, 1979; Ainsworth, Blehar, Waters, & Wall, 1978). In this procedure, an infant's behavior is observed in an unfamiliar room with toys, while the infant's mother and a stranger (an unfamiliar woman) move in and out of the room in a structured series of situations. The key observations focus on the infant's reaction to the mother's leaving and returning, both when the stranger is present and absent, and on the child exploring the situation (the room and the toys in it).

Types of attachment. Ainsworth and her colleagues found three types of attachment relationships—secure, insecure-avoidant, and insecure-ambivalent. **Secure attachment** is indicated by the infant exploring the situation freely in the presence of the mother, but displaying distress when the mother leaves, and responding enthusiastically when the mother returns. **Insecure-avoidant attachment** is indicated by exploration but minimal interest in the mother, the infant showing little distress when the mother leaves, and avoiding her when she returns. **Insecure-ambivalent attachment** is indicated by the infant seeking closeness to the mother and not exploring the situation, high levels of distress when the mother leaves, and ambivalent behavior when she returns by alternately clinging to and pushing away from her. About two-thirds of the infants studied are found to have a secure attachment, and the other third insecure attachments. Cross-cultural research indicates that these proportions may vary across different cultures, but the majority of infants worldwide seem to form secure attachments. Later researchers have added a fourth type of insecure attachment, **insecure-disorganized (disoriented) attachment,** which is indicated by the infant's confusion when the mother leaves and when she returns. The infant acts disoriented, seems overwhelmed by the situation, and does not demonstrate a consistent way of coping with it (Main & Solomon, 1990).

Before putting the infants in the Strange Situation series, researchers observed the infant–mother relationship at home during the first 6 months of an infant's life. From such observations, they found that the sensitivity of the mother is the major determinant of the quality of the attachment relationship. A mother who is sensitive and responsive to an infant's needs is more likely to develop a secure attachment with the infant. Although the mother's caregiver style is primary, does the infant also contribute to the attachment formation? The answer is yes. Each of us is born with a **temperament,** a set of innate tendencies or dispositions that lead us to behave in certain ways. Our temperament is fundamental to both our personality development and also how we interact with others (our social development). The temperaments of infants vary greatly. Some infants are more responsive, more active, and happier than others. How an infant's temperament matches the childrearing expectations and personality of his caregiver is important in forming the attachment relationship. A good match or fit between the two enhances the probability of a secure attachment.

The type of attachment that is formed is important to later development. Secure attachments in infancy have been linked to higher levels of cognitive functioning and social competence in childhood (Jacobsen & Hoffman, 1997; Schneider, Atkinson, & Tardif, 2001). This doesn't mean, however, that the type of attachment cannot

secure attachment The type of attachment indicated by the infant exploring freely in the presence of the mother in the Ainsworth Strange Situation procedure, displaying distress when the mother leaves, and responding enthusiastically when she returns.

insecure-avoidant attachment The type of attachment indicated by the infant exploring with little interest in the mother in the Ainsworth Strange Situation procedure, showing only minimal distress when the mother leaves, and avoiding her when she returns.

insecure-ambivalent attachment The type of attachment indicated by the infant not exploring but seeking closeness to the mother in the Ainsworth Strange Situation procedure, showing high levels of distress when the mother leaves, and ambivalent behavior when she returns—by alternately clinging to and pushing away from her.

insecure-disorganized (disoriented) attachment The type of attachment indicated by the infant's confusion when the mother leaves and returns in the Ainsworth Strange Situation procedure. The infant acts disoriented, seems overwhelmed by the situation, and does not demonstrate a consistent way of coping with it.

temperament The set of innate tendencies or dispositions that lead a person to behave in certain ways.

authoritarian parenting A style of parenting in which the parents are demanding, expect unquestioned obedience, are not responsive to their children's desires, and communicate poorly with their children.

authoritative parenting A style of parenting in which the parents are demanding, but set rational limits for their children and communicate well with their children.

permissive parenting A style of parenting in which the parents make few demands and are overly responsive to their children's desires, letting their children do pretty much as they please.

uninvolved parenting A style of parenting in which the parents minimize both the time they spend with their children and their emotional involvement with them and provide for their children's basic needs, but little else.

change or that an insecure attachment cannot be overcome by later experiences. As family circumstances change, interactions change and so may the type of attachment. For example, divorce might put a child into day care, or remarriage might bring another caring adult into the family. This brings us to a very important question in our present-day society of working mothers and single parents: Is day care detrimental to the formation of secure attachments and therefore to cognitive and social development? The general answer is no. Children in day care seem to be generally as well off as those who are raised at home (Erel, Oberman, & Yirmiya, 2000; NICHD Early Child Care Research Network, 1997, 2001). In addition, there do not seem to be any significant differences in social competence later in school for children raised in day care versus at home (NICHD Early Child Care Research Network, 2008). However, the effects of day care for a particular child are moderated by many variables, such as the age of the child when starting day care, the number of hours of day care per week, and the quality of the day care. Researchers all agree about one point—the quality of day care matters in that children in high-quality day care will do better later in school, both academically and socially, than children in low-quality day care (Belsky et al., 2007; Li, Farkas, Duncan, Burchinal, & Vandell, 2013). But what does high-quality day care entail? According to Berger (2016), high-quality day care has five characteristics—adequate attention to each child, encouragement of language and sensorimotor development, attention to health and safety of the child, professional caregivers who have experience and degrees/certificates in early childhood education, and warm, responsive caregiving.

Parenting styles. Attachment formation in infants is important in shaping later development. But how do parenting styles impact development in children and adolescents? Diana Baumrind (1971, 1991) has identified four styles of parenting—authoritarian, authoritative, permissive, and uninvolved (Baumrind, 1971, 1991). **Authoritarian parents** are demanding, expect unquestioned obedience, are not responsive to their children's desires, and communicate poorly with their children. Rules are made by the parents and enforced with punishment, which is sometimes physical. **Authoritative parents** are demanding but set rational limits for their children and communicate well with their children. There are rules that are consistently enforced, but the parents explain the reasons for the rules to the children and consider the children's point of view. **Permissive parents** make few demands and are overly responsive to their children's desires, letting their children do pretty much as they please. There are few rules, and punishment is rare. **Uninvolved parents** minimize both the time they spend with the children and their emotional involvement with them.

Courtesy of Diana Baumrind

Diana Baumrind

They provide for their children's basic needs but little else. These parenting styles have been related to differences in cognitive and social development. Authoritative parenting seems to have the most positive effect on a child's development (Baumrind, 1996). The children of authoritative parents are not only the most independent, happy, and self-reliant, but also the most academically successful and socially competent. Decades of research have consistently shown that the authoritative parenting style is associated with higher social and academic competence. This strong relationship between parenting style and child development was, however, primarily established based on studies of white, middle-class families. Thus, parenting style effects may vary across different ethnic and cultural groups because development is impacted not only by the immediate family but also by the broader cultural context in which the child lives (Bronfenbrenner, 1993). Nonetheless, studies of families in more than 200 cultures around the world have confirmed the social and academic benefits of authoritative parenting (for example, Sorkhabi, 2005). Regardless of how overwhelming these findings seem, we need to exercise some caution because these findings are correlational in nature. The researchers found a strong positive relationship between authoritative parenting and successful childhood outcomes. Thus, as we learned in Chapter 1, there may be third variables involved in this relationship between authoritative parenting and childhood competence. It is also important to realize that this is a situation in which it is ethically impossible to gather experimental data on possible causal factors in this relationship. Hence, correlational studies are our best source of information for examining this relationship.

So far we have discussed social development for the infant and child in terms of attachment and parenting styles, but such development involves others as well, such as friends and teachers. Friends become increasingly important and assume different functions as children age (Furman & Bierman, 1984; Simpkins, Parke, Flyr, & Wild, 2006). Early friendships are primarily due to children having similar play interests or living close together. As adolescence approaches, however, friendships begin to serve more important emotional needs, and friends provide emotional support for one another. Despite the increasing importance of friends, adolescents still value their relationships with their parents and try to uphold parental standards on major issues such as careers and education. In addition to friends, children are also part of a larger social peer network in which the social status of members varies (Asher, 1983; Jiang & Cillessen, 2005). Popular children tend to be liked by most other children and have good social skills. Children who are rejected by their peers, however, lack these social skills and often tend to be either aggressive or withdrawn. Rejected children are at increased risk for both emotional and social difficulties (Buhs & Ladd, 2001).

Theory of Mind

One of the most important social developments that occurs in early childhood is in the area of social cognition—the development of a **theory of mind.** Theory of mind refers

theory of mind The understanding of the mental and emotional states of both ourselves and others.

to the understanding of the mental and emotional states of both ourselves and others. In order to have a theory of mind, children must realize that other people do not necessarily think the same thoughts, have the same beliefs, or feel the same emotions that they themselves do. Whenever we interact with others, we interpret and explain their behavior in terms of their beliefs, desires, and emotions. If a friend is angry, we might explain it by attributing it to his or her belief that we did something to upset them. It is difficult to imagine what social relationships would be like if we were unable to infer the mental and emotional states of others.

While there are many aspects of theory of mind development that begin in infancy and early childhood, one critical theory of mind accomplishment is the understanding of false beliefs (recognizing that others can have beliefs about the world that are wrong) that typically develops between 4 and 5 years of age. To test for this understanding, researchers use false-belief problems in which another person believes something to be true that the child knows is false. The question is whether the child thinks that the other person will act in accord with his false belief or with the child's correct understanding of the situation. These problems reveal whether the child has the understanding that different people can have different beliefs about the same situation. For example, in an unexpected location task designed to assess false-belief understanding, a child sees a ball being hidden in a box by Big Bird and then Big Bird leaves the room to play outside. Next, the child observes Cookie Monster move the ball to a toy chest. The child is then asked where Big Bird will think the ball is when he comes back in from playing. A 5-year-old can accurately predict that Big Bird will think it is in the original box even though the child knows it is in the toy chest. That is, the child understands that different people can have different beliefs about the same situation. A 3-year old typically does not understand this and would incorrectly predict that Big Bird would think it is in the toy chest, because younger children believe that everyone thinks like they do. Such findings are extremely robust and have been observed with different problems and in different cultures (Wellman, Cross, & Watson, 2001).

The early emergence of theory of mind understanding has led some researchers to suggest that there is a biological basis for this knowledge (Baron-Cohen, 2000). The

DENNIS THE MENACE

Dennis The Menace © 1990 North American Syndicate

5-23

"I KNOW WHAT I THINK, BUT WHAT'S IMPORTANT IS WHAT MY MOM THINKS I THINK!"

developmental disorder of autism, in which children are primarily character-ized by difficulty in social interactions, supports this biological view of theory of mind (Frith, 2003). What might be the biological basis for theory of mind development? We have already learned about one possibility. Remember, in Chapter 4 we learned that mirror neuron systems *may* provide the neural basis for imitation learning and play a role in empathy and the understanding of the intentions and emotions of others. Thus, early mirror neuron system deficits might cascade into developmental impairments in imitation learning and subsequently in theory of mind development, leading to autism (Iacoboni & Dapretto, 2006; Williams, Whiten, Suddendorf, & Perrett, 2001). For example, Dapretto et al. (2006) had high-functioning children with autism and normal control children undergo fMRI while imitating emotional expres-sions. For the children with autism, they found little activity in brain regions associated with mirror neurons. For the children without autism, however, these regions were active, suggesting that a dysfunctional mirror neuron sys-tem may underlie the social deficits observed in autism. We must remember, however, that this is presently just a hypothesis and that, as we discussed in Chapter 4, researchers not only disagree about the presence of mirror neu-ron systems in humans but also, if they do exist, about what exactly they do. Clearly, more research must be conducted before any firm conclusions about a biological basis for theory of mind can be made.

We have primarily focused on social develop-ment during childhood and adolescence but social development continues throughout our lives. This is why we now turn to Erik Erikson's stage theory of how we develop throughout our life, from birth to old age.

Erik Erikson

Erikson's Psychosocial Stage Theory of Development

Erik Erikson's psychosocial stage theory covers the whole life span. Like Vygotsky, Erikson emphasized the impact of society and culture upon development, but Erikson's theory is different because it consid-ered both personality development and social devel-opment. We discuss it here rather than in the next chapter, with the other personality theories, because it is a developmental theory. In fact, Erikson's inclu-sion of the three stages of adulthood in his theory has played a major role in the increased amount of research on all parts of the life span—not just on childhood and adolescence. However, Erikson's the-

Ted Streshinsky/Time Life Pictures/Getty Images

ory has been criticized because of the lack of solid experimental data to support it. Erikson used only observational data, which is a criticism that can be leveled against most personality theories.

Erikson divided the life span into eight stages of development, summarized in Table 7.5 (Erikson, 1950, 1963, 1968, 1980). The first five stages cover infancy, childhood, and adolescence, where Freud's theory of personality development (discussed in the next chapter) and Piaget's theory of cognitive development end. Erikson's last three stages go beyond Freud and Piaget and deal with the three stages of adulthood (young, middle, and late).

Erikson viewed our social-personality development as the product of our social interactions and the choices we make in life. At each stage, there is a major psychosocial issue or crisis that has to be resolved. Think of each stage as a "fork in the road" choice whose resolution greatly impacts our development.

Table 7.5 Erikson's Psychosocial Stages	
Stage (age range)	**Stage Description**
Trust vs. mistrust (birth to 1 year)	Infants learn that they can or cannot trust others to take care of their basic needs.
Autonomy vs. shame and doubt (1 to 2 years)	Children learn to be self-sufficient in many activities such as toilet training, walking, and exploring. If restrained too much, they learn to doubt their abilities and feel shame.
Initiative vs. guilt (3 to 5 years)	Children learn to assume more responsibility by taking initiative but will feel guilty if they overstep limits set by parents.
Industry vs. inferiority (5 years to puberty)	Children learn to be competent by mastering new intellectual, social, and physical skills or feel inferior if they fail to develop these skills.
Identity vs. role confusion (adolescence)	Adolescents develop a sense of identity by experimenting with different roles. No role experimentation may result in role confusion.
Intimacy vs. isolation (young adulthood)	Young adults form intimate relationships with others or become isolated because of a failure to do so.
Generativity vs. stagnation (middle adulthood)	Middle-aged adults feel they are helping the next generation through their work and child rearing, or they stagnate because they feel that they are not helping.
Integrity vs. despair (late adulthood)	Older adults assess their lives and develop a sense of integrity if they find their lives have been meaningful, and a sense of despair if their lives do not seem meaningful.

Each stage is named after the two sides of the issue relevant in that stage. For example, the first stage is trust versus mistrust. In this stage, infants in the first year of life are wrestling with the issue of whether they can trust or not trust others to take care of them. The resolution of each stage can end up on either side of the issue. The infant can leave the first stage either generally trusting or generally mistrusting the world. When an issue is successfully resolved, the person increases in social competence. Erikson felt that the resolution of each stage greatly impacted our personal development. Table 7.5 includes the possible resolutions for each stage.

Erikson's best-known concept, identity crisis, is part of his fifth stage. The main task of this stage is the development of a sense of identity—to figure out who we are, what we value, and where we are headed in life. As adolescents, we are confused about our identity. The distress created by the confusion is what Erikson meant by identity crisis. For most adolescents, however, it's more of a search or exploration than a crisis. Teenagers experiment with different identities in the search to find their own. If you are a traditional-age college student, you may have just experienced or are still experiencing this search. Attending college and searching for a major and a career path may delay the resolution of this stage. Finding our true selves is clearly not easy. We usually explore many alternative identities before finding one that is satisfactory.

This identity stage is critical to becoming a productive adult, but development doesn't end with its resolution. Probably the greatest impact of Erikson's theory is that it expanded the study of developmental psychology past adolescence into the stages of adulthood. In young adulthood (from the end of adolescence to the beginning of middle age), a person establishes independence from her parents and begins to function as a mature, productive adult. Having established her own identity, a person is ready to establish a shared identity with another person, leading to an intimate relationship. This sequence in Erikson's theory (intimacy issues following identity issues) turns out to be most applicable to men and career-oriented women (Dyk & Adams, 1990). Many women may solve these issues in reverse order or simultaneously. For example, a woman may marry and have children and then confront the identity issues when her children become adults.

The crisis in middle adulthood (from about age 40 to age 60) is concerned with generativity versus stagnation. "Generativity" is being concerned with the next generation and producing something of lasting value to society. Generative activity comes in many forms. In addition to making lasting contributions to society, which most of us will not do, generative activity includes rearing children, engaging in meaningful work, mentoring younger workers, and contributing to civic organizations.

In Erikson's final stage, late adulthood, we conduct reviews of our lives, looking back at our lives to assess how well we have lived them. If we are satisfied, we gain a sense of integrity and the ability to face death. If not, we despair and look back with a sense of sadness and regret, and we fear death.

Section Summary

The most influential theory of moral development is Kohlberg's stage theory of moral reasoning. Using moral dilemmas, Kohlberg proposed three levels of reasoning— preconventional, conventional, and postconventional. The first level is self-oriented, and the emphasis is on avoiding punishment and looking out for one's own needs. At the conventional level, reasoning is guided by social approval and being a dutiful citizen. At the highest postconventional level, morality is based on universal ethical principles and the realization that society's laws are only a social contract, which can be broken if they violate these more global principles. Research indicates that proceeding through the stages is related to age and cognitive development, but that most people do not reach the postconventional stage of reasoning. The theory is criticized for being based on moral reasoning and not moral behavior (since these may be very different); for being biased against women, who may focus more on a morality of care than a morality of justice; and for being biased toward Western moral values.

Social development begins with attachment, the strong emotional bond formed between an infant and his mother or primary caregiver. Harry Harlow's studies with infant monkeys and surrogate mothers found that contact comfort, and not reinforcement from nourishment, is the crucial element in attachment formation. Using Mary Ainsworth's Strange Situation procedure, researchers have identified four types of attachment—secure, insecure-avoidant, insecure-ambivalent, and insecure-disorganized. The sensitivity of the caregiver to the infant and how well an infant's temperament matches the child-rearing expectations and personality of the caregiver are important to attachment formation. The majority of infants worldwide form secure attachments, and this type of attachment has been linked to higher levels of social competence and cognitive functioning in childhood. With respect to parenting styles, authoritative parenting—in which the parents are demanding but rational in setting limits for their children and communicate well with their children—seems to have the most positive effect on social and cognitive development. Recent research, however, indicates that parenting style effects may vary across ethnic and cultural groups. Friends are also important to social development, especially during adolescence when friendships serve important emotional needs.

One of the most important social developments that occurs in early childhood is the development of a theory of mind, the understanding of the mental and emotional states of both ourselves and others. One critical accomplishment in theory of mind development is the understanding of false beliefs around 4 to 5 years of age. To test for this understanding, researchers use false-belief problems in which another person believes something to be true that the child knows is false. If the child has the understanding of false beliefs, he will predict that the other person will act in accord with his false belief and not the child's correct understanding of the situation. Children without an understanding of false beliefs would make just the opposite prediction. The early emergence of theory of mind development has led some researchers to suggest that there is a biological basis for it. Mirror neuron systems are a possibility for this basis because they seem to provide the neural basis for imitation learning and play a role in empathy and the understanding of the intentions and emotions of others. Thus, early mirror neuron system deficits might lead to developmental impairments in imitation learning and subsequently theory of mind development, leading to social disorders such as autism.

With respect to social development across the life span, Erik Erikson developed an eight-stage theory of social and personality development. In each stage, there is a major psychosocial issue with two sides that has to be resolved. If the stage is resolved successfully, the person leaves the stage on the positive side of the stage issue. For example, the infant in the first year of life is dealing with the issue of trust versus mistrust. If resolved successfully, the infant will leave this stage trusting the world. Erikson stressed the fifth stage, in which a sense of identity must be developed during adolescence. This is the stage during which the identity crisis occurs. Erikson's theory is unusual in that it includes the three stages of adulthood. This inclusion played a major role in leading developmental psychologists to expand their focus to development across the entire life span.

ConceptCheck | 3

Describe how Kohlberg would classify the following response explaining why Heinz should not steal the drug. "You shouldn't steal the drug because you'll be caught and sent to jail if you do. If you do get away with it, your conscience would bother you thinking how the police would catch up with you any minute."

Explain why an infant's temperament is important to the process of attachment formation.

Explain the differences between authoritarian and authoritative parenting styles.

In the false-belief problem described in the text involving Big Bird and Cookie Monster, how will a child who does not have an understanding of false beliefs answer, and why will he answer in this way? How will he answer if he has an understanding of false beliefs, and why will he answer in this way?

Explain what Erikson meant by psychosocial issue or crisis.

Study Guide

Chapter Key Terms

You should know the definitions of the following key terms from the chapter. They are listed in the order in which they appear in the chapter. For those you do not know, return to the relevant section of the chapter to learn them. When you think that you know all of the terms, complete the matching exercise based on these key terms.

developmental psychology
zygote
gene
chromosomes
identical (monozygotic) twins
fraternal (dizygotic) twins
teratogens
fetal alcohol syndrome (FAS)
sucking reflex
rooting reflex
habituation
phonemes
baby talk (parentese)
babbling
holophrase
overextension
underextension
telegraphic speech
assimilation
accommodation

sensorimotor stage
object permanence
preoperational stage
egocentrism
conservation
reversibility
centration
concrete operational stage
formal operational stage
information-processing
   approach to cognitive
   development
zone of proximal development
scaffolding
cross-sectional study
longitudinal study
cohort effects
preconventional level
   of moral reasoning

conventional level of moral
   reasoning
postconventional level of moral
   reasoning
attachment
secure attachment
insecure-avoidant attachment
insecure-ambivalent attachment
insecure-disorganized
   (disoriented) attachment
temperament
authoritarian parenting
authoritative parenting
permissive parenting
uninvolved parenting
theory of mind

Key Terms Exercise

Identify the correct term for each of the following definitions. The answers to this exercise follow the answers to the ConceptChecks at the end of the chapter.

1. The knowledge that an object exists independent of perceptual contact with it.

2. An innate human reflex that leads infants to turn their mouth toward anything that touches their cheeks and search for something to suck on.

3. The fertilized egg that is formed from the union of the sperm and egg cells in human reproduction.

4. Piaget's term for the modification of present schemas to fit with new experiences.

   _____

5. A style of parenting in which the parents are demanding, but set rational limits for their children and communicate well with their children.

   _____

6. The type of attachment indicated by the infant exploring freely in the presence of the mother in the Ainsworth Strange Situation procedure, but displaying distress when the mother leaves, and responding enthusiastically when she returns.

   _____

7. The different format of speech that adults use when talking with babies that involves the use of shorter sentences with a higher, more melodious pitch.

   _____

8. Agents such as drugs, viruses, diseases, and physical conditions that impair prenatal development and lead to birth defects and sometimes death.

   _____

9. A study in which the performance of the same group of participants is examined at different ages.

   _____

10. According to Vygotsky, the difference between what a child can actually do and what the child could do with the help of others.

   _____

11. The smallest distinctive speech sounds in a language.

   _____

12. Using two-word sentences with mainly nouns and verbs.

   _____

13. The knowledge that the quantitative properties of objects (such as mass and number) remain the same despite changes in appearance.

   _____

14. A style of teaching in which the teacher adjusts the level of help in relation to the child's level of performance while orienting the child toward the upper level of his or her zone of proximal development.

   _____

15. The set of innate tendencies or dispositions that lead a person to behave in certain ways.

   _____

Practice Test Questions

The following are practice multiple-choice test questions on some of the chapter content. The answers are given after the Key Terms Exercise answers at the end of the chapter. If you guessed on a question or incorrectly answered a question, restudy the relevant section of the chapter.

1. In human conception, another name for the fertilized egg is _____.
   a. gene
   b. zygote
   c. chromosome
   d. teratogen

2. At about 6 or 7 months of age, an infant starts rhythmically repeating various syllables. This is called _____.
   a. baby talk
   b. holophrase
   c. telegraphic speech
   d. babbling

3. According to Piaget's theory of cognitive development, children are in the _____ stage if they have symbolic ability but lack conservation.
   a. sensorimotor
   b. preoperational
   c. concrete operational
   d. formal operational

4. According to Piaget, _____ is the interpretation of new experiences in terms of present schemas, and _____ is the modification of present schemas to fit with new experiences.

   a. assimilation; accommodation

   b. accommodation; assimilation

   c. reversibility; centration

   d. centration; reversibility

5. Vygotsky's term for the difference between what a child can actually do and what the child can do with the help of others is _____.

   a. zone of proximal development

   b. erogenous zone

   c. scaffolding

   d. cohort effect

6. In a _____ study, people of different ages are studied at one point in time and compared with one another.

   a. cross-sectional

   b. longitudinal

   c. habituation

   d. scaffolding

7. According to Kohlberg, a person who complies with rules and laws to avoid punishment is in the _____ level of moral development.

   a. preconventional

   b. conventional

   c. postconventional

   d. authoritarian

8. According to Ainsworth, a child who shows little distress when the mother leaves in the Srange Situation procedure and neglects her when she returns has developed a(n) _____ attachment.

   a. secure

   b. insecure-disorganized

   c. insecure-ambivalent

   d. insecure-avoidant

9. Which of the following parenting styles is most positively related to academic success, happiness, independence, and self-confidence?

   a. authoritative

   b. authoritarian

   c. permissive

   d. indifferent

10. According to Erikson's psychosocial theory, _____ is the issue that a person faces during adolescence.

    a. initiative versus guilt

    b. industry versus inferiority

    c. identity versus role confusion

    d. intimacy versus isolation

11. During the _____ stage of prenatal development (the final stage starting about two months after conception), the body structures and organs complete their growth.

    a. embryonic

    b. fetal

    c. germinal

    d. zygote

12. A decrease in the physiological responding to a stimulus once it becomes familiar is called _____.

    a. assimilation

    b. centration

    c. habituation

    d. conservation

13. Johnny, who is only 4 years old, stands in front of you blocking your view of the television screen, and he does not realize that he is doing so. He thinks that his view is the same as yours. Johnny is displaying _____ and is in Piaget's _____ stage of cognitive development.

    a. egocentrism; concrete

    b. egocentrism; preoperational

    c. centration; concrete

    d. centration; preoperational

14. Michelle, who is 18 months old, has a pet dog named Sam. After she learns the name of her dog, she calls all of the dogs she sees Sam. Michelle is demonstrating _____.
    a. babbling
    b. holophrase
    c. underextension
    d. overextension

15. Studies of intelligence in adulthood reveal that fluid intelligence abilities _____ with age, and crystallized intelligence abilities _____ with age.
    a. increase; increase
    b. increase; decrease
    c. decrease; increase
    d. decrease; decrease

Chapter ConceptCheck Answers

ConceptCheck | 1

- Teratogens are agents such as drugs, viruses, and diseases and conditions such as malnutrition that impair prenatal development and lead to birth defects or even death. Thus, they are not due to heredity (nature). They are prenatal environmental factors, and therefore their effects are due to nurture.

- Habituation, a decrease in physiological responding to a stimulus once it becomes familiar, is used to determine what stimuli an infant can perceptually discriminate. The inference is that if an infant looks longer at a new stimulus than an old one, then the infant must be able to perceive the difference. In addition to looking, researchers use other measures such as changes in the rates of sucking on a pacifier and the infant's heart rate.

ConceptCheck | 2

- Overextension and underextension in language development involve using a word too broadly or too narrowly, respectively. Through experience we learn to extend a word's meaning correctly. Overextension can be viewed as overassimilation—incorrectly attempting to assimilate the new object into the existing schema for the word when accommodation is necessary.

Underextension can be viewed as underassimilation—failing to assimilate the new object into the existing schema for the word. In overextension, the child assimilates when he needs to accommodate, and in underextension, the child does not assimilate when he needs to assimilate.

- A child who thought that a pizza cut into eight slices was more than the same pizza cut into six slices would be in the preoperational stage, because she is not demonstrating knowledge of conservation. She is centering her attention on the number of slices and not the size of the slices.

- Together these two concepts, zone of proximal development and scaffolding, make up a teaching method. First, the zone of proximal development (the difference between what a child can actually do and what the child could do with help) is determined. Then scaffolding (adjusting the level of help in relation to the child's level of performance) is used to structure and guide the learning to the upper level of the child's zone of proximal development.

- In a cross-sectional study, groups of participants of different ages are studied at one point in time. In a longitudinal study, one group of participants is studied at many different points in time as the group ages. The cross-sectional method is less time-consuming and expensive but subject to cohort effects created by factors unique to each generation in the study. Because the same participants are tested at different ages, the longitudinal method is not subject to such effects; but due to participant attrition, sample-group changes over time may impact the results.

ConceptCheck | 3

- The response indicates that Heinz should not steal the drug because he would be caught and sent to jail—punished. Even if he weren't caught, his conscience would punish him. Thus, Kohlberg would classify this explanation for not stealing the drug as reflective of Stage 1 (punishment orientation) in which people comply with rules in order to avoid punishment.

- An infant's temperament is the set of innate dispositions that lead him to behave in a certain way. It determines the infant's responsiveness in interactions with caregivers, how happy he is, how much he cries, and so on. The temperaments of infants vary greatly. Those that fit the child-rearing expectations and personality of the caregivers likely facilitate attachment formation. Difficult infants probably do not.

- Authoritarian parents are demanding and expect unquestioned obedience, are not responsive to their children's desires, and do not communicate well with their children. Authoritative parents, however, are demanding but reasonably so. Rather than demanding blind obedience, they explain the reasoning behind rules. Unlike authoritarian parents, they both are responsive to and communicate well with their children.

- A child without understanding of false beliefs would predict that Big Bird will look for the ball in the toy chest where Cookie Monster has rehidden it, because the child does not understand that others can have beliefs that disagree with his. If the child has an understanding of false beliefs, he would predict that Big Bird will look in the box where he had earlier put the ball because he realizes that others can have beliefs that disagree with his.

- Erikson thought that at each stage there is a major psychosocial issue or crisis (e.g., identity versus role confusion) that has to be resolved and whose resolution greatly impacts one's development. For each crisis, there is a positive adaptive resolution and a negative maladaptive resolution. When an issue is positively resolved, social competence increases and one is more adequately prepared for the next issue.

Answers to Key Terms Exercise

1. object permanence
2. rooting reflex
3. zygote
4. accommodation
5. authoritative parenting
6. secure attachment
7. baby talk (parentese)
8. teratogens
9. longitudinal study
10. zone of proximal development
11. phonemes
12. telegraphic speech
13. conservation
14. scaffolding
15. temperament

Answers to Practice Test Questions

1. b; zygote
2. d; babbling
3. b; preoperational
4. a; assimilation; accommodation
5. a; zone of proximal development
6. a; cross-sectional
7. a; preconventional
8. d; insecure-avoidant
9. a; authoritative
10. c; identity versus role confusion
11. b; fetal
12. c; habituation
13. b; egocentrism; preoperational
14. d; overextension
15. c; decrease; increase

Courtesy of Jackie Saccoccio and 11R, NY

8

Personality Theories and Assessment

As with intelligence, psychologists cannot agree upon a definition of *personality,* a word that we all use and whose meaning we think we know. In its everyday usage, personality is an individual's characteristic ways of acting and thinking. If I asked you to describe the personality of your best friend or your mother, you probably would respond with a set of adjectives that capture the defining characteristics (prominent qualities) of that person's behavior, such as caring, independent, and honest. You would also probably assume that these behavioral characteristics originate from within the person, that they are internally based. For our purposes, this is a satisfactory definition of **personality**—a person's internally based characteristic ways of acting and thinking.

> **personality** A person's internally based characteristic ways of acting and thinking.

Psychologists call such internally based characteristics "personality traits." Each trait corresponds to a continuum on which one end is the behavioral extreme for that characteristic and the other end is its opposite. For example, the extremes for caring would be "very caring" and "very uncaring." These trait dimensions are the building blocks of personality. Individuals' personalities correspond to their patterns of traits, leading to personality differences between people. But what causes these differences? What makes us the way that we are?

Throughout history, all sorts of theories of personality differences have been proposed. For example, the ancient Greeks thought that one's mental health (personality) was a function of the balance of four humors, or bodily fluids—black bile, yellow bile, blood, and phlegm. According to Franz Gall's phrenology theory in the early nineteenth century, personality was determined by the contours and bumps of a person's head. In the twentieth century, William Sheldon's theory proposed that personality is tied to one's body type. As you might guess, none of these theories proved very satisfactory.

Today, there are many theoretical approaches to the study of personality, but we will limit our discussion to the four major types of theories—psychoanalytic, humanistic, social-cognitive, and trait. These theories vary greatly in how they explain personality differences and in what aspects of personality they emphasize and study. Psychoanalytic theories emphasize the interaction of unconscious forces and childhood experiences in determining personality development. Humanistic theories emphasize the personal growth motive. Social-cognitive theories emphasize the importance of thought processes and interactions with others. Trait theories emphasize the role of basic personality dimensions. Because our descriptions of these theories will focus on what each one emphasizes, there will not be as much continuity as you might like across these discussions. Unfortunately, this is unavoidable given the diverse nature of these approaches.

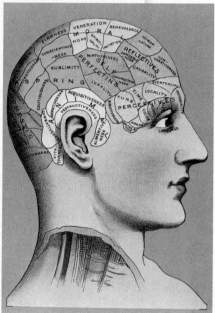

© Corbis

In the early nineteenth century, Franz Gall developed the phrenology theory of personality, which assumed that a person's personality could be determined by measuring the bumps on his skull. Areas that he believed were associated with particular personality traits are indicated in this phrenology chart. Although Gall's idea that brain functions, such as language, tend to be localized is true (as we learned in Chapter 2), the size of the bumps on a person's head has nothing to do with their personality.

Three of these four theoretical approaches also focus on problems in personality development; they have thus led to the development of therapies (based on the theories) to treat such problems. The prime example is psychoanalysis, developed by Freud; the humanistic approach and the social-cognitive approach have also led to well-known styles of therapy. We will discuss all of these therapies in Chapter 10, Abnormal Psychology.

The trait approach is not a therapeutic approach; it is more of a descriptive approach to personality. Its primary aim is to identify the set of traits—behavioral dimensions—necessary to describe human personality. Instead of leading to styles of therapy, trait theories often lead to personality tests designed to measure their theorized dimensions of personality. This is why the trait approach is paired with personality assessment in the final section of this chapter. We will treat the other three theoretical approaches in the order that they appeared historically—psychoanalytic followed by humanistic and social-cognitive. The humanistic approach and the social-cognitive approach were both reactions to the earlier psychoanalytic and behavioral approaches; therefore, we have paired them together in the second section. We begin with Freud's psychoanalytic theory of personality, which influenced not only psychological theorizing about personality but also twentieth-century culture.

The Psychoanalytic Approach to Personality

Freud developed his landmark psychoanalytic theory of personality starting in the late nineteenth century and continuing until his death in 1939. His first solo authored book, *The Interpretation of Dreams*, came out in 1900 and was followed by more than 20 other volumes. Freud's psychoanalytic theory has been so influential that many of its important concepts—id, ego, defense mechanisms, Oedipus conflict, Freudian slip, and so on—have become part of our culture. Freud's theory is usually referred to as classical psychoanalytic theory. This distinguishes it from both other psychoanalytic theories developed by Freud's disciples and from contemporary psychodynamic theories (personality theories with a psychoanalytic base). The theories of Freud's disciples are usually called neo-Freudian theories ("neo" is Greek for new). The neo-Freudian theories shared many assumptions with classical Freudian theory, but differed in one or more important ways. Modern psychodynamic theories have veered even further away from Freud's original work. They still emphasize the importance of childhood experiences, unconscious thought processes, and addressing inner conflicts, but they don't use much of Freud's terminology nor do they focus on sex as the origin of personality. In this chapter, we will first discuss Freud's classical psychoanalytic theory and then describe some prominent neo-Freudian theories of personality.

Freudian Classical Psychoanalytic Theory of Personality

Freud received a medical degree from the University of Vienna and established a practice as a clinical neurologist treating patients with emotional disorders.

Through his work with these patients, Freud became convinced that sex was a primary cause of emotional problems (Freud, 1905/1953b). Sex, including infantile sexuality, became a critical component of his personality theory (Freud 1900/1953a, 1901/1960, 1916 & 1917/1963, 1933/1964). To help you understand Freud's theory, we will consider its three main elements: (1) different levels of awareness, with an emphasis on the role of the unconscious; (2) the dynamic interplay between the three parts of the personality—id, ego, and superego; and (3) the psychosexual stage theory of personality development.

Sigmund Freud

Freud's three levels of awareness. According to Freud, the mind has three levels of awareness—the conscious, the preconscious, and the unconscious. This three-part division of awareness is Freud's famous iceberg model of the mind (Figure 8.1). The iceberg's visible

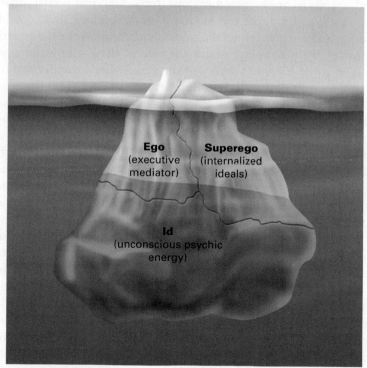

Conscious mind
(present awareness)

Preconscious mind
(outside awareness but accessible)

Unconscious mind
(not accessible)

Figure 8.1 | Freud's Iceberg Model of the Mind | In the iceberg model of the mind, the small part above water is our conscious mind; the part just below the surface is the preconscious; and the major portion, hidden below water, is the unconscious. A person has access only to the conscious and preconscious levels of awareness. The conscious mind is what the person is presently thinking about, and the preconscious mind is information that the person could bring into conscious awareness.

conscious mind Freud's term for what we are presently aware of.

preconscious mind Freud's term for what is stored in one's memory that one is not presently aware of but can access.

unconscious mind Freud's term for the part of our mind that we cannot become aware of.

id The part of the personality that a person is born with, where the biological instinctual drives reside, and that is located totally in the unconscious mind.

pleasure principle The principle of seeking immediate gratification for instinctual drives without concern for the consequences.

tip above the surface is the **conscious mind,** what you are presently aware of. In memory terms, this is your short-term memory. It is what you are thinking about right now. The part of the iceberg just beneath the surface is the **preconscious mind,** what is stored in your memory that you are not presently aware of but can gain access to. In memory terms, this is your long-term memory. For example, you are not presently thinking about your birthday, but if I asked you what day your birthday was, you could bring that information from the preconscious to the conscious level of awareness.

It is the third level of awareness, the unconscious, that Freud emphasized in his personality theory. In Freud's iceberg model, the large base of the iceberg that is hidden deep beneath the surface is the **unconscious mind,** the part of our mind that we cannot freely access. Freud believed this area contains the primary motivations for all of our actions and feelings, including our biological instinctual drives (such as for food and sex) and our repressed unacceptable thoughts, memories, and feelings, especially unresolved conflicts from our early childhood experiences. To better understand the role of these motivations, we need to become familiar with Freud's theory of the personality structure and his psychosexual stage theory of personality development.

Freud's three-part personality structure. Freud divided the personality structure into three parts—id, ego, and superego. These are mental processes or systems and not actual physical structures. Freud believed that personality is the product of the dynamic interaction of these three systems. The id is the original personality, the only part present at birth and the part out of which the other two parts of our personality emerge. As you can see in Figure 8.1, the id resides entirely in the unconscious part of the mind. The **id** includes biological instinctual drives, the primitive parts of personality located in the unconscious. Freud grouped these instinctual drives into life instincts (survival, reproduction, and pleasure drives such as for food, water, and sex) and death instincts (destructive and aggressive drives that are detrimental to survival). Freud downplayed the death instincts in his theory and emphasized the life instincts, especially sex. The id contains psychic energy, which attempts to satisfy these instinctual drives according to the **pleasure principle**—immediate gratification for these drives without concern for the consequences. Thus, the id is like a spoiled child, totally self-centered and focused on satisfying these drives. For example, if you were hungry, the id, using the pleasure principle, would lead you to take any food that is available without concern for whom it belongs to.

Obviously the id cannot operate totally unchecked. We cannot go around taking anything we want to satisfy the id's drives. Our behavior is constrained by social norms and laws. We have to buy food from markets, stores, and restaurants.

Our personality develops as we find ways to meet our needs within these social constraints. The second part of the personality structure, the **ego,** starts developing during the first year or so of life in order to find realistic outlets for the id's needs. Because the ego emerges out of the id, it derives its psychic energy from the id. The ego has the task of protecting the personality while ensuring that the id's drives are satisfied.

ego The part of the personality that starts developing in the first year or so of life in order to find realistic outlets for the id's instinctual drives.

reality principle The principle of finding gratification for instinctual drives within the constraints of reality (norms of society).

superego The part of the personality that represents one's conscience and idealized standards of behavior.

defense mechanism A process used by the ego to distort reality and protect a person from anxiety.

The ego, then, is the pragmatic part of the personality; it weighs the risks of an action before acting. The ego uses the **reality principle**—finding gratification for instinctual drives within the constraints of reality (the norms and laws of society). In order to do this, the ego spans all three levels of awareness (see Figure 8.1). Because of its ties to the id, part of the ego must be located in the unconscious; and because of its ties to reality (the external world), part of it must be in the conscious and preconscious. The ego uses memory and conscious thought processes, such as reasoning, to carry out its job.

The ego functions as the manager or executive of the personality. It must mediate not only between the instinctual drives of the id and reality but also between these drives and the third part of the personality structure, the **superego,** which represents the conscience and idealized standards of behavior in a particular culture. The superego emerges during childhood and, like the ego, develops from id energy and spans all levels of awareness. It tells the ego how one ought to act. Thus, the superego might be said to act in accordance with a morality principle. For example, if the id hunger drive demanded satisfaction, and the ego had found a way to steal some food without being caught, the superego would threaten to overwhelm the individual with guilt and shame for such an act. Inevitably, the demands of the superego and the id will come into conflict, and the ego will have to resolve this turmoil within the constraints of reality. This is not an easy task.

Here is why the ego's job is so difficult. Imagine that your parents are making conflicting demands on you. For example, when you were deciding which college to attend, let's say your father wanted you to attend a state university and your mother wanted you to attend her private college alma mater. Imagine also that your boyfriend or girlfriend is adding a third level of conflicting demands (wanting to go to school together at the local community college). You want to satisfy all three, but because the demands are conflicting, it is not possible. You get anxious, because there is no good resolution to the conflict. This is what often happens to the ego in its role as mediator between its three masters (id, superego, and reality). To prevent being overcome with anxiety, the ego uses what Freud called **defense mechanisms,** processes that distort reality and protect us from anxiety (Freud, 1936). The ego has many different defense mechanisms available for such self-deception, including repression, denial, displacement, and rationalization. Table 8.1 (page 338) provides descriptions and examples of several defense mechanisms.

Table 8.1	Some of Freud's Defense Mechanisms	
Defense Mechanism	**Description**	**Example**
Repression	Unknowingly placing an unpleasant memory or thought in the unconscious	Not remembering a traumatic incident in which you witnessed a crime
Regression	Reverting back to immature behavior from an earlier stage of development	Throwing temper tantrums as an adult when you don't get your way
Denial	Refusing to acknowledge anxiety-provoking realities	Refusing to accept evidence that your spouse is having an affair
Displacement	Redirecting unacceptable feelings from the original source to a safer, substitute target	Taking your anger toward your boss out on your spouse or children by yelling at them and not your boss
Sublimation	Replacing socially unacceptable impulses with socially acceptable behavior	Channeling aggressive drives into playing football or inappropriate sexual desires into art
Reaction formation	Acting in exactly the opposite way to one's unacceptable impulses	Being overprotective of and lavishing attention on an unwanted child
Projection	Attributing one's own unacceptable feelings and thoughts to others and not yourself	Accusing your boyfriend of cheating on you because you have felt like cheating on him
Rationalization	Creating false excuses for one's unacceptable feelings, thoughts, or behavior	Justifying cheating on an exam by saying that everyone else cheats

Freud thought of repression as the primary defense mechanism. He believed that repression, along with other defense mechanisms, helps us deal with anxiety. If we are unaware of unacceptable feelings, memories, and thoughts (they have been put in our unconscious), then we cannot be anxious about them. But it is important to remember that Freud proposed that repression occurs automatically—without conscious awareness. Once repressed, we have no conscious memory that the thought, event, or impulse ever existed. Although defense mechanisms may indeed help us with anxiety, we now know that we may also become dependent upon them. They may prevent us from facing our problems and dealing with them. The best defense mechanism may be using no defense mechanisms. Facing up to problems may allow us to see that reality is not as bad as we thought, and that consciously working to change reality is more beneficial than distorting it.

Freud believed that unhealthy personalities develop not only when we become too dependent upon defense mechanisms, but also when the id or superego is unusually strong or the ego is unusually weak. In such cases, the ego cannot control the other two processes. For example, a person with a weak ego would not be able to hold the id drives in check, possibly leading to a self-centered personality. Or, a person with an overly strong superego would be too concerned with morality, possibly leading to a guilt-ridden personality. A healthy personality, according to Freud's personality structure, is one in which none of the three personality systems (id, ego, and superego) is dominating, allowing the three systems to interact in a relatively harmonious way.

"Look, call it denial if you like, but I think what goes on in my personal life is none of my own damn business."

In addition to imbalances between the three personality parts, Freud stressed the importance of our early childhood experiences in determining our adult personality traits. In fact, he thought that our experiences during the first 6 years or so of life were critical in the development of our adult personality. To understand exactly how Freud proposed that early childhood experiences impact personality, we now turn to a consideration of his psychosexual stage theory.

Freud's psychosexual stage theory. Freud did not spend much time observing children to help him develop his psychosexual stage theory of personality development. Freud's psychosexual stage theory was developed chiefly from his own childhood memories and from his years of interactions with his patients and their case studies, which included their childhood memories.

Two key concepts in his psychosexual theory are erogenous zone and fixation. An **erogenous zone** is the area of the body where the id's pleasure-seeking psychic energy is focused during a particular stage of psychosexual development. The erogenous zone feels good when stimulated in various ways. Thus, the erogenous zones are the body areas where instinctual satisfaction can be obtained. Each of Freud's psychosexual stages is named after the erogenous zone involved, and a change in location of the erogenous zone designates the beginning of a new stage. For example, the first stage is called the oral stage, and the erogenous zone is the mouth area, so pleasure is derived from oral activities such as sucking. Freud proposed five stages—oral, anal, phallic, latency, and genital. They are outlined in Table 8.2 (page 340), with the erogenous zone for each stage indicated.

Freud's concept of fixation is important in understanding how he believed our childhood experiences impact our adult personality. A **fixation** occurs when a portion of the id's pleasure-seeking energy remains in an earlier psychosexual stage because of excessive or insufficient gratification of our instinctual needs during that stage of development. A person who is overindulged will want to stay and not move on, while a person who is frustrated has difficulty moving on because his needs are not met. The stronger the fixation, the more of the id's pleasure-seeking energy remains in

erogenous zone The area of the body where the id's pleasure-seeking energies are focused during a particular stage of psychosexual development.

fixation Some of the id's pleasure-seeking energies remaining stuck in a psychosexual stage due to excessive or insufficient gratification of instinctual needs.

Table 8.2	Freud's Psychosexual Stages of Personality Development	
Stage (age range)	**Erogenous Zone**	**Activity Focus**
Oral (birth to 1-1/2 years)	Mouth, lips, and tongue	Sucking, biting, and chewing
Anal (1-1/2 to 3 years)	Anus	Bowel retention and elimination
Phallic (3 to 6 years)	Genitals	Genital stimulation, attraction to opposite-sex parent and later identifying with same-sex parent to learn gender role and sense of morality
Latency (6 years to puberty)	No erogenous zone	Cognitive and social development
Genital (puberty through adulthood)	Genitals	Development of sexual relationships, moving toward intimate adult relationships

that stage. Such fixations continue throughout the person's life and impact his behavior and personality traits. For example, a person who is fixated in the oral stage because of excessive gratification may become overly concerned with oral activities such as smoking, eating, and drinking. Because his oral needs have been overindulged, such a person may continue to depend upon others to meet his needs and thus have a dependent personality. Such a person is also likely to be gullible or willing to "swallow" anything. We will consider some other examples of fixation as we describe the five stages.

In the **oral stage** (from birth to 18 months), the erogenous zones are the mouth, lips, and tongue, and the child derives pleasure from oral activities such as sucking, biting, and chewing. As already pointed out, a fixation would lead to having a preoccupation with oral behaviors, such as smoking, gum chewing, over-eating, or even talking too much. Freud himself had such a preoccupation with smoking. He smoked 20 or so cigars a day and had numerous operations for cancer in his mouth, which eventually led to his death (Larsen & Buss, 2000). Many other personality characteristics can also stem from oral fixations. For example, a fixation created by too little gratification might lead to an excessively mistrustful person. The deprived infant has presumably learned that the world cannot be trusted to provide for basic needs.

oral stage of psychosexual development The first stage in Freud's theory (from birth to 18 months), in which the erogenous zones are the mouth, lips, and tongue, and the child derives pleasure from oral activities such as sucking, biting, and chewing.

anal stage of psychosexual development The second stage in Freud's theory (from 18 months to 3 years), in which the erogenous zone is the anus, and the child derives pleasure from stimulation of the anal region through having and withholding bowel movements.

In the **anal stage** (from about 18 months to 3 years), the erogenous zone is the anus, and the child derives pleasure from stimulation of the anal region through having and withholding bowel movements. Toilet training and the issue of control are major concerns in this stage. Parents try to get the child to have self-control during toilet training. Freud believed that fixations during this stage depend upon how toilet training is approached by the parents. Such fixations can lead to two famous adult personalities, anal retentive and anal expulsive. Both are reactions to harsh toilet training in which the parents admonish and punish the child for failures. If the child reacts to this harsh toilet training by trying to get even with the parents and withholding bowel movements, an anal-retentive personality with the traits of orderliness, neatness, stinginess, and obstinacy develops. The anal-expulsive personality develops when children rebel against harsh training and have bowel movements whenever and wherever they please. Such people tend to be sloppy, disorderly, and possibly even destructive and cruel.

In the **phallic stage** (from age 3 to 6 years), the erogenous zone is located at the genitals, and the child derives pleasure from genital stimulation. According to Freud, there is much psychological conflict in this stage, including the Oedipus conflict for boys. In the **Oedipus conflict,** the little boy becomes sexually attracted to his mother and fears the father (his rival) will find out and castrate him. This parallels the Greek tragedy *Oedipus Rex,* in which Oedipus unknowingly kills his father, marries his mother, and then realizes what he's done and gouges his eyes out as punishment. Freud was much less confident about the existence of a comparable Electra conflict for girls, in which a girl is supposedly attracted to her father due to penis envy.

Freud believed that children resolve the conflicts in this stage by repressing their desire for the opposite-sex parent and identifying with the same-sex parent. It is in this process of **identification** that Freud believed children adopt the characteristics of the same-sex parent and learn their gender roles. For example, a little boy would adopt the behaviors and attitudes of his father. According to Freud, unsuccessful resolution of these conflicts would result in a child having a conflicted gender role, sexual relationship problems with the opposite sex, and possibly a homosexual orientation. It is also during this identification process that the superego develops, as a child learns his sense of morality by adopting the attitudes and values of his parents.

Freud considered the final two stages of his psychosexual theory the least important for personality development. He assumed that how a child progresses through the first three stages pretty much determined the child's adult personality. In the **latency stage** (from about age 6

"During the next stage of my development, Dad, I'll be drawing closer to my mother—I'll get back to you in my teens."

Lee Lorenz/The New Yorker Collection/The Cartoon Bank

phallic stage of psychosexual development The third stage in Freud's theory (from 3 to 6 years), in which the erogenous zone is located at the genitals, and the child derives pleasure from genital stimulation.

Oedipus conflict A phallic stage conflict for a boy in which the boy becomes sexually attracted to his mother and fears his father will find out and castrate him.

identification The process by which children adopt the characteristics of the same-sex parent and learn their gender role and sense of morality.

latency stage of psychosexual development The fourth stage in Freud's theory (from 6 years old to puberty), in which there is no erogenous zone, sexual feelings are repressed, and the focus is on cognitive and social development.

genital stage of psychosexual development The fifth stage in Freud's theory (from puberty through adulthood), in which the erogenous zone is at the genitals, and the child develops sexual relationships, moving toward intimate adult relationships.

to puberty), there is no erogenous zone, sexual drives become less active, and the focus is on cognitive and social development. A child of this age is most interested in school, sports, hobbies, and in developing friendships with other children of the same sex. In the **genital stage** (from puberty through adulthood), the erogenous zone is at the genitals again, and Freud believed that in this stage a person develops sexual relationships in a move toward intimate adult relationships.

Evaluation of Freud's psychoanalytic theory of personality. Freud's ideas were controversial when he first proposed them and have remained controversial over the past century. Let's consider some of the criticisms of his major concepts. First, consider Freud's "unconscious" level of awareness. Because this concept is not accessible to anyone, it is impossible to examine scientifically and thus cannot be experimentally tested. We can't observe and study a factor that we are not aware of. This criticism does not deny that unconscious processing greatly impacts thinking and behavior. On the contrary, it acknowledges that the impact is great. Think back to Chapter 3, on the human senses and perception, to Chapter 5, on memory, and to Chapter 6, on thinking. Our conscious level of awareness of these important processes is like Freud's "tip of the iceberg." We have learned, however, that this iceberg is not a storehouse of instinctual drives, conflicts, and repressed memories and desires as Freud proposed. It is the location of all of our cognitive processes and the knowledge base they use—the center of our information processing. Freud was correct in pointing to unconscious processing as crucial, but he was incorrect about its role and the nature of its importance.

Freud was also correct in pointing to the importance of early childhood experience, but he was again incorrect about the nature of its importance. There is little evidence that psychosexual stages impact development, but there is evidence that many of the concepts we discussed in the last chapter, such as the connection between the type of attachment an infant forms and parenting style, are important. What about Freud's main defense mechanism, repression? Contemporary memory researchers think that it seldom, if ever, occurs (Holmes, 1990; Loftus & Ketcham, 1994; McNally, 2003). Remember the discussion of so-called recovered memories in Chapter 5, on memory? We understand today how Freud's questioning during therapy may have created such "repressed" memories in his patients. Do the other defense mechanisms fare any better? There is evidence that we do use certain defense mechanisms to ward off anxiety, though we do not necessarily do so unconsciously.

We must remember that Freud started developing his theory over 100 years ago. Our world and the state of psychological research knowledge were very different then. So, it is not surprising that Freud's theory doesn't stand up very well today. What is surprising is that he could develop a theory from such a scant database, a theory that has had such great impact on our thinking and culture.

In 1999 he was on the cover of a special issue of *Time* magazine commemorating the 100 greatest thinkers and scientists of the twentieth century. We can only speculate on what his theory would be like if he had started in 1990 rather than 1890.

Neo-Freudian Theories of Personality

Even Freud's own circle of psychoanalysts disagreed with him on some aspects of his theory. These disagreements led them to develop psychoanalytic theories that accepted most of Freud's basic ideas but differed from Freud in one or more important ways. They became known as neo-Freudian psychoanalytic theorists. In addition to Erik Erikson, whose psychosocial stage theory of development was described in the last chapter, the major neo-Freudian theorists were Carl Jung, Alfred Adler, and Karen Horney (pronounced HORN-eye). In general, these three neo-Freudian theorists, like Erikson, thought that Freud placed too much importance on psychosexual development and sexual drives and not enough emphasis on social and cultural influences on the development of personality. We discuss Jung first because, other than Freud, he is the best-known psychoanalytic theorist.

Jung's collective unconscious. Carl Jung extended Freud's notion of the unconscious to include not only the personal unconscious—each individual's instinctual drives and repressed memories and conflicts—but also the collective unconscious, the accumulated universal experiences of humankind. Each of us inherits this same cumulative storehouse of all human experience that is manifested in archetypes—symbolic images of all of the important themes in the history of humankind (such as God, the mother, and the hero). The archetypes in the collective unconscious are why myths and legends in very diverse cultures tend to have common themes. In addition to these shared universal archetypes, each of us inherits more specific ones that guide our individual personality development. Jung's theoretical concepts are rather mystical and not really scientific. His interest in the mystical side of life greatly influenced his theory, and his concepts, such as the collective unconscious and archetypes, are beyond empirical verification. These symbolic, mystical aspects of Jung's theory may be why it has been more popular in the fields of religion, anthropology, and literature than in psychology.

Personality psychologists, however, have pursued some other aspects of Jung's theory. Most prominently, Jung proposed two main personality attitudes—extraversion and introversion. People's attitudes focus them toward the external, objective world (extraversion) or toward the inner, subjective world (introversion). Along with these two general outlooks, Jung proposed four functions (or cognitive styles)—sensing and intuiting for gathering information and thinking and feeling

Carl Jung

Alfred Adler

for evaluating information. Across individuals, the development of these four functions varies, with one of them being dominant. These two attitudes and four functions lead to eight possible personality types. These eight types were the basis for a personality test, the Myers-Briggs Type Indicator, developed in the 1920s by Katherine Briggs and her daughter, Isabel Myers. This test has been the primary tool for research on Jung's personality types, and it is still in use today (Myers & McCaulley, 1985). In addition, Jung's two personality attitudes, extraversion and introversion, play a central role in contemporary trait theories of personality, which we will discuss in the last section of this chapter.

Adler's striving for superiority. Another neo-Freudian theorist, Alfred Adler, disagreed with Freud's assumption that the main motivation in personality development is the satisfaction of sexual urges. Adler thought that the main motivation is what he termed "striving for superiority," the need to overcome the sense of inferiority that we feel as infants, given our totally helpless and dependent state. Adler believed that these feelings of inferiority serve as our basic motivation. They lead us to grow and strive toward success. A healthy person learns to cope with these feelings, becomes competent, and develops a sense of self-esteem. Parental love and support help a child overcome her initial feelings of inferiority. Adler used the phrase "inferiority complex" to describe the strong feelings felt by those who never overcome the initial feeling of inferiority. People with an inferiority complex often have unloving, neglectful, or indifferent parents. The complex leads to feelings of worthlessness and a mistrust of others. Adler also defined what he termed a "superiority complex," an exaggerated opinion of one's abilities. This leads to a self-centered, vain person.

Horney and the need for security. Like Adler, Karen Horney focused on our early social experiences with our parents, not on instinctual biological drives. Unlike Adler, Horney's focus was on dealing with our need for security rather than a sense of inferiority. Remember the importance of a secure attachment for infants that we discussed in the last chapter, on human development? According to Horney's theory, a child's caregivers must provide a sense of security for a healthy personality to develop. Children whose parents do not lead them to feel secure would suffer from what Horney called "basic anxiety," a feeling of helplessness and insecurity in a hostile world. This basic anxiety about personal relationships may lead to neurotic behavior and a disordered personality (Horney, 1937). Horney differentiated three neurotic personality patterns—moving toward people (a compliant, submissive person), moving against people (an aggressive, domineering person), and moving away from people (a detached, aloof person). This focus of Horney and other

Karen Horney

neo-Freudian theorists on the importance of interpersonal relationships, both in childhood and in adulthood, continues in contemporary psychodynamic theory (Westen, 1998).

Section Summary

In the late nineteenth and early twentieth centuries, Freud developed his psychoanalytic theory of personality. He divided the mind into three levels of awareness—conscious, preconscious, and unconscious—with the unconscious (the part that we cannot become aware of) being the most important in his theory. It is the unconscious that contains life and death instinctual drives, the primary motivators for all of our actions and feelings. In addition, there are three parts of the personality structure—the id (which contains the instinctual drives and is located totally in the unconscious), the ego (the manager of the personality), and the superego (our conscience and sense of morality). The ego and the superego span all three levels of awareness. The ego attempts to find gratification for the id's instinctual drives within the constraints of the superego and reality (societal laws and norms). When the ego cannot achieve this difficult task, we become anxious. To combat such anxiety, Freud suggested that we use defense mechanisms, which protect us from anxiety by distorting reality. The primary defense mechanism is repression, unknowingly placing an unpleasant memory or thought in the unconscious, where it cannot bother us.

Freud also emphasized the importance of early childhood experience in his theory. He proposed that how successfully a child progresses through the early psychosexual stages greatly impacts his personality development. Freud proposed five psychosexual stages, with the first three being most important to our personality development. The stages—in order, with the erogenous zone (pleasure center) indicated for that stage—are oral (mouth), anal (anus), phallic (genitals), latency (no erogenous zone), and genital (genitals). A fixation, which occurs when some of the id's pleasure-seeking energies remain in a stage because of excessive or insufficient gratification, influences a person's behavior and personality for the rest of her life. For example, a person with an oral fixation will seek physical pleasure from oral activities and may be overly dependent and gullible. The important Oedipus conflict for boys (and Electra conflict for girls) in which the child is attracted to the opposite-sex parent occurs in the phallic stage of development from about age 3 to age 6. Resolution of this conflict leads the child to identify with the same-sex parent and learn his or her proper gender role and sense of morality.

Neo-Freudian theorists were psychoanalytic theorists who agreed with much of Freud's theory but disagreed with some of Freud's key assumptions, which led them to develop their own versions of psychoanalytic theory. For example, Carl Jung theorized that, in addition to the personal unconscious, we have a collective unconscious that contains the accumulated experiences of humankind. Alfred Adler proposed that the main motivation was not sexual, but rather a striving for superiority in which we must overcome the sense of inferiority that we feel as infants. Failure to do so leads to an inferiority complex. Karen Horney focused her attention on our need for security as infants, rather than our sense of inferiority. She argued that if our caregivers do not help us to gain a feeling of security, we suffer from a sense of basic anxiety, which leads to various types of personality problems.

ConceptCheck | 1

Explain, according to Freudian theory, why the ego has such a difficult job.

Explain the difference between Freud's two defense mechanisms—reaction formation and projection.

Explain how fixations in psychosexual development affect adult behavior and personality.

The Humanistic Approach and the Social-Cognitive Approach to Personality

Humanistic theories of personality developed during the 1960s as part of the general humanistic movement in psychology. The humanistic movement was in response to the deterministic psychoanalytic and strict behavioral psychological approaches that dominated psychology and the study of personality at that time. As we just discussed, the classical psychoanalytic approach assumes that personality is a product of how the id's unconscious instinctual drives find satisfaction, especially during the first three psychosexual stages. The strict behavioral approach assumes that our personality and behavior are merely products of our environment, as a result of classical and operant conditioning (discussed in Chapter 4). Our personality is determined by our behavior and is conditioned by environmental events. According to both approaches, we are not in charge of our behavior and personality development. According to the psychoanalytic approach, our unconscious instinctual drives are the major motivators of our behavior and personality development. According to the behavioral approach, the environment motivates and controls our actions. In contrast, the humanistic approach emphasizes conscious free will in one's actions, the uniqueness of the individual person, and personal growth. Unlike the psychoanalytic approach's focus on our personality problems, the humanistic approach centers on the positive motivations for our actions and development, especially personal growth. To familiarize you with this approach, we will describe the theories of the two major humanistic proponents, Abraham Maslow and Carl Rogers.

At about the same time as the humanists, social-cognitive theorists rebelled against the narrowness of the strict behavioral approach to the development of personality. The behavioral approach limited itself to the factors of classical and operant conditioning for learning behaviors (personality). Social-cognitive theorists agreed that conditioning was important, but thought that the situation was more complex than that. Remember, Albert Bandura's work on social (observational) learning in Chapter 4 demonstrated our ability to learn from observing others without direct reinforcement, which meant that social and cognitive factors were involved in learning. The social-cognitive approach includes social and cognitive factors along with conditioning to explain personality development. Thus, the strict behavioral approach to personality is subsumed under the more extensive social-cognitive approach. Because of this, the social-cognitive approach is sometimes referred to as the social-learning approach and the cognitive-behavioral approach. We refer to it as the social-cognitive approach here in order to note its emphasis on these two types of factors in personality development. We will describe some of the theoretical concepts of two important social-cognitive theorists, Albert Bandura and Julian Rotter, to illustrate why they think social and cognitive factors are important in personality development.

> **hierarchy of needs** The motivational component in Maslow's theory of personality, in which our innate needs that motivate our behavior are hierarchically arranged in a pyramid shape. From bottom to top, the needs are physiological, safety, belonging and love, esteem, and self-actualization.

The Humanistic Approach to Personality

Abraham Maslow is considered the father of the humanistic movement. He studied the lives of very healthy and creative people to develop his theory of personality. His main theoretical emphases were psychological health and reaching one's full potential. In describing how one goes about reaching one's full potential, Maslow proposed a hierarchy of needs that motivate our behavior in this quest. Because of the motivating role of these various types of needs, Maslow's personality theory is also considered a theory of motivation.

Abraham Maslow

Maslow's hierarchy of needs. An overview of Maslow's motivational hierarchy of needs, which is often depicted as a pyramid-like structure, is given in Figure 8.2. The **hierarchy of needs** is an arrangement of the innate needs that motivate behavior, from the strongest needs at the bottom of the pyramid to the

Self-actualization need
Need to live up to one's fullest unique potential

Esteem needs
Need for self-esteem, achievement, competence, and independence

Belongingness and love needs
Need to love and be loved, to belong and be accepted

Safety needs
Need to feel safe, secure, and stable

Physiological needs
Need to satisfy hunger and thirst

Figure 8.2 | Maslow's Hierarchy of Needs | Needs are organized hierarchically into levels, with more pressing basic needs at the bottom of the pyramid. The level at which a person is investing most of his effort is the most important one at that particular point in time.

weakest needs at the top of the pyramid (Maslow, 1968, 1970). From bottom to top, the needs are physiological, safety, belonging and love, esteem, and self-actualization. For obvious practical reasons, motivation proceeds from the bottom of the hierarchy to the top; lower needs are more urgent and have to be satisfied before higher needs can even be considered. On average, people seem to work their way up the hierarchy, but they also work on several levels simultaneously. The level at which the person is investing most of his effort is the one most important to a person at a particular point in time.

As you move up in the hierarchy, the needs become more human and less basic. The most basic needs are physiological needs (such as for food and water); therefore, they form the base of the pyramid structure. At the next level, the needs to feel safe, secure, and out of danger are also relevant to our survival, but not quite as basic as physiological needs. At the next level in the hierarchy, however, needs begin to have social aspects. Love and belongingness needs (needs for affection, acceptance, family relationships, and companionship) are met through interactions with other people. Self-esteem needs at the next level in the hierarchy are concerned with achievement, mastery, and gaining appreciation from others for our achievements, as well as developing a positive self-image.

These first four levels of needs are more deficiency-based needs, stemming from deprivation, while self-actualization at the top of the hierarchy is a growth-based need. **Self-actualization** is the fullest realization of a person's potential, becoming all that one can be. According to Maslow, the characteristics of self-actualized people include accepting themselves, others, and the natural world for what they are; having a need for privacy and only a few very close, emotional relationships; and being autonomous and independent, unquestionably democratic, and very creative. In addition, self-actualized people have what Maslow termed "peak experiences"—moments of deep insight in which you experience whatever you are doing as fully as possible. In peak experiences, you are deeply immersed in what you are doing and feel a sense of awe and wonder. Peak experiences might, for example, arise from great music or art, or from intense feelings of love.

Maslow based his description of self-actualization on his study of about 50 people who he deemed "self-actualized." Some, such as Albert Einstein and Eleanor Roosevelt, were living, so he studied them through interviews and personality tests, but others, such as Thomas Jefferson and Abraham Lincoln, were not, so he used biographies and historical records to study them. Maslow was rather vague about how he conducted these "studies," however. Maslow's theory has been criticized for being based on nonempirical, imprecise studies of a small number of people that he subjectively selected as self-actualized (Smith, 1978). His theory may have been biased toward his own idea of a healthy, self-actualized person. Regardless of these criticisms, his theory popularized the humanistic movement and led many psychologists to focus on human potential and the positive side of humankind. Carl Rogers, the other major proponent of the humanistic approach, also focused on self-actualization. Unlike Maslow, however, Rogers based his theory upon his clinical work.

self-actualization The fullest realization of a person's potential.

Rogers's self theory. Freud's psychoanalytic theory of personality led to psychoanalysis, a type of psychotherapy used to help those suffering personality problems. Carl Rogers's self theory of personality led to another influential style of psychotherapy, client-centered (or person-centered) therapy (Rogers, 1951, 1961), which we will discuss in Chapter 10, on abnormal psychology. It is interesting to note that Rogers was a clinician in an academic setting during most of the time he was developing his theory (Schultz, 2001). His clients were not like those of psychotherapists in the private sector; he mainly dealt with young, bright people with adjustment problems. Keep this in mind as we consider his theory, since his clinical experiences likely guided its development.

Carl Rogers

Like Maslow, Rogers emphasized self-actualization, the development of one's fullest potential. He believed that this was the fundamental drive for humans. Sometimes we have difficulty in this actualization process, though, and this is the source of personality problems. How does this happen? Like Freud, Rogers believed that early experience was important, but for very different reasons. He thought that we have a strong need for positive regard—to be accepted by and have the affection of others, especially the significant others in our life. Our parents (or caregivers) set up conditions of worth, the behaviors and attitudes for which they will give us positive regard. Infants and children develop their self-concept in relation to these **conditions of worth** in order to be liked and accepted by others and feel a sense of self-worth.

"Just remember, son, it dosn't matter whether you win or lose—unless you want Daddy's love."

Meeting the conditions of worth continues throughout our lives. We want to be regarded positively by others, so we meet their conditions. There's a problem, though. In meeting these conditions of worth, we may develop a self-concept of what others think we should be. The problem is that this self-concept might not be the same as our true, ideal self, and thus would deter self-actualization. This conflict is created by conditional positive regard, so Rogers developed the concept of **unconditional positive regard**—acceptance and approval without conditions. In addition to giving us unconditional positive regard (liking us no matter what we are like), it is important that others be empathetic (able to truly understand our feelings) and genuine with respect to their own feelings if we are to self-actualize. As we will learn in Chapter 10, these characteristics are critical elements in Rogers's client-centered therapy. Rogers's self theory is summarized in Figure 8.3 (page 350).

Rogers's theory, like Freud's theory, is based on clinical experience and is important mainly because of its application

conditions of worth The behaviors and attitudes for which other people, starting with our parents, will give us positive regard.

unconditional positive regard Unconditional acceptance and approval of a person by others.

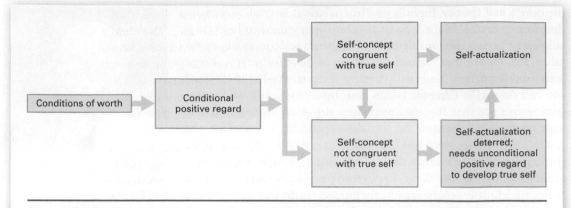

Figure 8.3 | Carl Rogers's Self Theory | According to Carl Rogers, the development of your self-concept is impacted by the conditions of worth set up by those people who are important to you. Their conditional positive regard may lead you to develop a self-concept that is congruent with your true self, thereby allowing you to self-actualize; or it may lead to a conflict between your developed self-concept and your true self. If there is a conflict, then you will need unconditional positive regard in order to develop your true self and self-actualize.

to therapy. Neither theory is research-based. The social-cognitive approach, which we will discuss next, is research-based. It combines elements of three of the major research perspectives—the cognitive, behavioral, and sociocultural approaches. The social-cognitive approach stresses that personality development involves learning that occurs in a social context and is mediated by cognitive processes. Let's see how.

The Social-Cognitive Approach to Personality

Social-cognitive theorists agree with behaviorists that learning through environmental conditioning contributes to personality development. However, they think that social learning (modeling) and cognitive processes, such as perception and thinking, are also involved and are actually more important to the development of our personality. To understand how modeling and cognitive processes are involved, we'll first consider the work of Albert Bandura, one of the main proponents of the social-cognitive approach.

Bandura's self-system. Bandura proposed that the behaviors that define one's personality are a product of a person's self-system (Bandura, 1973, 1986). This **self-system** is the set of cognitive processes by which a person observes, evaluates, and regulates her behavior. Social learning illustrates how this system works. Children observe the various behaviors of the models in their social environment, especially those of their parents. Given this observational learning, children may then choose, at some later time, to imitate these behaviors, especially if they were reinforced earlier. If these behaviors continue to be reinforced, children

self-system The set of cognitive processes by which a person observes, evaluates, and regulates her behavior.

may then incorporate them into their personality. This means that there is self-direction (the child consciously chooses which behaviors to imitate). The child's behavior is not just automatically elicited by environmental stimuli. People observe and interpret the effects of not only their own behavior, but also the behavior of others. Then they act in accordance with their assessment of whether the behavior will be reinforced or not. We do not respond mechanically to the environment; we choose our behaviors based on our expectations of reinforcement or punishment.

Bandura also proposed that people observe their own behavior and judge its effectiveness relative to their own standards (Bandura, 1997). This self-evaluation process impacts our sense of **self-efficacy**—a judgment of one's effectiveness in dealing with particular situations. Success increases our sense of self-efficacy; failure decreases it. According to Bandura, our sense of self-efficacy plays a major role in determining our behavior. People generally low in self-efficacy tend to be depressed and anxious and feel helpless. People generally high in self-efficacy are confident and positive in their outlook and have little self doubt. They also have greater persistence in working to attain goals and usually achieve greater success than those with low self-efficacy. Self-efficacy parallels the story of the little engine that could. To do something, you have to think you can do it.

Rotter's locus of control. Bandura's self-efficacy concept is similar to locus of control, a concept proposed by another social-cognitive theorist, Julian Rotter. According to Rotter, locus of control refers to a person's perception of the extent to which he controls what happens to him (Rotter, 1966, 1990). "Locus" means place. There are two major places that control can reside—outside you or within you. **External locus of control** refers to the perception that chance or external forces beyond your personal control determine your fate. **Internal locus of control** refers to the perception that you control your own fate. How is locus of control different from self-efficacy? People with an internal locus of control perceive their success as dependent upon their own actions, but they may or may not feel that they have the competence (efficacy) to bring about successful outcomes in various situations. For example, students may think that their own study preparation determines their exam performance, but they may not think that they have satisfactory study skills to produce good exam performance. For those with external locus of control, the self-efficacy concept isn't as relevant because such people believe that the outcomes of their actions are not affected by their actions.

Why is Rotter's locus of control concept important? Research has shown that people with an internal locus of control are psychologically and physically better off. They are more successful in school, healthier, and better able to cope with the stresses of life (Lachman & Weaver, 1998). In addition, an external locus of control may contribute to **learned helplessness,** a sense of hopelessness in which

self-efficacy A judgment of one's effectiveness in dealing with particular situations.

external locus of control The perception that chance or external forces beyond one's personal control determine one's fate.

internal locus of control The perception that one controls one's own individual fate.

learned helplessness A sense of hopelessness in which a person thinks that he is unable to prevent aversive events.

individuals think that they are unable to prevent unpleasant events (Seligman, 1975). But how does this happen? What goes on in the minds of those who become helpless? To understand, we first need to consider self-perception and the attribution process.

Self-perception. Given the impact of self-efficacy and locus of control, positive self-perception is important to healthy behavior. Our behavior, however, does not always lead to good outcomes. How, then, do we deal with poor outcomes and maintain positive self-perception? To understand how we do so, we need to understand **attribution,** the process by which we explain our own behavior and that of others. There are two types of attributions, internal and external. An internal attribution means that the outcome is attributed to the person. An external attribution means that the outcome is attributed to factors outside the person. Let's consider an example. You fail a psychology exam. Why? An internal attribution gives you the blame. For example, you might say, "I just didn't study enough." An external attribution would place the blame elsewhere. For example, you might say, "I knew the material, but that exam was unfair." In this case, you tend to make an external attribution. Why?

We place the blame elsewhere in order to protect our self-esteem. This attribution bias is called the **self-serving bias,** the tendency to make attributions so that one can perceive oneself favorably. If the outcome of our behavior is positive, we take credit for it (make an internal attribution). However, if the outcome is negative, we place the blame elsewhere (make an external attribution). The research evidence indicating that we use the self-serving bias is overwhelming (Myers, 2013). Think about it. Don't most of us think that we are above average in intelligence, attractiveness, and other positive characteristics? But most people can't be above average, can they? These self-enhancing perceptions created by the self-serving bias serve to maintain our self-esteem. This bias is adaptive because it protects us from falling prey to learned helplessness and depression. When negative events happen, we don't blame ourselves. Instead, we make external attributions and place the blame elsewhere.

So what type of explanatory style might lead us toward learned helplessness and depression? A pessimistic explanatory style is one answer (Peterson, Maier, & Seligman, 1993). First, the attributions of people using a pessimistic explanatory style tend to show a pattern that is the opposite of those generated by self-serving bias. Negative outcomes are given internal explanations ("I don't have any ability"), and positive outcomes external explanations ("I just got lucky"). There is more to it, however. Pessimistic explanations also tend to

---

attribution The process by which we explain our own behavior and that of others.

self-serving bias The tendency to make attributions so that one can perceive oneself favorably.

---

be stable (the person thinks that the outcome causes are permanent) and global (the causes affect most situations). Think about a person using a pessimistic explanatory style when experiencing a series of negative events. Not only would such a person blame himself (internal), but he would also think that such negative events would continue (stable) and impact most aspects of his life (global). Such thinking could easily lead to the perception of an external locus of control and learned help-lessness followed by depression. Indeed, much research has supported the relationship between styles of attribution, helplessness, and depression (Peterson & Seligman, 1984; Rotenberg, Costa, Trueman, & Lattimore, 2012; Seligman et al., 1988). In addition, uncontrollable negative events have been found to lead to lower serotonin and norepinephrine activity in rats (Wu et al., 1999), the activity pattern observed for these neurotransmitters in the brains of people diagnosed with depression.

Section Summary

The humanistic approach to the study of personality developed as part of the humanistic movement in the 1960s in response to the rather deterministic psychoanalytic and behavioral approaches that dominated psychology at that time. In contrast to these two approaches, the humanistic theorists emphasized conscious free will in one's development and the importance of self-actualization, the fullest realization of our potential, as a major motivator of our behavior. Based on his studies of very healthy and creative people, humanistic theorist Abraham Maslow developed a hierarchy of needs that motivate our behavior and development. From bottom to top, the needs are physiological, safety, belonging and love, esteem, and self-actualization. Motivation proceeds from the bottom of the hierarchy to the top, because a person cannot work toward self-actualization until the lower-level needs are met. Carl Rogers, the other major humanistic theorist, also focused on self-actualization as a major human motivation. According to Rogers, for a person to be self-actualized, the people in that person's life must set up conditions of worth that lead the person's developed self-concept to match her true self or they must give unconditional positive regard—acceptance and approval without conditions—which will allow the person to develop into her true self.

The social-cognitive approach to personality arose out of disenchantment with the rather narrow strict behavioral approach. Social-cognitive theorists agree that learning through conditioning is important, but that social learning (modeling) and cognitive processes are more important to the development of personality. For example, Albert Bandura proposed a self-system, a set of cognitive processes by which a person observes, evaluates, and regulates her behavior. Our sense of self-efficacy (our evaluation of our effectiveness in particular situations) is a key element in Bandura's theory for maintaining a healthy personality.

Julian Rotter's locus of control concept also demonstrates the importance of cognitive processing to psychological health. An external locus of control is the perception that chance or external forces beyond our personal control determine our fate. An internal locus of control is the perception that we control our own fate. People with an internal locus of control do better in school, are healthier, and are better able to cope with the stresses of life. To maintain positive self-evaluation, we also use self-serving bias in our explanations of our behavior. If the outcome of our behavior is positive, we take credit for it; if it is not, we do not. This bias is adaptive and protects us from depression. In contrast, a pessimistic explanatory style—in which we take the blame for negative outcomes and not positive ones, and see these outcomes as both stable and global—is maladaptive and will likely lead to feelings of learned helplessness and depression.

ConceptCheck | 2

Explain which needs, according to Maslow, must be satisfied before a person can worry about self-actualization.

Explain why, according to Rogers's self theory, unconditional positive regard is important.

Explain how the social-cognitive concepts of self-efficacy and locus of control are similar.

Trait Theories of Personality and Personality Assessment

As we pointed out at the beginning of this chapter, personality **traits** are internally based, relatively stable characteristics that define an individual's personality. Traits are continuous dimensions, and people vary from each other along the dimensions for each of the various traits that make up personality. But what are the specific traits that make up human personality? Think about all of the adjectives that can describe a person. There are thousands, but this doesn't mean that thousands of traits are necessary to describe human personality. Trait theories attempt to discover exactly how many traits are necessary. You will be surprised to find out that the major trait theories propose that this number is rather small. How are such numbers derived?

Trait theorists use factor analysis (and other statistical techniques) to tell them how many basic personality factors (or traits) are needed to describe human personality, as well as what these factors are. Remember, factor analysis is the statistical tool from Chapter 6 that we used to discuss the question of whether intelligence was one ability or many. Factor analysis identifies clusters of test items (in this case, on a personality test) that measure the same factor (trait). Allport and Odbert (1936) did the initial analyses, starting with 18,000 words that could be used to describe humans. Their analyses left them with around 200 clusters. Later trait researchers have reduced this number considerably; the consensus number of necessary traits is only five.

In this section, we'll consider two major trait theories that were developed using factor analysis, Hans Eysenck's three-factor theory and the Five Factor Model of personality. We'll also discuss personality assessment, because personality tests are often developed to assess a theorist's proposed basic traits. The major uses for personality tests, however, are to diagnose personality problems, to aid in counseling, and to aid in making personnel decisions; therefore, we'll focus our discussion on the two main types of personality tests used, personality inventories and projective tests.

traits The relatively stable internally based characteristics that describe a person.

Trait Theories of Personality

According to trait theorists, basic traits are the building blocks of personality. Each trait is a dimension, a continuum ranging from one extreme of the dimension to the other. A person can fall at either extreme or anywhere in between on the continuum. An individual's personality stems from the amount of each trait that he has. This is analogous to the trichromatic theory of color vision that we discussed in Chapter 3. Remember that according to the trichromatic theory, all of the thousands of different colors that we can perceive stem from different proportions of the three primaries (red, green, and blue). In trait theories, all personalities stem from different proportions of the basic traits.

The number and kind of personality traits. Different theorists have come up with different answers to the question of how many basic personality traits there are and even what they are. For example, using factor analysis, early trait researcher Raymond Cattell found that 16 traits were necessary (Cattell, 1950, 1965). More recently, Hans Eysenck, also using factor analysis, has argued for only three trait dimensions (Eysenck, 1982; Eysenck & Eysenck, 1985). There are two major reasons for the different numbers—the level of abstraction and the type of data. First, the number of traits depends upon the level of abstraction in the factor analysis. For example, if you factored Cattell's 16 traits further, you would probably get something closer to Eysenck's three higher-order factors (Digman, 1990). This means that Eysenck's theory is at a more general and inclusive level of abstraction than Cattell's theory. More important, the number of traits depends upon which databases and what types of data different theorists use in their factor analysis. Different data could, of course, lead to different traits, as well as a different number of traits. Surprisingly, contemporary trait researchers have reached something of a consensus about the number and the nature of the basic personality traits. The three traits proposed by Eysenck are insufficient, and the 16-factor theory of Cattell is needlessly complex (McCrae, 2011). The consensus number is five, and these five traits (or factors) are referred to as the "Big Five." First, we'll discuss Eysenck's three-factor theory, because he (unlike most trait theorists) proposes actual causal explanations for his traits, and then we'll discuss the Five Factor Model of personality.

Eysenck's three-factor theory. Hans Eysenck's three trait dimensions are extraversion–introversion, neuroticism–emotional stability, and psychoticism–impulse control. These are continuous dimensions, with extraversion, neuroticism, and psychoticism, respectively, at the high ends. Eysenck argues that these three traits are determined by heredity and proposes biological bases for each one of them (Eysenck, 1990, 1997). We will briefly discuss some of the proposed biological mechanisms for each of Eysenck's three trait dimensions so you can see why this is a biological trait theory of personality.

Extraversion and introversion have their normal meanings, indicating differences in sociability. Extraverts are gregarious, outgoing people with lots of friends; introverts are those who are quiet, are more introspective, and tend to avoid social interaction. For example, in a study of students going off to college, the extraverted ones struck up new friendships more quickly than the introverted ones (Asendorpf & Wilpers, 1998). The main proposed biological mechanism for the extraversion–introversion trait is variance in the normal level of cortical arousal (neuronal activity) in a person. According to Eysenck, an introvert has a higher resting level of arousal in the brain than an extravert because of differences in their reticular formations. Remember, as you learned in Chapter 2, the reticular formation is responsible for our different levels of arousal. According to Eysenck, the brains of introverts are sufficiently active normally, but an extravert has to seek out external stimulation in order to raise the level of arousal in the brain to a more optimal level. Brain-scan studies have generally provided support for this contention. Introverts are typically found to show more cortical arousal compared with extraverts (Hagemann et al., 2009).

People who are high on the neuroticism–emotional stability dimension tend to be overly anxious, emotionally unstable, and easily upset; people who are low on this dimension tend to be calm and emotionally stable. People high on this dimension experience more lingering negative emotional states in their daily lives and suffer from higher rates of anxiety and depression (Widiger, 2009). Eysenck proposes differences in the limbic system, which plays a major role in regulating our emotions, and the sympathetic nervous system, which controls the body when it is in a stressful situation, as the main biological bases for this trait. People high on the neuroticism trait tend to have greater activity in their limbic system and a more reactive sympathetic nervous system, causing them to be on average more anxious and to become even more emotionally aroused and upset when they are threatened or find themselves in stressful situations.

The psychoticism–impulse control trait dimension is concerned with aggressiveness, impulsiveness, empathy (seeing situations from other people's perspectives), and antisocial behavior. According to Krueger and Walton (2008), *psychoticism* seems to have been a poor choice of labels given its exaggerated image of pathology, so *disinhibition* might be a better label for the high end of this dimension. Eysenck assumes that the relevant biological mechanisms for this trait include a person's levels of testosterone and MAO, a neurotransmitter inhibitor. For example, a high level of testosterone and a low level of MAO lead to behavior that tends to be aggressive, impulsive, antisocial, or lacking in empathy (disinhibited behavior reflective of the high end of this dimension).

Eysenck's specific biological assumptions make his theory rather easy to test experimentally. Thus, it has generated much research, literally thousands of studies (Geen, 1997), and the findings have been fairly supportive. However, most research on personality traits seems to indicate that five factors, rather than three, are necessary to describe personality (Funder, 2001; Goldberg, 1990; John, 1990; McCrae & Costa, 2003; Wiggins, 1996). Unlike Eysenck, five-factor theorists use only the high end of each trait dimension to identify the factor. So how do you get to five from Eysenck's three factors? Eysenck's extraversion and neuroticism factors are retained, but his psychoticism factor is broken into two parts, conscientiousness and agreeableness, and an openness factor is added (Nettle, 2007). Now let's take a closer look at the Five Factor Model of personality.

The Five Factor Model of personality. The Five Factor Model of personality was formulated by Robert McCrae and Paul Costa (McCrae & Costa, 1999). The descriptions of the high and low ends of the five trait dimensions (called the Big Five) given in Table 8.3 will provide you with a brief overview of the five proposed factors. To remember the five factors, try forming acronyms using their first letters. Order is not important. You could use OCEAN (Openness, Conscientiousness, Extraversion, Agreeableness, and Neuroticism) or CANOE (Conscientiousness, Agreeableness, Neuroticism, Openness, and Extraversion). Similarly, you might use PEN to remember Eysenck's Big Three traits (Psychoticism, Extraversion, and Neuroticism).

We already briefly discussed extraversion and neuroticism when we described Eysenck's trait theory, so let's see what conscientiousness, openness, and agreeableness entail and what real-world behaviors they are related to. Conscientiousness is a tendency to show self-discipline, dependability, and organization and to prefer planned versus spontaneous behavior. Conscientiousness is positively correlated with high school and college GPAs (Noftle & Robins, 2007) and is linked to living a healthier and longer life (Bogg & Roberts, 2004; Kern & Friedman, 2008; Roberts, Smith, Jackson, & Edmonds, 2009). Openness (often referred to as openness to experience) reflects a person's degree of intellectual curiosity, creativity, and preference for novelty and variety. A person who scores high on the openness factor is willing to try new things, is imaginative, and tends to have liberal values and be open-minded (McCrae & Sutin, 2009). High scorers on openness also tend to score high on intelligence tests and the SAT Verbal test (Noftle & Robins, 2007; Sharp, Reynolds, Pedersen, & Gatz, 2010). Agreeableness is the tendency to be compassionate and cooperative rather than suspicious and antagonistic toward others. People who score high on the agreeableness factor tend to be friendly, altruistic, empathetic, and to have an optimistic view of human nature (Graziano, Habashi, Sheese, & Tobin, 2007). Variation in agreeableness also correlates well

	Table 8.3 The Big Five Personality Trait Dimensions	
Low End of Dimension	**Trait Dimension**	**High End of Dimension**
Conforming, practical, narrow interests, closed to new ideas	Openness	Independent, imaginative, broad interests, receptive to new ideas
Disorganized, undependable, careless, impulsive	Conscientiousness	Well-organized, dependable, careful, disciplined
Reclusive, quiet, aloof, cautious	Extraversion	Sociable, talkative, friendly, adventurous
Tough-minded, rude, irritable, ruthless	Agreeableness	Sympathetic, polite, good-natured, soft-hearted
Calm, secure, relaxed, self-satisfied	Neuroticism	Emotional, insecure, nervous, self-pitying

with the variation in social-cognitive theory of mind functioning in adults, with high scorers performing better on theory of mind tasks (Nettle & Liddle, 2008).

According to Costa and McCrae (1993, p. 302), the Five Factor Model "is the Christmas tree on which findings of stability, heritability, consensual validation, cross-cultural invariance, and predictive validity are hung like ornaments." Indeed, recent research indicates that these five factors may be universal. They have been observed across gender, and in many diverse languages (such as English, Korean, and Turkish) and cultures (including American, Hispanic, European, African, and Asian cultures), and not just in Western industrialized societies (McCrae & Costa, 1997, 2001; McCrae et al., 2004; Schmidt, Allik, McCrae, & Benet-Martinez, 2007). In addition, research has found that the Big Five factors have about a 50% heritability rate across several cultures (Bouchard & McGue, 2003; Jang et al; 2006; Loehlin, 1992; Loehlin, McCrae, Costa, & John, 1998), indicating a strong genetic basis. The Big Five factors also seem consistent from about age 30 to late adulthood (Costa & McCrae, 1988) and are generally consistent across situations (Buss, 2001). Given their general consistency over time and situations, some psychologists think that each trait must be associated with a specific pattern of brain behavior or structure (e.g., Canli, 2006). In fact, DeYoung et al. (2010) have proposed a theory of the biological bases of the Big Five personality factors and found supporting evidence using magnetic resonance imaging for four of the five factors.

Given the importance of the Big Five factors, Robert McCrae and Paul Costa have developed personality inventory assessment instruments, the NEO-PI-R, the NEO-PI-3, and the NEO-FFI, which provide personality profiles of these five factors (Costa & McCrae, 1985, 1992, 2008; McCrae, Costa, & Martin, 2005). Rammstedt and John (2007) have developed a 10-item, 1-minute-or-less measure of the NEO-PI-R that retains significant levels of reliability and validity. An adapted version of their test is given in Table 8.4. Go ahead and take the test. It will help you to get a better understanding of not only the Big Five personality traits but also personality inventories in general and how they differ from the better-known projective personality tests. After taking the test and before going on to read about personality assessment, review Table 8.5 (page 360), which summarizes all of the theoretical approaches to personality that we have discussed. Make sure that you know and understand the various theorists and their key concepts.

Person–situation controversy. In 1968, personality theorist Walter Mischel argued that situations and not personality traits determine a person's behavior. He pointed out that the correlation between a person's assessed traits and their behavior in personality laboratory studies was very weak and that a person's behavior was situation-dependent—a person's behavior varies in accordance with the situation and will vary across situations. Mischel's work led to what is known as the person–situation controversy in personality theory. Do traits or situations best predict behavior? Seymour Epstein (1979) answered Mischel's criticism by pointing out that Mischel's conclusions were based on looking at the relationship between traits and small slices of a person's behavior in laboratory research studies. Epstein argued that accurate assessment of the relationship between a person's

Table 8.4 — Big Five Inventory-10 (BFI-10)

Instruction: For each of the 10 statements that follow, rate how well each one describes your personality from 1 (Disagree strongly) to 5 (Agree strongly).

I see myself as someone who ...	Disagree strongly	Disagree a little	Neither agree nor disagree	Agree a little	Agree strongly
1. ... is reserved	1	2	3	4	5
2. ... is generally trusting	1	2	3	4	5
3. ... tends to be lazy	1	2	3	4	5
4. ... is relaxed, handles stress well	1	2	3	4	5
5. ... has few artistic interests	1	2	3	4	5
6. ... is outgoing, sociable	1	2	3	4	5
7. ... tends to find fault with others	1	2	3	4	5
8. ... does a thorough job	1	2	3	4	5
9. ... gets nervous easily	1	2	3	4	5
10. ... has an active imagination	1	2	3	4	5

To assess your tendencies toward the five factors in the Five Factor Model of personality, use the following scoring instructions. Your score on each factor can vary from 2 (Low) to 10 (High).

Extraversion	1R, 6 (R means that this item should be reverse scored; 1 = 5, 2 = 5, 3 = 3, 4 = 1, 5 = 1; for example, a 1 on Item 1 and a 5 on Item 6 would indicate a high Extraversion score of 10)
Agreeableness	2, 7R
Conscientiousness	3R, 8
Neuroticism	4R, 9
Openness	5R, 10

(Adapted from "Measuring personality in one minute or less: A 10-item version of the Big Five Inventory in English and German," by B. Rammstedt and O. P. John, *Journal of Research in Personality, 41*(2007), 203–212.)

traits and behavior requires assessment of a person's behavior over time and many different situations and not just single instances of behavior; a person's average behavior across time and situations will reflect his traits. Epstein argued that traits are general behavioral tendencies and not invariable predictors of behavior. Subsequent research has supported Epstein's argument (Funder, 2001). Research has

Table 8.5	Major Personality Theoretical Approaches	
Theoretical Approach	**Theorist**	**Key Concepts**
Psychoanalytic	Sigmund Freud	Id, ego, superego
		Conscious, preconscious, unconscious
		Pleasure principle, reality principle
		Defense mechanisms
		Psychosexual stages—oral, anal, phallic, latency, genital
		Erogenous zone, fixation
	Carl Jung	Collective unconscious, archetypes
	Alfred Adler	Striving for superiority, inferiority complex
	Karen Horney	Need for security, basic anxiety
Humanistic	Abraham Maslow	Hierarchy of needs, self-actualization
	Carl Rogers	Conditions of worth, unconditional positive regard, self-actualization
Social-cognitive	Albert Bandura	Self-system, self-efficacy
	Julian Rotter	Locus of control
Trait	Hans Eysenck	Three factors:
		Extraversion–Introversion
		Neuroticism–Emotional Stability
		Psychoticism–Impulse Control
	Robert McCrae and Paul Costa	Five Factor Model:
		Openness
		Conscientiousness
		Extraversion
		Agreeableness
		Neuroticism

also found that traits are relatively stable across time from childhood on (Roberts & DelVecchio, 2000). Please note, though, that this does not mean that traits are immutable. Although traits are generally consistent across time, there is evidence of trait change during the period of childhood through young adulthood, especially in the latter stage of development (Caspi, Roberts, & Shiner, 2005), and to a lesser degree from middle adulthood on (Helson, Jones, & Kwan, 2002).

Personality Assessment

Personality tests are a major tool in personality trait research, but the main uses of personality tests are to aid in diagnosing people with problems, in counseling, and in making personnel decisions. There are many types of personality tests, but we will focus on two, personality inventories and projective tests. Most of the other types of personality tests have more limited use. For example, Carl Rogers and humanistic psychologists have developed questionnaires that only address the self-concept, and Julian Rotter has developed a test that specifically assesses locus of control.

Personality inventories. A **personality inventory** is designed to measure multiple traits or, in some cases, disorders. It is a series of questions or statements for which the test taker must indicate whether they apply to him or not. The typical response format is True–False or Yes–No. Often a third response category of Can't Say or Uncertain is included. The assumption is that the person both can and will provide an accurate self-report. These tests include items dealing with specific behaviors, attitudes, interests, and values. We will discuss the MMPI, the Minnesota Multiphasic Personality Inventory (Hathaway & McKinley, 1943), revised to become the MMPI-2 in 1989 (Butcher, Dahlstrom, Graham, Tellegen, & Kaemmer, 1989). It is the most used personality test in the world (Weiner & Greene, 2008), and it has been translated into more than 100 languages.

The MMPI-2 uses a True–False–Cannot Say format with 567 simple statements (such as "I like to cook") and takes about 60 to 90 minutes to complete. Most of the statements are from the original MMPI. Some were reworded to update the item content and to eliminate sexist language, and most of the questions pertaining to religion and sexual practices were eliminated (Ben-Porath & Butcher, 1989). The MMPI was developed to be a measure of abnormal personality, with 10 clinical scales. Many of the test statements have obvious connections to disorders, such as "I believe I am being plotted against," but many are just simple ordinary statements, such as "I am neither gaining nor losing weight."

The MMPI test statements were chosen in the same way that Binet and Simon chose test items for their first valid test of intelligence (discussed in Chapter 6). Binet and Simon developed a large pool of possible test items and then chose only those items that differentiated fast and slow learners. Similarly, a large pool of possible test items (simple statements of all types) was developed, and then only those items that were answered differently (by a representative sample of people suffering from a specific disorder versus a group of normal people) were chosen for the test. It didn't matter what each group responded or what the content of the statement happened to be; what mattered was that the two groups generally responded to the item in opposite ways. Thus, the test developers were only concerned with whether, and not why, the items were answered differently by the groups. This test construction method allowed the test developers to choose items that clearly identified the response patterns of people with 10 different disorders (for example, depression or schizophrenia).

The MMPI and MMPI-2 are scored by a computer, which then generates a profile of the test taker on 10 clinical

personality inventory An objective personality test that uses a series of questions or statements for which the test taker must indicate whether they apply to her or not.

projective test A personality test that uses a series of ambiguous stimuli to which the test taker must respond about her perceptions of the stimuli.

(disorder) scales. There are also test statements that comprise the basis for three validity scales, which attempt to detect test takers who are trying to cover up problems and fake profiles or who were careless in their responding. For example, there is a lie detection scale that assesses the extent to which the test taker is lying to create a particular test profile. The lie scale is based on responses to a set of test items such as "I get angry sometimes," to which most people would respond "True." The profile for a person consistently answering "False" to these questions would be invalidated.

Personality inventories like the MMPI are objective tests and are objectively scored by a computer. The computer converts the test taker's responses into a personality profile for the trait or disorder dimensions that the test is measuring. This is why the MMPI has been so popular in clinical settings for making diagnoses of personality problems. Its test construction method leads to good predictive validity for its clinical scales (Garb, Florio, & Grove, 1998), and its objective scoring procedure leads to reliability in interpretation. Projective personality tests, which we will discuss next, do not have good validity or reliability, but are widely used.

Projective tests. The chances are that when personality tests are mentioned, you think of the Rorschach Inkblot Test, a projective personality test. In contrast with personality inventories, a **projective test** is a series of ambiguous stimuli, such as inkblots, to which the test taker must respond about his perceptions of the stimuli. An objective response format is not used. Test takers are asked to describe the stimulus or tell a story about it. We will discuss the two most used projective tests, the Rorschach Inkblot Test and the Thematic Apperception Test (TAT).

Projective tests aren't administered, scored, or interpreted in the same way as the MMPI, MMPI-2, and other objective personality inventories. They are not as objective, especially with respect to interpretation. The most popular and widely used projective test is the Rorschach Inkblot Test (often referred to as The Rorschach), which Swiss psychiatrist Hermann Rorschach included as part of

Roz Chast/The New Yorker Collection/The Cartoon Bank

a monograph in 1921 (Rorschach, 1921/1942). Actually Rorschach never intended this to be a test of personality. He created it for use as a diagnostic tool for schizophrenia. Sadly, in 1922, the year after his monograph was published, he died from appendicitis; he was only 37 years old. There are only 10 symmetric inkblots used in the test. Five are in black ink, two in black and red ink, and three are multicolored. All have a white background. The test taker is asked what he sees in each inkblot, though the inkblots are ambiguous and have no inherent meaning. The examiner then goes through the cards and asks the test taker to clarify his responses by identifying the various parts of the inkblot that led to the response.

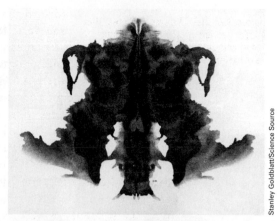

One of the ten inkblots on the Rorschach Inkblot Test.

Stanley Goldblatt/Science Source

The assumption is that the test taker's responses are projections of his personal conflicts and personality dynamics. This means that the test taker's responses have to be interpreted, which makes the test scoring subjective and creates great variability among test scorers. In fact, one could view the test scorer's interpretations as projections themselves. The Rorschach Inkblot Test has been widely used (Watkins, Campbell, Nieberding, & Hallmark, 1995), but many researchers have questioned its scoring system and hence its reliability and validity (e.g., Dawes, 1994; Lilienfeld, Wood, & Garb, 2000), leading to a call for a moratorium on its use (Garb, 1999). However, recently Mihura, Meyer, Dumitrascu, and Bombel (2013) reported their findings for meta-analyses of the validity studies using externally assessed criteria (e.g., psychiatric diagnoses) for the 65 main variables assessed by the Rorschach. The resulting estimated validity coefficients were very supportive for the majority of these variables. The strongest validity was observed for those variables that target cognitive processes, such as perception.

Some leading Rorschach critics promptly responded to Mihura et al.'s meta-analytic findings and validity claims. Wood, Garb, Nezworski, Lilienfeld, & Duke (2015; cf. Mihura, Meyer, Bombel, & Dumitrascu, 2015) concluded that Mihura et al.'s meta-analyses for the cognitive variables (e.g., *Conventional Form,* which assesses the tendency to perceive the world as others do) were trustworthy and thus lifted their moratorium on the use of these variables in research and applied settings. However, given the results of some new meta-analyses that they conducted, Wood et al. did not lift their moratorium on the use of the noncognitive variables (e.g., *Suicide Constellation,* which assesses suicide risk) for which Mihura et al. had found varying levels of support. They thought that although there was some support for these variables, it was still insufficient. Hence, the validity of these noncognitive variables remains debatable.

Science Source

One of the ambiguous picture cards used in the TAT.

In addition, a new Rorschach scoring system, Rorschach Performance Assessment System, R-PAS, has been published (Meyer, Viglione, Mihura, Erard, & Erdberg, 2011). This scoring system also utilizes normative data so the results are reported in a manner similar to using standard deviation scores like those used for intelligence tests that we discussed in Chapter 6 (page 269). Given that this new assessment system only selected Rorschach variables that have been empirically supported in the research literature, it should help to increase the test's reliability and validity in the future.

Now let's consider another popular projective test, the Thematic Apperception Test (TAT), developed by Henry Murray and his colleagues in the 1930s (Morgan & Murray, 1935). The TAT consists of 31 cards (the original version had only 20), 30 with black and white pictures of ambiguous settings and one blank card (the ultimate in ambiguity). Only 10 or so of the 31 cards are used in an individual testing session. The test taker is told that this is a storytelling test and that for each picture he has to make up a story. He is to tell what has happened before, what is happening now, what the people are feeling and thinking, and how things will turn out. In scoring these responses, the scorer looks for recurring themes in the feelings, relationships, and motives of the characters in the created stories. However, it has yet to be demonstrated that the TAT scoring (interpretation) is either reliable or valid (Lilienfeld, Wood, & Garb, 2000). You are probably wondering why these two projective tests have been used so much and are so popular if the TAT has no demonstrated reliability or validity and if these essential test characteristics have only recently been demonstrated for some of the variables assessed by the Rorschach Inkblot Test. Therapists who use them and other projective personality tests tend to believe that such tests allow them to explore aspects of the test taker's personality that the reliable and valid objective personality tests do not. These therapists tend to be psychoanalysts who believe projections are meaningful; therefore, the tests' subjective nature is not problematic for them.

Section Summary

The trait approach to personality attempts to identify the basic traits (dimensions) we need to describe human personality. These traits are the building blocks of personality. Given the basic traits, each person's personality can be viewed as her unique combination of values on these basic personality dimensions. Using factor analysis and other statistical techniques, trait theorists have proposed theories with varying numbers of basic dimensions. For example, Hans Eysenck has proposed three dimensions—psychoticism, extraversion, and neuroticism. Recent trait research indicates that five factors (the Big Five—openness, conscientiousness, extraversion, agreeableness, and neuroticism) are necessary. These five factors seem to be relatively stable throughout adulthood, with young adulthood being the most likely period of trait change. The five factors also appear to be consistent across gender and many diverse languages and cultures. However, it is important to remember that although our behavior is generally consistent with our traits, sometimes situations lead us to act counter to our traits.

To assess personality, psychologists make use of two types of tests—personality inventories and projective tests. A personality inventory is a set of questions or statements for which the test taker must indicate whether they apply to her or not. Such objective tests usually employ a True–False–Cannot Say format. The most used personality inventory is the MMPI/MMPI-2. These tests have predictive validity for diagnosing personality problems on 10 clinical scales, since the items on these tests were chosen because they differentiated normal people from people diagnosed with the 10 disorders. Projective tests are more subjective tests in which the test taker must respond about her perceptions of a series of ambiguous stimuli. The assumption is that the test taker's responses are projections of her personal conflicts and personality dynamics. Though widely used, projective tests vary with respect to their reliability and validity. Of the two that we discussed, the Rorschach Inkblot Test has been found to be reliable and valid for some of the variables that it measures (mainly, the cognitive-perceptual variables), but it is still lacking overall on these two dimensions. However, a new assessment system for the Rorschach Inkblot Test, the R-PAS, has recently been developed. It only uses variables that have been empirically supported, which should help to increase the test's reliability and validity in future studies. The other major projective test that we discussed, the TAT, has not yet been shown to be reliable or valid. It is important to note, though, that many users of these projective tests are not concerned about their subjective nature because they have a psychoanalytic orientation and thus believe that projections are meaningful and allow insight into a person's personality that reliable and valid objective personality tests do not.

ConceptCheck | 3

Explain why factor analysis can lead to different numbers of basic personality dimensions.

Explain how the test-construction method used to develop the MMPI ensures predictive validity for the test.

Study Guide

Chapter Key Terms

You should know the definitions of the following key terms from the chapter. They are listed in the order in which they appear in the chapter. For those you do not know, return to the relevant section of the chapter to learn them. When you think that you know all of the terms, complete the matching exercise based on these key terms.

personality
conscious mind
preconscious mind
unconscious mind
id
pleasure principle
ego
reality principle
superego
defense mechanism
erogenous zone
fixation
oral stage of psychosexual development

anal stage of psychosexual development
phallic stage of psychosexual development
Oedipus conflict
identification
latency stage of psychosexual development
genital stage of psychosexual development
hierarchy of needs
self-actualization
conditions of worth
unconditional positive regard

self-system
self-efficacy
external locus of control
internal locus of control
learned helplessness
attribution
self-serving bias
traits
personality inventory
projective test

Key Terms Exercise

Identify the correct term for each of the following definitions. The answers to this exercise follow the answers to the ConceptChecks at the end of the chapter.

1. A process used by the ego to distort reality and protect a person from anxiety.

_____

2. Unconditional acceptance and approval of a person by others.

_____

3. A judgment of one's effectiveness in dealing with particular situations.

_____

4. The third psychosexual stage in Freud's theory (from ages 3 to 6 years old) in which the erogenous zone is located at the genitals, and the child derives pleasure from genital stimulation.

_____

5. The principle of finding gratification for instinctual drives within the constraints of reality (norms of society).

_____

6. The part of the personality that a person is born with and that contains the biological instinctual drives and is located in the unconscious mind.

_____

7. The process by which children adopt the characteristics of the same-sex parent and learn their gender role and sense of morality.

_____

8. The tendency to make attributions so that one can perceive oneself favorably.

_____

9. A personality test that uses a series of ambiguous stimuli to which the test takers must respond about their perceptions of the stimuli.

_____

10. The perception that chance or external forces beyond one's individual control determine one's fate.

_____

11. Freud's term for the area of the body where the id's pleasure-seeking energies are focused during a particular stage of psychosexual development.

_____

12. The behaviors and attitudes for which other people, starting with our parents, will give us positive regard.

_____

13. Freud's term for what is stored in our memories that we are not presently aware of but can access.

_____

14. The process by which we explain our own behavior and that of others.

_____

15. Freud's term for the part of the personality that represents one's conscience and idealized standards of behavior.

_____

Practice Test Questions

The following are practice multiple-choice test questions on some of the chapter content. The answers are given after the Key Terms Exercise answers at the end of the chapter. If you guessed on a question or incorrectly answered a question, restudy the relevant section of the chapter.

1. According to Freud, the _____, the executive of the personality, is located _____
   a. ego; entirely in the unconscious
   b. ego; in all three levels of awareness
   c. superego; entirely in the unconscious
   d. superego; in all three levels of awareness

2. A woman has unacceptable feelings of hatred toward her mother, but lavishes attention and love on her. Freud would say that this is an example of _____.
   a. projection
   b. reaction formation
   c. displacement
   d. sublimation

3. Which of the following neo-Freudian theorists proposed "striving for superiority" as the primary motivation for personality development?
   a. Carl Jung
   b. Karen Horney
   c. Alfred Adler
   d. Erik Erikson

4. In Maslow's hierarchy of needs, _____ needs are at the bottom of the hierarchy, and _____ needs are at the top.
   a. physiological; self-actualization
   b. self-actualization; physiological
   c. safety; belonging and love
   d. belonging and love; safety

5. In Rogers's self theory, which of the following contributes greatly to one's self-actualization?
   a. conditional positive regard
   b. unconditional positive regard
   c. an internal locus of control
   d. an external locus of control

6. "Self-efficacy" is the answer to which of the following questions?
   a. What is the fullest realization of a person's potential?
   b. What is a sense of one's effectiveness in dealing with a particular situation?
   c. What is the perception that one controls one's own fate?
   d. What is the tendency to make attributions so that one can view one's self favorably?

7. After losing a tennis match, which of the following comments is a person most likely to make if self-serving bias is operating?
   a. "I should have practiced more."
   b. "I made too many unforced errors."
   c. "My opponent had the advantage of playing on his home court."
   d. "My mental concentration was lacking."

8. Which of the following theoretical approaches uses factor analysis to determine the number of factors necessary to describe human personality?
   a. the psychoanalytic approach
   b. the trait approach
   c. the humanistic approach
   d. the social-cognitive approach

9. Which one of Eysenck's three personality factors is not one of the "Big Five" factors?
   a. openness
   b. neuroticism
   c. psychoticism
   d. agreeableness

10. Which of the following personality tests uses True–False items and generates a profile of the test taker on 10 clinical scales?
    a. MMPI-2
    b. Rorschach Inkblot Test
    c. TAT
    d. all of the above

11. According to social-cognitive personality theorists, which of the following is least likely to lead to depression?
    a. low sense of self-esteem
    b. self-serving bias
    c. external locus of control
    d. learned helplessness

12. Which of the following trait dimensions is one of the "Big Five" personality dimensional labels?
    a. aggressiveness
    b. effectiveness
    c. cheerfulness
    d. openness

13. Inferiority complex is to basic anxiety as _____ is to _____.
    a. Adler; Horney
    b. Horney; Adler
    c. Jung; Horney
    d. Horney; Jung

14. Imagine a patient who was just diagnosed with a serious illness. According to Julian Rotter, if the patient has a strong internal locus of control, what is the patient's most likely response to the situation?
    a. "Whatever happens, it is in God's hands."
    b. "I'll just do what the doctor says and trust his judgment."
    c. "Whether I make it or not is just a matter of luck."
    d. "I want to learn about this illness and work to fight it."

15. Glenn's room looks like a tornado hit it. He is incredibly messy. His car is filled with old pizza boxes, last month's newspapers, and dirty laundry. According to Freud, Glenn is most likely fixated at the _____ stage.
    a. phallic
    b. oral
    c. anal
    d. genital

Chapter ConceptCheck Answers

ConceptCheck | 1

- According to Freud, the ego is the executive of the personality in that it must find acceptable ways within reality (society's norms) and the constraints of the superego to satisfy the instinctual drives of the id. Finding such ways is not easy, and the ego may not be able to do its job.

- In reaction formation, the ego transforms the unacceptable impulses and behavior into their opposites; in projection they are projected onto other people. For example, consider thoughts of homosexuality in a man. In reaction formation, the man would become just the opposite in his behavior, romantically overly interested in the opposite sex. However, in projection, the homosexual feelings would be projected onto other men. He would see homosexual tendencies in other men and think they were gay, but he would not think this about himself.

- According to Freud, as a child progresses through the first three psychosexual stages (oral, anal, and phallic), he may become fixated in a stage when there is an unresolved conflict in that stage. If fixated, part of the id's pleasure-seeking energy remains at that erogenous zone and continues throughout the person's life. Thus, it will show up in the child's adult personality. For example, anal fixations will lead to the anal retentive or expulsive personality types.

ConceptCheck | 2

- In Maslow's hierarchy of needs, physiological, safety, belonging and love, and esteem needs have to be satisfied before the highest level need for self-actualization can be met.

- Positive regard for a person should be unconditional so that the person is free to develop her true self and thus work toward self-actualization. If our positive regard for a person is conditionalized (we set up conditions of worth for that person), then the person develops a self-concept of what others think she should be. This self may be very different from the person's true self and thus prevent self-actualization.

- Both self-efficacy and locus of control are cognitive judgments about our effectiveness in dealing with the situations that occur in our lives. Whereas self-efficacy is a person's judgment of his effectiveness in dealing with particular situations, locus of control is a more global judgment of how much a person controls what happens to him. Both a low general sense of self-efficacy and an external locus of control (i.e., the perception that forces beyond one's control determine one's fate) often lead to depression.

ConceptCheck | 3

- There are two major reasons that factor analysis can lead to different numbers of basic personality dimensions. The first concerns the level of abstraction at which a theorist uses the analysis. Some theorists have used a level of analysis in which some of the dimensions are still correlated (Cattell); others (Eysenck) have used higher-order factors that are not correlated. Thus, theorists may use different levels of inclusiveness, with those using more global levels leading to fewer factors. Second, and independent of level of abstraction, is what data are being analyzed. Different theorists have examined different databases. Obviously, varying input will lead to varying results, even with the same type of analysis.

- The test construction method used to develop the MMPI involves only choosing test items that clearly differentiate the responding of two distinct groups. In the case of the MMPI, test items were chosen that were responded to differently by representative samples of people with 1 of 10 different disorders versus normal people. Thus, predictive validity is ensured because only test items that definitely differentiate test takers according to the purpose of the test are chosen. In the case of the MMPI, this means that various clinical personality problems, such as depression or schizophrenia, can be detected by comparing a test taker's response pattern to those of the disordered groups.

Answers to Key Terms Exercise

1. defense mechanism
2. unconditional positive regard
3. self-efficacy
4. phallic stage of psychosexual development
5. reality principle
6. id
7. identification
8. self-serving bias
9. projective test
10. external locus of control
11. erogenous zone
12. conditions of worth
13. preconscious
14. attribution
15. superego

Answers to Practice Test Questions

1. b; ego; in all three levels of awareness
2. b; reaction formation
3. c; Alfred Adler
4. a; physiological; self-actualization
5. b; unconditional positive regard
6. b; What is a sense of one's effectiveness in dealing with a particular situation?
7. c; "My opponent had the advantage of playing on his home court."
8. b; the trait approach
9. c; psychoticism
10. a; MMPI-2
11. b; self-serving bias
12. d; openness
13. a; Adler; Horney
14. d; "I want to learn about this illness and work to fight it."
15. c; anal

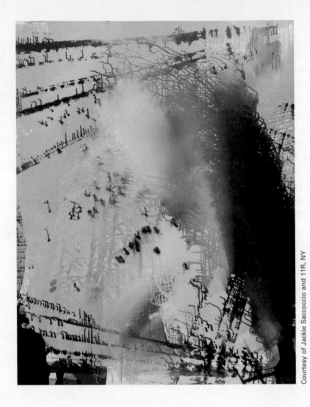

Courtesy of Jackie Saccoccio and 11R, NY

9

Social Psychology

**How Others Influence
Our Behavior**
Why We Conform
Why We Comply
Why We Obey
How Groups Influence Us

**How We Think About
Our Own And Others'
Behavior**
How We Make Attributions
How Our Behavior Affects
Our Attitudes

Humans are social animals. We affect one another's thoughts and actions, and how we do so is the topic of this chapter. This research area is called **social psychology**—the scientific study of how we influence one another's behavior and think-

ing. To understand what is meant by such social influence, we'll consider two real-world incidents in which social forces influenced behavior, and then, later in the chapter, we'll return to each incident to see how social psychologists explain them.

The first incident is the brutal rape and murder of Kitty Genovese in New York City in 1964 (briefly discussed in Chapter 1). Kitty Genovese was returning home from work late one night, when she was attacked in front of her apartment building. The attack was a prolonged one over a half-hour period in which the attacker left and came back. Kitty screamed for help and struggled with the knife-wielding attacker, but no help was forthcoming. Some apartment residents saw the attack, and others heard her screams and pleas for help. Exactly how many residents witnessed the attack is not clear. A recent analysis by Manning, Levine, and Collins (2007) of the court transcripts of the murder trial, an examination of other legal documents associated with the case, and a review

Kitty Genovese

of research carried out by a local historian and lawyer familiar with the case revealed a much different account of what happened than was depicted in the *New York Times* story that was described in Chapter 1. Their analysis indicated that the number of witnesses who actually saw the attack was considerably less than 38 (probably only a half dozen or so at most); that possibly a few more witnesses heard something; that none of the witnesses actually saw the stabbing; that the first attack was very brief because the attacker was temporarily scared away by the shouting of at least one of the witnesses; that the second, more prolonged, fatal attack occurred out of view and earshot of all but one witness, who chose not to intervene; that at least one person actually called the police after the first attack but the police did not respond to the call; and that a 70-year-old female neighbor of Kitty's actually left her apartment and went to the crime scene without knowing whether or not the murderer had fled (Lemann, 2014; Manning et al., 2007). With respect to the first call to the police, there was no 911 system in 1964, and calls from this area were not always welcomed by the police because of a bar there that had a reputation for trouble. In sum, Manning et al. showed that all of the key features of the *New York Times* report of the murder were inaccurate. Regardless, Kitty's cries for help went unanswered until it was too late. Someone finally called the police after the attacker had left, and they responded this time, but Kitty died soon thereafter on her way to the hospital. It is important to realize that social psychology researchers in 1964 did not know that the *New York Times* version of the attack was rife with errors. Thus, they conducted research to try to explain why 38 witnesses watched a killer stalk and stab a woman in a prolonged attack that lasted over 30 minutes and not one witness telephoned the police or intervened until it was too late. Media accounts blamed apathy created by a big-city culture for the many bystanders' failure to help (Rosenthal, 1964).

Based on their experiments, social psychology researchers, however, provided a very different explanation of the bystanders' behavior. We will describe this explanation in the section on social influence, when we discuss bystander intervention. Incidentally, Winston Moseley, the man who killed Kitty Genovese, died in prison in 2016. He was 81 and had been incarcerated for the past 52 years.

The second incident occurred in 1978, when over 900 people who were members of Reverend Jim Jones's Peoples Temple religious cult in Jonestown, Guyana (South America), committed mass suicide by drinking cyanide-laced Kool-Aid (though some sources say it was Flavor-Aid, a drink mix similar to Kool-Aid). These were Americans who had moved with Jones from San Francisco to Jonestown in 1977. Jonestown parents not only drank the poisoned Kool-Aid, but they also gave it to their infant children to drink. Strangely, the mass suicide occurred in a fairly orderly fashion as one person after another drank the poison. Hundreds of people went into convulsions and died within minutes. What social forces made so few of these people willing to disobey Reverend Jones's command for this unified act of mass suicide? We will return to this question in the social influence section, when we discuss obedience.

What if you had been one of those people who witnessed Kitty Genovese's murder? Would you have intervened or called the police? If you are like most people, you probably think that you would have done so. Similarly, most people would probably say that they would not have drunk the poison at Jonestown. However, the vast majority did so. Why is there at times this discrepancy between what we say we would do and what we actually do? Social psychologists would say that when we just think about what our behavior would be in such a situation, we are not subject to the social forces that are operating in the actual situation. If you're in the situation, however, social forces are operating and may guide your behavior in a different way. In summary, situational social forces greatly influence our behavior and thinking. Keep this in mind as we discuss various types of social influence and social thinking.

How Others Influence Our Behavior

Social influence research examines how other people and the social forces they create influence an individual's behavior. There are many types of social influence, including conformity, compliance, obedience, and group influences. In this section, we will discuss all of these types of social influence. We start with conformity.

Why We Conform

Conformity is usually defined as a change in behavior, belief, or both to conform to a group norm as a result of real or imagined group pressure. The word *conformity* has a negative connotation. We don't like to be thought of as conformists. However, conformity research indicates that humans have a strong tendency to conform. To understand the two major types of social influence leading to conformity (informational social influence and

conformity A change in behavior, belief, or both to conform to a group norm as a result of real or imagined group pressure.

normative social influence), we'll consider two classic studies on conformity: Muzafer Sherif's study using the autokinetic effect and Solomon Asch's study using a line-length judgment task.

The Sherif study and informational social influence. In Sherif's study, the participants thought that they were part of a visual perception experiment (Sherif, 1937). Participants in completely dark rooms were exposed to a stationary point of light and asked to estimate the distance the light moved. Thanks to an illusion called the autokinetic effect, a stationary point of light appears to move in a dark room because there is no frame of reference and our eyes spontaneously move. How far and in what direction the light appears to move varies widely among different people. During the first session in Sherif's study, each participant was alone in the dark room when making his judgments. Then, during the next three sessions, he was in the room with two other participants and could hear the others' estimates of the illusory light movement. What happened?

The average of the individual estimates varied greatly during the first session. Over the next three group sessions, however, the individual estimates converged on a common group norm (see Figure 9.1). All of the participants in the group

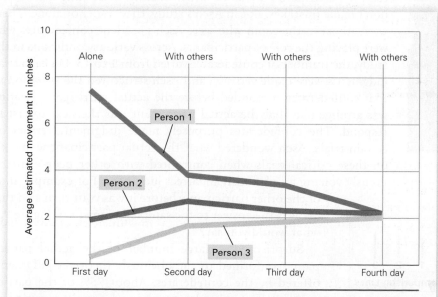

Figure 9.1 | Results of Sherif's Study of Conformity | When the three participants in Sherif's study were alone in the laboratory room on the first day, their estimates of the apparent movement of the stationary point of light varied greatly. However, once they were all together in the laboratory room from the second through the fourth day and could hear one another, their estimates converged. By the fourth day, they were all making the same judgments. (Data from Sherif, M. & Sherif, C.W. (1969) *Social Psychology*. New York: Harper and Row, p. 209.)

informational social influence
Influence stemming from the need for information in situations in which the correct action or judgment is uncertain.

ended up making the same estimates. What do you think would happen if you brought the participants back a year later and had them make estimates again while alone? Would their estimates regress back to their earlier individual estimates or stay at the group norm? Surprisingly, they stay at the group norm (Rohrer, Baron, Hoffman, & Swander, 1954).

To understand why conformity was observed in Sherif's study, we need to consider **informational social influence.** This effect stems from our desire to be right in situations in which the correct action or judgment is not obvious and we need information. In Sherif's study, participants needed information because of the illusory nature of the judgment; thus, their conformity was due to informational social influence. When a task is ambiguous or difficult and we want to be correct, we look to others for information. But what about conformity when information about the correct way to proceed is not needed? To understand this type of conformity, we need to consider Asch's study on line-length judgment and normative social influence.

Solomon Asch

The Asch study and normative social influence. Student participants in Asch's study made line-length judgments similar to the one in Figure 9.2 (Asch, 1955, 1956). These line-length judgments are easy. If participants are alone when making these judgments, they don't make mistakes. But in Asch's study, they were not alone. There were others in the room who were Asch's student confederates who were playing the role of participants. Across various conditions in the study, the number of confederates varied from 1 to 15. On each trial, judgments were made verbally, and Asch structured the situation so that confederates responded before the actual participant. Seating was arranged so that the actual participant was the next to last to respond. The confederates purposely made judgmental errors on certain trials. Asch wondered what the actual participant would do on these critical trials when confronted with other people unanimously voicing an obviously incorrect judgment. For example, if all of the other participants before it was your turn said that "1" was the answer to the sample judgment in Figure 9.2, what would you say?

Surprisingly, a large number of the actual participants conformed to the obviously incorrect judgments offered by the confederates. About 75% of the participants conformed at least once, and overall, participants conformed 37% of the time. Asch's results have been replicated many times and in many different countries (Bond & Smith, 1996). The correct answers are clear in the Asch judgment task, and there are no obvious reasons to conform. The students in the experimental room didn't know one another, and they were all of the same

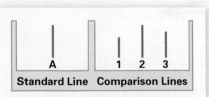

Figure 9.2 | An Example of Asch's Line-Length Judgment Task | The task is to judge which one of the comparison lines (1, 2, or 3) is the same length as the standard line on the left.

Asch's Conformity Study | This is a photograph taken from one of Asch's conformity experiments. The student in the middle (#6) is the actual participant. The other participants are confederates of the experimenter. As you can see, the actual participant is perplexed by the obviously incorrect responses of the confederate participants on this trial.

status. The judgment task was incredibly easy. Why, then, was any conformity observed?

The reason for the conformity observed in Asch's study is **normative social influence,** an effect stemming from our desire to gain the approval and to avoid the disapproval of others. We change our behavior to meet the expectations of others and to get the acceptance of others. We go along with the crowd. But Asch, who died in 1996, always wondered whether the subjects who conformed did so only out of normative needs, knowing that their answers were wrong, or whether they did so because the social pressure of the situation also actually changed their perceptions to agree with the group—what the confederates said changed what the participants saw (Blakeslee, 2005). Berns et al. (2005) found some evidence that the latter may possibly be the case. Using fMRI (see Chapter 2), they scanned subjects' brain activity while participating in an Asch-type conformity experiment employing a mental rotation task instead of a line-length judgment task. As in Asch's studies, conformity was observed. Subjects gave the group's incorrect answers (conformed) 41% of the time. Surprisingly, the brain activity for conforming responses was in the cortical areas dedicated to visual and spatial awareness, regions devoted to perception. However, the brain activity for independent responses was in the cortical areas devoted to emotion, such as the amygdala, indicating that nonconformity creates an emotional cost. These findings led the study's lead author, Gregory Berns, to conclude that, "We like to think that seeing is believing, but the study's findings show that seeing is believing what the group tells you to believe" (Blakeslee, 2005). This conclusion seems much too strong given the limitations on deciding the exact nature of the visual processing leading to the activity in the indicated brain areas. Although it can be concluded that different brain areas were active during conforming

normative social influence Influence stemming from our desire to gain the approval and to avoid the disapproval of others.

versus nonconforming responding, clearly, more research is needed before it can be concluded that the conformers actually changed their perceptions.

The finding by Berns et al. (2005) that the brain activity for independent responses indicated that nonconformity had an emotional cost, however, fits with Asch's belief that a shared reality is the foundation of social behavior, and people become very upset when it is violated, as it was on the critical trials in Asch's experiment (Gilchrist, 2015). According to Gilchrist, we feel the greatest distress when we find ourselves isolated on highly unambiguous properties of our shared reality, such as the line-length judgments in Asch's study. Interestingly, Gilchrist relates the situation on critical trials to the intense debate that arose over The Dress color controversy (white and gold perceivers vs. blue and black perceivers) that we discussed in Chapter 3. Remember, those dramatically different perceptions of the dress's color are thought to have stemmed from subjective differences among people in color constancy perception created by the brain's determination of the illumination source for the dress. We take color as a highly unambiguous property of reality. Hence, our shared view of reality was violated when confronted with perceptions of the colors of the dress different from our own, leading to the ensuing heated, emotional debate about the colors of the dress. Similarly, participants in Asch's experiment were confronted with a violation of shared reality created by the obviously incorrect judgments of the other participants to an unambiguous property of the reality (line length), which led them to be emotionally upset.

Although Asch's study found some evidence for conformity stemming from normative social influence, it is important to remember that most of the time, most of the subjects in Asch's study responded independently (gave correct answers) on the critical trials. For example, whereas 37% of the responses on critical trials were conforming (incorrect), 63% were independent (correct) responses (Asch, 1956). In addition, Asch reported that 25% of the participants never conformed, and only 5% conformed on all critical trials. Thus, 5 times as many participants were consistently independent as were consistently conforming, and although 75% of the subjects conformed at least once, 95% of the participants gave independent responses at least once. In sum, the subjects in Asch's study truly tended to respond independently more often than in a conforming manner. Even Asch was struck by the rate at which subjects responded independently (Friend, Rafferty, & Bramel, 1990). Friend et al. maintain that when Asch's work first appeared, it was taken as evidence of the powers of independence, but with the passing years, it has been represented as a study of conformity. In sum, Asch's study led to two complementary findings. Normative social influence leads some people to conform even in performing a nonambiguous task, but the majority of people, although emotionally affected, are not swayed in this situation by such influence. Next we will consider some factors that impact the amount of conformity observed.

Situational, cultural, and gender factors that impact conformity. Asch and other conformity researchers have found many situational factors that affect whether we conform. Let's consider three. (1) Unanimity of the group is important. It's difficult to be a minority of one, but not two. For example, Asch found that the amount of conformity drops considerably if just one of the confederate participants gives an answer—right or wrong—that differs from the rest of the group. (2) The mode of responding (voting aloud versus secret ballot) is also important. In Asch's study, if the actual participant did not have to respond aloud after hearing the group's responses, but rather could write his response, the amount of conformity dropped dramatically. So, in the various groups to which you belong, be sure to use secret ballots when voting on issues if you want the true opinions of your group members. (3) Finally, more conformity is observed from a person who is of lesser status than the other group members or who is attracted to the group and wants to be a part of it. These situational factors are especially effective in driving conformity when there is a probationary period for attaining group membership.

Cultural factors also seem to impact the amount of conformity that is observed. As mentioned earlier, Bond and Smith (1996) conducted a meta-analysis of 133 conformity studies drawn from 17 countries using an Asch-type line-length judgment task to investigate whether the level of conformity had changed over time and whether it is related cross-culturally to individualism–collectivism. Broadly defined, individualism emphasizes individual needs and achievement. Collectivism, in contrast, emphasizes group needs, thereby encouraging conformity and discouraging dissent with the group. Analyzing just the studies conducted in the United States, they found that the amount of conformity had declined since the 1950s, paralleling the change in our culture toward more individualism. Similarly, they found that collectivist countries (e.g., Hong Kong) tended to show higher levels of conformity than individualist countries (e.g., the United States). Thus, whereas Asch's basic conformity findings have been replicated in many different countries, cultural factors do play a role in determining the amount of conformity that is observed.

In their meta-analysis, Bond and Smith (1996) also found evidence for gender differences in conformity. They observed a higher level of conformity for female participants, which is consistent with earlier reviews of conformity studies (e.g., Eagly & Carli, 1981). They also found that this gender difference in conformity had not narrowed over time. Mori and Arai (2010) recently replicated this gender difference finding, using a very clever presentation technique, called the fMORI technique, that eliminates the need for confederates. This technique allowed the researchers to present different stimuli to the minority participants and the majority participants on critical trials without their awareness. The top part of the standard lines appeared in either green or magenta so that the two groups of participants would see them differently when wearing different types of polarizing sunglasses that filtered either green or magenta to make the lines appear longer or shorter. Mori and Arai's study, incorporating a new presentation technique, testifies to the continuing interest in Asch's conformity research, which is more than a half-century old.

Why We Comply

Conformity is a form of social influence in which people change their behavior or attitudes in order to adhere to a group norm. **Compliance** is acting in accordance to a direct request from another person or group. Think about how often others—your parents, roommates, friends, salespeople, and so on—make requests of you. Social psychologists have identified many different techniques that help others to achieve compliance with such requests. Salespeople, fundraisers, politicians, and anyone else who wants to get people to say "yes" use these compliance techniques. After reading this section you should be much more aware of how other people—especially salespeople—attempt to get you to comply with their requests. Of course, you'll also be better equipped to get other people to comply with your requests. As we discuss these compliance techniques, note how each one involves two requests, and how it is the second request with which the person wants compliance. We'll start our discussion with a compliance technique that you have probably encountered—the foot-in-the-door technique.

The foot-in-the-door technique. In the **foot-in-the-door technique,** compliance to a large request is gained by preceding it with a very small request. The tendency is for people who have complied with the small request to comply with the next, larger request. The principle is simply to start small and build. One classic experimental demonstration of this technique involved a large, ugly sign about driving carefully (Freedman & Fraser, 1966). People were asked directly if this ugly sign could be put in their front yards, and the vast majority of them refused. However, the majority of the people who had complied with a much smaller request two weeks earlier (for example, to sign a safe-driving petition) agreed to have the large, ugly sign put in their yard. The smaller request had served as the "foot in the door."

In another study, people who were first asked to wear a pin publicizing a cancer fund-raising drive and then later asked to donate to a cancer charity were far more likely to donate to the cancer charity than were people who were asked only to contribute to the charity (Pliner, Hart, Kohl, & Saari, 1974). Why does the foot-in-the-door technique work? Its success seems to be partially due to our behavior (complying with the initial request) affecting our attitudes both to be more positive about helping and to view ourselves as generally charitable people. In addition, once we have made a commitment (such as signing a safe-driving petition), we feel pressure to remain consistent (putting up the large ugly sign) with this earlier commitment.

compliance Acting in accordance with a direct request from another person or group.

foot-in-the-door technique Compliance to a large request is gained by preceding it with a very small request.

This technique was used by the Chinese Communists during the Korean War on prisoners of war to help brainwash them about Communism (Ornstein, 1991). Many prisoners returning after the war had praise for the Chinese Communists. This attitude had been cultivated by having the prisoners first do small things like writing out some questions and then the pro-Communist answers, which they might just copy from a notebook, and then later writing essays in the guise of students summarizing the Communist position on various issues such as poverty. Just as the participants' attitudes changed in the Freedman and Fraser study and they later agreed to put the big, ugly sign in their yard, the POWs became more sympathetic to the Communist cause. The foot-in-the-door technique is a very powerful technique. Watch out for compliance requests of increasing size. Say no, before it is too late to do so.

> **door-in-the-face technique**
> Compliance is gained by starting with a large, unreasonable request that is turned down and following it with a more reasonable, smaller request.

The door-in-the-face technique. The door-in-the-face technique is the opposite of the foot-in-the-door technique (Cialdini, Vincent, Lewis, Catalan, Wheeler, & Danby, 1975). In the **door-in-the-face technique,** compliance is gained by starting with a large, unreasonable request that is turned down and following it with a more reasonable, smaller request. The person who is asked to comply appears to be slamming the door in the face of the person making the large request. It is the smaller request, however, that the person making the two requests wants all along. For example, imagine that one of your friends asked you to watch his pet for a month while he is out of town. You refuse. Then your friend asks for what he really wanted, which was for you to watch the pet over the following weekend. You agree. What has happened? You've succumbed to the door-in-the-face technique.

The success of the door-in-the-face technique is probably due to our tendency toward reciprocity, making mutual concessions. The person making the requests appears to have made a concession by moving to the much smaller request. Shouldn't we reciprocate and comply with this smaller request? Fear that others won't view us as fair, helpful, and concerned for others likely also plays a role in this compliance technique's success. The door-in-the-face technique seems to have even been involved in G. Gordon Liddy getting the Watergate burglary approved by the Committee for the Re-election of the President, abbreviated CRP, but often mocked by the acronym CREEP (Cialdini, 1993). The committee approved Liddy's plan with a bare bones $250,000 budget, after they had disapproved plans with $1 million and $500,000 proposed budgets. The only committee person who opposed acceptance had not been present for the previous two more

BLONDIE

costly proposal meetings. Thus, he was able to see the irrationality of the plan and was not subject to the door-in-the-face reciprocity influence felt by other committee members.

The low-ball technique. Consider the following scenario (Cialdini, 1993). You go to buy a new car. The salesperson gives you a great price, much better than you ever imagined. You go into the salesperson's office and start filling out the sales forms and arranging for financing. The salesperson then says that before completing the forms, she forgot that she has to get approval from her sales manager. She leaves for a few minutes and returns looking rather glum. She says, regretfully, that the sales manager said that he couldn't give you that great price you thought you had. The sales price has to be a higher one. What do most people do in this situation? You probably are thinking that you wouldn't buy the car. However, research on this compliance tactic, called the low-ball technique, indicates that it does work—people buy the car at the higher price (Cialdini, Cacioppo, Bassett, & Miller, 1978).

In the **low-ball technique,** compliance to a costly request is achieved by first getting compliance to an attractive, less costly request and then reneging on it. This is similar to the foot-in-the-door technique in that a second, larger request is the one desired. In the low-ball technique, however, the first request is one that is very attractive to you. You are not making a concession (as in the foot-in-the-door technique), but rather getting a good deal. However, the "good" part of the deal is then taken away. Why does the low-ball technique work? The answer is that many of us feel obligated to go through with the deal after we have agreed to the earlier deal (request) even if the deal has changed for the worse. This is similar to the pressure we feel to remain consistent in our commitment that helps drive the foot-in-the-door technique. So remember, if somebody tries to use the low-ball technique on you, walk away. You are not obligated to comply with the new request.

The that's-not-all technique. There's another compliance technique, which is often used in television infomercials. Just after the price for the product is given and before you can decide yes or no about it, the announcer says, "But wait, that's not all, there's more," and the price is lowered or more merchandise is included, or both, in order to sweeten the deal. Sometimes an initial price is not even given. Rather, the announcer says something like, "How much would you pay for this incredible product?" and then goes on to sweeten the deal before you can answer. As in the low-ball technique, the final offer is the one that was planned from the start. However, you are more likely to comply and take the deal after all of the buildup than if this "better" deal were offered directly (Burger, 1986). This technique is called the **that's-not-all technique**—to gain compliance, a planned second request with additional benefits is made before a response to a first request can be made. Like the

low-ball technique Compliance to a costly request is gained by first getting compliance to an attractive, less costly request but then reneging on it.

that's-not-all technique Compliance to a planned second request with additional benefits is gained by presenting this request before a response can be made to a first request.

Table 9.1	Four Compliance Techniques		
Technique	**1st Request**	**2nd Request**	**Major Reason for Compliance**
Foot-in-the-door	Small	Larger	Consistency
Door-in-the-face	Large	Smaller	Reciprocity
Low-ball	Attractive	Less attractive	Consistency
That's-not-all	Attractive	More attractive	Reciprocity

door-in-the-face technique, salespeople also use this technique. For example, before you can answer yes or no to a price offered by a car salesperson, he throws in some "bonus options" for the car. As in the door-in-the-face technique, reciprocity is at work here. The seller has made a concession (the bonus options), so shouldn't you reciprocate by taking the offer, complying? We often do.

In summary, each of these compliance techniques involves two requests (see Table 9.1). In the foot-in-the-door technique, a small request is followed by a larger request. In the door-in-the-face technique, a large request is followed by a smaller request. In the low-ball technique, an attractive first request is taken back and followed by a less-attractive request. In the that's-not-all technique, a more attractive request is made before a response can be given to an initial request. In all cases, the person making the requests is attempting to manipulate you with the first request. It is the second request for which compliance is desired. The foot-in-the-door and low-ball techniques both lead to commitment to the first request with the hope that the person will feel pressure to remain true to his initial commitment and accede to the second request. The other two techniques involve reciprocity. Once the other person has made a concession (or accepted our refusal in the door-in-the-face technique) or done us a favor (or offered an even better deal in the that's-not-all technique), we think we should reciprocate and accede to the second request.

Why We Obey

Compliance is agreeing to a request from a person. **Obedience** is following the commands of a person in authority. Obedience is sometimes constructive and beneficial to us. It would be difficult for a society to exist, for instance, without obedience to its laws. Young children need to obey their caretakers for their own well-being. Obedience can also be destructive, though. There are many real-world examples of its destructive nature. Consider Nazi Germany, in which millions of innocent people were murdered, or the My Lai massacre in Vietnam, in which American soldiers killed hundreds of innocent children, women, and old people. In the My Lai massacre, the soldiers were ordered to shoot the innocent

obedience Following the commands of a person in authority.

Stanley Milgram

villagers, and they did. The phrase "I was only following orders" usually surfaces in such cases. When confronted with these atrocities, we wonder what type of person could do such horrible things. At times, however, it may be the situational social forces, and not the person, that should bear more of the responsibility for the actions. Just as we found that situational factors can lead us to conform and comply, can we find that such social forces can sometimes lead us to commit acts of destructive obedience?

Milgram's basic experimental procedure. The largest empirical study examining the possibility of social forces as causes of destructive obedience was Stanley Milgram's obedience study done at Yale University in the early 1960s (Milgram, 1963, 1965, 1974). It is arguably the most famous and most controversial study in psychology. After over 50 years, the debate about the ethical, methodological, and theoretical issues of the study shows no signs of abating. The fascination with Milgram's study outside of psychology has also continued, as evidenced by the recent release of *Experimenter,* a 2015 theatrical film about Milgram and the obedience study that starred Peter Sarsgaard and Winona Ryder. This is not the first film made about this study. *The Tenth Level,* a 1976 CBS television movie starring William Shatner, was also about Milgram and the obedience experiments. Because of the study's notoriety both within and outside psychology, we will describe Milgram's experimental procedure and findings in more detail than usual. We start with a description of Milgram's basic experimental procedure.

Let's consider Milgram's basic experimental procedure from the perspective of a participant in the study. Imagine that you have volunteered to be in an experiment on learning and memory. You show up at the assigned time and place, where you encounter two men, the experimenter and another participant, a middle-aged man. The experimenter explains that the study is examining the effects of punishment by electric shock on learning, specifically learning a list of word pairs (for example, blue–box). The teacher will read the list of word pairs to the learner, and then the testing will begin. The learner will have to indicate for each of the first words in the word pairs, which of four words had originally been paired with it on the list. The learner will press one of four switches, which will light up one of the four answer boxes located on top of the shock generator. The teacher will then inform the learner if he is correct. If not correct, the teacher will tell the learner the correct answer, shock the learner via the shock generator, and go on to the next test pair. The experimenter further explains that the two participants will draw slips for the roles of teacher and learner. The other participant draws "learner," making you the teacher. You accompany the learner to an adjoining room where he is strapped into a chair with one arm hooked up to the shock generator in the other room. The shock levels in the experiment will range from 15 to 450 volts. The experimenter explains that high levels of shock need to be used in order for the study to be a valid test of its effectiveness as punishment.

The experimenter gives you a sample shock of 45 volts so that you have some idea of the intensity of the various shock levels.

You return to the other room with the experimenter and sit down at the shock generator. It is big—3 feet long with a height and depth of 16 inches. It has an array of buttons, dials, and switches. There is a switch for each level of shock, starting at 15 volts and going up to 450 volts in 15-volt increments. There are also some labels below the switches—"Slight Shock," "Very Strong Shock," "Danger: Severe Shock," and, under the last two switches, "XXX" in red. The experimenter reminds you that when the learner makes a mistake on the word-pair task, you are to administer the shock by pushing the appropriate switch. You are to start with 15 volts for the first wrong answer and increase the shock level by 15 volts for each one after that.

After some preliminary practice trials to ensure that you and the learner understand the task, the experiment begins. The learner makes some errors, and you administer the appropriate shock each time he does. Nothing else happens except for a few groans from the learner until at 120 volts the learner cries out that the shocks really hurt. As the shock level increases, you hear him cry out, and his screams escalate with the increasing voltage. At higher levels, he protests and says that he no longer wants to participate and that he isn't going to respond anymore. After 330 volts, he doesn't respond. You turn to the experimenter to see what to do. The experimenter says to treat a nonresponse as a wrong answer and to continue with the experiment. The learner never responds again.

This is a summary of the situation that Milgram's participants confronted. What would you do? If you are like most people, you say you would stop at a rather low level of shock. Milgram asked various types of people (college students, nonstudent adults, and psychiatrists) what they thought they and other people would do. Inevitably, the response was that they would stop at a fairly low level of shock, less than 150 volts, that other people would also do so, and that virtually no one would go to the end of the shock generator. The psychiatrists said that maybe one person in a thousand would do so.

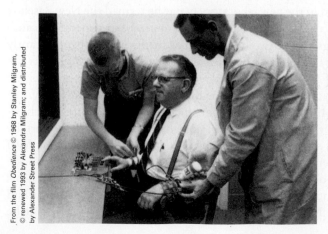

These photos from Milgram's obedience studies show the shock generator that the teacher used and the learner being strapped into a chair and fitted with electrodes.

Milgram's findings. As you have probably guessed, Milgram (1963) didn't find what these people predicted. For the experimental conditions just described, almost two out of every three participants (62.5%) continued to obey the experimenter and administered the maximum possible shock (450 volts). Milgram also found that the experimental situation generated considerable tension and emotional strain in the participants. Many participants showed signs of such tension—sweating, trembling, stuttering, biting their lips, and so on. Milgram attributed this tension to the conflict between our ingrained disposition not to harm others and the equally compelling tendency to obey authority. Surprisingly, Milgram had observed a similar 65% obedience rate in an experiment he conducted earlier in which the learner made no vocal protests but rather just pounded the laboratory wall in protest at 300 volts and stopped pounding and responding after 315 volts. Although a 65% obedience rate seems startlingly high for such limited learner feedback, Milgram found in a pilot study that without any auditory input (no vocal protests or pounding the wall), virtually every participant continued to obey the experimenter and administered the maximum possible shock (Milgram, 1965).

Because he had to change the laboratory in which he was conducting the obedience study after four experiments, Milgram felt it necessary to conduct a replication experiment using the conditions we initially described with different participants to determine if the new laboratory, which was much more modest and in the basement of the building, had any impact on his findings (Milgram, 1974). He added one small change to the script—the learner mentions a slight heart condition before the experiment and again during his protests (see Table 9.2). Milgram thought that this heart problem might provide additional justification for disobeying. It did not. He replicated his earlier 62.5% finding—this time 65% administered the maximum shock. The mentions of the heart condition had no significant impact on the obedience rate. There is a sad irony here in that the learner did have a heart problem and died from it about three years later (Blass, 2009). Before changing laboratories, Milgram used the experiment with no mention of a heart condition (what he termed the Voice-Feedback experiment) as the baseline for two more experiments and then used the replication experiment with the mention of a heart condition conducted in the new laboratory (what he termed the New Baseline experiment) thereafter as the baseline for the remaining 18 experiments. Because the obedience rate findings for the two baseline experiments were not significantly different and the finding for the New Baseline experiment (65%) was used as the baseline for almost all of Milgram's other experiments, we will refer to it as the baseline obedience rate in the remainder of the discussion of Milgram's study.

Do you realize how Milgram used the foot-in-the-door technique in achieving a high rate of obedience (Gilbert, 1981)? He had the participant start by administering very small shocks (beginning at 15 volts) and increased the level slowly (in 15-volt increments). The learner didn't protest these mild, early shocks. The teacher had already obeyed several times by the time the learner started his protests (at 120 volts), and by the time the shock level was high, the teacher had obeyed numerous times. Milgram's results might have been very different if he

Table 9.2	Examples of the Learner's Protests in Milgram's New Baseline Experiment in Which the Learner Has a Heart Condition
120 volts	Ugh! Hey, this really hurts.
150 volts	Ugh!!! Experimenter! That's all. Get me out of here. I told you I had heart trouble. My heart's starting to bother me now. Get me out of here, please. My heart's starting to bother me. I refuse to go on. Let me out.
210 volts	Ugh!! Experimenter! Get me out of here. I've had enough. I won't be in the experiment any more.
270 volt	(*Agonized scream.*) Let me out of here. Let me out of here. Let me out of here. Let me out. Do you hear? Let me out of here.
300 volts	(*Agonized scream.*) I absolutely refuse to answer any more. Get me out of here. You can't hold me here. Get me out. Get me out of here.
315 volts	(*Intensely agonized scream.*) I told you I refuse to answer. I'm no longer part of this experiment.
330 volts	(*Intense and prolonged agonized scream.*) Let me out of here. Let me out of here. My heart's bothering me. Let me out, I tell you. (Hysterically) Let me out of here. Let me out of here. You have no right to hold me here. Let me out! Let me out! Let me out! Let me out of here! Let me out! Let me out!

For the complete schedule of protests, see Milgram (1974), pp. 56–57.

would have had participants start at a high level of shock or if the learner had protested the first few small shocks.

There are some additional procedural aspects of Milgram's experiments that you should know before we discuss some of Milgram's other findings. All of the experiments were conducted at Yale University except for two conducted in Bridgeport, Connecticut, and, except for one experiment, the participants were men, from age 20 to 50, who were volunteers solicited from the New Haven or Bridgeport communities and paid $4, plus 50¢ bus fare, for their participation. The drawing was rigged so that the true participants always drew the role of teacher. The teacher only thought he was administering the shocks. The learner was never actually shocked. The only real shock administered was the sample shock given to the teacher before the experiment began. Both the learner and the experimenter were two local men that Milgram had hired to play those roles. In actuality, the experimenter was a 31-year-old high school biology teacher, and the learner was a 47-year-old accountant. Milgram personally trained them for weeks prior to the study to make sure that they were as convincing as possible in their roles. For standardization purposes, however, the learner's responses to the shocks were prerecorded on tape with each protest coordinated to a particular voltage level on the shock generator, and the learner's responses to the test items followed a preset pattern of right and wrong answers.

In addition, if at any time the teacher protested or expressed doubt about continuing, the experimenter was supposed to use a series of four standardized prods to encourage the participant to continue. These prods were to be delivered in the following sequence: "Please continue," or "Please go on"; "The experiment requires that you continue"; "It is absolutely essential that you continue"; and "You have no other choice, you must go on." If after the fourth prod, the participant refused to continue, the participant would be classified as disobedient, the experimental session terminated, and the voltage at which the participant stopped noted. There were also two special prods to be used in special situations. First, if the participant asked if the learner was liable to suffer permanent physical injury, the experimenter was to say: "Although the shocks may be painful, there is no permanent tissue damage, so please go on." If necessary, this would be followed by prods 2, 3, and 4. Second, if the participant said that the learner did not want to go on, the experimenter was to reply: "Whether the learner likes it or not, you must go on until he has learned all the word pairs correctly. So please go on." Again, if necessary, this would be followed by prods 2, 3, and 4.

Overall, Milgram conducted 23 experiments with a total of 780 participants. Perry (2013) provides a chronological list with descriptions of all of Milgram's experiments. The other 20 experiments that we haven't discussed examined variants of the baseline condition to determine the impact of various situational factors (social forces) on the obedience rate observed. Remember, the baseline obedience rate was 65%. Thus, the impact of a situational factor is assessed by how much it increases or decreases this 65% baseline obedience rate.

According to Milgram, an important situational factor is the physical presence of the experimenter (the person with authority). He found that if the experimenter left the laboratory and gave his commands over the telephone, the obedience rate dropped to 20.5%. The closeness of the teacher and the learner is also important (as the auditory input indicated). Remember, virtually every participant administered the maximum shock when the learner did not vocally protest or pound the wall, but only about two of every three participants did so when the teacher could hear the learner's protests or pounding. In another experiment, Milgram made the teacher and learner even closer by having them both in the same room instead of different rooms, and obedience rate dropped to 40%. It dropped even further, to 30%, when the teacher had to administer the shock directly by forcing the learner's hand onto a shock plate. This means that obedience decreases as the teacher and learner are physically closer to each other. Interestingly, though, the maximum obedience rate doesn't drop to 0% even when they touch; it is still 30%.

To check whether the location of the experiments, prestigious Yale University, contributed to the high

The teacher is administering the shock to the learner by directly forcing the learner's arm on the shock plate. Even in this situation, maximal obedience was still 30%.

obedience rate in the baseline condition, Milgram ran the baseline condition in a rundown office building in nearby Bridgeport, Connecticut, completely dissociated from Yale. The obedience rate went down. Milgram found an obedience rate of 47.5%. Hence, Milgram concluded that the prestige and authority of the university setting did contribute some to the baseline obedience rate, but not nearly as much as the presence of the experimenter or the closeness of the teacher and the learner. None of these factors, however, lowered the obedience rate below 20%, but it dropped to 10% in an experiment with two confederate disobedient teachers modeling disobedience for the participant teacher. To get the obedience rate to 0%, Milgram had to set up a situation with two experimenters who at some point during the experiment disagreed. One said to stop the experiment, while the other said to continue. In this case, when one of the people in authority said to stop, all of the participant teachers stopped.

What about getting the obedience rate to increase from that observed in the baseline condition? Milgram tried to do that by taking the direct responsibility for shocking away from the learner. Instead, the teacher only pushed the switch on the shock generator to indicate to another teacher (another confederate) in the room with the learner how much shock to administer. With this direct responsibility for shocking the learner lifted off of their shoulders, almost all of the participants (92.5%) obeyed the experimenter and administered the maximum shock level. This finding and all of the others that we have discussed are summarized in Table 9.3 (page 388), so that you can compare them.

Following his first publication about the obedience experiments in which he described the findings for the baseline condition with no mention of a heart condition (Milgram, 1963), Milgram was surprised by the first published response by his peers (Baumrind, 1964) because it focused on his treatment of his participants and methodology and not his results. Baumrind severely criticized Milgram for his unethical treatment of the participants. She argued that he inflicted emotional harm, possibly irreparable, on the participants by placing them in an extremely traumatic situation in which they believed they were harming another human being and that the gain in knowledge from Milgram's study did not outweigh the distress his participants had endured. In his rebuttal to Baumrind (1964), Milgram (1964) reported that when the experimental session was over, the participants were immediately debriefed and told that the learner was not actually shocked. He also reported the findings of a questionnaire sent to all experimental participants about a year later along with a study report, asking them to reflect on their experience during the experiment. Milgram reported that most participants in the obedience experiments had positive feelings about their participation. This positive reaction of most participants toward the experiments probably seems odd to you given the aversive nature of their experiences in the study. Why did they later feel so positive about such a negative experience? We will give an explanation of these seemingly contradictory questionnaire data later when we discuss the engaged-followership reinterpretation of Milgram's findings. Milgram also reported that 9 months

Table 9.3	Results for Some of Milgram's Experimental Conditions
Experimental Conditions	**Percent of Maximum Obedience Observed**
Teacher and learner in different rooms, no auditory input (pilot study)	100
Teacher does not have direct responsibility for administering shock	92.5
Teacher and learner in different rooms and learner pounds wall at 300 volts and stops pounding and responding after 315 volts	65
Baseline condition—teacher and learner in different rooms, escalated vocal protests, and nonresponding after 330 volts	62.5; 65 in replication with learner mentioning heart condition before and during the experiment
Baseline condition but female participants	65
In office building in Bridgeport, Connecticut	47.5
Teacher and learner in same room	40
Teacher and learner in same room and teacher has to force learner's hand onto shock plate	30
Experimenter not present	20.5
Two models of disobedience	10
Two experimenters who disagree	0

after the experiments, he had a psychiatrist interview 40 participants with the aim of identifying any who might have been harmed by the experiment and that the psychiatrist reported that he found no harm in any of the participants he interviewed. Milgram's reply, however, didn't satisfy Baumrind and other critics of his unethical methods and treatment of the participants, and this ethical controversy continued on into the 1970s and beyond.

Baumrind (1964) also argued that Milgram's findings did not have external validity (the extent to which the results of a study can be generalized to other situations and to other people) and thus, contrary to Milgram's claims, could not be used to explain real-world atrocities, such as the Holocaust. Orne and Holland (1968; cf. Milgram's rebuttal, 1972) agreed with Baumrind about the lack of external validity. They also argued that, given the experimental methodology used by Milgram, it was likely that many of Milgram's participants did not believe that they were really administering shocks to the learner, resulting in the high rate of obedience that was observed. This would indicate that there was also a lack of internal validity in that Milgram wasn't studying what he thought he was studying. In their opinion, Milgram was too concerned with participants' behavior and not enough with their perception of the situation. Participants in an experiment are concerned with being good subjects and acting in a manner that they perceive is expected of them. Orne and Holland reported some data that Orne and Evans

(1965) had collected that indicated that the vast majority of participants (84%) would comply with an experimenter's instructions to perform dangerous tasks, such as retrieving a coin from what appeared to be nitric acid, if they thought that they were participating in an experiment because they assumed that things were not at all as they appeared to be. However, participants who were not told they were participating in an experiment declined to perform these tasks. Hence, the participants in Milgram's study knew they were participating in a scientific experiment and likely acted as they did because they too assumed that things were not as they appeared and that the learner was not actually being shocked. This is a trust issue—the participants trusted that the experimenter and Yale University would not let the learner be seriously harmed. Laurent (1987) pointed out a congruent finding in a Milgram replication at the prestigious Max Planck Institute in Germany—"the subjects . . . seem to have felt that the Max Planck Institute would not let anything dreadful happen" (Mantell & Panzarella, 1976, p. 244). Brannigan, Nicholson, and Cherry (2015) recently reiterated this criticism and echoed Orne and Holland's argument: "The key point is that participants knew they were participating in a *psychology* experiment—a social space akin to a magician's stage, one that licenses all sorts of atypical behavior and unexpected occurrences, but which also brings with it the strong expectation that nobody will be harmed. Many participants indicated that this awareness influenced their actions . . ." (p. 556, italics in original). Like the ethical criticisms, criticisms concerned with the lack of internal or external validity continued on for decades (e.g., Fenigstein, 2015; Laurent, 1987; Lutsky, 1995; Mixon, 1976; Parker, 2000; Patten, 1977). Now, over 50 years later, new ethical and methodological criticisms have surfaced with some new discoveries about Milgram's experiments and his reporting of them. We discuss these next.

Recent revelations about Milgram's obedience experiments. Recent analyses of the materials in the Milgram archives at Yale's Sterling Memorial Library related to the obedience experiments have resulted in serious criticisms of both Milgram's experiments and his reporting of them. These archival materials include audio recordings of the actual experiments; transcripts of participants' conversations with the psychiatrist; participants' questionnaire responses; and the notes, documentation, and correspondence accumulated during the obedience experiments. Gina Perry spent more than 4 years not only analyzing these archival materials but also conducting personal interviews with former participants, experts familiar with the research, and relatives of the men who served as the experimenter and learner in the experiments. Her research resulted in a book, *Behind the Shock Machine,* in which she summarizes her findings and criticisms of both Milgram and the obedience experiments (Perry, 2013). We will discuss Perry's main criticisms and incorporate some of the criticisms of other archival researchers within this discussion. We'll start with her revelation about the debriefing procedure that Milgram reported that he used.

Perry found that the archival materials reveal a somewhat different account of the debriefing than was reported by Milgram. Perry discovered that the majority of participants were *not* appropriately debriefed in a timely manner as Milgram claimed in his reply to Baumrind (Milgram, 1964) or later in his 1974 book that summarized many of the obedience experiments. According to Perry, the majority of participants did *not* learn that they did not actually shock the learner until almost a year later. Based on the participants' comments on the questionnaire that Milgram had sent to them 9 months after the experiments, about three-fourths of the participants were not told the full story until they received the study report that Milgram sent to them with the questionnaire, but, as Perry points out, some may not have read or even received the report and thus would have never known that the learner was not actually shocked. Perry is not the only researcher criticizing Milgram's inadequate debriefing of participants. Nicholson (2011), for example, analyzed the Milgram archival materials and, like Perry, concluded that Milgram misrepresented the extent and efficacy of his debriefing procedures, the risk posed by the experiment, and the harm done to his participants. According to Nicholson, Milgram most likely deliberately misrepresented the post-experimental debriefing in his published work to protect his credibility as a responsible researcher and the ethical integrity and possible future of the obedience experiments. Although we will never know with certainty why Milgram misrepresented the debriefing process, he clearly did so.

Perry's analysis also discovered another significant discrepancy with what Milgram reported in his publications and what the archival materials reveal actually happened. Remember, according to Milgram, if at any time the teacher protested or expressed doubt about continuing, the experimenter was supposed to use a series of four standardized prods to encourage the participant to continue, and if after the fourth prod, the participant refused to continue, the session was terminated and the participant classified as disobedient. Perry analyzed the archival audiotapes for two experiments, an early one in the experimental sequence (the third experiment in which the teacher and learner were in the same room) and a later one (the twentieth experiment in which the participants were women). The audiotapes tell a very different story about the experimenter's use of prods than Milgram told. The experimenter definitely did not follow the controlled script for using the four prods and took on a much more active role in getting participants to continue in the experiment. Perry found that in the early experiment, the experimenter followed the script for the first part of the experiment, but toward the end he was straying far from the script and was urging the teacher time and time again to continue, saying that they must go on. This off-script prodding was even more prevalent in the later experiment with women as teachers. By this time in the experimental sequence, the experimenter was adept at applying pressure and coercing the teachers. He would parry the teachers' protests, escalate the pressure by inventing more coercive prods, and engage in arguments with the teacher about continuing on in the experiment. For example, the experimenter insisted that one woman continue 26 times and other women 14 times, 11 times, and 9 times instead of ending the session after the fourth standard prod was given. Perry concluded that there was definitely a mismatch between Milgram's description of the experimenter's use of prods and the audiotape evidence of what actually transpired.

Gibson (2013) also conducted an analysis of the audiotapes of two of Milgram's experiments (the second experiment which was the original baseline condition, and, like Perry, the later experiment with women as participants), and his conclusions agree with Perry's. Gibson draws attention to the verbal exchanges between the experimenter and the teacher, especially the experimenter's creative arguments designed to convince and persuade the participants to continue the experiment, leading to radical departures from the supposed standardized use of the four prods. Likewise, Russell (2009, p. 182), who studied the audiotapes from the two experiments conducted in Bridgeport, points out that the experimenter often invented his own, far more stressful prods and described the experimenter's invented prods as "great feats of bottom-up innovation . . . to bring about what he sensed his boss desired." Thus, the experimenter's deviations from the script may have been driven by **experimenter bias** (a process in which the person performing the research influences the results in order to portray a certain outcome). Perry also noted that Milgram appears to have tacitly allowed the experimenter the license to improvise because he watched a number of the experimental conditions through a one-way mirror. In a similar vein, Russell pointed out that, given the regularity with which the experimenter strayed from the script and the fact that Milgram seems to have never attempted to correct him, Milgram probably approved of the experimenter's actions. In sum, the experimenter's behavior with respect to prodding the participants was clearly not standardized as Milgram claimed, and his deviations from the standardized prodding protocol reported by Milgram may have been driven by experimenter

experimenter bias A process in which the person performing the research influences the results in order to portray a certain outcome.

bias and tacitly approved by Milgram. Thus, we need to add a caveat to the findings given in Table 9.3—these findings were likely influenced to varying extents by experimenter bias.

Perry (2013) also found that Milgram did not report the findings of all 23 of the experiments that he conducted and thus may have selectively chosen to report only findings that supported his interpretation of the results. Of particular interest is the unreported Relationship experiment, which Russell (2014) has referred to as possibly the most controversial experiment that Milgram conducted. Milgram conducted a second experiment in Bridgeport, Connecticut, but he never reported it. The participants were 20 pairs of men (one serving as teacher and the other as learner) who were related in some way or knew each other well (a relative, a close acquaintance, or a neighbor). After the learner was strapped in and the teacher and experimenter left the room, Milgram came in and explained to the learner about the experimental ruse and coached him on how to vocalize like the confederate learner had done in the baseline condition in response to the supposed shocks. There was one other important difference between this experiment and the others that Milgram conducted (Rochat & Blass, 2014). The learner's protests were aimed at the teacher and not the experimenter. What happened? Did teachers inflict pain on a relative, friend, or neighbor? No, they did not. Milgram found a high rate of *dis*obedience, 85%, demonstrating that when a participant believed someone close to them was being hurt, they disobeyed. Perry argues that Milgram probably decided against publishing this result not only because it contradicted his overall emphasis on obedience in his publications, but also because it would be difficult to defend ethically, especially given the ethical firestorm that had arisen over the research that Milgram had reported in 1963.

Perry (2013; also see Parker, 2000) discovered evidence in the archives that a large number of participants had expressed doubts about the experimental setup and cover story in their responses to Milgram's questionnaire. This agrees with Orne and Holland's (1968) trust argument that we discussed earlier. This argument predicted that the obedience rate would be a function of the participants' belief that the learner was actually being shocked. Perry (2013) discovered in the archival materials that Milgram had his research assistant, Taketo Murata, compile an analysis that examined this prediction, but chose not to publish it. The analysis was an experiment-by-experiment breakdown of the degree of shock given by participants who were certain that the learner was being shocked versus that given by participants who had doubts about this. In 18 of the 23 experiments, the participants who fully believed that the learner was being shocked gave lower levels of shock than the participants who expressed doubts about the learner being shocked. In addition, Murata found that in all 23 experiments, the participants most likely to *dis*obey were those who said that they believed the learner was being shocked. The analysis also revealed that the believability varied across conditions, and interestingly, roughly two-thirds of the participants in the New Baseline experiment doubted that the shocks were real, which maps perfectly onto the 65% obedience rate that was observed for this experiment.

Thus, it is no surprise that Milgram decided not to publish Murata's analysis, again seemingly reporting only findings that supported his interpretation of the results. Hence, using the belief-response data from the follow-up questionnaire that he sent out almost a year after the experiments were over, Milgram (1972, 1974) argued that three-quarters of his participants acted under the belief that they were administering painful shocks. However, as Perry and others before her (e.g., Parker, 2000; Patten, 1977) have pointed out, Milgram's questionable numerical conclusion stems from his inclusion of the 24% of the participants who had expressed *some* doubt about whether the learner was getting shocked. Perry argued that it was more truthful to say that half of the participants believed the shocks were real and about two-thirds of them disobeyed the experimenter.

You may be wondering what Milgram's response has been to these recent criticisms. Sadly, we will never know what his response might have been. He died of a heart attack in 1984 at the age of 51. However, Diana Baumrind, Milgram's first critic, has reviewed Perry's book and concluded that, given Perry's findings, Milgram's version of the obedience experiments "can never again be accepted as the whole truth" (2015, p. 695). In addition to these recent criticisms that challenge both the validity of Milgram's obedience experiments and the ethical behavior of Milgram in misrepresenting the experiments in his publications, a partial replication of Milgram's New Baseline experiment has recently been conducted, and its findings have led to the conclusion that Milgram's findings were not the result of the participants' obeying the orders of an authority figure, but rather *dis*obeying them. Related to this conclusion, a new explanation of Milgram's findings has been proposed. We discuss the replication and new explanation next.

A recent replication and a new explanation of Milgram's findings. The American Psychological Association tightened its ethical standards for research with the publication of its comprehensive "Ethical Principles in the Conduct of Research with Human Participants" in 1973. Based on this publication, researchers now had to obtain informed consent from potential participants. This meant that participants had to be informed of the purpose of the experiment and what was involved so that they could weigh the risks before deciding whether to participate in the study. Even if they did give their consent, they were also given the right to withdraw from an experiment after it had started if they chose to do so. In addition, in 1975 the U.S. Department of Health, Education, and Welfare began requiring that all research with human participants be reviewed and approved by institutional review boards before being conducted. An institutional review board at a university or college is a committee of faculty and staff members that screens all research proposals involving human participants in order to ensure the well-being of the participants. Thus, Milgram-type obedience research, with its potential to cause harm to participants and its use of deception that prevented informed consent, was curtailed. There have been a half dozen or so replication studies of Milgram's baseline condition conducted in other countries, such as Jordan and West Germany (for a summary, see Blass, 2004, Table C.1).

Interestingly, Milgram's findings were not replicated in the study conducted in the country most like the United States—Australia (Kilham & Mann, 1974). The overall obedience rate was only 28%, and a gender difference was observed. The obedience rate for men (40%) was significantly greater than that for women (16%). Recently, some researchers began to wonder if Milgram's findings could be replicated here in this country. Aren't we more aware now of the dangers of blindly following authority than people were in the early 1960s? If so, wouldn't participants now disobey more often than Milgram's participants?

To answer such questions, Burger (2009) conducted a partial replication of Milgram's New Baseline experiment. His participants were men and women who responded to newspaper advertisements and flyers distributed locally. Their ages ranged from 20 to 81 years, with a mean age of 42.9 years. Obviously, some changes to ensure the welfare of the participants were necessary in order to obtain permission from the Santa Clara University Institutional Review Board to run the study (Burger, 2007). For example, potential participants that a clinical psychologist deemed particularly vulnerable to stress were screened out. The main procedural change was that once participants pressed the 150-volt switch and started to read the next test item, the experiment was stopped. The 150-volt point was chosen because in Milgram's study, once participants went past 150 volts, the vast majority continued to obey up to the highest shock level. In a meta-analysis of data from eight of Milgram's obedience experiments, Packer (2008) also found that the 150-volt point was the critical juncture for disobedience (the voltage level at which participants were most likely to disobey the experimenter). This is likely due to the fact that it was at the 150-volt point that the learner began to verbally complain. Hence, in Burger's study, it was a reasonable assumption that the percentage of participants that go past 150 volts was a good estimate of the percentage that would go to the end of the shock generator. Of course, the experimenter also ended the experiment when a participant refused to continue after hearing all four of the experimenter's prods. What do you think Burger found? Almost 67% of the men pressed the 150-volt switch, and about 73% of the women did so. Although these percentages have to be adjusted down slightly because not every participant in Milgram's study who went past 150 volts maximally obeyed, these results are very close to Milgram's finding of 65% obedience for both men and women in the baseline condition. Even with such adjustments, Burger's findings indicate that people reacted in this laboratory obedience situation today much like they did almost 50 years ago in Milgram's original study. Burger, however, quizzically did not conclude that his participants were displaying obedience, but rather *dis*obedience (Burger, Girgis, & Manning, 2011). Why did he conclude this?

Burger (2009) pointed out that *only* the fourth prod, "You have no other choice, you must go on" truly constitutes an order, and in an analysis of the participants' comments and reactions in his partial replication study (reported in Burger et al., 2011), it was found that this prod did not elicit any obedience because not a single participant continued after receiving it. This finding begs the question as to whether this occurred in Milgram's experiments. Fortunately, Gibson

(2013) did a rhetorical analysis of the archival recorded interactions between the experimenter and participants in two of Milgram's experiments, providing us with an answer to this question. Consistent with Burger's conclusion, Gibson's analysis revealed that the experimenter's most order-like prods were overwhelmingly resisted by the participants. Thus, rather than showing that Milgram's participants were obeying orders of those in authority, Milgram's experiments seem to provide evidence of the opposite, that orders from an authority lead to disobedience and that the obedience that Milgram observed was due to other factors.

Related to Burger's conclusion, Alex Haslam, Stephen Reicher, and their colleagues have proposed that Milgram's "obedient" participants were motivated not by orders but by appeals to science and that their behavior needs to be reconceptualized as an act of "engaged followership" with the experimenter and the scientific community and not as a product of blind obedience to authority (Haslam, Reicher, & Birney, 2014; Haslam, Reicher, Millard, & McDonald, 2015). The level of obedience in each of Milgram's experiments is thus predicated upon the extent of the participants' acceptance of the experimenter's scientific goals and the leadership exhibited by the experimenter in pursuing these goals, leading participants to identify with the experimenter and become engaged in helping him achieve his scientific goals. Haslam and Reicher further propose that the participants in Milgram's experiments may also opt to identify with the learner and not the experimenter, leading them to "disobedient" behavior. Hence, the perturbing process of deciding which identification to make leads to the anxiety and upset witnessed in Milgram's participants. Which identification participants tend to make is determined mainly by which identification a particular experimental setting favors. In line with this analysis, Haslam and Reicher note that one can explain the variance observed for the obedience rate in Milgram's various experiments (from 0% to 100%) by examining how the situational factors in each experiment favor each type of identification (that is, the relative extent of identification with the experimenter versus identification with the learner). In fact, Reicher, Haslam, and Smith (2012) have shown that estimations of the levels of identification with the experimenter and with the learner made by both expert social psychologists and nonexpert college students for Milgram's descriptions of 15 of his experiments are strong significant predictors of the level of obedience found in each of the experiments. In agreement with the engaged-followership explanation, identification with the experimenter was a strong positive predictor of the level of obedience observed, and identification with the learner was a strong negative predictor of the level of obedience observed.

Haslam, Reicher, and Birney (2014) also point out that there was a confound in Milgram's study and Burger's partial replication between the content of the prods and the order in which they were presented in that it is unclear whether the observed resistance to the fourth prod was the consequence of it being an order or that it came fourth after the other three prods had already been resisted. Possibly the participants were just tired of being prodded or were already committed to resisting when the fourth prod was given. They argue that the second prod,

"The experiment requires that you continue," is the one that relates most to their engaged-followership proposed explanation because it indicates that continuing is essential to the success of the experiment and hence, science. In a very cleverly designed analogue of the Milgram basic procedure with 30 steps, each involving progressively more toxic responses, Haslam, Reicher, and Birney demonstrated that continuation and completion of an objectionable task was positively predicted by the extent to which prods appealed to scientific goals but not by the extent that the prods were seen as orders. In agreement with Burger's finding, the participants were far more inclined to disobey an order than to follow it.

As a further test of their engaged-followership explanation, Haslam, Reicher, and Millard (2015) used immersive digital realism (IDR) to restage and reexamine Milgram's New Baseline experiment and four more of his obedience experiments. The IDR methodology circumvents the ethical barriers to conducting obedience research using Milgram's original procedure with volunteer participants. In brief, this IDR used professional actors who deeply immerse themselves into portraying fictional characters in a film. A film director was hired to work with the actors in developing their characters before the filming. In this case, their characters were participants in the Milgram experiments being restaged and filmed in a faithful reproduction of the original laboratory environment, including the ominous shock generator. The film director, however, only informed the actors that their characters would be participants in a social psychology experiment in the film. They were not given any information about the nature or design of the Milgram experiments. Because the actors could differentiate the character's behavior in the experiment from their own, any ethical issues were avoided. Following the digital filming of each restaged experiment, the actors were thoroughly debriefed and provided complete information about the study and its aims. Post-experimental interviews were also conducted and used to assess the participants' relative identification with the experimenter and the learner in each experiment. Validating the use of the IDR, a strong correlation was found between the maximum level of shock administered in these restaged experiments and the mean maximum shock administered in the corresponding original experiments. Consistent with the engaged-followership explanation, relative identification with the experimenter versus the learner as assessed in the interviews was a good predictor of the maximum shock that participants administered in each experiment. In addition, as Burger found, there was near universal refusal by participants to continue after being given Milgram's fourth prod ("You have no other choice, you must continue").

Interestingly, Haslam and Reicher's engaged-followership proposal not only provides an explanation of both Milgram's results and Burger's replication findings, it also provides an explanation of the discrepancy that we described earlier between the extremely stressful and aversive experimental experience of the participants and their positive feelings toward the experiments that they expressed in their questionnaire responses about their participation. In an analysis of the Yale archival questionnaire data from Milgram's study, Haslam, Reicher, Millard, and McDonald (2015) showed that the participants were engaged with the science of the experiments and that they saw science—especially science at prestigious Yale University—as a "social good," and being associated with this made them feel good. It is critical, as Haslam et al. point out, to realize that the participants' questionnaire responses were made quite some time after their participation, so the stressful experimental situation that they experienced almost a year earlier was in the past, and the debriefing report that accompanied the questionnaire reminded them of the scientific goals of the study. In sum, led by this reminder of the study's scientific goals, the participants felt as if they had contributed to scientific progress, and this gave meaning to their participation, transforming the unpleasant, stressful experimental experience into something to feel good about when they completed the questionnaires.

It should now be clear that Milgram's obedience study was and still is very controversial. Recent criticisms based on analyses of the Yale archival materials have brought to light important new methodological and ethical concerns with both Milgram's study and his reporting of it, questioning both the validity of the experiments and Milgram's ethics in reporting them. Another recent interesting development is that Milgram's interpretation of his findings in terms of people following the orders of an authority that lead to acts of destructive obedience now seems misguided. There are social forces that have an impact on the participants, but they are not the ones Milgram proposed. The new engaged-followership inter- pretation that posits that the participants' "obedient" behavior was motivated by their active identification with the experimenter and science or the learner does a better job of explaining Milgram's findings. In sum, a half-century later, questions about the ethical, methodological, and theoretical aspects of Milgram's obedience experiments and his findings still linger. Nonetheless, one point seems certain— Milgram wasn't really studying destructive obedience. Such obedience, however, has been studied in a real-world, nonlaboratory setting involving doctors and nurses. Let's see how this was done and what was found.

The "Astroten" study. A fascinating aspect of the "Astroten" study on destructive obedience is that the participants did not even know they were in the study (the ultimate experimental deception). The participants in this study were nurses at work, on duty alone in a hospital ward (Hofling, Brotzman, Dalrymple, Graves, & Pierce, 1966). Each nurse received a call from a person using the name of a staff doctor not personally known by the nurse. The doctor ordered the nurse to give a dose exceeding the maximum daily dosage of an unauthorized medication ("Astroten") to an actual patient in the ward. This order violated many hospital rules—medication orders need to be given in person and not over the phone, it was a clear overdose, and the medication was not even authorized. Twenty-two nurses, in different hospitals and at different times, were confronted with such an order. What do you think they did? Remember that this was not a laboratory study like Milgram's. These were real nurses who were on duty in hospitals doing their jobs. Twenty-one of the twenty-two nurses did not question the order and went to give the medication, though they were intercepted before getting to the patient. Now what do you think that the researchers found when they asked other nurses and nursing students what they would do in such a situation? Of course, they said the opposite of what the nurses actually did. Nearly all of them (31 out of 33) said that they would have refused to give the medication, demonstrating the power of situational forces on obedience.

However, as with Milgram's studies, there are problems with Hofling et al.'s (1966) Astroten study. In addition to the obvious ethical problems, such as people participating in a study without even knowing they are in a study, Rank and Jacobson (1977) pointed out other problematic aspects of the Astroten study. The situation that was created in the Astroten study was far from a normal hospital situation. The nurses had no knowledge of the medication involved, and they had no opportunity to seek advice from another nurse or doctor. So Rank and Jacobson replicated the Astroten study but modified the situation so that it was more akin to a normal hospital scenario. An actual known doctor on the hospital staff telephoned in an instruction to administer Valium at three times the recommended dosage, and other nurses were working so that the nurse who took the call could consult with someone if she chose to do so. Their findings were dramatically different from those found in the Astroten study. All 18 nurses in the study accepted the order, 12 of the 18 nurses procured the drug, but only 2 out of 18 nurses prepared to give the drug as ordered. They concluded that if nurses are aware of the toxic effects of a drug and allowed to interact normally with other nurses and staff, most nurses will not administer a drug overdose merely because a doctor orders it. More recently though, Krackow and Blass (1995) conducted a survey study of registered nurses on the subject of carrying out a physician's order that could have harmful consequences for the patient. Nearly half (46%) of the nurses who completed the survey reported that they had carried out such orders, but they assigned most of the responsibility to the physicians and little to themselves. These findings are truly worrisome, because these were real patients who, through blind obedience, were placed into potentially life-threatening situations. Thus, across all of these studies some nurses (ranging from roughly 11% to almost 100%) would have carried out or did carry out doctors' orders that would harm their patients (destructive obedience). Next we will discuss a real-world case of destructive obedience in which the participants inflicted harm not on others but rather on themselves.

The Jonestown massacre. Given the findings of destructive obedience in the research on the authority relationship between nurses and doctors, the Jonestown mass suicide orchestrated by the charismatic Reverend Jim Jones should be a little easier to understand. Jones was not only an authority figure to his followers, he was also their leader. Using various compliance techniques, Jones fostered unquestioned faith in himself as the cult leader and discouraged individualism. For example, using the foot-in-the-door technique, he slowly increased the financial support required of Peoples Temple members until they had turned over essentially everything they had (Levine, 2003). He even used the door-in-the-face

The Jonestown Massacre | These are the dead bodies of some of the over 900 members of Reverend Jim Jones's religious cult in Jonestown, Guyana, who committed mass suicide by drinking cyanide-laced Kool-Aid.

and foot-in-the-door techniques to recruit members (Ornstein, 1991). He had his recruiters ask people walking by to help the poor. When they refused, the recruiters then asked them just to donate five minutes of their time to put letters in envelopes (door-in-the-face). Once they agreed to do this small task, they were then given information about future, related charitable work. After completing the small task, they then returned later to do more work as a function of the consistency aspect of the foot-in-the-door technique. As they contributed more and more of their time, they became more involved in the Peoples Temple and were then more easily persuaded to join.

There is one situational factor leading to the Jonestown tragedy that is not so obvious, though—the importance of Jones moving his almost 1,000 followers from San Francisco to the rain forests of Guyana, an alien environment in the jungle of an unfamiliar country (Cialdini, 1993). In such an uncertain environment, the followers would look to the actions of others (informational social influence) to guide their own actions. The Jonestown followers looked to the settlement leaders and other followers, which then helped Jones to manage such a large group of followers. With this in mind, think about the day of the commanded suicide. Why was the mass suicide so orderly, and why did the people seem so willing to commit suicide? The most fanatical followers stepped forward immediately and drank the poison. Because people looked to others to define the correct response, they followed the lead of those who promptly, using syringes, injected the poison into their children's throats and then willingly drank the poisoned Kool-Aid. In other words, drinking the poison seemed to be the correct thing to do. This situation reflects a "herd mentality," getting some members going in the right direction so that others will follow like cattle being led to the slaughterhouse. The phrase "drinking the Kool-Aid" later became synonymous with such blind allegiance. Over 900 people were found dead, one-third of them children. There were roughly 30 survivors who managed to escape without being shot or were away from the compound when the mass suicide occurred. Did Reverend Jones drink the Kool-Aid? No, he was found dead from a single gunshot to the head, probably self-inflicted.

How Groups Influence Us

Usually when we think of groups, we think of formalized groups such as committees, sororities and fraternities, classes, or trial juries. Social psychologists, however, have studied the influences of all sorts of groups, from less formal ones, such as an audience at some event, to these more formal ones. Our discussion of the influences of such groups begins with one of the earliest ones that was studied, social facilitation.

Social facilitation. How would your behavior be affected by the presence of other people, such as an audience? Do you think the audience would help or hinder? One of the earliest findings for such situations was social facilitation, improvement in performance in the presence of others. This social facilitative effect is limited, however, to familiar tasks for which the person's response is automatic (such as doing simple arithmetic problems). When people are faced with difficult unfamiliar tasks that they have not mastered (such as solving a complex maze), performance is hindered by the presence of others. Why? One explanation proposes that the presence of others increases a person's drive and arousal, and research studies have found that under increased arousal, people tend to give whatever response is dominant (most likely) in that situation (Bond & Titus, 1983; Zajonc, 1965). This means that when the task is very familiar or simple, the dominant response tends to be the correct one; thus performance improves. When the task is unfamiliar or complex, however, the dominant response is likely not the correct one; thus performance is hindered. This means that people who are very skilled at what they do will usually do better in front of an audience than by themselves, and those who are novices will tend to do worse. This is why it is more accurate to define **social facilitation** as facilitation of the dominant response on a task due to social arousal, leading to improved performance on simple or well-learned tasks and worse performance on complex or unlearned tasks when other people are present.

social facilitation Facilitation of a dominant response on a task due to social arousal, leading to improved performance on simple or well-learned tasks and worse performance on complex or unlearned tasks when other people are present.

social loafing The tendency to exert less effort when working in a group toward a common goal than when individually working toward the goal.

Social loafing and the diffusion of responsibility. Social facilitation occurs for people on tasks for which they can be evaluated individually. Social loafing occurs when people are pooling their efforts to achieve a common goal (Karau & Williams, 1993). **Social loafing** is the tendency for people to exert less effort when working toward a common goal in a group than when individually accountable. Social loafing is doing as little as you can get away with. Think about the various group projects that you have participated in, both in school and outside of school. Didn't some members contribute very little to the group effort? Why? A major reason is the **diffusion of responsibility**—the responsibility for the task is diffused across all members of the group; therefore, individual accountability is lessened.

Behavior often changes when individual responsibility is lifted. Remember that in Milgram's study the maximum obedience rate increased to almost 100% when the direct responsibility for administering the shock was lifted from the teacher's shoulders. This diffusion of responsibility can also explain why social loafing tends to increase as the size of the group increases (Latané, Williams, & Harkins, 1979). The larger the group, the less likely it is that a social loafer will be detected, and the more the responsibility for the task gets diffused. Think about students working together on a group project for a shared grade. Social loafing will be greater when the group size is seven or eight than when it is only two or three. However, for group tasks in which individual contributions are identifiable and evaluated, social loafing decreases (Williams, Harkins, & Latané, 1981; Harkins & Jackson, 1985). Thus, in a group project for a shared grade, social loafing decreases if each group member is assigned and responsible for a specific part of the project.

The bystander effect and the Kitty Genovese case. Now let's think about the Kitty Genovese case described at the beginning of this chapter. Given the *New York Times* 38-witnesses account of the murder with no one intervening until it was too late, subsequent media coverage described it as a sad consequence of big-city apathy. Experiments by John Darley, Bibb Latané, and other social psychologists, however, indicate that it wasn't apathy, but rather that the diffusion of responsibility, as in social loafing, played a major role in this failure to help (Latané & Darley, 1970; Latané & Nida, 1981). Conducting experiments in which people were faced with emergency situations, Darley and Latané found what they termed the **bystander effect**—the probability of an individual helping in an emergency is greater when there is only one bystander than when there are many bystanders.

To understand this effect, Darley and Latané developed a model of the intervention process in emergencies. According to this model, for a person to intervene in an emergency, he must make not just one, but a series of decisions, and only one set of choices will lead him to take action. In addition, these decisions are typically made under conditions of stress, urgency, and threat of possible harm. The decisions to be made are (1) noticing the relevant event or not, (2) defining the event as an emergency or not, (3) feeling personal responsibility for helping or not, and (4) having accepted responsibility for helping, deciding what form of assistance he should give (direct or indirect intervention). If the event is not noticed or not defined as an emergency or if the

diffusion of responsibility The lessening of individual responsibility for a task when responsibility for the task is spread across the members of a group.

bystander effect The probability of a person's helping in an emergency is greater when there are no other bystanders than when there are other bystanders.

bystander does not take responsibility for helping, he will not intervene. Darley and Latané's research (e.g., Latané & Darley, 1968, and Latané & Rodin, 1969) demonstrated that the presence of other bystanders negatively influenced all of these decisions, leading to the bystander effect.

Let's take a closer look at one of these experiments (Darley & Latané, 1968) to help you better understand the bystander effect. Imagine that you are asked to participate in a study examining the adjustments you've experienced in attending college. You show up for the experiment, are led to a booth, and are told that you are going to participate in a round-robin discussion of adjustment problems over the laboratory intercom. You put on earphones so that you can hear the other participants, but you cannot see them. The experimenter explains that this is to guarantee each student's anonymity. The experimenter tells you that when a light in the booth goes on, it is your turn to talk. She also says that she wants the discussion not to be inhibited by her presence, so she is not going to listen to the discussion. The study begins. The first student talks about how anxious he has been since coming to college and that sometimes the anxiety is so overwhelming, he has epileptic seizures. Another student talks about the difficulty she's had in deciding on a major and how she misses her boyfriend who stayed at home to go to college. It's your turn, and you talk about your adjustment problems. The discussion then returns to the first student, and as he is talking, he seems to be getting very anxious. Suddenly, he starts having a seizure and cries out for help. What would you do?

Like most people, you would likely say that you would go to help him. However, this is not what was found. Whether a participant went for help depended upon how many other students the participant thought were available to help the student having the seizure (the bystander effect). Darley and Latané manipulated this number, so there were zero, one, or four others. In actuality, there were no other students present; the dialogue was all tape-recorded. There was only one participant. The percentage of participants who attempted to help before the victim's cries for help ended decreased dramatically as the presumed number of bystanders increased, from 85% when alone to only 31% when four other bystanders who could help were assumed to be present. The probability of helping decreased as the responsibility for helping was diffused across more participants. Those participants who did not go for help were not apathetic, however. They were very upset and seemed to be in a state of conflict, even though they did not leave the booth to help. They appeared to want to help, but the situational forces (the presumed presence of other bystanders and the resulting diffusion of responsibility) led them not to do so. The bystander effect has been replicated many times for many different types of emergencies. Latané and Nida (1981) analyzed almost 50 bystander intervention studies with thousands of participants and found that bystanders were more likely to help when alone than with others about 90% of the time.

Now let's see how Darley and Latané's bystander effect can be applied to the Kitty Genovese case as reported in the *New York Times*. The responsibility for helping was diffused across the supposed witnesses to the attack. Because the bystanders did not communicate with one another, each bystander likely assumed that someone else had called the police, so they didn't need to do so. However, after much time had elapsed and the police had not arrived, one of these bystanders likely decided that no one had intervened so he called the police, but it was too late. But how would Darley and Latané explain the bystander who did call the police early on in the attack? According to the Darley and Latané bystander intervention model that we described earlier, a bystander has to make a series of decisions that determine whether he will intervene or not intervene. Unlike the other bystanders, the bystander who called the police must have decided to take responsibility for helping and then decided to intervene indirectly by calling the police. Sadly, the police did not come. Similarly, the bystander who shouted at the attacker during the first attack must have decided to indirectly intervene.

It is important to understand that bystanders to an emergency have to make decisions under conditions of stress and urgency and thus sometimes may make decisions that are regretted later. Even if a bystander decides to take responsibility and act, deciding whether to intervene directly or indirectly is extremely difficult because of the possibility in some situations that he, too, could be harmed if he tries to directly intervene. The neighbor who actually left her apartment and went to the crime scene did decide to intervene directly, risking harm to herself, but the murderer had already fled. These bystanders' interventions do not invalidate the bystander effect. The bystander effect describes what typically happens as the number of bystanders to an emergency increases; the bystander effect is not, however, what invariably happens. Remember, the remaining bystanders to the murder did nothing. For example, the only witness to the second fatal attack did not call the police but rather called a friend to ask what to do. The friend told him to get out of there, and he did, by sneaking out a back window in his apartment (Lemann, 2014). Why the differences in bystander reactions? A bystander's actions are not entirely controlled by the situational forces; dispositional factors (personality traits) also impact the bystander's behavior. In the discussion of trait theories of personality in the last chapter, we pointed out that there was a situational influence on whether a person's behavior reflected a particular trait. Similarly, there is a dispositional influence on a person's behavior when he is subject to strong situational forces. The critical thing to remember as a bystander, especially in situations in which you do not know what other bystanders are doing, is you should not assume that someone else is going to help. The bystander effect tells us that this assumption will likely lead to no one helping.

Deindividuation. Diffusion of responsibility also seems to play a role in **deindividuation,** the loss of self-awareness and self-restraint in a group situation that fosters arousal and anonymity. The responsibility for the group's actions is defused across all the members of the group. Deindividuation can be

> **deindividuation** The loss of self-awareness and self-restraint in a group situation that fosters arousal and anonymity.

Pat Sullivan/AP Photo

Deindividuation and the Ku Klux Klan | The uniform of Ku Klux Klan members, especially the hood, fosters deindividuation, the loss of self-awareness and self-restraint in a group situation that fosters arousal and anonymity. Deindividuation increases the likelihood that members will forget their moral values and act without thinking.

thought of as combining the increased arousal in social facilitation with the diminished sense of responsibility in social loafing. Deindividuated people feel less restrained, and therefore may forget their moral values and act spontaneously without thinking. The result can be damaging, as seen in mob violence, riots, and vandalism. In one experiment on deindividuation, college women wearing Ku Klux Klan–type white hoods and coats delivered twice as much shock to helpless victims than did similar women not wearing Klan clothing who were identifiable by name tags (Zimbardo, 1970). Once people lose their sense of individual responsibility, feel anonymous, and are aroused, they are capable of terrible things.

Group polarization and groupthink. Two other group influences, group polarization and groupthink, apply to more structured, task-oriented group situations (such as committees and panels). **Group polarization** is the strengthening of a group's prevailing opinion about a topic following group discussion of the topic. The group members already share the same opinion on an issue, and when they discuss it among themselves, this opinion is further strengthened as members gain additional information from other members in support of the opinion. This means that the initially held view becomes even more polarized following group discussion.

In addition to this informational influence of the group discussion, there is a type of normative influence. Because we want others to like us, we may express stronger views on a topic after learning that other group members share our opinion. Both informational and normative influences lead members to stronger, more extreme opinions. A real-life example is the accentuation phenomenon in college students—initial differences in college students become more accentuated over time (Myers, 2002). For example, students who do not belong to fraternities and sororities tend to be more liberal politically, and this difference grows during college at least partially because group members reinforce and polarize one another's views. Group polarization for some groups may lead to destructive behavior, encouraging group members to go further out on a limb through mutual reinforcement. For example, group polarization within community gangs tends to increase the rate of their criminal behavior. Within terrorist organizations, group polarization leads to more extreme acts of violence. Alternatively, association with a quiet, nonviolent group, such as a quilter's guild, strengthens a person's tendency toward quieter, more peaceful behavior. In summary, group polarization may exaggerate prevailing attitudes among group members, leading to more extreme behavior.

group polarization The strengthening of a group's prevailing opinion about a topic following group discussion about the topic.

Groupthink is a mode of group thinking that impairs decision making; the desire for group harmony overrides a realistic appraisal of the possible decisions. The primary concern is to maintain group consensus. Pressure is put on group members to go along with the group's view and external information that disagrees with the group's view is suppressed, which leads to the illusion of unanimity. Groupthink also leads to an illusion of infallibility—the belief that the group cannot make mistakes.

"All those in favor say 'Aye.'"
"Aye."   "Aye."   "Aye."   "Aye."   "Aye."

Given such illusory thinking, it is not surprising that groupthink often leads to very bad decisions and poor solutions to problems (Janis, 1972, 1983). The failure to anticipate Pearl Harbor, the disastrous Bay of Pigs invasion of Cuba, and the space shuttle *Challenger* disaster are a few examples of real-world bad decisions that have been linked to groupthink. In the case of the *Challenger* disaster, for example, the engineers who made the shuttle's rocket boosters opposed the launch because of dangers posed by the cold temperatures to the seals between the rocket segments (Esser & Lindoerfer, 1989). However, the engineers were unsuccessful in arguing their case with the group of NASA officials, who were suffering from an illusion of infallibility. To maintain an illusion of unanimity, these officials didn't bother to make the top NASA executive who made the final launch decision aware of the engineers' concerns. The result was tragedy.

> **groupthink** A mode of group thinking that impairs decision making, because the desire for group harmony overrides a realistic appraisal of the possible decision alternatives.

Sadly, the NASA groupthink mentality reared its head again with the space shuttle *Columbia* disaster. It appears that NASA management again ignored safety warnings from engineers about probable technical problems. The *Columbia* accident investigation board strongly recommended that NASA change its "culture of invincibility." To prevent groupthink from impacting your group decisions, make your group aware of groupthink and its dangers, and then take explicit steps to ensure that minority opinions, critiques of proposed group actions, and alternative courses of action are openly presented and fairly evaluated.

The *Challenger* Explosion | Groupthink has been linked to the *Challenger* disaster. NASA officials, who were suffering from an illusion of infallibility, ignored the warnings of engineers who opposed the launch because of dangers posed by the cold temperatures to the seals between the rocket segments.

Section Summary

In this section, we discussed many types of social influence, how people and the social forces they create influence a person's thinking and behavior. Conformity—a change in behavior, belief, or both to conform to a group norm as a result of real or imagined group pressure—is usually due to either normative social influence or informational social influence. Normative social influence leads people to conform to gain the approval and avoid the disapproval of others. Informational social influence leads people to conform to gain information from others in an uncertain situation. Several situational factors impact the amount of conformity that is observed. For example, nonconsensus among group members reduces the amount of conformity, and responding aloud versus anonymously increases conformity. In addition, culture and gender impact the amount of conformity observed. Collectivist cultures tend to lead to more conformity than individualistic cultures, and women conform more than men.

In conformity, people change their behavior or attitudes to adhere to a group norm, but in compliance, people act in accordance with a direct request from another person or group. We discussed four techniques used to obtain compliance. Each technique involves two requests, and it is always the second request for which compliance is desired. In the foot-in-the-door technique, a small request is followed by the desired larger request. In the door-in-the-face technique, a large first request is followed by the desired second smaller request. In the low-ball technique, an attractive first request is followed by the desired and less attractive second request. In the that's-not-all technique, the desired and more attractive second request is made before a response can be made to an initial request. The foot-in-the-door and low-ball techniques work mainly because the person has committed to the first request and complies with the second in order to remain consistent. The door-in-the-face and that's-not-all techniques work mainly because of reciprocity. Because the other person has made a concession on the first request, we comply with the second in order to reciprocate.

Stanley Milgram conducted 23 experiments at Yale University in the early 1960s in an attempt to study destructive obedience in an empirical setting. Milgram argued that his findings indicated our willingness to commit acts of destructive obedience, bringing harm to others through our obedient behavior. He also identified numerous situational factors that influenced the amount of obedience observed. For example, a very high rate of obedience is observed when the direct responsibility for one's acts is removed, but less obedience is observed when we view models of disobedience. Milgram's study, however, has become a contentious classic in that the validity of the study, Milgram's explanation of his findings, and the accuracy of Milgram's publications about the study have all been challenged by critics. Many of these criticisms stem from analyses of the experimental materials, such as audiotapes of the experiments, available in the Milgram archives at Yale. In addition, analyses of the results of the recent Milgram partial replication, the original experiments, and some recent related empirical work indicate that the obedience experiments were probably not about destructive obedience but rather about engaged followership (participants' behavior is motivated by appeals to science, leading participants to become engaged in helping the experimenter achieve his scientific goals). However, obedience studies in the real world, specifically the doctor–nurse relationship, have found varying amounts of destructive obedience, and the overall conclusion is that nurses' obedience to doctors' orders can lead to patient harm.

Even the mere presence of other people can influence our behavior. This is demonstrated in social facilitation, an improvement in simple or well-learned tasks but worse performance on complex or unlearned tasks when other people are observing us. Some group influences occur when the responsibility for a task is diffused across all members of the group. For example, social loafing is the tendency for people to exert less effort when working in a group toward a common goal than when individually accountable. Social loafing increases as the size of the group increases and decreases when each group member feels more responsible for his contribution to the group effort. Diffusion of responsibility also contributes to the bystander effect, the greater probability of an individual helping in an emergency when there is only one bystander versus when there are many bystanders. Diffusion of responsibility also contributes to deindividuation, the loss of self-awareness and self-restraint in a group situation that promotes arousal and anonymity. The results of deindividuation can be tragic, such as mob violence and rioting.

Two other group influences, group polarization and groupthink, apply to more structured, task-oriented situations, and refer to effects on the group's decision making. Group polarization is the strengthening of a group's prevailing opinion following group discussion of the topic. Like-minded group members reinforce their shared beliefs, which leads to more extreme attitudes and behavior among all group members. Groupthink is a mode of group thinking that impairs decision making. It stems from the group's illusion of infallibility and its desire for group harmony, which override a realistic appraisal of decision alternatives, often leading to bad decisions.

ConceptCheck | 1

Explain the difference between normative social influence and informational social influence.

Explain how both the door-in-the-face technique and the that's-not-all technique involve reciprocity.

Milgram found that 0% of the participants continued in the experiment when one of two experimenters said to stop. Based on this finding, predict what he found when he had two experimenters disagree, but the one who said to stop was substituting for a participant and serving as the learner. Explain the rationale for your prediction.

According to the bystander effect, explain why you would be more likely to be helped if your car broke down on a little-traveled country road than on an interstate highway.

How We Think About Our Own and Others' Behavior

Social thinking is concerned with how we view our own attitudes and behavior and those of others. We will discuss two of the major areas of research on social thinking—attributions and attitudes. First, we will examine **attribution,** the process (briefly discussed in Chapter 8) by which we explain our own

attribution The process by which we explain our own behavior and that of others.

behavior and the behavior of others. In other words, what do we perceive to be the causes of our behavior and that of others? Is the behavior due to internal causes (the person) or external causes (the situation)? Remember, we show a self-serving bias when it comes to explaining our own behavior. In this section, we will revisit this bias and examine two other biases in the attribution process (the fundamental attribution error and the actor-observer bias). The second major topic to be discussed is the relationship between our attitudes and our behavior. For example, do our attitudes drive our behavior, does our behavior determine our attitudes, or is it some of both? We will also consider the impact of role-playing on our attitudes and behavior.

How We Make Attributions

Imagine it's the first cold day in the fall, and you're standing in a long line for coffee at the student union coffee shop. All of a sudden, a person at the head of the line drops her cup of coffee. You turn to your friend and say "What a klutz!" inferring that this behavior is characteristic of that person. You are making an internal (dispositional) attribution, attributing the cause of dropping the cup of coffee to the person. But what if it had been you who had dropped the cup of coffee? Chances are you would have said something like, "Boy was that cup hot!" making an external (situational) attribution by inferring that dropping the cup wasn't your fault. We have different biases in the attributions we make for behavior we observe versus our own behavior. Let's look first at being an observer.

Attributions for the behavior of others. As an observer, we tend to commit the fundamental attribution error (Ross, 1977). The **fundamental attribution error** is the tendency as an observer to overestimate internal dispositional influences and underestimate external situational influences on others' behavior. Simply put, observers are biased in that they tend to attribute others' behavior to them and not the situation they are in. In the coffee example, we tend to make an internal attribution (the person is a klutz) and ignore possible external situational factors, such as the cup being really hot or slippery. The fundamental attribution error tends to show up even in experiments in which the participants are told that people are only faking a particular type of behavior. For example, in one experiment participants were told that a person was only pretending to be friendly or to be unfriendly (Napolitan & Goethals, 1979). Even with this knowledge, participants still inferred that the person they met in the experiment was actually like the way he or she acted, either friendly or unfriendly.

fundamental attribution error The tendency as an observer to overestimate dispositional influences and underestimate situational influences on others' behavior.

Think about the participants in Milgram's obedience experiments. On first learning of their destructive obedient behavior, didn't you think the teachers were horrible human beings? How could they treat fellow humans in that way? Or consider the teachers themselves in these experiments. When the learners kept making mistakes, the teachers may have thought the learners were incredibly stupid and so deserved the shocks. People who have been raped are sometimes blamed for provoking the rape, and people who are homeless are often blamed for their poverty-stricken state. Placing blame in this manner involves the **just-world hypothesis,** the assumption that the world is just and that people get what they deserve (Lerner, 1980). Beware of just-world reasoning. It is not valid, but is often used to justify cruelty to others.

The fundamental attribution error impacts our impressions of other people. There are two related concepts that you should also be aware of when forming impressions of others—the primacy effect and the self-fulfilling prophecy. In the **primacy effect,** early information is weighted more heavily than later information in forming an impression of another person. Beware of this effect when meeting someone new. Develop your impression slowly and carefully by gathering more information across time and from many different situations. Also be careful about the initial impressions that you make on people. Given the power of the primacy effect, your later behavior may not be able to change their initial impression of you. Try to be your true self when you first meet someone so that the primacy effect will be more accurate.

In the **self-fulfilling prophecy,** our expectations of a person elicit behavior from that person that confirms our expectations. In other words, our behavior encourages the person to act in accordance with our expectations (Jones, 1977; Rosenthal & Jacobson, 1968). For example, if you think someone is uncooperative, you may act hostile and not be very cooperative in your interactions with that person. Given your hostile behavior, the person responds by being uncooperative, confirming your expectations. The person may not really be uncooperative, however, and may only act this way in response to your behavior. However, your expectations will have been confirmed, and you will think that the person is uncooperative. Self-fulfilling prophecy is related to our tendency toward confirmation bias in hypothesis testing (see Chapter 6). Rather than acting in a manner that confirms your expectations, act in the opposite way (in the example, instead of being uncooperative, be cooperative) and see what happens. You may be surprised.

Attributions for our own behavior. Now let's consider our own behavior and making attributions. Our attribution process is biased in a different way when we are actors and not observers. Think about the example where you dropped the cup of coffee (you were the actor). You don't make a dispositional attribution ("I'm clumsy"). You make a situational attribution ("The cup was slippery"). As actors we tend to have what's called the **actor-observer bias,** the tendency to attribute our own behavior to situational influences, but to attribute the behavior of others to dispositional influences. Why this difference in attributional bias? As observers, our attention is focused on the person, so we see him as the cause of the action. As actors, our attention is focused on the situation, so we see the situation as the cause of the action.

just-world hypothesis The assumption that the world is just and that people get what they deserve.

primacy effect Information gathered early is weighted more heavily than information gathered later in forming an impression of another person.

self-fulfilling prophecy Our behavior leads a person to act in accordance with our expectations for that person.

actor-observer bias The tendency to overestimate situational influences on our own behavior, but to overestimate dispositional influences on the behavior of others.

We are more aware of situational factors as actors than as observers. This explanation is supported by the fact that we are less susceptible to the bias toward dispositional attributions with our friends and relatives, people whom we know well.

We described another attribution bias in the last chapter, the **self-serving bias**—the tendency to make attributions so that one can perceive oneself favorably. As actors, we tend to overestimate dispositional influences when the outcome of our behavior is positive and to overestimate situational influences when the outcome of our behavior is negative. In the last chapter, we were discussing this bias's role as a defense mechanism against depression. In this chapter, let's look at how self-serving bias qualifies the actor-observer bias. It defines the type of attribution we make as actors based on the nature of the outcome of our actions. Think about our reaction to a test grade. If we do well, we think that we studied hard and knew the material, both dispositional factors. If we don't do well, then we may blame the test and the teacher ("What a tricky exam," or "That test was not a good indicator of what I know"). We take credit for our successes but not our failures. Teachers also have this bias. For example, if the class does poorly on a test, the teacher thinks that the test she made up was just fine, but that the students weren't motivated or didn't study. It is important to realize that the self-serving bias and the other attribution biases do not speak to the correctness of the attributions we make, but only to the types of attributions we tend to make. This means that our attributions will be sometimes correct and sometimes incorrect.

The self-serving bias also leads us to see ourselves as "above average" when we compare ourselves with others on positive dimensions, such as intelligence and attractiveness. This tendency is exemplified in Garrison Keillor's fictional Lake Wobegon community, where "All the women are strong, all the men are good-looking, and all the children are above average." We tend to rate ourselves unreasonably high on dimensions that we value (Mezulis, Abramson, Hyde, & Hankin, 2004). Think about it. If you were asked to compare yourself with other people on intelligence, what would you say? If you respond like most people, you would say "above average." However, most people cannot be "above average." Many of us have to be average or below average. Intelligence, like most human traits, is normally distributed with about half of us below average, about half of us above average, and the rest of us average.

The self-serving bias also influences our estimates of the extent to which other people think and act as we do. This leads to two effects—the false consensus effect and the false uniqueness effect (Myers, 2013). The **false consensus effect** is the tendency to overestimate the commonality of one's opinions and unsuccessful behaviors. Let's consider two examples. If you like classical music, you tend to overestimate the number of people who also like classical music, or if you fail all of your midterm exams, you tend to overestimate the number of students who also failed all of their midterms. You tend to think that your opinion and your negative behavior are the consensus opinion and behavior.

self-serving bias The tendency to make attributions so that one can perceive oneself favorably.

false consensus effect The tendency to overestimate the commonality of one's opinions and unsuccessful behaviors.

Table 9.4	**Attributional Biases**
Bias	**Description**
Fundamental attribution error	The tendency to overestimate dispositional influences and to underestimate situational influences on others' behavior
Actor-observer bias	The tendency to overestimate situational influences on our own behavior but to overestimate dispositional influences on others' behavior (*Note:* This bias is qualified by self-serving bias when explaining our own behavior)
Self-serving bias	The tendency to make attributions so that one can perceive oneself favorably; we tend to overestimate dispositional influences on our behavior when the outcome is positive and to overestimate situational influences when the outcome is negative

The **false uniqueness effect** is the tendency to underestimate the commonality of one's abilities and successful behaviors. For example, if you are a good pool player, you tend to think that few other people are. Or, if you just aced your psychology exam, you think few students did so. You think your abilities and successful behaviors are unique. The false consensus effect and the false uniqueness effect relate to the self-protective function of the self-serving bias. We want to protect and enhance our view of ourselves, our self-esteem.

All three major attributional biases (the fundamental attribution error, the actor-observer bias, and the self-serving bias) are summarized in Table 9.4.

How Our Behavior Affects Our Attitudes

In this section, we are going to consider our attitudes. In simple terms, **attitudes** are evaluative reactions (positive or negative) toward things, events, and other people. Our attitudes are our beliefs and opinions. What do you think of the Republican political party, abortion, Twitter, or rap music? Have you changed any of your attitudes during your life, especially since you have been in college? Most of us do. Our attitudes often determine our behavior, but this is not always the case.

When our behavior contradicts our attitudes. Our attitudes tend to guide our behavior when the attitudes are ones that we feel strongly about, when we are consciously aware of our attitudes, and when outside influences on our behavior are not strong. For example, you may think that studying is the top priority for a student. If you do, you

false uniqueness effect The tendency to underestimate the commonality of one's abilities and successful behaviors.

attitudes Evaluative reactions (positive or negative) toward objects, events, and other people.

will likely get your studying done before engaging in other activities. However, if there is a lot of pressure from your roommates and friends to stop studying and go out partying, you may abandon studying for partying. But what happens when our attitudes don't guide our behavior and there isn't a lot of outside influence on our behavior? To help you understand the answer to this question, we'll consider a classic study (Festinger & Carlsmith, 1959).

Imagine that you are a participant in an experiment. You show up at the laboratory at the assigned time, and the experiment turns out to be incredibly boring. For an hour, you perform various boring tasks, such as turning pegs on a pegboard over and over again or organizing spools in a box, dumping them out, and then organizing them again. When the hour is over, the experimenter explains to you that the experiment is concerned with the effects of a person's expectations on their task performance and that you were in the control group. The experimenter is upset because his student assistant hasn't shown up. She was supposed to pose as a student who has just participated in the experiment and tell the next participant who is waiting outside that this experiment was really enjoyable. The experimenter asks if you can help him out by doing this, and for doing so, he can pay you. His budget is small, though, so he can only pay you $1. Regardless, you agree to help him out and go outside and tell the waiting participant (who is really a confederate of the experimenter and not a true participant) how enjoyable and interesting the experiment was.

Before you leave, another person who is studying students' reactions to experiments asks you to complete a questionnaire about how much you enjoyed the earlier experimental tasks. How would you rate these earlier incredibly boring tasks? You are probably thinking that you would rate them as very boring, because they were. However, this isn't what researchers observed. Participants' behavior (rating the tasks) did not follow their attitude (the tasks were boring). Participants who were paid only $1 for helping out the experimenter (by lying about the nature of the experimental tasks to the next supposed participant) rated the tasks as fairly enjoyable. We need to compare this finding with the results for another group of participants who received $20 for lying about the experiment. Their behavior did follow their attitude about the tasks. They rated the tasks as boring. This is what researchers also found for another group of participants who were never asked to help out the experimenter and lie. They also rated the tasks as boring. So why did the participants who lied for $1 not rate the tasks as boring?

Before answering this question, let's consider another part of this experiment. After rating the task, participants met again with the experimenter to be debriefed, and were told the true nature of the study. Following the debriefing, the experimenter asks you to give back the money he paid you. What would you do if you were in the $20 group? You are probably saying, "No way," but remember the studies on obedience and the high rates of obedience that were observed. What actually happened? Just like all of the participants agreed to lie (whether for $1 or $20), all of the participants gave back the money, showing once again our tendency to be obedient and comply with requests of those in authority. Now let's think about why the $1 group rated the tasks differently than the $20 group.

Festinger's cognitive dissonance theory. Their behavior can be explained by Leon Festinger's **cognitive dissonance theory,** which proposes that people change their attitudes to reduce the cognitive discomfort created by inconsistencies between their attitudes and their behavior (Festinger, 1957). Let's consider a real-life example before applying this theory to the participants who were paid $1 for lying. Think about people who smoke. Most smokers have the attitude (believe) that smoking is dangerous to their health, but they continue to smoke. Cognitive dissonance theory says that smokers feel cognitive discomfort because of the inconsistency between their attitude about smoking (dangerous to their health) and their behavior (continuing to

Leon Festinger

Karen Zebulon/Bentley Historical Library, University of Michigan

smoke). To reduce this cognitive disharmony, either the attitude or the behavior has to change. According to the cognitive dissonance theory, many smokers change their attitude so that it is no longer inconsistent with their behavior. For example, a smoker may now believe that the medical evidence isn't really conclusive. The change in the attitude eliminates the inconsistency and the dissonance it created. So now let's apply cognitive dissonance theory to the participants in the boring tasks study who lied for $1. Why did they rate the tasks as enjoyable? Their attitude was that the tasks were incredibly boring, but this was inconsistent with their behavior, lying about the tasks for only $1. This inconsistency would cause them to have cognitive dissonance. To reduce this dissonance, the participants changed their attitude to be that the tasks were fairly enjoyable. Now the inconsistency and resulting dissonance are gone.

A key aspect of cognitive dissonance theory is that we don't suffer dissonance if we have sufficient justification for our behavior (the participants who were paid $20 in the study) or our behavior is coerced. Also, cognitive dissonance sometimes changes the strength of an attitude so that it is consistent with past behavior. Think about important decisions that you have made in the past, for example, which college to attend. Cognitive dissonance theory says that once you make such a tough decision, you will strengthen your commitment to that choice in order to reduce cognitive dissonance. Indeed, the attractiveness of the alternate choices fades with the dissonance (you don't understand why you ever were attracted to the other schools) as you find confirming evidence of the correctness of your choice (you like your classes and teachers) and ignore evidence to the contrary (such as your school not being as highly rated as the other schools). Carol Tavris and

> **cognitive dissonance theory** A theory developed by Leon Festinger that assumes people have a tendency to change their attitudes to reduce the cognitive discomfort created by inconsistencies between their attitudes and their behavior.

Elliot Aronson (2007) provide numerous real-world examples of this cognitive dissonance–driven justification of our decisions, beliefs, and actions in their illuminating book, *Mistakes Were Made (But Not By Me)*. Recent research by Egan, Santos, and Bloom (2007) indicates that such decision rationalization even appears in children and nonhuman primates.

Bem's self-perception theory. There have been hundreds of studies on cognitive dissonance, but there is an alternative theoretical explanation for the results of some of these studies—Daryl Bem's **self-perception theory,** which proposes that when we are unsure of our attitudes we infer them by examining our behavior and the context in which it occurs (Bem, 1972). According to Bem, we are not trying to reduce cognitive dissonance, but are merely engaged in the normal attribution process that we discussed earlier in this chapter. We are making self-attributions. Self-perception theory would say that the participants who lied for $1 in the boring tasks experiment were unsure of their attitudes toward the tasks. They would examine their behavior (lying for $1) and infer that the tasks must have been fairly enjoyable and interesting or else they would not have said that they were for only $1. Those paid $20 for lying would not be unsure about their attitude toward the boring tasks, because they were paid so much to lie about them. According to self-perception theory, people don't change their attitude because of their behavior but rather use their behavior to infer their attitude. People are motivated to explain their behavior, not to reduce dissonance. According to self-perception theory, there is no dissonance to be reduced.

So which theory is better? Neither is really a better theory than the other. Both theories have merit and both seem to operate—but in different situations. This is similar to our earlier discussion of color vision theories, the trichromatic-color theory and the opponent-process theory in Chapter 3. Remember that trichromatic-color theory operates at the receptor cell level and opponent-process theory at the post-receptor cell level in the visual pathways. Cognitive dissonance theory seems to be the best explanation for behavior that contradicts well-defined attitudes. Such behavior creates mental discomfort, and we change our attitudes to reduce it. Self-perception theory explains situations in which our attitudes are not well-defined; we infer our attitudes from our behavior. As with the color vision theories, both cognitive dissonance theory and self-perception theory operate, but at different times.

The impact of role-playing. Now let's consider one final factor that impacts the complex relationship between our attitudes and our behavior—role-playing. We all have various social roles that we play—student, teacher, friend, son or daughter, parent, employee, and so on. Each role is defined by a socially expected pattern of behavior, and these definitions have an impact on both our behavior and our attitudes. Given the power of roles on behavior, think about how each of the various roles you play each day impacts

self-perception theory A theory developed by Daryl Bem that assumes that when we are unsure of our attitudes, we infer them by examining our behavior and the context in which it occurs.

your own attitudes and behavior. They are powerful influences. As social psychologist David Myers has observed, "we are likely not only to think ourselves into a way of acting but also to act ourselves into a way of thinking" (Myers, 2002, p. 136).

The Stanford prison experiment (SPE) conducted in 1971 at Stanford University by Philip Zimbardo has often been viewed as a dramatic example of the power of roles, specifically prison guard and prisoner (Haney, Banks, & Zimbardo, 1973; Zimbardo, 2007; Zimbardo, Maslach, & Haney, 1999). Like Milgram's obedience study, the SPE is another famous, controversial psychological study that has become a contentious classic. Thus, as we did for Milgram's study, we will cover the SPE in more detail than usual. Also, like Milgram's study, the SPE has remained in the public eye from the initial publications about it until the present. Curiously, it was also dramatized in 2015 in a theatrical film, *The Stanford Prison Experiment*, starring Billy Crudup as Zimbardo. Even stranger, the creators of these two contentious classics, Milgram and Zimbardo, were high school classmates at James Monroe High School in the Bronx in the late 1940s. It is highly unlikely that anyone back then could have predicted that Milgram and Zimbardo would both become famous social psychologists and conduct such controversial research. As with Milgram's study and his interpretation of its results, much criticism has surfaced in response to both the SPE itself and Zimbardo's interpretation of its results, casting doubt on the validity of the study, its findings, and the conclusions that have been drawn from the findings. In addition, a more recent prison study, known as the BBC Prison Study, has been conducted (Haslam & Reicher, 2005; Reicher & Haslam, 2006), and its results differ greatly from those of the SPE. We will first briefly describe the SPE, consider some of the methodological criticisms of it, and then describe the BBC Prison Study, its results, and the interpretation of these results.

First, you should realize that although Zimbardo's study is referred to as an experiment (hence, the E in SPE), it really is not an experiment in the sense that we described in Chapter 1. It would be more aptly described as a simulation study, specifically a psychological simulation of prison life. So what did Zimbardo do? He recruited male college students to participate in the study and renovated the basement in the Stanford University psychology building to be a mock prison. Any volunteers with prior arrests or any with medical or mental problems were disqualified from participating. Following psychological assessments and in-depth interviews, 24 volunteers were chosen and then randomly assigned to the role of prisoner or guard (12 as guards and 12 as prisoners). The guards were given uniforms and billy clubs and instructed to enforce the rules of the mock prison. The prisoners were arrested, booked, locked in cells, and had to wear humiliating clothing (smocks with no undergarments). Such clothing was used in an attempt to simulate the emasculating feeling of being a prisoner. How did the roles of prisoner and prison guard impact the attitudes and behavior of the participants? Some of the participants began to take their respective roles too seriously. After only one day of role-playing, some of the guards started treating the prisoners cruelly. Some of the prisoners rebelled, and others began to break down.

What was only supposed to be role-playing seemed to become reality. The guards' treatment of the prisoners became both harsh and degrading. For example, some prisoners were made to clean out toilets with their bare hands. Some prisoners began to hate the guards, and some of them were on the verge of emotional collapse. The situation worsened to such a degree that Zimbardo said that he had to stop the study after six days. According to Zimbardo, due to the power of their situational roles, the participating college students had truly "become" guards and prisoners. The roles transformed their attitudes and behavior. In sum, the abusive guards were not "bad apples." It was the "bad barrel" of the Stanford prison (the situation) that temporarily transformed them.

Let's consider Zimbardo's situational account of the SPE results. First, it is not clear that the SPE participants behaved in ways consistent with their roles because of their natural acceptance of situational role requirements. It seems more likely that their behavior was due to the active leadership provided by Zimbardo (e.g., Banyard, 2007; Haslam & Reicher, 2012). Zimbardo served as prison superintendent and gave the guards an orientation that seems, in retrospect, to provide clear guidance about how they should behave. Zimbardo (2007) recounted the following from this orientation:

> We can create boredom. We can create a sense of frustration. We can create fear in them, to some degree. We can create a notion of the arbitrariness that governs their lives, which are totally controlled by us, by the system, by you, me. . . . They'll have no privacy at all, there will be constant surveillance—nothing they do will go unobserved. They will have no freedom of action. They will be able to do nothing and say nothing that we don't permit. We're going to take away their individuality in various ways. . . . In general, what all this should create in them is a sense of powerlessness. We have total power in the situation. They have none. (p. 55)

As Banyard (2007) pointed out, notice the use of pronouns in this orientation. Zimbardo puts himself with the guards ("we") and gives clear instructions for the hostile environment that "we" are going to create for "them." Thus, Zimbardo's leadership may have legitimized oppression in the SPE. Banyard concludes that, "It is not, as Zimbardo suggests, the guards who wrote their own scripts on the blank canvas of the SPE, but Zimbardo who creates the script of terror. . . ." (2007, p. 494). But Zimbardo's guidance continued past the orientation. Via his silence, Zimbardo provided tacit approval of the abusive guards' behavior, thereby confirming to them that they were behaving as they should. He also specifically instructed his prison warden (a research assistant) to chastise the guards who were not behaving like the "bad" guards (Zimbardo, 2007). With respect to Zimbardo's active role in the SPE, some recent comments by one the guards in the SPE, John Mark, are relevant (Ratnesar, 2011). Mark said:

> I didn't think it was ever meant to go the full two weeks. I think Zimbardo wanted to create a dramatic crescendo, and then end it as quickly as possible. I felt that throughout the experiment, he knew what he wanted and then tried to shape the experiment—by how it was constructed, and how it played out—to

fit the conclusion that he had already worked out. He wanted to be able to say that college students, people from middle-class backgrounds—people will turn on each other just because they're given a role and given power. Based on my experience, and what I saw and what I felt, I think that was a real stretch. I don't think the actual events match up with the bold headline. I never did, and I haven't changed my opinion.

Mark's sentiments are echoed by Carlo Prescott, an African-American ex-con who was the SPE's chief consultant on real prisons (Zimbardo, 2007), in his 2005 letter in *The Stanford Daily* entitled "The Lie of the Stanford Prison Experiment." He expressed regret for his involvement and disclosed that it was he and not the guards who came up with the abusive and humiliating behaviors displayed by the guards. He wrote:

> My opinion, based on my observations, was that Zimbardo began with a pre-formed blockbuster conclusion and designed an experiment to "prove" that conclusion . . . ideas such as bags being placed over the heads of prisoners, inmates being bound together with chains and buckets being used in place of toilets in their cells were all experiences of mine at the old "Spanish Jail" section of San Quentin and which I dutifully shared with the Stanford Prison Experiment brain trust months before the experiment started. . . . How can Zimbardo . . . express horror at the behavior of the "guards" when they were merely doing what Zimbardo and others, myself included, encouraged them to do at the outset or frankly established as ground rules?

That Zimbardo's strong involvement and guidance (experimenter bias) may have been critical to the SPE outcome is also supported by some findings for simulated prison environments in a study conducted in Australia by Lovibond, Mithiran, and Adams (1979). These researchers found that changes in the experimental prison regime produced dramatic changes in the relations between guards and prisoners. In a more liberal prison condition (essentially the opposite of what Zimbardo created) in which security was maintained in a manner that allowed prisoners to retain their self-respect and in a participatory condition in which prisoners were treated as individuals and included in the decision-making process, the behavior of the guards and prisoners was rather benign and very dissimilar from the dramatic behavioral outcomes observed in the SPE.

Zimbardo's guard orientation that essentially told the guards how he wanted them to behave, his tacit approval of the abusive guards' later abusive behavior, and the prison warden's talks with some of the nonabusive guards about being more abusive are excellent examples of demand characteristics (Orne, 1962). **Demand characteristics** are cues in the experimental environment that make participants aware of what the experimenter expects to find and how participants are expected to act. Demand characteristics can impact the outcome of an experiment because participants may alter their behavior to conform to the experimenter's expectations. Hence, given the blatant demand characteristics of

demand characteristics Cues in the experimental environment that make participants aware of what the experimenters expect to find (their hypothesis) and how participants are expected to act.

the SPE, it should not be surprising that some of the guards became "bad" guards. Banuazizi and Movahedi (1975) provide data that indicate that the SPE would have likely been confounded by demand characteristics even if Zimbardo had not been so actively involved in the study. They mailed students a questionnaire that included a brief description of the procedures followed in the SPE and some open-ended questions to determine their awareness of the experimental hypothesis and their expectancies regarding the outcomes of the experiment. Of the 150 students responding, a vast majority determined the experiment's purpose was to show that normal people placed into the positions of guards and prisoners would act like real guards and prisoners and predicted that the behavior of the guards toward prisoners would be oppressive, hostile, etc., and that prisoners would react in passive or defiant ways or both. These findings indicate that the demand characteristics inherent in the SPE's design were fairly obvious, so it is not surprising that the guards and prisoners acted in the ways they did.

Given the strong demand characteristics available in the SPE and Zimbardo's blatant guidance, what is surprising is that only a few of the guards (about one-third) were "bad" guards (Zimbardo, 2007). The rest were "strict but fair" guards and "good" guards (those that sided with the prisoners). This finding obviously runs counter to Zimbardo's simplistic situational explanation of the SPE results and shows that dispositional factors (personality traits) contributed to the results. Given that dispositional factors played a role in the behavior of the guards, is it possible that the "bad" guards were, using Zimbardo's metaphor, "bad apples"? That is, is there anything unusual about the type of person who would volunteer to participate in a study like the SPE? If so, then participant self-selection may have occurred in the SPE. This means that the participants selectively volunteered for the SPE because they were attracted to a prison study because of their personalities. Carnahan and McFarland's (2007) findings suggest that this is a distinct possibility. They recruited students in two ways: (1) for a psychological study of prison life using a virtually identical newspaper advertisement as used in the SPE, and (2) for just a psychological study, an identical ad but without the mention of prison life. Carnahan and McFarland found that those who volunteered to participate in the prison life study tended to be more aggressive, authoritarian, socially dominant, and Machiavellian and less empathetic and altruistic than those who volunteered for the more innocuous experiment. Thus, counter to what Zimbardo argued, it could be that the barrel was not bad but that some of the "apples" (the "bad" guards) were already "bad" before being put in the barrel (the Stanford prison).

It is clear that the SPE had serious methodological shortcomings—the presence of experimenter bias and strong demand characteristics and possibly participant self-selection—that prevent any sound conclusions being drawn from its results. Because of this, some textbook authors do not even cover the SPE in their texts (e.g., Gray, 2013). Unfortunately, textbook authors who do cover the SPE tend not to cover its shortcomings; hence, teachers tend not to cover them in their courses (Bartels, Milovich, & Moussier, 2016). Because of its renown both within and outside of psychology, we discussed the SPE and its methodological shortcomings so that you would be aware of these shortcomings and how they invalidate Zimbardo's conclusions about the results of the study. It is important, though, that you realize that this does not mean that social roles are not important influences on our behavior; they definitely are (Greenberg, Schmader, Arndt, & Landau, 2015). It is just that the SPE is not a cogent demonstration of their influence. It is also worth noting that Zimbardo served as an expert witness in the trial of one of the abusive prison guards at Abu Ghraib, the U.S. military prison in Iraq (Zimbardo, 2007). He argued that situational pressures, as he claimed in the SPE, led the soldier to commit the abusive acts. His argument, however, failed, and the soldier was reduced to the lowest rank and given a harsh prison sentence and a dishonorable discharge. The prosecutor's winning argument was that individuals are responsible for their own behavior and that the abusive guards' immoral, evil behavior

This is what I hear when people cite the Zimbardo prison experiment.

stemmed from their dispositions (they were "bad apples"). Next, we would like to make you are aware of a more recent prison study that was conducted, one that you likely have not heard about but that is methodologically sounder than the SPE.

Two British social psychologists, Alexander Haslam and Stephen Reicher (the proponents of the engaged-followership explanation of Milgram's findings that we discussed earlier in the chapter), in collaboration with the British Broadcasting Corporation (BBC), re-created the SPE, but with ethical procedures that ensured that the study would not harm participants (Haslam & Reicher, 2005, Haslam & Reicher, 2012; Reicher & Haslam, 2006). This study has become known as the BBC Prison Study. It was filmed by the BBC and televised in 2002. As in the SPE, the male volunteer participants were randomly assigned to the roles of guards and prisoners within a custom-built prison setting. However, unlike Zimbardo and his colleagues, Haslam and Reicher took no leadership role in the study (in particular, they did not instruct their guards to subjugate the prisoners to their will in the way that Zimbardo did). Hence, the fact that the guards' and prisoners' behavior diverged markedly from that in the SPE bolsters the argument that demand characteristics (and Zimbardo's leadership) were likely responsible for the outcome of the SPE.

So what happened in the BBC Prison Study? The guards failed to identify with their role and were reluctant to impose their authority. The prisoners, however, did form a cohesive group identity, leading them to rebel and overthrow the established regime after six days. Hence, rather than brutal guards and passive prisoners, ambivalent guards and rebellious prisoners materialized. The guards and the prisoners then formed a single self-governing, egalitarian commune, but the commune disintegrated after a short time, because again some participants did not want to discipline those who broke the commune's rules. Following the

The guards and prisoners who participated in the BBC Prison Study.

collapse of the communal system, some former prisoners and former guards proposed a coup in which they would become the new guards, creating a more hard-line prisoner–guard divide and using force, if necessary, to maintain it. At this point, Haslam and Reicher brought the study to a close on the eighth day. Haslam and Reicher interpreted their findings in terms of social identity theory, in that power resides in the ability of a group to establish a sense of shared identity. This group power can be used for a positive purpose, as illustrated by the prisoners in the BBC prison study, or for a negative one, as illustrated by the guards in the SPE. They concluded that people do not automatically assume roles that are given to them, as was suggested by the Zimbardo's account of the SPE, and that tyranny arises from a complex process in which group failure and powerlessness lead group members to identify with authoritarian regimes and their leaders (a process that was short-circuited in the SPE because, from the outset, Zimbardo encouraged identification with his own authoritarian leadership). Of course, it may be argued that the guards in the BBC Prison Study failed to display the brutality of the SPE guards because their behavior was filmed and would ultimately be broadcast on television. Against this, Haslam and Reicher (2012) noted that toward the end of the study, once a group of new guards had come to identify with their role, they proved very willing to oppress prisoners. Indeed, here the regime that was in ascendancy closely resembled that in the SPE. However, the participants had arrived at that point because they believed in the authoritarian regime they were implementing and not because they were blindly conforming to role.

Section Summary

In this section, we considered social thinking by examining how we make attributions, explanations for our own behavior and the behavior of others, and the relationship between our attitudes and our behavior. Attribution is a biased process. As observers, we commit the fundamental attribution error, tending to overestimate dispositional influences and underestimate situational influences upon others' behavior. This error seems to stem from our attention being focused on the person, so we see her as the cause of the action. When we view our own behavior, however, we fall prey to the actor-observer bias, the tendency to attribute our own behavior to situational influences, and not dispositional influences, as we do when we observe the behavior of others. The actor-observer bias stems from focusing our attention, as actors, on the situation and not on ourselves.

The actor-observer bias, however, is qualified by the self-serving bias, the tendency to make attributions so that we can perceive ourselves favorably and protect our self-esteem. As actors, we tend to overestimate dispositional influences when the outcome of our behavior is positive and to overestimate situational influences when the outcome is negative. Self-serving bias also leads us to rate ourselves as "above average" in comparison to others on positive dimensions, such as intelligence and attractiveness. It also leads to two other effects—the false consensus effect (overestimating the commonality of one's attitudes and unsuccessful behaviors) and the false uniqueness effect (underestimating the commonality of one's abilities and successful behaviors).

Attitudes are our evaluative reactions (positive or negative) toward objects, events, and other people. They are most likely to guide our behavior when we feel strongly about them, are consciously aware of them, and when outside influences on our behavior are minimized. Sometimes, however, our behavior contradicts our attitudes, and this situation often leads to attitudinal change. A major explanation for such attitudinal change is cognitive dissonance theory—we change our attitude to reduce the cognitive dissonance created by the inconsistency between the attitude and the behavior. Such change doesn't occur if we have sufficient justification for our behavior, however. A competing theory, self-perception theory, argues that dissonance is not involved. Self-perception theory proposes that we are just unsure about our attitude, so we infer it from our behavior. We are merely making self-attributions. Both theories seem to operate but in different situations. For well-defined attitudes, cognitive dissonance theory seems to be the better explanation; for weakly defined attitudes, self-perception theory is the better explanation.

Both our attitudes and our behavior also seem to be greatly affected by the roles we play. These roles are defined, and the definitions greatly influence our actions and our attitudes. Zimbardo has argued that the impact of the roles of guard and prisoner on the behavior and attitudes of male college students was dramatically demonstrated in the SPE. However, there has been much methodological criticism of the SPE, questioning both its validity and Zimbardo's situationist interpretation of its findings. The findings seem more a product of the demand characteristics in the study and not the social forces of the prisoner and guard roles. In addition, a new prison study was conducted more recently, Haslam and Reicher's BBC Prison Study. The results of the BBC Prison Study suggest that people do not automatically assume roles that are given to them as Zimbardo argued and that it is powerlessness and the failure of groups to form identities that may lead to tyranny.

ConceptCheck | 2

Explain how the actor-observer bias qualifies the fundamental attribution error and how self-serving bias qualifies the actor-observer bias.

Explain the difference between the false consensus effect and the false uniqueness effect.

Explain when cognitive dissonance theory is a better explanation of the relationship between our behavior and our attitudes and when self-perception theory is a better explanation of this relationship.

Study Guide

Chapter Key Terms

You should know the definitions of the following key terms from the chapter. They are listed in the order in which they appear in the chapter. For those you do not know, return to the relevant section of the chapter to learn them. When you think that you know all of the terms, complete the matching exercise based on these key terms.

social psychology
conformity
informational social
  influence
normative social influence
compliance
foot-in-the-door technique
door-in-the-face technique
low-ball technique
that's-not-all technique
obedience

experimenter bias
social facilitation
social loafing
diffusion of responsibility
bystander effect
deindividuation
group polarization
groupthink
attribution
fundamental attribution
  error

just-world hypothesis
primacy effect
self-fulfilling prophecy
actor-observer bias
self-serving bias
false consensus effect
false uniqueness effect
attitudes
cognitive dissonance theory
self-perception theory
demand characteristics

Key Terms Exercise

Identify the correct term for each of the following definitions. The answers to this exercise follow the answers to the ConceptChecks at the end of the chapter.

1. Compliance to a large request is gained by preceding it with a very small request.

   _____

2. Influence stemming from the need for information in situations in which the correct action or judgment is uncertain.

   _____

3. The tendency to underestimate the commonality of one's abilities and successful behaviors.

   _____

4. A mode of group thinking that impairs decision making because the desire for group

harmony overrides a realistic appraisal of the possible decision alternatives.

   _____

5. The loss of self-awareness and self-restraint in a group situation that fosters arousal and anonymity.

   _____

6. The tendency to exert less effort when working in a group toward a goal than when individually working toward a goal.

   _____

7. Following the commands of a person in authority.

   _____

8. The probability of a person helping in an emergency is greater when there are no other bystanders than when there are other bystanders.

   _____

9. The tendency as an observer to overestimate internal dispositional influences and underestimate situational influences upon others' behavior.

   _____

10. A theory developed by Festinger that assumes people have a tendency to change their attitudes to reduce the cognitive discomfort created by inconsistencies between their attitudes and their behavior.

    _____

11. The assumption that the world is just and that people get what they deserve.

    _____

12. In impression formation, information gathered early is weighted more heavily than information gathered later in forming an impression of another person.

    _____

13. Compliance to a costly request is gained by first getting compliance to an attractive, less costly request but then reneging on it.

    _____

14. The lessening of individual responsibility for a task when responsibility for the task is spread across the members of a group.

    _____

15. A change in behavior, belief, or both to conform to a group norm as a result of real or imagined pressure.

    _____

Practice Test Questions

The following are practice multiple-choice test questions on some of the chapter content. The answers are given after the Key Terms Exercise answers at the end of the chapter. If you guessed on a question or incorrectly answered a question, restudy the relevant section of the chapter.

1. The conformity demonstrated in Sherif's study using the autokinetic effect stems from _____.
   a. actor-observer bias
   b. self-serving bias
   c. informational social influence
   d. normative social influence

2. Which of the following factors increases conformity?
   a. group is not unanimous
   b. responding secretly
   c. correct action is not clear
   d. being of higher status than other group members

3. Which of the following compliance techniques involves gaining compliance to a much larger request by preceding it with a much smaller request?
   a. that's-not-all technique
   b. door-in-the-face technique
   c. low-ball technique
   d. foot-in-the-door technique

4. Which of the following situational factors in Milgram's shock experiments led to the highest maximum obedience rate?
   a. experiment conducted in a rundown office building
   b. two co-teachers disobey experimenter
   c. experimenter not present
   d. teacher has to force learner's hand onto shock plate

5. _____ is the strengthening of a group's prevailing opinion on a topic following group discussion of the topic.
   a. Deindividuation
   b. Group polarization
   c. Groupthink
   d. Social facilitation

6. Facilitation of a dominant response on a task due to social arousal is called _____.
   a. deindividuation
   b. social facilitation
   c. social loafing
   d. the bystander effect

7. When committing the fundamental attribution error, we tend to _____ the influence of dispositional factors and _____ the influence of situational factors.
   a. overestimate; overestimate
   b. overestimate; underestimate
   c. underestimate; overestimate
   d. underestimate; underestimate

8. With the self-serving bias, we tend to make _____ attributions for our failures and _____ attributions for our successes.
   a. dispositional; dispositional
   b. dispositional; situational
   c. situational; dispositional
   d. situational; situational

9. Bill likes country music; therefore, he thinks that most people like country music. Bill's behavior is an example of the _____.
   a. fundamental attribution error
   b. actor-observer bias
   c. false consensus effect
   d. false uniqueness effect

10. Two groups of children are told to not play with a very attractive toy in a playroom. One group is threatened very severely, while the other group is only threatened mildly. Neither group played with the toy. According to cognitive dissonance theory, which group(s) should later still rate the toy as very attractive?
    a. severe threat group
    b. mild threat group
    c. neither group
    d. both groups

11. Which two compliance techniques involve the rule of reciprocity?
    a. foot-in-the-door and door-in-the-face
    b. low-ball and that's-not-all
    c. foot-in-the-door and low-ball
    d. door-in-the-face and that's-not-all

12. Conformity is higher for a person when the group _____ the person's responses and when the person is of _____ status than the other group members.
    a. hears; lesser
    b. does not hear; lesser
    c. hears; higher
    d. does not hear; higher

13. The bystander effect refers to the finding that an observer of an emergency is less likely to help if the _____.
    a. emergency takes place in a big city
    b. emergency is being observed by other people

c. observer has just endured a frustrating experience
d. observer has been exposed to many similar emergencies in the past

14. Which of the following comments is most likely to be made by the leader of a group characterized by groupthink?
    a. "We have been united on matters in the past, and I hope that will continue."
    b. "We will need some outside experts to critique our decisions."
    c. "It's important for each of us individually to think critically about this issue."
    d. "We should probably divide into subgroups and arrive at independent decisions."

15. When our expectations of a person elicit behavior from that person that confirms our expectations, this is a case of _____.
    a. self-serving bias
    b. actor-observer bias
    c. deindividuation
    d. self-fulfilling prophecy

Chapter ConceptCheck Answers

ConceptCheck | 1

- The main difference between normative social influence and informational social influence concerns the need for information. When normative social influence is operating, information is not necessary for the judgment task. The correct answer or action is clear. People are conforming to gain the approval of others in the group and avoid their disapproval. When informational social influence is operating, however, people conform because they need information as to what the correct answer or action is. Conformity in this case is due to the need for information, which we use to guide our behavior.

- In the door-in-the-face technique, the other person accepts your refusal to the first request, so you reciprocate by agreeing to her second smaller request, the one she wanted you to comply with. In the that's-not-all technique, you think that the other person has done you a favor by giving you an even better deal with the second request, so you reciprocate and do her a favor and agree to the second request.

- If you predicted that the result was the same (0% maximum obedience), you are wrong. The result was the same as in Milgram's New Baseline experiment, 65% maximum obedience. An explanation involves how we view persons of authority who lose their authority (being demoted). In a sense, by agreeing to serve as the learner, the experimenter gave up his authority, and the teachers no longer viewed him as an authority figure. He had been demoted.

- According to the bystander effect, you would be more likely to receive help on the little-traveled country road, because any passing bystander would feel the responsibility for helping you. She would realize that there was no one else available to help you, so she would do so. On a busy interstate highway, however, the responsibility for stopping to help is diffused across hundreds of people passing by, each thinking that someone else would help you.

ConceptCheck | 2

- The actor-observer bias qualifies the fundamental attribution error because it says that the type of attribution we tend to make depends upon whether we are actors making attributions about our own behavior or observers making attributions about others' behavior. The actor-observer bias leads us as actors to make situational attributions; the fundamental attribution error leads us, as observers, to make dispositional attributions. The actor-observer bias is qualified, however, by the self-serving bias, which says that the type of attribution we make for our own actions depends upon whether the outcome is positive or negative. If positive, we tend to make dispositional attributions; if negative, we tend to make situational attributions.

- The false consensus effect pertains to situations in which we tend to overestimate the commonality of our opinions and unsuccessful behaviors. The false uniqueness effect pertains to situations in which we tend to underestimate the commonality of our abilities and successful behaviors. According to these effects, we think others share our opinions and unsuccessful behaviors but do not share our abilities and successful behaviors. These effects both stem from the self-serving bias, which helps to protect our self-esteem.

- Cognitive dissonance theory seems to be the better explanation for situations in which our attitudes are well-defined. With well-defined attitudes, our contradictory behavior creates dissonance; therefore, we tend to change our attitude to make it fit with our behavior. Self-perception theory seems to be the better explanation for situations in which our attitudes are weakly defined. We make self-attributions using our behavior to infer our attitudes.

Answers to Key Terms Exercise

1. foot-in-the-door technique
2. informational social influence
3. false uniqueness effect
4. groupthink
5. deindividuation
6. social loafing
7. obedience
8. bystander effect
9. fundamental attribution error
10. cognitive dissonance theory
11. just-world hypothesis
12. primacy effect
13. low-ball technique
14. diffusion of responsibility
15. conformity

Answers to Practice Test Questions

1. c; informational social influence
2. c; correct action is not clear
3. d; foot-in-the-door technique
4. a; experiment conducted in a rundown office building
5. b; Group polarization
6. b; social facilitation
7. b; overestimate; underestimate
8. c; situational; dispositional
9. c; false consensus effect
10. a; severe threat group
11. d; door-in-the-face and that's-not-all
12. a; hears; lesser
13. b; emergency is being observed by other people
14. a; "We have been united on matters in the past, and I hope that will continue."
15. d; self-fulfilling prophecy

10

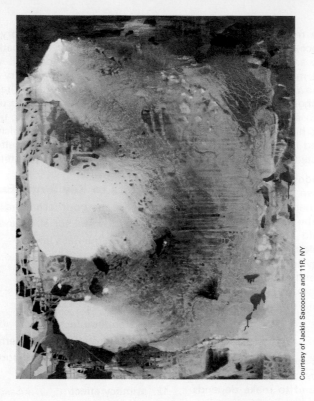

Courtesy of Jackie Saccoccio and 11R, NY

Abnormal Psychology

The scientific study of mental disorders and their treatment is called **abnormal psychology**. In this chapter, we will detail some of the major types of disorders and then describe the various types of therapy available to treat them. We will also consider the important question of whether these therapies are truly effective in treating disorders. First, however, we need to consider the diagnosis and classification processes so that you understand how disordered behavior and thinking are identified.

The Diagnosis and Classification of Mental Disorders

When psychologists say that the behavior and thinking of someone with a disorder are "abnormal," what do they mean? How do psychologists decide when someone's behavior or thinking has crossed over the line from normal to abnormal? First, it is important to realize that psychologists do not use the terms *sane* and *insane* in their decisions about the normality or abnormality of a person's behavior and thinking. These are primarily legal terms that are used to assess responsibility in a criminal case. A person accused of a crime can plead "not guilty by reason of insanity." The person acknowledges that he committed the crime, but argues that he is not responsible for it because of mental illness. There is a misperception that this defense is overused and used most frequently in heinous crimes. This misperception is likely due to the defense's frequent occurrence on television and in movies and the high profile nature of some of the cases in which it is used. However, research (Borum & Fulero, 1999, for example) has found that it rarely occurs in real life (less than 1% of felony cases) and is even more rarely successful (about 15% to 20% of the time).

So how do psychologists go about deciding whether a person's behavior and thinking are abnormal, that he is suffering from a mental disorder? They use four key criteria. It is important to realize that if a person's behavior or thinking meets one or more of these criteria, this does not necessarily mean that the person is suffering from a disorder. This will become clear as we discuss each of the criteria, which can be posed as questions.

First, is the behavior or thinking atypical (statistically infrequent)? Of course, not all statistically infrequent behavior or thinking is abnormal. Consider skydiving. That's an atypical behavior in our society, but it does not mean that a person who skydives has a disorder. Having hallucinations, however, is an atypical behavior that likely does reflect a disorder.

Second, is the behavior or thinking maladaptive? Maladaptive behavior or thinking prevents the person from successfully functioning and adapting to life's demands. Thus, a disordered person is not able to function in daily life. For example, being afraid to leave one's home is atypical and maladaptive behavior that would interfere with daily functioning.

Third, is the person or are others distressed by the behavior or thinking? Perhaps a young man is attempting, but failing, to make a living doing odd street stunts. His behavior is atypical and maladaptive (he will soon be penniless), but if he is not disturbed and if his stunts are not disturbing others, then he is not considered disordered.

Fourth, is the behavior or thinking rational? For example, a fear of birds might be so strong that even thinking about them causes great anxiety. The person may realize that this atypical, maladaptive, disturbing fear is not rational but still be unable to suppress the anxiety, and he would therefore be considered disordered.

The Diagnostic and Statistical Manual of Mental Disorders

These criteria help to determine whether a person's behavior and thinking may be "abnormal," but how do we know exactly what disorder the person has? The *Diagnostic and Statistical Manual of Mental Disorders,* **Fifth Edition (DSM-5),** published in 2013 by the American Psychiatric Association (APA), is the most widely used diagnostic system for mental disorders, informally referred to as "the bible of mental disorders." The intent of the DSM-5 is to serve both as a guide and an aid in the accurate diagnosis and treatment of mental disorders. It bases the classification of each disorder upon behavioral and psychological symptoms and defines the diagnostic guidelines for each disorder. The APA published the DSM-5 in print and also plans to publish it as a "living document" that can be updated as new research emerges. These incremental updates will be online and identified with decimals; i.e., DSM-5.1, DSM-5.2, and so on. Previous editions of the DSM were labeled using Roman numerals (e.g., DSM-IV), but the APA changed to Arabic numerals to facilitate the labeling of the versions of the living document.

The *Diagnostic and Statistical Manual of Mental Disorders* (DSM) first appeared in 1952, was only 86 pages long, and described about 60 disorders (Cordón, 2005), whereas the DSM-5 is almost 1,000 pages long and describes approximately 400 disorders. Why has the number of disorders in the DSM increased so dramatically, causing the DSM to go from a thin, spiral-bound book to a weighty tome across its five editions? A major reason is that over the last 60 years or so, we have learned a lot about various disorders and how to differentiate them, leading to more and more disorder classifications over successive versions of the DSM. This ability to make better differentiations between disorders has also led to more diagnostic reliability. In fact, the framers of the DSM-5 followed procedures in the development of the manual that would lead to it having greater reliability than previous editions, which were at best only moderately reliable (Regier, Narrow, Kuhl, & Kupfer, 2011). For example, they conducted extensive reviews of research, consulted with numerous clinicians about diagnostic difficulties, and

Diagnostic and Statistical Manual of Mental Disorders, Fifth Edition (DSM-5) The current version of the American Psychiatric Association's diagnostic and classification guidelines for mental disorders.

developed new categories and diagnostic criteria for categories that in the past have not been reliable. Thus, a major strength of the DSM-5 is that clinicians using it should be able to make more reliable classifications, which means that clinicians should more frequently agree on a particular diagnosis for a particular patient. The DSM-5 framers also conducted extensive research to ensure its validity. They were mainly concerned with the DSM-5's predictive validity (discussed in Chapter 6), the ability to predict future symptoms and behavior of the people classified in the various disorder categories. Thus, as with its reliability, the DSM-5's validity should be greater. Despite these efforts of the framers of DSM-5, some critics still have concerns about its reliability and validity (Frances, 2013; Freedman et al., 2013).

In addition to these concerns about its reliability and validity, the DSM-5 has been heavily criticized on other dimensions, causing quite a kerfuffle among mental health professionals (e.g., Frances, 2013; Greenberg, 2013). A major criticism is that disorder classification in the DSM-5 is out of control, leading many aspects of normal behavior and ordinary life to fit the criteria for diagnosis of a mental disorder. For example, mental decline that goes a bit beyond normal

DIAGNOSTIC AND STATISTICAL MANUAL OF MENTAL DISORDERS
FIFTH EDITION
DSM-5™
AMERICAN PSYCHIATRIC ASSOCIATION

The DSM-5 (published in 2013) is the latest version of the *Diagnostic and Statistical Manual of Mental Disorders* (DSM), the most widely used diagnostic system for mental disorders. The DSM is a living document that will be updated as new research emerges.

aging may now be given the new DSM-5 diagnosis of "mild neurocognitive disorder" (giving "senior moments" clinical significance) and children who have recurrent temper outbursts may be given the new DSM-5 diagnosis of "disruptive mood dysregulation disorder." The DSM-5 has also eliminated the bereavement exclusion for the diagnosis of major depressive disorder. Past versions of the DSM excluded people who had lost a loved one from receiving this diagnosis for the first two months of their bereavement. Thus, many people undergoing a normal grief reaction to the loss of a loved one may now receive a diagnosis of major depressive disorder. Allen Frances, who served as chairman of the DSM-IV task force, argues that the new diagnoses in the DSM-5 turn "everyday anxiety, eccentricity, forgetting, and bad eating habits into mental disorders" (Frances, 2013, pp. xv–xvi). According to Frances, such overdiagnosis will lead not only to a bonanza for the pharmaceutical industry but also to great costs (e.g., unnecessary and possibly harmful drug therapy) for all of the false-positive patients (people falsely diagnosed as having a mental disorder). Remember, we discussed the costs of false positives in the context of medical screening tests in Chapter 6.

BREVITY By Guy & Rodd

Dan Thompson/Universal Press UClick

This is a disorder that the framers of the DSM-5 seem to have missed.

According to critics such as Frances, the DSM-5 with its excessively wide diagnostic net creates an analogous situation in psychiatric diagnosis.

In spite of all of its possible flaws, the DSM-5 serves many useful purposes. It provides a common language and useable classification system for clinicians and clinical researchers to describe, discuss, evaluate, treat, and conduct research on mental disorders. It also serves an important practical purpose—health insurance companies require a DSM-5 disorder classification before paying for therapy. The DSM-5 should be thought of as a work in progress. As our knowledge about mental disorders evolves, so will the DSM. For now, however, the DSM-5 is the classification system in use; so, how does it work?

The DSM-5 has abandoned the multiaxial diagnostic system used in the DSM-IV and moved to a nonaxial assessment system in which a diagnosis requires a clinician to identify the disorder (or disorders) indicated by the person's symptoms along with dimensional judgments on the severity of the person's present symptoms and impairment. The DSM-5 provides specific diagnostic criteria, the key clinical features, and background information (such as prevalence rates) for approximately 400 disorders. Some disorders share certain symptoms, so the DSM-5 clusters these disorders into a major category. For example, several disorders that share anxiety as a symptom, such as phobic and panic disorders, are categorized as anxiety disorders. There are 20 major categories in the DSM-5. We will consider some disorders from six of these categories—Anxiety Disorders, Obsessive-Compulsive and Related Disorders, Depressive Disorders, Bipolar and Related Disorders, Schizophrenia Spectrum and Other Psychotic Disorders, and Personality Disorders. It is important to remember that the DSM-5 classification system applies to a pattern of symptoms and not to the person, so it refers, for example, to "a person with schizophrenia" and not a "schizophrenic."

Labeling People with Mental Disorders

In classifying mental disorders, regardless of the system used, labels are attached to people, possibly leading to a disquieting effect—negatively biasing our perception of these people in terms of the labels. Our perception may no longer be objective. Think about the words that are often used to describe people with mental disorders—for example, "crazy," "lunatic," "deranged," "insane," or "mad." These words have strong negative connotations. Similarly, diagnostic disorder labels may lead to negative perceptions and interpretations of a person's behavior in terms of the label. The label may guide our perception. In sum, it seems tenable that labeling mental disorders may lead to a stigmatizing effect, but is there evidence that it actually does?

There is a famous participant observational study that we briefly mentioned in Chapter 1 that deals with this possible perceptual-biasing effect of labeling (Rosenhan, 1973). Like Milgram's obedience study and Zimbardo's Stanford prison study discussed in Chapter 9, Rosenhan's "On Being Sane in Insane Places" study is a contentious classic. Between 1969 and 1972, David L. Rosenhan, then a psychology professor at Swarthmore College, and seven others (a psychology graduate student, three psychologists, a pediatrician, a housewife, and a painter) went to several different hospitals in five states and tried to gain admission. They each faked a major symptom of schizophrenic disorders: auditory hallucinations (hearing voices). The voice in these cases was saying the words "empty," "hollow," and "thud." Other than this sole symptom, the researchers acted normal and only lied about their true identities. First, they wanted to see whether they would be admitted given this singular symptom. Second, they wanted to see what would happen after they were admitted if they acted normal and said that they no longer heard the voices and that they were feeling normal again. According to Rosenhan, here's what happened. In brief, all of the pseudopatients (fake patients) were admitted, one diagnosed with manic depression and all the others with schizophrenia. They were placed in psychiatric wards where they remained for periods ranging from 8 to 52 days. Rosenhan argued that their subsequent normal behavior was misinterpreted in terms of their diagnoses, illustrating the perceptual biasing of labels. For example, one person's excessive note taking was interpreted as a function of his illness when, in fact, he was just trying to take notes to document the study. What kind of treatment did they receive? For the most part, they were given antipsychotic medications—an estimated 2,100 pills, though only two were taken. The pseudopatients just pretended to take the pills, pocketed them, and flushed them down the toilet. Ironically, some of the true patients realized that the pseudopatients were not true patients, but according to Rosenhan, the staff, guided by the diagnostic labels, did not. Even when the pseudopatients were released (an average stay of 19 days), they all had psychiatric labels on record upon discharge from the hospitals.

Rosenhan's bold interpretations of his findings did not go unchallenged. As Ruscio (2004, 2015) points out, there was a flurry of responses starting with a series of letters published in *Science* in 1973 and continuing with a special section of the *Journal of Abnormal Psychology* in 1975 devoted to responses to Rosenhan's contentions. Several detailed critiques, such as Millon (1975), Spitzer (1975, 1976), and Weiner (1975), also followed. According to Ruscio, these critics argued that Rosenhan used seriously flawed methodology, ignored relevant data, and reached unsound conclusions and that the greatest difficulty in accepting Rosenhan's conclusions revolved around the discharge diagnoses for the pseudopatients. All but one were diagnosed with "schizophrenia in remission." The other pseudopatient was diagnosed with "manic depression in remission." Spitzer (1976) provided data that indicated that these classifications were rarely used in psychiatric hospitals at the time of Rosenhan's study. Given this, Spitzer argues that this almost unaminous agreement across diagnosticians in very different settings and for different patients (1) contradicts Rosenhan's assertion that diagnoses are unreliable and (2) indicates that the clinicians' initial diagnoses of psychosis appear *not* to have significantly influenced their perceptions because their discharge diagnoses appear to have been based on their observation of the absence of the psychotic symptoms in the patients. Hence, according to his critics, Rosenhan's own findings suggest that the clinical decisions about the pseudopatients relied more on their *post*-diagnostic behavior than their initial diagnoses. It is also worth noting that Spitzer asked Rosenhan for access to his data to verify his conclusions, but he never received them. In addition, there is a substantial body of labeling research that indicates that the claim that psychiatric labels per se cause harm by stigmatizing people is a myth (Lilienfeld, Lynn, Ruscio, & Beyerstein, 2010). This does not mean that a stigma of mental illness does not exist, it does. The stigma, however, is more a product of other factors such as the behaviors of those given psychiatric labels and not the labels themselves (Ruscio, 2004). Finally, it is important to realize that in spite of all the scathing criticism of it, Rosenhan's study did draw attention to possible problems in the classification (diagnosis and labeling) of mental disorders. As already discussed, claims of such problems have persisted and followed the development of the DSM throughout its history and are especially prevalent for the DSM-5 (e.g., Frances, 2013, and Greenberg, 2013).

There was, however, a second study reported in Rosenhan (1973) that is not often mentioned, but it is interesting because it provides a clear demonstration of perceptual set, which we discussed in Chapter 3. The staff of a well-known research and teaching hospital, which was aware of the results of Rosenhan's initial study, claimed that similar errors would not be made at their hospital. In response, Rosenhan set up a test for them. He informed them that over a three-month period, one or more pseudopatients would attempt to gain admission to the hospital and that the staff should rate every incoming patient with respect to the likelihood that they were pseudopatients. What happened? Out of the 193 real patients who came to the hospital for admittance with symptoms of a disorder, 83 (43%) were either suspected or confidently judged to be a pseudopatient by at least one psychiatrist or staff member. However, Rosenhan had not sent any pseudopatients. All of the patients that the staff had judged or suspected to be pseudopatients were real patients. Rosenhan got the psychiatrists and staff members perceptually set to see pseudopatients, and so they did even when none came to the hospital. Remember from Chapter 3, seeing is believing, but it isn't always believing correctly.

Our perception of people with disorders is further complicated by the misrepresentation of disordered people on television and in other media. They are often depicted as violent and dangerous to others when the vast majority of people with disorders are not a threat to anyone except maybe themselves (Applebaum, 2004; Lilienfeld et al., 2010; Teplin, 1985). In addition, because these media depictions are typically very dramatic, they tend to stick in our memories and hence may lead us to think that such incidents are more prevalent than they really are, because of our use of the availability heuristic that we discussed in Chapter 6. They are not prevalent. We also need to be aware that these incidents are not representative of the behavior of the vast majority of people with mental disorders. Most people with mental disorders are experiencing a troubled period in their lives and are just finding it difficult to adjust. We need labels in order to know how to treat people with these disorders and for health professionals to communicate with one another about such disorders as well as to conduct research on them, but there is much more to a person than a label. Remember to distinguish between the person and the label.

Now that we have a general understanding of the diagnostic classification system and its strengths and weaknesses, we will consider some of the specific mental disorders (labels) that are identified in the DSM-5.

Section Summary

In this section, we first discussed the criteria for classifying behavior and thinking as abnormal and then how mental disorders are diagnosed and classified. The criteria for abnormality are that one's behavior and thinking are atypical, maladaptive, cause distress, and are not rational. The most widely used diagnostic system is the *Diagnostic and Statistical Manual of Mental Disorders,* Fifth Edition (DSM-5). The DSM-5 bases classification upon behavioral and psychological symptoms and provides diagnostic guidelines for about 400 disorders. Because some disorders share certain symptoms, the DSM-5 clusters the disorders into 20 major categories, such as Anxiety Disorders and Depressive Disorders. The DSM-5 should be viewed as a work in progress and will also be published as a living document, with future versions such as DSM-5.1, DSM-5.2, etc. as new research findings emerge.

A major strength of the DSM-5 is that it was developed to be more reliable and valid than previous editions. Regardless, the DSM-5 has been criticized for casting too wide a diagnostic net, possibly leading to normal behavior being classified as abnormal. In spite of its possible flaws, the DSM-5 reflects the current state of our knowledge about mental disorders and serves very important functions, both in clinical practice and in research. It provides a common language and useable classification system for clinicians and clinical researchers to describe, discuss, evaluate, treat, and conduct research on mental disorders. It also serves an important practical purpose—health insurance companies require a DSM-5 classification before paying for therapy. Thus, disorder classification is essential for many purposes. It is also important to remember that disorder classification (attaching psychiatric labels to people) does not bring harm to people by stigmatizing them. Our perception of people with disorders is biased, though, by the media's misrepresentation of people with disorders as violent and dangerous when most are not a threat to anyone except possibly themselves.

ConceptCheck | 1

Explain what the DSM-5 is.

Explain why, although it is controversial, classifying mental disorders by attaching labels to the disorders is necessary.

Six Major Categories of Mental Disorders

As you read this section, beware of the "medical school syndrome"—the tendency to think that you have a disease (disorder in our case) when you read about its symptoms. Symptoms are behaviors or mental processes that indicate the presence of a disorder. The symptoms of many disorders often involve behavior and thinking that we all experience, which may lead us to think we have the disorders. To prevent such misdiagnoses, remember the criteria that we discussed for distinguishing abnormal behavior and thinking. For example, we all get anxious or depressed (symptoms of several different disorders) at different times in our lives for understandable reasons, such as an upcoming presentation or a death in the family. These feelings of anxiety and depression only become symptoms of a disorder when they prevent us from functioning normally. We are suffering from a disorder only if our reactions to life's challenges become atypical, maladaptive, disturbing to ourselves or others, and irrational.

What causes such abnormal behavior and thinking? Most causal explanations for mental disorders are tied to the four major research approaches—biological, behavioral, cognitive, and sociocultural. None of these approaches has proven consistently better at explaining all of the various disorders, though particular approaches are sometimes better for specific disorders. Even in these cases, however, it appears best to formulate an explanation in terms of more than one kind of cause. This is usually referred to as the **biopsychosocial approach**—explaining abnormality as the result of the interaction among biological, psychological (behavioral and cognitive), and sociocultural factors. As we consider various disorders, we will provide some examples of this type of explanation. Table 10.1 outlines the six major categories of disorders, along with the specific mental disorders within each category that we will consider.

biopsychosocial approach Explaining abnormality as the result of the interaction among biological, psychological (behavioral and cognitive), and sociocultural factors.

anxiety disorders Disorders that share features of excessive fear and anxiety and related behavioral disturbances, such as avoidance behaviors.

Anxiety Disorders

We all have experienced anxiety. Don't you get anxious at exam times, especially at final exam time? Most students do. How do you feel when you are about to give an oral presentation? Anxiety usually presents itself again. These are normal reactions, not signs of a disorder. **Anxiety disorders** are disorders that share features of excessive fear and anxiety and related behavioral disturbances, such as avoidance behaviors

Table 10.1	Six Major Categories of Mental Disorders and the Specific Disorders to Be Considered in Each Category
Major Category	**Specific Disorder(s) Within Category**
Anxiety disorders	Specific phobia, social anxiety disorder (social phobia), agoraphobia, panic disorder, generalized anxiety disorder
Obsessive-compulsive and related disorders	Obsessive-compulsive disorder, hoarding disorder, excoriation (skin-pulling) disorder, trichotillomania (hair-pulling disorder)
Depressive disorders	Major depressive disorder
Bipolar and related disorders	Bipolar disorder
Schizophrenia spectrum and other psychotic disorders	Schizophrenia
Personality disorders	Avoidant personality disorder, schizoid personality disorder, antisocial personality disorder

(APA, 2013). In anxiety disorders, the anxiety and fear often occur inexplicably and are so intense that they prevent the person from functioning normally in daily life. The specific anxiety disorders differ from one another in the types of objects and situations that induce the excessive fear and anxiety. Because anxiety disorders are some of the most common disorders in the United States (Hollander & Simeon, 2011; cf. Horwitz & Wakefield, 2012), we'll discuss several different anxiety disorders—specific phobia, social anxiety disorder (social phobia), agoraphobia, panic disorder, and generalized anxiety disorder.

Specific phobia. According to the DSM-5, a **specific phobia** is indicated by a marked and persistent fear of specific objects or situations (such as snakes or heights) that is excessive and unreasonable. In the United States, the overall prevalence rate for specific phobia ranges from 7% to 9%, with a higher prevalence rate in teenagers and a lower prevalence rate in older adults (APA, 2013). More than 12% of people in the United States develop a specific phobia at some point during their lives, and having a specific phobia is about twice as prevalent in women versus men and in African and Hispanic Americans (born in the United States) versus White Americans (Comer, 2014). A selection of specific phobias is given in Table 10.2 (page 436). A person with a specific phobia realizes that the fear is excessive and unreasonable but cannot control it. Both the avoidance of the object or situation and the anxious anticipation of encountering the object or situation interfere with the person's daily life. This is important. Many of us have fears of such things as heights, snakes, and spiders, but we do not have a disorder. The anxiety and fear are not to the degree that they interfere with normal functioning and lead us to behave in maladaptive and irrational ways.

specific phobia An anxiety disorder indicated by a marked and persistent fear of specific objects or situations that is excessive and unreasonable.

Table 10.2	A Selection of Specific Phobias
Phobia	**Specific Fear**
Acrophobia	Fear of heights
Aerophobia	Fear of flying
Agyrophobia	Fear of crossing streets
Arachnophobia	Fear of spiders
Claustrophobia	Fear of closed spaces
Cynophobia	Fear of dogs
Gamophobia	Fear of marriage
Gephyrophobia	Fear of crossing bridges
Hydrophobia	Fear of water
Ophidiophobia	Fear of snakes
Ornithophobia	Fear of birds
Pyrophobia	Fear of fire
Thanatophobia	Fear of death
Xenophobia	Fear of strangers
Zoophobia	Fear of animals

To emphasize this difference, consider this brief description of a case of a woman with a specific phobia of birds. She became housebound because of her fear of encountering a bird. Any noises that she heard within the house she thought were birds that had somehow gotten in. Even without encountering an actual bird, the dreaded anticipation of doing so completely controlled her behavior. When she did leave her house, she would carefully back out of her driveway so that she did not hit a bird; she feared that the birds would retaliate if she did. She realized that such cognitive activity was beyond the capabilities of birds, but she could not control her fear. Her behavior and thinking were clearly abnormal.

What causes a specific phobia? One biopsychosocial answer involves both behavioral and biological factors. We learn phobias through classical conditioning and are biologically predisposed to learn some fears more easily than others. We are conditioned to fear a specific object or situation. Remember Watson and Rayner's study described in Chapter 4 in which they classically conditioned Little Albert to fear white rats? Behavioral psychologists believe that the fears in specific phobias are learned the same way, but through stressful experiences in the real world, especially during early childhood. For example, a fear of birds might be due to the stressful experience of seeing Alfred Hitchcock's movie *The Birds* (in which birds savagely attack humans) at a young age. You should also remember from Chapter 4 that biological preparedness constrains learning. Certain associations (such as taste and sickness) are easy to learn, while others (such as taste and electric shock) are very difficult. This biological preparedness shows up with specific phobias in that fears that seem to have more evolutionary survival value, such as fear of heights, are more frequent than ones that do not, such as fear of marriage (McNally, 1987). It is also more difficult to extinguish fears that have more evolutionary survival value (Davey, 1995).

"Stephen's fear of heights is particularly bad today."

Social anxiety disorder (social phobia) and agoraphobia. Most phobias are classified as specific phobias, but the DSM-5 describes two broader types of phobias: social anxiety disorder (previously labeled social phobia in the DSM-IV) and agoraphobia. **Social anxiety disorder** is a marked, irrational, and persistent fear of one or more social performance situations in which embarrassment may occur and in which there is exposure to unfamiliar people or scrutiny by others. Again this is more than the normal anxiety before giving a presentation. The fear is excessive, unreasonable, and interferes with the person's normal functioning. For example, the person may fear eating in public and will have great difficulty managing lunch at work; she will reject all lunch and dinner invitations, greatly limiting her social opportunities. The fear may be specific to one particular social situation (such as eating in public) or more general (such as functioning inadequately with respect to all behavior in front of others), leading to the avoidance of most social situations.

Social anxiety disorder is different from **agoraphobia,** the fear of being in places or situations from which escape may be difficult or embarrassing. The name of this disorder literally means fear of the marketplace; in Greek, "agora" means marketplace, and "phobia" means fear. In addition to the marketplace, situations commonly feared in agoraphobia include being in a crowd, standing in a line, and traveling in a crowded bus or train or in a car in heavy traffic. To avoid these situations, people with agoraphobia usually won't leave the security of their home. Surveys reveal that about 7% of people in the United States suffer from social anxiety disorder in any given year but only about 2% from agoraphobia (Kessler, Ruscio, Shear, & Wittchen, 2010; NIMH, 2011). Just as for

social anxiety disorder An anxiety disorder indicated by a marked and persistent fear of one or more social performance situations in which embarrassment may occur and in which there is exposure to unfamiliar people or scrutiny by others.

agoraphobia An anxiety disorder indicated by a marked and persistent fear of being in places or situations from which escape may be difficult or embarrassing.

specific phobias, a behavioral-evolutionary explanation seems indicated for agoraphobia. However, the leading explanation for social anxiety disorder is cognitive—people with this disorder have negative social beliefs about themselves, such as that they are socially inadequate and that their behavior in social situations will inevitably lead to disasters (e.g., Heimberg, Brozovich, & Rapee, 2010; Rosenberg, Ledley, & Heimberg, 2010). Anticipating that such disasters will occur, people with social anxiety disorder try to avoid social situations, and when they are in a social situation, they suffer increased anxiety, which leads to a negative assessment of how poorly they have acted, increasing their fear of future social situations.

Panic disorder. **Panic disorder** is a condition in which a person experiences recurrent panic attacks—sudden onsets of intense fear. A panic attack includes symptoms such as trembling, sweating, heart palpitations, chest pain, shortness of breath, and feelings of choking and dizziness. The person is overrun with anxiety and fear. Some panic attacks occur when a person is faced with a dreaded situation (such as going to the dentist), but others occur without any apparent reason. Only about 2% to 3% of adolescents and adults suffer from panic disorder each year, and it is twice as common in women as in men (APA, 2013).

Biological explanations of panic disorder involve abnormal neurotransmitter activity, especially that of norepinephrine, and improper functioning of a panic brain circuit, which includes the amygdala, hypothalamus, and some other areas in the brain. Cognitive explanations involve panic-prone people who are overly sensitive to bodily sensations. Such people misinterpret these sensations as signs of a medical catastrophe, plunging them into a panic attack. Panic disorder is also often accompanied by agoraphobia. One explanation of panic disorder with agoraphobia is the fear-of-fear hypothesis: Agoraphobia is the result of the fear of having a panic attack in a public place. According to this hypothesis, agoraphobia is a case of classical conditioning in which the fear-avoidance response is a conditioned response to the initial panic attack.

panic disorder An anxiety disorder in which a person experiences recurrent panic attacks.

generalized anxiety disorder An anxiety disorder in which a person has excessive, global anxiety and worries that he cannot control, occurring more days than not for at least a period of 6 months.

Generalized anxiety disorder. Panic attacks occur suddenly in panic disorder. In generalized anxiety disorder, the anxiety is chronic and lasts for months. **Generalized anxiety disorder** is a disorder in which a person has excessive, global anxiety that he cannot control, occurring more days than not for at least 6 months (APA, 2013). The person just cannot stop worrying, and the anxiety is general—it is not tied to specific objects or situations as it is in a phobic disorder. The problem is sometimes described as free-floating anxiety. About 6% of us will develop a generalized anxiety disorder in our lifetimes, and it is diagnosed twice as often in women than men (APA, 2013). Recent biological research has indicated that generalized anxiety disorder may be related to a biochemical dysfunction in the brain involving GABA, a neurotransmitter that we discussed in Chapter 2. Remember, GABA is the major inhibitory neurotransmitter, which means that it causes neurons to stop generating impulses. In anxiety and fear situations, more and more neurons get excited. After a while, this state of excitability in a normal person triggers the release of GABA to reduce the level of neuronal firing back to normal, which reduces the feelings of anxiety. A person with generalized anxiety disorder may have problems activating GABA, and therefore the feelings of anxiety are not reduced.

Obsessive-Compulsive and Related Disorders

Obsessive-compulsive and related disorders is a new major category in the DSM-5. In the DSM-IV, obsessive-compulsive disorder was classified as an anxiety disorder. In this new category, obsessive-compulsive disorder is grouped with some related disorders, such as excoriation (skin-picking) disorder and trichotillomania (hair-pulling) disorder. These disorders are related to obsessive-compulsive disorder because of the compulsive nature of the behaviors involved and the obsessive-like concerns that trigger these behaviors. We will focus our discussion on obsessive-compulsive disorder and then briefly describe a few of the related disorders. None of the disorders in this category is as prevalent as the anxiety disorders that we discussed.

Obsessive-compulsive disorder. A person with **obsessive-compulsive disorder** experiences recurrent obsessions or compulsions that are recognized by the person as excessive or unreasonable, but consume considerable time and cause significant distress and disruption in the person's daily life.

Album/Oronoz /SuperStock

The Scream by Edvard Munch. This painting is typically interpreted as illustrating the intense terror in a panic attack. According to the text Munch carved into the work's gilded frame for the second of the four colored versions that he painted, the painting stems from an actual incident in Munch's life. Munch and two friends were walking on a bridge at sunset when Munch actually experienced the enormous anxiety and melancholy that he brought to life in the painting. He said that he was trembling with fright and felt the great scream in nature.

obsessive-compulsive disorder
A disorder in which the person experiences recurrent obsessions or compulsions that are perceived by the person as excessive or unreasonable, but cause significant distress and disruption in the person's daily life.

obsession A persistent intrusive thought, idea, impulse, or image that causes anxiety.

compulsion A repetitive and rigid behavior that a person feels compelled to perform in order to reduce anxiety.

Some people with obsessive-compulsive disorder experience only obsessions or only compulsions, but most suffer both. An **obsession** is a persistent intrusive thought, idea, impulse, or image that causes anxiety. A **compulsion** is a repetitive and rigid behavior that a person feels compelled to perform in order to reduce anxiety. The most common obsessions are concerned with contamination through germs, dirt, or other toxic substances, and the fear that something terrible, such as death or illness, is going to occur; the most frequent compulsions are excessive hand washing, bathing, and grooming (Rapoport, 1989). The 12-month prevalence of obsessive-compulsive disorder is only 1.2% (APA, 2013).

It is important to realize that many people experience minor obsessions (e.g., a pervasive worry about upcoming exams) or compulsions (e.g., arranging their desks in a certain way), but they do not have this disorder. People with obsessive-compulsive disorder cannot function in their daily lives, because their obsessions and compulsions consume most of the day and prevent a normal life. People who don't have this disorder might go back to check to make sure that the stove was turned off once (or even twice), but a person with an obsessive-compulsive disorder might check 50 times and in a very ritualistic manner. This is a checking compulsion—the person checks the same thing over and over again, usually a set number of times and in a particular manner. Similarly, people who suffer from a cleaning compulsion feel compelled to keep cleaning themselves. Such people might spend their day washing their hands, taking showers, and engaging in other cleaning activities. Compulsions are usually tied to obsessions. For example, the cleaning compulsion is usually tied to a contamination obsession in which people are overly concerned with avoiding contamination. To reduce the anxiety stemming from the fear of contamination, they feel compelled to keep cleaning themselves.

Snapshots at jasonlove.com

© Jason Love

It is not known for sure what causes obsessive-compulsive disorder, but recent research suggests that a neurotransmitter imbalance involving serotonin may be involved. Antidepressant drugs that only increase serotonin activity (SSRIs) help many patients with obsessive-compulsive disorder (Rapoport, 1991). Serotonin activity has also been linked to parts of the brain that may be related to the disorder—the orbital region of the frontal cortex (the cortical area just above the eyes), the caudate nuclei (areas in the basal ganglia), the thalamus, the amygdala, and the cingulate cortex (the communication conduit between the prefrontal lobes and the limbic system). These parts make up a brain circuit that is involved in filtering out irrelevant information and disengaging attention, which are certainly central aspects of obsessive-compulsive disorder (Seligman, Walker, & Rosenhan, 2001). One explanation may be that serotonin works to stabilize activity in these areas. One truly bizarre case of obsessive-compulsive disorder highlights the importance of the frontal lobe region. A man with obsessive-compulsive disorder became severely depressed and attempted suicide. He shot himself in the head, but fortunately survived and was cured of his disorder. The bullet had removed some of his orbital frontal cortex and his disorder with it.

Obsessive-compulsive related disorders. We will briefly describe three of these disorders—hoarding disorder, excoriation (skin-picking) disorder, and trichotillomania (hair-pulling disorder). At present, explanations for these related disorders are similar to those we discussed for obsessive-compulsive disorder. It is hoped that by being grouped with obsessive-compulsive disorder in the DSM-5, these disorders will be researched more, leading to more disorder-specific explanations.

Hoarding disorder reflects a persistent difficulty in discarding or parting with possessions due to a perceived need to save the items and the distress associated with discarding them. This need to save items results in an extraordinary accumulation of clutter. Parts of the home may become inaccessible because of the stacks of clutter occupying those areas. Sofas, beds, and other pieces of furniture may be unusable, because they are filled with stacks of hoarded items. Such clutter may not only impair personal and social functioning but also result in fire hazards and unhealthy sanitary conditions. Prevalence rates for hoarding disorder are not available, but it appears to be more prevalent in older adults than younger adults (APA, 2013). About 75% of individuals with hoarding disorder also have an anxiety or depressive disorder, with the most common being major depressive disorder (APA, 2013). Having another disorder is important, because it may often be the main reason for consultation. Individuals with hoarding disorder seldom seek consultation for hoarding symptoms.

People with excoriation (skin-picking) disorder keep picking at their skin, leading to sores and other skin problems, as well as, in some cases, lesions. Most people with this disorder pick with their fingers and center their focus on one area of the body, most often the face. However, other areas, such as the arms and legs, are also common focal points for this disorder. The skin-picking is usually triggered and accompanied by anxiety and stress. People with excoriation disorder often spend significant amounts of time on their picking behavior, sometimes several hours per day. The lifetime prevalence for excoriation is only 1% to 2%, and 75% or more of the people with this disorder are women (APA, 2013).

People with trichotillomania (hair-pulling disorder) continually pull out hair from the scalp or other areas of the body. The hair-pulling typically is only focused on one body part, most often the scalp, eyebrows, or eyelids, and done one hair at a time, sometimes in a ritualistic manner. Like excoriation, trichotillomania is triggered and accompanied by anxiety or stress. The hair-pulling may occur in brief episodes throughout the day or during less frequent but more sustained periods that can continue for hours. Women are more frequently affected with trichotillomania than men, at a ratio of approximately 10 to 1 (APA, 2013).

Depressive Disorders

Depressive disorders involve the presence of sad, empty, or irritable mood, accompanied by somatic and cognitive changes that significantly affect the individual's capacity to function. Major depressive disorder (sometimes called unipolar depression) represents the classic condition in this category, so it is the depressive disorder that we will discuss.

Major depressive disorder. When people say that they are depressed, they usually are referring to their feelings of sadness and downward mood following a stressful life event (such as the breakup of a relationship or the loss of a job). Such mood changes are understandable and over time usually right themselves. A major depressive disorder, however, is debilitating, has an impact on every part of a person's life, and usually doesn't right itself. To be classified as having a **major depressive disorder,** a person must have experienced one or more major depressive episodes. A **major depressive episode** is characterized by symptoms such as feelings of intense hopelessness, low self-esteem, and worthlessness; extreme fatigue; dramatic changes in eating and sleeping behavior; inability to concentrate; and greatly diminished interest in family, friends, and activities for a period of 2 weeks or more. Such people are not just down in the dumps, but rather are in a snowballing downward spiral that lasts for weeks. They lose interest in everything, even their life. Suicide is strongly related to depression and can occur at any point during or after a major depressive episode. Any comments about suicide made by people suffering a major depression should be taken seriously.

depressive disorders Disorders that involve the presence of sad, empty, or irritable mood, accompanied by somatic and cognitive changes that significantly affect the individual's capacity to function.

major depressive disorder A depressive disorder in which the person has experienced one or more major depressive episodes.

major depressive episode An episode characterized by symptoms such as feelings of intense hopelessness, low self-esteem and worthlessness, extreme fatigue, dramatic changes in eating and sleeping behavior, inability to concentrate, and greatly diminished interest in family, friends, and activities for a period of 2 weeks or more.

The 12-month prevalence is 7%, but this prevalence in the 18- to 29-year-old age group is three times greater than that in individuals age 60 years or older (APA, 2013). Major depressive disorder is also more common among poor people than wealthy people (Sareen, Afifi, McMillan, & Asmundson, 2011). About 19% of all adults suffer a major depressive disorder at some point in their lives. Women suffer from major depressive disorders about twice as often as men (Kessler et al., 2003), and this gender difference seems to be true worldwide (Weissman et al., 1996). Recent research suggests that this gender difference for depression may be due to biological differences (Westly, 2010). The sex hormones estrogen and testosterone have different effects on the neurotransmitters involved in mood (serotonin, norepinephrine, and dopamine), leading to a difference in both emotional reaction and symptomology in women and men. The primary emotional symptom for women is sadness; but for men, it is anger often paired with irritability. Thus, female depression will be seen as depression, but male depression may be mistakenly seen as some other emotional problem, such as general frustration, and not the serious disorder that it is. This difference, along with the fact that women are more likely than men to seek help, almost certainly contributes to the gender difference in the clinical prevalence rates for depression.

There is also a recent argument that the high prevalence rate for depression is spurious, in that it is due to overdiagnosis caused by insufficient diagnostic criteria (Horwitz & Wakefield, 2007). True mental disorders are usually rare, with very low prevalence rates, but depression has a high prevalence rate. According to Andrews and Thomson (2009, 2010), the fact that depression has a high prevalence rate poses an evolutionary paradox, because the pressures of evolution should have led our brains to resist such a high rate of malfunction. Andrews and Thomson propose that much of what is diagnosed as depression should not be thought of as a true mental disorder (a brain malfunction) but rather as an evolutionary mental adaptation (stress response mechanism) that focuses the mind to better solve the complex life problems that brought about the troubled state. This is an intriguing hypothesis with implications not only for the diagnostic criteria for this disorder but also for the therapeutic approaches to treat it.

Traditional explanations of major depressive disorder propose both biological and psychological factors as causes. A leading biological explanation involves neurotransmitter imbalances, primarily inadequate serotonin and norepinephrine activity. Antidepressant drugs (to be discussed later in the chapter) are the most common treatment for such imbalances. There is also evidence of a genetic predisposition for this disorder (Levinson & Nichols, 2014; Tsuang & Faraone, 1990). The likelihood of one identical twin getting a disorder given that the other identical twin has the disorder is the concordance rate for identical twins for the disorder. McGuffin, Katz, Watkins, and Rutherford (1996) looked at almost 200 pairs of twins and found that the concordance rate for identical twins is 46%, which is significantly greater than the 20% found for fraternal twins. Adoption studies have also implicated a genetic predisposition, at least for major depressive disorder (Kamali & McInnis, 2011). The biological parents of adoptees who had been diagnosed with this disorder were found to have a higher incidence of severe depression than the biological parents of adoptees who had not been diagnosed with this disorder.

Brain researchers have recently proposed a brain circuit responsible for unipolar depression (Treadway & Pizzagalli, 2014). Brain-imaging studies indicate that the parts of the circuit are the hippocampus, amygdala, prefrontal cortex (all discussed in Chapter 2), and an area of the brain that we did not discuss in Chapter 2, Brodmann Area 25, located in the cerebral cortex under the corpus callosum. Although this research indicates that these areas likely each play a role in this disorder, their exact roles have not yet been determined. However, much of the recent research has been focused on Brodmann Area 25's role (Eggers, 2014; Schiferle, 2013). Activity in this area seems to ebb and flow with episodes of depression. When depression subsides, activity decreases; when depression resumes, activity increases. Helen Mayberg and her colleagues at Emory University believe that this area functions as sort of a "depression switch," a kind of juncture box whose malfunction leads to depression (Dodds, 2006; Mayberg et al., 2000). Mayberg's group has even demonstrated that deep-brain stimulation in Brodmann Area 25 can be effective in treating severe intractable depression (Mayberg et al., 2005).

There are a panoply of other biological theories about depression and treatments for it. An interesting one involves a toxin, botulinum poison, which we discussed in Chapter 2. Remember, an extremely mild form of this poison is used in Botox treatments for facial wrinkling. Depending upon the injection site, particular facial expression muscles are paralyzed temporarily. According to this theory, information flows both ways in the circuit connecting the brain with these facial muscles. The brain monitors the emotional valence (expression) of the face and responds by generating the appropriate feeling, and conversely, the brain can direct the facial muscles to generate specific expressions depending upon what the brain judges our emotional state to be. This theory is congruent with the theories of emotion that we discussed in Chapter 2. Remember, for example, that the Schachter and Singer two-factor theory proposed that our cognitive appraisal (by the brain) of our physiological and behavioral responses leads the brain to identify the relevant emotion, resulting in the appropriate emotional feeling. Hence, this new theory of treatment for depression proposes that if the frowning muscles (the corrugator and procerus muscles) are paralyzed so we cannot frown, then the brain will generate a more positive emotional feeling, relieving our depression to some extent. Indeed, some recent studies have shown that if we cannot frown (because of Botox treatments), then it is harder for us to stay depressed. For example, Finzi and Rosenthal (2014) found that 6 weeks after injection, 52% of those diagnosed with major depression showed relief from depression versus only 15% of those who received a saline placebo. This theory fits with other findings that use facial feedback in similar ways. For example, light therapy that stimulates the eyes sends signals directly to the brain via the optic nerve to treat seasonal depression. Research on this theory is still in the early stages, so whether Botox injections will prove to be a truly useful treatment for depression remains an unanswered question until further research answers it.

It is clear, however, that major depressive disorder is not totally biological in origin. Thus, nonbiological factors are also seen as causes in major depressive disorder. For example, cognitive factors have been found to be important. The person's perceptual and cognitive processes are assumed to be faulty, causing the depression. We discussed an example of such faulty cognitive processing in Chapter 8. Remember the pessimistic explanatory style in which a person explains negative events in terms of internal (her own fault), stable (here to stay), and global (applies to all aspects of her life) causes. Such a style, paired with a series of negative events in a person's life, will lead to learned helplessness and depression. Thus, the cause of the person's depression is her own thinking, in this case how she makes attributions. Cognitive therapies, which we will discuss later in this chapter, attempt to replace such maladaptive thinking with more adaptive thinking that will not lead to depression. These therapies have been shown to be just as effective as drug therapy in treating depression (DeRubeis et al., 2005).

Bipolar and Related Disorders

Major depressive disorder is often referred to as unipolar depression or a unipolar disorder to contrast it with bipolar disorder, another disorder in which the person's mood takes dramatic mood swings between depression and mania. Such disorders used to be called "manic–depressive" disorders. Experiencing a mania is not just having an "up" day. A **manic episode** is a period of at least a week of abnormally elevated mood in which the person experiences such symptoms as inflated self-esteem with grandiose delusions, a decreased need for sleep, constant talking, distractibility, restlessness, and poor judgment. The person's behavior becomes maladaptive and interferes with daily functioning.

"Now that I've swung back to depression, I'm truly sorry for what I did when I was manic."

Consider the following behavior of a person experiencing a manic episode. A postal worker stayed up all night and then went off normally to work in the morning. He returned later that morning, however, having quit his job, withdrawn all of the family savings, and spent it on fish and aquariums. He told his wife that, the night before, he had discovered a way to keep fish alive forever. He then ran off to canvass the neighborhood for possible sales. This person showed poor judgment and a decreased need for sleep, and his behavior disrupted his normal functioning (he quit his job). In the beginning, milder stages of a manic episode, some people become not only more energetic but also more creative, until the episode accelerates and their behavior deteriorates.

There is no diagnosis for mania alone. It is part of a **bipolar disorder** in which recurrent cycles of depressive and manic episodes occur. A bipolar disorder is an emotional roller coaster, with the person's mood swinging from manic highs to depressive lows. There are two types of bipolar disorder. In Bipolar I disorder, the person has both major manic and depressive episodes. In Bipolar II disorder, the person has full-blown depressive episodes, but the manic episodes are milder. Bipolar I disorder is more common than Bipolar II disorder, but both disorders are rare and only affect less than 1% of the population (APA, 2013; Kessler et al., 1994).

Because the concordance rate for identical twins for bipolar disorder is so strong, 70% (Tsuang & Faraone, 1990), biological causal explanations are the most common. In fact, researchers are presently working on identifying the specific

manic episode An episode characterized by abnormally elevated mood in which the person experiences symptoms such as inflated self-esteem with grandiose delusions, a decreased need for sleep, constant talking, distractibility, restlessness, and poor judgment for a period of at least a week.

bipolar disorder A disorder in which recurrent cycles of depressive and manic episodes occur.

genes that make a person vulnerable to bipolar disorder. As with major depressive disorder, the biological predisposition shows up as neurotransmitter imbalances. In this case, the imbalances swing between inadequate activity (depression) and too much activity (mania). The most common treatment is drug therapy, and the specific drugs used will be discussed later in the chapter.

Schizophrenia Spectrum and Other Psychotic Disorders

We will only be discussing schizophrenia from this category. It is the disorder that people are usually thinking of when they use words such as "insane" and "deranged." More people are institutionalized with schizophrenia than with any other disorder, and schizophrenia is much more difficult to successfully treat than other mental disorders. Thankfully, only about 1% of the population suffers from this disorder (Gottesman, 1991). The onset of schizophrenia is usually in late adolescence or early adulthood. Men and women are equally likely to develop schizophrenia, but it tends to strike men earlier and more severely (Lindenmayer & Khan, 2012). Schizophrenia is more common in the lower socioeconomic classes than in the higher ones, and also for those who are single, separated, or divorced (Sareen et al., 2011). In addition, people with schizophrenia have an increased risk of suicide, with an estimated 25% attempting suicide (Kasckow, Felmet, & Zisook, 2011).

Schizophrenia is referred to as a **psychotic disorder,** because it is characterized by a loss of contact with reality. The word "schizophrenia" is Greek in origin and literally means "split mind." This is not a bad description; in a person with schizophrenia, mental functions become split from one another and the person becomes detached from reality. The person has trouble distinguishing reality from his own distorted view of the world. This splitting of mental functions, however, has led to the confusion of schizophrenia with "split personality" or multiple personality disorder (now called dissociative identity disorder in the DSM-5), but these are very different disorders. In schizophrenia, the split is between the mental functions and their contact with reality; in multiple personality disorder, one's personality is split into two or more distinct personalities.

The symptoms of schizophrenia. The symptoms of schizophrenia vary greatly, but they are typically divided into three categories—positive, negative, and disorganized. This use of the terms "positive" and "negative" is consistent with their use in Chapter 4, on learning. Positive means that something has been added, and negative means that something has been removed.

Positive symptoms are the more active symptoms that reflect an excess or distortion of normal thinking or behavior, including **hallucinations** (false sensory perceptions) and **delusions** (false beliefs). Hallucinations are usually auditory,

psychotic disorder A disorder characterized by a loss of contact with reality.

hallucination A false sensory perception.

delusion A false belief.

hearing voices that aren't really there. Remember, the fake patients in Rosenhan's study said that they heard voices and were admitted and diagnosed as having a schizophrenic disorder. Delusions fall into several categories, such as delusions of persecution (for example, believing that one is the victim of conspiracies) or delusions of grandeur (for example, believing that one is a person of great importance, such as Jesus Christ or Napoleon). Hallucinations and delusions are referred to as positive symptoms because they refer to things that have been added.

Negative symptoms are deficits or losses in emotion, speech, energy level, social activity, and even basic drives such as hunger and thirst. For example, many people with schizophrenia suffer a flat affect in which there is a marked lack of emotional expressiveness. Their faces show no expression, and they speak in a monotone. Similarly, there may be a serious reduction in their quantity and quality of speech. People suffering from schizophrenia may also lose their energy and become extremely apathetic—they are not able to start a task, much less finish one.

Disorganized symptoms include nonsensical speech and behavior and inappropriate emotion. Disorganized speech sounds like a "word salad," with unconnected words incoherently spoken together and a shifting from one topic to another without any apparent connections. One thought does not follow the other. Those who show inappropriate emotion may smile when given terrible news. Their emotional reactions seem unsuited to the situation.

Behavior may also be catatonic—physical actions that do not appear to be goal-directed, such as assuming and maintaining postures and remaining motionless for a long period of time. Catatonic behavior takes extreme forms ranging from immobility to hyperactivity (such as rocking constantly).

According to the DSM-5, **schizophrenia** is the presence, most of the time during at least a 1-month period, of at least two of the following symptoms—hallucinations, delusions, disorganized speech, grossly abnormal psychomotor activity (including catatonic behavior), or any negative symptom (such as loss of emotion). In addition, functioning in daily life is markedly below that prior to the onset of the symptoms, and the signs of this disturbance must occur for at least 6 months, including the period of at least 1 month when at least two of the symptoms are present.

Clinicians have used the various types of symptoms of schizophrenia and their course of development to make distinctions between types of schizophrenia. One such distinction, between chronic and acute schizophrenia, deals with how quickly the symptoms developed. In chronic schizophrenia, there is a long period of development, over years, and the decline in the person's behavior and thinking occurs gradually. In acute schizophrenia, there is a sudden onset of symptoms that usually can be attributed to a crisis in the person's life, and the person functioned normally before the crisis with no clinical signs of the disorder. Acute schizophrenia is more of a reactive disorder, and recovery is much more likely.

schizophrenia A psychotic disorder in which at least two of the following symptoms are present most of the time during a 1-month period—hallucinations, delusions, disorganized speech, disorganized or catatonic behavior, or negative symptoms such as loss of emotion.

Another distinction is between Type I and II schizophrenia (Crow, 1985). Type I is characterized by positive symptoms, and Type II by negative symptoms. Type I is similar to acute schizophrenia: The person has usually functioned relatively normally before the disorder strikes, and there is a higher likelihood of recovery. People with Type I schizophrenia respond better to drug therapy than do those with Type II. This difference may be because the positive symptoms of Type I result from neurotransmitter imbalances, which are affected by drugs, whereas the more permanent structural abnormalities in the brain that produce the negative symptoms of Type II are not as affected by drugs.

The causes of schizophrenia. Schizophrenia seems to have many different causes, and we do not have a very good understanding of any of them. Hypothesized causes inevitably involve a genetic or biological predisposition factor. There definitely appears to be a genetic predisposition to some schizophrenia; it seems to run in families, with the concordance rate for identical twins similar to that for a major depression, about 50% (DeLisi, 1997; Gottesman, 1991). This is significantly greater than the 17% concordance rate for fraternal twins. In addition, recently the biggest-ever genetic study of mental illness identified 128 gene variants associated with schizophrenia in 108 distinct areas in the human genome (Schizophrenic Working Group of the Psychiatric Genomics Consortium, 2014). This research project compared the genomes of almost 37,000 people with schizophrenia with those of more than 113,000 people without schizophrenia. One promising finding has already emerged from this line of research. Dhindsa and Goldstein (2016) found that people who had a deviant form of a gene, called *C4,* had a higher prevalence of schizophrenia. This gene plays a key role in pruning back synapses during adolescence and early adulthood in order to speed up cognitive processing by getting rid of weak and redundant connections that are no longer needed. A deviant *C4* gene, however, causes this pruning process to run amok, leading to excessive pruning and a decline in cognitive functioning (sudden slippage in mental acuity and memory and so on) that is typically first observed during this time period in people who develop schizophrenia. Such excessive pruning also fits the brain-imagery finding that in people with schizophrenia certain brain regions, such as the prefrontal cortex, have fewer synaptic connections because this pruning activity during adolescence and early adulthood takes place primarily in the prefrontal cortex, where thinking and planning skills are centered. Carrying a gene variant that leads to overaggressive pruning, however, is hardly enough to cause schizophrenia by itself. Other factors, both biological and non-biological, are almost certainly involved. It is also probably the case that different variant genes might be involved in the different types of schizophrenia or that schizophrenia is a polygenic disorder caused by a combination of gene defects (e.g., Sanders, Duan, & Gejman, 2012). In sum, it appears that deviant genes are involved in the development of schizophrenia, but the major questions of which ones are involved and how they each contribute via interactions with one another and nongenetic factors remain questions to be answered by future research.

Nongenetic biological factors also likely play a role in the development of schizophrenia. One hypothesis involves prenatal factors, such as viral infections (Brown, 2006; Washington, 2015). Research has found that people are at increased risk for schizophrenia if there was a flu epidemic during the middle of their fetal development (Takei, Van Os, & Murray, 1995; Wright, Takei, Rifkin, & Murray, 1995). There is even a birth-month effect for schizophrenia. People born in the winter/spring months (January to April) following the fall/winter flu season are more likely to develop schizophrenia, because it is more likely that they were exposed to a flu virus during fetal development (Torrey, Miller, Rawlings, & Yolken, 1997). According to the viral hypothesis, the invading virus impairs fetal brain development, making people more susceptible to developing schizophrenia later in life. The viral hypothesis is further supported by the finding that the 50% concordance rate in identical twins is the result of a 60% chance for identical twins that share the same placenta (about two-thirds of identical twins), but only a 10% chance for identical twins with separate placentas (Davis & Phelps, 1995). It is certainly more likely that a viral infection would affect both twins in the same placenta rather than twins in separate placentas.

Prenatal or early postnatal exposure to several other viruses (e.g., herpes simplex virus) has also been associated with the later development of schizophrenia (Yolken & Torrey, 1995). Even exposure to house cats has been proposed as a risk factor for the development of schizophrenia (Torrey, Rawlings, & Yolken, 2000; Torrey & Yolken, 1995; Yolken, Dickerson, & Torrey, 2009). Infectious parasites hosted by cats, *Toxoplasma gondii* (*T. gondii*), are transmitted through ingestion or inhalation of the parasite's eggs that are shed with the infected cat's feces into litter boxes, the yard, and elsewhere. For example, this could occur through hand-to-mouth contact following gardening or cleaning a cat's litter box. According to this viral zoonosis hypothesis, the *T. gondii* invade the brain and upset its chemistry, creating the psychotic behaviors recognized as schizophrenia. This may sound far-fetched to you, but many significant correlational findings supporting this hypothesis have been observed. For example, individuals with schizophrenia have an increased prevalence of antibodies to *T. gondii* in their blood (Torrey, Bartko, Lun, & Yolken, 2007; Torrey, Bartko, & Yolken, 2012; Torrey & Yolken, 2003). This increased prevalence has been observed for both prenatal and early postnatal exposure to *T. gondii* (Mortensen et al., 2007). Should cat owners panic? Probably not, but keeping basic hygienic precautions in mind is highly recommended.

Given these possible genetic, prenatal, and postnatal factors, what might be the organic problems that the person is predisposed to develop? There are two good answers—neurotransmitter imbalances and brain abnormalities. People with schizophrenia have elevated levels of dopamine activity in certain areas in the brain (Davis, Kahn, Ko, & Davidson, 1991). Autopsy and brain-scan research indicate that the brains of people with schizophrenia have an excess of dopamine receptors. In addition, drugs that decrease dopamine activity reduce schizophrenic symptoms, and drugs that increase dopamine activity seem to heighten the symptoms of people with schizophrenia and produce schizophrenic symptoms in people who do not have schizophrenia. Such findings led to the development of antipsychotic drugs that are dopamine antagonists (reduce the level of dopamine activity) and help control the symptoms in many people with schizophrenia, especially those with Type I. We will discuss these antipsychotic drugs later in the chapter.

Two psychedelic drugs, phencyclidine (PCP) and ketamine, have also provided some insight into the neurochemistry of schizophrenia (Julien, 2011). These two drugs produce schizophrenia-type symptoms, such as a general motor slowing and reduced speech and other cognitive deficits. The underlying neurochemical action for these drugs is antagonistic, the blocking of glutamate receptors, especially one type of receptor that plays a critical role in brain development and neural processing in general (Javitt & Coyle, 2007). Remember from Chapter 2, glutamate is the major excitatory neurotransmitter in our nervous system. The ability of PCP and ketamine to induce schizophrenia-type symptoms suggests that the actions of these drugs replicate disturbances in the brains of people with schizophrenia. Thus, a glutamate dysfunction has been proposed as a contributor to the development of schizophrenia, especially the negative symptoms and cognitive impairments that are observed (Goff & Coyle, 2001). According to this hypothesis, excessive release of glutamate destroys neurons, especially in the frontal lobes, leading to cortical damage and triggering the mental deterioration observed in schizophrenia. Hence, glutamate neurotransmission has become a promising target for antipsychotic drug development, and antipsychotic drugs that impact glutamate activity levels are presently undergoing clinical trials (Stone, 2011).

Various structural brain abnormalities have also been found in people with schizophrenia, especially those suffering from Type II and chronic schizophrenia (Buchanan & Carpenter, 1997; Weyandt, 2006). I'll mention a few. For example, brain scans of people with schizophrenia often indicate shrunken cerebral tissue and enlarged fluid-filled areas. Some brain areas (the thalamus) seem to be smaller than normal, and, as we have already mentioned, the prefrontal cortex has fewer synaptic connections and is less active. Because structural brain abnormalities have not been observed using multiple brain-imaging methods in the nonpsychotic siblings of people with schizophrenia, these abnormalities may be due to nongenetic factors (Boos et al., 2012). Prenatal factors, such as the viral infections we discussed, and postnatal factors, such as oxygen deprivation arising from birth complications, likely play a role in the development of some of these brain abnormalities (Cannon, 1997; Wright et al., 1995).

vulnerability–stress model A biopsychosocial explanation of schizophrenia that proposes that genetic, prenatal, and postnatal biological factors render a person vulnerable to schizophrenia, but environmental stress determines whether it develops or not.

Even given all of this biological evidence, biopsychosocial explanations are necessary to explain all of the evidence accumulated about schizophrenia. A popular biopsychosocial explanation is the **vulnerability–stress model**—genetic, prenatal, and postnatal biological factors render a person vulnerable to schizophrenia, but environmental stress determines whether it develops or not (Gottesman, 1991). According to the vulnerability–stress model, we vary in our vulnerability to schizophrenia. A person's level of vulnerability interacts with the stressful social-cognitive events in his life to determine the likelihood of schizophrenia. Remember that schizophrenia typically strikes in late adolescence/early adulthood, which are periods with unusually high stress levels. There is also some evidence that dysfunctional family environments may be a contributing stress factor (Fowles, 1992).

In summary, there has been much research on the causes of schizophrenia, but we still do not have many clear answers. The only certainty is that schizophrenia is a disabling disorder with many causes. As pointed out in the DSM-5, schizophrenia is a heterogeneous mental disorder and people with schizophrenia will vary substantially in their symptomology. Explanations inevitably involve a biological component, making drug therapy the predominant treatment for schizophrenia, both historically and at present. Although these drugs (called antipsychotics) work well for some people with schizophrenia, many people stop taking them after a year or so because of bad side effects. A recent study (Morrison et al., 2014), however, found that a treatment program using psychotherapy (talk therapy) for those who had stopped taking their medications led to significant improvement versus those not receiving the therapy. In addition, Kane et al. (2015) found that the combination of hybrid cognitive-behavioral psychotherapy and drug therapy was superior to drug therapy alone as early treatment for people diagnosed with their first episode of schizophrenia. These recent studies indicate that combining psychotherapy and drug therapy, especially early on in the treatment process, may be the best way to proceed. We will discuss various types of psychotherapy and drug therapy, including antipsychotics, later on in the chapter.

Personality Disorders

A **personality disorder** is characterized by inflexible, long-standing personality traits that lead to behavior that deviates from cultural norms and results in distress or impairment. The DSM-5 identifies 10 personality disorders divided into three clusters based on their symptoms (APA, 2013). One cluster of three disorders (the avoidant, dependent, and obsessive-compulsive personality disorders) involves highly anxious or fearful behavior patterns. For example, a person with an avoidant personality disorder is so overwhelmed by feelings of inadequacy and rejection that social situations are avoided. A second cluster of three (the paranoid, schizoid, and the schizotypal personality disorders) involves eccentric or odd behavior patterns. For example, a person with a schizoid personality disorder totally avoids social relationships and contact. The last cluster of four disorders (the antisocial, borderline, histrionic, and narcissistic personality disorders) involves excessively dramatic, emotional, or erratic behavior patterns. For example, a person with an antisocial personality disorder shows total disregard for the rights of others and the moral rules of the culture.

personality disorder A disorder characterized by inflexible, long-standing personality traits that lead to behavior that impairs social functioning and deviates from cultural norms.

A person with antisocial personality disorder used to be referred to as a psychopath or sociopath. If you would like to learn more about these disorders, Millon, Millon, Meagher, and Grossman (2004) provide detailed coverage of all 10 personality disorders and their development.

Personality disorders usually begin in childhood or adolescence and persist in a stable form throughout adulthood. It has been estimated that 9% to 13% of adults in the United States have a personality disorder (Comer, 2014). Personality disorders are fairly resistant to treatment and change. They need to be diagnosed, however, because they give the clinician a more complete understanding of the patient's behavior and may complicate the treatment for a patient with another mental disorder. In addition, because the symptoms of the 10 personality disorders overlap so much, clinicians sometimes diagnose a person to have more than one personality disorder. This symptom overlap also leads clinicians to disagree about which personality disorder is the correct diagnosis, questioning the reliability of the DSM-5 definitions of these disorders.

Section Summary

In this section, we discussed six major categories of mental disorders—anxiety disorders, obsessive-compulsive and related disorders, depressive disorders, bipolar and related disorders, schizophrenia spectrum and other psychotic disorders, and personality disorders. Anxiety disorders involve excessive fear and anxiety. For each of the anxiety disorders, anxiety is involved in a different way. Panic attacks (being overwhelmed by anxiety and fear) occur suddenly in panic disorder, but the anxiety is chronic and global in generalized anxiety disorder. In specific phobia disorder, there is a marked and persistent fear of specific objects or situations that is excessive and unreasonable. There are two broader types of phobias, however—social anxiety disorder and agoraphobia. Social anxiety disorder involves a fear of social performance situations in which there is exposure to unfamiliar people or scrutiny by others, and agoraphobia involves a fear of being in places or situations from which escape may be difficult or embarrassing. Causal explanations of anxiety disorders typically involve both behavioral and biological factors.

In obsessive-compulsive disorder, the person experiences recurrent obsessions (persistent thoughts that cause anxiety) and compulsions (repetitive and rigid behaviors that have to be performed to alleviate anxiety). It is not known what causes obsessive-compulsive disorder, but recent research indicates a biochemical lack of serotonin activity in several parts of the brain. Obsessive-compulsive-related disorders include hoarding disorder, excoriation (skin-picking) disorder, and trichotillomania (hair-pulling) disorder.

Depressive disorders involve the presence of sad, empty, or irritable mood that impacts the individual's capacity to function. The changes in the person's emotional mood are excessive and unwarranted. The most common depressive disorder is major depressive disorder, which involves at least one major depressive episode. It is twice as frequent in women as in men. Sometimes this disorder is referred to as unipolar depression in order to contrast it with bipolar disorder, in which the person has recurrent cycles of depressive and manic (elevated mood) episodes. The concordance rate (the likelihood that one identical twin will get the disorder if the other twin has it) is substantial for both disorders, about 50% for depression and 70% for bipolar disorder. Neurotransmitter imbalances seem to be involved in both disorders, and cognitive factors are involved in major depressive disorder.

Schizophrenia is the most serious disorder discussed in this chapter. It is a psychotic disorder, which means that the person loses contact with reality. Clinicians divide schizophrenic symptoms into three categories—positive, negative, and disorganized. Schizophrenia seems to be a very heterogeneous disorder with many possible causes. Biological abnormalities in people with schizophrenia range from deviant gene patterns and elevated dopamine activity levels to shrunken cerebral tissue, and there is also evidence that prenatal viral infections and birth complications may be involved. A popular biopsychosocial explanation of schizophrenia is the vulnerability–stress model, which proposes that genetic, prenatal, and postnatal biological factors render a person vulnerable to schizophrenia, but environmental stress determines whether it develops or not.

Personality disorders are characterized by inflexible, long-standing personality traits that lead to behavior that impairs social functioning and deviates from cultural norms. The DSM-5 identifies 10 personality disorders. They fall into three clusters, each characterized by a group of problematic personality symptoms. One cluster of disorders involves highly anxious or fearful behavior patterns; one involves eccentric or odd behavior patterns; and the third involves excessively dramatic, emotional, or erratic behavior patterns. Personality disorders are fairly resistant to treatment and change.

ConceptCheck | 2

Explain what is meant by the biopsychosocial approach and then describe a biopsychosocial explanation for specific phobic disorders.

Explain how the two anxiety disorders, specific phobia and generalized anxiety disorder, are different.

Explain how the concordance rates for identical twins for a major depressive disorder and for schizophrenia indicate that more than biological causes are responsible for these disorders.

Explain the difference between schizophrenia and "split personality."

The Treatment of Mental Disorders

Before discussing treatment for disorders (types of therapy), we need to describe the various types of mental health professionals who treat disorders. Table 10.3 (page 454) lists most of the major types of mental health professionals, along with the type of credential and the typical kinds of problems they treat. States have licensing requirements for these various mental health professionals, and it is important to verify that a therapist is licensed. There is also one major difference between psychiatrists and the other health professionals. Psychiatrists are medical doctors. This means that psychiatrists can write prescriptions for medical

Table 10.3	Different Types of Mental Health Professionals
Type	**Credential and Job Description**
Clinical psychologist	Doctoral degree in clinical psychology; provides therapy for people with mental disorders
Counseling psychologist	Doctoral degree in psychological or educational counseling; counsels people with milder problems such as academic, job, and relationship problems
Psychiatrist	Medical degree with residency in mental health; provides therapy for people with mental disorders and is the only type of therapist who can prescribe drugs or other biomedical treatment
Psychoanalyst	Any of the above types of credential, but with training in psychoanalysis from a psychoanalytic institute; provides psychoanalytic therapy for psychological disorders
Clinical social worker	Master's or doctoral degree in social work with specialized training in counseling; provides help with social problems, such as family problems

treatment of patients. This is especially important because drug therapy is the major type of treatment for many disorders. To circumvent this prescription-writing problem, nonpsychiatrist mental health professionals typically work in a collaborative practice with medical doctors.

There are two major types of therapy: biomedical and psychological. **Biomedical therapy** involves the use of biological interventions, such as drugs, to treat disorders. **Psychotherapy** involves the use of psychological interventions to treat disorders. Psychotherapy is what we normally think of as therapy. There is a dialogue and interaction between the person and the therapist. They talk to each other. This is why psychotherapy is sometimes referred to as "talk therapy." The nature of the "talk" varies with the approach of the therapist. The behavioral, cognitive, psychoanalytic, and humanistic approaches all lead to different styles of psychotherapy. In biomedical therapy, however, a drug or some other type of biological intervention is used to treat disorders. The interaction is biological, not interpersonal. As with psychotherapy, there are different types of biomedical therapy—drug therapy, electroconvulsive therapy, and psychosurgery. We must remember though that this either-or distinction between biomedical therapy and psychotherapy is somewhat obscured by the fact that psychotherapy does lead to changes that take place in the brain. So the end result (changes in the brain) is the same for both types of therapy, but the means for achieving this result are different. We will first consider biomedical therapies and then the major types of psychotherapy.

biomedical therapy The use of biological interventions, such as drugs, to treat mental disorders.

psychotherapy The use of psychological interventions to treat mental disorders.

Biomedical Therapies

Biomedical therapies for disorders have a long history, reaching back hundreds of years. Looking back, these earlier treatments may seem inhumane and cruel, but remember that we are assessing these treatments given our current state of medical and psychological knowledge, which is far superior to that available when such treatments were used. Let's consider a couple of examples.

Possibly the earliest biological treatment was trephining, which was done in the Middle Ages. In this primitive treatment, a trephine (stone tool) was used to cut away a section of the person's skull, supposedly to let evil spirits exit the body, thus freeing the person from the disorder. A treatment device from the early 1800s was called the "tranquilizing chair." This device was designed by Benjamin Rush, the "father of American psychiatry," who actually instituted many humane reforms in the treatment of mental patients (Gamwell & Tomes, 1995). The treatment called for patients to be strapped into a tranquilizing chair, with the head enclosed inside a box, for long periods of time. The restriction of activity and stimulation was supposed to have a calming effect by restricting the flow of blood to the patient's brain. Such "therapies" seem absurd to us today, as does the fact

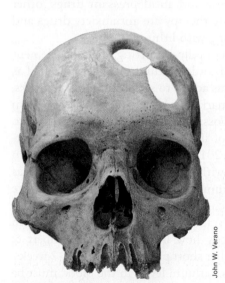

Primitive Biological Therapy | The two holes in this ancient skull illustrate trephining—cutting away sections of a person's skull to let evil spirits exit the body, thus freeing the person from a disorder.

The Tranquilizing Chair | This treatment device was designed by Benjamin Rush, the "father of American psychiatry," in the early 1800s. Supposedly the restriction of the patient's activity and stimulation would have a calming effect by restricting the blood flow to the patient's brain. Although it seems barbaric today, it was intended as a humane alternative to the straitjacket at that time. In actuality, it did neither harm nor good.

that well into the nineteenth century, many mental patients were still being kept in chains in asylums, untreated. The history of therapy is a rather sad one.

Even the more contemporary biomedical treatments exist in an atmosphere of controversy. Most people have strong, negative feelings about shock therapy, and the most frequently used biomedical treatment, drug therapy, is shrouded in conflict (Barber, 2008; Moncrieff, 2009; Valenstein, 1988). Why? Biomedical treatments are very different from undergoing psychotherapy. Direct biological interventions have a more powerful downside, because they involve possibly serious medical side effects. For example, high levels of some drugs in the blood are toxic and may even be fatal. Careful monitoring is essential. As we discuss the major types of biomedical treatments, we will include discussion of some of these potential problems. We start with drug therapy.

Drug therapy. The drugs used to treat mental disorders are referred to as psychotropic drugs, and they are among the very best sellers for drug companies, with about 300 million prescriptions written for them yearly in the United States (Frances, 2013). Leading the way are antipsychotic drugs with sales of $18 billion a year and antidepressant drugs with sales of $12 billion a year. Surprisingly, primary care providers, not psychiatrists, write the majority of these prescriptions (DuBosar, 2009). In addition to antipsychotic and antidepressant drugs, other major psychotropic medications used in drug therapy are antianxiety drugs and lithium. We will discuss all of these, beginning with lithium.

Lithium is not a drug, but rather a naturally occurring metallic element (a mineral salt) that is used to treat bipolar disorder. Lithium was actually sold as a substitute for table salt in the 1940s and was added to some commercial drinks, such as 7-Up, but the salt was taken off the market and the lithium removed from the drinks when reports of its toxicity and possible role in some deaths began to circulate (Valenstein, 1988). The discovery of lithium's effectiveness in combating bipolar disorder was accidental (Julien, 2011). Around 1950, John Cade, an Australian psychiatrist, injected guinea pigs with uric acid, which he thought was the cause of manic behavior, and mixed lithium with it so that the acid was more easily liquefied. Instead of becoming manic, the guinea pigs became lethargic. Later tests in humans showed that lithium stabilized the mood of patients with bipolar disorder. It is not understood exactly how lithium works (Lambert & Kinsley, 2005; Paulus, 2007), but within a rather short period of time, 1 to 2 weeks, it stabilizes mood in the majority of patients. Lithium levels in the blood must be monitored carefully, however, because of possible toxic effects—nausea, seizures, and even death (Moncrieff, 1997). Because of these possibly toxic side effects, anticonvulsants (drugs used to control epileptic seizures) are now sometimes prescribed instead for people with bipolar disorder. Anticonvulsants seem to reduce bipolar disorder symptoms but have less dangerous potential side effects.

lithium A naturally occurring element (a mineral salt) that is used to treat bipolar disorder.

antidepressant drugs Drugs used to treat depressive disorders.

Antidepressant drugs are drugs used to treat depressive disorders. There are many different types. The first antidepressants developed were monoamine oxidase (MAO) inhibitors and tricyclics (this name refers to the three-ring molecular structure of these drugs). MAO inhibitors increase the availability of the neurotransmitters norepinephrine, serotonin, and dopamine (which affect our mood) by preventing their breakdown (Advokat, Comaty, & Julien, 2014). Tricyclics make the neurotransmitters norepinephrine and serotonin more available by blocking their reuptake during synaptic gap activity (Advokat et al, 2014). Like lithium, the effects of both types of antidepressants were discovered accidentally when they were being tested for their impact on other problems (Comer, 2014). An MAO inhibitor was being tested as a possible treatment for tuberculosis when it was found to make the patients happier. In the case of tricyclics, their impact on depression was discovered when they were being tested as possible drugs to treat schizophrenia.

Research indicates that MAO inhibitors are fairly successful in combating depressive symptoms, but they are not used very often because of a potentially very dangerous side effect. Their interaction with several different foods and drinks may result in fatally high blood pressure. Tricyclics are prescribed more often than MAO inhibitors, because they are not subject to this potentially dangerous interaction. The most prescribed antidepressants by far, however, are the more recently developed selective serotonin reuptake inhibitors (SSRIs). Remember from Chapter 2 that their name describes how they achieve their effect—they selectively block the reuptake of serotonin in the synaptic gap, keeping the serotonin active and increasing its availability. The well-known antidepressant drugs Prozac, Zoloft, and Paxil are all SSRIs. The success rate of SSRIs in treatment is about the same as tricylics, but they are prescribed more often because of their milder side effects. Millions of prescriptions have been written for SSRIs, resulting in billions of dollars of sales. Prescriptions for the more recently developed selective serotonin and norepinephrine reuptake inhibitors (SSNRIs), such as Cymbalta and Effexor, which we discussed in Chapter 2, are also on the increase. None of these various types of antidepressants, however, have immediate effects. It typically takes 3 to 6 weeks to see improvement.

A recent survey study of about 12,000 people by the Centers for Disease Control and Prevention found some interesting results with respect to the use of antidepressants (Pratt, Brody, & Gu, 2011). First, the use of antidepressant drugs has soared nearly 400% since 1988, making antidepressants the most frequently used drugs by people ages 18–44. About 1 in 10 Americans aged 12 years and older were taking antidepressants during the period of the study, 2005–2008. As expected, because women are twice as likely to suffer from depression as men, women were more likely to be taking

"Of course your daddy loves you. He's on Prozac—he loves everybody."

antidepressants than were men, and this was true for every level of depression severity. The survey also found that nearly one in four women ages 40 to 59 were taking antidepressants, more than in any other age-sex group. Of concern, it was found that less than one-third of persons taking an antidepressant and less than one-half of those taking multiple antidepressants had seen a mental health professional in the past year, indicating a lack of follow-up care. This is further complicated by the fact that people who take antidepressants are usually taking them long term. About 60% of those taking antidepressants had taken them for 2 years or longer, and 14% had taken them for more than a decade.

There is a controversy about the effectiveness of antidepressant drugs, with some researchers arguing that antidepressants are just expensive, overused placebos. Indeed, some recent research indicates that much of their effectiveness can be accounted for by placebo effects—improvements due to the expectation of getting better (Kirsch, 2010; Kirsch et al., 2008). Remember from Chapter 1 that a placebo is an inert substance or treatment that is given to patients who believe that it is a real treatment for their problem. An especially intriguing finding is that placebos that lead to actual physical side effects also lead to larger placebo effects. These placebo effects have sometimes been found to be comparable to the improvement effects of antidepressant drugs (Kirsch, 2010). Some researchers believe that this means much, if not most, of the effect found with antidepressant drugs may be due to placebo effects. However, the difference between drug and placebo effects may vary as a function of symptom severity (Khan, Brodhead, Kolts, & Brown, 2005). A meta-analysis of antidepressant drug effects and depression severity found that the benefit of antidepressant drug versus placebo may be minimal or nonexistent, on average, in patients with mild or moderate symptoms, but it is significant for patients with very severe depression (Fournier et al., 2010).

How can we make sense of these placebo effects? One possibility involves neurogenesis, which we discussed in Chapter 2. Remember, neurogenesis, the growth of new neurons, has been observed in the hippocampus in the adult brain (Jacobs, van Praag, & Gage, 2000a, 2000b). The **neurogenesis theory of depression** assumes that neurogenesis in the hippocampus stops during depression, and when neurogenesis resumes, the depression lifts (Jacobs, 2004). The question, then, is how do we get neurogenesis to resume? There are many possibilities. Research has shown that SSRIs lead to increased neurogenesis in other animals. Both rats and monkeys given Prozac make more neurons than rats and monkeys not given Prozac (Perera et al., 2011). This also seems to be the case for humans taking antidepressants (Boldrini et al., 2009; Malberg & Schechter, 2005).

neurogenesis theory of depression
An explanation of depression that proposes that neurogenesis, the growth of new neurons, in the hippocampus stops during depression, and when it resumes, the depression lifts.

The time frame for neurogenesis also fits the time frame for SSRIs to have an impact on mood. It takes 3 to 6 weeks for new cells to mature, the same time it typically takes SSRIs to improve the mood of a patient. This means that, in the case of the SSRIs, the increased serotonin activity may be responsible for getting neurogenesis going again and lifting mood.

Remember, however, what we said about disorders being biopsychosocial phenomena. It is certainly plausible that psychological factors could also have an impact on neurogenesis. Positive thinking, in the form of a strong placebo effect, might also get neurogenesis going again, but possibly not sufficiently enough to deal with very severe depression. A similar claim could be made for the effectiveness of cognitive psychotherapies in which therapists turn the patient's negative thinking into more positive thinking. The neurogenesis theory is only in its formative stage, but it does provide a coherent framework for the many diverse improvement effects due to drugs, placebos, and psychotherapies.

Antianxiety drugs are drugs that treat anxiety problems and disorders. The best known antianxiety drugs, such as Valium and Xanax, are in a class of drugs called benzodiazepines. Benzodiazepines reduce anxiety by increasing the activity of the major inhibitory neurotransmitter GABA. They achieve their agonistic effect by facilitating GABA binding at GABA receptors (Advokat et al., 2014). When GABA's activity is increased, it reduces anxiety by slowing down and inhibiting neural activity, getting it back to normal levels. Unfortunately, recent evidence has shown that benzodiazepines have potentially dangerous side effects, such as physical dependence or fatal interactions with alcohol, but other types of nonbenzodiazepine antianxiety drugs have been developed with milder side effects. In addition, some antidepressant drugs, especially the SSRIs, have been very successful in treating anxiety disorders.

Antipsychotic drugs are drugs that reduce psychotic symptoms. The first antipsychotic drugs appeared in the 1950s and, as we discussed in Chapter 2, worked antagonistically by globally blocking receptor sites for dopamine, thereby reducing its activity. These drugs greatly reduced the positive symptoms of schizophrenia but had little impact on the negative symptoms. Antipsychotic drugs revolutionized the treatment of schizophrenia and greatly reduced the number of people with schizophrenia in mental institutions. These early drugs, along with those developed through the 1980s, are referred to as "traditional" antipsychotic drugs to distinguish them from the more recently developed "new generation" antipsychotic drugs.

The traditional drugs (for example, Thorazine and Stelazine) produce side effects in motor movement that are similar to the movement problems of Parkinson's disease. In addition, there is a long-term-use side effect of traditional antipsychotic drugs called **tardive dyskinesia** in which the patient has uncontrollable facial tics, grimaces, and other involuntary movements of the lips, jaw, and tongue. The new generation antipsychotic drugs (for example, Clozaril and Risperdal) are more selective about where in the brain they reduce dopamine activity; therefore, they do not produce the severe movement side effects such as tardive dyskinesia. They also have the advantage of helping some patients' negative schizophrenic symptoms. This may be due to the fact that these drugs also decrease the level of serotonin activity.

antianxiety drugs Drugs used to treat anxiety problems and disorders.

antipsychotic drugs Drugs used to treat psychotic disorders.

tardive dyskinesia A side effect of long-term use of traditional antipsychotic drugs causing the person to have uncontrollable facial tics, grimaces, and other involuntary movements of the lips, jaw, and tongue.

electroconvulsive therapy (ECT) A biomedical treatment for severe depression that involves electrically inducing a brief brain seizure.

Regrettably, the new generation antipsychotic drugs have other potentially dangerous side effects and have to be monitored very carefully (Folsom, Fleisher, & Depp, 2006). Such monitoring is expensive; therefore, traditional drugs are often prescribed instead. In addition, the initial optimism for the new generation drugs has been tempered by recent evidence that they do not lead to as much improvement as originally thought (Jones et al., 2006; Lieberman, Stroup, et al., 2005). A recent study of long-term antipsychotic treatment and brain volume also found a negative effect for both traditional and new generation antipsychotic drugs (Ho, Andreasen, Ziebell, Pierson, & Magnotta, 2011). Longer-term antipsychotic treatment was associated with smaller volumes of both brain tissue and gray matter. Other studies have found similar decreases in gray matter in the short term (Dazzan et al., 2005; Lieberman, Tollefson, et al., 2005). Thus, antipsychotic drugs may lead to loss of brain tissue or exacerbate declines in brain volume caused by schizophrenia.

A different type of new generation antipsychotic drug, trade name Abilify, is sometimes referred to as a "third generation" antipsychotic drug because of its neurochemical actions. It achieves its effects by stabilizing the levels of both dopamine and serotonin activity in certain areas of the brain. It blocks receptor sites for these two neurotransmitters when their activity levels are too high and stimulates these receptor sites when their activity levels are too low. Thus, it works in both antagonistic and agonistic ways, depending upon what type of effect is needed. This is why it is also sometimes called a "dopamine-serotonin system stabilizer." Clinical research thus far indicates that it is as effective as other new generation antipsychotic drugs and may have less severe side effects (DeLeon, Patel, & Crismon, 2004; Rivas-Vasquez, 2003). Given its neurochemical properties, Abilify is also used as treatment for bipolar disorder for those who have not responded to lithium and as an add-on to antidepressant therapy for major depressive disorder (Julien, 2011).

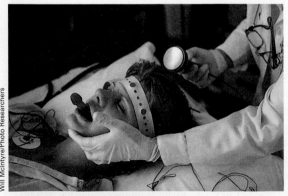

Electroconvulsive Therapy | The patient is given an anesthetic so that she is not conscious during the procedure, as well as muscle relaxants to minimize the convulsions.

Electroconvulsive therapy. Another type of biomedical therapy is **electroconvulsive therapy (ECT),** a last-resort treatment for the most severe cases of depression. ECT involves electrically inducing a brief brain seizure and is informally referred to as "shock therapy." ECT was introduced in 1938 in Italy by Ugo Cerletti as a possible treatment for schizophrenia, but it was later discovered to be effective only for depression (Impastato, 1960). The first use of ECT in the United States was in 1940, a couple of years later (Pulver, 1961). How is ECT administered? Electrodes are placed on one or both sides of the head, and a very brief electrical shock is administered, causing a brain seizure that makes the patient convulse for a few minutes. Patients are given anesthetics so that they are not conscious during the procedure, as well as muscle relaxants to minimize the convulsions.

About 80% of depressed patients improve with ECT (Glass, 2001), and they show improvement somewhat more rapidly with the use of ECT than with antidepressant drugs (Seligman, 1994). This more rapid effect makes ECT a valuable treatment for suicidal, severely depressed patients, especially those who have not responded to any other type of treatment. Strangely, after more than 50 years we still do not know how ECT works in treating depression. One explanation is that, like anti-depressant drugs, the electric shock increases the activity of serotonin and norepinephrine, which improves mood. ECT's effects also fit the speculative neurogenesis theory of depression. Like SSRIs, electroconvulsive shock increases neurogenesis in rats (Scott, Wojtowicz, & Burnham, 2000). This means that ECT may have an impact on neurogenesis and may do so a little more quickly than antidepressant drugs. Current research seems to indicate that ECT does not lead to any type of detectable brain damage or long-term cognitive impairment, but there is a memory-loss side effect for events just prior to and following the therapy (Calev, Guadino, Squires, Zervas, & Fink, 1995). Regardless

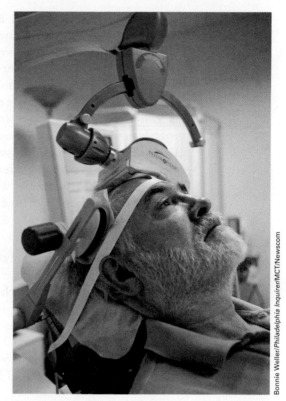

Bonnie Weller/*Philadelphia Inquirer*/MCT/Newscom

This man is undergoing transcranial magnetic stimulation (TMS) therapy for depression. The electromagnetic coil above his left frontal lobe is transmitting magnetic pulses to stimulate neuronal activity in that area of his brain.

of its clear success in treating severe depression, perhaps saving thousands of lives, ECT remains a controversial therapeutic technique because of its perceived barbaric nature. Interestingly, patients who have undergone ECT do not see it in such a negative light, and the vast majority report that they would undergo it again if their depression recurred (Goodman, Krahn, Smith, Rummans, & Pileggi, 1999; Pettinati, Tamburello, Ruetsch, & Kaplan, 1994). Much of the general public's sordid misconception of ECT likely stems from its inaccurate coverage in the entertainment media (Lilienfeld et al., 2010).

Because of the general public's negative image of ECT, alternative neurostimulation therapies for the severely depressed are being developed. One promising alternative is **transcranial magnetic stimulation (TMS).** In contrast with ECT, which transmits electrical impulses, TMS stimulates the brain with magnetic pulses via an electromagnetic coil placed on the patient's scalp above the left frontal lobe.

transcranial magnetic stimulation (TMS) A neurostimulation therapy in which the left frontal lobe is stimulated with magnetic pulses via an electromagnetic coil placed on the patient's scalp. It is only cleared for use in cases of severe depression for which traditional treatment has not helped.

psychosurgery A biomedical treatment in which specific areas of the brain are destroyed.

lobotomy A type of psychosurgery in which the neuronal connections of the frontal lobes to lower brain areas are severed.

This area is stimulated because brain scans of depressed patients show that it is relatively inactive. Typically a patient receives five treatments a week for 4 to 6 weeks. Unlike ECT, the patient is awake during TMS, and TMS does not produce any memory loss or other major side effects. Like ECT, it is not exactly clear how TMS works to alleviate depression, but it seems to do so by energizing neuronal activity in a depressed patient's relatively inactive left frontal lobe. Although some research has shown that it may be as effective as ECT in treating severely depressed patients for whom more traditional treatments have not helped (Grunhaus, Schreiber, Dolberg, Polak, & Dannon, 2003) and its use for this purpose has been approved, more research on this relatively new therapy and its effects is clearly needed.

Psychosurgery. An even more controversial biomedical therapy is **psychosurgery,** the destruction of specific areas in the brain. The most famous type of psychosurgery is the **lobotomy,** in which the neuronal connections of the frontal lobes to lower areas in the brain are severed. Egas Moniz, a Portuguese neurosurgeon who coined the term "psychosurgery," pioneered work on lobotomies for the treatment of schizophrenia (Valenstein, 1986). In fact, he won a Nobel Prize for Medicine in 1949 for his work. However, not everything went well for Moniz. Ten years earlier, he was almost killed by one of his patients—not one he had lobotomized though (Valenstein, 1986). The patient shot him four times, and one of the bullets became lodged in a vertebra and could not be removed because of the risk of damaging his spinal cord. He was wheelchair bound for the rest of his life (Jarrett, 2015). No good scientific rationale for why lobotomies should work, or scientific evidence that they did work, was ever put forth by Moniz or anyone else. Regardless, led by Dr. Walter Freeman, tens of thousands of lobotomies were done in the United States in the 1940s and 1950s (El-Hai, 2005). In 1945, Freeman developed the transorbital lobotomy technique—gaining access to the frontal lobes through the eye socket behind the eyeball via a tear duct with an ice-pick-like instrument (called a leucotome), he

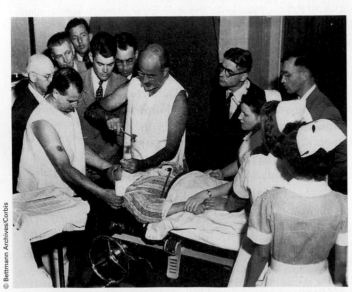

A Transorbital Lobotomy | Neurosurgeon Walter Freeman is performing a transorbital lobotomy in 1949. He is entering the patient's brain through his eye socket. Once he gains access to the brain, he will rotate the ice-pick-like instrument from side to side in order to destroy the targeted brain tissue.

pushed the leucotome about an inch and a half into the patient's frontal lobe and then moved the instrument from side to side, cutting the neural connections between the frontal lobes and the thalamus and other lower brain structures (Valenstein, 1986). Freeman didn't even do the lobotomies in hospital operating rooms. He would travel directly to the mental institutions with his bag and do several in one day. Because it renders the patient unconscious, ECT was often used as the anesthetic. Freeman traveled thousands of miles on psychosurgical road trips to over 20 states and performed nearly 3,500 lobotomies (El-Hai, 2001). Freeman's lobotomies were just part of a wave of psychosurgery that was used on 40,000 to 50,000 Americans until the late 1950s. The arrival of antipsychotic drugs in the 1950s thankfully replaced the lobotomy as the main treatment for schizophrenia. Unfortunately, these primitive procedures had already left thousands of victims in a zombielike, deteriorated state.

Psychosurgery is still around, but it is very different from the earlier primitive lobotomies (Vertosick, 1997). For example, cingulotomies, in which dime-sized holes are surgically lesioned (burnt) in specific areas of the cingulate gyrus in the frontal lobes, are sometimes performed on patients who are severely depressed or have obsessive-compulsive disorder and who have not responded to other types of treatment. The cingulate gyrus is part of the pathway between the frontal lobes and the limbic system structures that govern emotional reactions. These new procedures bear no resemblance to the earlier lobotomies. They are done in operating rooms, using magnetic resonance imaging to guide the surgery and computer-guided electrodes with minute precision to perform the surgery. Because it involves irreversible brain injury, psychosurgery is done very infrequently today. These procedures are used only in cases of serious disorders when all other treatments have failed, and only with the patient's permission.

Psychotherapies

In Chapter 8, one type of psychotherapy, psychoanalysis, developed by Sigmund Freud in the early 1900s, was briefly discussed. When thinking about psychoanalysis, we usually think of a patient lying on a couch with the therapist sitting behind the patient and taking notes about the patient's dreams and free associations. This is actually a fairly accurate description of classical psychoanalysis, but most types of psychotherapy are nothing like this. We'll discuss psychoanalysis first and then the other three major types of psychotherapy—humanistic, behavioral, and cognitive. Sometimes these four types of psychotherapy are divided according to their emphasis on insight or action. Psychoanalysis and humanistic therapies are usually referred to as insight therapies—they focus on the person achieving insight into (conscious awareness and understanding of) the causes of his behavior and thinking. In contrast, behavioral and cognitive therapies are usually referred to as action therapies—they focus on the actions of the person in changing his behavior or ways of thinking.

Psychoanalysis. Psychoanalysis is a style of psychotherapy, originally developed by Sigmund Freud, in which the therapist helps the person gain insight into the unconscious sources of his or her problems. Classical psychoanalysis, as developed by Freud, is very expensive and time consuming. A patient usually needs multiple sessions each week for a year or two to get to the source of her problems. Remember from Chapter 8 that Freud proposed that problems arise from repressed memories, fixations, and unresolved conflicts, mainly from early childhood. Such problems are repressed in the unconscious but continue to influence the person's behavior and thinking. The task for the psychoanalyst is to discover these underlying unconscious problems and then help the patient to gain insight into them. The difficulty with this is that the patient herself is not even privy to these unconscious problems. This means that the therapist has to identify conscious reflections of the underlying problems and interpret them. The major task of the psychoanalyst, then, is to interpret many sources of input—including free associations, resistances, dreams, and transferences—in order to find the unconscious roots of the person's problem.

Free association is a technique in which the patient spontaneously describes, without editing, all thoughts, feelings, or images that come to mind. For psychoanalysts, free association is like a verbal projective test. Psychoanalysts assume that free association does not just produce random thoughts but will provide clues to the unconscious conflicts leading to the patient's problems. This is especially true for resistances during free association. A **resistance** is a patient's unwillingness to discuss particular topics. For example, a patient might be free associating and say the word "mother." A resistance to this topic (his mother) would be indicated by the patient abruptly halting the association process and falling silent. The patient might also miss a therapy appointment to avoid talking about a particular topic (such as his mother) or change the subject to avoid discussion of the topic. The psychoanalyst must detect these resistances and interpret them.

The psychoanalyst also interprets the patient's dreams, which may provide clues to the underlying problem. According to Freud, psychological defenses are lowered during sleep; therefore, the unconscious conflicts are revealed symbolically in one's dreams. This means that dreams have two levels of meaning—the **manifest content,** the literal surface meaning of a dream, and the **latent content,** the underlying true meaning of a dream. It is the latent content that is important. For example, a king and queen in a dream could really represent the person's parents, or having a tooth extracted could represent castration. Another tool available to the therapist is the process of **transference,** which occurs when the patient acts toward the therapist as she did or does toward important figures

psychoanalysis A style of psychotherapy, originally developed by Sigmund Freud, in which the therapist helps the person gain insight into the unconscious sources of his or her problems.

free association A person spontaneously describes, without editing, all thoughts, feelings, or images that come to mind.

resistance A person's unwillingness to discuss a particular topic during therapy.

manifest content Freud's term for the literal surface meaning of a dream.

latent content Freud's term for the underlying true meaning of a dream.

transference When a person undergoing therapy acts toward the therapist as he or she did or does toward important figures in his or her life, such as his or her parents.

in her life, such as her parents. For example, if the patient hated her father when she was a child, she might transfer this hate relationship to the therapist. In this way transference is a reenactment of earlier or current conflicts with important figures in the patient's life. The patient's conflicted feelings toward these important figures are transferred to the therapist, and the therapist must detect and interpret these transferences.

Classical psychoanalysis requires a lot of time, because the therapist has to use these various indirect clues to build an interpretation of the patient's problem. It's similar to a detective trying to solve a case without any solid clues, such as the weapon, fingerprints, or DNA evidence. There's only vague circumstantial evidence. Using this evidence, the therapist builds an interpretation that helps the patient to gain insight into the problem. This classical style of psychoanalysis has been strongly criticized and has little empirical evidence supporting its efficacy. However, contemporary psychoanalytic therapy, usually referred to as psychodynamic therapy, has proved successful (Shedler, 2010). It is very different from Freud's psychoanalysis. The patient sits in a chair instead of lying on a couch, sessions are only once or twice a week, and the therapy may finish in months, instead of years. In addition, patients who receive psychodynamic therapy seem to maintain their therapeutic gains and continue to improve after the therapy ends.

Client-centered therapy. The most influential humanistic therapy is Carl Rogers's client-centered therapy, which is sometimes called person-centered therapy (Raskin & Rogers, 1995; Rogers, 1951). **Client-centered therapy** is a style of psychotherapy in which the therapist uses unconditional positive regard, genuineness, and empathy to help the person to gain insight into his true self-concept. Rogers and other humanists preferred to use the words "client" or "person" rather than "patient"; they thought that "patient" implied sickness, while "client" and "person" emphasized the importance of the clients' subjective views of themselves. Remember from Chapter 8 that Rogers assumed that conditions of worth set up by other people in the client's life have led the troubled person to develop a distorted self-concept, and that a person's perception of his self is critical to personality development and self-actualization (the fullest realization of one's potential). The therapeutic goal of client-centered therapy is to get the person on the road to self-actualization. To achieve this goal, the therapist is nondirective; she doesn't attempt to steer the dialogue in a certain direction. Instead, the client decides the direction of each session. The therapist's main task is to create the conditions that allow the client to gain insight into his true feelings and self-concept.

These conditions are exactly the same as those for healthy personality growth that were discussed in Chapter 8. The therapist should be accepting, genuine, and empathic. The therapist establishes an environment of acceptance by giving the client unconditional positive regard (accepting

> **client-centered therapy** A style of psychotherapy, developed by Carl Rogers, in which the therapist uses unconditional positive regard, genuineness, and empathy to help the person to gain insight into his or her true self-concept.

the client without any conditions upon his behavior). The therapist demonstrates genuineness by honestly sharing her own thoughts and feelings with the client. To achieve empathic understanding of the client's feelings, the therapist uses active listening to gain a sense of the client's feelings, and then uses mirroring to echo these feelings back to the client, so that the client can then get a clearer image of his true feelings. It is this realization of his true feelings that allows the client to get back on the road to personal growth and self-actualization. By creating a supportive environment, this style of therapy is very successful with people who are not suffering from a clinical disorder but who are motivated toward greater personal awareness and growth.

Behavioral therapy. Behavioral therapy is a style of psychotherapy in which the therapist uses the principles of classical and operant conditioning to change the person's behavior from maladaptive to adaptive. The assumption is that the behavioral symptoms (such as the irrational behavior of the woman with the specific phobia of birds) are the problem. Maladaptive behaviors have been learned, so they have to be unlearned, and more adaptive behaviors need to be learned instead. Behavioral therapies are based on either classical or operant conditioning. We'll first describe an example of one based on classical conditioning.

Remember the Little Albert classical conditioning study by Watson and Rayner that we mentioned earlier in this chapter when we were discussing phobic disorders. As we pointed out in Chapter 4, Albert's fear of white rats was never deconditioned, but one of Watson's former students, Mary Cover Jones, later showed that such a fear could be unlearned and replaced with a more adaptive relaxation response (Jones, 1924). Jones eliminated the fear of rabbits in a 3-year-old boy named Peter by gradually introducing a rabbit while Peter was eating. Peter's pleasure response while eating was incompatible with a fear response. Over time, Peter learned to be relaxed in the presence of a rabbit. Some consider this to be the first case of behavioral therapy. Jones's work led to the development of a set of classical conditioning therapies called counterconditioning techniques. In **counterconditioning,** a maladaptive response is replaced by an incompatible adaptive response. Counterconditioning therapies, such as systematic desensitization, virtual reality therapy, and flooding, have been especially successful in the treatment of anxiety disorders. These three counterconditioning therapies are referred to as exposure therapies because the patient is exposed at some point to the source of his anxiety.

Using Jones's idea that fear and relaxation are incompatible responses, Joseph Wolpe developed a behavioral therapy called systematic desensitization that is very effective in treating phobias (Wolpe, 1958). **Systematic desensitization** is a

behavioral therapy A style of psychotherapy in which the therapist uses the principles of classical and operant conditioning to change the person's behavior from maladaptive to adaptive.

counterconditioning A type of behavioral therapy in which a maladaptive response is replaced by an incompatible adaptive response.

systematic desensitization A counterconditioning exposure therapy in which a fear response to an object or situation is replaced with a relaxation response in a series of progressively increasing fear-arousing steps.

counterconditioning procedure in which a fear response to an object or situation is replaced with a relaxation response in a series of progressively increasing fear-arousing steps. The patient first develops a hierarchy of situations that evoke a fear response, from those that evoke slight fear on up to those that evoke tremendous fear. For example, a person who had a specific phobia of spiders might find that planning a picnic evoked slight fear because of the possibility that a spider might be encountered on the picnic. Seeing a picture of a spider would evoke more fear, seeing a spider on a wall 20 feet away even more. Having actual spiders crawl on her would be near the top of the hierarchy. These are just a few situations that span a possible hierarchy. Hierarchies have far more steps over which the fear increases gradually.

Once the hierarchy is set, the patient is then taught how to use various techniques to relax. Once this relaxation training is over, the therapy begins. The patient starts working through the hierarchy and attempts to relax at each step. First the patient relaxes in imagined situations in the hierarchy and later in the actual situations. With both imagined and actual situations, the anxiety level of the situation is increased slowly. At some of the later stages in the hierarchy, a model of the same sex and roughly same age may be brought in to demonstrate the behavior before the patient attempts it. For example, the model will touch the picture of a bird in a book before the patient is asked to do so. In brief, systematic desensitization teaches the patient to confront progressively increasing fear-provoking situations with the relaxation response.

Virtual reality therapy is similar to systematic desensitization, but the patient is exposed to computer simulations of his fears in a progressively anxiety-provoking manner. Wearing a motion-sensitive display helmet that projects a three-dimensional virtual world, the patient experiences seemingly real computer-generated images rather than imagined and actual situations as in systematic desensitization. When the patient achieves relaxation, the simulated scene becomes more fearful until the patient can relax in the simulated presence of the feared object or situation. Virtual reality therapy has been used successfully to treat specific phobias, social anxiety disorder, and some other anxiety disorders (Krijn, Emmelkamp, Olafsson, & Biemond, 2004).

Another counterconditioning exposure therapy, flooding, does not involve such gradual confrontation. In **flooding,** the patient is immediately exposed to the feared object or situation. For example, in the case of the spider phobia, the person would immediately have to confront live spiders. Flooding is often used instead of systematic desensitization when the fear is so strong that the person is unable to make much progress in systematic desensitization.

Behavioral therapies using operant conditioning principles reinforce desired behaviors and extinguish undesired behaviors. A good example is the token economy that we

virtual reality therapy A counterconditioning exposure therapy in which the patient is exposed in graduated steps to computer simulations of a feared object or situation.

flooding A counterconditioning exposure therapy in which the patient is immediately exposed to a feared object or situation.

cognitive therapy A style of psycho-therapy in which the therapist attempts to change the person's thinking from maladaptive to adaptive.

rational-emotive therapy A type of cognitive therapy, developed by Albert Ellis, in which the therapist directly confronts and challenges the person's unrealistic thoughts and beliefs to show that they are irrational.

discussed in Chapter 4. A token economy is an environment in which desired behaviors are reinforced with tokens (secondary reinforcers such as gold stars or stickers) that can be exchanged for rewards such as candy and television privileges. This technique is often used with groups of institutionalized people, such as those in mental health facilities. As such, it has been fairly successful in managing populations of people with autism spectrum disorder, intellectual disabilities, and schizophrenia. For example, if making one's bed is the desired behavior, it will be reinforced with tokens that can be exchanged for treats or privileges. A token economy is more of a way to manage the daily behavior of such people than a way to cure them, but we must remember that a behavioral therapist thinks that the maladaptive behavior is the problem.

Cognitive therapy. Behavioral therapies work to change the person's behavior; cognitive therapies work on the person's thinking. **Cognitive therapy** is a style of psychotherapy in which the therapist changes the person's thinking from maladaptive to adaptive. The assumption is that the person's thought processes and beliefs are maladaptive and need to change. The cognitive therapist identifies the irrational thoughts and unrealistic beliefs that need to change and then helps the person to execute that change. Two prominent cognitive therapies are Albert Ellis's rational-emotive therapy (Ellis, 1962, 1993, 1995) and Aaron Beck's cognitive therapy (Beck, 1976; Beck, 1995).

In Ellis's **rational-emotive therapy,** the therapist directly confronts and challenges the patient's unrealistic thoughts and beliefs to show that they are irrational. These irrational, unrealistic beliefs usually involve words such as "must," "always," and "every." Let's consider a simple example. A person might have the unrealistic belief that he must be perfect in everything he does. This is an unrealistic belief. He is doomed to failure, because no one can be perfect at everything they do. Instead of realizing that his belief is irrational, he will blame himself for the failure and become depressed. A rational-emotive therapist will show him the irrationality of his thinking and lead him to change his thinking to be more realistic. This is achieved by Ellis's ABC model. A refers to the Activating event (failure to be perfect at everything); B is the person's Belief about the event ("It's my fault; I'm a failure"); and C is the resulting emotional Consequence (depression). According to Ellis, A does not cause C; B causes C. Through rational-emotive therapy, the person comes to realize that he controls the emotional consequences because he controls the interpretation of the event.

Rational-emotive therapists are usually very direct and confrontational in getting their clients to see the errors of their thinking. Ellis has said that he does not think that a warm relationship between

© Bettmann/Corbis

Albert Ellis

therapist and client is essential to effective therapy. Aaron Beck's form of cognitive therapy has the same therapeutic goal as Ellis's rational-emotive therapy, but the therapeutic style is not as confrontational. A therapist using **Beck's cognitive therapy** works to develop a warm relationship with the person and has a person carefully consider the objective evidence for his beliefs in order to see the errors in his thinking. For example, to help a student who is depressed because he thinks he has blown his chances to get into medical school by not having a perfect grade point average, the therapist would have the student examine the statistics on how few students actually graduate with a perfect average and the grade point averages of students actually accepted to medical school. The therapist is like a good teacher, helping the person to discover the problems with his thinking. Regardless of the style differences, both types of cognitive therapy have been especially effective at treating major depressive disorders.

Courtesy of Aaron T. Beck, University of Pennsylvania Medical Center

Aaron T. Beck

Is psychotherapy effective? Now that you understand the four major approaches to psychotherapy, let's consider the question of whether it is effective or not. To assess the effectiveness of psychotherapy we must consider spontaneous remission, the tincture of time. **Spontaneous remission** is when a person gets better with the passage of time without receiving any therapy. Thus, spontaneous remission accounts for all of the factors that might lead to improvement other than receiving therapy. One such factor, for example, is regression toward the mean, which we discussed in Chapter 1. Extreme (disordered) behavior and thinking should be followed by more normal behavior and thinking. Another factor would be the beneficial effect of the support of family and friends, a type of informal therapy. And so on. In order to be considered effective then, improvement from psychotherapy must be significantly (statistically) greater than that due to spontaneous remission. To answer the question, researchers have used meta-analysis, a statistical technique discussed in Chapter 1 in which the results from many separate experimental studies on the same question are combined into one analysis to determine whether there is an overall effect. The results of a meta-analysis that included the results of 475 studies involving many different types of psychotherapy and thousands of participants revealed that psychotherapy is effective (Figure 10.1 on page 470). The average psychotherapy client is better off than about 80% of people not receiving any therapy (Smith, Glass, & Miller, 1980). A more recent meta-analysis of psychotherapy

Beck's cognitive therapy A type of cognitive therapy, developed by Aaron Beck, in which the therapist works to develop a warm relationship with the person and has the person carefully consider the evidence for his or her beliefs in order to see the errors in his or her thinking.

spontaneous remission Getting better with the passage of time without receiving any therapy.

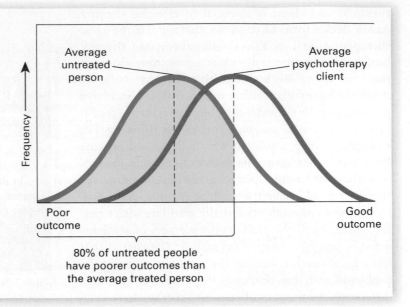

**Figure 10.1 |
Psychotherapy Versus
No Treatment** | These
two normal distributions
summarize the data of a
meta-analysis of 475 studies
on the effectiveness of psychotherapy. They show that
psychotherapy is effective—
the average psychotherapy
client was better off than 80%
of the people not receiving
therapy. (Data from Smith, M. L., Glass,
G. V., & Miller, T. I. (1980). *The benefits of
psychotherapy*. Baltimore, MD: Johns Hopkins
University Press.

effectiveness studies also confirms that psychotherapy helps (Shadish, Matt,
Navarro, & Phillips, 2000).

No one particular type of psychotherapy is superior to all of the others. Some
types of psychotherapy do, however, seem to be more effective in treating particular disorders. For example, behavioral therapies have been very successful in
treating phobias and other anxiety disorders. Also, cognitive therapies tend to
be very effective in treating depressive disorders. None of the psychotherapies,
however, have been very successful in treating schizophrenia, but, as mentioned
earlier in the chapter, some recent findings indicate that combining hybrid
cognitive–behavioral psychotherapy with drug therapy as early treatment for
people experiencing their first episode of schizophrenia is more effective than
drug therapy alone.

INSIDE WOODY ALLEN

Section Summary

There are two major categories of therapy: biomedical and psychological. Biomedical therapy involves the use of biological interventions, such as drugs, to treat disorders. Psychotherapy involves the use of psychological interventions to treat disorders. Psychotherapy is what we normally think of as therapy. In psychotherapy, there is an interaction between the person and the therapist. In biomedical therapy, the interaction is biological. There are three major types of biomedical therapy—drug therapy, shock therapy, and psychosurgery. There are four major types of psychotherapy—psychoanalytic, humanistic, behavioral, and cognitive.

The major medications are lithium, antidepressant drugs, antianxiety drugs, and antipsychotic drugs. Lithium, a naturally occurring mineral salt, is the main treatment for bipolar disorder. There are four types of antidepressants—MAO inhibitors, tricyclics, SSRIs, and SSNRIs. SSRIs, which work by selectively blocking the reuptake of serotonin, are prescribed most often. Antianxiety drugs are in a class of drugs called benzodiazepines; they reduce anxiety by stimulating GABA activity that inhibits the anxiety.

There are two types of antipsychotic drugs—traditional (those developed from the 1950s through the 1980s) and new generation (developed since the 1990s). The traditional antipsychotic drugs block receptor sites for dopamine, which globally lowers dopamine activity. Because of this, these traditional drugs produce side effects in motor movement that are similar to the movement problems of Parkinson's disease. In addition, there is a long-term-use side effect of traditional antipsychotic drugs, tardive dyskinesia, in which the person has uncontrollable facial movements. The new generation drugs do not have these side effects, but they do have to be monitored very carefully because of other dangerous side effects. Such monitoring is expensive; therefore, traditional antipsychotic drugs are often prescribed instead.

Electroconvulsive therapy (ECT) that involves electrically inducing a brief brain seizure is used almost exclusively to treat severe depression. We do not know how or why this therapy works, but it is a valuable treatment for severely depressed people who have not responded to other types of treatment because it leads to somewhat faster improvement than antidepressant drugs. Given its nature, however, ECT remains shrouded in controversy. An alternative neurostimulation therapy for the severely depressed, transcranial magnetic stimulation (TMS), is not as controversial as ECT and does not produce any major side effects, but more research on its effectiveness is needed.

Even more controversial is psychosurgery, in which specific areas in the brain are actually destroyed. The most famous type of psychosurgery is the lobotomy, in which the neuronal connections of the frontal lobes to lower areas in the brain are severed. No good evidence for why such operations should work or that they did was ever put forth. The arrival of antipsychotic drugs in the 1950s replaced the lobotomy as the main treatment for schizophrenia. Psychosurgery is still around, but it is very different from what it once was and is used very infrequently, only when all other treatments have failed.

Psychotherapies can be categorized into two types—insight or action. Psychoanalytic and humanistic therapies are insight therapies; they focus on the person achieving insight into the causes of her behavior and thinking. Behavioral and cognitive therapies are action therapies; they focus on the actions of the person in changing her behavior and ways of thinking. The main goal of psychoanalysis, as developed by Freud, is for the therapist to uncover the unconscious sources of the person's problems by interpreting the person's free associations, dreams, resistances, and transferences. The therapist then helps the person to gain insight into the unconscious sources of her problem with this interpretation. Such classical psychoanalysis takes a long time; therefore, contemporary psychoanalytic therapists take a more direct and interactive role, emphasizing the present more than the past in order to shorten the period of therapy.

The most influential humanistic therapy is Rogers's client-centered therapy in which the therapist uses unconditional positive regard, genuineness, and empathy to help the person to gain insight into her true self-concept and get on the path to self-actualization. The therapy is client-centered, and the client decides the direction of each session. The therapist's main task is to create the conditions that allow the client to discover her true feelings and self-concept.

In behavioral therapies, the therapist uses the principles of classical and operant conditioning to change the person's behavior from maladaptive to adaptive. The assumption is that the behavioral symptoms are the problem. These behaviors were learned; therefore, they need to be unlearned and more adaptive behaviors learned. Counterconditioning exposure therapies, such as systematic desensitization, virtual reality therapy, and flooding, have been especially effective in treating anxiety disorders such as phobias. Instead of changing the person's behavior, the cognitive therapist attempts to change the person's thinking from maladaptive to adaptive. Two major kinds of cognitive therapy are Ellis's rational-emotive therapy and Beck's cognitive therapy. Both have the same therapeutic goal—changing the person's thinking to be more rational—but the therapeutic styles are very different. Rational-emotive therapy is far more confrontational and direct in its approach. Regardless, both have been very successful in treating major depressive disorders.

Using meta-analysis, a statistical technique that pools the results from many separate experimental studies on the same question into one analysis to determine whether there is an overall effect, researchers have concluded that psychotherapy is more effective than no therapy. There is no one particular type of psychotherapy that is best for all disorders, however. Rather, some types of psychotherapy seem more effective in treating particular disorders. For example, behavioral therapies tend to be effective in treating anxiety disorders, and cognitive therapies are more effective in treating depression.

ConceptCheck | 3

Explain the difference between biomedical therapy and psychotherapy.

Explain how the neurogenesis theory of depression could be considered a biopsychosocial explanation.

Explain why the psychoanalyst can be thought of as a detective.

Explain the difference between behavioral therapy and cognitive therapy.

Explain why a control for spontaneous remission must be included in any assessment of the effectiveness of psychotherapy.

Study Guide

Chapter Key Terms

You should know the definitions of the following key terms from the chapter. They are listed in the order in which they appear in the chapter. For those you do not know, return to the relevant section of the chapter to learn them. When you think that you know all of the terms, complete the matching exercise based on these key terms.

abnormal psychology
Diagnostic and Statistical Manual of Mental Disorders, Fifth Edition (DSM-5)
biopsychosocial approach
anxiety disorders
specific phobia
social anxiety disorder
agoraphobia
panic disorder
generalized anxiety disorder
obsessive-compulsive disorder
obsession
compulsion
depressive disorders
major depressive disorder
major depressive episode
manic episode
bipolar disorder

psychotic disorder
hallucination
delusion
schizophrenia
vulnerability–stress model
personality disorder
biomedical therapy
psychotherapy
lithium
antidepressant drugs
neurogenesis theory of depression
antianxiety drugs
antipsychotic drugs
tardive dyskinesia
electroconvulsive therapy (ECT)
transcranial magnetic stimulation (TMS)

psychosurgery
lobotomy
psychoanalysis
free association
resistance
manifest content
latent content
transference
client-centered therapy
behavioral therapy
counterconditioning
systematic desensitization
virtual reality therapy
flooding
cognitive therapy
rational-emotive therapy
Beck's cognitive therapy
spontaneous remission

Key Terms Exercise

Identify the correct term for each of the following definitions. The answers to this exercise follow the answers to the ConceptChecks at the end of the chapter.

1. A repetitive and rigid behavior that a person feels compelled to perform in order to reduce anxiety.

2. An anxiety disorder indicated by a marked and persistent fear of being in places or situations from which escape might be difficult or embarrassing.

3. An explanation of schizophrenia that proposes that genetic, prenatal, and postnatal biological factors render a person vulnerable to schizophrenia, but environmental stress determines whether it develops or not.

4. A style of psychotherapy, developed by Carl Rogers, in which the therapist uses

473

unconditional positive regard, genuineness, and empathy to help the person to gain insight into his true self-concept.

_____

5. A counterconditioning exposure therapy in which a fear response to an object or situation is replaced with a relaxation response in a series of progressively increasing fear-arousing steps.

_____

6. Getting better with the passage of time without receiving any therapy.

_____

7. A type of cognitive therapy, developed by Albert Ellis, in which the therapist directly confronts and challenges the person's unrealistic thoughts and beliefs to show that they are irrational.

_____

8. A disorder characterized by inflexible, long-standing personality traits that lead to behavior that impairs social functioning and deviates from cultural norms.

_____

9. A false sensory perception.

_____

10. A disorder in which recurrent cycles of depressive and manic episodes occur.

_____

11. The current version of the American Psychiatric Association's diagnostic and classification guidelines for mental disorders.

_____

12. Explaining abnormality as the result of the interaction among biological, psychological (behavioral and cognitive), and social or cultural factors.

_____

13. An explanation of depression that proposes that the growth of new neurons in the hippocampus stops during depression, and when it resumes, the depression lifts.

_____

14. A person undergoing therapy acts toward the therapist as he or she did or does toward important figures in his or her life, such as parents.

_____

15. A side effect of long-term use of traditional antipsychotic drugs causing the person to have uncontrollable facial tics, grimaces, and other involuntary movements of the lips, jaw, and tongue.

_____

Practice Test Questions

The following are practice multiple-choice test questions on some of the chapter content. The answers are given after the Key Terms Exercise answers at the end of the chapter. If you guessed on a question or incorrectly answered a question, restudy the relevant section of the chapter.

1. Which of the following is a personality disorder?
   a. schizophrenia
   b. antisocial personality
   c. bipolar disorder
   d. generalized anxiety disorder

2. _____ is the fear of being in places or situations from which escape may be difficult or embarrassing.
   a. A specific phobia
   b. Agoraphobia
   c. Social anxiety disorder
   d. Panic disorder

3. Which of the following disorders has the highest concordance rate for identical twins?
   a. bipolar disorder
   b. schizophrenia
   c. major depressive disorder
   d. The concordance rates for all of the above are the same.

4. Which of the following disorders is a (are) psychotic disorder(s)?
   a. obsessive-compulsive disorder
   b. major depressive disorder
   c. schizophrenia
   d. all of the above

5. A false sensory perception is a(n) _____, and a false belief is a(n) _____.
   a. obsession; compulsion
   b. compulsion; obsession
   c. hallucination; delusion
   d. delusion; hallucination

6. Which of the following is (are) most often used to treat bipolar disorder?
   a. SSRIs
   b. lithium
   c. new generation antipsychotic drugs
   d. MAO inhibitors

7. Tardive dyskinesia is a side effect of long-term use of _____.
   a. SSRIs
   b. traditional antipsychotic drugs
   c. lithium
   d. tricyclics

8. A _____ therapist interprets resistances and transferences to discover a person's underlying problems.
   a. psychoanalytic
   b. client-centered
   c. behavioral
   d. cognitive

9. Maladaptive behavior is to maladaptive thinking as _____ is to _____.
   a. psychoanalysis; client-centered therapy
   b. client-centered therapy; psychoanalysis
   c. behavioral therapy; cognitive therapy
   d. cognitive therapy; behavioral therapy

10. Which of the following psychotherapies is most effective in treating phobic disorders?
    a. psychoanalysis
    b. cognitive therapy
    c. behavioral therapy
    d. client-centered therapy

11. _____ is a disorder in which the person has excessive global anxiety and worry that they cannot control for a period of at least 6 months.
    a. Agoraphobia
    b. Social phobia

c. Generalized anxiety disorder
    d. Panic disorder

12. Which of the following is a part of rational-emotive therapy?
    a. ABC model
    b. token economy
    c. free association
    d. flooding

13. Unconditional positive regard and empathy are to resistance and transference as _____ is to _____.
    a. rational-emotive therapy; Beck's cognitive therapy
    b. Beck's cognitive therapy; rational-emotive therapy
    c. psychoanalysis; client-centered therapy
    d. client-centered therapy; psychoanalysis

14. Which of the following is the best example of a biopsychosocial explanation of a mental disorder?
    a. the ABC model
    b. the vulnerability–stress model
    c. counterconditioning
    d. meta-analysis

15. Which of the following disorders is classified as an obsessive-compulsive related disorder?
    a. panic disorder
    b. trichotillomania
    c. agoraphobia
    d. social anxiety disorder

Chapter ConceptCheck Answers

ConceptCheck | 1

- The DSM-5 is the *Diagnostic and Statistical Manual of Mental Disorders,* Fifth Edition, published by the American Psychiatric Association. It is the most widely used diagnostic system for classifying mental disorders. Basing its classification upon behavioral and psychological symptoms, it provides reliable diagnostic guidelines for approximately 400 disorders, grouped into major categories that share particular symptoms.

- Diagnostic labels for mental disorders are necessary in order to identify the source of a person's problem and know how to treat it and for health professionals to both communicate with one another about and to conduct research on mental disorders. Such research helps to find the most successful treatments for each of the disorders. Without labels, such identification, communication, research, and treatment would not be possible.

ConceptCheck | 2

- A biopsychosocial explanation of a disorder entails explaining the problem as the result of the interaction of biological, psychological (behavioral and cognitive), and sociocultural factors. A good example is the explanation of specific phobia disorders in terms of a behavioral factor (classical conditioning) along with a biological predisposition to learn certain fears more easily. Thus, a psychological factor is involved in the learning of the fear but a biological factor determines which fears are easier to learn. Another good example is the vulnerability–stress model explanation of schizophrenia in which one's level of vulnerability to schizophrenia is determined by biological factors, but how much stress one experiences and how one copes psychologically with the stress determines whether or not one suffers from the disorder.

- The anxiety and fear in a specific phobia disorder are exactly as the label indicates. They are specific to a certain class of objects or situations. However, the anxiety and fear in generalized anxiety disorder are not specific, but rather global. The person has excessive anxiety and worries most of the time, and the anxiety is not tied to anything in particular.

- The concordance rates for identical twins for major depressive disorder and schizophrenia are only about 1 in 2 (50%). If only biological genetic factors were responsible for these disorders, these concordance rates would be 100%. Thus, psychological and sociocultural factors must play a role in causing these disorders.

- Schizophrenia is a psychotic disorder. This means the person loses contact with reality. Thus, the split is between the person's mental functions (perception, beliefs, and speech) and reality. In "split personality," which used to be called

multiple personality disorder and is now called dissociative identity disorder in the DSM-5, one's personality is split into two or more distinct personalities.

ConceptCheck | 3

- In biomedical therapy, there is a direct biological intervention, via drugs or ECT, which has an impact on the biochemistry of the nervous system, or psychosurgery, in which part of the brain is actually destroyed. There is no direct impact on the client's biology in psychotherapy. Psychological interventions (talk therapies) are used to treat disorders. However, successful psychotherapy may indirectly lead to biological changes in the client's neurochemistry through more positive thinking.

- The neurogenesis theory of depression can be considered a biopsychosocial explanation, because both biological and psychological factors can have an impact on the neurogenesis process that is assumed to eliminate the depression. Antidepressant drugs with their antagonistic effects on serotonin and norepinephrine are good examples of possible biological factors, and the positive thinking produced by cognitive psychotherapy is a good example of a psychological factor.

- A psychoanalyst can be thought of as a detective, because she has to interpret many clues to the client's problem. Discovering the client's problem is like solving a case. The sources of the psychoanalyst's clues are free association data, resistances, dream analysis, and transferences. The therapist uses these clues to interpret the person's problem (solve the case) and then uses this interpretation to help the person gain insight into the source of his problem.

- Both of these types of psychotherapies are very direct in their approach. However, behavioral therapies assume that the client's behavior is maladaptive and needs to be replaced with more adaptive behavior. Cognitive therapies instead hold that the client's thinking is maladaptive and needs to be replaced with more adaptive thinking. In brief, the behavioral therapist works to change the client's behavior, and the cognitive therapist works to change the client's thinking.

• Spontaneous remission is when a person gets better with the passage of time without receiving any therapy. Thus, if it were not considered when the effectiveness of psychotherapy is being evaluated, the researcher might incorrectly assume that the improvement was due to the psychotherapy and not to spontaneous remission. This is why the improvement in wellness for the psychotherapy group must be significantly (statistically) greater than the improvement for the spontaneous remission control group. If it is, then the psychotherapy has produced improvement that cannot be due to just spontaneous remission.

Answers to Key Terms Exercise

1. compulsion
2. agoraphobia
3. vulnerability–stress model
4. client-centered therapy
5. systematic desensitization
6. spontaneous remission
7. rational-emotive therapy
8. personality disorder
9. hallucination
10. bipolar disorder
11. *Diagnostic and Statistical Manual of Mental Disorders,* Fifth Edition (DSM-5)
12. biopsychosocial approach
13. neurogenesis theory of depression
14. transference
15. tardive dyskinesia

Answers to Practice Test Questions

1. b; antisocial personality
2. b; Agoraphobia
3. a; bipolar disorder
4. c; schizophrenia
5. c; hallucination; delusion
6. b; lithium
7. b; traditional antipsychotic drugs
8. a; psychoanalytic
9. c; behavioral therapy; cognitive therapy
10. c; behavioral therapy
11. c; Generalized anxiety disorder
12. a; ABC model
13. d; client-centered therapy; psychoanalysis
14. b; the vulnerability–stress model
15. b; trichotillomania

Glossary

abnormal psychology The scientific study of mental disorders and their treatment.

absolute threshold The minimum amount of energy in a sensory stimulus detected 50% of the time.

accommodation (1) In vision, the focusing of light waves from objects of different distances directly on the retina. (2) In Piagetian theory, Piaget's term for the modification of present schemas to fit with new experiences.

acetylcholine (ACh) A neurotransmitter involved in learning, memory, and muscle movement.

acquisition (1) In classical conditioning, acquiring a new response (the conditioned response) to the conditioned stimulus. (2) In operant conditioning, the strengthening of a reinforced operant response.

actor-observer bias The tendency to overestimate situational influences on our own behavior, but to overestimate dispositional influences on the behavior of others.

additive mixtures Direct mixtures of different wavelengths of light in which all of the wavelengths reach the retina and are added together.

agonist A drug or poison that increases the activity of one or more neurotransmitters.

agoraphobia An anxiety disorder indicated by a marked and persistent fear of being in places or situations from which escape may be difficult or embarrassing.

algorithm A step-by-step problem-solving procedure that guarantees a correct answer to a problem.

amnesic A person with severe memory deficits following brain surgery or injury.

amplitude The amount of energy in a wave, its intensity, which is the height of the wave at its crest.

amygdala A part of the brain that is involved in emotions by influencing aggression, anger, and fear and by providing the emotional element of our memories and the interpretation of emotional expressions in others.

anal stage of psychosexual development The second stage in Freud's theory (from 18 months to 3 years), in which the erogenous zone is the anus, and the child derives pleasure from stimulation of the anal region through having and withholding bowel movements.

anchoring and adjustment heuristic A heuristic for estimation problems in which one uses his or her initial estimate as an anchor estimate and then adjusts the anchor up or down (often insufficiently).

antagonist A drug or poison that decreases the activity of one or more neurotransmitters.

anterograde amnesia The inability to form new explicit long-term memories for events following surgery or trauma to the brain. Explicit memories formed before the surgery or trauma are left intact.

antianxiety drugs Drugs used to treat anxiety problems and disorders.

antidepressant drugs Drugs used to treat depressive disorders.

antipsychotic drugs Drugs used to treat psychotic disorders.

anxiety disorders Disorders that share features of excessive fear and anxiety and related behavioral disturbances, such as avoidance behaviors.

appetitive stimulus A stimulus that is pleasant.

arousal theory A theory of motivation that proposes that our behavior is motivated to maintain an optimal level of physiological arousal.

assimilation Piaget's term for the interpretation of new experiences in terms of present schemas.

association cortex All of the cerebral cortex except those areas devoted to primary sensory processing or motor processing. This is where all the higher-level cognitive processing that requires the association (integration) of information, such as perception and language, occurs.

attachment The lifelong emotional bond between infants and their mothers or other caregivers, formed during the first 6 months of life.

attitudes Evaluative reactions (positive or negative) toward objects, events, and other people.

attribution The process by which we explain our own behavior and that of others.

authoritarian parenting A style of parenting in which the parents are demanding, expect unquestioned obedience, are not responsive to their children's desires, and communicate poorly with their children.

authoritative parenting A style of parenting in which the parents are demanding, but set rational limits for their children and communicate well with their children.

automatic processing Memory processing that occurs subconsciously and does not require attention.

autonomic nervous system The part of the peripheral nervous system that regulates the functioning of our internal environment (glands and organs like the heart, lungs, and stomach).

availability heuristic A heuristic for judging the probability of an event by how available examples of the event are in memory (the more available, the more probable).

aversive stimulus A stimulus that is unpleasant.

axon The long, singular fiber projecting out of the cell body of a neuron, whose function is to conduct the neural impulse from the cell body to the axon terminals, triggering chemical communication with other neurons.

babbling The rhythmic repetition of various syllables including both consonants and vowels.

baby talk (parentese) The different format of speech that adults use when talking with babies that involves the use of shorter sentences with a higher, more melodious pitch.

basal ganglia A part of the brain that is involved in the initiation and execution of movements.

Beck's cognitive therapy A type of cognitive therapy, developed by Aaron Beck, in which the therapist works to develop a warm relationship with the person and has the person carefully consider the evidence for his or her beliefs in order to see the errors in his or her thinking.

behavior modification The application of classical and operant conditioning principles to eliminate undesirable behavior and to teach more desirable behavior.

behavioral perspective A research perspective whose major explanatory focus is how external environmental events condition observable behavior.

behavioral therapy A style of psychotherapy in which the therapist uses the principles of classical and operant conditioning to change the person's behavior from maladaptive to adaptive.

belief perseverance The tendency to cling to one's beliefs in the face of contradictory evidence.

biological perspective A research perspective whose major explanatory focus is how the brain, nervous system, and other physiological mechanisms produce behavior and mental processes.

biomedical therapy The use of biological interventions, such as drugs, to treat mental disorders.

biopsychosocial approach Explaining abnormality as the result of the interaction among biological, psychological (behavioral and cognitive), and sociocultural factors.

bipolar disorder A disorder in which recurrent cycles of depressive and manic episodes occur.

blindsight A condition in which a blind person has some spared visual capacities in the absence of any visual awareness.

blood–brain barrier A protective mechanism by which the blood capillaries supplying the brain create a barrier that prevents dangerous substances access to the brain.

bottom-up processing The processing of incoming sensory information as it travels up from the sensory structures to the brain.

Broca's area An area in the cerebral cortex responsible for fluent speech production. It is in the left frontal lobe of the majority of people, regardless of handedness.

bystander effect The probability of a person's helping in an emergency is greater when there are no other bystanders than when there are other bystanders.

Cannon-Bard theory A theory of emotion proposing that an emotion is determined from simultaneously occurring physiological arousal, behavioral responses, and cognitive appraisal.

case study A descriptive research method in which the researcher studies an individual in depth over an extended period of time.

cell body The part of the neuron that contains its nucleus and the other biological machinery to keep the cell alive and that decides whether to generate a neural impulse in order to pass incoming information on to other neurons.

central nervous system (CNS) The brain and spinal cord.

centration The tendency to focus on only one aspect of a problem at a time.

cerebellum A part of the brain involved in the coordination of our movements, sense of balance, and motor learning.

cerebral cortex The layers of interconnected cells covering the brain's two hemispheres. This is the control and information-processing center for the nervous system and where perception, memory, language, decision making, and all other higher-level cognitive processing occur.

chromosomes Molecules of DNA that hold the genetic instructions for every cell in the body.

chunk A meaningful unit in a person's memory.

classical conditioning Acquiring a new response (the conditioned response) to a previously neutral stimulus (the conditioned stimulus) that reliably signals the arrival of an unconditioned stimulus.

client-centered therapy A style of psychotherapy, developed by Carl Rogers, in which the therapist uses unconditional positive regard, genuineness, and empathy to help the person to gain insight into his or her true self-concept.

closure The Gestalt perceptual organizational principle that the brain completes (closes) incomplete figures to form meaningful objects.

cochlea A snail-shaped structure in the inner ear that contains the receptor cells for hearing.

cognitive dissonance theory A theory, developed by Leon Festinger, that assumes people have a tendency to change their attitudes to reduce the cognitive discomfort created by inconsistencies between their attitudes and their behavior.

cognitive perspective A research perspective whose major explanatory focus is how mental processes, such as perception, memory, and problem solving, work and impact behavior.

cognitive therapy A style of psychotherapy in which the therapist attempts to change the person's thinking from maladaptive to adaptive.

cohort effects People of a given age (cohorts) are affected by factors unique to their generation, leading to differences in performance between generations.

complementary colors Wavelengths of light that when added together produce white.

compliance Acting in accordance with a direct request from another person or group.

compulsion A repetitive and rigid behavior that a person feels compelled to perform in order to reduce anxiety.

concrete operational stage The third stage in Piaget's theory of cognitive development, from age 6 to 12, during which children gain a fuller understanding of conservation and other mental operations that allow them to think logically, but only about concrete events.

conditioned response (CR) The response that is elicited by the conditioned stimulus in classical conditioning.

conditioned stimulus (CS) The stimulus that comes to elicit a new response (the conditioned response) in classical conditioning.

conditions of worth The behaviors and attitudes for which other people, starting with our parents, will give us positive regard.

conduction deafness Hearing loss created by damage to one of the structures in the ear responsible for mechanically conducting the auditory information to the inner ear.

cones Receptor cells in the retina that are principally responsible for bright light and color vision.

confirmation bias The tendency to seek evidence that confirms one's beliefs.

conformity A change in behavior, belief, or both to conform to a group norm as a result of real or imagined group pressure.

conjunction fallacy Incorrectly judging the overlap of two uncertain events to be more probable than either of the two events.

conscious mind Freud's term for what we are presently aware of.

consciousness An individual's subjective awareness of their inner thinking and feeling and their external environment.

conservation The knowledge that the quantitative properties of objects (such as mass and number) remain the same despite changes in appearance.

contextual effect The use of the present context of sensory information to determine its meaning.

continuous schedule of reinforcement In operant conditioning, reinforcing the desired operant response each time it is made.

control group In an experiment, the group not exposed to the independent variable.

conventional level of moral reasoning The second level of reasoning in Kohlberg's theory of moral development in which moral reasoning is based on social rules and laws.

corpus callosum The bridge of neurons that connects the two cerebral hemispheres.

correlation coefficient A statistic that tells us the type and the strength of the relationship between two variables. The sign of the coefficient (+ or −) indicates the type of correlation—positive or negative, respectively. The absolute value of the coefficient (0.0 to 1.0) represents the strength of the correlation, with 1.0 being the maximum strength.

correlational study A research study in which two variables are measured to determine if they are related (how well either one predicts the other).

counterconditioning A type of behavioral therapy in which a maladaptive response is replaced by an incompatible adaptive response.

cross-sectional study A study in which the performances of groups of participants of different ages are compared with one another.

cue-dependent theory A theory of forgetting that proposes that forgetting is due to the unavailability of the retrieval cues necessary to locate the information in long-term memory.

cumulative record A record of the total number of operant responses over time that visually depicts the rate of responding.

dark adaptation The process by which the rods and cones through internal chemical changes become more and more sensitive to light in dim light conditions.

defense mechanism A process used by the ego to distort reality and protect a person from anxiety.

deindividuation The loss of self-awareness and self-restraint in a group situation that fosters arousal and anonymity.

delayed conditioning A classical conditioning procedure in which the conditioned stimulus precedes the unconditioned stimulus and remains present until after the unconditioned stimulus is presented so that the two stimuli occur together.

delusion A false belief.

demand characteristics Cues in the experimental environment that make participants aware of what the experimenters expect to find (their hypothesis) and how participants are expected to act.

dendrites Fibers projecting out of the cell body of a neuron whose function is to receive information from other neurons.

dependent variable In an experiment, a variable that is hypothesized to be affected by the independent variable and thus is measured by the experimenter.

depressive disorders Disorders that involve the presence of sad, empty, or irritable mood, accompanied by somatic and cognitive changes that significantly affect the individual's capacity to function.

depth perception Our ability to perceive the distance of objects from us.

descriptive methods Research methods whose main purpose is to provide objective and detailed descriptions of behavior and mental processes.

descriptive statistics Statistics that describe the results of a research study in a concise fashion.

developmental psychology The scientific study of biological, cognitive, social, and personality development across the life span.

deviation IQ score 100 plus or minus (15 × the number of standard deviations the person is from the raw score mean for their standardization group).

Diagnostic and Statistical Manual of Mental Disorders, Fifth Edition (DSM-5) The current version of the American Psychiatric Association's diagnostic and classification guidelines for mental disorders.

difference threshold The minimum difference between two sensory stimuli detected 50% of the time. The difference threshold is also sometimes referred to as the just noticeable difference, or jnd.

diffusion of responsibility The lessening of individual responsibility for a task when responsibility for the task is spread across the members of a group.

discriminative stimulus In operant conditioning, the stimulus that has to be present for the operant response to be reinforced.

distractor task A memory task in which a small amount of information is briefly presented and then the participant is distracted from rehearsing the information for a variable period of time, after which the participant has to recall the information.

door-in-the-face technique Compliance is gained by starting with a large, unreasonable request that is turned down and following it with a more reasonable, smaller request.

dopamine A neurotransmitter involved in arousal and mood states, thought processes, and physical movement.

double-blind procedure A control measure in an experiment in which neither the experimenters nor the participants know which participants are in the experimental and control groups.

drive-reduction theory A theory of motivation that proposes that our behavior is motivated to reduce drives (bodily tension states) created by unsatisfied bodily needs in order to return the body to a balanced internal state.

effortful processing Memory processing that occurs consciously and requires attention.

ego The part of the personality that starts developing in the first year or so of life in order to find realistic outlets for the id's instinctual drives.

egocentrism The inability to distinguish one's own perceptions, thoughts, and feelings from those of others.

elaborative rehearsal A type of rehearsal in short-term memory in which incoming information is related to information from long-term memory to encode it into long-term memory.

electroconvulsive therapy (ECT) A biomedical treatment for severe depression that involves electrically inducing a brief brain seizure.

emotion A complex psychological state that involves a state of physiological arousal, an outward behavioral expression of the emotion, and a cognitive appraisal of the situation to determine the specific emotion and its intensity.

encoding The process of moving information from one memory stage to the next (from sensory memory into short-term memory or from short-term memory to long-term memory).

encoding failure theory A theory of forgetting that proposes that forgetting is due to the failure to encode the information into long-term memory.

encoding specificity principle The principle that the environmental cues (both internal and external) present at the time information is encoded into long-term memory serve as the best retrieval cues for the information.

endocrine glandular system The body's other major communication system, in addition to the nervous system. Communication is achieved through hormones that are secreted by the endocrine glands and travel through the bloodstream to their target sites.

endorphins A group of neurotransmitters that are involved in pain relief and feelings of pleasure.

episodic memory Explicit memory for personal experiences.

erogenous zone The area of the body where the id's pleasure-seeking energies are focused during a particular stage of psychosexual development.

experiment A research method in which the researcher manipulates one or more independent variables and measures their effect on one or more dependent variables while controlling other potentially relevant variables.

experimental group In an experiment, the group exposed to the independent variable.

experimenter bias A process in which the person performing the research influences the results in order to portray a certain outcome.

explicit (declarative) memory Long-term memory for factual knowledge and personal experiences. This type of memory requires a conscious effort to remember and entails making declarations about the information remembered.

external locus of control The perception that chance or external forces beyond one's personal control determine one's fate.

extinction (1) In classical conditioning, the diminishing of the conditioned response when the unconditioned stimulus no longer follows the conditioned stimulus. (2) In operant conditioning, the diminishing of the operant response when it is no longer reinforced.

extrinsic motivation The desire to perform a behavior for external reinforcement.

factor analysis A statistical technique that identifies clusters of test items that measure the same ability (factor).

false consensus effect The tendency to overestimate the commonality of one's opinions and unsuccessful behaviors.

false memory An inaccurate memory that feels as real as an accurate memory.

false uniqueness effect The tendency to underestimate the commonality of one's abilities and successful behaviors.

farsightedness A visual problem in which the light waves from nearby objects come into focus behind the retina, blurring the images of these objects.

fetal alcohol syndrome (FAS) A syndrome affecting infants whose mothers consumed large amounts of alcohol during pregnancy, resulting in a range of severe effects including intellectual disability and facial abnormalities.

figure-and-ground principle The Gestalt perceptual organizational principle that the brain organizes sensory information into a figure or figures (the center of attention) and ground (the less distinct background).

fixation (1) In problem solving, the inability to create a new interpretation of a problem. (2) In Freudian theory, some of the id's pleasure-seeking energies remaining stuck in a psychosexual stage due to excessive gratification or frustration of instinctual needs.

fixed-interval schedule A partial schedule of reinforcement in which a reinforcer is delivered after the first response is given once a set interval of time has elapsed.

fixed-ratio schedule A partial schedule of reinforcement in which a reinforcer is delivered each time a fixed number of responses is made. The fixed number can be any number greater than one.

flooding A counterconditioning exposure therapy in which the patient is immediately exposed to a feared object or situation.

Flynn effect The finding that the average intelligence test score in the United States and other industrialized nations has improved steadily over the last century.

foot-in-the-door technique Compliance to a large request is gained by preceding it with a very small request.

formal operational stage The last stage in Piaget's theory of cognitive development, starting at age 12 or so, during which a child gains the capacity for hypothetical-deductive thought.

fovea A tiny pit in the center of the retina filled with cones.

fraternal (dizygotic) twins Twins that originate from the fertilization of two eggs at approximately the same time (two zygotes).

free association A person spontaneously describes, without editing, all thoughts, feelings, or images that come to mind.

free recall task A memory task in which a list of items is presented one at a time and then the participant is free to recall them in any order.

frequency The number of times a wave cycles in one second.

frequency distribution A depiction, in a table or figure, of the number of participants (frequency) receiving each score for a variable.

frequency theory A theory of pitch perception that assumes that the frequency of the sound wave is mimicked by the firing rate of the entire basilar membrane.

frontal lobe The area in each cerebral hemisphere in front of the central fissure and above the lateral fissure. The motor cortex is in this lobe.

functional fixedness The inability to see that an object can have a function other than its typical one in solving a problem.

functional magnetic resonance imaging (fMRI) A computerized image of the activity levels of various areas in the brain generated by detecting the amount of oxygen brought to each area.

fundamental attribution error The tendency as an observer to overestimate dispositional influences and underestimate situational influences on others' behavior.

GABA (gamma-aminobutyric acid) The main inhibitory neurotransmitter in the nervous system. It is involved in lowering arousal and anxiety and regulating movement.

gambler's fallacy Incorrectly believing that a chance process is self-correcting in that an event that has not occurred for a while is more likely to occur.

gene The basic unit of genetic instruction.

generalized anxiety disorder An anxiety disorder in which a person has excessive, global anxiety and worries that he cannot control, occurring more days than not for at least a period of 6 months.

genital stage of psychosexual development The fifth stage in Freud's theory (from puberty through adulthood), in which the erogenous zone is at the genitals, and the child develops sexual relationships, moving toward intimate adult relationships.

glial cells (glia) Cells in the nervous system that comprise the support system for the neurons.

glutamate The main excitatory neurotransmitter in the nervous system. It is involved in memory storage, pain perception, strokes, and schizophrenia.

group polarization The strengthening of a group's prevailing opinion about a topic following group discussion about the topic.

groupthink A mode of group thinking that impairs decision making, because the desire for group harmony overrides a realistic appraisal of the possible decision alternatives.

habituation A decrease in the physiological responding to a stimulus once it becomes familiar.

hair cells The receptor cells for hearing. They line the basilar membrane inside the cochlea.

hallucination A false sensory perception.

heritability An index of the degree that variation of a trait within a given population is due to heredity.

heuristic A problem-solving strategy that seems reasonable given one's past experience with solving problems, especially similar problems, but does not guarantee a correct answer to a problem.

hierarchy of needs The motivational component in Maslow's theory of personality, in which our innate needs that motivate our behavior are hierarchically arranged in a pyramid shape. From bottom to top, the needs are physiological, safety, belonging and love, esteem, and self-actualization.

hindsight bias (I-knew-it-all-along phenomenon) The tendency, after learning about an outcome, to be overconfident in one's ability to have predicted it.

hippocampus A part of the brain involved in the formation of memories.

holophrase A word used by an infant to express a complete idea.

hormone A chemical messenger that is produced by an endocrine gland and carried by the bloodstream to target tissues throughout the body.

hypothalamus A part of the brain that is involved in regulating basic drives such as eating, drinking, and having sex. It also directs the endocrine glandular system through its control of the pituitary gland and the autonomic nervous system to maintain the body's internal environment.

iconic memory The visual sensory register that holds an exact copy of the incoming visual input but only for a brief period of time, less than 1 second.

id The part of the personality that a person is born with, where the biological instinctual drives reside, and that is located totally in the unconscious mind.

identical (monozygotic) twins Twins that originate from the same zygote.

identification The process by which children adopt the characteristics of the same-sex parent and learn their gender role and sense of morality.

ill-defined problem A problem lacking clear specification of either the start state, goal state, or the processes for reaching the goal state.

illusory correlation The erroneous belief that two variables are statistically related when they actually are not.

implicit (nondeclarative) memory Long-term memory for procedural tasks, classical conditioning, and primary effects. This type of memory does not require conscious awareness or the need to make declarations about the information remembered.

incentive theory A theory of motivation that proposes that our behavior is motivated by incentives, external stimuli that we have learned to associate with reinforcement.

independent variable In an experiment, the variable that is a hypothesized cause and thus is manipulated by the experimenter.

infantile/child amnesia Our inability as adults to remember events that occurred in our lives before about 3 years of age.

inferential statistical analyses Statistical analyses that allow researchers to draw conclusions about the results of a study by determining the probability that the results are due to random variation (chance). The results are statistically significant if this probability is .05 or less.

informational social influence Influence stemming from the need for information in situations in which the correct action or judgment is uncertain.

information-processing approach to cognitive development An approach to studying cognitive development that assumes cognitive development is continuous and improves as children become more adept at processing information (taking in, storing, and using information).

insecure-ambivalent attachment The type of attachment indicated by the infant not exploring but seeking closeness to the mother in the Ainsworth strange situation procedure, showing high levels of distress when the mother leaves, and ambivalent behavior when she returns—by alternately clinging to and pushing away from her.

insecure-avoidant attachment The type of attachment indicated by the infant exploring with little interest in the mother in the Ainsworth strange situation procedure, showing only minimal distress when the mother leaves, and avoiding her when she returns.

insecure-disorganized (disoriented) attachment The type of attachment indicated by the infant's confusion when the mother leaves and returns in the Ainsworth strange situation procedure. The infant acts disoriented, seems overwhelmed by the situation, and does not demonstrate a consistent way of coping with it.

insight A new way to interpret a problem that immediately yields the solution.

instinctual drift The tendency for an animal to drift back from a learned operant response to an innate, instinctual response to an object.

intelligence quotient (IQ) (mental age/chronological age) $\times$ 100.

interference theory A theory of forgetting that proposes that forgetting is due to other information in memory interfering and thereby making the to-be-remembered information inaccessible.

internal locus of control The perception that one controls one's own individual fate.

interneurons Neurons that integrate information within the central nervous system through their communication with each other and between sensory and motor neurons in the spinal cord.

interposition A monocular depth cue referring to the fact that if one object partially blocks our view of another, we perceive it as closer to us.

intrinsic motivation The desire to perform a behavior for its own sake.

James-Lange theory A theory of emotion proposing that an emotion is determined from a cognitive appraisal of the physiological arousal and behavioral responses, which occur first.

just-world hypothesis The assumption that the world is just and that people get what they deserve.

L-dopa A drug for Parkinson's disease that contains the precursors to dopamine so that once it is in the brain, it will be converted to dopamine.

latency stage of psychosexual development The fourth stage in Freud's theory (from 6 years old to puberty), in which there is no erogenous zone, sexual feelings are repressed, and the focus is on cognitive and social development.

latent content Freud's term for the underlying true meaning of a dream.

latent learning Learning that occurs but is not demonstrated until there is incentive to do so.

law of effect A principle developed by Edward Thorndike that says that any behavior that results in satisfying consequences tends to be repeated and that any behavior that results in unsatisfying consequences tends not to be repeated.

learned helplessness A sense of hopelessness in which a person thinks that he is unable to prevent aversive events.

left-skewed distribution An asymmetric frequency distribution in which there are some unusually low scores that distort the mean to be less than the median.

levels-of-processing theory A theory of information processing in memory that assumes that semantic processing, especially elaborative semantic processing, leads to better long-term memory.

limbic system A group of brain structures (hypothalamus, hippocampus, and amygdala) that play an important role in our survival, memory, and emotions.

linear perspective A monocular depth cue referring to the fact that as parallel lines recede away from us, they appear to converge—the greater the distance, the more they seem to converge. Sometimes referred to as perspective convergence.

lithium A naturally occurring element (a mineral salt) that is used to treat bipolar disorder.

lobotomy A type of psychosurgery in which the neuronal connections of the frontal lobes to lower brain areas are severed.

long-term memory (LTM) The memory stage in which information is stored for a long period of time (perhaps permanently) and whose capacity is essentially unlimited.

longitudinal study A study in which performance of the same group of participants is examined at different ages.

low-ball technique Compliance to a costly request is gained by first getting compliance to an attractive, less costly request but then reneging on it.

maintenance rehearsal A type of rehearsal in short-term memory in which the information is repeated over and over again in order to maintain it.

major depressive disorder A depressive disorder in which the person has experienced one or more major depressive episodes.

major depressive episode An episode characterized by symptoms such as feelings of intense hopelessness, low self-esteem and worthlessness, extreme fatigue, dramatic changes in eating and sleeping behavior, inability to concentrate, and greatly diminished interest in family, friends, and activities for a period of 2 weeks or more.

manic episode An episode characterized by abnormally elevated mood in which the person experiences symptoms such as inflated self-esteem with grandiose delusions, a decreased need for sleep, constant talking, distractibility, restlessness, and poor judgment for a period of at least a week.

manifest content Freud's term for the literal surface meaning of a dream.

mean The numerical average of a distribution of scores.

means–end analysis heuristic A problem-solving heuristic in which the distance to the goal state is decreased systematically by breaking the problem down into subgoals and achieving these subgoals.

median The score positioned in the middle of a distribution of scores when all of the scores are arranged from lowest to highest.

medulla A brain stem structure involved in many essential body functions, such as heartbeat, breathing, blood pressure, digestion, and swallowing.

memory span The average number of items an individual can remember across a series of memory span trials.

memory span task A memory task in which the participant is given a series of items one at a time and then has to recall the items in the order in which they were presented.

mental set The tendency to use previously successful problem-solving strategies without considering others that are more appropriate for the current problem.

meta-analysis A statistical technique that combines the results of a large number of studies on one experimental question into one analysis to arrive at an overall conclusion.

method of loci A mnemonic in which sequential pieces of information to be remembered are encoded by associating them with sequential locations in a very familiar room or place and then the pieces of information are retrieved by mentally going around the room (place) and retrieving the piece at each location.

mirror neurons Neurons that fire both when performing an action and when observing another person perform that same action.

misinformation effect The distortion of a memory by exposure to misleading information.

mnemonic A memory aid.

mode The most frequently occurring score in a distribution of scores.

mood-congruence effect Tendency to retrieve experiences and information that are congruent with a person's current mood.

mood-dependent memory Long-term memory retrieval is best when a person's mood state at the time of encoding and retrieval of the information is the same.

motivation The set of internal and external factors that energize our behavior and direct it toward goals.

motor cortex The strip of cortex in each cerebral hemisphere in the frontal lobe directly in front of the central fissure, which allows us to move different parts of our body.

motor neurons Neurons in the peripheral nervous system that carry movement commands from the central nervous system out to the rest of the body.

myelin sheath An insulating layer covering an axon that allows for faster neural impulses.

naturalistic observation A descriptive research method in which the behavior of interest is observed in its natural setting, and the researcher does not intervene in the behavior being observed.

nearsightedness A visual problem in which the light waves from distant objects come into focus in front of the retina, blurring the images of these objects.

negative correlation An inverse relationship between two variables.

negative punishment Punishment in which an appetitive stimulus is removed.

negative reinforcement Reinforcement in which an aversive stimulus is removed.

nerve deafness Hearing loss created by damage to the hair cells or the auditory nerve fibers in the inner ear.

neurogenesis theory of depression An explanation of depression that proposes that neurogenesis, the growth of new neurons, in the hippocampus stops during depression, and when it resumes, the depression lifts.

neurons Cells that transmit information within the nervous system.

neuroscience The scientific study of the brain and nervous system.

neurotransmitter A naturally occurring chemical in the nervous system that specializes in transmitting information between neurons.

nocebo effect A negative placebo effect due to the expectation of adverse consequences from receiving treatment.

normal distribution A frequency distribution that is shaped like a bell. About 68% of the scores fall within 1 standard deviation of the mean, about 95% within 2 standard deviations of the mean, and over 99% within 3 standard deviations of the mean.

normative social influence Influence stemming from our desire to gain the approval and to avoid the disapproval of others.

obedience Following the commands of a person in authority.

object permanence The knowledge that an object exists independent of perceptual contact with it.

observational learning (modeling) Learning by observing others and imitating their behavior.

obsession A persistent intrusive thought, idea, impulse, or image that causes anxiety.

obsessive-compulsive disorder A disorder in which the person experiences recurrent obsessions or compulsions that are perceived by the person as excessive or unreasonable, but cause significant distress and disruption in the person's daily life.

occipital lobe The area located in the lower back of each cerebral hemisphere. The primary visual cortex is in this lobe.

Oedipus conflict A phallic stage conflict for a boy in which the boy becomes sexually attracted to his mother and fears his father will find out and castrate him.

operant conditioning Learning to associate behaviors with their consequences. Behaviors that are reinforced (lead to satisfying consequences) will be strengthened, and behaviors that are punished (lead to unsatisfying consequences) will be weakened.

operational definition A description of the operations or procedures that a researcher uses to manipulate or measure a variable.

opponent-process theory A theory of color vision that assumes that there are three opponent-process cell systems (red-green, blue-yellow, and black-white) that process color information after it has been processed by the cones. The colors in each system oppose one another in that if one color is stimulated, the other is inhibited.

oral stage of psychosexual development The first stage in Freud's theory (from birth to 18 months), in which the erogenous zones are the mouth, lips, and tongue, and the child derives pleasure from oral activities such as sucking, biting, and chewing.

overextension The application of a newly learned word to objects that are not included in the meaning of the word.

overjustification effect A decrease in an intrinsically motivated behavior after the behavior is extrinsically reinforced and then the reinforcement is discontinued.

panic disorder An anxiety disorder in which a person experiences recurrent panic attacks.

parasympathetic nervous system The part of the autonomic nervous system that returns the body to its normal resting state after having been highly aroused, as in an emergency.

parietal lobe The area in each cerebral hemisphere in back of the central fissure and above the lateral fissure. The somatosensory cortex is in this lobe.

Parkinson's disease A disease in which the person has movement problems such as muscle tremors, difficulty initiating movements, and rigidity of movement. These movement problems stem from a scarcity of dopamine in the basal ganglia.

partial-reinforcement effect The finding that operant responses that are reinforced on partial schedules are more resistant to extinction than those reinforced on a continuous schedule.

partial schedule of reinforcement In operant conditioning, reinforcing the desired operant response only part of the time.

participant observation A descriptive research method in which the observer becomes part of the group being observed.

peg-word system A mnemonic in which the items in a list to be remembered are associated with the sequential items in a memorized jingle and then the list is retrieved by going through the jingle and retrieving the associated items.

percentile rank The percentage of scores below a specific score in a distribution of scores.

perception The interpretation by the brain of sensory information.

perceptual constancy The perceptual stability of the size, shape, brightness, and color for familiar objects seen at varying distances, different angles, and under different lighting conditions.

perceptual set The interpretation of ambiguous sensory information in terms of how our past experiences have set us to perceive it.

peripheral nervous system (PNS) The part of the nervous system that links the central nervous system with the body's sensory receptors, muscles, and glands.

permissive parenting A style of parenting in which the parents make few demands and are overly responsive to their children's desires, letting their children do pretty much as they please.

person-who reasoning Questioning a well-established research finding because one knows a person who violates the finding.

personality A person's internally based characteristic ways of acting and thinking.

personality disorder A disorder characterized by inflexible, long-standing personality traits that lead to behavior that impairs social functioning and deviates from cultural norms.

personality inventory An objective personality test that uses a series of questions or statements for which the test taker must indicate whether they apply to her or not.

phallic stage of psychosexual development The third stage in Freud's theory (from 3 to 6 years), in which the erogenous zone is located at the genitals, and the child derives pleasure from genital stimulation.

phonemes The smallest distinctive speech sounds in a language.

pituitary gland The most influential gland in the endocrine glandular system. It releases hormones for human growth and hormones that direct other endocrine glands to release their hormones.

place theory A theory of pitch perception that assumes that there is a specific location along the basilar membrane that will maximally respond to a particular frequency, thereby indicating the pitch to the brain. As this location goes down the basilar membrane from the oval window, the pitch goes down from 20,000 Hz to 20 Hz.

placebo An inactive pill or a treatment that has no known effects.

placebo effect Improvement due to the expectation of improving because of receiving treatment.

placebo group A control group of participants who believe they are receiving treatment, but who are only receiving a placebo.

pleasure principle The principle of seeking immediate gratification for instinctual drives without concern for the consequences.

pons A brain stem structure that serves as a bridge between the cerebellum and the rest of the brain and is involved in sleep and dreaming.

population The entire group of people that a researcher is studying.

positive correlation A direct relationship between two variables.

positive punishment Punishment in which an aversive stimulus is presented.

positive reinforcement Reinforcement in which an appetitive stimulus is presented.

positron emission tomography (PET) scans A visual display of the activity levels in various areas in the brain generated by detecting the amount of positron emission created by the metabolization of radioactive glucose in each area.

postconventional level of moral reasoning The last level of reasoning in Kohlberg's theory of moral development in which moral reasoning is based on self-chosen universal ethical principles (with human rights taking precedence over laws) and the avoidance of self-condemnation for violating such principles.

preconscious mind Freud's term for what is stored in one's memory that one is not presently aware of but can access.

preconventional level of moral reasoning The first level of reasoning in Kohlberg's theory of moral development in which moral reasoning is based on avoiding punishment and looking out for your own welfare and needs.

Premack principle The principle that the opportunity to perform a highly frequent behavior can reinforce a less frequent behavior.

preoperational stage The second stage in Piaget's theory of cognitive development, from age 2 to 6, during which the child's thinking becomes more symbolic and language-based, but remains egocentric and lacks the mental operations that allow logical thinking.

primacy effect (1) In memory, the superior recall of the early portion of a list relative to the middle of the list in a one-trial free recall task. (2) In impression formation, information gathered early is weighted more heavily than information gathered later in forming an impression of another person.

primary reinforcer A stimulus that is innately reinforcing.

priming The implicit influence of an earlier presented stimulus on the response to a later stimulus. This influence is independent of conscious memory for the earlier stimulus.

proactive interference The disruptive effect of prior learning on the retrieval of new information.

procedural memory Implicit memory for cognitive and motor tasks that have a physical procedural aspect to them.

projective test A personality test that uses a series of ambiguous stimuli to which the test taker must respond about her perceptions of the stimuli.

psychoanalysis A style of psychotherapy, originally developed by Sigmund Freud, in which the therapist helps the person gain insight into the unconscious sources of his or her problems.

psychology The science of behavior and mental processes.

psychosurgery A biomedical treatment in which specific areas of the brain are destroyed.

psychotherapy The use of psychological interventions to treat mental disorders.

psychotic disorder A disorder characterized by a loss of contact with reality.

punisher A stimulus that decreases the probability of a prior response.

punishment The process by which the probability of a response is decreased by the presentation of a punisher.

random assignment A control measure in which participants are randomly assigned to groups in order to equalize participant characteristics across the various groups in an experiment.

random sampling A sampling technique that obtains a representative sample of a population by ensuring that each individual in a population has an equal opportunity to be in the sample.

range The difference between the highest and lowest scores in a distribution of scores.

rational-emotive therapy A type of cognitive therapy, developed by Albert Ellis, in which the therapist directly confronts and challenges the person's unrealistic thoughts and beliefs to show that they are irrational.

reaction range The genetically determined limits for an individual's intelligence.

reality principle The principle of finding gratification for instinctual drives within the constraints of reality (norms of society).

recall A measure of long-term memory retrieval that requires the reproduction of the information with essentially no retrieval cues.

recency effect The superior recall of the latter portion of a list relative to the middle of the list in a one-trial free recall task.

recognition A measure of long-term memory retrieval that only requires the identification of the information in the presence of retrieval cues.

reflex A stimulus-response pair in which the stimulus (the unconditioned stimulus) automatically elicits the response (the unconditioned response).

regression toward the mean The tendency for extreme or unusual values on one variable to be matched on average with less extreme values on the other variable when the two variables are not perfectly correlated.

reinforcement The process by which the probability of a response is increased by the presentation of a reinforcer.

reinforcer A stimulus that increases the probability of a prior response.

relearning The savings method of measuring long-term memory retrieval in which the measure is the amount of time saved when learning information for the second time.

reliability The extent to which the scores for a test are consistent.

REM (rapid eye movement) sleep The stage of sleep that is characterized by rapid eye movements and brain wave patterns that resemble those for an awake state and in which most dreaming occurs. REM sleep is sometimes referred to as paradoxical sleep because the bodily muscles are immobilized but much of the brain is highly active.

representativeness heuristic A heuristic for judging the probability of membership in a category by how well an object resembles (is representative of) that category (the more representative, the more probable).

resistance A person's unwillingness to discuss a particular topic during therapy.

reticular formation A network of neurons running up the center of the brain stem that is responsible for our different levels of arousal and consciousness.

retina The light-sensitive layer of the eye that is composed of three layers of cells—ganglion, bipolar, and receptor (rods and cones).

retinal disparity A binocular depth cue referring to the fact that as the disparity (difference) between the two retinal images of an object increases, the distance of the object from us decreases.

retrieval The process of bringing information stored in long-term memory into short-term memory.

retroactive interference The disruptive effect of new learning on the retrieval of old information.

retrograde amnesia The disruption of memory for the past, especially episodic information for events before, especially just before, surgery or trauma to the brain.

reversibility The knowledge that reversing a transformation brings about the conditions that existed before the transformation.

right-skewed distribution An asymmetric frequency distribution in which there are some unusually high scores that distort the mean to be greater than the median.

rods Receptor cells in the retina that are principally responsible for dim light and achromatic vision.

rooting reflex An innate human reflex that leads infants to turn their mouth toward anything that touches their cheeks and search for something to suck on.

sample The subset of a population that actually participates in a research study.

scaffolding According to Vygotsky, a style of teaching in which the teacher adjusts the level of help in relation to the child's level of performance while orienting the child's learning toward the upper level of his or her zone of proximal development.

scatterplot A visual depiction of correlational data in which each data point represents the scores on the two variables for each participant.

Schachter-Singer two-factor theory A theory of emotion proposing that an emotion is determined by cognitive appraisal of the physiological arousal and the entire environmental situation.

schemas Frameworks for our knowledge about people, objects, events, and actions that allow us to organize and interpret information about our world.

schizophrenia A psychotic disorder in which at least two of the following symptoms are present most of the time during a 1-month period—hallucinations, delusions, disorganized speech, disorganized or catatonic behavior, or negative symptoms such as loss of emotion.

secondary reinforcer A stimulus that gains its reinforcing property through learning.

secure attachment The type of attachment indicated by the infant exploring freely in the presence of the mother in the Ainsworth strange situation procedure, displaying distress when the mother leaves, and responding enthusiastically when she returns.

selective serotonin and norepinephrine reuptake inhibitors (SSNRIs) Antidepressant drugs that achieve their agonistic effect on serotonin and norepinephrine by selectively blocking their reuptake.

selective serotonin reuptake inhibitors (SSRIs) Antidepressant drugs that achieve their agonistic effect on serotonin by selectively blocking its reuptake.

self-actualization The fullest realization of a person's potential.

self-efficacy A judgment of one's effectiveness in dealing with particular situations.

self-fulfilling prophecy Our behavior leads a person to act in accordance with our expectations for that person.

self-perception theory A theory, developed by Daryl Bem, that assumes that when we are unsure of our attitudes, we infer them by examining our behavior and the context in which it occurs.

self-reference effect The superior long-term memory for information related to oneself at time of encoding into long-term memory.

self-serving bias The tendency to make attributions so that one can perceive oneself favorably.

self-system The set of cognitive processes by which a person observes, evaluates, and regulates her behavior.

semantic memory Explicit memory for factual knowledge.

sensation The initial information gathering and recoding by the sensory structures.

sensorimotor stage The first stage in Piaget's theory of cognitive development, from birth to about age 2, during which infants learn about the world through their sensory and motor interactions with it and develop object permanence.

sensory adaptation Our sensitivity to unchanging and repetitious stimuli disappears over time.

sensory memory (SM) The set of sensory registers, one for each of our senses, that serve as holding places for incoming sensory information until it can be attended to, interpreted, and encoded into short-term memory.

sensory neurons Neurons in the peripheral nervous system that carry information to the central nervous system from sensory receptors, muscles, and glands.

serotonin and norepinephrine Neurotransmitters involved in levels of arousal and mood, sleep, and eating.

shaping Training a human or animal to make an operant response by reinforcing successive approximations of the desired response.

short-term memory (STM) The memory stage with a small capacity (7 ± 2 chunks) and brief duration (< 30 seconds) that we are consciously aware of and in which we do our problem solving, reasoning, and decision making.

signal detection theory A theory that assumes that the detection of faint sensory stimuli depends not only upon a person's physiological sensitivity to a stimulus but also upon his decision criterion for detection, which is based on nonsensory factors.

social anxiety disorder An anxiety disorder indicated by a marked and persistent fear of one or more social performance situations in which embarrassment may occur and in which there is exposure to unfamiliar people or scrutiny by others.

social facilitation Facilitation of a dominant response on a task due to social arousal, leading to improved performance on simple or well-learned tasks and worse performance on complex or unlearned tasks when other people are present.

social loafing The tendency to exert less effort when working in a group toward a common goal than when individually working toward the goal.

social psychology The scientific study of how we influence one another's behavior and thinking.

sociocultural perspective A research perspective whose major explanatory focus is how other people and the cultural context impact behavior and mental processes.

somatic (skeletal) nervous system The part of the peripheral nervous system that carries sensory input from receptors to the central nervous system and relays commands from the central nervous system to skeletal muscles to control their movement.

somatosensory cortex The strip of cortex in each cerebral hemisphere in the parietal lobe directly in back of the central fissure, which allows us to sense pressure, temperature, and pain in different parts of our body as well as the position of our body parts.

source misattribution Attributing a memory to the wrong source, resulting in a false memory.

spacing (distributed study) effect Superior long-term memory for spaced study versus massed study (cramming).

specific phobia An anxiety disorder indicated by a marked and persistent fear of specific objects or situations that is excessive and unreasonable.

Sperling's full-report procedure An experimental procedure in which, following the brief presentation of a matrix of unrelated consonants, the participant has to attempt to recall all of the letters in the matrix.

Sperling's partial-report procedure An experimental procedure in which, following the brief presentation of a matrix of unrelated consonants, the participant is given an auditory cue about which row of the matrix to recall.

spinal cord The conduit between the brain and the peripheral nervous system for incoming sensory data and outgoing movement commands to the muscles.

spinal reflex A simple automatic action of the spinal cord not requiring involvement of the brain, such as the knee-jerk reflex.

spontaneous recovery (1) In classical conditioning, a partial recovery in strength of the conditioned response following a break during extinction training. (2) In operant conditioning, the temporary recovery of the operant response following a break during extinction training.

spontaneous remission Getting better with the passage of time without receiving any therapy.

spurious correlation A correlation in which the variables are related through their relationship with one or more other variables but not through a causal mechanism.

standard deviation The average extent that the scores vary from the mean for a distribution of scores.

standardization The process that allows test scores to be interpreted by providing test norms.

state-dependent memory Long-term memory retrieval is best when a person's physiological state at the time of encoding and retrieval of the information is the same.

Stevens's power law The perceived magnitude of a stimulus is equal to its actual physical intensity raised to some constant power. The constant power is different for each type of sensory judgment.

stimulus discrimination (1) In classical conditioning, the elicitation of the conditioned response only by the conditioned stimulus or only by a small set of highly similar stimuli that includes the conditioned stimulus. (2) In operant conditioning, learning to give the operant response only in the presence of the discriminative stimulus.

stimulus generalization (1) In classical conditioning, the elicitation of the conditioned response to stimuli that are similar to the conditioned stimulus. The more similar the stimulus is to the conditioned stimulus, the stronger the response. (2) In operant conditioning, giving the operant response in the presence of stimuli similar to the discriminative stimulus. The more similar the stimulus is to the discriminative stimulus, the higher the operant response rate.

storage The process of maintaining information in a memory stage.

storage decay theory A theory of forgetting that proposes that forgetting is due to the decay of the biological representation of the information and that periodic usage of the information will help to maintain it in storage.

subjective contour A line or shape that is perceived to be present but does not really exist. The brain creates it during perception.

subtractive mixtures Mixtures of wavelengths of light in which some wavelengths are absorbed (subtracted) and so do not get reflected from the mixtures to the retina.

sucking reflex An innate human reflex that leads infants to suck anything that touches their lips.

superego The part of the personality that represents one's conscience and idealized standards of behavior.

survey research A descriptive research method in which the researcher uses questionnaires and interviews to collect information about the behavior, beliefs, and attitudes of particular groups of people.

sympathetic nervous system The part of the autonomic nervous system that is in control when we are highly aroused, as in an emergency, and need to prepare for defensive action.

synaptic gap (synapse) The microscopic gap between neurons across which neurotransmitters travel to carry their messages to other neurons.

systematic desensitization A counterconditioning exposure therapy in which a fear response to an object or situation is replaced with a relaxation response in a series of progressively increasing fear-arousing steps.

tardive dyskinesia A side effect of long-term use of traditional antipsychotic drugs causing the person to have uncontrollable facial tics, grimaces, and other involuntary movements of the lips, jaw, and tongue.

telegraphic speech Using two-word sentences with mainly nouns and verbs.

temperament The set of innate tendencies or dispositions that lead a person to behave in certain ways.

temporal integration procedure An experimental procedure in which two meaningless visual patterns that produce a meaningful pattern if integrated are presented sequentially with the time delay between their presentations varied.

temporal lobe The area in each cerebral hemisphere located beneath the lateral fissure. The primary auditory cortex is in this lobe.

teratogens Environmental agents such as drugs and viruses, diseases, and physical conditions that impair prenatal development and lead to birth defects and sometimes death.

thalamus A part of the brain that serves as a relay station for incoming sensory information.

that's-not-all technique Compliance to a planned second request with additional benefits is gained by presenting this request before a response can be made to a first request.

theory of mind The understanding of the mental and emotional states of both ourselves and others.

thinking The processing of information to solve problems and make judgments and decisions.

third-variable problem An explanation of a correlation between two variables in terms of another (third) variable that could possibly be responsible for the observed relationship between the two variables.

tip-of-the-tongue (TOT) phenomenon The failure to recall specific information from memory combined with partial recall and the feeling that recall is imminent.

top-down processing The brain's use of knowledge, beliefs, and expectations to interpret sensory information.

trace conditioning A classical conditioning procedure in which the conditioned stimulus precedes the unconditioned stimulus but is removed before the unconditioned stimulus is presented so that the two stimuli do not occur together.

traits The relatively stable internally based characteristics that describe a person.

transcranial magnetic stimulation (TMS) A neurostimulation therapy in which the left frontal lobe is stimulated with magnetic pulses via an electromagnetic coil placed on the patient's scalp. It is only cleared for use in cases of severe depression for which traditional treatment has not helped.

transduction The conversion of physical energy into neural signals that the brain can understand.

transference When a person undergoing therapy acts toward the therapist as he or she did or does toward important figures in his or her life, such as his or her parents.

trichromatic theory A theory of color vision that assumes that there are three types of cones, each only activated by wavelength ranges of light corresponding roughly to blue, green, and red. It further assumes that all of the various colors that we can see are mixtures of various levels of activation of the three types of cones. If all three are equally activated, we see white.

unconditional positive regard Unconditional acceptance and approval of a person by others.

unconditioned response (UCR) The response in a reflex that is automatically elicited by the unconditioned stimulus.

unconditioned stimulus (UCS) The stimulus in a reflex that automatically elicits an unconditioned response.

unconscious mind Freud's term for the part of our mind that we cannot become aware of.

underextension The failure to apply a new word more generally to objects that are included within the meaning of the word.

uninvolved parenting A style of parenting in which the parents minimize both the time they spend with their children and their emotional involvement with them and provide for their children's basic needs, but little else.

validity The extent to which a test measures what it is supposed to measure or predicts what it is supposed to predict.

variable Any factor that can take on more than one value.

variable-interval schedule A partial schedule of reinforcement in which the time that must elapse on each trial before a response will lead to the delivery of a reinforcer varies from trial to trial but averages to a set time across trials.

variable-ratio schedule A partial schedule of reinforcement in which the number of responses it takes to obtain a reinforcer varies on each trial but averages to a set number across trials.

virtual reality therapy A counterconditioning exposure therapy in which the patient is exposed in graduated steps to computer simulations of a feared object or situation.

volley principle Cells taking turns firing will increase the maximum firing rate for a group of cells.

vulnerability–stress model A biopsychosocial explanation of schizophrenia that proposes that genetic, prenatal, and postnatal biological factors render a person vulnerable to schizophrenia, but environmental stress determines whether it develops or not.

wavelength The distance in one cycle of a wave, from one crest to the next.

Weber's law For each type of sensory judgment that we can make, the measured difference threshold is a constant fraction of the standard stimulus value used to measure it. This constant fraction is different for each type of sensory judgment.

well-defined problem A problem with clear specifications of the start state, goal state, and the processes for reaching the goal state.

Wernicke's area An area in the cerebral cortex responsible for comprehension of speech and text. It is in the left temporal lobe of the majority of people, regardless of handedness.

working backward heuristic A problem-solving heuristic in which one attempts to solve a problem by working from the goal state back to the start state.

working memory A more detailed version of short-term memory that includes the mechanisms that allow short-term memory to accomplish its tasks.

Yerkes-Dodson law A law describing the relationship between the amount of arousal and the performance quality on a task—increasing arousal up to some optimal level increases performance quality on a task, but increasing arousal past this point is detrimental to performance.

zone of proximal development According to Vygotsky, the difference between what a child can actually do and what the child could do with the help of others.

zygote The fertilized egg that is formed from the union of the sperm and egg cells in human reproduction.

References

Abraham, C. (2001). *Possessing genius: The bizarre odyssey of Einstein's brain.* Cambridge, England: Icon Books Ltd.

Ackerman, D. (2004). *An alchemy of mind: The marvel and mystery of the brain.* New York: Scribner.

Adams, J. L. (1986). *Conceptual blockbusting* (3rd ed.). Reading, MA: Addison-Wesley.

Adolph, K. E., Kretch, K. S., & LoBue, V. (2014). Fear of heights in infants? *Current Directions in Psychological Science, 23,* 60–66.

Advokat, C. D., Comaty, J. E., & Julien, R. M. (2014). *Julien's primer of drug action: A comprehensive guide to the actions, uses, and side effects of psychoactive drugs* (13th ed.). New York: Worth.

Ainsworth, M. D. S. (1979). Infant-mother attachment. *American Psychologist, 34,* 932–937.

Ainsworth, M. D. S., Blehar, M. C., Waters, E., & Wall, S. (1978). *Patterns of attachment: A psychological study of the Strange Situation.* Hillsdale, NJ: Erlbaum.

Akers, K. G., Martinez-Canabal, A., Restivo, L., Yiu, A. P., De Cristofaro, A., Hsiang, H.-L., . . . Frankland, P. W. (2014). Hippocampal neurogenesis regulates forgetting during adulthood and infancy. *Science, 344,* 598–602.

Allen, C. T., & Shimp, T. A. (1990). On using classical conditioning methods for researching the impact of ad-evoked feelings. In S. J. Agnes, J. A. Edell, & T. M. Dubitsky (Eds.), *Emotion in advertising: Theoretical and practical explanations (*pp. 19–34). New York: Quorum Books.

Allport, G. W., & Odbert, H. S. (1936). Trait-names: A psycholexical study. *Psychological Monographs, 47* (Whole No. 1).

Allyon, T., & Azrin, N. H. (1968). *The token economy.* New York: Appleton-Century-Crofts.

American Academy of Pediatrics. (2009). Policy statement—Media violence. *Pediatrics, 124,* 1495–1503. doi:10.1542/peds.2009.2146

American Psychiatric Association. (1952). *Diagnostic and statistical manual of mental disorders.* Washington, DC: Author.

American Psychiatric Association. (1994). *Diagnostic and statistical manual of mental disorders* (4th ed.). Washington, DC: Author.

American Psychiatric Association. (2013). *Diagnostic and statistical manual of mental disorders* (5th ed.). Washington, DC: Author.

Andersen, A. N., Wohlfahrt, J., Christens, P., Olsen, J., & Melbe, M. (2000). Maternal age and fetal loss: Population based linkage study. *British Medical Journal, 320,* 1708–1712.

Anderson, C. (2008). *The long tail: Why the future of business is selling less of more.* New York: Hyperion.

Anderson, C. A., Berkowitz, L., Donnerstein, E., Huesmann, L. R., Johnson, J. D., Linz, D., . . . Wartella, E. (2003). The influence of media violence on youth. *Psychological Science in the Public Interest, 4*(3) [Whole issue].

Anderson, C. A., Lepper, M. R., & Ross, L. (1980). Perseverance of social theories: The role of explanations in the persistence of discredited information. *Journal of Personality and Social Psychology, 39,* 1037–1049.

Anderson, C. A., Shibuya, A., Ihori, N., Swing, E. L., Bushman, B. J., Sakamoto, A., . . . Saleem, M. (2010). Violent video game effects on aggression, empathy, and prosocial behavior in Eastern and Western countries. *Psychological Bulletin, 136,* 151–173.

Andrews, P. W., & Thomson, J. A. (2009). The bright side of being blue: Depression as an adaptation for analyzing complex problems. *Psychological Review, 116,* 620–654.

Andrews, P. W., & Thomson, J. A. (2010, January/February). Depression's evolutionary roots. *Scientific American MIND, 20,* 56–61.

Annese, J., Schenker-Ahmed, N. M., Bartsch, H., Maechler, P., Sheh, C., Thomas, N., . . . Corkin, S. (2014). Postmortem examination of patient H. M.'s brain based on histological sectioning and digital 3D reconstruction. *Nature Communications, 5,* Article Number 3122. doi:10.1038/ncomms4122

Applebaum, P. S. (2004). One madman keeping loaded guns: Misconceptions of mental illness and their legal consequences. *Psychiatric Services, 55,* 1105–1106.

Asch, S. E. (1955, November). Opinions and social pressure. *Scientific American, 193,* 31–35.

Asch, S. E. (1956). Studies of independence and conformity: A minority of one against a unanimous majority. *Psychological Monographs: General and Applied, 70*(9,Whole No. 416).

Asendorpf, J. B., & Wilpers, S. (1998). Personality effects on social relationships. *Journal of Personality and Social Psychology, 74,* 1531–1544.

Asher, S. R. (1983). Social competence and peer status: Recent advances and future directions. *Child Development, 54,* 1427–1434.

Atkinson, R. C., & Shiffrin, R. M. (1968). Human memory: A proposed system and its control processes. In K. W. Spence & J. T. Spence (Eds.), *The psychology of learning and motivation: Advances in research and theory* (Vol. 2, pp. 89–195). New York: Academic Press.

Azevedo, F. A., Carvalho, L. R. B., Grinberg, L. T., Farfel, J. M., Ferretti, R. E., Leite, R. E., . . . Herculano-Houzel, S. (2009). Equal numbers of neuronal and nonneuronal cells make the human brain an isometrically scaled-up primate brain. *Journal of Comparative Neurology, 513,* 532–541.

Baddeley, A. D. (2007). *Working memory, thought, and action.* New York: Oxford University Press.

Baddeley, A. D. (2012). Working memory: Theories, models, and controversies. *Annual Review of Psychology, 63,* 1–29.

Baddeley, A. D., & Hitch, G. J. (1974). Working memory. In G. Bower (Ed.), *Recent advances in learning and memory* (Vol. 8, pp. 47–90). New York: Academic Press.

Bahrick, H. P. (1984). Semantic memory content in permastore: Fifty years of memory for Spanish learned in school. *Journal of Experimental Psychology: General, 113,* 1–29.

Baillargeon, R. (1987). Object permanence in 3.5- and 4.5-month-old infants. *Developmental Psychology, 23,* 655–664.

Baillargeon, R. (1993). The object-concept revisited: New directions in the investigation of infants' physical knowledge. In C. E. Granrud (Ed.), *Visual perception and cognition in infancy* (pp. 265–315). Hillsdale, NJ: Erlbaum.

Baillargeon, R. (2002). The acquisition of physical knowledge in infancy: A summary in eight lessons. In U. Goswami (Ed.), *Handbook of childhood cognitive development* (pp. 47–83). Malden, MA: Blackwell.

Baldwin, D. A., & Moses, L. J. (2001). Links between social understanding and early word learning: Challenges to current accounts. *Social Development, 10,* 309–329.

Bandura, A. (1965). Influences of models' reinforcement contingencies on the acquisition of imitative responses. *Journal of Personality and Social Psychology, 1,* 589–593.

Bandura, A. (1973). *Social learning theory.* Englewood Cliffs, NJ: Prentice Hall.

Bandura, A. (1986). *Social functions of thought and action: A social-cognitive theory.* Englewood Cliffs, NJ: Prentice Hall.

Bandura, A. (1997). *Self-efficacy: The exercise of control.* New York: W. H. Freeman.

Bandura, A., Ross, D., & Ross, S. A. (1961). Transmission of aggression through imitation of aggressive models. *Journal of Abnormal and Social Psychology, 63,* 575–582.

Bandura, A., Ross, D., & Ross, S. A. (1963a). Imitation of film-mediated aggressive models. *Journal of Abnormal and Social Psychology, 66,* 3–11.

Bandura, A., Ross, D., & Ross, S. A. (1963b). Vicarious reinforcement and imitative learning. *Journal of Abnormal and Social Psychology, 67,* 601–607.

Bangasser, D. A., Waxler, D. E., Santollo, J., & Shors, T. J. (2006). Trace conditioning and the hippocampus: The importance of contiguity. *The Journal of Neuroscience, 26,* 8702–8706.

Banuazizi, A., & Movahedi, S. (1975). Interpersonal dynamics in a simulated prison: A methodological analysis. *American Psychologist, 30,* 152–160.

Banyard, P. (2007). Tyranny and the tyrant: From Stanford to Abu Ghraib. [Review of the book *The Lucifer effect: Understanding how good people turn evil*, by P. Zimbardo]. *The Psychologist, 20,* 494–495.

Bar, M., & Biederman, I. (1998). Subliminal visual priming. *Psychological Science, 9,* 464–469.

Barber, C. (2008). *Comfortably numb: How psychiatry is medicating a nation.* New York: Pantheon Books.

Bard, P. (1934). On emotional expression after decortication with some remarks on certain theoretical views. *Psychological Review, 41,* 309–329.

Baron-Cohen, S. (2000). Theory of mind and autism: A fifteen year review. In S. Baron-Cohen, H. Tager-Flusberg, & D. J. Cohen (Eds.), *Understanding other minds: Perspectives from developmental cognitive neuroscience* (pp. 3–20). New York: Oxford University Press.

Barres, B. A. (2008). The mystery and magic of glia: A perspective on their roles in health and disease. *Neuron, 60,* 430–440.

Bartels, J. M., Milovich, M. M., & Moussier, S. (2016). Coverage of the Stanford prison experiment in introductory psychology courses: A survey of introductory psychology instructors. *Teaching of Psychology, 43,* 136–141.

Bartlett, F. C. (1932). *Remembering: A study in experimental and social psychology.* Cambridge, UK: Cambridge University Press.

Bartlett, J. C., & Searcy, J. (1993). Inversion and configuration of faces. *Cognitive Psychology, 25,* 281–316.

Bartlett, T. (2014, June 6). The search for psychology's lost boy. *Chronicle of Higher Education, 60,* B6–B10.

Bates, S. C. (2004). Coverage: Findings from a national survey of introductory psychology syllabi. In D. V. Doty (Chair), *What to leave in and out of introductory psychology.* Symposium conducted at the 112th convention of the American Psychological Association, Honolulu, Hawaii.

Baumrind, D. (1964). Some thoughts on ethics of research: After reading Milgram's "Behavioral study of obedience." *American Psychologist, 19,* 421–423.

Baumrind, D. (1971). Current patterns of parental authority. *Developmental Psychology Monograph, 4,* 1–103.

Baumrind, D. (1991). The influence of parenting style on adolescent competence and substance abuse. *Journal of Early Adolescence, 11,* 56–95.

Baumrind, D. (1996). The discipline controversy revisited. *Family Relations, 45,* 405–414.

Baumrind, D. (2015). When subjects become objects: The lies behind the Milgram legend. *Theory & Psychology, 25,* 690–698.

Beck, A. T. (1976). *Cognitive therapy and the emotional disorders.* New York: International Universities Press.

Beck, J. S. (1995). *Cognitive therapy: Basics and beyond* (2nd ed.). New York: Guilford.

Békésy, G. von (1960). *Experiments in hearing.* New York: McGraw-Hill.

Bellisi, M., Pfister-Genskow, M., Maret, S., Keles, S., Tonino, G., & Cirelli, C. (2013). Effects of sleep and wake on oligodentrocytes and their precursors. *Journal of Neuroscience, 33,* 14288–14300.

Belmont, L., & Marolla, F. A. (1973). Birth order, family size and intelligence. *Science, 182,* 1096–1101.

Belsky, J., Vandell, D. L., Burchinal, M., Clarke-Stewart, K. A., McCartney, K., & Tresch Owen, M. (2007). Are there long-term effects of early child care? *Child Development, 78,* 681–701.

Bem, D. J. (1972). Self-perception theory. In L. Berkowitz (Ed.), *Advances in experimental social psychology* (Vol. 6, pp. 1–62). New York: Academic Press.

Benedetti, F. (2014). *Placebo effects* (2nd ed.). New York: Oxford University Press.

Benedetti, F., Lanotte, M., Lopiano, L., & Colloca, L. (2007). When words are painful: Unraveling the mechanisms of the nocebo effect. *Neuroscience, 147,* 260–271.

Ben-Porath, Y. S., & Butcher, J. N. (1989). The comparability of MMPI and MMPI-2 scales and profiles. *Psychological Assessment: A Journal of Consulting and Clinical Psychology, 1,* 345–347.

Berger, K. S. (2006). *The developing person through childhood* (4th ed.). New York: Worth.

Berger, K. S. (2016). *The developing person through childhood* (7th ed.). New York: Worth.

Berns, G. S., Chappelow, J., Zin, C. F., Pagnoni, G., Martin-Skurski, M. E., & Richards, J. (2005). Neurobiological correlates of social conformity and independence during mental rotation. *Biological Psychiatry, 58,* 245–253.

Bertenthal, B. I., Campos, J. J., & Barrett, K. C. (1984). Self-produced locomotion: An organizer of emotional, cognitive, and social development in infancy. In R. N. Emde & R. J. Harmon (Eds.), *Continuities and discontinuities in development* (pp. 175–210). New York: Plenum Press.

Besson, M., Faita, F., Peretz, L., Bonnel, A. M., & Requin, J. (1998). Singing in the brain: Independence of lyrics and tunes. *Psychological Science, 9,* 494–498.

Bigelow, H. J. (1850). Dr. Harlow's case of recovery from the passage of an iron bar through the head. *American Journal of the Medical Sciences, 20,* 13–22.

Binkofski, F., & Buccino, G. (2007, June/July). Therapeutic reflection. *Scientific American MIND, 18,* 78–81.

Birdsong, D., & Molis, M. (2001). On the evidence for maturational constraints in second-language acquisition. *Journal of Memory and Language, 44,* 235–249.

Blake, A. B., Nazarian, M., & Castel, A. D. (2015). The Apple of the mind's eye: Everyday attention, metamemory, and reconstructive memory for the Apple logo. *The Quarterly Journal of Experimental Psychology, 68,* 858–865.

Blakeslee, S. (2005, June 28). What other people say may change what you see. *The New York Times.* Retrieved from www.nytimes.com/2005/06/28 /science/28brai.html

Blakeslee, S., & Blakeslee, M. (2008). *The body has a mind of its own.* New York: Random House.

Blank, H., Musch, J., & Pohl, R. F. (2007). Hindsight bias: On being wise after the event. *Social Cognition, 25,* 1–9.

Blaser, E., & Kaldy, Z. (2010). Infants get five stars on iconic memory tests: A partial report test of 6-month-old infants' iconic memory. *Psychological Science, 21,* 1643–1645.

Blass, T. (1999). The Milgram paradigm after 35 years: Some things we now know about obedience to authority. *Journal of Applied Social Psychology, 29,* 955–978.

Blass, T. (2004). *The man who shocked the world: The life and legacy of Stanley Milgram.* New York: Basic Books.

Blass, T. (2009). From New Haven to Santa Clara: A historical perspective on the Milgram obedience experiments. *American Psychologist, 64,* 37–45.

Blastland, M., & Dilnot, A. (2009). *The numbers game: The commonsense guide to understanding numbers in the news, in politics, and in life.* New York: Gotham Books.

Bogg, T., & Roberts, B. W. (2004). Conscientiousness and health-related behaviors: A meta-analysis of the leading behavioral contributors to mortality. *Psychological Bulletin, 130,* 887–919.

Boldrini, M., Underwood, M. D., Hen, R., Rosoklija, G. B., Dwork, A. J., Mann, J. J., & Arango, V. (2009). Antidepressants increase neural progenitor cells in the human hippocampus. *Neuropsychopharmacology, 34,* 2376–2389.

Bond, C. E., Jr., & Titus, L. J. (1983). Social facilitation: A meta-analysis of 24 studies. *Psychological Bulletin, 94,* 265–292.

Bond, R., & Smith, P. B. (1996). Culture and conformity: A meta-analysis of studies using Asch's (1952b,

1956) line judgment task. *Psychological Bulletin, 119,* 111–137.

Boos, H. B., Cahn, W., van Haren, N. E., Derks, E. M., Brouwer, R. M., Schnack, H. G., . . . Kahn, R. S. (2012). Focal and global brain measurements in siblings of patients with schizophrenia. *Schizophrenia Bulletin, 38,* 814–825.

Borum, R., & Fulero, S. M. (1999). Empirical research on the insanity defense and attempted reforms: Evidence toward informed policy. *Law and Human Behavior, 23,* 375–394.

Botwinick, J. (1961). Husband and father-in-law: A reversible figure. *American Journal of Psychology, 74,* 312–313.

Bouchard, T. J., Jr., & McGue, M. (1981). Familial studies of intelligence: A review. *Science, 212,* 1055–1059.

Bouchard, T. J., Jr., & McGue, M. (2003). Genetic and environmental influences on human psychological differences. *Journal of Neurobiology, 54,* 4–45.

Bouchard, T. J., Jr., Lykken, D. T., McGue, M., Segal, N. L., & Tellegen, A. (1990). Sources of human psychological differences: The Minnesota Study of twins reared apart. *Science, 250,* 223–228.

Bouton, M. E. (1994). Context, ambiguity, and classical conditioning. *Current Directions in Psychological Science, 13,* 148–151.

Bower, J. M., & Parsons, L. M. (2007). Rethinking the "lesser brain." In F. E. Bloom (Ed.), *Best of the brain from Scientific American: Mind, matter, and tomorrow's brain* (pp. 90–101). New York: Dana Press.

Bowlby, J. (1969). *Attachment and loss: Vol. 1. Attachment.* New York: Basic Books.

Boynton, R. M. (1988). Color vision. *Annual Review of Psychology, 39,* 69–100.

Bradley, D. R., Dumais, S. T., & Petry, H. M. (1976). Reply to Cavonius. *Nature, 261,* 78.

Brang, D., & Ramachandran, V. S. (2011). Survival of the synesthesia gene: Why do people hear colors and taste words? *PLoS Biology 9*(11): e1001205. doi:10.1371/ journal.pbio.1001205

Brannigan, A., Nicholson, I., & Cherry, F. (2015). Introduction to the special issue: Unplugging the Milgram machine. In A. Brannigan, F. Cherry, & I. Nicholson (Eds.), Unplugging the Milgram machine [Special issue]. *Theory and Psychology, 25,* 551–563.

Bregman, E. O. (1934). An attempt to modify the emotional attitudes of infants by the conditioned response technique. *Journal of Genetic Psychology, 45,* 169–198.

Breland, K., & Breland, M. (1961). The misbehavior of organisms. *American Psychologist, 16,* 681–684.

Bronfenbrenner, U. (1993). The ecology of cognitive development: Research models and fugitive findings. In R. H. Wozniak & K. W. Fischer (Eds.), *Development in context* (pp. 3–44). Hillsdale, NJ: Erlbaum.

Bronfenbrenner, U., & Mahoney, M. A. (1975). The structure and verification of hypotheses. In U. Bronfenbrenner & M. A. Mahoney (Eds.), *Influences on human development* (2nd ed., pp. 3–39). Hillsdale, IL: Dryden Press.

Brooks, R., & Meltzoff, A. N. (2008). Infant gaze following and pointing predict accelerated vocabulary growth through two years of age: A longitudinal, growth curve modeling study. *Journal of Child Language, 35,* 207–220.

Brown, A. S. (2006). Prenatal infection as a risk factor for schizophrenia. *Schizophrenia Bulletin, 32,* 200–202.

Brown, J. (1958). Some tests of the decay theory of immediate memory. *Quarterly Journal of Experimental Psychology, 10,* 12–21.

Brown, R., & McNeill, D. (1966). The "tip-of-the-tongue" phenomenon. *Journal of Verbal Learning and Verbal Behavior, 5,* 325–337.

Brynie, F. H. (2009). *Brain sense: The science of the senses and how we process the world around us.* New York: AMACOM.

Buchanan, R. W., & Carpenter, W. T. (1997). The neuroanatomies of schizophrenia. *Schizophrenia Bulletin, 23,* 367–372.

Buckley, K. W. (1989). *Mechanical man: John Broadus Watson and the beginning of behaviorism.* New York: Guilford.

Buhs, E., & Ladd, G. (2001). Peer rejection as an antecedent of young children's school adjustment: An examination of mediating processes. *Developmental Psychology, 37,* 550–560.

Buonomano, D. (2011). *Brain bugs: How the brain's flaws shape our lives.* New York: W. W. Norton.

Burger, J. M. (1986). Increasing compliance by improving the deal: The that's-not-all technique. *Journal of Personality and Social Psychology, 51,* 277–283.

Burger, J. M. (2007, December). Replicating Milgram. *APS Observer, 20,* 15–17.

Burger, J. M. (2009). Replicating Milgram: Would people still obey today? *American Psychologist, 64,* 1–11.

Burger, J. M., Girgis, Z. M., & Manning, C. C. (2011). In their own words: Explaining obedience to authority through an examination of participants' comments. *Social Psychological and Personality Science, 2,* 460–466.

Burt, R. K., Balabanov, R., Han, X., Sharrack, B., Morgan, A., Quigley, K., . . . Burman, J. (2015). Association of nonmyeloablative hematopoietic stem cell transplantation with neurological disability in patients with relapsing-remitting multiple schlerosis. *JAMA, 313,* 275–284.

Bushman, B. J., & Huesmann, L. R. (2001). Effects of televised violence on aggression. In D. Singer & J. Singer (Eds.), *Handbook of children and the media* (pp. 223–254). Thousand Oaks, CA: Sage.

Bushman, B. J., & Huesmann, L. R. (2010). Aggression. In S. T. Fiske, D. T. Gilbert, & G. Lindsey (Eds.), *Handbook of social psychology* (5th ed., pp. 833–863). New York: Wiley.

Buss, A. H. (2001). *Psychological dimensions of the self.* Thousand Oaks, CA: Sage.

Butcher, J. N., Dahlstrom, W. G., Graham, J. R., Tellegen, A., & Kaemmer, B. (1989). *Manual for the restandardized Minnesota Multiphasic Personality Inventory: MMPI-2.* Minneapolis, MN: University of Minnesota Press.

Calev, A., Gaudino, E. A., Squires, N. K., Zervas, I. M., & Fink, M. (1995). ECT and non-memory cognition: A review. *British Journal of Clinical Psychology, 34,* 505–515.

Campos, J. J., Anderson, D., Barbu-Roth, M., Hubbard, E., Hertenstein, M., & Witherington, D. (2000). Travel broadens the mind. *Infancy, 1,* 149–219.

Campos, J. J., Bertenthal, B. I., & Kermoian, R. (1992). Early experience and emotional development: The emergence of wariness of heights. *Psychological Science, 3,* 61–64.

Canli, T. (2006). *Biology of personality and individual differences.* New York: Guilford Press.

Cannon, T. D. (1997). On the nature and mechanisms of obstetric influence in schizophrenia: A review and synthesis of epidemiologic studies. *International Review of Psychiatry, 9,* 387–397.

Cannon, W. B. (1927). The James-Lange theory of emotions: A critical examination and an alternative theory. *American Journal of Psychology, 39,* 106–124.

Carnahan, T., & McFarland, S. (2007). Revisiting the Stanford Prison Experiment: Could participants' self-selection have led to the cruelty? *Personality and Social Psychology Bulletin, 33,* 603–614.

Caspi, A., Roberts, B. W., & Shiner, R. L. (2005). Personality development: Stability and change. *Annual Review of Psychology, 56,* 453–484.

Cattaneo, L., & Rizzolatti, G. (2009). The mirror neuron system. *Archives of Neurology, 66,* 557–560.

Cattell, R. B. (1950). *Personality: A systematic, theoretical, and factual study.* New York: McGraw-Hill.

Cattell, R. B. (1965). *The scientific analysis of personality.* Baltimore, MD: Penguin.

Cattell, R. B. (1987). *Intelligence: Its structure, growth and action.* Amsterdam, NL: Elsevier.

Cepeda, N. J., Pashler, H., Vul, E., Wixted, J. T., & Rohrer, D. (2006). Distributed practice in verbal recall tasks: A review and quantitative synthesis. *Psychological Bulletin, 132,* 354–380.

Chapman, G. B., & Bornstein, B. H. (1996). The more you ask for, the more you get: Anchoring in personal injury verdicts. *Applied Cognitive Psychology, 10,* 519–540.

Chapman, L. J. (1967). Illusory correlation in observational report. *Journal of Verbal Learning and Verbal Behavior, 6,* 151–155.

Chapman, L. J., & Chapman, J. P. (1967). Genesis of popular but erroneous psychodiagnostic observations. *Journal of Abnormal Psychology, 72,* 193–204.

Chase, W. G., & Simon, H. A. (1973). Perception in chess. *Cognitive Psychology, 4,* 55–81.

Chi, R. P., & Snyder, A. W. (2011). Facilitate insight by non-invasive brain stimulation. *PLoS ONE 6*(2), e16655. doi:10.1371/journal.pone.0016655

Chi, R. P., & Snyder, A. W. (2012). Brain stimulation enables the solution of an inherently difficult problem. *Neuroscience Letters, 515,* 121–124.

Chomsky, N. (1965). *Aspects of the theory of syntax.* Cambridge, MA: MIT Press.

Churchland, P. S., & Ramachandran, V. S. (1996). Filling in: Why Dennett is wrong. In K. Atkins (Ed.), *Perception* (pp. 132–157). Oxford, England: Oxford University Press.

Cialdini, R. B. (1993). *Influence: Science and practice* (3rd ed.). New York: HarperCollins.

Cialdini, R. B., Cacioppo, J. T., Bassett, R., & Miller, J. A. (1978). Low-ball procedure for producing compliance: Commitment then cost. *Journal of Personality and Social Psychology, 36,* 463–476.

Cialdini, R. B., Vincent, J. E., Lewis, S. K., Catalan, J., Wheeler, D., & Danby, B. L. (1975). Reciprocal concession procedure for inducing compliance: The door-in-the-face technique. *Journal of Personality and Social Psychology, 31,* 206–215.

Clark, R. E., & Squire, L. R. (1998). Classical conditioning and brain systems: The role of awareness. *Science, 280,* 77–91.

Cleary, A. M. (2008). Recognition memory, familiarity, and déjà vu experiences. *Current Directions in Psychological Science, 17,* 353–357.

Cohen, L. B., & Marks, K. S. (2002). How infants process addition and subtraction events. *Developmental Science, 5,* 186–201.

Cohen, N. J., & Eichenbaum, H. (1993). *Memory, amnesia, and the hippocampal system.* Cambridge, MA: MIT Press.

Comer, R. J. (2014). *Fundamentals of abnormal psychology* (7th ed.). New York: Worth.

Corballis, M. C. (2007). The dual-brain myth. In S. Della Sala (Ed.), *Tall tales about the mind and brain: Separating fact from fiction* (pp. 291–314). New York: Oxford University Press.

Cordón, L. A. (2005). *Popular psychology: An encyclopedia.* Westport, CT: Greenwood Press.

Coren, S. (1993). *Sleep thieves: An eye-opening exploration into the science and mysteries of sleep.* New York: Free Press.

Coren, S., Ward, L. M., & Enns, J. T. (2004). *Sensation and perception* (6th ed.). New York: Wiley.

Corina, D. P. (1998). The processing of sign language: Evidence from aphasia. In B. Stemmer & H. A. Whittaker (Eds.), *Handbook of neurolinguistics* (pp. 313–329). San Diego: Academic Press.

Corkin, S. (1968). Acquisition of a motor skill after bilateral medial temporal lobe excision. *Neuropsychologia, 6,* 255–265.

Corkin, S. (1984). Lasting consequences of bilateral and medial temporal lobectomy: Clinical course and experimental findings in H. M. *Seminars in Neurology, 4,* 249–259.

Corkin, S. (2002). What's new with the amnesic patient H. M.? *Nature Reviews Neuroscience, 3,* 153–160.

Corkin, S. (2013). *Permanent present tense: The unforgettable life of the amnesic patient, H. M.* New York: Basic Books.

Corkin, S., Amaral, D., Gonzalez, A., Johnson, K., & Hyman, B. (1997). H. M.'s medial temporal lobe lesion: Findings from magnetic resonance imaging. *Journal of Neuroscience, 17,* 3964–3979.

Costa, P. T., Jr., & McCrae, R. R. (1985). *The NEO Personality Inventory manual.* Odessa, FL: Psychological Assessment Resources.

Costa, P. T., Jr., & McCrae, R. R. (1988). Personality in adulthood: A six-year longitudinal study of self-reports and spouse ratings on the NEO Personality Inventory. *Journal of Personality and Social Psychology, 54,* 853–863.

Costa, P. T., Jr., & McCrae, R. R. (1992). *Revised NEO Personality Inventory (NEO PI) and NEO Five Factor Inventory (NEO FFI) professional manual.* Odessa, FL: Psychological Assessment Resources.

Costa, P. T., Jr., & McCrae, R. R. (1993). Bullish on personality psychology. *The Psychologist, 6,* 302–303.

Costa, P. T., Jr., & McCrae, R. R. (2008). The NEO inventories. In R. P. Archer & S. R. Smith (Eds.). *Personality assessment* (pp. 213–246). New York: Routledge.

Cowey, A. (2010). The blindsight saga. *Experimental Brain Research, 200,* 3–24.

Craik, F. I. M., & Lockhart, R. S. (1972). Levels of processing: A framework for memory research. *Journal of Verbal Learning and Verbal Behavior, 11,* 671–684.

Craik, F. I. M., & Tulving, E. (1975). Depth of processing and the retention of words in episodic memory. *Journal of Experimental Psychology: General, 104,* 268–294.

Crow, T. J. (1985). The two-syndrome concept: Origins and current status. *Schizophrenia Bulletin, 11,* 471–485.

Damasio, A. R., Grabowski, T. J., Bechara, A., Damasio, H., Ponto, L., Parvizi, J., & Hichma, R. D. (2000). Subcortical and cortical brain activity during the feeling of self-generated emotions. *Nature Neuroscience, 3,* 1049–1056.

Dapretto, M., Davies, M. S., Pfeifer, J. H., Scott, A. A., Sigman, M., Bookheimer, S. Y., & Iacoboni, M. (2006). Understanding emotions in others: Mirror neuron dysfunction in children with autism spectrum disorders. *Nature Neuroscience, 9,* 28–30.

Darley, J. M., & Latané, B. (1968). Bystander intervention in emergencies: Diffusion of responsibility. *Journal of Personality and Social Psychology, 8,* 377–383.

Darwin, C. J., Turvey, M. T., & Crowder, R. G. (1972). An auditory analogue of the Sperling partial-report procedure. *Cognitive Psychology, 3,* 255–267.

Dasen, P. R. (1994). Culture and cognitive development from a Piagetian perspective. In W. J. Lonner & R. S. Malpass (Eds.), *Psychology and culture* (pp. 145–149). Needham Heights, MA: Allyn & Bacon.

Davey, G. C. L. (1995). Classical conditioning and the acquisition of human fears and phobias: A review and synthesis of the literature. *Advances in Behavior Research and Therapy, 14,* 29–66.

Davis, J. O., & Phelps, J. A. (1995). Twins with schizophrenia: Genes or germs? *Schizophrenia Bulletin, 21,* 13–18.

Davis, K. L., Kahn, R. S., Ko, G., & Davidson, M. (1991). Dopamine in schizophrenia: A review and reconceptualization. *American Journal of Psychiatry, 148,* 1474–1486.

Dawes, R. M. (1994). *House of cards: Psychology and psychotherapy built on myth.* New York: Free Press.

Dawson, E., Gilovich, T., & Regan, D. T. (2002). Motivated reasoning and performance on the Wason selection task. *Personality and Social Psychology Bulletin, 28,* 1379–1387.

Dazzan, P., Morgan, K. D., Orr, K., Hutchinson, G., Chitnis, X., Suckling, J., . . . Murray, R. M. (2005). Different effects of typical and atypical antipsychotics on grey matter in first episode psychosis: The Aesop study. *Neuropsychopharmacology, 30,* 765–774.

DeCasper, A. J., & Fifer, W. P. (1980). Of human bonding: Newborns prefer their mothers' voices. *Science, 208,* 1174–1176.

DeCasper, A. J., & Spence, M. J. (1986). Prenatal maternal speech influences newborns' perception of speech sounds. *Infant Behavior and Development, 9,* 133–150.

Deci, E. L., Koestner, R., & Ryan, R. M. (1999). A meta-analytic review of experiments examining the effect of extrinsic rewards on intrinsic motivation. *Psychological Bulletin, 125,* 637–668.

Dehaene, S. (2014). *Consciousness and the brain: Deciphering how the brain codes our thoughts.* New York: Viking.

DeLeon, A., Patel, N. C., & Crismon, M. L. (2004). Aripiprazole: A comprehensive review of its pharmacology, clinical efficacy, and tolerability. *Clinical Therapeutics, 26,* 649–666.

Delis, D. C., Robertson, L. C., & Efron, R. (1986). Hemispheric specialization of memory for visual hierarchical stimuli. *Neuropsychologica, 24,* 205–214.

DeLisi, L. E. (1997). The genetics of schizophrenia. *Schizophrenia Research, 28,* 163–175.

Dement, W. C. (1999). *The promise of sleep.* New York: Delacorte Press.

DeRubeis, R. J., Hollon, S., Amsterdam, J., Shelton, R., Young, P., Salomon, R., . . . Gallop, R. (2005). Cognitive therapy vs medications in the treatment of moderate to severe depression. *Archives of General Psychiatry, 62,* 409–416.

DeValois, R. L., & DeValois, K. K. (1975). Neural coding of color. In E. C. Carterette & M. P. Friedman (Eds.), *Handbook of perception* (Vol. 5, pp. 117–166). New York: Academic Press.

DeYoung, C. G., Hirsh, J. B., Shane, M. S., Papadermetris, X., Rajeevan, N., & Gray, J. R. (2010). Testing predictions from personality neuroscience: Brain structure and the Big Five. *Psychological Science, 2,* 820–828.

Dhindsa, R. S., & Goldstein, D. B. (2016, January 27). Schizophrenia: From genetics to physiology at last. *Nature.* Advance online publication. doi:10.1038/nature/6874

Diamond, M. C., Scheibel, A. B., Murphy, G. M., & Harvey, T. (1985). On the brain of a scientist: Albert Einstein. *Experimental Neurology, 88,* 198–204.

Digman, J. M. (1990). Personality structure: Emergence of the five-factor model. *Annual Review of Psychology, 41,* 417–440.

Dinberg, U., & Thunberg, M. (1998). Rapid facial reactions to emotional facial expressions. *Psychological Science, 11,* 86–89.

Dirix, C. E. H., Nijhuis, J. G., Jongsma, H. W., & Hornstra, G. (2009). Aspects of fetal learning and memory. *Child Development, 80,* 1251–1258.

Dodds, D. (2006, April 2). A depression switch? *New York Times Magazine.* Retrieved from www .nytimes.com/2006/04/02/magazine/02depression .html?pagewanted=all

Domhoff, G. W. (1996). *Finding meaning in dreams: A quantitative approach.* New York: Plenum.

Domhoff, G. W. (2003). *The scientific study of dreams: Neural networks, cognitive development, and content analysis.* Washington, DC: American Psychological Association.

Domhoff, G. W. (2011). The neural substrate for dreaming: Is it a subsystem of the default network? *Consciousness and Cognition, 20,* 1163–1174.

Dougherty, R. F., Koch, V. M., Brewer, A. A., Fischer, B., Modersitzki, J., & Wandell, B. A. (2003). Visual field representations and locations of visual areas V1/2/3 in human visual cortex. *Journal of Vision, 3,* 586–598.

Dowling, J. E. (1998). *Creating mind: How the brain works.* New York: Norton.

Druckman, D., & Swets, J. A. (1988). *Enhancing human performance: Issues, theories, and techniques.* Washington, DC: National Academy Press.

DuBosar, R. (2009, November). Psychotropic drug prescriptions by medical specialty. *ACP Internist.* Retrieved from www.acpinternist.org /archives/2009/11/national-trends.htm

DuJardin, J., Guerrien, A., & LeConte, P. (1990). Sleep, brain activation, and cognition. *Physiology and Behavior, 47,* 1271–1278.

Duncker, K. (1945). On problem solving. *Psychological Monographs, 58* (Whole No. 270).

Dyk, P. H., & Adams, G. R. (1990). Identity and intimacy: An initial investigation of three theoretical models using cross-lag panel correlations. *Journal of Youth and Adolescence, 19,* 91–100.

Eagleman, D. (2011). *Incognito: The secret lives of the brain.* New York: Pantheon Books.

Eagly, A. H., & Carli, L. L. (1981). Sex of researchers and sex-typed communication as determinants of sex differences in influenceability: A meta-analysis of social influence studies. *Psychological Bulletin, 90,* 1–20.

Ebbinghaus, H. (1964). *Memory: A contribution to experimental psychology* (H. A. Ruger & C. E. Bussenius, Trans.). New York: Dover. (Original work published 1885)

Eddy, D. M. (1982). Probabilistic reasoning in clinical medicine: Problems and opportunities. In D. Kahneman, P. Slovic, & A. Tversky (Eds.), *Judgment under uncertainty: Heuristics and biases* (pp. 249–267). Cambridge: Cambridge University Press.

Egan, L. C., Santos, L. R., & Bloom, P. (2007). The origins of cognitive dissonance: Evidence from children and monkeys. *Psychological Science, 18,* 978–983.

Eggers, A. E. (2014). Treatment of depression with deep brain stimulation works by altering in specific ways the conscious perception of the core symptoms of sadness or anhedonia, not by modulating network circuitry. *Medical Hypotheses, 83,* 62–64.

Eich, E. (1995). Searching for mood dependent memory. *Psychological Science, 6,* 67–75.

Eisenberger, R., & Cameron, J. (1996). Detrimental effects of rewards: Reality or myth? *American Psychologist, 51,* 1153–1166.

Ekstrom, A. D., Kahana, M. J., Caplan, J. B., Fields, T. A., Isham, E. A., Newman, E. L., & Fried, I. (2003). Cellular networks underlying human spatial navigation. *Nature, 425,* 184–188.

El-Hai, J. (2001, February). The lobotomist. *Washington Post Magazine, 124*(55), 16–20, 30–31.

El-Hai, J. (2005). *The lobotomist: A maverick medical genius and his tragic quest to rid the world of mental illness.* Hoboken, NJ: John Wiley & Sons, Inc.

Ellis, A. (1962). *Reason and emotion in psychotherapy.* New York: Lyle Stuart.

Ellis, A. (1993). Reflections on rational-emotive therapy. *Journal of Counseling and Clinical Psychology, 61,* 199–201.

Ellis, A. (1995). Rational emotive behavior therapy. In R. J. Corsini & D. Wedding (Eds.), *Current psychotherapies* (5th ed., pp. 162–196). Itasca, IL: Peacock.

Elman, J. L., Bates, E. A., Johnson, M., Karmiloff-Smith, A., Paisi, D., & Plunkett, K. (1996). *Rethinking innateness: A connectionist perspective on development.* Cambridge, MA: MIT Press.

Engel, S. A. (1999). Using neuroimaging to measure mental representations: Finding color-opponent neurons in visual cortex. *Current Directions in Psychological Science, 8,* 23–27.

Engle, R. W. (2002). Working memory capacity as executive attention. *Current Directions in Psychological Science, 11,* 19–23.

Epstein, S. (1979). The stability of behavior. I. On predicting most of the people much of the time. *Journal of Personality and Social Psychology, 37,* 1097–1126.

Erel, O., Oberman, Y., & Yirmiya, N. (2000). Maternal versus nonmaternal care and seven domains of children's development. *Psychological Bulletin, 126,* 727–747.

Eriksen, C. W., & Collins, J. F. (1967). Some temporal characteristics of visual pattern recognition. *Journal of Experimental Psychology, 74,* 476–484.

Erikson, E. H. (1950). *Childhood and society.* New York: Norton.

Erikson, E. H. (1963). *Childhood and society* (2nd ed.). New York: Norton.

Erikson, E. H. (1968). *Identity: Youth and crisis.* New York: Norton.

Erikson, E. H. (1980). *Identity and the life cycle.* New York: Norton.

Eriksson, P. S., Perfilieva, E., Björk-Eriksson, T., Alborn, A., Nordborg, C., Peterson, D. A., & Gage, F. H. (1998). Neurogenesis in the adult human hippocampus. *Nature Medicine, 4,* 1313–1317.

Ertelt, D., Small, S., Solodkin, A., Dettmers, C., McNamara, A., Binofski, F., & Buccino, G. (2007), Action observation has a positive impact on rehabilitation of motor deficits after stroke. *NeuroImage, 36,* 164–173.

Esser, J. K., & Lindoerfer, J. S. (1989). Groupthink and the space shuttle *Challenger* accident: Toward a quantitative case analysis. *Journal of Behavioral Decision Making, 2,* 167–177.

Etscorn, E., & Stephens, R. (1973). Establishment of conditioned taste aversions with a 24-hour CS-US interval. *Physiological Psychology, 1,* 251–253.

Evans, J. St B. T. (2008). Dual-processing accounts of reasoning, judgment, and social cognition. *Annual Review of Psychology, 59,* 255–278.

Evans, J. St B. T. (2010). *Thinking twice: Two minds in one brain.* New York: Oxford University Press.

Eysenck, H. J. (1982). *Personality, genetics, and behavior.* New York: Praeger.

Eysenck, H. J. (1990). Biological dimensions of personality. In L. A. Pervin (Ed.), *Handbook of personality: Theory and research* (pp. 244–276). New York: Guilford Press.

Eysenck, H. J. (1997). Personality and experimental psychology: The unification of psychology and the possibility of a paradigm. *Journal of Personality and Social Psychology, 73,* 1224–1237.

Eysenck, H. J., & Eysenck, M. W. (1985). *Personality and individual differences.* New York: Plenum.

Falk, D., Lepore, F. E., & Noe, A. (2013). The cerebral cortex of Albert Einstein: A description and preliminary analysis of unpublished photographs. *Brain, 136,* 1304–1327. doi:10.1093/brain/aws295

Fancher, R. E. (1985). *The intelligence men: Makers of the IQ controversy.* New York: Norton.

Fantz, R. L. (1961, May). The origin of form perception. *Scientific American, 204,* 66–72.

Fantz, R. L. (1963). Pattern vision in newborn infants. *Science, 140,* 296–297.

Fenigstein, A. (2015). Milgram's shock experiments and the Nazi perpetrators: A contrarian perspective on the role of obedience pressures during the Holocaust. In A. Brannigan, F. Cherry, & I. Nicholson (Eds.), Unplugging the Milgram machine [Special issue]. *Theory and Psychology, 25,* 581–598.

Ferguson, C. J., & Kilburn, J. (2009). The public health risks of media violence: A meta-analytic review. *Journal of Pediatrics, 154,* 759–763.

Ferguson, C. J., & Kilburn, J. (2010). Much ado about nothing: The misestimation and overinterpretation of violent video game effects in Eastern and Western nations: Comment on Anderson et al. (2010). *Psychological Bulletin, 136,* 174–178.

Fernald, A. (1993). Approval and disapproval: Infant responsiveness to vocal affect in familiar and unfamiliar languages. *Child Development, 64,* 657–674.

Festinger, L. (1957). *A theory of cognitive dissonance.* Stanford, CA: Stanford University Press.

Festinger, L., & Carlsmith, J. M. (1959). Cognitive consequences of forced compliance. *Journal of Abnormal and Social Psychology, 38,* 203–210.

Field, T. M., Cohen, D., Garcia, R., & Greenberg, R. (1984). Mother-stranger face discrimination by the newborn. *Infant Behavior and Development, 7,* 19–25.

Fields, R. D. (2009). *The other brain: From dementia to schizophrenia, how new discoveries about the brain are revolutionizing medicine and science.* New York: Simon & Schuster.

Fields, R. D. (2011, May/June). The hidden brain. *Scientific American MIND, 22,* 52–59.

Fineman, M. (1996). *The nature of visual illusion.* Mineola, NY: Dover Publications.

Fink, G. R., Halligan, P. W., Marshall, J. C., Frith, C. D., Frackowiak, R. S. J., & Dolan, R. J. (1996). Where in the brain does visual attention select the forest and the trees? *Nature, 382,* 626–628.

Finkelstein, A., Derdikman, D., Rubin, A., Foerster, J. N., Las, L., & Ulanovsky, N. (2014). Three-dimensional head-direction coding in the bat brain. *Nature, 517,* 159–164.

Finzi, E., & Rosenthal, N. E. (2014). Treatment of depression with onabotulinumtoxinA: A randomized, double-blind, placebo controlled trial. *Journal of Psychiatric Research, 52,* 1–6.

Fleischman, J. (2002). *Phineas Gage: A gruesome but true story about brain science.* Boston: Houghton Mifflin.

Flynn, J. R. (1987). Massive IQ gains in 14 nations: What IQ tests really measure. *Psychological Bulletin, 101,* 171–191.

Flynn, J. R. (1999). Searching for justice: The discovery of IQ gains over time. *American Psychologist, 54,* 5–20.

Flynn, J. R. (2007). *What is intelligence?: Beyond the Flynn effect.* New York: Cambridge University Press.

Flynn, J. R. (2012). *Are we getting smarter? Rising IQ in the twenty-first century.* New York: Cambridge University Press.

Foer, J. (2011). *Moonwalking with Einstein: The art and science of remembering everything.* New York: Penguin Press.

Folsom, D. P., Fleisher, A. S., & Depp, C. A. (2006). Schizophrenia. In D. V. Jeste & J. H. Friedman (Eds.), *Psychiatry for neurologists* (pp. 59–66). Totowa, NJ: Humana Press.

Fossey, D. (1983). *Gorillas in the mist.* Boston: Houghton Mifflin.

Foster, M. (1897). *A textbook of physiology, Part III* (7th ed.). New York: The Macmillan Company.

Fournier, J. C., DeRubeis, R. J., Hollon, S. D., Dimidjian, S., Amsterdam, J. D., Shelton, R. C., & Fawcett, J. (2010). Antidepressant drug effects and depression severity: A patient-level meta-analysis. *JAMA, 303,* 47–53.

Fowles, D. C. (1992). Schizophrenia: Diathesis-stress revisited. *Annual Review of Psychology, 43,* 303–336.

Frances, A. (2013). *Saving normal: An insider's revolt against out-of-control psychiatric diagnosis, DSM-5, big pharma, and the medicalization of ordinary life.* New York: HarperCollins.

Freedman, J. L., & Fraser, S. C. (1966). Compliance without pressure: The foot-in-the-door technique. *Journal of Personality and Social Psychology, 4,* 195–202.

Freedman, R., Lewis, D. A., Michels, R., Pine, D. S., Schultz, S. K., Tamminga, C. A., . . . Yager, J. (2013). The initial field trials of DSM-5: New blooms and old thorns. *American Journal of Psychiatry, 170,* 1-5.

Frenda, S. J., Nichols, R. M., & Loftus, E. F. (2011). Current issues and advances in misinformation research. *Current Directions in Psychological Science, 20,* 20-23.

Freud, A. (1936). *The ego and the mechanisms of defense* (C. Baines, Trans.). New York: International Universities Press.

Freud, S. (1953a). The interpretation of dreams. In J. Strachey (Ed. & Trans.), *The standard edition of the complete psychological works of Sigmund Freud* (Vols. 4 & 5). London, England: Hogarth. (Original work published 1900)

Freud, S. (1953b). Three essays on sexuality. In J. Strachey (Ed. & Trans.), *The standard edition of the complete psychological works of Sigmund Freud* (Vol. 7). London, England: Hogarth. (Original work published 1905)

Freud, S. (1960). Psychopathology of everyday life. In J. Strachey (Ed. & Trans.), *The standard edition of the complete psychological works of Sigmund Freud* (Vol. 6). London, England: Hogarth. (Original work published 1901)

Freud, S. (1963). Introductory lectures on psychoanalysis. In J. Strachey (Ed. & Trans.), *The standard edition of the complete psychological works of Sigmund Freud* (Vols. 15 & 16). London, England: Hogarth. (Original work published 1916 & 1917)

Freud, S. (1964). New introductory lectures on psycho-analysis. In J. Strachey (Ed. & Trans.), *The standard edition of the complete psychological works of Sigmund Freud* (Vol. 22). London, England: Hogarth. (Original work published 1933)

Friend, R., Rafferty, Y., & Bramel, D. (1990). A puzzling misinterpretation of the Asch "conformity" study. *European Journal of Social Psychology, 20,* 29-44.

Frith, U. (2003). *Autism: Explaining the enigma* (2nd ed.). New York: Wiley-Blackwell.

Fromkin, V., Krasjen, S., Curtiss, S., Rigler, D., & Rigler, M. (1974). The development of language in Genie: A case of language acquisition beyond the "critical period." *Brain & Language, 1,* 81-107.

Funder, D. C. (2001). Personality. *Annual Review of Psychology, 52,* 197-221.

Furman, W., & Biermam, K. L. (1984). Children's conceptions of friendship: A multi-method study of developmental changes. *Developmental Psychology, 20,* 925-931.

Fyhn, M., Molden, S., Witter, M. P., Moser, E. I., & Moser, M. B. (2004) Spatial representation in the entorhinal cortex. *Science, 305,* 1258-1264.

Gabrieli, J. D. E., Corkin, S., Mickel, S. F., & Growdon, J. H. (1993). Intact acquisition and long-term retention of mirror-tracing skill in Alzheimer's disease and in global amnesia. *Behavioral Neuroscience, 107,* 899-910.

Gabrieli, J. D. E., Keane, M. M., & Corkin, S. (1987). Acquisition of problem-solving skills in global amnesia. *Society for Neuroscience Abstracts, 12,* 1455.

Gage, F. H. (2003, September). Brain, repair yourself. *Scientific American, 289,* 46-53.

Galak, J., LeBoeuf, R. A., Nelson, L. D., & Simmons, J. P. (2012). Correcting the past: Failures to replicate psi. *Journal of Personality and Social Psychology, 103,* 933-948.

Galanter, E. (1962). Contemporary psychophysics. In R. Brown, E. Galanter, E. H. Hess, & G. Mandler (Eds.), *New directions in psychology* (Vol. 1, pp. 87-156). New York: Holt, Rinehart, & Winston.

Gallese, V., Gernsbacher, M. A., Heyes, C., Hickok, G., & Iacoboni, M. (2011). Mirror neuron forum. *Perspectives on Psychological Science, 6,* 369-407.

Gamwell, L., & Tomes, N. (1995). *Madness in America: Cultural and medicinal perceptions of mental illness before 1914.* Ithaca, NY: Cornell University Press.

Gansberg, M. (1964, March 27). 37 who saw murder didn't call the police: Apathy at stabbing of Queens woman shocks inspector. *The New York Times,* p. 1.

Garb, H. N. (1999). Call for a moratorium on the use of the Rorschach inkblot test in clinical and forensic settings. *Assessment, 6,* 313-315.

Garb, H. N., Florio, C. M., & Grove, W. M. (1998). The validity of the Rorschach and the Minnesota Multiphasic Personality Inventory: Results from meta-analyses. *Psychological Science, 9,* 402-404.

Garcia, J. (2003). Psychology is not an enclave. In R. J. Sternberg (Ed.), *Defying the crowd: Stories of those who battled the establishment and won* (pp. 67-77). Washington, DC: American Psychological Association.

Garcia, J., Kimeldorf, D. J., Hunt, E. L., & Davies, B. P. (1956). Food and water consumption of rats during exposure to gamma radiation. *Radiation Research, 4,* 33–41.

Garcia, J., & Koelling, R. A. (1966). Relation of cue to consequence in avoidance learning. *Psychonomic Science, 4,* 123–124.

Gardner, H. (1983). *Frames of mind: The theory of multiple intelligences.* New York: Basic Books.

Gardner, H. (1993). *Multiple intelligences: The theory in practice.* New York: Basic Books.

Gardner, H. (1999). *Intelligence reframed.* New York: Basic Books.

Gardner, H., Kornhaber, M. L., & Wake, W. K. (1996). *Intelligence: Multiple perspectives.* Fort Worth, TX: Harcourt.

Garry, M., Manning, C. G., Loftus, E. F., & Sherman, S. J. (1996). Imagination inflation: Imagining a childhood event inflates confidence that it occurred. *Psychonomic Bulletin & Review, 3,* 208–214.

Gazzaniga, M. S. (1992). *Nature's mind.* New York: Basic Books.

Gazzaniga, M. S. (2005). Forty-five years of split-brain research and still going strong. *Nature Reviews Neuroscience, 6,* 653–659.

Gazzaniga, M. S. (2008). *Human: The science behind what makes us unique.* New York: HarperCollins.

Gazzaniga, M. S. (2015). *Tales from both sides of the brain: A life in neuroscience.* New York: HarperCollins.

Gazzaniga, M. S., Bogen, J. E., & Sperry, R. W. (1962). Some functional effects of sectioning the cerebral commissures in man. *PNAS, 48,* 1765–1769.

Gazzaniga, M. S., Fendrich, R., & Wesainger, C. M. (1994). Blind-sight reconsidered. *Current Directions in Psychological Science, 3,* 93–95.

Gazzaniga, M. S., Ivry, R. B., & Mangun, G. R. (2002). *Cognitive neuroscience: The biology of the mind* (2nd ed.). New York: Norton.

Geen, R. G. (1997). Psychophysiological approaches to personality. In R. Hogan, J. Johnson, & S. Briggs (Eds.), *Handbook of personality psychology* (pp. 387–414). San Diego, CA: Academic Press.

Gegenfurtner, K. R., & Kiper, D. C. (2003). Color vision. *Annual Review of Neuroscience, 26,* 181–206.

Gescheider, G. A. (1976). *Psychophysics: Method and theory.* Hillsdale, NJ: Erlbaum.

Ghim, H. (1990). Evidence for perceptual organization in infants: Perception of subjective contours by young infants. *Infant Behavior and Development, 13,* 221–248.

Gibson, E. J., & Walk, R. D. (1960, April). The "visual cliff." *Scientific American, 202,* 80–92.

Gibson, S. (2013). Milgram's obedience experiments: A rhetorical analysis. *British Journal of Social Psychology, 52,* 290–309.

Gigerenzer, G. (2002). *Calculated risks: How to know when numbers deceive you.* New York: Simon & Schuster.

Gigerenzer, G. (2004). Dread risk, September 11, and fatal traffic accidents. *Psychological Science, 15,* 286–287.

Gigerenzer, G. (2006). Out of the frying pan into the fire: Behavioral reactions to terrorist attacks. *Risk Analysis, 26,* 347–351.

Gigerenzer, G., & Edwards, A. G. K. (2003). Simple tools for understanding risk: From innumeracy to insight. *British Medical Journal, 307,* 741–744.

Gigerenzer, G., Gaissmaier, W., Kurz-Milcke, E., Schwartz, L. M., & Woloshin, S. (2007). Helping doctors and patients make sense of health statistics. *Psychological Science in the Public Interest, 8,* 53–96.

Gigerenzer, G., & Hoffrage, U. (1995). How to improve Bayesian reasoning without instruction: Frequency formats. *Psychological Review, 102,* 684–704.

Gilbert, D. T., King, K. G., Pettigrew, S., & Wilson, T. (2016). Comment on "Estimating the reproducibility of psychological science." *Science, 351,* 1037.

Gilbert, S. J. (1981). Another look at the Milgram obedience studies: The role of the gradated series of shocks. *Personality and Social Psychology Bulletin, 7,* 690–695.

Gilchrist, A. (2015). Perception and the social psychology of "The Dress." *Perception, 44,* 229–231. doi:10.1068/p4403ed

Gilhooly, K. J. (1996). *Thinking: Directed, undirected and creative* (3rd ed.). London, England: Academic Press.

Gilligan, T. (2009). The new data on prostate cancer screening: What should we do now? *Cleveland Clinic Journal of Medicine, 76,* 446–448.

Gilovich, T. (1991). *How we know what isn't so: The fallibility of human reason in everyday life.* New York: Free Press.

Glanzer, M., & Cunitz, A. R. (1966). Two storage mechanisms in free recall. *Journal of Verbal Learning and Verbal Behavior, 5,* 351–360.

Glass, R. M. (2001). Electroconvulsive therapy: Time to bring it out of the shadows. *JAMA, 285,* 1346–1348.

Gluck, M. A., Mercado, E., & Myers, C. E. (2011). *Learning and memory: From brain to behavior* (2nd ed.). New York: Worth.

Glucksberg, S., & Cowen, G. N., Jr. (1970). Memory for nonattended auditory material. *Cognitive Psychology, 1,* 149–156.

Godden, D. R., & Baddeley, A. D. (1975). Context-dependent memory in two natural environments: On land and underwater. *British Journal of Psychology, 66,* 325–331.

Goel, V., & Grafman, J. (1995). Are the frontal lobes implicated in "planning" functions? Interpreting data from the Tower of Hanoi. *Neuropsychologica, 33,* 623–642.

Goff, D. C., & Coyle, J. T. (2001). The emerging role of glutamate in the pathophysiology and treatment of schizophrenia. *American Journal of Psychiatry, 158,* 1367–1377.

Goff, L. M., & Roediger, H. L., III. (1998). Imagination inflation for action events: Repeated imaginings lead to illusory recollections. *Memory & Cognition, 26,* 20–33.

Goldberg, L. R. (1990). An alternative "description of personality": The big-five factor structure. *Journal of Social and Personality Psychology, 59,* 1216–1229.

Goldstein, E. B. (2007). *Sensation and perception* (7th ed.). Belmont, CA: Thomson Wadsworth.

Golinkoff, R. M., & Hirsch-Pasek, K. (2006). Baby wordsmith: From associationist to social sophisticate. *Current Directions in Psychological Science, 15,* 30–33.

Gonsalves, B., Reber, P. J., Gitelman, D. R., Parrish, T. B., Mesulam, M.-M, & Paller, K. A. (2004). Neural evidence that vivid imagining can lead to false remembering. *Psychological Science, 15,* 655–659.

Goodall, J. (1986). *The chimpanzees of Gombe: Patterns of behavior.* Boston: Belknap Press of Harvard University Press.

Goodman, J. A., Krahn, L. E., Smith, G. E., Rummans, T. A., & Pileggi, T. S. (1999, October). Patient satisfaction with electroconvulsive therapy. *Mayo Clinic Proceedings, 74,* 967–971.

Gottesman, I. I. (1991). *Schizophrenia genesis.* New York: W. H. Freeman.

Gottfredson, L. S. (1997). Mainstream science on intelligence: An editorial with 52 signatories, history, and bibliography. *Intelligence, 24,* 13–23.

Gottfredson, L. S. (2002a). Where and why g matters: Not a mystery. *Human Performance, 15,* 25–46.

Gottfredson, L. S. (2002b). g: Highly general and highly practiced. In R. J. Sternberg & E. L. Grigorenko (Eds.), *The general factor of intelligence: How general is it?* (pp. 331–380). Mahwah, NJ: Erlbaum.

Gottfredson, L. S. (2009). Logical fallacies used to dismiss evidence on intelligence testing. In R. Phelps (Ed.). *Correcting fallacies about educational and psychological testing* (pp. 11–65). Washington, DC: American Psychological Association.

Gould, S. J. (1985, June). The median isn't the message. *Discover, 6,* 40–42.

Graf, P., Squire, L. R., & Mandler, G. (1984). The information that amnesic patients do not forget. *Journal of Experimental Psychology: Learning, Memory, and Cognition, 10,* 164–178.

Gray, P. (2013, October 18). Why Zimbardo's prison experiment isn't in my textbook [Web log comment]. Retrieved from www.psychologytoday.com/blog /freedom-learn/201310/why-zimbardo-s-prison -experiment-isn-t-in-my-textbook

Graziano, W. G., Habashi, M. M., Sheese, B. E., & Tobin, R. M. (2007). Agreeableness, empathy, and helping: A person x situation perspective. *Journal of Personality and Social Psychology, 93,* 583–599.

Green, D. M., & Swets, J. A. (1966). *Signal detection theory and psychophysics.* New York: Wiley.

Green, J. T., & Woodruff-Pak, D. S. (2000). Eyeblink classical conditioning: Hippocampal formation is for neutral stimulus associations as cerebellum is for asso-ciation-response. *Psychological Bulletin, 126,* 138–158.

Greenberg, G. (2013). *The book of woe and the unmaking of psychiatry.* New York: Penguin.

Greenberg, J., Schmader, T., Arndt, J., & Landau, M. (2015). *Social psychology: The science of everyday life.* New York: Worth.

Greenough, W. T., Black, J. E., & Wallace, C. S. (1987). Experience and brain development. *Child Development, 58,* 539–559.

Greenwald, A. G., Draine, S. C., & Abrams, R. L. (1996). Three cognitive markers of unconscious semantic activation. *Science, 273,* 1699–1702.

Greenwald, A. G., Klinger, M. R., & Schuh, E. S. (1995). Activation by marginally perceptible ("subliminal") stimuli: Dissociation of unconscious from conscious cognition. *Journal of Experimental Psychology: General, 124,* 22–42.

Greenwald, A. G., Spangenberg, E. R., Pratkanis, A. R., & Eskenazi, J. (1991). Double-blind tests of subliminal self-help audiotapes. *Psychological Science, 2,* 119–122.

Gregory, R. L. (1968, November). Visual illusions. *Scientific American, 219,* 66–76.

Gregory, R. L. (1970). *The intelligent eye.* New York: McGraw-Hill.

Gregory, R. L. (2009). *Seeing through illusions.* New York: Oxford University Press.

Greuter, T. (2007, August/September). Forgetting faces. *Scientific American MIND, 18,* 68–73.

Griggs, R. A. (2003). Helping students gain insight into mental set. *Teaching of Psychology, 30,* 143–145.

Griggs, R. A. (2015). Psychology's lost boy: Will the real Little Albert please stand up? *Teaching of Psychology, 42,* 14–18.

Griggs, R. A., & Cox, J. R. (1982). The elusive thematic materials effect in Wason's selection task. *British Journal of Psychology, 73,* 407–420.

Grimes, T., Anderson, J. A., & Bergen, L. (2008). *Media violence and aggression: Science and ideology.* Thousand Oaks, CA: Sage.

Grossman, R. P., & Till, B. D. (1998). The persistence of classically conditioned brand attitudes. *Journal of Advertising, 27,* 23–31.

Gruneberg, M. M., & Herrmann, D. J. (1997). *Your memory for life.* London: Blanford.

Grunhaus, L., Schreiber, S., Dolberg, O. T., Polak, D., & Dannon, P. N. (2003). A randomized controlled comparison of electroconvulsive therapy and repetitive transcranial magnetic stimulation in severe and resistant nonpsychotic major depression. *Biological Psychiatry, 53,* 324–331.

Guerra, N. G., Huesmann, L. R., & Spindler, A. (2003). Community violence exposure, social cognition, and aggression among urban elementary school children. *Child Development, 74,* 1561–1576.

Gurung, R. A. R., Hackathorn, J., Enns, C., Frantz, S., Cacioppo, J. T., & Freeman, J. E. (2016). Strengthening introductory psychology: A new model for teaching the introductory course. *American Psychologist, 71,* 112–124.

Hadjikhani, N., & de Gelder, B. (2002). Neural basis of prosopagnosia: An fMRI study. *Human Brain Mapping, 16,* 176–182.

Hafting, T., Fyhn, M., Molden, S., Moser, M. B., & Moser, E. I. (2005). Microstructure of spatial map in the entorhinal cortex. *Nature, 436,* 801–806.

Hagemann, D., Hewig, J., Walker, C., Schankin, A., Danner, D., & Naumann, E. (2009). Positive evidence for Eysenck's arousal hypothesis: A combined EEG and MRI study with multiple measurement occasions. *Personality and Individual Differences, 47,* 717–721.

Hallinan, J. T. (2009). *Why we make mistakes: How we look without seeing, forget things in seconds, and are all pretty sure we are above average.* New York: Broadway Books.

Hamilton, A. (2013). Reflecting on the mirror neuron system in autism: A systematic review of current theories. *Developmental Cognitive Neuroscience, 3,* 91–105.

Haney, C., Banks, C., & Zimbardo, P. (1973). A study of prisoners and guards in a simulated prison. *Naval Research Reviews, 9,* 1–17. Washington, DC: Office of Naval Research. [Reprinted in E. Aronson (Ed.), *Readings about the social animal* (3rd ed., pp. 52–67). San Francisco: W. H. Freeman.]

Harkins, S. G., & Jackson, J. M. (1985). The role of evaluation in eliminating social loafing. *Personality and Social Psychology Bulletin, 11,* 457–465.

Harlow, H. F. (1959, June). Love in infant monkeys. *Scientific American, 200,* 68–74.

Harlow, H. F., & Harlow, M. K. (1962, November). Social deprivation in monkeys. *Scientific American, 207,* 136–146.

Harlow, H. F., & Zimmerman, R. R. (1959). Affectional responses in the infant monkey. *Science, 130,* 421–432.

Harris, J. R. (1998). *The nurture assumption: Why children turn out the way they do.* New York: Free Press.

Hartigan, J. A., & Wigdor, A. K. (Eds.). (1989). *Fairness in employment testing: Validity generalization, minority issues, and the General Aptitude Test Battery.* Washington, DC: National Academy Press.

Hartshorne, J. K., & Germine, L. T. (2015). When does cognitive functioning peak? The asynchronous rise and fall of different cognitive abilities across the life span. *Psychological Science, 26,* 433–443.

Hasan, Y., Bègue, L., Scharkow, M., & Bushman, B. J. (2013). The more you play, the more aggressive you become: A long-term experimental study of cumulative violent video game effects on hostile expectations and aggressive behavior. *Journal of Experimental Social Psychology, 49,* 224–227.

Hasher, L., & Zacks, R. T. (1979). Automatic and effortful processes in memory. *Journal of Experimental Psychology: General, 108,* 356–388.

Haslam, S. A., & Reicher, S. (2005, October) The psychology of tyranny. *Scientific American MIND, 6,* 41–51.

Haslam, S. A., & Reicher, S. (2012). Tyranny: Revisiting Zimbardo's Stanford prison experiment. In J. R. Smith & S. A. Haslam (Eds.), *Social psychology: Revisiting the classic studies* (pp. 126–141). Thousand Oaks, CA: Sage.

Haslam, S. A., Reicher, S., & Birney, M. E. (2014). Nothing by mere authority: Evidence that in an experimental analogue of the Milgram paradigm participants are motivated not by orders but by appeals to science. *Journal of Social Issues, 70,* 473–488.

Haslam, S. A., Reicher, S., & Millard, K. (2015, March). Shock treatment: Using immersive digital realism to restage and re-examine Milgram's "Obedience to Authority" research. *PLoS ONE, 10*(3), e109015. doi:10.1371/journal.pone.0109015

Haslam, S. A., Reicher, S., Millard, K., & McDonald, R. (2015). "Happy to have been of service": The Yale archive as window into the engaged followership of participants in Milgram's "obedience" experiments. *British Journal of Social Psychology, 54,* 55–83.

Hathaway, S. R., & McKinley, J. C. (1943). *MMPI manual.* New York: Psychological Corporation.

Häuser, W., Hansen, E., & Enck, P. (2012). Nocebo phenomena in medicine. *Deutsches Ärzteblatt International, 109,* 459–465.

Hefferline, R. F., Keenan, B., & Harford, R. A. (1959). Escape and avoidance conditioning in human subjects without their observation of the response. *Science, 130,* 1338–1339.

Heimberg, R. G., Brozovich, F. A., & Rapee, R. M. (2010). A cognitive-behavioral model of social anxiety disorder: Update and extension. In S. G. Hofmann & P. M. DiBartolo (Eds.), *Social anxiety: Clinical, developmental, and social perspectives* (2nd ed., pp. 395–422). New York: Academic Press.

Hellige, J. B. (1993). Unity of thought and action: Varieties of interaction between the left and right cerebral hemispheres. *Current Directions in Psychological Science, 2,* 21–25.

Helson, R. C., Jones, C., & Kwan, V. (2002). Personality change over 40 years of adulthood: Hierarchical linear modeling analyses of two longitudinal samples. *Journal of Personality and Social Psychology, 89,* 752–766.

Herculano-Houzel, S. (2014). The glia/neuron ratio: How it varies uniformly across brain structures and what that means for brain physiology and evolution. *Glia, 62,* 1377–1391.

Herrnstein, R. J., & Murray, C. (1994). *The bell curve: Intelligence and class in American life.* New York: Free Press.

Hickok, G. (2014). *The myth of mirror neurons: The real neuroscience of communication and cognition.* New York: W. W. Norton.

Hilgetag, C. C., & Barbas, H. (2009). Are there ten times more glia than neurons in the brain? *Brain Structure and Function, 213,* 365–366.

Hill, W. E. (1915, November) My wife and my mother-in-law. *Puck, 16,* 1.

Hilts, P. F. (1995). *Memory's ghost: The strange tale of Mr. M and the nature of memory.* New York: Simon & Schuster.

Hite, S. (1987). *Women and love: A cultural revolution in progress.* New York: Knopf.

Ho, B.-C., Andreasen, N. C., Ziebell, S., Pierson, R., & Magnotta, V. (2011). Long-term antipsychotic treatment and brain volumes: A longitudinal study of first-episode schizophrenia. *Archives of General Psychiatry, 68,* 127–138.

Hobson, J. A. (2003) *Dreaming: An introduction to the science of sleep.* New York: Oxford.

Hobson, J. A., & McCarley, R. W. (1977). The brain as a dream generator: An activation-synthesis hypothesis of the dream process. *American Journal of Psychiatry, 134,* 1335–1348.

Hobson, J. A., Pace-Scott, E. F., & Stickgold, R. (2000). Dreaming and the brain: Toward a cognitive neuroscience of conscious states. *Behavioral and Brain Sciences, 23,* 793–842.

Hoffrage, U., & Gigerenzer, G. (1998). Using natural frequencies to improve diagnostic inferences. *Academic Medicine, 73,* 538–540.

Hofling, C. K., Brotzman, E., Dalrymple, S., Graves, N., & Pierce, C. M. (1966). An experimental study in nurse-physician relationships. *Journal of Nervous and Mental Disease, 143,* 171–180.

Hoffman, D. D. (1998). *Visual intelligence: How we create what we see.* New York: W. W. Norton.

Hofmann, W., De Houwer, J., Perugini, M., Baeyens, F., & Crombez, G. (2010). Evaluative conditioning in humans: A meta-analysis. *Psychological Bulletin, 136,* 390–421.

Hogben, J. H., & Di Lollo, V. (1974). Perceptual integration and perceptual segregation of brief visual stimuli. *Vision Research, 14,* 1059–1069.

Hollander, E., & Simeon, D. (2011). Anxiety disorders. In R. E. Hales, S. C. Yudofsky, & G. O. Gabbard (Eds.), *Essentials of psychiatry* (3rd ed., pp. 185–228). Arlington, VA: American Psychiatric Association.

Holmes, D. S. (1990). The evidence for repression: An examination of sixty years of research. In J. L. Singer (Ed.), *Repression and dissociation: Implications for personality theory, psychopathology, and health* (pp. 85–102). Chicago: University of Chicago Press.

Holsti, L., Grunau, R., & Whitfield, M. (2002). Developmental coordination disorder in extremely low birth weight children at nine years. *Journal of Developmental and Behavioral Pediatrics, 23,* 9–15.

Hood, B. M. (2009). *Supersense: Why we believe in the unbelievable.* New York: HarperCollins.

Horn, J. (1982). The aging of cognitive abilities. In B. B. Wolman (Ed.), *Handbook of developmental psychology* (pp. 847–870). Englewood Cliffs, NJ: Prentice Hall.

Horn, J., & Cattell, R. B. (1966). Refinement and test of the theory of fluid and crystallized general intelligences. *Journal of Educational Psychology, 57,* 253–270.

Horn, J. L., & Cattell, R. B. (1967). Age differences in fluid and crystallized intelligence. *Acta Psychologica, 26,* 107–129.

Horney, K. (1937). *The neurotic personality of our time.* New York: Norton.

Horwitz, A. V., & Wakefield, J. C. (2007). *The loss of sadness: How psychiatry transformed normal sorrow into depressive disorder.* New York: Oxford University Press.

Horwitz, A. V., & Wakefield, J. C. (2012). *All we have to fear: Psychiatry's transformation of natural anxieties into mental disorders.* New York: Oxford University Press.

Hubel, D. H., & Wiesel, T. N. (2004). *Brain and visual perception: The story of a 25-year collaboration.* New York: Oxford University Press.

Huesmann, L. R. (2007). The impact of electronic media violence: Scientific theory and research. *Journal of Adolescent Health, 41*(6, Suppl. 1), S6–S13.

Huesmann, L. R. (2010). Nailing the coffin shut on doubts that violent video games stimulate aggression: Comment on Anderson et al. (2010). *Psychological Bulletin, 136,* 179–181.

Huff, D. (1954). *How to lie with statistics.* New York: Norton.

Hunt, M. (1993). *The story of psychology.* New York: Doubleday.

Hurvich, L. M., & Jameson, D. (1957). An opponent-process theory of color vision. *Psychological Review, 63,* 384–404.

Huston, A. C., Donnerstein, E., Fairchild, H., Feshbach, N. D., Katz, P. A., & Murray, J. P., . . . Zuckerman, D. (1992). *Big world, small screen: The role of television in American Society.* Lincoln, NE: University of Nebraska Press.

Iacoboni, M. (2005). Neural mechanisms of imitation. *Current Opinion in Neurobiology, 15,* 632–637.

Iacoboni, M. (2009a). Imitation, empathy, and mirror neurons. *Annual Review of Psychology, 60,* 653–670.

Iacoboni, M. (2009b). *Mirroring people: The science of empathy and how we connect with others.* New York: Picador.

Iacoboni, M., & Dapretto, M. (2006). The mirror neuron system and the consequences of its dysfunction. *Nature Reviews Neuroscience, 7,* 942–951.

Impastato, D. J. (1960). The story of the first electroshock treatment. *American Journal of Psychiatry, 116,* 1113–1114.

Inhelder, B., & Piaget, J. (1958). *The growth of logical thinking from childhood to adolescence* (A. Parsons & S. Milgram, Trans.). New York: Basic Books.

Izard, C. E. (1990). Facial expressions and the regulation of emotions. *Journal of Personality and Social Psychology, 58,* 487–498.

Jackson, S. L. (2016). *Research methods and statistics: A critical thinking approach* (5th ed.). Boston, MA: Cengage Learning.

Jacobs, B. L. (2004). Depression: The brain finally gets into the act. *Current Directions in Psychological Science, 13,* 103–106.

Jacobs, B. L., van Praag, H., & Gage, F. H. (2000a). Adult brain neurogenesis and psychiatry: A novel theory of depression. *Molecular Psychiatry, 5,* 262–269.

Jacobs, B. L., van Praag, H., & Gage, F. H. (2000b, July/August). Depression and the birth and death of brain cells. *American Scientist, 88,* 340–345.

Jacobs, J., Weidemann, C. T., Miller, J. F., Solway, A., Burke, J. F., Wei, X.-X., . . . Kahana, M. J. (2013). Direct recordings of grid-like neuronal activity in human spatial navigation. *Nature Neuroscience, 16,* 1188–1190.

Jacobsen, T., & Hoffman, V. (1997). Children's attachment representations: Longitudinal relations to school behavior and academic competency in middle childhood and adolescence. *Developmental Psychology, 33,* 703–710.

Jang, K. L., Livesley, W. J., Ando, J., Yamagata, S., Suzuki, A., Angleitner, A., . . . Spinath, F. (2006). Behavioral genetics of the higher-order factors of the Big Five. *Personality and Individual Differences, 41,* 261–272.

Janis, I. L. (1972). *Victims of groupthink.* Boston: Houghton Mifflin.

Janis, I. L. (1983). *Groupthink: Psychological studies of policy decisions and fiascoes* (2nd ed.). Boston: Houghton Mifflin.

Jarrett, C. (2015). *Great myths of the brain.* West Sussex, UK: Wiley-Blackwell.

Javitt, D. C., & Coyle, J. T. (2007). Decoding schizophrenia. In F. E. Bloom (Ed.), *Best of the brain from Scientific American: Mind, matter, and tomorrow's brain* (pp. 157–168). New York: Dana Press.

Jiang, X., & Cillessen, A. (2005). Stability of continuous measures of sociometric status: A meta-analysis. *Developmental Review, 25,* 1–25.

John, O. P. (1990). The "Big Five" factor taxonomy: Dimensions of personality in the natural language and in questionnaires. In L. A. Pervin (Ed.), *Handbook of personality: Theory and research* (pp. 66–100). New York: Guilford.

Johnson, J., & Newport, E. (1989). Critical period effects in second language learning: The influence of maturational state on the acquisition of English as a second language. *Cognitive Psychology, 21,* 60–99.

Johnson, V. E. (2013). Revised standards for statistical evidence. *PNAS, 110,* 19313–19317. doi:10.1073/pnas.13134767110

Johnson, V. E. (2014). Reply to Gelman, Gaudert, Pericchi: More reasons to revise standards for statistical evidence. *PNAS, 111,* E1936–E1937. doi:10.1073/pnas.1400338111

Jones, M. C. (1924). A laboratory study of fear: The case of Peter. *Pedagogical Seminary, 31,* 308–315.

Jones, P. B., Davies, L. M., Barnes, T. R. E., Davies, L., Dunn, G., Lloyd, H., . . . Lewis, S. W. (2006). Randomized controlled trial of effect on quality of life of second generation versus first generation antipsychotic drugs in schizophrenia (CUtLASS 1). *Archives of General Psychiatry, 63,* 1079–1087.

Jones, R. A. (1977). *Self-fulfilling prophecies.* Hillsdale, NJ: Erlbaum.

Jones, S. S. (2007). Imitation in infancy: The development of mimicry. *Psychological Science, 18,* 593–599.

Julien, R. M. (2011). *A primer of drug action* (12th ed.). New York: W. H. Freeman.

Kahneman, D. (2011). *Thinking, fast and slow.* New York: Farrar, Straus and Giroux.

Kahneman, D., & Tversky, A. (1973). On the psychology of prediction. *Psychological Review, 80,* 237–251.

Kail, R. (1991). Developmental change in speed of processing during childhood and adolescence. *Psychological Bulletin, 109,* 490–501.

Kaku, M. (2014). *The future of the mind: The scientific quest to understand, enhance, and empower the mind.* New York: Doubleday.

Kalat, J. W. (2007). *Biological psychology* (9th ed.). Belmont, CA: Wadsworth.

Kamali, M., & McInnis, M. G. (2011). Genetics of mood disorders: General principles and potential applications for treatment resistant depression. In J. F. Greden, M. B. Riba, & M. G. McInnis (Eds.), *Treatment resistant depression: A roadmap for effective care* (pp. 293–308). Arlington, VA: American Psychiatric Association.

Kam-Hansen, S., Jakubowski, M., Kelley, J. M., Kirsch, I., Hoaglin, D. C., Kaptchuk, J., & Burstein, R. (2014). Altered placebo and drug labeling changes the outcome of episodic migraine attacks. *Science Translational Medicine, 6,* 218ra5. doi:10.1126/scitranslmed.3006175

Kane, J. M., Robinson, D. G., Schooler, N. R., Mueser, K. T., Penn, D. L., Rosenheck, R. A., . . . Heinssen, R. K. (2015). Comprehensive versus usual community care for first-episode psychosis: 2-year outcomes from the NIMH RAISE early treatment program. *The American Journal of Psychiatry Online.* Retrieved from http://ajp.psychiatryonline.org /doi/10.1176/appi.ajp.2015.15050632

Kanizsa, G. (1976, April). Subjective contours. *Scientific American, 234,* 48–52.

Kanwisher, N. (2006). Neuroscience: What's in a face? *Science, 311,* 617–618.

Kanwisher, N., McDermott, J., & Chun, M. M. (1997). The fusiform face area: A module in human extrastriate cortex specialized for face perception. *Journal of Neuroscience, 17,* 4302–4311.

Kanwisher, N., & Yovel, G. (2009). Cortical specialization for face perception in humans. In G. G. Berntson & J. T. Cacioppo (Eds.), *Handbook of neuroscience for the behavioral sciences* (Vol. 2, pp. 841–851). Hoboken, NJ: Wiley.

Kaptchuk, T. J., Friedlander, E., Kelley, J. M., Sanchez, M. N., Kokkotou, E., Singer, J. P., . . . Lembo, A. J. (2010). Placebos without deception: A randomized controlled trial in irritable bowel syndrome. *PLoS ONE 5*(12), e15591. doi:10.1371 /journal.pone.0015591

Karau, S. J., & Williams, K. D. (1993). Social loafing: A meta-analytic review and theoretical integration. *Journal of Personality and Social Psychology, 65,* 681–706.

Kasckow, J., Felmet, K., & Zisook, S. (2011). Managing suicide risk in patients with schizophrenia. *CNS Drugs, 25,* 129–143.

Kaufman, A. S. (2000). Tests of intelligence. In R. J. Sternberg (Ed.), *Handbook of intelligence* (pp. 445–476). New York: Cambridge University Press.

Kaufman, A. S. (2009). *IQ testing 101.* New York: Springer.

Kean, S. (2014). Phineas Gage, neuroscience's most famous patient. Retrieved from www.slate.com /articles/health_and_science/science/2014/05/phineas _gage_neuroscience_case_true_story_of_famous _frontal_lobe_patient.html

Kazdin, A. E. (2001). *Behavior modification in applied settings* (6th ed.). Belmont, CA: Wadsworth.

Keating, N. L., & Pace, L. E. (2015). New guidelines for breast cancer screening in US women. *JAMA, 314,* 1569–1571.

Kellman, P. J., & Arterberry, M. E. (1998). *The cradle of knowledge: Development of perception in infancy.* Cambridge, MA: MIT Press.

Kellman, P. J., & Banks, M. S. (1998). Infant visual perception. In W. Damon (Series Ed.) & R. Siegler & D. Kuhn (Vol. Eds.), *Handbook of child psychology: Vol. 2. Cognition, perception, and language* (5th ed., pp. 103–146). New York: Wiley.

Kempermann, G., & Gage, F. H. (1999, May). New nerve cells for the adult brain. *Scientific American, 280,* 48–53.

Kennedy, W. P. (1961). The nocebo reaction. *Medical World, 95,* 203–205.

Kern, M. I., & Friedman, H. S. (2008). Do conscientious individuals live longer? A quantitative review. *Health Psychology, 27,* 505–512.

Kessler, R. C., Berglund, P., Demler, O., Jin, R., Koretz, D., Merikangas, K. R., . . . Wang, P. S. (2003). The epidemiology of major depressive disorder: Results from the National Comorbidity Survey Replication (NCS-R). *JAMA, 289,* 3095–3105.

Kessler, R. C., McGonagle, K. A., Zhao, S., Nelson, C. B., Hughes, M., Eshleman, S., . . . Kendler, K. S. (1994). Lifetime and 12-month prevalence of DSM-III-R psychiatric disorders in the United States. *Archives of General Psychology, 51,* 8–19.

Kessler, R. C., Ruscio, A. M., Shear, K., & Wittchen, H.-U. (2010). Epidemiology of anxiety disorders. In M. B. Stein & T. Steckler (Eds.). *Behavioral neurobiology of anxiety and its treatment: Current topics in behavioral neurosciences* (pp. 21–35). New York: Springer Science + Business Media.

Keysers, C., & Gazzola, V. (2010). Social neuroscience: Mirror neurons recorded in humans. *Current Biology, 20,* R353–R354.

Khan, A., Brodhead, A. E., Kolts, R. L., & Brown, W. A. (2005). Severity of depressive symptoms and response to antidepressants and placebo in antidepressant trials. *Journal of Psychiatric Research, 39,* 146–150.

Kilham, W., & Mann, L. (1974). Level of destructive obedience as a function of transmitter and executant roles in the Milgram obedience paradigm. *Journal of Personality and Social Psychology, 29,* 696–702.

Kingdom, F. A. A., Yoonessi, A., & Gheorghiu, E. (2007). The leaning tower illusion: A new illusion of perspective. *Perception, 36,* 475–477.

Kirkpatrick, E. A. (1894). An experimental study of memory. *Psychological Review, 1,* 602–609.

Kirsch, I. (2010). *The emperor's new drugs: Exploding the antidepressant myth.* New York: Basic Books.

Kirsch, I., Deacon, B. J., Huedo-Medina, T. B., Scoboria, A., Moore, T. J., & Johnson, B. T. (2008). Initial severity and antidepressant benefits: A meta-analysis of data submitted to the Food and Drug Administration. *PLoS Medicine, 5*(2), e45.

Klein, S. B., & Kihlstrom, J. F. (1998). On bridging the gap between social-personality psychology and neuropsychology. *Personality and Social Psychology Review, 2,* 228–242.

Klüver, H., & Bucy, P. C. (1939). Preliminary analysis of functions of the temporal lobes in monkeys. *Archives of Neurology and Psychiatry, 42,* 979–1000.

Knight, D. C., Nguyen, H. T., & Bandettini, P. A. (2003). Expression of conditional fear with and without awareness. *PNAS, 100,* 15280–15283.

Knoblich, G., & Oellinger, M. (2006, October/November). Aha! The Eureka moment. *Scientific American MIND, 17,* 38–43.

Knowlton, B. J., Squire, L. R., Paulsen, J. S., Swerdlow, N. R., Swenson, M., & Butters, N. (1996). Dissociations within nondeclarative memory in Huntington's disease. *Neuropsychology, 10,* 538–548.

Kohlberg, L. (1976). Moral stages and moralization: The cognitive-developmental approach. In T. Lickona (Ed.), *Moral development and behavior: Theory, research, and social issues* (pp. 31–53). New York: Holt, Rinehart, & Winston.

Kohlberg, L. (1984). *Essays on moral development, Vol. 2. The psychology of moral development: The nature and validity of moral stages.* San Francisco: Harper & Row.

Kolb, B., & Whishaw, I. Q. (2001). *An introduction to brain and behavior.* New York: Worth.

Koob, A. (2009). *The root of thought.* Upper Saddle River, NJ: Pearson Education.

Kotowicz, Z. (2007). The strange case of Phineas Gage. *History of the Human Sciences, 10,* 115–131.

Krackow, A., & Blass, T. (1995). When nurses obey or defy inappropriate physician orders: Attributional differences. *Journal of Social Behavior, 10,* 585–594.

Kraut, A. M. (2003). *Goldberger's war: The life and work of a public health crusader.* New York: Hill and Wang.

Krebs, H., Hogan, N., Hening, W., Adamovich, S., & Poizner, H. (2001). Procedural motor learning in Parkinson's disease. *Experimental Brain Research, 141,* 425–437.

Krijn, M., Emmelkamp, P. M. G., Olafsson, R. P., & Biemond, R. (2004). Virtual reality therapy of anxiety disorders: A review. *Clinical Psychology Review, 24,* 259–281.

Krueger, R. F., & Walton, K. E. (2008). Introduction to the special issue. In R. F. Krueger & K. E. Walton (Eds.), A neo-Eysenckian personality psychology for the 21st century: Conceptualization, etiology, structure, and clinical implications [Special issue]. *Journal of Personality, 76,* 1347–1354.

Kruger, J., Savitsky, K., & Gilovich, T. (1999, March/April). Superstition and the regression effect. *Skeptical Inquirer, 23,* 24–29.

Krupa, D. J., Thompson, J. K., & Thompson, R. F. (1993). Localization of a memory trace in the mammalian brain. *Science, 260,* 989–991.

Kuhl, P. K. (2004). Early language acquisition: Cracking the speech code. *Nature Reviews Neuroscience, 5,* 831–843.

Kuhl, P. K., Tsao, F.-M., & Liu, H. M. (2003). Foreign-language experience in infancy: Effects of short-term exposure and social interaction on phonetic learning. *PNAS, 100,* 9096–9101.

Lachman, M. E., & Weaver, S. L. (1998). The sense of control as a moderator of social class differences in health and well-being. *Journal of Personality and Social Psychology, 74,* 763–773.

Lafer-Sousa, R., Hermann, K. L., & Conway, B. R. (2015). Striking individual differences in color perception uncovered by "the dress" photograph. *Current Biology, 25,* R545–R546.

Lambert, K., & Kinsley, C. H. (2005). *Clinical neuroscience: The neurobiological foundations of mental health.* New York: Worth.

Lang, P. J. (1994). The varieties of emotional experience: A meditation on the James-Lange theory. *Psychological Review, 101,* 211–221.

Lange, C. G., & James, W. (1922). *The emotions* (I. A. Haupt, Trans.). Baltimore, MD: Williams & Wilkins.

Langer, E. J. (1989). *Mindfulness.* Reading, MA: Addison-Wesley.

Langer, E. J. (1997). *The power of mindful learning.* Reading, MA: Addison-Wesley.

Lansford, J. E. (2012). Aggression: Beyond Bandura's Bobo doll studies. In A. M. Slater & P. C. Quinn (Eds.). *Developmental psychology: Revisiting the classic studies* (pp. 176–190). Thousand Oaks, CA: Sage.

Larsen, R. J., & Buss, D. M. (2000). *Personality psychology: Domains of knowledge about human nature.* New York: McGraw-Hill.

Latané, B., & Darley, J. M. (1968). Group inhibition of bystander intervention. *Journal of Personality and Social Psychology, 10,* 215–221.

Latané, B., & Darley, J. M. (1970). *The unresponsive bystander: Why doesn't he help?* New York: Appleton-Century-Crofts.

Latané, B., & Nida, S. (1981). Ten years of research on group size and helping. *Psychological Bulletin, 89,* 308–324.

Latané, B., & Rodin, J. (1969). A lady in distress: Inhibiting effects of friends and strangers on bystander intervention. *Journal of Experimental Social Psychology, 5,* 189–202.

Latané, B., Williams, K. D., & Harkins, S. G. (1979). Many hands make light work: The causes and consequences of social loafing. *Journal of Personality and Social Psychology, 37,* 822–832.

Laurent, J. (1987). Milgram's shocking experiments: A case in the social construction of "science." *Indian Journal of History of Science, 22,* 247–272.

Lawson, T. J. (2002). *Everyday statistical reasoning: Possibilities and pitfalls.* Pacific Grove, CA: Wadsworth.

LeDoux, J. E. (1996). *The emotional brain: The mysterious underpinnings of emotional life.* New York: Simon & Schuster.

LeDoux, J. E. (2000). Emotional circuits in the brain. *Annual Review of Neuroscience, 23,* 155–184.

LeDoux, J. E. (2002). *Synaptic self: How our brains become who we are.* New York: Viking Penguin.

Legrenzi, P., & Umiltà, C. (2011). *Neuromania: On the limits of brain science.* New York: Oxford University Press.

Lehrer, J. (2007). *Proust was a neuroscientist.* New York: Houghton Mifflin Harcourt.

Lehrer, J. (2009). *How we decide.* New York: Houghton Mifflin Harcourt.

Lemann, N. (2014, March 10). A call for help. *The New Yorker, 90,* 73.

Leo, I., & Simion, F. (2009). Face processing at birth: A Thatcher illusion study. *Developmental Science, 12,* 492–498.

Lepore, F. E. (2001, Winter). Dissecting genius: Einstein's brain and the search for the neural basis of intellect. *Cerebrum, 3,* 11–26. Retrieved from www.dana.org/news/cerebrum/detail.aspx?id=3032

Lepper, M. R., Greene, D., & Nisbett, R. E. (1973). Undermining children's intrinsic interest with extrinsic rewards. *Journal of Personality and Social Psychology, 28,* 129–137.

Lepper, M. R., & Henderlong, J. (2000). Turning "play" into "work" and "work" into "play": 25 years of research on intrinsic versus extrinsic motivation. In C. Sansone & J. M. Havackiewicz (Eds.), *Intrinsic and extrinsic motivation: The search for optimal motivation and performance* (pp. 257–307). San Diego: Academic Press.

Lerner, M. J. (1980). *The belief in a just world: A fundamental delusion.* New York: Plenum.

Leung, A. K.-y., Kim, S., Polman, E., Ong, L. S., Qiu, L., Goncalo, J. A., & Sanchez-Burks, J. (2012). Embodied metaphors and creative "acts." *Psychological Science, 23,* 502–509.

Levenson, R. W. (1992). Autonomic nervous system differences among emotions. *Psychological Science, 3,* 23–27.

Levine, R. (2003). *The power of persuasion: How we're bought and sold.* New York: Wiley.

Levinson, D. E., & Nichols, W. E. (2014). *Major depression and genetics.* Stanford, CA: Stanford School of Medicine.

Levitt, S. D., & Dubner, S. J. (2009). *Super freakonomics: Global cooling, patriotic prostitutes and why suicide bombers should buy life insurance.* New York: HarperCollins.

Li, C. (1975). *Path analysis: A primer.* Pacific Grove, CA: Boxwood Press.

Li, W., Farkas, G., Duncan, G. J., Burchinal, M. R., & Vandell, D. L. (2013). Timing of high-quality day care and cognitive, language, and preacademic development. *Developmental Psychology, 49,* 1440–1451.

Lichtenstein, S., Slovic, P., Fischhoff, B., Layman, M., & Combs, B. (1978). Judged frequency of lethal events. *Journal of Experimental Psychology: Human Learning and Memory, 4,* 551–578.

Lieberman, J. A., Stroup, T. S., McEvoy, J. P., Swartz, M. S., Rosenheck, R. A., Perkins, D. O., . . . Lewis, S. W. (2005). Effectiveness of antipsychotic drugs in patients with chronic schizophrenia. *New England Journal of Medicine, 353,* 1209–1223.

Lieberman, J. A., Tollefson, G. D., Charles, C., Zipursky, R., Sharma, T., Kahn, R. S., . . . Tohen, M. (2005). Antipsychotic drug effects on brain morphology in first-episode psychosis. *Archives of General Psychiatry, 62,* 361–370.

Lilienfeld, S. O., Lynn, S. J., Ruscio, J., Beyerstein, B. L. (2010). *50 great myths of popular psychology: Shattering widespread misconceptions about human behavior.* Malden, MA: Wiley-Blackwell.

Lilienfeld, S. O., Wood, J. M., & Garb, H. N. (2000). The scientific status of projective techniques. *Psychological Science in the Public Interest, 1,* 27–66.

Lindenmayer, J. P., & Khan, A. (2012). Psychopathology. In J. A. Lieberman, T. S. Stroup, & D. O. Perkins (Eds.), *Essentials of schizophrenia* (pp. 11–54). Arlington, VA: American Psychiatric Publishing.

Lindner, I., Echterhoff, G., Davidson, P. S. R., & Brand, M. (2010). Observation inflation: Your actions become mine. *Psychological Science, 21,* 1291–1299.

Lingnau, A., Gesierich, B., & Caramazza, A. (2009). Asymmetric fMRI adaptation reveals no evidence for mirror neurons in humans. *PNAS, 106,* 9925–9930.

Linn, R. L. (1982). Admissions testing on trial. *American Psychologist, 37,* 279–291.

Livingstone, M. (2002). *Vision and art: The biology of seeing.* New York: Abrams.

Loehlin, J. C. (1992). *Genes and environment in personality development.* Newbury Park, CA: Sage.

Loehlin, J. C., McCrae, R. R., Costa, P. T., Jr., & John, O. P. (1998). Heritabilities of common and measure-specific components of the Big Five personality factors. *Journal of Research in Personality, 32,* 431–453.

Loftus, E. F. (2001, November). Imagining the past. *The Psychologist, 14,* 584–587.

Loftus, E. F. (2005). Planting misinformation in the human mind: A 30-year investigation of the malleability of memory. *Learning and Memory, 12,* 361–366.

Loftus, E. F., Coan, J., & Pickrell, J. E. (1996). Manufacturing false memories using bits of reality. In L. Reder (Ed.), *Implicit memory and metacognition* (pp. 195–220). Mahwah, NJ: Erlbaum.

Loftus, E. F., & Ketcham, K. (1991). *Witness for the defense.* New York: St. Martin's.

Loftus, E. F., & Ketcham, K. (1994). *The myth of repressed memory: False memories and accusations of sexual abuse.* New York: St. Martin's.

Loftus, E. F., & Palmer, J. C. (1974). Reconstruction of automobile destruction: An example of the interaction between language and memory. *Journal of Verbal Learning and Verbal Behavior, 13,* 585–589.

Lourenco, O., & Machado, A. (1996). In defense of Piaget's theory: A reply to 10 common criticisms. *Psychological Review, 103,* 143–164.

Lovibond, S. H., Mithiran, X., & Adams, W. G. (1979). The effects of three experimental prison environments on the behavior of non-convict volunteer subjects. *Australian Psychologist, 14,* 273–287.

Lutsky, N. (1995). When is "obedience" obedience? Conceptual and historical commentary. *Journal of Social Issues, 51,* 55–65.

Lynch, G., & Granger, R. (2008). *Big brain: The origins and future of human intelligence.* New York: Palgrave Macmillan.

MacFarlane, A. (1975). Olfaction in the development of social preferences in the human neonate. *Parent-infant interaction* (CIBA Foundation Symposium, No. 33). Amsterdam, NL: Elsevier.

Macknik, S. L., & Martinez-Conde, S. (2015, July/August). Unraveling "The Dress." *Scientific American MIND, 26,* 19–21.

Macmillan, M. (2000). *An odd kind of fame: Stories of Phineas Gage.* Cambridge, MA: MIT Press.

Macmillan, M., & Lena, M. L. (2010). Rehabilitating Phineas Gage. *Neuropsychological Rehabilitation, 20,* 641–658.

Maguire, E. A., Valentine, E. R., Wilding, J. M., & Kapur, N. (2003). Routes to remembering: The brains behind superior memory. *Nature Neuroscience, 6,* 90–95.

Mahler, D. A., Cunningham, L. N., Skrinar, G. S., Kraemer, W. J., & Colice, G. L. (1989). Beta-endorphin activity and hypercapnic ventilatory responsiveness after marathon running. *Journal of Applied Physiology, 66,* 2431–2436.

Main, M., & Solomon, J. (1990). Procedures for identifying infants as disorganized/disoriented during the Ainsworth Strange Situation. In M. T. Greenberg, D. Cicchetti, & E. M. Cummings (Eds.), *Attachment in the preschool years* (pp. 121–160) Chicago: University of Chicago Press.

Malberg, J. E., & Schechter, L. E. (2005). Increasing hippocampal neurogenesis: A novel mechanism for antidepressant drugs. *Current Pharmaceutical Design, 11,* 145–155.

Manning, R., Levine, M., & Collins, A. (2007). The Kitty Genovese murder and the social psychology of helping: The parable of 38 witnesses. *American Psychologist, 62,* 555–562.

Mantell, D. M., & Panzarella, R. (1976). Obedience and responsibility. *British Journal of Social and Clinical Psychology, 15,* 239–245.

Marcel, A. (1983). Conscious and unconscious perception: Experiments on visual masking and word recognition. *Cognitive Psychology, 15,* 197–237.

Marchant, J. (2016, January 6). A placebo treatment for pain. *The New York Times,* p. 5. Retrieved from www.nytimes.com/2016/01/10/opinion/sunday/a-placebo-treatment-for-pain.html?_r=0

Marmor, M. F. (2006). Ophthalmology and art: Simulation of Monet's cataracts and Degas retinal disease. *Archives of Ophthalmology, 124,* 1764–1769.

Martinez-Conde, S., & Macknik, S. L. (2010, Summer). The neuroscience of illusion. *Scientific American MIND, 20,* 4–7.

Maslow, A. H. (1968). *Toward a psychology of being* (2nd ed.). New York: Harper & Row.

Maslow, A. H. (1970). *Motivation and personality* (2nd ed.). New York: Harper & Row.

Mayberg, H. S., Brannan, S. K., Tekell, J. L., Silva, J. A., Mahurin, R. K., McGinnis, S., & Jerabek, P. A. (2000). Regional metabolic effects of fluoxetine in major depression: Serial changes and relationship to clinical response. *Biological Psychiatry, 48,* 830–843.

Mayberg, H. S., Lozano, A. M., Voon, V., McNeely, H. E., Seminowicz, D., Hamani, C., . . . Kennedy, S. H. (2005). Deep brain stimulation for treatment-resistant depression. *Neuron, 45,* 651–660.

Matlin, M. W., & Foley, H. J. (1997). *Sensation and perception* (4th ed.). Needham Heights, MA: Allyn and Bacon.

Mazur, J. E. (1998). *Learning and behavior* (4th ed.). Upper Saddle River, NJ: Prentice-Hall.

McCrae, R. R. (2011). Personality theories for the 21st century. *Teaching of Psychology, 38,* 209–214.

McCrae, R. R., & Costa, P. T., Jr. (1997). Personality trait structure as a human universal. *American Psychologist, 52,* 509–516.

McCrae, R. R., & Costa, P. T., Jr. (1999). A five-factor theory of personality. In L. A. Perrin & O. P. John (Eds.), *Handbook of personality: Theory and research* (pp. 139–153). New York: Guilford.

McCrae, R. R., & Costa, P. T., Jr. (2003). *Personality in adulthood: A five-factor theory perspective* (2nd ed.). New York: Guilford.

McCrae, R. R., Costa, P. T., Jr., & Martin, T. A. (2005). The NEO-PI-3: A more readable revised NEO personality inventory. *Journal of Personality Assessment, 84,* 261–270.

McCrae, R. R., Costa, P. T., Jr., Martin, T. A., Oryol, V. E., Rukavishnikow, A. A., Senin, I. G., . . . Urbanek, T. (2004). Consensual validation of personality traits across cultures. *Journal of Research in Personality, 38,* 179–201.

McCrae, R. R., & Sutin, A. R. (2009). Openness to experience. In M. R. Leary & R. H. Hoyle (Eds.), *Handbook of individual differences in social behavior* (pp. 257–273). New York: Guilford.

McGue, M., Bouchard, T. J., Jr., Iacono, W. G., & Lykken, D. T. (1993). Behavioral genetics of cognitive ability: A life-span perspective. In R. Plomin & G. E. McClearn (Eds.), *Nature, nurture, and psychology* (pp. 59–76). Washington, DC: American Psychological Association.

McGuffin, P., Katz, R., Watkins, S., & Rutherford, J. (1996). A hospital-based twin study of the heritability of DSM-IV unipolar depression. *Archives of General Psychiatry, 53,* 129–136.

McGurk, H., & MacDonald, J. (1976). Hearing lips and seeing voices. *Nature, 264,* 746–748.

McKinnon, J. W., & Renner, J. W. (1971). Are colleges concerned with intellectual development? *American Journal of Psychology, 39,* 1047–1052.

McNally, R. J. (1987). Preparedness and phobias: A review. *Psychological Bulletin, 101,* 283–303.

McNally, R. J. (2003). *Remembering trauma.* Cambridge, MA: Harvard University Press.

Messer, W. S., & Griggs, R. A. (1989). Student belief and involvement in the paranormal and performance in introductory psychology. *Teaching of Psychology, 16,* 187–191.

Meyer, G. J., Viglione, D. J., Mihura, J. L., Erard, R. E., & Erdberg, P. (2011). *Rorschach Performance Assessment System: Administration, coding, interpretation, and technical manual.* Toledo, OH: Author.

Mezulis, A. H., Abramson, L. Y., Hyde, J. S., & Hankin, B. L. (2004). Is there a universal positivity bias in attributions? A meta-analytic review of individual, developmental, and cultural differences in self-serving attributional bias. *Psychological Bulletin, 130,* 711–747.

Milgram, S. (1963). Behavioral study of obedience. *Journal of Abnormal and Social Psychology, 67,* 371–378.

Milgram, S. (1964). Issues in the study of obedience: A reply to Baumrind. *American Psychologist, 19,* 848–852.

Milgram, S. (1965). Some conditions of obedience and disobedience. *Human Relations, 18,* 57–76.

Milgram, S. (1972). Interpreting obedience: Error and evidence—a reply to Orne and Holland. In A. G. Miller (Ed.), *The social psychology of psychological research* (pp. 138–154). New York, NY: Free Press.

Milgram, S. (1974). *Obedience to authority.* New York: Harper & Row.

Mihura, J. L., Meyer, G. J., Dumitrascu, N., & Bombel, G. (2013). The validity of individual Rorschach variables: Systematic reviews and meta-analyses of the comprehensive system. *Psychological Bulletin, 139,* 548–605.

Mihura, J. L., Meyer, G. J., Bombel, G., & Dumitrascu, N. (2015). Standards, accuracy, and questions of bias in Rorschach meta-analyses: Reply to Wood, Garb, Nezworski, Lilienfeld, and Duke (2015). *Psychological Bulletin, 141,* 250–260.

Miller, B., & Gentile, B. F. (1998). Introductory course content and goals. *Teaching of Psychology, 25,* 89–96.

Miller, G. (2005). How are memories stored and retrieved? *Science, 309,* 92.

Miller, G. A. (1956). The magical number seven, plus or minus two: Some limits on our capacity for processing information. *Psychological Review, 63,* 81–97.

Miller, G. A. (1962). *Psychology: The science of mental life.* New York: Penguin Books.

Miller, P. H. (2011). *Theories of developmental psychology* (5th ed.). New York: Worth.

Millon, T. (1975). Reflections of Rosenhan's "On being sane in insane places." *Journal of Abnormal Psychology, 84,* 456–461.

Millon, T., Millon, C. M., Meagher, S., & Grossman, S. (2004). *Personality disorders in modern life* (2nd ed.). New York: Wiley.

Milton, J., & Wiseman, R. (1999). Does psi exist? Lack of replication of an anomalous process of information transfer. *Psychological Bulletin, 125,* 387–391.

Mingroni, M. A. (2014). Future efforts in Flynn effect research: Balancing reductionism with holism. *Journal of Intelligence, 2,* 122–155.

Mischel, W. (1968). *Personality and assessment.* New York: Wiley.

Mixon, D. (1976). Studying feignable behavior. *Representative Research in Social Psychology, 7,* 89–104.

Miyake, A., & Shah, P. (Eds.). (1999). *Models of working memory: Mechanisms of active maintenance and executive control.* New York: Cambridge University Press.

Mlodinow, L. (2008). *The drunkard's walk: How randomness rules our lives.* New York: Pantheon Books.

Moncrieff, J. (1997). Lithium: Evidence reconsidered. *British Journal of Psychiatry, 171,* 113–119.

Moncrieff, J. (2009). *The myth of the chemical cure: A critique of psychiatric drug treatment* (Rev. ed.). New York: Palgrave Macmillan.

Moonesinghe, R., Khoury, M. J., & Janssens, A. C. J. W. (2007). Most published research findings are false—But a little replication goes a long way. *PLoS Med 4*(2), e28. doi:10.1371/journal.pmed.0040028

Moore, T. E. (1988). The case against subliminal manipulation. *Psychology and Marketing, 5,* 297–316.

Moore, T. E. (1992, November/December). Subliminal perception: Facts and fallacies. *Skeptical Inquirer, 16,* 273–281.

Morgan, C. D., & Murray, H. A. (1935). A method for investigating fantasies: The Thematic Apperception Test. *Archives of Neurology and Psychiatry, 34,* 289–306.

Mori, K., & Arai, M. (2010). No need to fake it: Reproduction of the Asch experiment without confederates. *International Journal of Psychology, 45,* 390–397.

Morris, J. S., Öhman, A., & Dolan, R. J. (1998). Conscious and unconscious emotional learning in the human amygdala. *Nature, 393,* 467–470.

Morris, R. G., Miotto, E. C., Feigenbaum, J. D., Bullock, P., & Polkey, C. E. (1997). The effect of goal-subgoal conflict on planning ability after frontal- and temporal-lobe lesions in humans. *Neuropsychologica, 35,* 1147–1157.

Morrison, A. P., Turkington, D., Pyle, M., Spencer, H., Brabban, A., Dunn, G., . . . Hutton, P. (2014). Cognitive therapy for people with schizophrenia spectrum disorders not taking antipsychotic drugs: A single-blind randomized trial. *The Lancet, 383,* 1395–1403.

Mortensen, P. B., Norgaard-Pedersen, B., Waltoft, B. L., Sorensen, T. L., Hougaard, D., & Yolken, R. H. (2007). Early infections of *Toxoplasma gondii* and the later development of schizophrenia. *Schizophrenia Bulletin, 33,* 741–744.

Moruzzi, G., & Magoun, H. W. (1949). Brain stem reticular formation and activation of the EEG. *Electroencephalography and Clinical Neurophysiology, 1,* 455–473.

Moser, M.-B., & Moser, E. L. (2016, January). Where am I? Where am I going? *Scientific American, 314,* 26–33.

Moshman, D., & Franks, B. A. (1986). Development of the concept of inferential validity. *Child Development, 57,* 153–165.

Moyer, V. A. (2012, July). Screening for prostate cancer: U.S. Preventive Services Task Force recommendation statement. *Annals of Internal Medicine, 157*(2), 1–44.

Mukamel, R., Ekstrom, A. D., Kaplan, J., Iacoboni, M., & Fried, I. (2010). Single-neuron responses in humans during execution and observation of actions. *Current Biology, 20,* 750–756.

Murray, J. P. (2008). Media violence: The effects are both real and strong. *American Behavioral Scientist, 51,* 1212–1230.

Myers, D. G. (2001, December). Do we fear the right things? *APS Observer, 14,* 3.

Myers, D. G. (2002). *Social psychology* (7th ed.). New York: McGraw-Hill.

Myers, D. G. (2013). *Social psychology* (11th ed.). New York: McGraw-Hill.

Myers, I. B., & McCaulley, M. H. (1985). *Manual: A guide to the development and use of the Myers-Briggs Type Indicator.* Palo Alto, CA: Consulting Psychologists Press.

Napolitan, D. A., & Goethals, G. R. (1979). The attribution of friendliness. *Journal of Experimental Social Psychology, 15,* 105–113.

Navon, D. (1977). Forest before trees: The precedence of global features in visual perception. *Cognitive Psychology, 9,* 353–383.

Nicholson, I. (2011). "Torture at Yale": Experimental subjects, laboratory torment and the "rehabilitation" of Milgram's "Obedience to Authority." *Theory & Psychology, 21,* 737–761.

Nielsen, J. A., Zielinski, B. A., Ferguson, M. A., Lainhart, J. E., & Anderson, J. S. (2013). An evaluation of the left-brain vs. right-brain hypothesis with resting state connectivity magnetic resonance imaging. *PLoS ONE 8*(8): e71275. doi:10.1371/journal.pone.0071275

Neimark, J. (1996, January). The diva of disclosure, memory researcher Elizabeth Loftus. *Psychology Today, 29,* 48–80.

Neisser, U. (Ed.). (1998). *The rising curve: Long-term gains in IQ and related measures.* Washington, DC: American Psychological Association.

Neisser, U., Boodoo, G., Bouchard, T. J., Jr., Boykin, A. W., Brody, N., Ceci, S. J., . . . Urbina, S. (1996). Intelligence: Knowns and unknowns. *American Psychologist, 51,* 77–101.

Nettle, D. (2007). *Personality: What makes you the way you are.* New York: Oxford University Press.

Nettle, D., & Liddle, B. (2008). Agreeableness is related to social-cognitive, but not social-perceptual, theory of mind. *European Journal of Personality, 22,* 323–335.

Newport, E. (1991). Contrasting concepts of the critical period for language. In S. Carey & R. Gelman (Eds.), *The epigenesis of mind: Essays on biology and cognition* (pp. 111–132). Hillsdale, NJ: Erlbaum.

NICHD Early Child Care Research Network. (1997). The effects of infant child care on infant-mother attachment security: Results of the NICHD Study of Early Child Care. *Child Development, 68,* 860–879.

NICHD Early Child Care Research Network. (2001). Child-care and family predictors of preschool attachment and stability from infancy. *Developmental Psychology, 37,* 347–862.

NICHD Early Child Care Research Network. (2008). Social competence with peers in third grade: Associations with earlier peer experiences in child care. *Social Development, 17,* 419–453.

NIMH (National Institute of Mental Health). (2011). *Agoraphobia among adults.* Bethesda, MD: Author.

Nickerson, R. S. (1998). Confirmation bias: A ubiquitous phenomenon in many guises. *Review of General Psychology, 2,* 175–220.

Nickerson, R. S., & Adams, M. J. (1979). Long-term memory for a common object. *Cognitive Psychology, 11,* 287–307.

Niemi, M. (2009, February/March). Cure in the mind. *Scientific American MIND, 20,* 42–49.

Nir, Y., & Tonino, G. (2010). Dreaming and the brain: From phenomenology to neurophysiology. *Trends in Cognitive Science, 14,* 88–100.

Nisbett, R. E. (2015). *Mindware: Tools for smart thinking.* New York: Farrar, Straus, and Giroux.

Nisbett, R. E., & Ross, L. (1980). *Human inference: Strategies and shortcomings of social judgment.* Englewood Cliffs, NJ: Prentice-Hall.

Noftle, E. E., & Robins, R. W. (2007). Personality predictors of academic outcomes: Big Five correlates of GPS and SAT scores. *Journal of Personality and Social Psychology, 93,* 116–130.

Noice, T., & Noice, H. (1997). *The nature of expertise in professional acting: A cognitive view.* Mahwah, NJ: Erlbaum.

Oatley, K., & Duncan, E. (1994). The experience of emotions in everyday life. *Cognition and Emotion, 8,* 369–381.

Öhman, A., & Mineka, S. (2001). Fear, phobias, and preparedness: Toward an evolved module of fear and fear learning. *Psychology Review, 108,* 483–522.

O'Kane, G., Kensinger, E. A., & Corkin, S. (2004). Evidence for semantic learning in profound amnesia: An investigation with patient H. M. *Hippocampus, 14,* 417–425.

O'Keefe, J. (1976). Place units in the hippocampus of the freely moving rat. *Experimental Neurology, 51,* 78–109.

O'Keefe, J., & Dostrovsky, J. (1971). The hippocampus as a spatial map. Preliminary evidence from unit activity in the freely-moving rat. *Brain Research, 34,* 171–175.

Olson, M. A., & Fazio, R. H. (2001). Implicit attitude formation through classical conditioning. *Psychological Science, 12,* 413–417.

Olsson, A., & Phelps, E. A. (2004). Learned fear of "unseen" faces after Pavlovian, observational, and instructed fear. *Psychological Science, 15,* 822–828.

Open Science Collaboration. (2015, August 28). Estimating the reproducibility of psychological science. *Science, 349,* No. 6251. doi:10.1126/science.aac4716

Orne, M. T. (1962) On the social psychology of the psychological experiment: With particular references to demand characteristics and their implications. *American Psychologist, 17,* 776–783.

Orne, M. T., & Evans, F. J. (1965). Social control in the psychological experiment: Antisocial behavior and hypnosis. *Journal of Personality and Social Psychology, 1,* 189–200.

Orne, M. T., & Holland, C. C. (1968). On the ecological validity of laboratory deceptions. *International Journal of Psychiatry, 6,* 282–293.

Ornstein, R. (1991). *The evolution of consciousness: Of Darwin, Freud, and cranial fire—the origins of the way we think.* Englewood Cliffs, NJ: Prentice-Hall.

Osherson, D. N., & Markman, E. M. (1975). Language and the ability to evaluate contradictions and tautologies. *Cognition, 2,* 213–226.

Otsuka, Y., Yanagi, K., & Watanabe, S. (2009). Discriminative and reinforcing stimulus properties of music for rats. *Behavioural Processes, 80,* 121–127.

Packer, D. J. (2008). Identifying systematic disobedience in Milgram's obedience experiments: A meta-analytic review. *Perspectives on Psychological Science, 3,* 301–304.

Papanastasiou, E., Stone, J. M., & Shergill, S. (2013). When the drugs don't work: The potential of glutamatergic antipsychotics in schizophrenia. *British Journal of Psychiatry, 202,* 91–93.

Parents Television Council. (2007, January 10). *Dying to entertain: Violence on prime time broadcast TV, 1998 to 2006* [Special Report]. Retrieved from w2.parentstv.org

Parker, I. (2000, Autumn). Obedience. *Granta, 71,* 99–125.

Pascual-Leone, J. (1989). Constructive problems for constructive theories: The current relevance of Piaget's work and a critique of information-processing simulation psychology. In R. Kluwe & H. Spada (Eds.), *Developmental models of thinking* (pp. 263–296). New York: Academic Press.

Paterniti, M. (2000). *Driving Mr. Albert: A trip across America with Einstein's brain.* New York: Random House.

Patten, S. C. (1977). Milgram's shocking experiments. *Philosophy, 52,* 425–440.

Paulos, J. A. (2003). *A mathematician plays the stock market.* New York: Basic Books.

Paulos, J. A. (2006, August 6). Who's counting: It's mean to ignore the median. Retrieved from www.abcnews.com/Technology/WhosCounting

Paulus, J. (2007, April/May). Lithium's healing power. *Scientific American MIND, 18,* 70–75.

Pavlov, I. P. (1960). *Conditioned reflexes: An investigation of the physiological activity of the cerebral cortex* (G.V. Anrep, Trans.). New York: Dover. (Original work published 1927)

Payne, D. G., & Wenger, M. J. (1996). Practice effects in memory: Data, theory, and unanswered questions. In D. Herrmann, C. McEvoy, C. Hertzog, P. Hertel, & M. K. Johnson (Eds.), *Basic and applied memory research: Practical applications* (Vol. 2, pp. 123–138). Mahwah, NJ: Erlbaum.

Peciña, M., Azhar, H., Love, T. M., Lu, T., Frederickson, B. L., Stohler, C. S., & Zubieta, J. K. (2013). Personality trait predictors of placebo analgesia and neurobiological correlates. *Neuropsychopharmacology, 38,* 639–646.

Penfield, W., & Boldrey, E. (1937). Somatic motor and sensory representation in the cerebral cortex of man as studied by electrical stimulation. *Brain, 60,* 389.

Penfield, W., & Rasmussen, T. (1968). *The cerebral cortex of man: A clinical study of localization of function.* New York: Hafner.

Perera, T. D., Dwork, A. J., Keegan, K. A., Thirumangalakudi, L., Lipira, C. M., Joyce, N., . . . Coplan, J. D. (2011). Necessity of hippocampal neurogenesis for the therapeutic action of antidepressants in adult nonhuman primates. *PLoS ONE 6*(4), e17600. doi:10.1371/journal.pone.0017600

Perry, G. (2013). *Behind the shock machine: The untold story of the notorious Milgram psychology experiments.* New York: The New Press.

Pert, C. B. (1997). *Molecules of emotion.* New York: Simon & Schuster.

Pert, C. B., & Snyder, S. H. (1973). Opiate receptors: Demonstration in the nervous tissue. *Science, 179,* 1011–1014.

Pessiglione, M., Petrovic, P., Daunizeau, J., Palminteri, S., Dolan, R. J., & Frith, C. D. (2008). Subliminal instrumental conditioning demonstrated in the human brain. *Neuron, 59,* 561–567.

Petersen, G. L., Finnerup, N. B., Colloca, L., Amanzio, M., Price, D. D., Jensen, T. S., & Vase, L. (2014). The magnitude of nocebo effects in pain: A meta-analysis. *Pain, 155,* 1426–1434.

Peterson, C., Maier, S. F., & Seligman, M. E. P. (1993). *Learned helplessness: A theory for the age of personal control.* New York: Oxford University Press.

Peterson, C., & Seligman, M. E. P. (1984). Causal explanations as a risk factor for depression: Theory and evidence. *Psychological Review, 91,* 347–374.

Peterson, L. R., & Peterson, M. J. (1959). Short-term retention of individual verbal items. *Journal of Experimental Psychology, 58,* 193–198.

Pettinati, H. M., Tamburello, B. A., Ruetsch, C. R., & Kaplan, F. N. (1994). Patient attitudes toward electroconvulsive therapy. *Psychopharmacology Bulletin, 30,* 471–475.

Phipps, M., Blume, J., & DeMonner, S. (2002). Young maternal age associated with increased risk of post-neonatal death. *Obstetrics and Gynecology, 100,* 481–486.

Piaget, J. (1929). *The child's conception of the world.* New York: Harcourt, Brace. (Original work published 1926)

Piaget, J. (1932). *The moral judgment of the child.* New York: Harcourt, Brace.

Piaget, J. (1952). *The origins of intelligence in children.* New York: International Universities Press. (Original work published 1936)

Piaget, J. (1972). Intellectual evolution from adolescence to adulthood. *Human Development, 15,* 1–12.

Piaget, J. (1983). Piaget's theory. In P. H. Mussen (Series Ed.) and W. Kessen (Vol. Ed.), *Handbook of child*

psychology: Vol. 1. History, theory, and methods (4th ed., pp. 103–126). New York: Wiley.

Pietschnig, J., & Voracek, M. (2015). One century of global IQ gains: A formal meta-analysis of the Flynn effect (1909–2013). *Perspectives on Psychological Science, 10,* 282–306.

Pinker, S. (1994). *The language instinct: How the mind creates language.* New York: William Morrow.

Pliner, P., Hart, H., Kohl, J., & Saari, D. (1974). Compliance without pressure: Some further data on the foot-in-the-door technique. *Journal of Experimental Social Psychology, 10,* 17–22.

Plomin, R., DeFries, J. C., McClearn, G. E., & Rutter, M. (1997). *Behavioral genetics.* New York: W. H. Freeman.

Plous, S. (1993). *The psychology of judgment and decision making.* New York: McGraw-Hill.

Porter, D., & Neuringer, A. (1984). Musical discriminations by pigeons. *Journal of Experimental Psychology: Animal Behavior Processes, 10,* 138–148.

Powell, R. A., Digdon, N., Harris, B., & Smithson, C. (2014). Correcting the record on Watson, Rayner, and Little Albert: Albert Barger as "psychology's lost boy." *American Psychologist, 69,* 600–611.

Powell, R. A., Symbaluk, D. G., & MacDonald, S. E. (2002). *Introduction to learning & behavior.* Belmont, CA: Wadsworth.

Pratkanis, A. R. (1992, Spring). The cargo-cult science of subliminal persuasion. *Skeptical Inquirer, 16,* 260–272.

Pratkanis, A. R., & Greenwald, A. G. (1988). Recent perspectives on unconscious processing: Still no marketing applications. *Psychology and Marketing, 5,* 337–353.

Pratt, L. A., Brody, D. J., & Gu, Q. (2011, October). *Antidepressant use in persons aged 12 and over: United States, 2005–2008.* (NCHS data brief, No. 76). Hyattsville, MD: National Center for Health Statistics. Retrieved from www.cdc.gov/nchs/data/databriefs/db76.htm

Premack, D. (1959). Toward empirical behavior laws: I. Positive reinforcement. *Psychological Review, 66,* 219–233.

Premack, D. (1965). Reinforcement theory. In D. Levine (Ed.), *Nebraska Symposium on Motivation* (Vol. 13, pp. 123–180). Lincoln, NE: University of Nebraska.

Prescott, C. (April 28, 2005). The lie of the Stanford prison experiment. *Stanford Daily,* in News section. Posted at: http://valtinsblog.blogspot.com.au/2012/03/lie-of-the-stanford-prison-experiment.html

Ptito, A., & Leh, S. E. (2007). Neural substrates of blindsight after hemispherectomy. *Neuroscientist, 13,* 506–518.

Pulver, S. E. (1961). The first electroconvulsive treatment given in the United States. *American Journal of Psychiatry, 117,* 845.

Ramachandran, V. W. (1992, May). Blind spots. *Scientific American, 266,* 86–91.

Ramachandran, V. W., & Blakeslee, S. (1998). *Phantoms in the brain: Probing the mysteries of the human mind.* New York: William Morrow and Company, Inc.

Ramachandran, V. W., & Gregory, R. L. (1991). Perceptual filling in of artificially induced scotomas in human vision. *Nature, 350,* 699–702.

Rammstedt, B., & John, O. P. (2007). Measuring personality in one minute or less: A 10-item short version of the Big Five Inventory in English and German. *Journal of Research in Personality, 41,* 203–212.

Rank, S. G., & Jacobson, C. K. (1977). Hospital nurses' compliance with medication overdose orders: A failure to replicate. *Journal of Health and Social Behavior, 18,* 188–193.

Raphael, B. (1976). *The thinking computer.* San Francisco: W. H. Freeman.

Rapoport, J. L. (1989, March). The biology of obsessions and compulsions. *Scientific American, 260,* 83–89.

Rapoport, J. L. (1991). Recent advances in obsessive-compulsive disorder. *Neuropsychopharmacology, 5,* 1–10.

Rapport, R. (2005). *Nerve endings: The discovery of the synapse.* New York: W. W. Norton.

Raskin, N. J., & Rogers, C. R. (1995). Person-centered therapy. In R. J. Corsini & D. Wedding (Eds.), *Current psychotherapies* (5th ed., pp. 144–149). Itasca, IL: Peacock.

Ratey, J. J. (2001). *A user's guide to the brain: Perception, attention, and the four theaters of the brain.* New York: Pantheon.

Ratiu, P., Talos, I.-F., Haker, S., Lieberman, D., & Everett, P. (2004). The tale of Phineas Gage, digitally remastered. *Journal of Neurotrauma, 21,* 637–643.

Ratnesar, R. (2011, July/August). The menace within. *Stanford Alumni Magazine*. Available at http://alumni.stanford.edu/get/page/magazine/article/?article_id=40741

Reber, P. (2010, May/June). Ask the Brains. *Scientific American MIND, 21,* 70.

Redelmeier, D. A., & Tversky, A. (1996). On the belief that arthritis pain is related to the weather. *PNAS, 93,* 2895–2896.

Regier, D. A., Narrow, W. E., Kuhl, E. A., & Kupfer, D. J. (Eds.). (2011). *The conceptual evolution of DSM-5.* Arlington, VA: American Psychiatric Association.

Reicher, S., & Haslam, S. A. (2006). Rethinking the psychology of tyranny: The BBC prison study. *British Journal of Social Psychology, 45,* 1–40.

Reicher, S., Haslam, S. A., & Smith, J. R. (2012). Working toward the experimenter: Reconceptualizing obedience within the Milgram paradigm as identification-based followership. *Perspectives on Psychological Science, 7,* 315–324.

Rescorla, R. A. (1988). Pavlovian conditioning: It's not what you think it is. *American Psychologist, 43,* 151–160.

Rescorla, R. A. (1996). Preservation of Pavlovian associations through extinction. *Quarterly Journal of Experimental Psychology, 49B,* 245–258.

Restak, R., & Kim, S. (2010). *The playful brain: The surprising science of how puzzles improve your mind.* New York: Penguin Group.

Restle, F. (1970). Moon illusion explained on the basis of relative size. *Science, 167,* 1092–1096.

Reuter-Lorenz, P. A., & Miller, A. C. (1998). The cognitive neuroscience of human laterality: Lessons from the bisected brain. *Current Directions in Psychological Science, 15,* 15–20.

Reverberi, C., Toraldo, A., D'Agostini, S., & Skrap, M. (2005). Better without (lateral) frontal cortex? Insight problems solved by frontal patients. *Brain, 128,* 2882–2890.

Ridley-Johnson, R., Cooper, H., & Chance, J. (1983). The relation of children's television viewing to school achievement and IQ. *Journal of Educational Research, 76,* 294–297.

Rief, W., Nestoriuc, Y., Weiss, S., Welzel, E., Barsky, A. J., & Hofmann, S. G. (2009). Meta-analysis of the placebo response in antidepressant trials. *Journal of Affective Disorders, 118,* 1–8.

Rilling, J. K., & Insel, T. R. (1998). Evolution of the cerebellum in primates: Differences in relative volume among monkeys, apes, and humans. *Brain, Behavior, and Evolution, 52,* 308.

Rinck, M. (1999). Memory for everyday objects: Where are the digits on numerical keypads? *Applied Cognitive Psychology, 13,* 329–350.

Ritov, I. (1996). Anchoring in simulated competitive market negotiation. *Organizational Behavior and Human Decision Processes, 67,* 16–25.

Rivas-Vasquez, R. A. (2003). Aripiprazole: A novel antipsychotic with dopamine stabilizing properties. *Professional Psychology: Research and Practice, 34,* 108–111.

Rizzolatti, G., & Arbib, M. A. (1998). Language within our grasp. *Trends in Neuroscience, 21,* 188–194.

Rizzolatti, G., & Craighero, L. (2004). The mirror-neuron system. *Annual Review of Neuroscience, 27,* 169–192.

Roberts, B. W., & DelVecchio, W. F. (2000). The rank-order consistency of personality traits from childhood to old age: A quantitative review of longitudinal studies. *Psychological Bulletin, 126,* 3–25.

Roberts, B. W., Smith, J., Jackson, J. J., & Edmonds, G. (2009). Compensatory conscientiousness and health in older couples. *Psychological Science, 20,* 553–559.

Rochat, F., & Blass, T. (2014). The "Bring a Friend" condition: A report and analysis of Milgram's unpublished Condition 24. *Journal of Social Issues, 70,* 456–472.

Roediger, H. L., & Karpicke, J. D. (2006). Test-enhanced learning: Taking memory tests improves long-term retention. *Psychological Science, 17,* 249–255.

Roese, N. J., & Vohs, K. D. (2012). Hindsight bias. *Perspectives on Psychological Science, 7,* 411–426.

Rogers, C. R. (1951). *Client-centered therapy: Its current practices, implications, and theory.* Boston: Houghton Mifflin.

Rogers, C. R. (1961). *On becoming a person: A therapist's view of psychotherapy.* Boston: Houghton Mifflin.

Rogers, T. B., Kuiper, N. A., & Kirker, W. S. (1977). Self-reference and the encoding of personal information. *Journal of Personality and Social Psychology, 35,* 677–688.

Rohrer, D., & Taylor, K. (2006). The effects of overlapping and distributed practise on the retention of mathematics knowledge. *Applied Cognitive Psychology, 20,* 1209–1224.

Rohrer, J. H., Baron, S. H., Hoffman, E. L., & Swander, D. V. (1954). The stability of autokinetic judgments. *Journal of Abnormal and Social Psychology, 49*, 595–597.

Rorschach, H. (1942). *Psychodiagnostik* (Hans Huber, Trans.). Bern, Switzerland: Verlag. (Original work published in 1921)

Rosch, E. H. (1973). Natural categories. *Cognitive Psychology, 4*, 328–350.

Rosenberg, A., Ledley, D. R., & Heimberg, R. G. (2010). Social anxiety disorder. In D. McKay, J. S. Abramowitz & S. Taylor (Eds.), *Cognitive-behavioral therapy for refractory cases: Turning failure into success* (pp. 65–88). Washington, DC: American Psychological Association.

Rosenhan, D. L. (1973). On being sane in insane places. *Science, 179*, 250–258.

Rosenthal, A. M. (1964). *Thirty-eight witnesses: The Kitty Genovese case.* New York: McGraw-Hill.

Rosenthal, R. (1966). *Experimenter effects in behavioral research.* New York: Appleton-Century-Crofts.

Rosenthal, R. (1994). Interpersonal expectancy effects: A 30-year perspective. *Current Directions in Psychological Science, 3*, 176–179.

Rosenthal, R., & Jacobson, L. (1968). *Pygmalion in the classroom: Teacher expectation and pupils' intellectual development.* New York: Holt, Rinehart & Winston.

Ross, L. (1977). The intuitive psychologist and his shortcomings: Distortions in the attribution process. In L. Berkowitz (Ed.), *Advances in experimental social psychology* (Vol. 10, pp. 173–220). New York: Academic Press.

Rotenberg, K. J., Costa, P., Trueman, M., & Lattimore, P. (2012). An interactional test of the reformulated helplessness theory of depression in women receiving clinical treatment for eating disorders. *Eating Behaviors, 13*, 264–266.

Rotter, J. B. (1966). Generalized expectancies for internal versus external control of reinforcement. *Psychological Monographs, 80* (1, Whole No. 609).

Rotter, J. B. (1990). Internal versus external control of reinforcement: A case history of a variable. *American Psychologist, 45*, 489–493.

Rubin, D. C., & Konstis, T. C. (1983). A schema for common cents. *Memory & Cognition, 11*, 335–341.

Rubin, E. (2001). Figure and ground. In S. Yantis (Ed.), *Visual perception: Essential readings* (pp. 225–230). Philadelphia: Psychology Press. (Original work published 1921)

Rubin, N. (2001). Figure and ground in the brain. *Nature Neuroscience, 4*, 857–858.

Rundus, D., & Atkinson, R. C. (1970). Rehearsal processes in free recall: A procedure for direct observation. *Journal of Verbal Learning and Verbal Behavior, 9*, 99–105.

Ruscio, J. (2004). Diagnosis and the behaviors they denote: A critical evaluation of the labeling theory of mental illness. *The Scientific Review of Mental Health Practice, 3*, 5–22.

Ruscio, J. (2015). Rosenhan pseudopatient study. In R. L. Cautin & S. O. Lilienfeld (Eds.), *The encyclopedia of clinical psychology* (p. 425). New York: Wiley.

Russell, N. (2009). *Stanley Milgram's obedience to authority experiments: Towards an understanding of their relevance in explaining aspects of the Nazi Holocaust.* University of Wellington, Australia. Retrieved from http://researcharchive.vuw.ac.nz/handle/10063/1091

Russell, N. (2014). Stanley Milgram's obedience to authority "relationship" condition: Some methodological and theoretical implications. *Social Sciences, 3*, 194–214.

Sabbagh, L. (2006, August/September). The teen brain, hard at work. No, Really. *Scientific American MIND, 17*, 20–25.

Sackett, P. R., Bornerman, M. J., & Connelly, B. J. (2008). High-stakes testing in higher education and employment: Appraising the evidence for validity and fairness. *American Psychologist, 63*, 215–227.

Sackett, P. R., Schmitt, N., Ellingson, J. E., & Kabin, M. B. (2001). High-stakes testing in employment, credentialing, and higher education: Prospects in a post-affirmative action world. *American Psychologist, 56*, 302–318.

Sanders, A. R., Duan, J., & Gejman, P. V. (2012). Schizophrenia genetics: What have learned from genome-wide association studies? In A. S. Brown & P. H. Patterson (Eds.), *The origins of schizophrenia* (pp. 175–209). New York: Columbia University Press.

Sareen, J., Afifi, T. O., McMillan, K. A., & Asmundson, G. J. G. (2011). Relationship between household income and mental disorders: Findings from a population-based longitudinal study. *Archives of General Psychiatry, 68*, 419–426.

Sargolini, F., Fyhn, M., Hafting, T., McNaughton, B. L., Witter, M. P., Moser, M. B., & Moser, E. I. (2006). Conjunctive representation of position, direction, and velocity in the entorhinal cortex. *Science, 312,* 758–762.

Satel, S. L., & Lilienfeld, S. O. (2013). *Brainwashed: The seductive appeal of mindless neuroscience.* New York: Basic Books.

Saufley, W. H., Otaka, S. R., & Bavaresco, J. L. (1985). Context effects: Classroom tests and context independence. *Memory and Cognition, 13,* 522–528.

Schachter, S., & Singer, J. E. (1962). Cognitive, social, and physiological determinants of emotional state. *Psychological Review, 69,* 379–399.

Schacter, D. L. (1996). *Searching for memory: The brain, the mind, and the past.* New York: Basic Books.

Schacter, D. L. (2000). *The seven sins of memory: How the mind forgets and remembers.* New York: Houghton Mifflin.

Schafe, G. E., Sollars, S. I., & Bernstein, I. L. (1995). The CS-UCS interval and taste aversion learning: A brief look. *Behavioral Neuroscience, 109,* 799–802.

Schaie, K. W. (1994). The life course of adult intellectual development. *American Psychologist, 49,* 304–313.

Schaie, K. W. (1995). *Intellectual development in adulthood: The Seattle Longitudinal Study.* New York: Cambridge University Press.

Schank, R. C., & Abelson, R. P. (1977). *Scripts, plans, goals, and understanding: An inquiry into human knowledge structures.* Hillsdale, NJ: Erlbaum.

Schiferle, E. (2013). An impulse of hope for individuals with treatment-resistant depression. *Columbia Science Review.* Retrieved from http://csrspreadscience.wordpress.com/2013/11/05

Schizophrenia Working Group of the Psychiatric Genomics Consortium. (2014). Biological insights from 108 schizophrenia-associated genetic loci. *Nature, 511,* 421–427.

Schmid, M. C., Mrowka, S. W., Turchi, J., Saunders, R. C., Wilke, M., Peters, A. J., . . . Leopold, D. A. (2010). Blindsight depends on the lateral geniculate nucleus. *Nature, 466,* 373–377.

Schmidt, D. P., Allik, J., McCrae, R. R., & Benet-Martinez, V. (2007). The geographic distribution of big five personality traits: Patterns and profiles of human self-description across 56 nations. *Journal of Cross-Cultural Psychology, 38,* 173–212.

Schmidt, F. L., & Hunter, J. E. (1998). The validity and utility of selection methods in personnel psychology: Practical and theoretical implications of 85 years of research findings. *Psychological Bulletin, 124,* 262–274.

Schneider, B. H., Atkinson, L., & Tardif, C. (2001). Child-parent attachment and children's peer relations: A quantitative review. *Developmental Psychology, 37,* 86–100.

Schneider, W. (1993). Domain-specific knowledge and memory performance in children. *Educational Psychology Review, 5,* 257–273.

Schultz, D. (2001). *Theories of personality* (7th ed.). Pacific Grove, CA: Brooks/Cole.

Shultz, S., & Vouloumanos, A. (2010). Three-month-olds prefer speech to other naturally occurring signals. *Language Learning and Development, 6,* 241–257.

Schwartz, N. (1999). Self-reports: How the questions shape the answers. *American Psychologist, 54,* 93–105.

Schwartzkopf, D. S., Song, C., & Rees, G. (2011). The surface area of human V1 predicts the subjective experience of object size. *Nature Neuroscience, 14,* 28–30.

Scott, B. W., Wojtowicz, J. M., & Burnham, W. M. (2000). Neurogenesis in the dentate gyrus of the rat following electroconvulsive shock seizures. *Experimental Neurology, 165,* 231–236.

Scoville, W. B., & Milner, B. (1957). Loss of recent memory after bilateral hippocampal lesions. *Journal of Neurology, Neurosurgery and Psychiatry, 20,* 11–21.

Segall, M. H., Campbell, D. T., & Herskovits, M. J. (1963). Cultural differences in the perception of geometric illusions. *Science, 193,* 769–771.

Segall, M. H., Campbell, D. T., & Herskovits, M. J. (1966). *The influence of culture on visual perception.* Indianapolis, IN: Bobbs-Merrill.

Segall, M. H., Dasen, P. R., Berry, J. W., & Poortinga, Y. H. (1990). *Human behavior in a global perspective: An introduction to cross-cultural psychology.* New York: Pergamon.

Seligman, M. E. P. (1971). Phobias and preparedness. *Behavior Therapy, 2,* 307–320.

Seligman, M. E. P. (1975). *Helplessness: On depression, development, and death.* San Francisco: W. H. Freeman.

Seligman, M. E. P. (1994). *What you can change and what you can't: The ultimate guide to self-improvement.* New York: Knopf.

Seligman, M. E. P., Castellon, C., Cacciola, J., Schulman, P., Luborsky, L., Ollove, M., & Downing, R. (1988). Explanatory style change during cognitive therapy for unipolar depression. *Journal of Abnormal Psychology, 97,* 13–18.

Seligman, M. E. P., Walker, E. F., & Rosenhan, D. L. (2001). *Abnormal psychology* (4th ed.). New York: Norton.

Senfor, A. J., Van Petten, C., & Kutas, M. (2002). Episodic action memory for real objects: An ERP investigation with perform, watch and imagine action encoding tasks versus a non-action encoding task. *Journal of Cognitive Neuroscience, 14,* 402–419.

Senghas, A., & Coppola, M. (2001). Children creating language: How Nicaraguan sign language acquired a spatial grammar. *Psychological Science, 12,* 323–328.

Sergent, J., Ohta, S., & MacDonald, B. (1992). Functional neuroanatomy of face and object processing: A positron emission tomography study. *Brain, 115,* 15–36.

Seung, S. (2012). *Connectome: How the brain's wiring makes us who we are.* New York: Houghton Mifflin Harcourt.

Shadish, W. R., Matt, G. E., Navarro, A. M., & Phillips, G. (2000). The effects of psychological therapies under clinically representative conditions: A meta-analysis. *Psychological Bulletin, 126,* 512–529.

Sharman, S. J., Garry, M., & Beuke, C. J. (2004). Imagination or exposure causes imagination inflation. *American Journal of Psychology, 117,* 157–168.

Sharp, E. S., Reynolds, C. A., Pedersen, N. L., & Gatz, M. (2010). Cognitive engagement and cognitive aging: Is openness protective? *Psychology and Aging, 25,* 60–73.

Shedler, J. (2010). The efficacy of psychodynamic psychotherapy. *American Psychologist, 63,* 98–109.

Sheingold, K. (1973). Developmental differences in intake and storage of visual information. *Journal of Experimental Child Psychology, 16,* 1–11.

Shepard, R. N. (1990). *Mind sights: Original visual illusions, ambiguities, and other anomalies.* New York: W. H. Freeman.

Sherif, M. (1937). An experimental approach to the study of attitudes. *Sociometry, 1,* 90–98.

Sherif, M., & Sherif, C. W. (1969). *Social psychology.* New York: Harper and Row.

Shermer, M. (2008, October/November). Why you should be skeptical of brain scans. *Scientific American MIND, 19,* 66–71.

Silver, N. (2012). *The signal and the noise: Why so many predictions fail—but some don't.* New York: Penguin.

Simpkins, S., Parke, R., Flyr, M., & Wild, M. (2006). Similarities in children's and early adolescents' perceptions of friendship qualities across development, gender, and friendship qualities. *Journal of Early Adolescence, 26,* 491–508.

Siu, A. L. (2016). Screening for breast cancer: U. S. Preventive Services Task Force recommendation statement. *Annals of Internal Medicine, 164,* 279–296.

Skinner, B. F. (1938). *The behavior of organisms: An experimental analysis.* New York: Appleton-Century-Crofts.

Skinner, B. F. (1956). A case history in the scientific method. *American Psychologist, 45,* 1206–1210.

Skotko, B. G., Kensinger, E. A., Locascio, J. J., Einstein, G., Rubin, D. C., Tupler, L. A., . . . Corkin, S. (2004). Puzzling thoughts for H. M.: Can new semantic information be anchored to old semantic memories? *Neuropsychology, 18,* 756–769.

Slater, M. D., Henry, K. L., Swaim, R. C., & Anderson, L. L. (2003). Violent media content and aggressiveness in adolescents: A downward spiral model. *Communication Research, 30,* 713–736.

Slovic, P., & Fischhoff, B. (1977). On the psychology of experimental surprises. *Journal of Experimental Psychology: Human Perception and Performance, 3,* 544–551.

Smith, M. B. (1978). Psychology and values. *Journal of Social Issues, 34,* 181–199.

Smith, C. N., & Squire, L. R. (2009). Medial temporal lobe activity during retrieval of semantic memory is related to the age of the memory. *The Journal of Neuroscience, 29,* 930–938.

Smith, M. L., Glass, G. V., & Miller, T. I. (1980). *The benefits of psychotherapy.* Baltimore, MD: Johns Hopkins University Press.

Smith, S. M., Glenberg, A., & Bjork, R. A. (1978). Environmental context and human memory. *Memory and Cognition, 6,* 342–353.

Snarey, J. R. (1985). Cross-cultural universality of social-moral development: A critical review of Kohlbergian research. *Psychological Bulletin, 97,* 202–232.

Sorkhabi, N. (2005). Applicability of Baumrind's parent typology to collective cultures: Analysis of cultural explanations of parent socialization effects. *International Journal of Behavioral Development, 29,* 552–563.

Soussignan, R. (2002). Duchenne smile, emotional experience, and autonomic reactivity: A test of the facial-feedback hypothesis. *Emotion, 2,* 52–74.

Spearman, C. (1927). *The abilities of man.* New York: Macmillan.

Spence, M. J., & Freeman, M. S. (1996). Newborn infants prefer the low-pass filtered voice, but not the maternal whispered voice. *Infant Behavior and Development, 19,* 199–212.

Sperling, G. (1960). The information available in brief visual presentations. *Psychological Monographs, 74* (Whole No. 498).

Spitzer, R. L. (1975). On pseudoscience in science, logic in remission, and psychiatric diagnosis: A critique of Rosenhan's "On being sane in insane places." *Journal of Abnormal Psychology, 84,* 442–452.

Spitzer, R. L. (1976). More on pseudoscience in science and the case for psychiatric diagnosis: A critique of D. L. Rosenhan's "On being sane in insane places" and "The contextual nature of psychiatric diagnosis." *Archives of General Psychiatry, 33,* 459–470.

Springer, S. P., & Deutsch, G. (1998). *Left brain, right brain* (5th ed.). New York: W. H. Freeman.

Squire, L. R. (2004). Memory systems of the brain: A brief history and current perspective. *Neurobiology of Learning and Memory, 82,* 171–177.

Squire, L. R. (2009). The legacy of patient H. M. for neuroscience. *Neuron, 61,* 6–9.

Squire, L. R., & Cohen, N. J. (1984). Human memory and amnesia. In G. Lynch, J. L. McGaugh, & N. M. Weinberger (Eds.), *Neurobiology of learning and memory* (pp. 3–64). New York: Guilford Press.

Staddon, J. E. R., & Ettinger, R. H. (1989). *Learning: An introduction to the principles of adaptive behavior.* San Diego: Harcourt.

Stanovich, K. E. (2009a, November/December). Rational and irrational thought: The thinking that IQ tests miss. *Scientific American MIND, 20,* 34–39.

Stanovich, K. E. (2009b). *What intelligence tests miss: The psychology of rational thought.* New Haven, CT: Yale University Press.

Stanovich, K. E. (2010). *How to think straight about psychology* (9th ed.). Needham Heights, MA: Allyn and Bacon.

Stanovich, K. E., & West, R. F. (2000). Individual differences in reasoning: Implications for the rationality debate. *Behavioral and Brain Sciences, 23,* 645–665.

Stern, W. (1914). *The psychological methods of testing intelligence* (G. M. Whipple, Trans.). Baltimore, MD: Warrick and York.

Sternberg, R. J. (1985). *Beyond IQ: A triarchic theory of intelligence.* New York: Cambridge University Press.

Sternberg, R. J. (1988). *The triarchic mind: A new theory of human intelligence.* New York: Viking.

Sternberg, R. J. (1999). The theory of successful intelligence. *Review of General Psychology, 3,* 292–316.

Sternberg, R. J., & Davidson, J. E. (1982, June). The mind of the puzzler. *Psychology Today, 16,* 37–44.

Stevens, S. S. (1962). The surprising simplicity of sensory metrics. *American Psychologist, 17,* 29–39.

Stevens, S. S. (1975). *Psychophysics: Introduction to its perceptual, neural, and social prospects.* New York: Wiley.

Stevenson, H. W., Chen, C., & Lee, S. (1993). Mathematics achievement of Chinese, Japanese, and American schoolchildren: Ten years later. *Science, 259,* 53–58.

Stevenson, H. W., & Stigler, J. W. (1992). *The learning gap.* New York: Summit.

Stewart, N. (2009). The cost of anchoring. *Psychological Science, 20,* 39–41.

Stewart, V. M. (1973). Tests of the "carpentered world" hypothesis by race and environment in America and Zambia. *International Journal of Psychology, 8,* 83–94.

Stewart-Williams, S. (2004). The placebo puzzle: Putting together the pieces. *Health Psychology, 23,* 198–206.

Stickgold, R., & Ellenbogen, J. M. (2009, August/September). Quiet! Sleeping brain at work. *Scientific American MIND, 19,* 22–29.

Stickgold, R., Hobson, J. A., Fosse, R., & Fosse, M. (2001). Sleep, learning, and dreams: Off-line memory reprocessing. *Science, 294,* 1052–1057.

Stone, J. M. (2011). Glutamatergic antipsychotic drugs: A new dawn in the treatment of schizophrenia? *Therapeutic Advances in Psychopharmacology, 1,* 5–18.

Stone, V. E., Nisenson, L., Eliassen, J. C., & Gazzaniga, M. S. (1996). Left hemisphere representations of emotional facial expressions. *Neuropsychologica, 34,* 23–29.

Sweeney, M. S. (2009). *Brain: The complete mind.* Washington, DC: National Geographic.

Sweeney, M. S. (2011). *Brain works: The mind-bending science of how you see, what you think, and who you are.* Washington, DC: National Geographic.

Swets, J. A. (1964). *Signal detection and recognition by human observers.* New York: Wiley.

Symons, C. S., & Johnson, B. T. (1997). The self-reference effect in memory: A meta-analysis. *Psychological Bulletin, 121,* 371–394.

Takei, N., Van Os, J., & Murray, R. M. (1995). Maternal exposure to influenza and risk of schizophrenia: A 22 year study from the Netherlands. *Journal of Psychiatric Research, 29,* 435–445.

Talmi, D., Grady, C. L., Goshen-Gottstein, Y., & Moscovitch, M. (2005). Neuroimaging the serial position curve: A test of single-store versus dual-store models. *Psychological Science, 16,* 716–723.

Tammet, D. (2009). *Embracing the wide sky: A tour across the horizons of the mind.* New York: Free Press.

Tang, S., & Hall, V. C. (1995). The overjustification effect: A meta-analysis. *Applied Cognitive Psychology, 9,* 365–404.

Tavris, C. A. (2014, October). Teaching contentious classics. *APS Observer, 27*(8). Retrieved from www.psychologicalscience.org/index.php/publications/observer/2014/october-14/teaching-contentious-classics.html

Tavris, C., & Aronson, E. (2007). *Mistakes were made (but not by me): Why we justify foolish beliefs, bad decisions, and hurtful acts.* New York: Harcourt.

Teghtsoonian, R. (1971). On the exponents in Stevens's law and the constant in Ekman's law. *Psychological Review, 78,* 71–80.

Teigen, K. H. (1986). Old truths or fresh insights? A study of students' evaluation of proverbs. *British Journal of Social Psychology, 25,* 43–50.

Teplin, L. A. (1985). The criminality of the mentally ill: A deadly misconception. *American Journal of Psychiatry, 142,* 593–598.

Terman, L. M. (1916). *The measurement of intelligence.* Boston: Houghton Mifflin.

Thaler, R., & Sunstein, C. (2008). *Nudge: Improving decisions about health, wealth, and happiness.* New Haven, CT: Yale University Press.

Thelen, E. (1995). Motor development: A new synthesis. *American Psychologist, 50,* 79–95.

Thomas, A. K., Bulevich, J. B., & Loftus, E. F. (2003). Exploring the role of repetition and sensory elaboration in the imagination inflation effect. *Memory & Cognition, 31,* 630–640.

Thompson, P. (1980). Margaret Thatcher: A new illusion. *Perception, 9,* 483–484.

Thompson, R. F. (2000). *The brain: A neuroscience primer* (3rd ed.). New York: Worth.

Thorndike, E. L. (1898). Animal intelligence: An experimental study of the associative processes in animals. *Psychological Review Monograph Supplement, 2* (No. 8).

Thorndike, E. L. (1911). *Animal intelligence: Experimental studies.* New York: Macmillan.

Thurstone, L. L. (1938). *Primary mental abilities.* Chicago: University of Chicago Press.

Tilburt, J. C., Emanuel, E. J., Kaptchuk, T. J., Curlin, F. A., & Miller, F. G. (2008, October 23). Prescribing placebo treatments: Results of a national survey of US internists and rheumatologists. *British Medical Journal, 337,* a1938. doi:10.1136/bmj.a1938

Tolman, E. C., & Honzik, C. H. (1930a). Degrees of hunger, reward and non-reward, and maze learning in rats. *University of California Publications in Psychology, 4,* 241–256.

Tolman, E. C., & Honzik, C. H. (1930b). "Insight" in rats. *University of California Publications in Psychology, 4,* 215–232.

Tolman, E. C., & Honzik, C. H. (1930c). Introduction and removal of reward, and maze performance in rats. *University of California Publications in Psychology, 4,* 257–275.

Tomasello, M. (2003). *Constructing a language: A usage-based theory of language acquisition.* Cambridge, MA: Harvard University Press.

Tomasello, M., Strosberg, R., & Akhtar, N. (1996). Eighteen-month-old children learn words in non-ostensive contexts. *Journal of Child Language, 23,* 157–176.

Tong, F., Nakayama, K., Moscovitch, M., Weinrib, O., & Kanwisher, N. (2000). Response properties of the human fusiform face area. *Cognitive Neuropsychology, 17,* 257–279.

Torrey, E. F., Bartko, J. J., Lun, Z.-R., & Yolken, R. H. (2007). Antibodies to *Toxoplasma gondii* in patients with schizophrenia: A meta-analysis. *Schizophrenia Bulletin, 33,* 729–736.

Torrey, E. F., Bartko, J. J., & Yolken, R. H. (2012). *Toxoplasma gondii* and other risk factors for schizophrenia: An update. *Schizophrenia Bulletin, 38,* 642–647.

Torrey, E. F., Miller, J., Rawlings, R., & Yolken, R. H. (1997). Seasonality of births in schizophrenia and bipolar disorder: A review of the literature. *Schizophrenia Research, 28,* 1–38.

Torrey, E. F., Rawlings, R., & Yolken, R. H. (2000). The antecedents of psychoses: A case-control study of selected risk factors. *Schizophrenia Research, 46,* 17–23.

Torrey, E. F., & Yolken, R. H. (1995). Could schizophrenia be a viral zoonosis transmitted from house cats? *Schizophrenia Bulletin, 21,* 167–171.

Torrey, E. F., & Yolken, R. H. (2003). *Toxoplasma gondii* and schizophrenia. *Emerging Infectious Diseases, 9,* 1375–1380.

Tovee, M. J., Rolls, E., & Ramachandran, V. S. (1996). Rapid visual learning in neurons in the primate visual cortex. *Neuroreport, 7,* 2757–2760.

Trahan, L., Stuebing, K. K., Hiscock, M. K., & Fletcher, J. M. (2014). The Flynn effect: A meta-analysis. *Psychological Bulletin, 140,* 1332–1360.

Tranel, D., & Damasio, A. R. (1985). Knowledge without awareness: An autonomic index of facial expression by prosopagnosics. *Science, 228,* 1453–1454.

Trappey, C. (1996). A meta-analysis of consumer choice and subliminal advertising. *Psychology and Marketing, 13,* 517–530.

Treadway, M. T., & Pizzagalli, D. A. (2014). Imaging the pathophysiology of major depressive disorder—from localist models to circuit-based analysis. *Biology of Mood & Anxiety Disorders, 4,* 5.

Tsuang, M. T., & Faraone, S. V. (1990). *The genetics of mood disorders.* Baltimore, MD: Johns Hopkins University Press.

Tuddenham, R. D. (1948). Soldier intelligence in World Wars I and II. *American Psychologist, 3,* 54–56.

Tulving, E. (1972). Episodic and semantic memory. In E. Tulving & W. Donaldson (Eds.), *Organization of memory* (pp. 381–403). New York: Academic Press.

Tulving, E. (1974, January/February). Cue-dependent forgetting. *American Scientist, 62,* 74–82.

Tulving, E. (1983). *Elements of episodic memory.* New York: Oxford University Press.

Tulving, E., Schacter, D. L., & Stark, H. (1982). Priming effects in word-fragment completion are independent of recognition memory. *Journal of Experimental Psychology: Learning, Memory, and Cognition, 8,* 336–342.

Tuttle, A. H., Tohyama, S., Ramsay, T., Kimmelman, J., Schweinhardt, P. Bennett, G. J., & Mogil, J. S. (2015). Increasing placebo responses over time in U.S. clinical trials of neuropathic pain. *Pain, 156,* 2616–2626.

Tversky, A., & Kahneman, D. (1971). Belief in the law of small numbers. *Psychological Bulletin, 76,* 105–110.

Tversky, A., & Kahneman, D. (1973). Availability: A heuristic for judging frequency and probability. *Cognitive Psychology, 5,* 207–232.

Tversky, A., & Kahneman, D. (1974). Judgment under uncertainty: Heuristics and biases. *Science, 185,* 1124–1131.

Tversky, A., & Kahneman, D. (1983). Extensional versus intuitive reasoning: The conjunction fallacy in probability judgment. *Psychological Review, 90,* 293–315.

Twitmyer, E. B. (1974). A study of the knee jerk. *Journal of Experimental Psychology, 103,* 1047–1066.

Uttal, W. (2003). *The new phrenology: The limits of localizing cognitive processes in the brain.* Cambridge, MA: MIT Press.

Valenstein, E. S. (1986). *Great and desperate cures: The rise and decline of psychosurgery and other radical treatments.* New York: Basic Books.

Valenstein, E. S. (1988). *Blaming the brain: The truth about drugs and mental health.* New York: Free Press.

Valenstein, E. S. (2005). *The war of the soups and sparks: The discovery of neurotransmitters and the dispute over how nerves communicate.* New York: Columbia University Press.

Valenza, E., Simion, F., Cassia, V. M., & Umiltà, C. (1996). Face preferences at birth. *Journal of Experimental Psychology: Human Perception & Performance, 22,* 892–903.

Van Horn, J. D., Irinia, A., Torgerson, C. M., Chambers, M., Kikinis, R., & Toga, A. W. (2012). Mapping connectivity damage in the case of Phineas Gage. *PLoS ONE, 7*(5), e37454. doi:10.1371/journal.pone.0037454

van Praag, H., Schinder, A. F., Christie, B. R., Toni, N., Palmer, T. D., & Gage, F. H. (2002). Functional neurogenesis in the adult hippocampus. *Nature, 415,* 1030–1034.

Vasta, R., Miller, S. A., & Ellis, S. (2004). *Child psychology* (4th ed.). New York: Wiley.

Vertosick, F. T., Jr. (1997, October). Lobotomy's back. *Discover, 18,* 66–68, 70–72.

Vigen, T. (2015). *Spurious correlations: Correlation does not equal causation.* New York: Hachette Books.

von der Heydt, R., Peterhans, E., & Baumgartner, G. (1984). Illusory contours and cortical neuron responses. *Science, 224,* 1260–1262.

Vygotsky, L. S. (1978). *Mind in society: The development of higher psychological processes.* Cambridge, MA: Harvard University Press. (Original work published 1930, 1933, & 1935)

Vygotsky, L. S. (1986). *Thought and language.* Cambridge, MA: MIT Press. (Original work published 1934)

Vyse, S. A. (1997). *Believing in magic: The psychology of superstition.* New York: Oxford University Press.

Waber, R. L., Shiv, B., Carmon, Z., & Ariely, D. (2008). Commercial features of placebo and therapeutic efficacy. *Journal of the American Medical Association, 299,* 1016–1017.

Wald, G. (1964). The receptors of human color vision. *Science, 145,* 1007–1017.

Waldman, M., Nicholson, S., Adilov, N., & Williams, J. (2008). Autism prevalence and precipitation rates in California, Oregon, and Washington counties. *Archives of Pediatric and Adolescent Medicine, 162,* 1026–1034.

Walsh, D. A., & Thompson, L. W. (1978). Age differences in visual sensory memory. *Journal of Gerontology, 33,* 383–387.

Washington, H. A. (2015). *Infectious madness: The surprising science of how we "catch" mental illness.* New York: Little, Brown & Co.

Wason, P. C. (1960). On the failure to eliminate hypotheses in a conceptual task. *The Quarterly Journal of Experimental Psychology, 12,* 129–140.

Wason, P. C. (1966). Reasoning. In B. M. Foss (Ed.), *New horizons in psychology* (pp. 135–151). Harmondsworth, ENG: Penguin.

Wason, P. C. (1968). Reasoning about a rule. *The Quarterly Journal of Experimental Psychology, 20,* 273–281.

Watanabe, S., Sakamoto, J., & Wakita, M. (1995). Pigeons' discrimination of painting by Monet and Picasso. *Journal of the Experimental Analysis of Behavior, 63,* 165–174.

Watkins, C. E., Campbell, V. L., Nieberding, R., & Hallmark, R. (1995). Contemporary practice of psychological assessment by clinical psychologists. *Professional Psychology: Research and Practice, 26,* 54–60.

Watson, J. B. (1913). Psychology as the behaviorist views it. *Psychological Review, 20,* 158–177.

Watson, J. B. (1919). *Psychology from the standpoint of the behaviorist.* Philadelphia: Lippincott.

Watson, J. B., & Rayner, R. (1920). Conditioned emotional reactions. *Journal of Experimental Psychology, 3,* 1–14.

Weiner, B. (1975). "On being sane in insane places": A process (attributional) analysis and critique. *Journal of Abnormal Psychology, 84,* 433–441.

Weiner, I. B., & Greene, R. L. (2008). *Handbook of personality assessment.* New York: Wiley.

Weisberg, R., & Alba, J. W. (1981). An examination of the alleged role of "fixation" in the solution of several "insight" problems. *Journal of Experimental Psychology: General, 110,* 169–192.

Weiskrantz, L. (2009). *Blindsight: A case study spanning 35 years and new developments.* New York: Oxford University Press.

Weiskrantz, L., Warrington, E. K., Sanders, M. D., & Marshall, J. (1974). Visual capacity in the hemianopic field following a restricted occipital ablation. *Brain, 97,* 709–728.

Weissman, M. M., Bland, R. C., Canino, G. J., Faravelli, C., Greenwald, S., Hwu, H. G., . . . Yeh, E. K. (1996). Cross-national epidemiology of major depression and bipolar disorder. *Journal of the American Medical Association, 276,* 293–299.

Weisstein, E. W. (2009). Young girl-old woman illusion. From *MathWorld*—A Wolfram Web Resource. Retrieved from www.mathworld.wolfram.com/YoungGirl-OldWomanIllusion.html

Wellman, H. M., Cross, D., & Watson, J. (2001). Meta-analysis of theory-of-mind development: The truth about false belief. *Child Development, 72,* 655–684.

Werner, L. A. (2007). Human auditory development. In P. Dallos & D. Oertel (Eds.), *The senses: A comprehensive reference: Vol. 3. Audition* (pp. 871–894). St. Louis, MO: Elsevier.

Westen, D. (1998). The scientific legacy of Sigmund Freud: Toward a psychodynamically informed psychological science. *Psychological Bulletin, 124,* 333–371.

Westly, E. (2010, May/June). Different shades of blue. *Scientific American MIND, 21,* 30–37.

Weyandt, L. L. (2006). *The physiological basis of cognitive and behavioral disorders.* Mahwah, NJ: Erlbaum.

Wheelan, C. (2013). *Naked statistics: Stripping the dread from the data.* New York: W. W. Norton & Company.

Whitehurst, G. J., & Valdez-Menchaca, M. C. (1988). What is the role of reinforcement in early language acquisition? *Child Development, 59,* 430–440.

Wickelgren, W. A. (1974). *How to solve problems: Elements of a theory of problems and problem solving.* San Francisco: W. H. Freeman.

Widiger, T. A. (2009). Neuroticism. In M. R. Leary & R. H. Hoyle (Eds.), *Handbook of individual differences in social behavior* (pp. 129–146). New York: Guilford.

Wigdor, A. K., & Garner, W. R. (Eds.). (1982). *Ability testing: Uses, consequences, and controversies.* Washington, DC: National Academy Press.

Wiggins, J. S. (Ed.). (1996). *The five-factor model of personality: Theoretical perspectives.* New York: Guilford.

Wilcoxon, H. C., Dragoin, W. B., & Kral, P. A. (1971). Illness-induced aversions in rats and quail: Relative salience of visual and gustatory cues. *Science, 171,* 826–828.

Wilgus, B., & Wilgus, J. (2009). Face to face with Phineas Gage. *Journal of the History of the Neurosciences, 18,* 340–345.

Williams, H., Conway, M. A., & Cohen, G. (2008). Autobiographical memory. In G. Cohen & M. A. Conway (Eds.), *Memory in the real world* (pp. 21–90). New York: Psychology Press.

Williams, J. H., Whiten, A., Suddendorf, T., & Perrett, D. I. (2001). Imitation, mirror neurons and autism. *Neuroscience and Biobehavioral Review, 25,* 287–295.

Williams, K. D., Harkins, S. G., & Latané, B. (1981). Identifiability as a deterrent to social loafing: Two cheering experiments. *Journal of Personality and Social Psychology, 40,* 303–311.

Williams, R. L. (2013). Overview of the Flynn effect. *Intelligence, 41,* 753–764.

Wilmer, J. B., Germine, L., Chabris, C. F., Chatterjee, G., Williams, M., Loken, E., . . . Duchaine, B. (2010). Human face recognition ability is specific and highly heritable. *PNAS, 107,* 5238–5241.

Witelson, S. F., Kigar, D. L., & Harvey, T. (1999). The exceptional brain of Albert Einstein. *Lancet, 363,* 2149–2158.

Woloshin, S., Schwartz, L. M., & Welch, H. G. (2008). *Know your chances: Understanding health statistics.* Berkeley, CA: University of California Press.

Wolpe, J. (1958). *Psychotherapy by reciprocal inhibition.* Stanford, CA: Stanford University Press.

Wong, K. F. E., & Kwong, J. Y. Y. (2000). Is 7300 m equal to 7.3 km? Same semantics but different anchoring effects. *Organizational Behavior and Human Decision Processes, 82,* 314–333.

Wongupparaj, P., Kumari, V., & Morris, R. G. (2015). A cross-temporal meta-analysis of Raven's Progressive Matrices: Age groups and developing and developed countries. *Intelligence, 49,* 1–9.

Wood, J. M., Garb, H. N., Nezworski, M. T., Lilienfeld, S. O., & Duke, M. C. (2015). A second look at the validity of widely used Rorschach indices: Comment on Mihura, Meyer, Dumitrascu, and Bombel (2013). *Psychological Bulletin, 141,* 236–249.

Woodruff-Pak, D. S. (1993). Eyeblink classical conditioning in H. M.: Delay and trace paradigms. *Behavioral Neuroscience, 107,* 911–925.

Wright, P., Takei, N., Rifkin, L., & Murray, R. M. (1995). Maternal influenza, obstetric complications, and schizophrenia. *American Journal of Psychiatry, 152,* 1714–1720.

Wu, J., Kramer, G. L., Kram, M., Steciuk, M., Crawford, I. L., & Petty, F. (1999). Serotonin and learned helplessness: A regional study of 5-HR-sub(1A), 5-HT-sub(2A) receptors and the serotonin transport site in rat brain. *Journal of Psychiatric Research, 33,* 17–22.

Wynn, K. (1992). Addition and subtraction by human infants. *Nature, 358,* 749–750.

Xie, L., Kang, H., Xu, Q., Chen, M. J., Liao, Y., Thiyagarajan, M., . . . Nedergaard, M. (2013). Sleep drives metabolic clearance from the adult brain. *Science, 342,* 373–377.

Xu, Y., & Corkin, S. (2001). H. M. revisits the Tower of Hanoi puzzle. *Neuropsychology, 15,* 69–79.

Yantis, S. (2014). *Sensation and perception.* New York: Worth.

Yates, F. A. (1966). *The art of memory.* Chicago: University of Chicago Press.

Yerkes, R. M., & Dodson, J. D. (1908). The relation of strength of stimulus to rapidity of habit-formation. *Journal of Comparative and Neurological Psychology, 18,* 459–482.

Yolken, R. H., Dickerson, F. B., & Torrey, E. F. (2009). Toxoplasma and schizophrenia. *Parasite Immunology, 31,* 706–715.

Yolken, R. H., & Torrey, E. F. (1995). Viruses, schizophrenia, and bipolar disorder. *Clinical Microbiology Reviews, 8,* 131–145.

Yovel, G., Tambini, A., & Brandman, T. (2008). The asymmetry of the fusiform face area is a stable characteristic that underlies the left-visual field superiority for faces. *Neuropsychologia, 46,* 3061–3068.

Yuhas, D., & Jabr, F. (2012, June 13). Know your neurons: What is the ratio of glia to neurons in the brain? Retrieved from http://blogs.scientificamerican.com/brainwaves/know-your-neurons-what-is-the-ratio-of-glia-to-neurons-in-the-brain/

Zajonc, R. B. (1965). Social facilitation. *Science, 149,* 269–274.

Zimbardo, P. G. (1970). The human choice: Individuation, reason, and order versus deindividuation, impulse, and chaos. In W. J. Arnold & D. Levine (Eds.), *Nebraska Symposium on Motivation, 1969* (pp. 237–307). Lincoln, NE: University of Nebraska Press.

Zimbardo, P. (2007). *The Lucifer effect: Understanding how good people turn evil.* New York: Random House.

Zimbardo, P., Maslach, C., & Haney, C. (1999). Reflections on the Stanford prison experiment: Genesis, transformations, consequences. In T. Blass (Ed.), *Obedience to authority: Current perspectives on the Milgram paradigm* (pp. 193–237). Mahwah, NJ: Erlbaum.

Zuckerman, M. (1979). *Sensation seeking: Beyond the optimal level of arousal.* Hillsdale, NJ: Erlbaum.

Zwislocki, J. J. (1981, March/April). Sound analysis in the ear: A history of discoveries. *American Scientist, 69,* 184–192.

Name Index

Note: Page numbers followed by f indicate figures; those followed by t indicate tables.

Subject Index

Note: Page numbers followed by f indicate figures; those followed by t indicate tables.

Abilify, 460
abnormal psychology, 396–472. *See also* mental disorders; therapy
absolute threshold, 103–104, 103f, 110
Abu Ghraib prison, 419
accommodation
  in Piaget's theory, 300
  in vision, 112
acetylcholine (ACh)
  Alzheimer's disease and, 50
  definition and overview of, 50–51
  Huntington's chorea and, 68
  poisons influencing, 50–51
  summary of functions, 54t
acquisition
  in classical conditioning, 158–159, 159f, 162t
  of language, 5–6, 296–299, 311
  in operant conditioning, 170, 171–172, 172f
acrophobia, 436t
activation-synthesis theory of dreaming, 90
actor-observer bias, 409–410, 411t, 420–421
acupuncture, endorphins and, 53
acute schizophrenia, 447
adaptation
  dark, 117
  in Piaget's theory, 300
  sensory, 109
additive color mixtures, 118, 119, 119f
Adelson's checker shadow illusion, 135–136, 135f
Adler's striving for superiority, 344, 344f
adolescent(s)
  approximate age range, 287t
  formal operations in, 304–305
  identity crisis of, 323
  identity vs. role confusion stage and, 322t

adoption studies
  of depression, 443
  of intelligence, 275
adrenal glands, 59, 60f
adrenalin, 59
adulthood
  intelligence changes in, 272, 308–310, 310t
  late, 287t, 323
  middle, 287t, 323
  young, 287t, 323
advertising, classical conditioning and, 147
aerophobia, 436t
afterimages, 119, 120
age, vision and, 291–294
aggression
  in Eysenck's three-factor personality theory, 356
  media violence's relationship with, 191–192, 194
  modeling of, 189–191
aging
  intelligence influenced by, 272, 308–310, 310t, 312
  vision and, 114
agonists, 50, 51, 52
agoraphobia, 437–438
agreeableness, in Five Factor Model of personality, 357–358, 357t
agyrophobia, 436t
Aha! experience, 246
alcohol
  effect on the brain, 67, 68
  and state-dependent memory, 221
  as teratogen, 290
algorithms, 247–248, 252
alternate-form reliability, 270
Alzheimer's disease
  acetylcholine and, 50
  glial cells and, 45
ambiguous subjective contours, 133–134, 133f
American Psychiatric Association, DSM-5 and, 428–430
American Psychological Association, 1
  ethical standards of, 393
American schoolchildren, test score gap vs. Asian schoolchildren, 276

amnesia, 9–10, 69, 212–215
  anterograde, 213
  infantile/child, 214–215
  retrograde, 213
amnesics, 212, 213–214, 251
amphetamines, 52
amplitude, of waveforms, 111, 111f
amygdala, 66, 66f, 68, 69–70, 69f, 70t, 89, 375, 438, 440
anal stage, in Freudian theory, 340–341, 340t
anal-expulsive personality, 341
anal-retentive personality, 341
analytical intelligence, 273
anchoring and adjustment heuristic, 249, 252
antagonists, 50, 51, 52
anterior temporal lobes, 246–247
anterograde amnesia, 213–215
  practice effect and problem solving in, 251
antianxiety drugs, 22, 52–53, 459, 471
anticonvulsants, 456
antidepressants, 52, 456–459
  for major depressive disorder, 443, 456–458
  for obsessive-compulsive disorder, 440–441
antipsychotics, 52, 459–460, 471
antisocial personality disorder, 451–452
anvil (bone), 121, 122f
anxiety
  basic, 344
  defense mechanisms and, 337–338
  GABA and, 52–53, 439
anxiety disorders
  agoraphobia, 437–438
  definition of, 434–435
  drugs treating, 22, 52–53, 459, 471
  generalized, 438–439
  overview of, 434–439, 435t, 436t, 439f
  panic disorder, 438
  social anxiety disorder, 437–438
  specific phobia, 435–437, 436t
  summary of, 452